CONTEMPORARY BRITISH POLITICS

Also by Bill Coxall

Politics, Compromise and Conflict in Liberal Democracy
Parties and Pressure Groups

Also edited by Lynton Robins

Introductory Political Science
The American Way
Political Institutions in Britain
Politics and Policy-Making in Britain

Contemporary British Politics

An Introduction

Bill Coxall and Lynton Robins

MACMILLAN

First published 1989
Reprinted with corrections 1989
Reprinted with new postscript 1990
Reprinted with revised postscript 1991
Reprinted 1991

Published by
MACMILLAN EDUCATION LTD
Houndmills, Basingstoke, Hampshire RG21 2XS
and London
Companies and representatives
throughout the world

Typeset by Latimer Trend & Company Ltd, Plymouth

Printed in Hong Kong

British Library Cataloguing in Publication Data
Coxall, W. N. (William Norman)
Contemporary British politics.
1. Great Britain. Politics.
I. Title   II. Robins, Lynton
320.941
ISBN 0–333–46440–0 (hardcover)
ISBN 0–333–34046–9 (paperback)

This book is dedicated to
Hazel and Vivien

Contents

PART I   POLITICS, SOCIETY AND THE STATE

PART II   INSTITUTIONS AND PARTICIPATION

PART III   ISSUES AND THE POLICY PROCESS

v

PART IV   BRITISH GOVERNMENT AND POLITICS RECONSIDERED: THEORIES AND TENDENCIES

List of Exhibits

List of Figures

List of Tables

Preface

Traditionally, textbooks on British government and politics have focused on institutions and behaviour whilst ignoring or paying mere lip-service to the controversies and issues which are the stuff of politics. This book seeks to remedy that omission. It is based on the conviction that political institutions and issues are inseparable and need to be discussed together. Accordingly, Parts II and III which deal respectively with institutions, participation, and issues form the core of the book. The authors also believe that, to be fully comprehensible, such a discussion requires context. Hence Part I establishes a framework consisting of the concept of politics, the major shaping influences of culture and ideology together with a brief analysis of the leading types of government to be found in the modern world of states. Put simply and somewhat schematically, where textbooks of the 1970s moved beyond a formal constitutional and institutional subject-matter to deal with political behaviour (parties, pressure groups and the media) we have sought a further expansion of the political universe to encompass ideologies and controversies in addition to the more conventional content. Part IV aims to bring the concerns of Parts I–III of the book together: it first explores ideological approaches (pluralist and Marxist) to understanding the political system before concluding with an analysis of the impact of Thatcherism upon the agenda of British politics.

The book is designed to be of particular use to A level and BTEC students but the authors will be disappointed if it is not of value to others also, including first-year undergraduate students and even that elusive person, the general reader.

BILL COXALL
LYNTON ROBINS

A postscript has been added in this reprint covering the events in 1988, 1989 and 1990.

Acknowledgements

The authors and publishers wish to thank the following who have kindly given permission for the use of copyright material:

John Ardill for article 'Aerosol carbon blamed for hole in ozone layer', *The Guardian*, 7 August 1987.

Curtis Brown Group Ltd for table adapted from David Butler and Dennis Kavanagh, *The British General Election of October 1974*, p. 215. Copyright © 1975 by David Butler and Dennis Kavanagh.

The Economist for two tables from their 31 May 1986 issue.

Gower publishing Group for material from J. Westergaard and H. Resler, *Class in a Capitalist Society*, Heinemann, 1975.

The Guardian for extracts from various issues of *The Guardian*.

Harper & Row, Publisher, Inc., for a figure from Anthony Downs, *Economic Theory of Democracy*, p. 118. Copyright © 1957 by Harper & Row.

The Controller of Her Majesty's Stationery Office for Crown copyright material from *Social Trends* and *Employment Gazette*.

The Independent for extract from various editions of *The Independent*.

Longman Inc., for adapted tables from Philip Norton, *The Commons in Perspective*. Copyright © 1981 by Longman, Inc.; and Philip Norton, *The British Polity*. Copyright © by Longman, Inc.

Macmillan Publishers Ltd for material from S. Hall *et al*, *Policing the Crisis*, 1978, pp. 53–4; D. Butler and D. Kavanagh, *The British General Election of 1983;* L. Robins, T. Brennan and S. Sutton, *People and Politics in Britain*, 1985; M. Moran, *Politics and Society in Britain*.

The Observer for table, 'How the EEC Works', *The Observer*, 18 November 1974.

Oxford University Press for table from M. Burch and M. Moran, 'The Changing British Political Elite 1945–1983', *Parlimentary Affairs*, 138, Winter 1985, p. 15.

Penguin Books Ltd for table from David J. Smith, *Racial Disadvantage in Britain*. Copyright © PEP 1977.

Pergamon Books Ltd for table from A. Heath, R. Jowell and J. Curtice, *How Britain Votes*, 1985; p. 20.

The Press Association Ltd for material used in *The Guardian*, 1 July 1986, 'BBC "obsessive and biased" on South Africa'.

Routledge & Kegan Paul for tables from Glasgow University Media Group, *Bad News*, 1976.

The Statistical Office of the European Communities for *Eurostat* data.

Jonathan Steele for articles 'Peace Movement influenced talks', *The Guardian*, 19 September 1987.

Teaching Politics for material from various issues of *Teaching Politics*.

Unwin Hyman Ltd for table from A. H. Hanson, *Nationalization: A Book of Readings*, 1963, p. 36.

Brian Wilson for article 'The £4000 early warning', *The Guardian*, 21 September 1987.

Cecil Woolf, Publishers, for an extract from C. Woolf and J. Moorcroft Wilson, *Authors Take Sides on the Falklands*, 1982, pp. 10–12.

Every effort has been made to trace all the copyright-holders, but if any have been inadvertently overlooked the publishers will be pleased to make the necessary arrangement at the first opportunity.

Part I
Politics, Society and the State

1

What is Politics?

In seeking an understanding of the nature of politics we begin by considering those features of human society out of which the need for politics arises. We then move on to examine whether, as some people allege, certain spheres of human life are inherently non-political. In this section, we ask and seek to answer the question 'What makes a disagreement political?' The chapter ends by analysing the role of violence in politics. Is politics a particular non-violent way of resolving disagreements or does it comprehend all methods including force?

Politics arises out of a basic feature of human social life: the fact of differing interests and viewpoints. Differences of material interest develop because we live in a world of scarcity, and not abundance. In a 'Big Rock Candy Mountain' Utopia, where objects of need and desire were as freely available as the air we breathe, there would be no problem because we could all have everything we wanted. The real world, however, is not like that. It is one of limited resources, which are always more or less unevenly divided. And this is the case wherever we look, equally true of states within the world community (Table 1.1 and Exhibit 1.1) and of social groups within each national community (Tables 1.2 and 1.3). Of course, logically, no disagreement, let alone conflict, *need* flow from this situation if, for example, each individual, social group and State were perfectly satisfied with the distribution of international and national resources and were prepared to put up with

TABLE 1.1
World inequality

	1980 GNP per capita $
Developing countries	670
Low income countries	270
Middle income countries	1 500
Industrial market economies	10 630

Source: Derived from *World Development Report, 1987*, Oxford, University Press (1987) p. 171

3

Exhibit 1.1   The North–South divide

Just under a third of the world's population lives in the North, with over four-fifths of the world's income at its disposal ... The number of people suffering from malnutrition is still 500 million and the number of those living in 'absolute poverty' is around 800 million ... enough food is being produced worldwide ... but famine disasters such as the African catastrophes still occur. Every minute, thirty children die for lack of food and clean water ... The export to the Third World of the East–West conflict, and the increasing militarization of the Third World, severely encumber the development process ... In Africa as a whole (south of the Sahara) we may say that: 150–450 million are suffering from inadequate nutrition; 30–35 million face the threat of famine. Expectation of life has indeed risen, even in the Third World, but is still not much above 40 in a number of countries. In 1984 the USA had one doctor to 520 people, the Federal Republic of Germany had one to 450, but in Indonesia the ratio was one to 11 500, in Mali one to 32 000, and in Ethiopia one doctor to 58 000 people ... In 1983/4 29 per cent of the population of the world were unable to read and write. In 24 countries, over 70 per cent of adults could not read and write. In the developing countries, 300 million children between the ages of six and eleven do not go to school at all. And half of those who do go to school leave before the end of their second year.

Source: Willy Brandt, *World Armament and World Hunger* (first published 1985, translated by Anthea Bell, Gollancz, 1986) pp. 86, 49–50, 62, 72, 160.

---

shortage and inequality. But such a situation is a figment of the imagination. In practice, few *are* content and the world we actually inhabit is one of competition, often severe, for scarce resources. Each individual or group can only get more at the expense of everyone else. And it is this which creates the political problem – that of settling competing claims upon a limited economic product. Politics, it has been said, crudely but not inaccurately, is concerned with 'who gets what, when and how'. It is the arena where conflicts arising from such disagreements are fought out. Its role is to aggregate, adjust and

TABLE 1.2

Inequality in the United Kingdom: distribution of original and disposable household income, 1984 (percentages)

	Groups of households				
	Bottom fifth	Next fifth	Middle fifth	Next fifth	Top fifth
Original income	0.3	6.1	17.5	27.5	48.6
Disposable income	6.7	11.7	17.5	24.4	39.7

Source: as per Table 1.3

TABLE 1.3
Inequality in the United Kingdom:
distribution of wealth, 1984

Percentage of marketable wealth owned by:

Most wealthy	1%	21
Most wealthy	5%	39
Most wealthy	10%	52
Most wealthy	25%	75
Most wealthy	50%	93

Source: derived from *Social Trends*, no. 17, London, HMSO (1987) p. 17

settle (although it can never finally resolve) these conflicts. It has been an important aspect of the life of all societies that have existed in history and is likely to be an important part of all societies that will or might exist. It is as ineliminable a characteristic of human existence as food, sex or play.

The disagreements that lead to the need for politics arise from differences of viewpoint as well as economic conflicts. There are disagreements because customs, moralities and ultimate goals differ. These differences, in turn, may reflect divisions of class, religion and race. They are expressed in membership of a variety of social institutions – such as clubs, trade unions, business and professional associations, political parties and churches. For modern societies are not monolithic structures but present, on the contrary, a very considerable diversity. Pluralism – of beliefs and social groupings – is a fact, and it is by means of politics that the disagreements which flow from this fact are either reconciled or fail to be reconciled. Many of these differences stem from those systems of opposed beliefs which we call *ideologies* – for example nationalism, liberalism, anarchism, communism and fascism. These belief systems – or ideologies – shape a great deal of political action in the modern world. However, differences which call for political solution may, and often do, arise on less exalted grounds than ideology. Opinions may differ about the *truth* of a proposition (statement, theory, hypothesis) depending on its degree of elaboration and complexity, and about the *merits* of a thing (person, institution, decision, action). Controversy occurs because of the frequent need to make judgements of fact without conclusive evidence and judgements of value without conclusive reasons (Exhibit 1.2, Britain, Argentina and the Falklands/Malvinas).

None of this is meant to imply that disagreement is more common or intrinsic a feature of human communities than is agreement. If it were, no common life would be possible: we should merely clash and rebound from each other like robots. In fact, we do have many things in common with other members of the community we inhabit. A shared nationality is perhaps the

Exhibit 1.2   Britain, Argentina and the Falklands

On 2 April 1982 Argentine troops landed on the Falkland Islands and within a short time were in possession of the Island. Britain's response was the despatch of a Task Force which, after some severe fighting in which over 1000 men lost their lives, by 15 June 1982 had recaptured the Islands. The war divided opinion in Britain and its range is well demonstrated by a survey of 150 authors conducted while the war was actually taking place. The writers were asked two questions: 'Are you for, or against, our Government's response to the Argentine annexation of the Falkland Islands?' and 'How, in your view, should the dispute in the South Atlantic be resolved?' Their responses were well summarised by the editors in their introduction and we have subdivided these summaries into various categories in order to illustrate more clearly the complex factual and moral judgements which enter into the making of political decisions.

(a) *How opinion divided*

'What struck us from the beginning was the low proportion of those who were neutral, less than 10 per cent. It was also noticeable that, at the outset, opinion was almost equally divided between those for and against the Government's response. As time went on, however, those opposed to the Government increased until, in the final poll of 106, approximately 39 were for, 59 against and eight appeared to be neutral.'

(b) *The range of opinion on political/diplomatic strategies*

'The hard-line war party is represented, though its members are few. Then there are those who support the Government's despatch of the task force, and the use of it to retake the islands, but who would like to see Mrs Thatcher ready to negotiate. Next come those who back the sending of the task force but *not* the use of it. Finally there are those who oppose the whole exercise from start to finish, arguing that it was not worth the spilling of one drop of blood.'

(c) *The variety of attitudes*

(i) *On the role of the United Nations*   'Attitudes towards the United Nations ... vary widely. Some contributors are dismissive of it, while others firmly believe that the dispute provided an opportunity for the UN to develop as an effective institution for maintaining world peace.'

(ii) *National prestige*   'Some writers argue that national credibility and pride were at stake in the Falklands conflict, it was a "national humiliation *not* to be borne".'

(iii) *Right of self-defence against aggression*   'Some see it (the Argentine invasion of the Falklands) ultimately, as a threat to our survival. Aggression, they assert, must not be seen to pay ... Equally there are those who argue that it was not a situation comparable with the Second World War: to use one writer's words, "it was *not* a war of national survival" and therefore not justifiable.'

continued

Exhibit . . . *– continued*

(iv) *Resistance to dictators* 'A number of writers compare the Argentine junta with the leaders of Nazi Germany and conclude that, just as we had no choice but to fight Hitler, so we had to oppose Galtieri.'

(v) *Duty to the Falkland Islanders* 'Another argument put forward is our duty to the islanders: we could not abandon them to the not-so-tender mercies of a Fascist regime. On the other side there are those who argue that we could safely do precisely that, pointing to the sizeable Welsh and Scots communities in Argentina, or compensate each islander so handsomely that they [*sic*] could choose where they wished to live.'

(vi) *Legal entitlement* 'A number of writers refer to the historical and legal aspect of the conflict. Surprisingly few of them question the legality of Britain's claim to sovereignty, though both the *Sunday Times* and *The Times* carried articles on the secret doubts of the Foreign Office concerning our legal title over a long period of time.'

(vii) *Moral right* 'One of the strongest arguments in favour of the Government's action is that it was a matter of "principle". We could not allow a large country to walk in and take over a small one. In answer to this various cases are cited to show that this Government was not preoccupied with "principle" when the people concerned were black, as are the Diego Garcians. Nor were previous governments ready to help Greek Cypriots against "Fascist" Turkey. East Timor provides yet another example.'

(viii) *Pacifism* 'One frequent theme to emerge from these pieces is the necessity for pacifism, particularly in a nuclear age. Holders of this view are not confined to those who oppose the Government's action. Paradoxically several supporters of military action to retake the islands also subscribe to the notion that settling disputes by war is an anachronism.'

(ix) *Judgements on the motives of both governments* 'Another pervasive theme is what one author calls "bonapartism" in both governments. That is, the device by which leaders deflect criticism of their domestic policies by pointing to glories abroad. Even more sinister motives were perceived by some for the Government's response, such as the testing of new weapons, both for "defence" and as a shop-window for our arms industry, and a test of the preparedness of the nation . . . The nearest the contributors come to unanimity is in their condemnation of the junta.'

(x) *Criticism of the British Government's handling of the crisis* Contributors were 'almost equally' unanimous in 'their reservations about our own Government's handling of the situation' and these criticisms included 'allowing the crisis to develop in the first place', 'their willingness to sell arms to the Argentines up to the last moment' and Mrs Thatcher's 'bellicose demeanour', with the sinking of the Belgrano 35 miles outside the exclusion zone seen as 'a deliberate act of provocation' which made further negotiations with the Argentines fruitless. Many people suggest that an appeal to the International

continued

Exhibit . . .   *– continued*

Court, together with sanctions and a blockade, should have been tried before sending the task force and that the Government was too anxious to engage in hostilities.

(xi) *The costs of the military action*   'Yet another consideration that arises is not merely the cost of the campaign and the future garrison, but also the expense involved in the Government's implicit commitment to develop the islands. This seems to some writers shameful in view of the drastic cuts imposed by the Government in education, health and other social services for financial reasons.'

(d) *Proposals for a solution to the crisis*

'Solutions to the problem range from retaining the islands with a strong garrison for as long as necessary, to negotiating a settlement either as soon as possible or after feelings have been allowed to cool down. Several people would like to see the UN called in to arbitrate and a few suggest partition as the most sensible answer.'

Source: C. Woolf and J. Moorcroft Wilson, *Authors Take Sides on the Falklands* (Cecil Woolf Publishers, 1982) pp. 10–12

---

most significant factor, overriding differences of class and religion to bind members of the same territorial State together. Often, also, as we shall see, a considerable degree of consensus exists on the decision-making procedure, or constitution, even if this is rarely complete. Again, material interdependence is another source of identity of interest: we may not be able to agree on the relative worth in terms of financial reward of various occupations – of doctors, nurses, teachers, solicitors, miners and dustmen; we can agree that these jobs are essential and that the community as a whole is poorer if one or the other fails to carry out its tasks properly.

But this takes us only part of the way towards an understanding of the nature of politics. We now need to be more precise in specifying what is meant by such terms as 'groups', 'disagreement' and the 'expression' and 'settlement' of disagreements in this context. In particular, we need to ask three important questions. First, do all human social groupings have a political aspect and even if so do we nonetheless accord some groups a special status when we think about politics? Second, assuming that not all disagreements are political, by what criteria do we place a dispute in this category? What makes a controversy 'political'? Third, does politics involve a particular way of seeking to settle controversies – for example, the non-violent way of verbal persuasion – or can it include all methods of articulating and resolving conflicts?

DO ALL SOCIAL GROUPS POSSESS POLITICS?

In one sense, the answer to this question must be 'yes'. It is common practice to refer to subordinate groups in society as having a political element. We speak, for example, of the 'politics' of a school, of a company, of a civil service department, even of the 'politics' of the family. Clearly, the well-established usage involved here goes beyond a mere manner of speaking. In fact, it has a two-fold justification:

1. social subgroups contain structured patterns of relationships culminating in *decision-procedures*.
2. it makes sense because these structures involve relationships of *authority*, *power* and *influence*, terms which are themselves, as we shall see, pre-eminently political.

All social groups – from a trade union to the United Nations – possess a decision-procedure of some kind. *Decision-procedure* means a method of reaching collective decisions about what rules to have, how to change them once in existence, and how to apply them. This basic or fundamental rule which prescribes the form by which policy and executive decisions shall be taken is usually called the *constitution*. In a club, society or association, a constitution normally lays down such matters as the purposes of the organisation, the conditions of membership and, above all, the way in which its officials are to be selected. In other words, it will make provision for the *government* of the association. The need for government springs from the fact that in life decisions have constantly to be made and made now, not at some indefinite point in the future. Considerations of time and practicality have to be taken into account. Some matters are postponable; others, such as what action to take with regard to an unruly member, must be made quickly. Nor is it generally practicable to consult the entire membership on matters of urgency and routine. The constitution therefore designates who in an association may take such decisions and the procedures to be followed in reaching them. The 'politics' of the organisation may be said to consist in the attempts to influence the procedures and outcomes of its decision-making process. Of course, the decision-making process of an organisation may be, and normally is, broader and more complex than a single document or set of written documents. As we shall see later, unofficial and informal processes can be as important constituents of a decision-procedure as are written rules. But this point does not affect the matter at issue here. Politics includes the effort to affect all aspects of a collective decision-making process, both formal and informal.

So far the discussion has focused upon voluntary subgroups in society – organisations like a youth club, a choral society or a political party, which people decide to join for specific purposes. But similar conclusions with regard to their political aspect may be drawn about institutions and groups named at the outset of this section such as schools, companies, government departments and the family. All of these have a non-voluntary, 'unchosen' character yet all possess structures conceived in terms of patterns of relationships and roles and, in particular, all have decision-making processes. Their structured nature together with their possession of a method of arriving at decisions binding upon their members, however informal this may be, distinguishes them from more random social aggregates like a bus queue or a birthday party. They may therefore be said to contain a political element so that it makes sense, for example, to speak of the politics of Keele University, of ICI and of Whitehall.

All but the most random of social groupings are also political in another sense. There is *competition* to influence collective decisions. The phrase most commonly invoked to describe this feature of their existence is 'struggle for power'. The English political philosopher, Thomas Hobbes, writing in the seventeenth century, found the motive springs of this struggle in man's restlessness and ambition, in 'a general inclination of all mankind, a perpetual and restless desire of power after power, that ceaseth only in death'. There is competition both to achieve the positions of authority within a group or organisation and also among the ordinary members, employees and so on, to influence the possessors of authority. Indeed, the concept of power is so fundamental in the study of politics that it requires careful consideration at the outset. In particular, we need to distinguish three related terms which are often confused – 'authority', 'power' and 'influence'.

Authority

The term 'authority' is generally employed to designate the rightful use of power. It refers to power that is conferred by a rule and exercised in accordance with rules. A party secretary, a judge or a teacher, indeed anyone with an 'official' position within an organisation or society, may be said to be 'in authority' because a rule in a system of rules authorises each to give orders. So long as the authority continues to act within his legally defined sphere, those to whom he or she issues commands (however crudely or subtly) are required to obey. They may not, in fact, do so, but we should not regard their refusal to obey orders as justified unless the authority himself had abused or exceeded his jurisdiction. The word 'authority' in its legal sense refers not to any personal characteristics of its possessor but to the qualities of an *office*. When the term of office ends, the authority disappears. Of course, as already implied, a considerable part of the meaning of 'authority' is normative rather than descriptive. It refers to what should be, rather than what is, the case. A policeman who is overpowered by a criminal does not cease to be an authority. He simply lacks control over events. But it is at this point that we need a word other than 'authority' if we are to describe the realities of the situation adequately.

Power

That term is 'power' which, to a much greater extent than 'authority', has an empirical and descriptive connotation. Power, in the words of Michael Oakshott, is 'the ability to procure . . . a wished-for response in the conduct of another' although he adds that this effect can never be achieved with certainty because power as a social relationship must always contain an element of uncertainty and unpredictability. Indeed, against much in our common usage and ways of thought which suggests that power is a *possession* – as, for example, when we speak of '*X*' or '*Y*', the President of Ford Corporation or the Chairman of ICI as a powerful individual – it is worth emphasising the extent to which power is a *relationship*. Thus, whereas the concept of authority focuses upon the *entitlement* of an agent to issue commands, the word 'power' points to the way in which orders are received. It draws attention to whether they are actually obeyed. It constantly brings us back to the *consequences* of the competition for control which is always taking place. Power and authority come together where commands can be described as not only rightful in the sense that the issuer is authorised to make them but also effective in the sense that they are carried out by those who receive them. But they move apart in cases where we say that although a group undoubtedly has *power* in the sense it can impose its will on others even against opposition – as the Mafia, for example, can maim, kill and generally terrorise its enemies into submission – it has no *authority* to do so. This does not mean, of course, that the exercise of power necessarily involves force, although not infrequently it does. Equally, however, money, status, intelligence, education, knowledge, time, social connections and organisation can all influence group decisions and consequently may be identified as important political resources.

Influence

To a very considerable extent in modern industrialised societies the exercise of power depends upon the ability to persuade people to behave in one way rather than another. The word 'influence' is useful here because it directs attention to the *process* by which opinions are changed and behaviour altered. It points beyond a purely formal analysis of a structure of authority in terms of institutions and offices to the complex interplay between people within institutions and between institutions and groups outside. The politics of any institution appears rather like an iceberg even to those who try to follow it closely; nine-tenths of it lies beneath the surface, hidden from view. The term 'influence' directs attention to the ways in which collective decisions are moulded by a whole range of individuals and organisations other than – but of course not excluding – the formal authorities.

It is now convenient to summarise these three terms. In the neat formulations of J. R. Lucas:

> 'Someone or some group has *authority* if it follows from his saying "Let X happen" that X ought to happen.'
> 'Someone or some group has *power* if it follows from his saying "Let X happen" that X does happen.'
> 'Someone or group has *influence* if the result of his saying "Let X happen" is that others say "Let X happen".' (Lucas, *The Principles of Politics, 1967 [italics ours]*.

Politics, then, is about collective decision-making by groups, the political relationships of whose members are appropriately characterised by the terms 'authority', 'power' and 'influence'. But although this takes us some of the way towards an understanding of the subject, it does not take us far enough. Etymology enables us to complete the definition. 'Politics' derives from the Greek word *polis* meaning 'city-state'. This term had a broader significance than the modern word 'state'; it meant state and church rolled into one. But the word has the merit in this context of directing attention to a dimension of meaning which has remained absolutely central to the word 'politics'. In its most fundamental sense, it relates to matters of State or the government of the State. Its concern, then, is not primarily with individuals in their private lives – as members of voluntary groups or in the family circle (although, as we have seen, these relationships do have a political aspect). Its major reference is to individuals in their *public* relationships, as holding office in and seeking to influence affairs of *State*.

THE STATE

The term 'State' refers to the supreme law-making authority within a particular geographical area. The concept first emerged in the sixteenth century to denote a novel form of association claiming sovereignty and exercising power within a given territory. Three characteristics of this new entity are of special importance here:

1. The State is a *compulsory* form of association. Membership of a State, although not of a particular one, is obligatory. Indeed, although change of citizenship is normally possible, it is also difficult, and most remain as citizens of the State in which they are born.
2. It is *comprehensive*. It stands above and includes all partial associations and groups within its territory, giving or denying them rights of legal existence, regulating their powers over their members and helping to settle their disputes.
3. The State is *a sovereign body* possessing extreme powers of coercion over its members. Alone among associations, the State may imprison us and, in

the ultimate analysis, it may have the right to take our lives. Modern States conscript, punish, and even put to death their citizens. Of course, the possession by the State of supreme sanctions over its members does not mean that it is the sole wielder of force in a particular community. It merely means that the State has the ultimate responsibility for deciding by whom force may be used (parents, schools, sportsmen) and to what degree, and for controlling and punishing the illegitimate users of violence (criminals, terrorists).

Quite clearly, these characteristics place the State in a completely different category to the other forms of association considered so far. Moreover, its possession of these characteristics transforms the significance of *those features which it shares* with voluntary and subordinate social groups and associations. To non-members, the decision-making procedures no less than the actual processes of the competition for authority, power and influence of a particular family, club, society, association, union or company are of no direct significance. But the constitution of the State and the struggle for power within it between individuals, groups and classes must concern us all because we are all citizens. Like it or not and whether we interest ourselves in public affairs or not, the nature of the regime and the outcome of the competition for power must affect us because of the non-voluntary, inclusive and sovereign nature of the State. We may choose whether or not to join a club; we cannot choose whether or not to be citizens of a State. In the modern world, there is no escaping it.

The answer to our first question is now clear. Whereas partial associations have political aspects, such secondary, limited groupings are not our major concern when we think of 'politics'. Rather, the term 'politics' inevitably centres upon decision-making within the only 'society' which touches us all – the community of communities – the State.

WHAT MAKES A DISAGREEMENT POLITICAL?

The analysis to date – which has concentrated upon isolating a specifically 'political' element in the activities of social groups – also takes us far towards answering our second and third questions. Perhaps the best approach to the second problem – what makes a controversy political – is via a number of commonly expressed opinions. It is often said, for example, that religion, art, education or sport should either never become matters of political contro- versy or, in so far as they already are so, should be taken out of political debate. The suggestion implicit in such remarks is that these spheres of human activity are inherently non-political. There is the further, pejorative, implication that they are sullied by being made 'political' since they naturally inhabit a finer, purer air. What should we make of this contention? Our principal comment must be that it appears to misunderstand the nature of politics. This, as we have seen, involves a competitive struggle between individuals and groups who disagree about ultimate goals and collective priorities, material and non-material. Potentially, any matter at all may become a subject of public debate. Nothing exists in a watertight compartment sealed off from the political arena. Thus, art, we may say, ought not to be directly political in the sense that the State demands commitment to a particular ideology from its artists. But in so far as artists, freely, express visions of society, either negative or positive, in so far as they uncoercedly make anarchist or Fascist statements in their art, they necessarily engage in politics. Art may enter politics in another more mundane sense. In the modern world, a considerable amount of patronage of the arts is conducted through the State. Exactly what priority to give to the arts as against other claimants upon the public revenue – agriculture, industry or defence, for example – is therefore a political decision. Again, to contend that education should be kept out of politics is to suggest by implication that society as a whole should not concern itself with the upbringing of its citizens. In fact, it both has to, and does, and differing views on the organisation and content of education reflect differing sets of moral values. Thus, some give highest priority to the maintenance of a private sector (the moral principle being the freedom to choose); others place the emphasis upon the attainment of a common education for all (the ethic invoked being a more integrated and less divided society). Finally, many people criticise sporting boycotts – for example, preventing cricketers from playing in South Africa or athletes from competing in the Moscow Olympics in 1980 – for (wrongly, in their view) bringing politics into sport. But politics is already in sport. In the West, athletes train with facilities provided by governments and, in the Eastern bloc countries, they are wholly State-supported. Above all, sporting achievement is one facet of international rivalry between States. The gesture of withdrawing from sporting contacts as a sign of disapproval of a country's foreign policy (the Soviet invasion of Afghanistan) or domestic affairs (apartheid in South Africa) may be criticised for being unfair to athletes but not for politicising the unpolitical.

This does not mean that it is not to be regretted when activities like athletics or cricket become the means of making political gestures, weapons in the international rivalry of States (although as instruments of persuasion not sending athletes or cricketers is infinitely preferable to sending gunboats). Nor is it to argue that art and literature do not suffer when they become too overtly politicised. Soviet 'Realist' artists and political writers like Gentile in Mussolini's Fascist Italy who allow themselves to become the tame ideologues of a regime deserve their reputation as mere propagandists. What it does contend is twofold:

1. The conditions under which a whole range of human social activities considered as 'unpolitical' by nature (art, sport, religion, education) are

practised depend ultimately upon political decision. The main reason for this is not that governments provide facilities for them, although this is often the case. It is rather that the decision to establish and maintain a voluntary sphere of life for the free and unimpeded practice of these activities is itself a political decision and depends for its existence upon a continuing public commitment. In other words, it rests upon the particular system of moral values embodied in the Liberal State, which has developed in Western societies over the past 200 years. This point that the rights of individuals and groups to practise these activities are inherently a matter for political decision can be simply illustrated. In the sixteenth century, the State imposed religious uniformity on its citizens, a practice which in succeeding centuries gradually gave way to toleration of a variety of religious denominations, which now possess the right to worship as they please. But the decision to tolerate, – as formerly to prosecute and even persecute, for non-observance of a State-ordained creed, – is a political one. It now becomes clear that those who maintain that politics should be kept out of a particular activity are expressing a (liberal) political preference, which itself reflects the conventional division between State – an area of compulsory activity – and Society – the sphere of voluntary activity – that has grown up in the West since the eighteenth century. Equally, it is clear that the division itself depends upon a prior political guarantee (by the State) and that the boundaries of this division may from time to time shift.

2. Sometimes the desire to keep politics out of a particular activity arises out of a simple distaste for controversy and disagreement and a wish that it would stop (e.g. the resentment of businessmen, educationalists and the medical profession at political interference). But these demands are in themselves political. What they require by implication is that public discussion of these affairs in terms of preferences and priorities should cease in favour of administration by their practitioners. But there is no such thing as 'pure' administration unsullied by ideas and values. In practice, the 'experts' would have to make 'political' decisions' – allocate scarce resources between the various parts of their enterprises – and engage in political activities – lobby governments for a greater share of the public funds to be devoted to their concerns. A matter becomes political not because of the malign intent of politicians but because disagreement exists about it – e.g. how much 'private' medical practice to allow, and on what terms; or about a claim to a particular share of public expenditure. The differences of opinion and the clashes of interest which demand and generally receive public resolution in free societies do not cease if they are ignored or driven underground. The public may see little of it but controversy over collective goals still takes place in 'closed' societies like the USSR (over the relative importance to be attached to defence, investment and current consumption, for example). It merely takes place

within a different constitutional framework – the single party in a one-party State. As J. B. D. Miller writes in *The Nature of Politics* (1962) 'Politics will never stop because social reconciliation and agreement will never be complete' (p. 19). It will never be complete for three fundamental reasons: first, because material resources are likely to remain scarce and their distribution at any given moment will be unacceptable to some; second, because our images of the 'good society', our 'Utopias', will almost certainly continue to diverge; and, finally, because, however much we eliminate irrelevant factors like wealth and status of birth from the struggle for positions of authority, these remain in their nature limited and, therefore, subject to competition. (The office of Prime Minister is a *positional* good – if I get it, you cannot have it, and vice versa.) For these reasons, disagreement, competition and the need for politics are likely to be with us for a long time yet. The idea that the world can be rid of politics and its practitioners reflects a secret desire for a kind of conflict-free, unchanging society that has never existed nor is ever likely to.

IS POLITICS A PARTICULAR (NON-VIOLENT) WAY OF EXPRESSING AND RESOLVING SOCIAL CONFLICTS, OR DOES IT COMPREHEND ALL SUCH METHODS (INCLUDING FORCE)?

'What words mean few can say, but with words we govern men', said Disraeli. Language is fundamental to politics. How could it be otherwise in a sphere of activity wholly concerned with persuasion? How else could the expression of varying viewpoints and the search for common ground be conducted except through talk and writing, verbal and written communications? One has only to consider the great variety of forms taken by political discourse to realise how central words are to politics. Slogan, speech, lecture, article, pamphlet, tract, polemic – the list is a lengthy one. Speech is the essence of politics. Greek writers realised this: Aristotle's *Rhetoric* is about the art of political argument. Moreover, this linkage of politics with oral and literary fluency took strong root. The first European Chair of Politics, founded at Uppsala in 1622, was in 'Statesmanship and Eloquence'.

Some writers have been so impressed with the centrality of words to politics that they have sought to define politics in terms of verbal communication. In other words, they have equated politics with *a particular (peaceful) method* of expressing and settling disagreements. Thus, Bernard Crick writes:

> If the argument is, then, that politics is simply the activity by which government is made possible when differing interests in an area to be governed grow powerful enough to need to be conciliated, the obvious objection will be: 'why do certain interests have to be conciliated?' And the answer is, of course, that they do not have to be. Other paths are always open. *Politics is simply when they are conciliated – that solution to the problem of order which chooses conciliation rather than violence*

and coercion, and chooses it as an effective way by which varying interests can discover that level of compromise best suited to their common interest in survival (Crick, *In Defence of Politics*, 1982, p. 30) [*italics ours*].

This contention gains support, first, from much in the European tradition of theorising about politics. *Political* rule, to Aristotle, was that method of ordering the affairs of a community which sought to draw all interests into government rather than a system in which one group overwhelmed all the others and ruled in its own interest alone. Indeed, the word 'politician', although increasingly signifying simply a person who engages in politics as a profession or career, does retain something of its earlier meaning as a kind of broker of interests, someone whose developed skills of articulacy were put to the service of expressing and mediating between the differing interests in a community. Second, this understanding of politics gets some endorsement from contemporary usage.

For example, on occasions when countries become bogged down in struggles against terrorists like the British Government with the IRA in Northern Ireland or in wars like the one fought by the Americans in Vietnam in the early 1970s, it is often said that ultimately there will have to be a *political* solution. In the long run, the various parties to the dispute will have to sit down round a table and seek to resolve their differences by bandying words rather than by firing bullets. In both these well-established usages of the terms 'politics' and 'political', the contrast is with *force*. Thus, 'political *rule*', 'polity' or – as it is sometimes called – 'mixed government', contrasts with 'tyranny', 'oligarchy' or even (in the sense in which Aristotle used the words to signify the rule of the poor in their own interest) 'democracy'. A political *solution* or *method* (discussion) is opposed to the use of violence (terrorism, war) in the settlement of conflicts.

However, this value-loaded understanding of politics is clearly at variance with the more neutral definition offered so far and, equally clearly, incompatible with it. Politics is here defined as the arena where social disagreements are expressed, and conflicts are reconciled or fail to be reconciled. This process may be peaceful or violent. In the real world, as is only too obvious, violence is everywhere. Just consider. The States which had experienced no political killing in the post-war period up to 1975 can be numbered on fewer than the fingers of one hand: New Zealand, Fiji and Iceland. At that date (1975) perhaps as many as half of the world's regimes owed their existence to a violent stroke within the previous generation. Between 1969 and 1976 political violence in Northern Ireland accounted for 1700 deaths; when the numbers of wounded are also taken into account, it meant that in Ulster more than one family in every six had had a relative killed or injured in the Troubles. During the 1970s, terrorist groups like the Provisional IRA, Baader–Meinhof and the Palestine Liberation Organisation and terrorist regimes like Uganda under Amin and Cambodia under Pol-Pot made violence central to the achievement of their policy ends.

However, it is unnecessary to invoke such extreme – in some cases pathological – examples in order to realise the close relationship that exists between power and violence. Will rather than force may be the basis of the State in the sense that ultimately it rests on public opinion. But since survival is the primary requirement of any State and since its enemies, internal and external, may at any time deploy violence against it, clearly force – its possession of and readiness to deploy weapons – always backs up the State. This is not, of course, to equate violence with power. Indeed, all States, if they are wise, will seek to minimise the violence they use. Excessive violence by the authorities may reduce their power by undermining public respect, as Mayor Daley's Chicago police and the French riot police demonstrated in the 1960s. But this is by the way. The point is that to exclude violence from our definition of politics would be to rule out from consideration a very high proportion of actual behaviour in the real world. It would eliminate from our vocabulary a number of concepts – revolution, rebellion, *coup d'état*, terrorism, repression – vital to any understanding of recurrent social phenomena. Violent means may be, and frequently are, used both in the maintenance and the overthrow of States and regimes. We need to adopt a conception of 'politics' which recognises this fact. None of this is in any way to justify violence, of course. It is simply to say that no conception of politics which ignored it as a major means of social change would be realistic. And it is also to suggest that to equate politics in general with the non-violent resolution of conflicts is to identify it (narrowly, as well as somewhat misleadingly, since these States ultimately depend upon force, too) with a particular type of political system, the liberal–democratic State.

SUMMARY

Disagreement is an inevitable feature of human groups and politics is the area of life in which such disagreements are expressed, modified and settled. Disagreements may arise out of differences of material interest and as a consequence of conflicts of belief and opinion. The existence of controversy and conflict in human groups does not preclude the existence of cooperation, solidarity and interdependence.

Politics is concerned with the machinery, processes and outcomes of collective decision-making by social creatures whose common life is characterised as much by disagreement over the allocation of resources and values as by interdependence, cooperation and mutual need. People in societies therefore require an authoritative centre of resource allocation, which, in turn is provided by a compulsory, comprehensive, territorial association possessing ultimate powers of coercion known as a 'State'. States themselves contain a pattern of offices (constitution), a set of decision-makers (government) and an apparatus of power (army, police).

The intrinsically non-political does not exist. All social activities are potential sources of disagreement and welfare, and also potential contributors to the resolution of disagreements; hence, all possess a political aspect. Even the decision to create a private–public division of spheres, with a predisposition towards non-intervention in the 'private' sphere (art, religion, family life) is a political decision, as would be any decision to by-pass it.

Politics as a concept cannot be identified with a non-violent competition for authority, power and influence over the allocation of goods and the determination of collective goals. In the world as it is, violence is constantly used to maintain and overthrow States, regimes and governments and we need a concept of politics broad enough to recognise this fact. We may say, therefore, that 'politics' includes all methods (violent and non-violent) of influencing the machinery, processes and outcomes of collective decision-making.

FURTHER READING

Crick, B. (1982) *In Defence of Politics*, Harmondsworth, Penguin, 2nd edn (expanded).
Duverger, M. (1966) *The Idea of Politics*, London, Methuen.
Lucas, J. R. (1966) *The Principles of Politics*, Oxford, University Press (paperback edn, 1985).
O'Sullivan, N. (ed.) (1983) *Revolutionary Theory and Political Reality*, Brighton, Wheatsheaf.
Renwick, A. and Swinburn, I. (1987) *Basic Political Concepts*, London, Hutchinson, 2nd (updated and expanded) edn.
Wilkinson, P. (1977) *Terrorism and the Liberal State*, London, Macmillan.

QUESTIONS

1. What is politics?
2. Critically examine the contention that politics ought to be 'kept out of sport'.

ASSIGNMENT

Conduct a case-study on how a particular national decision was made (it can involve either foreign affairs, e.g. the decision to join the Common Market or to resist the invasion of the Falklands, or domestic policy, e.g. the decision to privatise a particular industry or to resist a trade-union demand). Analyse the decision in terms of the standpoints of the main participants, the issues involved, the resources (e.g. money, expertise) upon which the 'sides' could call, the reasons why a particular outcome was reached, and the consequences – immediate and more far-reaching – for those concerned and for the community-at-large. What made the decision 'political'?

2

The Social Context of Politics

This chapter examines the nature of Britain's political culture, and the means by which that culture is passed from one generation to the next. The principal characteristics of the political culture are examined from contrasting viewpoints in order to assess whether it is based on a *consensus* regarding political values or on *conflict*. Political scientists have answered this question in different ways, and to help our assessment the concept of deference and the embourgeoisement thesis will be examined in order to see how far they explain political behaviour. Political scientists have also adopted differing views of the process by which the political culture is learnt. The concept of political socialisation is explored and the impact of the major agencies of socialisation on the way people learn about politics is considered. These agencies include the family, the educational system, peer groups and the mass media. Finally, political socialisation is examined in terms of which periods in an individual's lifetime are the critical ones in the learning process. The chapter concludes by considering the arguments of those who say early childhood is the time when the foundations of political values are laid, together with the alternative view that adolescence and early adulthood are the most important periods.

THE POLITICAL CULTURE

We have all heard people from other countries described in very general terms; for example, it has been said that 'Germans work hard' and 'Americans are friendly'. Such generalisations, or stereotypes, are very crude and common sense tells us that not all Germans work hard and not all Americans are friendly. At the same time there appears to be some truth in these generalisations since people from different countries share different characteristics. What these crude statements acknowledge is that people from different countries share distinctive cultures and have different social customs. A society's culture includes its customs, values, beliefs, ideas and the artefacts it produces. Attitudes towards such things as work, leisure, wealth, the role of women and the value of education in one society's culture might be significantly different from the attitudes and values found in another society's culture. This is also the case regarding attitudes found in different countries towards politics and the political system.

What is a political culture?

Political scientists have defined the concept of political culture in a number of different ways. For example, Roy Macridis has defined the political culture as being made up of the 'commonly shared goals and commonly accepted rules' of a society. Richard Rose has argued along rather different lines and stated that 'the political culture of England consists of those values, beliefs and emotions that give meaning to politics'.

We shall start from the point that the political culture of a country is part of that country's general culture. It is made up of the attitudes, values and beliefs held by the people about *how* their government should operate and *what* their government should do. People from different societies expect different behaviour and responses from their governments. For example the political culture found in most developed societies leads to people expecting their governments to respond to their social needs. The State is expected to provide education for the young, health care for the sick and to cope with the problems resulting from natural disasters such as floods or earthquake. In contrast, people from some less developed countries expect far less from their governments. They do not necessarily expect extensive provision of educational and health care services nor do they expect total relief in the wake of a natural disaster.

Not only do political cultures differ from each other, but there are also differences to be found within a single political culture. In their study of five democracies, *The Civic Culture* (1963), Gabriel Almond and Sidney Verba classified differences in political involvement and awareness. Some people might live in what they called a *parochial* political culture; they would be only dimly aware of government and hardly feel affected by its policies. Others might share a *subject* political culture in which individuals know about their government but do not expect to exert any influence over it. Despite this lack of influence, they may still give strong support to their government. Finally, Almond and Verba defined the *participant* political culture, in which people expect to act in ways which influence government. In Britain, which has largely a subject and participant political culture, there will nevertheless be a minority who have a parochial political culture.

Geographical and historical constraints

Britain's political culture is constantly changing but there are a number of constraints on the directions in which it is likely to develop. In other words, an understanding of Britain's contemporary political culture involves an understanding of its geography and history.

The English Channel has provided an important barrier between the British Isles and continental Europe. Mainland Britain has not been invaded since 1066. In sharp contrast, its close neighbour France was last invaded in

1940. It has been argued that Britain's relative isolation from Europe has produced an insular political outlook.

The way in which British people view Britain's role in the world is still influenced by our past. Today Britain is an important *regional* power, but in the recent past it was a *world* power. A little over half a century ago Britain ruled the largest empire that the world has ever known. Incredible as it may seem today, during the 1920s almost one fifth of the world's population lived under British rule. But the empire disappeared rapidly during the 1940s, 1950s and 1960s as member-countries gained their independence. British leaders were not very successful in adapting to play a much smaller part in world affairs. This led to an American, Dean Acheson, making the painful remark that Britain had lost an empire but had not yet found a role.

Britain's allies made it clear that they no longer saw Britain as a major force in world politics. The 'special relationship' which was said to exist between Britain and the USA weakened as other European countries, particularly Germany, recovered after the Second World War. If American leaders recognised London as the 'capital' of Europe during the 1940s and 1950s, Bonn was seen as the new capital of Europe during the 1960s. British leaders suffered a humiliating blow when Australia, New Zealand and the USA signed the ANZUS Pact. Despite complaints about not being invited to participate in this defence treaty, Britain remained excluded from it.

There were other defeats and humiliations that affected Britain's political culture. For example, the British government over-reacted when Egypt nationalised the Suez Canal in 1956. The canal was due to revert to Egyptian government ownership in 1968. Britain, France and Israel took military action in order to regain the canal. Many people considered that the government had acted wrongly and the British forces were withdrawn as a result of international pressure. The French felt let down by Britain, and this was one reason behind a further humiliation of Britain in 1963 and 1967 when Britain's membership of the EEC was blocked by the French veto.

The inability of the British people to adapt quickly enough to changing circumstances led to much self-examination. During the 1960s many books were published around the theme of 'what's wrong with Britain?' The authors questioned Britain's traditional values and at first argued for economic and social reform. Later they were to argue for political change.

Occasionally, events occur which bring to the fore aspects of the political culture which for many years seemed to be irrelevant or of sharply-declining importance. For example, the Falklands War, which resulted from the capture of the islands by Argentinian forces in 1982, generated a remarkable political atmosphere reminiscent of Britain's imperial past. The public followed the progress of a naval task force and greeted the final surrender of the Argentinian forces with an enthusiasm which dwarfed the national celebration of Britain's long-awaited entry into the EEC in 1973. Almost half a century before, Sir Winston Churchill had commented that if ever faced with a choice between 'Europe' and the 'open sea', Britain would always choose the open sea. In 1982, the British people revealed that despite Britain's vastly changed position in the world, there is an element in the political culture which still values the open sea and Britain's maritime tradition.

A homogeneous political culture based on consent?

Dennis Kavanagh pointed out that a number of myths need dispelling about the nature of political culture in Britain. For example, it has been argued that Britain's island position, the existence of national government for over 800 years, and the absence of invasion and settlement have produced people of similar stock who have developed a strong sense of national identity. This view of the political culture is a myth, so it is argued, because it ignores Scottish, Irish and Welsh nationalism which have weakened the sense of national identity. Also, it ignores the racial diversity that has resulted from the growth of Britain's ethnic communities (Kavanagh, 'New bottles for new wines: changing assumptions about British Politics', *Parliamentary Affairs*, 31, 1978, pp. 6–21). Notwithstanding this, some would argue that Kavanagh is overstating his argument. This is because Britain is seen as still retaining a homogeneous political culture. This view results from a perception that British people share a *core of common values*. Because people share similar values they live together in basic harmony and cooperate with each other to overcome the problems which result from economic scarcity. The core of common values includes contents such as the right to free speech, religious toleration, freedom of assembly, support of the parliamentary system of government and the right to own property. Not all people will hold all the values in the core but they will hold some of them. Also people will be attached to some values more intensely than to others. But the point of the argument remains that an overwhelming majority of the population hold enough of these values to enable us to talk of Britain having a homogeneous political culture.

According to this viewpoint, the existence of social class would not break up the homogeneous nature of Britain's political culture. This is because neither class war nor even class conflict exists in Britain. People from all social classes seem to agree that class divisions are inevitable, even desirable. Some sociologists have argued that an open class system works like a motor to make society work more efficiently. First, there is need for the division of labour to overcome economic scarcity and, second, social class gives people incentive to work hard. Individuals high in the social strata maintain their effort in order to keep their position. On the other hand, individuals in the working class are encouraged to increase their efforts in order to enjoy upward social mobility. In everyday life you may have heard of someone 'who worked hard in order to better himself'. This describes exactly how the social class system operates and how it meets with general approval.

Others have argued that the cleavage between the middle class and working class is neither very deep nor really significant in an understanding of the social structure. In short, the working class is a part of mainstream society and not an outside threat to it. Two explanations for this accommodation by the working class to *status quo* have been offered in the shape of (i) *the embourgeoisement thesis* and (ii) the *deferential worker*.

In response to three successive Conservative victories in the general elections of the 1950s, in each case with an increased margin, it was argued by some that the growing affluence of the working class was weakening traditional loyalties to the Labour Party. The embourgeoisement thesis suggested that, because the working class had 'never had it so good' as in the post-war years, its members were being absorbed into the middle class as their standards of living rose. More and more workers enjoyed what was previously thought of as a middle-class life-style – home ownership, car ownership, foreign holidays, bank accounts, and so on. What was more natural, it was asked, than for such affluent workers to begin seeing themselves as middle class and voting for the Conservatives? Their lives were in sharp contrast to those of their fathers and grandfathers, who were poorly paid, lived in rented, poorly furnished homes and who, as often as not, had never even been inside a bank. It was the older generation who had lived in relative poverty and insecurity who felt that society was a battle between 'them and us'. The process of enbourgeoisement shattered this conflict view of society which was shared by the majority of the working class during the 1920s and 1930s.

A study conducted in Luton, published as *The Affluent Worker* (1968), suggested that the embourgeoisement thesis was not an accurate explanation of the changes that were occurring in society. The research of John Goldthorpe and his colleagues revealed a 'new' generation of workers, but one which still joined trade unions and voted Labour. However, these 'privatised' workers were without feelings of class loyalty and solidarity. They did not join a union or vote Labour because of attitudes of working-class solidarity, but because they believed union membership and Labour support would increase their standard of living. In other words, they did these things for purely practical reasons. They were 'money-minded', and their political behaviour was guided by considerations of what action would increase their affluence most. Members of the working class who voted Tory clearly posed no threat to society. Political scientists have been fascinated by working-class Tories because their behaviour seemed 'deviant' in so far as they failed to support the political party established to protect their interests. Research by Eric Nordlinger in *The Working Class Tories* (1967) and by Robert McKenzie and Alan Silver in *Angels in Marble* (1968) attempted to solve the riddle of this seemingly irrational behaviour. Their findings revealed 'secular' or 'pragmatic' working-class Tories, who gave their support to the Conservatives because they believed that they would be better off under Conservative governments. But their research also revealed the existence of deferential working-class Tories.

Deference is a rather vague concept. It implies the acceptance of a social élite that is uniquely fitted to hold office. The typical image of a deferential is a cap-doffing worker who prefers to be governed by his betters. He sees society in terms of a power pyramid, and he happily accepts his place at the bottom. It has to be said that the study of rural workers in East Anglia, *The Deferential Worker* (1977) by H. Newby, failed to substantiate this image of the deferential. Indeed, agricultural workers often shared an undeferential 'them *versus* us' view of society.

Deference is no longer accepted as a satisfactory explanation of why some working-class individuals vote Tory. Neither can working-class Tories still be viewed as a 'deviant' section of society, as the results of the 1983 and 1987 general elections showed. In the former, 40 per cent of the skilled working class voted Conservative whilst only 32 per cent supported Labour. With the Labour Party's radical election manifesto out of step with public opinion, it could be argued that those who supported Labour were now the 'political deviants'.

The consensus view of politics recognises that all citizens have some power, although some may have more power than others. Power is fragmented, dispersed and found at all levels of society. No group or institution has sufficient power to dominate all other groups and institutions. Some political power is exercised on a mandate from the members of society. Politicians use this power to achieve the collective goals of society. Realising those goals involves a bargaining process at all levels.

The political parties in Britain encourage the development of a consensual political culture. None of the major parties is based firmly on support from one particular section of society. Labour, the Conservatives, the SLD and the SDP are all national parties. At one time, Labour could rely on support from the overwhelming majority of the working class but this, as we have seen, is no longer the case.

The politics of post-war Labour and Conservative governments have been so similar that political scientists have talked of 'consensus government'. This was particularly the case during the 1950s when journalists invented the word 'Butskellite' to describe the economic and social policies of the day. It was felt that the policies followed by the Conservative Chancellor 'Rab' Butler could hardly be distinguished from those supported by his Labour shadow, Hugh Gaitskell. Even during the 1980s, when partisan differences seemed more apparent between Labour and Conservative, there was considerable agreement beneath the surface. The Conservatives were attacked for pursuing monetarist policies, yet the first modern Chancellor to adopt monetarism was Labour's Denis Healey in 1976. Even during what appear to be periods of intense conflict in the House of Commons, the differences between Labour and Conservative economic policies in practice tend to be ones of degree rather than principle. Faced with similar problems, Labour and Conservative Chancellors have produced similar solutions and followed similar policies. For example, both Labour and Conservative Chancellors have privatised State assets in order to finance government spending. The scope of privatisation not the principle has divided the parties.

How might the party system reinforce the consensual nature of the political culture? In order to answer this question, it is necessary to make one assumption. This is that political attitudes are distributed 'normally' amongst the population in the same way as physical attributes such as height or weight. In a well-known and controversial book, *An Economic Theory of Democracy* (1957), Anthony Downs explores the electoral consequences of making this assumption for its impact on the political system (Figure 2.1).

In order to *maximise* votes in an election, the party of the Left and the party of the Right find themselves competing for the same floating votes around the vertical line *xy* in Figure 2.1. Since both parties are trying to attract the support of the same electors, they tend to offer similar policies. Consensus policies emerge, then, in the same way that rival commercial products aimed at the same section of the market come to make similar claims and even come to look similar.

During the 1980s, both Labour and the Tories appeared to desert the centre ground and each party moved towards the respective extremes of its

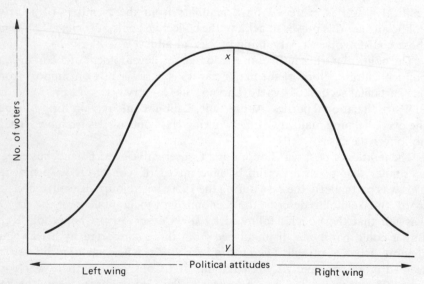

Source: A. Downs, *An Economic Theory of Democracy*, London, Harper & Row (1957) p. 118.

FIGURE 2.1   *The distribution of political attitudes among the electorate*

support. Labour represented 'Bennery' in the eyes of the electorate and the Conservative Party became the prisoner of 'Thatcherism'. Did this leave the British centre based on *xy* unrepresented by a political party? The model suggests that if people in the centre of political spectrum remain unrepresented by established parties, then new political formations will emerge to undertake this task. Therefore, on this theory it is no surprise that in 1981 a new centre party, the SDP, emerged and quickly formed an alliance with the Liberals. The phenomenal success of the SDP/Liberal Alliance in receiving around a quarter of the popular vote in the 1983 and 1987 General Elections revealed the durability and strength of the consensus in Britain's political culture.

The mass media reflect the consensual political culture in Britain with all the major newspapers sympathising with one or other of the major parliamentary parties. Some papers support a particular political party; others remain 'independent' whilst nevertheless taking a political position close to that of a parliamentary party.

Television and the newspapers tend to reflect the public's distaste of organisations which threaten to disrupt society. The media tend to attack individuals or organisations which threaten to shatter the calm of the consensus. For example, trade unions which disrupt the running of the country through strikes, or radical politicians whose policies go beyond sensible reform, are treated as 'political deviants' by the mass media. At times, newspapers are guilty of going too far in making demons out of such individuals. But the anger directed at individuals such as Tony Benn, Ken Livingstone or Arthur Scargill is a symptom of how widely and intensely the core of common values is held by the rest of society.

A diverse political culture based on conflict

If the consensus view of society sees any conflict as a temporary state of affairs, then the conflict view of society sees consensus as a temporary condition. Conflict theorists dismiss the idea of a core of common values and instead stress the diversity of values that exist in society. Since different groups have different values and are pursuing different political goals, conflict is to be expected. Conflict theorists point out that it is easy to exaggerate the extent of the consensus in British politics that lasted from the 1940s. There may have been a resurgence of conflict on the election of Mrs Thatcher to the leadership of the Conservative Party, but the seeds of conflict have always been present in the political system. For example, Mrs Thatcher's view of economic liberalism which supposedly shattered the old consensus was foreshadowed first by the resignation of Peter Thorneycroft, Enoch Powell and Nigel Birch from the Macmillan Government in 1957 because they believed that public expenditure should be cut, and, second, by the policies agreed by Edward Heath's Shadow Cabinet and outlined in the

Selsdon Park Hotel meeting in 1968. Inside the Labour Party, there have always been those who resisted consensus politics. Tony Benn's radicalism was foreshadowed by the Bevanite group in the 1950s and the Tribune group in the 1960s. In other words, the political conflict of the 1980s is nothing new.

Where does conflict in society originate? Exhibit 2.1 suggests one answer. It arises out of the scarcity of economic resources, and the fact that groups struggle to win extra resources from other groups. Usually, members of one group manage to monopolise economic resources and force all other groups into accepting their dominance. Society is not seen as being held together by a core of common values but by the power and force used by the dominant group. Conflict results from the great inequalities of wealth, power and opportunities in society. These inequalities are reflected in the existence of social classes. Although society can be divided along other lines, such as ethnic or gender, social class is recognised to be the most important grouping. Members of social classes tend to be winners or losers in social conflict. The winners benefit from conflict and enjoy more secure, more affluent, and more privileged life-styles than the losers. They are better housed, better fed, better educated and enjoy better health.

Political power is not regarded as being fragmented and dispersed throughout society. Rather it is located in the hands of a small ruling class. Political institutions such as Parliament are believed to be controlled by the ruling class. It is not easy to 'prove' this but the fact that there are few women, few blacks and few working-class individuals to be found within Westminster is used as evidence to support the argument of a ruling class. Even organisations originally set up to represent the interests of the working class – the Labour Party and the trade unions – are seen as being dominated by individuals who share the values of the ruling class. These individuals ensure that Labour and the unions follow 'moderate' policies which do not threaten the privileges of the ruling class.

The Butskellite politics of the 1950s were seen to reveal just how successfully the ruling class controls both the governing and opposition parties. The fact that Labour supporters did not feel betrayed by their party's Butskellite policies showed the extent to which the working-class subculture was manipulated in the interests of the ruling class.

How does the ruling class control the actions of other groups? Two important instruments of control in the hands of the ruling class are the educational system and the mass media. Both these instruments work towards creating a false consensus which supports the *status quo* and undermine the chances of an alternative ideology to capitalism from gaining public support. As we shall see, schooling can be used to legitimise the inequality which is to be found in wider society. In other words, the inequalities that exist between and within schools prepare pupils to accept inequalities in society as something normal. The education system is based

Exhibit 2.1 Britain as a class society

Class inequality is tenacious. Disparities in material conditions and security remain acute, against a background of rising levels of average welfare; and despite some compression of the range of economic inequality in exceptional circumstances, around the time of the two world wars of this century. Ownership of wealth in particular is still highly concentrated. Possession of small property that carries no power – housing for owner occupation, cars and household goods – is more widespread than it was. Not so ownership for profit – property in business shares and securities – some diffusion within families of the rich apart. Public provision for social security has been greatly expanded; so in general have most services and activities of the state. But this has occurred within a framework of policy and practice which leaves the cost of working-class welfare as a charge mainly on working-class earnings, and control of the machinery well away from the hands of rank-and-file labour. Levels of formal education in the population at large have been steadily stepped up by government action. Schools and colleges have been set more deliberately to the business of preparing and sorting young people for their places in the world of work. Yet, limited though the vision which inspires it is, the liberal goal of free opportunity according to individual merits is little nearer achievement. There is a good deal of social circulation, down as well as up; but marked still by sharp disparities of prospects in life according to class origin; and not much more of it well into the second half of this century than by the beginning of the first. As yet, channels of social mobility have changed far more than rates of flow. It is possible that rates, too, could rise: the balance between pressures for efficient use of talent and the restrictions of formal and informal inheritance is not unalterably fixed. But in the pervasive nature of class inequalities of condition and power, the balance is likely to shift only within rather narrow limits.

Private capital is the central force behind the persistence of these and related inequalities of life circumstances. In the simplest and most visible sense: because the concentration of high incomes in few hands arises in substantial part from a still sharper concentration of property in private ownership. Less directly but far more significantly: because the principles which govern allocation and use of most resources reflect the dominance of private capital. The routine assumptions that set the principal parameters of life and policy are capitalist. Ownership of property, however acquired, constitutes an automatic claim on resources and, in sufficient quantity, confers on its beneficiaries an effective right not to work. By contrast, the livelihood of non-owners – the great majority – is set by the terms on which they can sell their labour in the market; or they depend on state support which, at levels generally well below labour market earnings, imposes a penalty for not working, even on those who are retired because of old age or sickness. Production and investment, moreover, are determined by the imperatives associated with the institution of private property: by the search for maximum long-run return to capital in markets where demand itself is shaped by the capital- and market-formed pattern of income distribution.

John Westergaard and Henrietta Resler, *Class in a Capitalist Society: A Study of Contemporary Britain*, London, Heinemann (1975) pp. 343–4

on the ideology of competition and is seen as preparing young people for their widely differing roles in the capitalist system.

The mass media are perceived as being controlled by the ruling class. Most national newspapers are owned by large capitalist concerns which have an interest in the survival of the existing economic order. Newspapers, it is argued, project commercial values. It is not surprising, therefore, that almost all daily newspapers support either the Conservative or Labour parties. No paper supports left-wing Labour views. Television is tightly controlled by law and projects consensus values. The mass media fail to reflect the views of minorities. Minorities which threaten the *status quo*, such as women's lib, unilateral disarmers or trade unionists are discredited and presented in the media as irresponsible or even dangerous. Minorities such as Rastafarians which reject society's dominant values are simply ignored. Thus, the mass media do not so much reflect the views of their readers and viewers as create those views in the first place. The main message transmitted through the media is that there is no alternative to the present system.

POLITICAL SOCIALISATION

The process by which individuals learn the culture of their society is referred to as socialisation, and the process by which they learn their political culture is known as political socialisation. The first major study of the political socialisation process was Herbert Hyman's book, *Political Socialization* (1959). During the 1960s, there was a great deal of research into political socialisation in the political science departments of many American and some British universities. However, much of this research has since been criticised for being based on dubious assumptions and for employing shoddy research methods. As a consequence, academic interest in political socialisation has declined to a very great extent over recent years.

We have already seen that the political culture in Britain is a controversial subject and is understood in fundamentally different ways. The way the political culture is learnt is also defined in different ways. For example, Roberta Sigel reflects the consensus view of society when she states: 'political socialization refers to the process by which people learn to adopt the norms, values, attitudes, and behaviour accepted and practised by the ongoing system' (Sigel, *Learning about Politics*, 1970, p. xii). According to this definition, political socialisation is the learning of only those attitudes, values and behaviours which contribute to the basic stability of the existing political system. In other words, political socialisation is limited to the process of learning the core of common values which form society's consensus.

David Easton and Jack Dennis have defined political socialisation as the process by which *any* political values or behaviours are learnt. They argued that political socialisation consists of 'those developmental processes through which persons acquire political orientations and patterns of behaviour' (Easton and Dennis, *Children in the Political System* (1969) p. 7). Such orientations and patterns of behaviour may or may not contribute to the stability of the existing political order. In his study of politics in Northern Ireland, *Governing Without Consensus* (1971), Richard Rose explored how children were socialised into conflict. Children in one community learnt allegiance to the existing political system, whilst those in the other community learnt to oppose it.

The agencies of political socialisation

The sources which influence the political learning of an individual are known as the agencies of political socialisation. These agencies supply *information* and *judgements* about politics, and influence the individual's political *behaviour*. The most influential agencies are the family, education, peer groups, the mass media and important political events or experiences. We will consider four of these agencies separately, but in reality the influence of one agency will be modified in some way by the influence of other agencies. For example, an individual born into an upper middle-class family may receive messages about politics from his family, his public school and his friends which reinforce each other. But then he may be moved by seeing a play written by a radical playwright such as Alan Bleasdale or David Storey. He may then receive messages about poverty, unemployment or the need for social change which contradict most of what he has learnt from the other agencies. In other words, every individual stands in the middle of a network of social influences and we must not forget this when we analyse the agencies.

The family

In all societies, the family is a key agent in transmitting the political culture from one generation to the next. The importance of the family in political socialisation is easy to understand. The family is generally a small primary group in which deep emotional relationships exist between members. The deeper the emotional ties between people, the more influence is likely to be wielded. Also, the family has a near monopoly over access to its children in their formative years when the foundations of political belief are being laid. There may be no influence on very young children other than the family.

Some political scientists have argued that the family is like a political system in miniature. The parent–child relationship is hierarchic and this is where the child first learns to recognise authority. Parents and children cannot be equals during the early years of socialisation and so children experience power first hand. Parents are authoritative figures in the eyes of their children and wield power over them. The family is thus a power structure in which young children learn to play a subordinate role. However, in adolescence, the authority of parents may be rejected or challenged by teenagers who 'rebel' against their parents.

Robert Lane has suggested there are three ways in which a child's political outlook is influenced by the family:

1. by conscious or unconscious political indoctrination;
2. by placing the child in a particular social class and giving him particular cultural values;
3. by moulding the child's personality (Lane, *Political Man*, 1972, p. 6).

An example of conscious indoctrination in the family would be the political learning by children in the Protestant and Catholic communities in Northern Ireland. Children are deliberately made aware of their cultural identity. On the other hand, subconscious indoctrination may take place in the way children learn sex roles from their parents. For example, daughters learn what women's place in society is through observing and learning from their mothers.

The family also affects the political outlook of its children by placing them within a particular network of social and economic relations. The family has an ethnic, religious and class identity which is passed on to each child. With this will go a particular set of political orientations. Finally, the family plays an important role in developing the child's personality. An individual's personality conditions the way in which he will respond to political situations. The family is the major place in which a child develops his basic identity. His experience in the family may influence whether he develops an authoritarian personality (which includes attitudes of dominance towards subordinates and deference towards superiors) or a democratic personality (including warm attitudes towards other people and shared values). The family environment may influence a person's development of tough-minded (fatalistic, going by 'facts') or tender-minded (optimistic, believing in principles) political attitudes.

Education

Some argue that 'politics must be kept out of education' whilst others believe that education is a powerful ideological force which preserves the existing political order. Political-socialisation research findings confirm that education is a very political process and that schools help to reproduce the inequalities found in wider society.

In an advanced industrial society such as Britain, the major features of the educational system result from its task of producing a workforce able to fill roles in the economy. Education therefore reflects the structure of wider society and reproduces or recreates a stratified society. In his study of educational change in Britain during the last century, 'Education and social change in modern England' (1961), David Glass revealed two distinct sets of considerations which influenced schooling; one related to the middle class and the other to the working class. The main concern of secondary education for the middle class was that it should be successful in getting wealth and maintaining the social status of its pupils when they left school. Elementary education for the working class was designed to produce four responses: to 'gentle' the masses; to instil discipline; to obtain respect for private property and the social order; and to provide the instruction which was necessary for an industrial nation. Research conducted during the 1960s and 1970s revealed that different types of school were still producing different types of political beings. For example, P. R. Abramson found that public school pupils were more likely than others to develop feelings of social and political competence and political interest ('Political Socialisation in English and American Secondary Schools,' *The High School Journal*, 54, 1970, p. 72). Grammar school pupils were more likely to express political competence and political interest than pupils in comprehensive or secondary modern schools. 45 per cent of the public school sample were 'somewhat' or 'very' interested in politics. Only 37 per cent of grammar school pupils and 25 per cent of non-selected pupils expressed an interest in politics.

Some research findings have stirred up considerable controversy in the academic world. For example, a study by J. Dennis, L. Lindberg and D. J. McCrone (1971) revealed that English pupils exhibited far less support for the political system than did children in other countries. Another study which was criticised for its methods suggested that comprehensive and secondary modern pupils knew less about democracy than did pupils from grammar and public schools.

How does the educational system work in order to produce different political orientations amongst pupils? To answer this, we have to examine the way schools work. Institutions are organised to produce certain attitudes. Schools are complex institutions, which exhibit a network of formal relations and public goals together with informal relations and unofficial goals. Each school can be seen as a small political system, in which individuals and groups compete for power and resources. Viewed in this light the school timetable is not a neutral piece of paper but a political document which allocates resources. Ken Shaw (1980) has described it as a 'Bill of Rights' and argued that the inequalities built into the timetable reflect the inequalities found in society at large.

The school, then, has a power structure in which the hierarchy is more clearly defined than in the family. Again, unlike the family, the school has a bureaucracy to assist with the running of the organisation. Pupils learn to adapt to this power structure and bureaucracy through what is known as the 'hidden curriculum'.

The hidden curriculum is just as much a source of learning as the formal curriculum. 'Deferring to authority', 'knowing one's place', and 'waiting one's turn' are messages that go towards achieving conformity in the behaviour of pupils. In *Life in Classrooms* (1968) one sociologist, P. W. Jackson, has calculated that pupils spend over 1000 hours a year at school and for most of this time the teacher is talking or directing affairs. Lesson after lesson teaches pupils to expect to be passive and to obey authority – not exactly an appropriate political education for participating in politics later in life.

Of course not all pupils conform to the hidden curriculum. Another sociologist, Paul Willis, described the behaviour of 'the lads' at Hammertown Boys School. In his book, *Learning to Labour* (1977), he described ways in which the lads opposed school authority and rejected the rules of the school. The lads' behaviour constituted a counter-school culture, which attempted to give them power to control their lives at school.

Peer groups

Peer groups form another example of political socialisation within a primary group. These groups may be childhood play groups, friendship groups, or work groups. Membership of a group is likely to influence many things that an individual will learn, experience and think about. The peer group may provide an individual with much of his understanding of the political world, and how he fits into it. Peer groups act as reference groups; that is, individuals are guided by the attitudes and values of their close associates because they like or respect them.

If an individual admires a particular group and wishes to join that group, he is likely to begin to behave like the existing members of the group. *Anticipatory socialisation* refers to the way an individual learns to fit in with the views of a group that he hopes to join. An individual in a group may be made to conform with the attitudes of other members because he fears punishment, ridicule or rejection if he does not. On the factory floor workers involved in an industrial dispute may attempt to get one of their group to conform to the majority view by 'sending him to Coventry'. The only way that he will be readmitted to his work group is by changing his attitudes or behaviour.

Mass media

Contemporary research findings suggest that the mass media have a considerable role in the political socialisation process. This was not always the case since early research into the subject led to the conclusion that the media made little impact on political behaviour. This view of the media's role resulted from the way in which early social scientists understood the media to work. They believe that the influence of the mass media was indirect, because of the 'two-step flow' in the communication of information (see Figure 2.2).

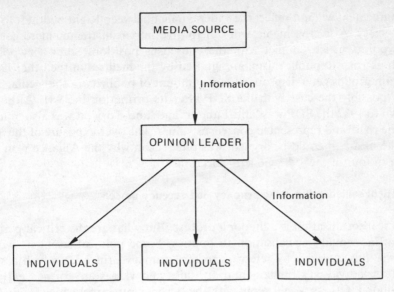

FIGURE 2.2　*The two-step model of the role of the media in the communication of information*

It was believed that information from the mass media – newspapers, radio and television – was not communicated directly to the public. Instead information was communicated via 'opinion leaders' who interpreted it before passing it on to the public. Opinion leaders were simply the most politically aware members of primary groups such as the family or peer groups. Because of the two-step flow via opinion leaders, it was felt that group values modified any influence that the media may have possessed.

This picture of communication resulted from fear expressed by some that the USA might become a Fascist State. Social scientists were keen to be reassured that any State propaganda machine in the USA would not give the power that Hitler wielded in Germany. The two-step-flow theory of communication allowed liberals to be confident that any unhealthy state propaganda would be countered by opinion leaders who held traditional American values. But, in reality, the mass media communicate directly and have a near monopoly over political information which is passed to the public.

The influence of the mass media will be considered in greater detail in Chapter 14. At this stage it is argued that the mass media in Britain help to create a consensus of opinion about politics. The media legitimise the political system and effectively prevent the growth of public support for radical change. Conflict is expressed in the mass media, but the media never reflect the actual extent of conflict that exists in parts of society. For example, although the editorial in the Conservative *Daily Telegraph* may differ from the line taken in the Labour-inclined *Daily Mirror* the extent of their disagreement will not reflect the wider conflict between Right and Left found in society. Also, the media will fail to give impartial treatment to certain viewpoints which conflict with the consensus position. Some viewpoints, such as Irish Republicanism, are ignored by the media. On the other hand, certain groups get a disproportionate amount of publicity in the media. This was possibly the case with the SDP after its formation in 1981. Although down to 1987 the SDP was 'anti-Labour' and 'anti-Tory', it was also 'middle of the road' and represented consensus values. The over-exposure of the SDP in the media, it could be argued, was one reason why the Alliance won one vote in four in the 1983 General Election.

Political socialisation – the primacy and recency models

Political socialisation is a life-long process. But what are the critical periods in an individual's socialisation to politics? Some political scientists would answer this question by referring to the 'primacy principle', which asserts that an individual's fundamental attitudes and values are formed early in childhood. Others would reply with the 'recency principle' which holds that the closer a learning experience is to adulthood, the greater its influence on political attitudes and behaviour will be.

The *primacy principle* assumes that the family is the most influential agency of socialisation. According to this theory, an individual's basic orientation towards authority is developed within the family. If the primacy principle is correct then the most critical period of political socialisation results in strong allegiance to the political system. This is because young children are highly dependent on adults and idealise authority figures. It is this early idealisation of authority that later produces strong support for the political system.

The *recency principle* assumes that peer groups and political experiences are more influential in the socialisation process than is early upbringing in the family. The recency model might explain Labour's increase in electoral support between 1918 and 1929 and the party's dramatic breakthrough in the 1945 General Election. The harsh experiences of two world wars and an economic depression provided an environment of hardship which influenced generations into supporting the party of change. In contrast, many of those in the generations who grew up during the affluent period of the 1960s and 1970s saw less reason for supporting Labour. In the 1983 General Election, fewer than one young person in three voted for Labour whereas 42 per cent voted for the Conservative party.

SUMMARY

This chapter has examined different ways in which Britain's political culture has been approached by political scientists. There is sharp disagreement

between them about whether Britain has a homogeneous political culture based on consent or a diverse political culture based on conflict. Although Britain is a multicultural society, political scientists also do not agree on whether it is politically multicultural. The ways in which young people learn the political culture was considered in terms of the concept of political socialisation and the agencies of socialisation. Although ideas concerning political socialisation have been criticised in recent years, it is still useful to think of political learning as taking place in the family, in school, through peer groups and the mass media. But which agencies are the most influential in the socialisation process and when they are influential, in terms of an individual's life cycle, remain open questions.

FURTHER READING

Abramson, P. R. (1970) 'Political Socialisation in English and American Secondary Schools', *The High School Journal*, vol. 54.

Dennis, J., Lindberg, L. and McCrone, D. J. (1971) 'Support for Nation and Government among English Schoolchildren', *British Journal of Political Science*, vol. I.

Glass, D. V. (1961) 'Location and Social Change in Modern England', in A. H. Halsey, J. Floud and C. A. Anderson, *Education, Economy and Society*, New York, Free Press.

Reid, I. (1981) *Social Class Differences in Britain: A Sourcebook*, Shepton Mallett, Open Books.

Robins, L. (1982) 'Political Socialisation in British Schools: Some Political and Sociological Approaches', in L. Robins (ed.) *Topics in British Politics*, London, Politics Association.

Shaw, K. E. (1980) 'The Timetable: A Bill of Rights?', *Teaching Politics*, vol. 9.

Stacey, B. (1978) *Political Socialisation in Western Society*, London, Edward Arnold.

Tapper, T. and Bowles, N. (1982) 'Working-class Tories: The Search for Theory', in L. Robins (ed.) *Topics in British Politics*, London, Politics Association.

QUESTIONS

1. Is Britain's political culture best described as being based on conflict or consensus?
2. Describe how the agencies of socialisation might operate to influence an individual's understanding of politics.
3. Why have 'working-class Conservatives' been a topic of greater interest than 'middle class radicals' to political scientists?

ASSIGNMENT

Political scientists have conducted a number of surveys which examine the links between the political awareness of pupils and the type of school attended. Construct a brief questionnaire which could be used to measure the extent of political knowledge that exists amongst Britain's 16-year-olds. As far as possible ensure that your questions are equally meaningful to young people who live in different parts of the country. Do not confine your questions to parliamentary topics and consider whether items on international politics would be appropriate. Finally, check that each question is clearly worded and that it cannot be interpreted in different ways.

3

Ideology and Politics

We noticed in Chapter 1 that politics not only involves public conflict over the distribution of scarce resources but also includes public competition between differing beliefs. These beliefs, when expressed as or forming part of systems of ideas, are called *ideologies*. It is the purpose of this chapter to look more closely at ideology. In particular, we shall be concerned with two questions. First, what is ideology and what is its political significance? Second, what are the leading doctrines of the major ideologies of the modern world and what form do they assume in the British context?

THE MEANING AND POLITICAL SIGNIFICANCE OF IDEOLOGY

An ideology is a belief-system which serves as a guide to action and the importance of ideologies in politics is that they shape political behaviour. They do this by providing pictures of the world which show how it has come to be as it is; how it is likely to change; what changes are desirable and undesirable; and how the former can be facilitated and the latter controlled. Ideologies appeal to people as members of particular social groups – governing, business, ethnic, racial, national, religious – as classes, and as sexes. They aim to extend such groupings (which includes adding to them sympathisers who are not actually 'members') and to build up their morale. The word 'extend' here calls for further explanation. It is obviously not possible for a Socialist to increase the actual numbers of the working class, for a Scottish Nationalist to make the population of Scotland greater than it is or for a feminist to augment the number of women in society. What each ideologist can, and does, strive to do is to enlist more workers, Scots and women to their respective causes. They try to effect both a shift in individual *perspectives* on the world and a more intense *identification* with a specific category of people. To the extent that they succeed, their 'target-groups' will probably, but not inevitably, behave differently towards other sections of society – workers towards 'bosses', Scots towards the English and women towards men in a 'male-dominated' society.

The core of a political ideology, then, is its commitment to some political ideal, be it national independence or resurgence, the social ownership of the means of production or the equality of the sexes. By supplying more-or-less

39

comprehensive justifications of principled convictions about the proper organisation of society, ideologies make politics more than a struggle for power and material benefits. Ideologies may be called upon to provide legitimacy both for forms of government (the Divine Right of the Monarchy until the eighteenth century; democracy today) and for economic systems (capitalism or communism). They endorse the existing social and political systems and also set goals that may yet be achieved. This is not meant to imply that ideology leads directly to political action. No straight line can be drawn between beliefs and action, the relationship between what we believe and what we do often being indirect, and usually subtle. Marx can no more be held responsible for the Bolshevik Revolution of 1917 than can Rousseau for the French Revolution. Nonetheless, it is true that in comparison with any academic discipline – history, for example, or philosophy or physics – which aims at *understanding*, the intention of ideology is to *persuade*. It was the ideologue in Marx who was speaking when he said that whereas in the past philosophers had sought to understand the world, the point was to *change* it. Ideology, then, aims to convince that this or that course of action is the right one; and it is, of course, true that we expect people to act upon their convictions. If they agree with Mill and yet do nothing about a freer and more tolerant society, they are (rightly) suspected of insincerity. Ideology need not act as a powerful influence upon political behaviour, but in practice it often does so.

We are now in a position to define ideology.

Definition

Ideology is any set of ideas about human nature, society and history which can gain the commitment of significant numbers of individuals for or against political change.

Two more points are worth making before we consider the main political ideologies in detail. First, the forms taken by ideology vary from country to country and from century to century. In the USSR, for example, there is an official ideology – Marxist–Leninism. The writings of Marx and Lenin are regarded as sacred texts and continually used as justifications of policy. Throughout Africa and Asia, nationalism has been the predominant ideology since 1945 – to rally peoples against the occupying power in anti-colonial liberation wars, to integrate disparate tribal elements in post-independence regimes and – often allied to some variant of Socialism – to mobilise the new country behind a drive to modernisation. In the West, liberal values are all-pervasive and deeply rooted and there is wide support for individualism, with its associated ideas and practices – freedom of conscience, speech and association, legal and political equality, the rights of private property, toleration, and the separation of State and civil society. Also, ideologies change their function over time, the same ideology appearing as revolutionary to one generation and being put to conservative purposes by later generations. Thus, liberalism was a revolutionary ideology in the late eighteenth century: as encapsulated in the slogans the 'rights of man' and 'liberty, equality, fraternity', it expressed the demands of the American and French Revolutionaries. By the mid-nineteenth, it had become the dominant ideology in Britain and the USA, the 'ideology of the age', but it was itself under attack from Socialists, the new enemies on the left. Revolutionary itself in the nineteenth century and the ideology of the second, Bolshevik, revolution in 1917, Marxism soon became, as we have seen, the official ideology of the USSR, serving a fundamentally conservative function.

Second, ideology is closely related to those versions of the past which also mould social and political behaviour – namely, myth and tradition. The link between ideology and myth can be simply illustrated by reference again to socialism, nationalism and feminism. Each of these ideologies seeks to mobilise and to spur to action the particular groups to which it appeals (respectively, the working class, the nation and women) and accordingly, as we have seen, allocates each a specific social role (respectively, to fight the capitalist, imperialist and male oppressor). The roles are invariably romanticised, being presented in a somewhat 'ideal' light, an idealisation which, extending into the past, involves a highly selective version of history – in short, the use of history as *myth*. Past moments of 'heroic' activity by the group in question receive especial stress: for example, the mass action in the streets of Paris in 1789 which overthrew the French old régime; Petrograd in 1917 which broke the tsarist autocracy (by Socialists); past battles (not always victorious) and charismatic leaders (by nationalists), and historical campaigns like the one for political equality led by the Suffragettes (by feminists). The point here is not that the episodes referred to are not true; they often do contain a great deal of truth. The point is rather the ideological intention of such exercises: there is no attempt to be critical, to depict the protagonists on the 'right' side in such struggles with all their failings, 'warts and all'; only to persuade. They appeal to the romantic in all of us, our liking for the heroic, our desire to be identified with a group in the achievement of a good cause, our sociability. Finally, and more briefly, ideology can make use of another selective version of a particular past – a political *tradition*. The concept of political tradition refers to those modes of political behaviour, a mixture of values and practices, which have come to be widely-accepted in a society. In Britain, for instance, the political tradition includes a respect for parliament as an institution, a belief in free speech, tolerance of what in many other countries (the USA for example) would be regarded as a very secretive system of government, and a repugnance for violent behaviour and behaviour which is outside the law. Calls for political action which run up against these norms almost invariably encounter difficulty, and at least part of the explanation for this is that conservatives may so easily invoke the traditional modes of behaviour against such proposals; that is, they can ideologise the political tradition. Thus, the proposal for proportional representation has to contend not only with the opposition of the party in government which is content with the electoral system by which it has gained power but also with the general public belief that the existing system 'works', a belief which the governing party itself, acting ideologically, seeks to mobilise.

We turn now to a consideration of the leading ideologies of the modern world – conservatism, nationalism, fascism, liberalism and socialism. For each ideology we provide a description of its leading tenets, or articles of belief, followed by a brief account of its significance in recent British political experience. Descriptions of each ideology focus particularly upon its conceptions of human nature; social class; nation; progress and history; and participation, power and authority. Our aim is to provide a picture – as vivid a one as possible – of *how the political universe appears in each ideology*. We phrase it this way deliberately, despite the temptation to write 'how each ideology views the political universe'. For, as David Manning has neatly put it, the liberal and Marxist understanding of capitalism are not two different views of the same thing, capitalism is two entirely different things in their view (Manning, *Liberalism*, p. 141). We begin with the world as seen by Conservatives.

Conservatism

There were Conservatives before the late eighteenth century but Conservatism as a modern political ideology began in the 1790s as a reaction against the French Revolution. It originated in opposition to political Radicalism, that is, to a particular set of doctrines about the nature of man, of society and of political change. These were respectively (and we shall encounter them directly in considering liberalism and socialism) the inherent goodness and rationality of man; the idea of society as a mere collection of isolated individuals; and, finally, the notion of the feasibility, and desirability, of radical (i.e. root and branch) political change, accomplished by revolutionary methods.

Modern Conservatism, which began as a European movement in resistance to the Radical ideology of the rights of man, continued in the nineteenth century in opposition to political and economic *Liberalism* and, in the twentieth century, has seen its main enemy as statist and totalitarian *Socialism*. As Noël O'Sullivan argues, nineteenth-century Conservatives opposed the idea that the only legitimate form of government is self-government, or democracy (the key political concept of nineteenth-century radical Liberalism), on two main grounds (O'Sullivan, *Conservatism* (1976) pp. 15–20). First, they maintained that taken to its logical conclusion, this doctrine leads to an uncompromising, intransigent type of politics in which the sole court of appeal is the desire or will of the individual. If the only acceptable limits or restraints on the individual members of a community are those they impose upon themselves, what happens when agreement breaks down? In principle, there is no reason why they need resort to force since they could agree beforehand to accept the majority decision. In practice, however, they often do so, and they are encouraged in this by the idea that their own wishes have paramount authority and all external authority is an imposition. Second, Conservatives felt that the concept of self-government focused attention too much upon the *origins* of the authority of a government at the expense of the wisdom, or otherwise, of its *decisions*, which in their view was the proper concern of citizens. The democratic ideology, therefore, could be used to sanction the rule of any petty tyrant who could lay claim to have received the support of the people in some way – however dubious – e.g. plebiscites. Nineteenth-century Conservatives opposed economic Liberalism (the doctrine of *laissez-faire*) on the grounds that its unrestricted application in the shape of the free market economy led to excessive and remediable suffering, especially of groups like women and children who could not defend themselves. For this, it drew upon its tradition of *paternalism*, which embodied the concern of the propertied sections of society for those worse off than themselves.

The 1920s brought a major reorientation of Conservatism in domestic politics, to face the assertion of class interest by organised labour together with the Socialist threat to use the State as an instrument of social levelling and, internationally, to counter the menace of totalitarianism consequent upon the Bolshevik Revolution. In accomplishing this change, Conservatism drew upon both Liberalism and Socialism. First, as institutional Liberalism (in the form of the Liberal Party) collapsed, Conservatism absorbed much of its ideology – in particular its support for the market economy, for preservation of the State/Society distinction and for the protection of the political liberty of the individual – deploying these values against Socialism in all its varieties. But it remained distinct from Liberalism in its endorsement of the strong centralised State, resisting, for example, all ideas of devolution and decentralisation. As a consequence of its traditional belief in firm and paternalistic government, twentieth-century Conservatism was the more easily able to adapt to the more interventionist (collectivist or 'Socialist') State which developed after 1945 in the form of the welfare state and the managed economy. At the same time as moving towards acceptance of some of the welfare goals of Labour, Conservatism remained distinct in its ideological sympathy for private enterprise in the 'mixed' economy. Since the late 1960s, as we shall see in more detail later, Conservative *policy* has tilted strongly towards reducing the role of the State. To sum up, although over two centuries, Conservatism has changed in certain ways – most notably in the character of the élite it has defended (from territorial–aristocratic to business–professional–managerial) and in the nature of the State it has been required to endorse (non-democratic and individualist to democratic and interventionist) – the fundamental elements of Conservative ideology remain: scepticism about the possibility of radical (and preference for gradual) change; belief in rule by an energetic and capable élite; and strongly patriotic support for the interests of the nation.

The following ideas and beliefs, held in differing combinations, with divergent emphases and varying intensity, by actual Conservatives, may be said to characterise British Conservatism as a modern ideology. The extent to which emphases may diverge is well-exemplified by Mrs Thatcher's Conservatism. To some, her radical rather than gradualist approach to change, her rejection of pragmatic in favour of conviction politics and her seeming contempt for constitutional checks and balances place her outside the Conservative tradition. However, her vigorous assertion of the merits of private property, the free market economy, a powerful State (national defence and policing) and of primary institutions like the family place her squarely in a Conservative tradition stretching back to Burke.

1   *Human fallibility*

A deep vein of pessimism runs through the Conservative concept of human nature. Against those who believe in its perfectibility, Conservatives stress the fixed, unchanging and irremediable imperfection of mankind. This frailty of humanity has two sides: moral and intellectual. Thus, morally, although the affective dimension of human nature underlies much which is of enduring social value – loyalty, bravery, faith, family feeling, for example – human beings are also creatures of anti-social passions which, unassisted, they are unable to control. This emphasis upon the moral flaw in human nature has in some Conservatives flowed from Christian belief in the sinfulness of mankind, but it does not logically have to do so, and in many cases it has not, secular Conservatives reaching the same conclusion by a different route. In any case, what matters here is not the origin of the belief but its consequences: a firm conviction that, since self-control alone is inadequate to the task, institutions outside the individual – church, law, government – are needed to keep the passions in check. Second, against those ideologies on the left which have emphasised human rationality and in general accorded a high place to reason in human affairs, Conservatives have repeatedly drawn attention to the limitations of the human mind, the intellectual fallibility of mankind. As Edmund Burke wrote: 'We are afraid to put men to live and trade each on his own private stock of reason; because we suspect that this stock in each man is small . . .' (Burke, *Reflections on the Revolution in France* 1790, p. 183). The imperfection of the political judgement of the individual contrasts with the wisdom of the community. Burke continues: 'and that the individuals would do better to avail themselves of the general bank and capital of nations, and of ages'. To a consideration of what Conservatives mean when they speak of the individual being foolish and the community wise, we now turn in the following two points.

2 *Traditionalism and the organic nature of society*

Conservatives use the metaphor of an organism when describing society. That is, they consider society to be more like a plant or a tree which has grown than a machine which has been constructed. Societies are not devised, created or built; they evolve. And what has evolved exists now because of its ability to satisfy human needs in some way. For Conservatives certain political conclusions follow from the organic concept of society:

(i) *traditionalism*: the present generation should respect its historical inheritance. Properly speaking, it is only a trustee for the society's language, culture and institutions and has an obligation to hand them on undamaged to future generations.

(ii) *social interdependence and unity*: the various groups, classes and institutions which compose a society have grown together so that the whole consists of a vast number of organically-related parts, each with its allotted role, like organs in a body. Hence Conservatives stress cooperation and partnership rather than disagreement and conflict as the way a society must develop.

The role of the politician is clear – he or she must seek to preserve and even improve the laws and institutions inherited from the past, but always cautiously, always in accordance with the way they have developed (in Burke's words, with an eye to the 'style' of the building) and being always careful to enhance partnership and minimise social discord.

3 *A preference for gradual change*

The concepts discussed under (1) and (2) provide the theoretical justification for the Conservative doctrine of change. Conservatives hold strong views both on the *kind* of change which is desirable and also upon the *manner* of change, how it should be conducted. Thus, against advocates of large-scale, even total, change, they advocate gradual improvement. Human reason is too fallible to provide blueprints for the perfect society: such designs are invariably abstract and remote from actual human experience. As the evidence of historical revolutions shows, radicals may aim to create a heaven on earth but invariably succeed in creating only a hell. They never accomplish their original purpose, but end with dictatorship or totalitarianism rather than freedom, and kill large numbers of people on the way to these grisly destinations. Rather than being an exact science, politics is an art.

Since each society is different, the action a ruler should take varies according to time, place and circumstance; in other words, according to the stage of a society's development, the way in which it has evolved (its history) and the state of public opinion. In the words of Anthony Quinton, politics, for the Conservative, is 'the expedient pursuit of the public advantage' (Quinton, *The Politics of Imperfection*, 1978, ch. 3). This implies a pragmatic attitude to change. Thus, what may be considered appropriate political action always accepts changes which are not reversible without unacceptable public upheaval: for example, democracy, resisted in eighteenth-century Britain, was acceptable by the twentieth century. In the minds of Conservatives, closely related to this preference for gradualness is a concern that change should be orderly. This concern takes the form of an emphasis upon the need to observe established procedures and existing constitutional forms when carrying out political changes.

4   *Rule by an élite*

Conservatives believe that rule by an élite is both inevitable and desirable. It is inevitable because inequality – of power and influence as well as of wealth and income – seems on the historical evidence to be structured into society. Attempts to eliminate inequality usually end in disaster with the emergence of an unwelcome form of élite – witness the Bolshevik Party in the USSR. It is desirable because the qualities – including intellectual ability – required by government are, in fact, unevenly spread throughout society. Only a relatively limited section, therefore, is capable of providing the leadership which society requires (even if this section is growing as educational opportunities expand). Rule by this élite is clearly in the interest of the general public, which wants the best government it can get. Elites (party, managerial and bureaucratic) must be accountable, responsive to public opinion and should govern according to established procedures. The rest of society equally has a duty to respond to the initiatives of the élite.

5   *Nationalism*

Conservatives are strongly patriotic, indeed nationalist, in their outlook. This perspective on the world is demonstrated in the very high political priority they accord to the preservation of the integrity of the 'nation' against internal separatist pressures and external threats. Distaste for behaviour which divides rather than binds together the nation, including that which exacerbates class hatred as well as ethnic disintegration; a pride in the nation's historical achievements – political, literary, scientific, military; and a permanent preoccupation with matters of national security and defence, which can include shame for policy episodes when the country's external posture was weak, e.g. appeasement. All these are aspects of an ideology which sees the 'nation' as the primary historical and political unit.

6 *Law, government and the Constitution*

Respect for the rule of law; a belief in the need for strong yet limited government; and the idea that power is conferred from above rather than originating from below are deeply-embedded in British Conservatism. The law deserves respect not only because of the value attaching to all historically-evolving institutions but also more pragmatically because it is a guarantee against disorder. Conservatives, typically, place great emphasis upon the maintenance of public order. As a consequence, and also because, like the rule of law, it is sanctioned by history as part of the British political tradition, Conservatives extol strong government and pay considerable attention to supporting the main policing and law-enforcing agencies.

The laws should be observed and government should have the power necessary to enforce its authority, but not at the expense of the liberties of the citizen. Conservatives are not *authoritarians*: the need itself to act within the law is one restraint upon government and guarantee of individual freedom. Another check – one borrowed from eighteenth-century liberalism – is the way in which organs of government balance each other within the State (Ministers, the two Houses of Parliament, Whitehall). The action of each is held to be restrained by having to gain the consent of or act in concert with another; this is the idea of the balanced constitution. Second, Conservatives believe in *limited government* (another Liberal legacy) – that is, in the preservation of a firm distinction between State and Society, public and private life, a boundary which has changed dramatically in the twentieth century.

Finally, for Conservatives, the British political tradition is a Tory tradition, a historical process by which authority in the Constitution has gradually spread out in ripples from a central (initially monarchical) power, first to take in parliament and then, from the eighteenth century, as a parliamentary monarchy with an aristocratic base, to absorb the middle and working classes in successive centuries. The point is that in the Conservative perception of the British Constitution authority flows from the top, sanctioned by historical precedent; it does not emanate from the people. As L. S. Amery has written in *Thoughts on the Constitution* (1953), British democracy is 'democracy by consent and not by delegation', government of, for and with but not *by* the people (cited by S. Beer, *Modern British Politics*, p. 95). Rulers rule, leaders lead; the ruled and the led, at elections and party conferences, endorse and consent (or not, as the case may be). Either way, a passive role is all that is required of them.

NATIONALISM

The core of nationalism as an ideology is reducible to four propositions. Nationalists believe that:

1. The world is naturally divided into nations.
2. Each nation has its own unique character resulting from its history and culture including, especially, its language.
3. Each nation should be independent or, at least, should possess a large measure of autonomy; only in running its own affairs can it achieve self-realisation.
4. The first loyalty, the primary allegiance of the individual, is to the nation-state.

As is immediately apparent, the central concept of nationalist ideology is the idea of the 'nation'. Its basic political doctrine flows from this idea: that each 'nation' should form itself into a State. It has proved to be a doctrine of striking potency in the modern world.

For the emergence of nationalism as an ideology, the era of the French Revolution (c.1789–1815) was decisive. During these years, three ideas fused to create the modern doctrine:

(i)   the concept of the State as a particular form of territorially based civil association;
(ii) the idea of the sovereignty of the people, popular government or democracy;
(iii) the definition of a 'people' or 'nation' in terms of its culture, including, especially, its language.

The Revolution itself brought about the combination of the first two of these ideas by extending the basis of a previously monarchical State ('*L'Etat, c'est moi*', stated Louis XIV) to include the whole people. 'The nation', according to the famous Declaration of the Rights of Man and of Citizens in 1789, 'is essentially the source of all sovereignty'. The case for democracy was certainly made in theory even though in practice voting rights were limited. Thus far, we have the concept of the democratic State but not as yet the doctrine of the democratic nation-State, despite the reference in the quotation to 'the nation'. The French at the time of the Revolution already lived in a 'nation-State' and had done for over 200 years. The point here is that because they could *assume* the existence of a French 'nation', they did not have to concern themselves with the question of how to *define* it. The problem of the character of the community that was to be the 'self' in 'self-government' could be, and was, left to others to solve.

For the doctrine of nationalism to emerge, a criterion or set of criteria, by which a 'nation' could be identified, had to be provided. Historically, it was the work of a number of German writers of the same period, of whom J. G. Herder was the most important, to suggest the distinguishing marks of a 'nation'. (Herder's main works were *Another Philosophy of History* (1774) and *Outlines of a Philosophy of the History of Man*, 1784–91. He died in 1803.) What characterised a 'people', in the eyes of Herder, was its possession of a unique culture – the distinctive blend of habits, customs, manners, literature, art, religion and notably language, which had grown up over the centuries. The building-blocks of modern nationalism – State, popular sovereignty, the nation as a self-conscious culturally defined entity – were now in place.

From these beginnings, nationalism spread rapidly in the next 200 years to encompass the entire world. It was aided by the remorseless erosion of small-scale (village) and primitive (tribal) communities by the tides of industrialisation and urbanisation and, in many areas of the world, by the weakening of the social observance of religion in a widespread process of secularisation. At the same time, middle- and upper-class loyalties had to be reorientated as cultural cosmopolitanism disintegrated and, more importantly, empires collapsed. The deeper consequence of these social and political developments was the need to discover new foci of loyalty, new frames of cultural identification, together with the rationale of a new social purpose, for large numbers of people, including élites, throughout the world. This the cultural concept of the 'nation', together with the political doctrine of nationalism, was able to supply.

Superficially, the idea of nationalism is similar to an older concept like *patriotism* (love of one's country, or *patria*) but it is distinguishable from it by its aggressive and sharply political frame of reference. As Orwell wrote, patriotism means 'devotion to a particular place, a particular way of life, which one believes to be the best in the world but has no wish to force upon other people. Patriotism is of its nature defensive both militarily and culturally.' Nor is nationalism to be identified with mere *national self-consciousness*, an awareness of separate identity by a nation, which pre-dates it by hundreds of years – although nationalism may develop and use such a feeling. In contrast to both patriotism and national self-consciousness, nationalism is a specific political doctrine which is directed almost invariably outside a particular country, asserting the claims of a particular nationality against an external force, an alien, an outsider. Thus, the discovery, revival, systematisation and propagandist expounding of historic national cultures normally culminates in the demand for political recognition in some shape or form – for example, by separation, federalism or devolution.

Chameleon-like, nationalism can change its ideological colour according to its surroundings. In the past 200 years it has kept company with all the other major political doctrines. Thus, in the nineteenth century, it was closely associated with *Liberalism*, and nationalist movements habitually demanded a free constitution as well as independence. Nationalism can also blend with *Conservatism*, as when in well-established nations such as the United Kingdom or France, politicians seek national regeneration by invoking the memory of heroic leaders like Churchill or of danger ultimately overcome like Dunkirk or, as de Gaulle did after 1958, by self-consciously appealing to 'The Fatherland and the dead.' If the association of nationalism with

Conservatism relies upon the idea of national greatness, its role in the ideology of the extreme right exploits the pernicious doctrine of racism. As a doctrine, as Hitler's *Mein Kampf* shows, *Fascism* first depicted the German nation (Teutons) as belonging to an Aryan master-race, next insisted that it keep itself racially pure and finally required it to purge itself of the alien Jewish element in its midst (see especially chapter 11 entitled 'Nation and Race'). In this way, aggressive nationalism was harnessed to virulent anti-Semitism. Nationalism has been related to *Socialism*, especially in the period since 1945, in two main ways. It was Lenin who did most to formulate a Marxist theory of nationalism, arguing that Socialists could assist nationalist movements without sacrificing their ultimate Socialist goal. In the past few decades, the Chinese, the Cubans and the Russians have given considerable assistance in the form of weapons, technical aid and advice to *independence struggles* against 'imperialists' in the Third World. Second, *post-independence regimes* have drawn upon Socialism – especially the Russian model of a centralised one-party State, in their bid to integrate their respective countries and to mobilise them behind a drive for economic modernisation. This does not mean that there is any logical or necessary connection between nationalism and these other ideologies; rather, it suggests that nationalism's own core doctrine – that the nation should form the basis of the State or at least receive direct constitutional acknowledgement of its existence – has in practice lent itself to amalgamation with other doctrines and ideas.

It is now useful to summarise the main forms which nationalism has taken in the modern world. Anthony D. Smith in his book *Nationalism in the Twentieth Century* has suggested a useful fourfold classification:

1. *Liberation struggles against empires*, their goal and frequent end being independence and the creation of a new State (Italy against the Habsburg Empire in the nineteenth century, Latin America in the nineteenth century and Afro-Asian countries in the twentieth century against the European empires);
2. *State 'renewal'*: the regeneration of an old-established State by an appeal to national pride, often, as in the case of Gaullism and the government of Mrs Thatcher in Britain after 1979, associating this with a quest for economic revitalisation;
3. *Nation-building in post-colonial societies*, which often face severe problems in containing fiercely divisive tribal loyalties; the mobilisation of support among the population for the new 'nation' (e.g. Kenya, Nigeria, Zimbabwe) is aimed both at weakening tribalism and, in combination with Socialist principles and methods, achieving economic modernisation;
4. *Ethnic separatism in old multinational States*. This is the most recent development in nationalism as a political doctrine, although based on old-established loyalties. Examples of the demand for greater autonomy within the multinational State include Bretons and Corsicans against the

French State, Basques against Spain and the Welsh and the Scots against the United Kingdom. It is a form of nationalism which our case-study of the United Kingdom as a multinational State now gives us the chance to examine more closely, along with further complexities of nationalist doctrine.

Nationalities and nationalism within the United Kingdom

Britain has traditionally been regarded as a unified political culture in which class differences provided the main dividing lines between Britons. The use of the English language; a two–three party system found everywhere but in Northern Ireland; the Protestant religion; a shared experience of the economic benefits of industrialisation; the modern media (TV, radio and press) and mass entertainments (films, pop music and professional sport) were all factors which drew the component parts of the United Kingdon together. These forces were – and still are – tending to produce cultural homogeneity, a flattening-out of regional differences. However, the upsurge of political support for nationalist parties in Scotland and Wales in the 1970s, together with a renewal of sectarian strife in Northern Ireland, brought the national divisions within the United Kingdom into the spotlight. It is to the cultural sources of these divisions and to the varieties of national consciousness they underpin that we now turn (see Chapter 11 for a discussion of the political impact of the nationalist parties and Chapter 24 for an examination of UK devolution as a political issue).

The United Kingdom of Great Britain and Northern Ireland – to give the British State its full designation – is the result of various acts of absorption by the Westminster Government. These expansionist measures – undertaken for motives of national security and economic advantage – successively brought Wales (1536), Scotland (1707) and Ireland (1801) under the rule of the English Crown. In this process, both Ireland and Scotland lost the separate parliaments which had met in Dublin and Edinburgh respectively; in Wales, no parliament existed at the time it was absorbed by the English State. Essentially, then, the United Kingdom dates from 1801, but it fragmented in 1922 when twenty-six of the thirty-two Irish provinces split away to form the Republic of Ireland. The other six northern provinces remained part of the UK. The United Kingdom is thus a multinational State which contains no fewer than five distinct 'national' groupings based on culture and ethnic origin: English, Scottish, Welsh and, in Northern Ireland, the Protestant majority group of English–Scottish descent and the Catholic minority of Celtic descent. Each resulted in a unique brand of national consciousness. In addition, the UK contains a broader State-centred source of national identification, over-arching the other national loyalties: the *British* nation. We take each 'nation' in turn.

British

With reference to nationality this is both a *legal* term, denoting the possession of citizenship, and also an indication of *cultural* affiliation. The distinction matters because, whilst all the component nations of the UK share a common citizenship, only the English, Welsh and Scots also identify (the latter two nations to varying degrees) with Britain as a cultural entity. Northern Ireland Unionists do not feel this sense of cultural identification, only a political loyalty to the British Crown and State.

English   Territorially, England is only approximately 50 per cent of the UK but this bald statistic does not take into account that this area includes the southern Midlands, South and South-east, the British 'heartland'. Territorially, demographically, militarily, economically, and, above all, politically, the English (about 80 per cent of the UK population, compared with 50 per cent in 1801) dominate the United Kingdom, and hence have tended to see 'England' and 'Britain' as virtually synonymous terms. This is most noticeable in the way in which British history has been written (at least until very recently) in terms of the expansion of the English (= British) State both within the British Isles and across the world in the foundation of transoceanic empire. The slow, gradual and, above all, successful nature of the process of English expansion; the absence from English history since the seventeenth century of major popular uprisings and, since the eleventh century, of invasion, despite the frequent threats of it; and the massive wealth generated by early industrialisation: all these factors have contributed to the conservative, traditional character of English nationalism. It is insular – until very recently it kept 'Europe' at arm's length while carrying out its imperial venture – and non-popular, which is not to be confused with 'unpopular', but simply means that English nationalism lacks any symbolic association of the people with the nation such as exists in the French celebration of the fall of the Bastille (14 July) or even the American celebration of Independence Day (4 July). What it celebrates are institutions and constitutional achievements (parliament, monarchy, common law) predominantly associated with élites together with moments of national deliverance from invasion – the defeat of the Spanish Armada, of Napoleon at Trafalgar and Waterloo, and of Hitler. The English national myth is (not unusually) 'freedom' ('Britons never, never shall be slaves') but because conquest and assimilation of the other 'nations' in the British Isles took place so early, the English habit is just subconsciously to include them in 'Britons' without considering – until the 1970s – the possibility of any claim for national freedom against them by peripheral countries.

Welsh   National consciousness in Wales is *cultural*, the idea of a people whose sense of its identity never found political expression in a State (cf.

Scotland) but rather took root in a historically evolving culture. In this historical experience, *language* and *religion* have been of decisive significance. In the nineteenth century, the character of the nation was shaped by its Nonconformist chapels where, often, the services were conducted in Welsh; by a Welsh-language newspaper press; by the struggle against English landlords in rural communities; and by the affront given to Welsh suscepti- bilities by the derogatory attitude to their language by the Westminster parliament as national education in English got under way. Nonetheless, despite the activities of Welsh Language groups to preserve and increase Welsh-speaking and the prominence of language in nationalist ideology, a sense of Welshness and an identification with Wales goes well beyond either language or religion. Only one-fifth of the population today are Welsh speakers compared with two-fifths in 1911 and less than half the community are Nonconformists. What unites Welsh people is an affection for the physical landscape of the country and for its cultural and social institutions – choirs, eisteddfods and rugby football; an enthusiasm for education (the demand for autonomous educational institutions, especially in further and higher education, was second only to disestablishment for the Welsh at the end of the last century); and a pride in their history, which stretches back over 1200 years to the first British inhabitants who resisted the Saxon invaders. But for all their strong sense of a distinct cultural identity, no other people in the British Isles are so disposed to think of themselves also as 'British'. More than the English – who equate 'British' and 'English', more than the Scots – who distinguish their national identity more sharply from 'British', and more than the peoples of Northern Ireland – who tend not to identify culturally with Britain at all, the Welsh possess a 'dual identity' both Welsh *and* British.

Scottish   A State in medieval and early modern times (James I of England (1601–25) was also James VI of Scotland and, for over a century before the Union, there was a dual monarchy), Scotland had more to lose than Wales by union with England (it became a 'dispossessed' nation), but also, by virtue of its former statehood, retained more control over its own administration at the Union. Unlike Ireland (until 1868) and Wales (until 1920) Scotland possessed its own established Church (Presbyterian) and, in addition, separate systems of law, education and local government. From 1885, the country had its own Secretary of State (Wales did not acquire its own Minister until 1964). Scotland also has its own newspaper press. A Scottish national society, therefore, enjoyed a considerable amount of practical independence in the eighteenth and nineteenth centuries. It is this fact which, taken together with its relatively large population ($5\frac{1}{4}$ m in 1971, compared with Wales, $2\frac{3}{4}$ m and Northern Ireland, $1\frac{1}{2}$ m) and the cultural self- confidence dating back to its role in the eighteenth century Enlightenment (when it produced a leading European philosopher, David Hume, as well as

Adam Smith, the founder of political economy) account for its ability to generate a significant nationalist movement in the 1970s, a movement triggered by the discovery of offshore oil. Language – the tiny amount of Gaelic-speaking is confined to the Highlands (only 1.8 per cent in 1971) – is of no significance in Scottish national consciousness; nor is the rather self-conscious literary movement associated with Hugh MacDiarmid earlier in the twentieth century. A historically-developed sense of and pride in a distinctive identity, to some extent linked with the culture of the great cities, Glasgow and Edinburgh, and stimulated in the twentieth century by mass sport, especially association football, typifies Scottish consciousness.

Irish   The national consciousness of the majority in Northern Ireland (65 per cent of the population) is based on the Protestant religion and ethnicity (descent from English–Scottish colonisers). It is expressed in unwavering support for the Crown, symbol of the 'British connection' (Loyalism). Although its roots go back to the late seventeenth century, Ulster national-ism really defined itself about one century ago in opposition to ethnic (Celtic) Catholic nationalism, which itself both stimulated and derived additional momentum from the Gaelic cultural revival at the end of the nineteenth century. The Partition of 1922, which saw the Catholic majority hiving off to form the Republic of Ireland, left a Catholic minority (35 per cent) in the North, thereby effectively transforming Ulster Protestant Unionism into a second (the first being British) 'possessive' nationalism in that region of the United Kingdom. In Northern Ireland, then, three nationalisms interact – British, Protestant Irish and Catholic Irish – with deadly consequences.

Summary

National identities and national consciousness take a variety of forms, as do the nationalist ideologies and movements they inspire. In the UK, key influences upon national consciousness have been *religion* (Catholicism – Eire, Protestant – Ulster Unionist; Nonconformist Protestantism – Wales; Presbyterianism – Scotland); *language* (Welsh in Wales; Gaelic in Ireland, but not in Scotland) and *historical relationships with the dominant power* (England). Note especially in this connection, the significance for Scottish national consciousness of the prior existence of a Scottish State and the significance of the lack of one for the cultural emphasis of Welsh nationalism. Intellectuals play a role in the creation of national consciousness – for example, by stimulating or seeking to stimulate literary revivals. National consciousness is compatible with other overlapping and contemporaneous loyalties (e.g. Welsh–British and Scots–British) but is also capable of generating intransigent and *non-negotiable* political demands (Ireland).

FASCISM

Fascism is an extreme right-wing ideology which rose to prominence in inter-
war Europe, especially in Germany and Italy, declined with the defeat and
death in war of Hitler and Mussolini and resurfaced in altered form in several
European countries in the 1970s. It is a compound of aggressive nationalism,
racialism, élitism and authoritarianism; it is both anti-Liberal and violently
anti-Communist. What follows is in essence a description of its German form
(racialism was not a feature of Italian Fascism) but some remarks are
included at the end about the far milder British versions of the creed, namely
Oswald Mosley's British Union of Fascists in the 1930s and the National
Front after 1967. We deal in turn with Fascist doctrines of human nature,
nation, society and government.

Human nature

To Fascists, human nature is malleable and they would wish to reshape it in a
different mould. The 'new man' of their ideal is a heroic individual, brave,
resolute, austere and self-sacrificing – in short, utterly dedicated to the service
of his Leader and Fatherland, even to the point of dying for them. In Fascist
ideology, this vital 'superman' stands in sharp contrast to the petty-minded,
squabbling mediocrities who typify liberal–democratic regimes and the
slavish herds inhabiting Communist States. The Fascist 'hero' is dynamic,
constantly prepared to test his beliefs in action against the nation's enemies,
internal and external: there is an overt appeal to violence and brutality in
Fascism. As Hitler wrote, describing an early 'action' by his 'Storm Detach-
ment' against the Socialists, 'we hit out right and left for ten minutes, and a
quarter of an hour later there was no more red to be seen in the streets' (A.
Hitler, *Mein Kampf*, p. 234). The sole desire of the Fascist is to achieve the
supremacy of his group, defined in national–racial terms. The appeal is to the
irrational side of human nature, to ties of blood and race, to the fighting
instincts; reason, intellect and moderation are despised. It is a warrior creed.
For the 'new woman' there is the more traditional role of bearing sons for the
Fatherland and of bringing up and supporting its 'heroes'.

Nation

Fascism exalts the consciousness of belonging to a particular group, the
nation. It thrives on the contrast it draws between the existing state of the
nation – 'hopelessly corrupted' by the Communists, traitors and Jews – and
an ideal, the true or authentic nation of its own imagining. The Nazi nation
was a myth made up of a romantic cult of a past full of gods and heroes and a
pseudo-biological notion of the Germans as an Aryan 'master race'. (No
Aryan race ever existed, 'master' or otherwise: 'Aryan' was simply a language

of one of the ancient Indian cultures. Its basic fictitiousness made no difference to the energising force of the concept of a powerful, pure and creative race.)

The goals for this Teutonic 'master race' were set by adding to its racialism the idea – which was very powerful in late nineteenth- and early twentieth-century culture – that nations, like biological organisms, were engaged in a continual struggle for survival and only 'proved themselves' by overcoming all rivals. Thus, internally, the nation must revitalise itself by purging itself of all alien elements in its midst, notably the Jews. The swastika, an ancient symbol of rebirth, became the emblem of this new Germany. Abroad, it adopted the expansionist pan-German programme of the unification of all Germans within the one Reich, if necessary by war against the Slavs in Eastern Europe. The deliberate aim of Fascism was and is to create a totally unified 'organic' community whose service is the highest duty of the individual. It seeks to achieve this total integration both by focusing upon the virtues possessed by the 'in-group' and by directing hatred against an 'out-group'.

Society and government

In Fascist ideology, loyalty to class is totally overridden by allegiance to the State. The organic Nation-State of its ideal absorbs all subordinate groups – capital and labour, family, Church, profession – and harmoniously integrates them into the national community itself. It is a 'mobilised society' in which the masses stand in permanent readiness for action behind goals set by its dynamic Leader. It is an authoritarian State which sets aside ordinary law in favour of organic Fascist law and suppresses civil and political freedom in the name of service to the great cause proclaimed by the Leader. Fascism as a doctrine of society is openly élitist, believing in the existence of, and seeking to recruit, 'superior' individuals who can transcend material drives in the pursuit of a spiritual ideal and subordinate selfish motives in the service of the community. This new élite (in part at least) selects itself by volunteering to join the Party. Fascism is contemptuous of parliamentary regimes for dithering indecisiveness and of Communist regimes for exalting the alleged needs of the working class above all else. With its uniformed ranks marching in step and its disciplined chants, the Nazi mass meeting forms a kind of miniature representation of the Fascist conception of an ideal national community. Here individual identity is submerged in that of a group possessed by a single purpose, inspired, united and energised, in an atmosphere of dramatic, tense expectancy, by a leader of overwhelming personality.

Fascism in Britain

An ideologically and politically weak version of this creed appeared in Britain in the 1930s associated with Oswald Mosley and his British Union of Fascists. Mosley's book, *The Greater Britain*, published in 1932, blends elements of Fascist thought in a mix calculated to appeal to a British readership. Two-thirds of it consists of Mosley's plan for British economic regeneration, 'Britain First', which combined the idea of the corporate state with protectionism to guarantee industry a large secure home market. The corporate state idea was derived especially from Italian Fascism and sought to overcome economic sectionalism by building capitalist and labour organisations into a hierarchical structure culminating in the supreme National Corporation. Mosley was thoroughly Fascist in seeking first to supercede the failed politicians and parties of the parliamentary system, the 'Old Gang', who, in his view, had completely failed to measure up to the contemporary 'crisis', and then to root out the major enemies of the State, the Communists. Anti-Semitism is not a theme of this book but there is little doubt either that he was prepared to attack the Jews opportunistically in his speeches or that his supporters in the BUF were virulently anti-Semitic. As well as calling for national regeneration under an authoritative State, Mosley also invoked other Fascist themes: a lofty conception of individual service to the State, whose citizens should live 'like athletes' vigorous in mind and body, and who would become, under the dynamic, forward-looking leadership of the Fascist Party, 'a disciplined army not a bewildered mob'. Mosley himself stressed the significance of the Second World War in bringing British Fascism to a halt but the more probable truth is that it never really got going, held back by the strong social support enjoyed by the parliamentary system, by the respect for political moderation felt by most British people, by the resilience of the British class system and, most important of all perhaps, by the modesty of the economic problem, grave as it was, compared with the situation in Germany after 1918.

By 1967, another racialist party of the extreme right had emerged: the National Front. Its political impact, organisation and detailed policies are examined in Chapter 11. Here it is sufficient to remark that its central ideological idea was a redefinition of the 'real' or 'authentic' British community in terms of colour, with 'whites' conceived as true Britons, and coloured people denied this identity, and blamed for a host of social problems in the tradition of Fascist 'scapegoating'.

LIBERALISM

Ideologies change through time but in important respects they also maintain their identities. As social and political organisation changes, and new ideologies appear, existing ideologies adapt their perceptions of the social and political world accordingly. They may even, as we have seen both with conservatism and nationalism, move closer to other ideologies. But, it needs also to be insisted that even in modifying themselves, they retain many similiarities with their former selves. Otherwise, it would not be possible, as it is, to continue to call them by the same names. Nor are such adaptations – hard as they sometimes make it to discern the body of beliefs under the different clothing – all that surprising. The sole alternative is to become out of date, and ultimately perish. Some ideologies simply cannot adapt (there are few Divine Right Monarchists today). Those that can change must try to do so.

This somewhat abstract introduction is especially necessary in the case of Liberalism since its history goes back at least 300 years during which time its character had undergone successive modifications. From being the attacker of monarchical, ecclesiastical and artistocratic authority in the eighteenth century, Liberalism has moved to social domination in the nineteenth century and thence to an uneasy existence in the shadow of Socialism in the twentieth century. In particular, its doctrine of the role of the State in society has changed considerably since 1880 in response both to the manifest failings of a society informed by its own economic philosophy (even though *laissez-faire* and the 'Minimal State' never did exist in their pure form) and also to Socialist doctrines calling for greater government intervention in society to alleviate poverty and increase social justice. But, considerable as these adaptations were, Liberalism has retained in the twentieth century its earlier – and fundamental – preoccupation with the freedom of the individual. Our analysis of British Liberalism focuses in turn upon its beliefs and doctrines concerning human nature, society, progress, government, participation, and nation.

Human nature

Liberal thought is individualist. It believes in the dignity, autonomy, rationality and self-development of each person. Ultimately, this idea of the supreme and intrinsic worth of each individual derives from Christianity although it no longer requires a religious world-view to justify it. Moreover, from Liberalism it has stretched out to inform many other ideologies. Not only do individuals merit respect as individuals (hence the evil of slavery, torture, violence and manipulation of other persons), they are also *autonomous*, or self-directing. They can draw up plans and make choices. They are moral agents able to shape their lives as they think fit. In forming their purposes, in deciding how to live their lives, in conducting their relationships with others, individuals make use of their reason. They can calculate, adapt means to ends, deploy logic, subject customs and institutions to critical examination, analyse, compare – in short, they possess *rationality*. Lastly,

Liberals drew upon Romanticism for their conception of human beings as creatures whose destiny is to develop their powers to the maximum extent possible. This seems vague – who can be sure they have fulfilled their potential? – but *self-development* nonetheless remains an aspiration of great power. After all, people are well aware when they are being *denied* opportunities to fulfil themselves, for whatever reason this may be. The concept of the individual in all its aspects is at the very heart of Liberalism, underlying its approach to society, State and government. Indeed, it is the only creed which appeals directly to the individual *as* an individual and not as member of some group, class or nation.

Society

There are two sets of relationships which concern us here: between the individual and society, and between society and the State. We consider them in turn.

Individual and society

In classical Liberalism (c.1760–1860), society is visualised simply as a collection of individuals. In this conception, the 'individual' appears strongly-etched in the foreground, 'society' as a rather dimly-perceived background. Liberal theory of this period is often criticised for over-emphasising the claims of the individual upon society and neglecting the legitimate demands of groups, classes and the community as a whole upon the individual. Certainly, Liberal economic doctrine in arguing for freedom of enterprise for the businessman (free contracts and free trade) undoubtedly sanctioned grossly unequal work-contracts between capital and labour which led to great evils. Equally, however, the liberating aims and consequences of Liberal ideas should be borne in mind together with the *universality* of its demands, which, even if they were not carried out for the whole society at the time, were potentially applicable to *all* members of it.

It needs to be remembered in particular that Liberalism when it first emerged in the writings of Locke, Paine, Bentham and the two Mills took as its major target the eradication of privilege in societies which had slavery and serfdom and in which aristocracies and established churches were strongly entrenched. In such a context, the liberal demands for *civil* liberty – for toleration of all creeds and for the extension of the freedoms of conscience, expression and association – and for *equality before the law*, irrespective of race, class or creed, were revolutionary in scope and impact.

In asserting these demands, the middle class of the time was perfectly aware that society was in fact composed of distinct groups and classes not only because of their own sufferings from aristocratic condescension but also because the claims they advanced, although couched in universal language (*the rights of man*), were invariably made on behalf of specific excluded groups, such as Quakers, Catholics, Nonconformists, property-owners, and so on. In addition, as John Stuart Mill's book *On Liberty* testifies, there was acute understanding amongst Liberals of the enormous power of social prejudice, convention and taboo to inhibit and frustrate individuals. Whilst the claims of 'society' were perhaps less neglected by Liberals in this phase than is often said, it remains true that the essential thrust of Liberal ideology is individualist. It is towards the inclusion in the laws of a society of a set of rights which individuals are held to possess merely by virtue of their humanity.

In the twentieth century, as society in general has become more 'collectivist', more conscious of political responsibility for all its members (the Welfare State) and also more aware of individuals as members of *groups*, these perceptions have influenced Liberalism. It has become the philosophy of the open, plural society – 'open', because there is widespread freedom of intellectual production and expression, and 'plural', because there is also widespread freedom for groups to exist, put their points of view and live according to their own principles.

Society and State

State–society relations may be more briefly treated notwithstanding their importance. Liberalism has always been concerned with the quality, and protection, of the private life of the individual. As the early nineteenth-century French Liberal, Benjamin Constant, wrote, 'Nearly all the enjoyments of the moderns are in their private lives'. The idea of a sphere of thought and action free from public interference is central to the Liberal vision of the good society. This conception is often described by the phrase 'negative liberty' – what we do *not* want the State to do to us. In this sense, 'society' is the arena of freedom, of voluntary activity, of personal relationships; the 'State' signifies the area of compulsion, involuntary activity, constraint.

Typically, in the twentieth century, as the State has vastly extended the scope of its responsibilities into 'society', Liberals have worried about the intrusion into individuals' rights – over conscription, for example, over the adoption of compulsory land use and planning powers which infringe individuals' rights to dispose of their property as they please, and, with the use of electronic 'bugging' devices and telephone tapping by the authorities, over the invasion of the home, the citadel of privacy itself. The Liberal nightmare is an extension of this fear: that the sphere of society will be completely swallowed up by the State which would be totalitarianism.

Progress

Liberalism's idea of progress is an outgrowth of its individualism. Societies prosper, in the Liberal view, in so far as they remove restrictions upon individual enterprise and unleash the energies and inventiveness of individuals. In the economic sphere, of course, the untrammelled capitalism of the nineteenth century is no longer defensible. The unfairness and inefficiency it produced were evident before 1900 and were described by New Liberals as well as by Socialists. It was true of course that under this system society had got richer but what was equally true was that the middle and upper classes' share of the national wealth had increased in massive disproportion to that of the working class and also that a third of the population lived at or near to the poverty line, as then defined. L. T. Hobhouse in his book *Liberalism* (1911) pointed out that for government to undertake responsibility to provide directly for the poorer class and to take steps to improve the working of the market for labour need not necessarily, as previously thought, undermine the initiative and sense of responsibility for their own welfare of individuals. Greater fairness could result in a more efficient society. In his thought, as in that of later Liberals like J. M. Keynes and W. H. Beveridge, the need was to increase the scope of government without sapping individual initiative: to keep a balance between what was done *for* individuals and what they still must do for themselves. As he phrased it 'the function of the State is to secure conditions upon which its citizens are able *to win by their own efforts* all that is necessary to a full civic efficiency' (Hobhouse, *Liberalism*, 1911, p. 83) [our italics].

This was the philosophy of a modified or regulated capitalist society. It anticipated by some half century the form of society based upon a 'mixed economy' (Welfare State plus Managed Economy, or as it has sometimes been called, 'welfare capitalism') which emerged after 1945. It was a society based upon the principle of equality of opportunity but not of equality. Its economic philosophy was that of Keynes, whose academic work as an economist, *The General Theory of Employment, Interest and Money* (1936), provided the techniques on which government economic management could be based. Keynes, as Roy Harrod tells us, 'was by nature a progressive and reformer ... He was not a great friend of the profit motive ... and came to hope that an economic system might be evolved in which it was curtailed. But he did not think it would be beneficial for the State to run industry and trade.' (Harrod, *Keynes*, 1963, pp. 332–3). Keynes thought that 'Liberals should turn their backs on the old doctrine of *laissez-faire* ... The State would have to intervene at many points. *Yet the structure of a free economy with its scope for individual initiative must be preserved. Keynes remained essentially an individualist*' (ibid. p. 354) [our italics]. This attitude was typical of the way Liberals redefined the meaning of social progress in the twentieth century. The State should provide a safety-net of social security but within what has been called 'the interstices of a capitalist economy', which, of course, as before, would depend upon entrepreneurial initiative for its effective working.

Another Liberal, William Beveridge, in his report on *Social Insurance and Allied Services* (1942), laid the foundations of the post-1945 Welfare State, as Keynes had provided the theoretical bases of the managed economy. The famous Report proposed a scheme of social insurance to cover all classes of society and recommended a national health service, family allowances, an improved educational system, better housing and the maintenance of employment. Beveridge's concern that the State should provide what Orwell called the preconditions of a 'decent' life by securing citizens against the various contingencies of childhood, sickness, unemployment and old age fits in well with the philosophy of the New Liberalism in its demand for an enlarged role for the State. But Beveridge, like other New Liberals, retained the older Liberal concern with the value of individual initiative, and the desire not to see it sapped in any way by State provision. Thus, in his view, much social welfare should continue to be done by *voluntary* agencies, groups and individuals. His social insurance scheme was designed to provide only a basic subsistence minimum. As 'a good Liberal', he believed that anything over and above the minimum should be left to the individual to provide through private insurance.

Government

The fundamental Liberal political idea is the idea of freedom. This conception has three aspects: freedom under the law, limited government, and government by consent. Underlying all three aspects is individualism: the notion that the basic purpose of law and government is to protect individual rights and to enhance individual interests. Since the philosophy was formulated against a background of the absolute power of kings, it naturally bears many signs of this experience. In essence, it is a doctrine of limits, a theory of control of the power of governments. This is because, for the Liberal, *any* government whatever its form, composition and goals, may abuse its power, become arbitrary, even authoritarian – at worst, degenerate into a dictatorship.

Freedom under the law

The principle of freedom under the law is directed to securing a government of laws, not men. This is impossible, of course, since judges will always be necessary to interpret the law. But the phrase catches well the ideological tendency of Liberalism, its fear of being subject to the capricious power of another and its corresponding desire to establish a set of objective external limits over everyone – the law. Where the law, conceived in these impersonal terms as a body of rules equally applicable to all, is sovereign, no one need fear the power of another – to defame his reputation, trespass upon his property or threaten or use violence against him. Protection of the person is the role of the civil and criminal law. As Locke wrote, 'where there is no law, there is no freedom. For liberty is to be free from restraint and violence by others, which cannot be where there is no law.' Freedom, in this sense, is the ability to do what the law does not prevent; and the corresponding duty to refrain from doing what it prohibits. But what happens when it is governments themselves which break the law?

Limited government

The idea of limited government, or constitutional freedom, is aimed at guaranteeing the liberty of individuals against their rulers. Historically, the attempt to make citizens more secure against governments has led to a number of constitutional emphases and devices, including the separation of powers, bicameralism, the Ombudsman, the rule of law, and the legalisation of political opposition. Some stress the creation of *internal* checks upon governments (e.g. the way in which one branch of government cannot proceed without the consent of another, as in the Constitution of the USA), others the establishment of *external* authorities to restrain executives (e.g. the Parliamentary Commissioner, or Ombudsman, who serves as a 'watchdog' of the public interest).

The point here is neither to give a comprehensive account of these approaches, nor to discuss their effectiveness; ultimately they all depend for their effective working upon a sympathetic political culture together with the preparedness of individuals and groups to defend their interests. It is simply to suggest that, whatever form this may take in different periods, the perennial concern of Liberals is with 'the taming of Leviathan', the protection of the individual against oppression by an over-mighty State. (See Chapters 10 on parliament and 15 on the legal system and redress, for a more detailed discussion of these institutions and mechanisms for the control of government.) In the twentieth century, Liberal political theory has focused increasingly on groups in society as a way of limiting the power of government – a pluralist approach to politics (see Chapter 13 on pressure groups).

Government by consent

Finally, for Liberals, government should be based upon individual consent. What legitimates government is free elections. In turn, elections produce representative bodies, or parliaments, which, it may be assumed, will then enact laws to which citizens may be taken to have assented. Representation, in Liberal theory, is of individuals; it is not of estates, classes or sectional groups of any kind. And since politics in the view of Liberals is primarily about the reconciliation of differences of opinion, government can be by discussion. Moreover, because in the Liberal perception of politics no irreconcilable conflicts exist, the state can be seen as a neutral agency whose role it is to carry out the majority view as policy.

Participation

Two streams of thought – one associated with Thomas Paine, the other with Jeremy Bentham – flow into Liberal views on political participation. Both wanted to maximise it, both may be regarded as favouring participatory democracy, but they justify it differently. For Paine and later Radicals, the possession of a vote is a natural right; it is the logical product of human equality. We should say today that it is a moral right. For Bentham and the Utilitarians, the vote is necessary for the defence of one's *interests*, an understandable emphasis against the aristocratic parliament of his day – the early nineteenth century – which, to Bentham's disgust, perpetually legislated in the interest of a class. No government can know the interests of a person as well as the person can, nor is likely to pursue them so single-mindedly. Hence, so the argument goes, the only way to ensure that government is in the general interest is to have a democratic system. Only in that way will government legislate, as Bentham put it, for 'the greatest happiness of the greatest number'.

Nation

The concept of the nation appears in Liberal thought in two main ways, one of which we have already noticed: first, in the argument for national self-government and independence (Liberal Nationalism); second, in the argument which would seek to contain and control – and perhaps ultimately supercede – the authority of the nation-state (Liberal Internationalism). Both derive from essentially Liberal principles notwithstanding the fact that, like Liberal arguments for democracy, for example, they also crop up in other ideologies. Thus, Liberal Nationalism is an extension to the nation of the Liberal concept of freedom, redefined as rule not by aliens, but by people like ourselves. It is worth pointing out that it may underlie not only arguments against empire (e.g. European empires in Africa and Asia in the twentieth century; Russian in Eastern Europe after 1945) but also arguments in favour of the devolution of power to national units within the multinational State. Ultimately, Liberal Internationalism – with its idealistic goal of an international community in which national identities are transcended (e.g. the idea of the League of Nations, the United Nations and of federally-organised regional groups of nations) – rests upon a typical Liberal view of the individual, shorn of subordinate loyalties, as 'a citizen of the world'. It is much reinforced by the Liberal preference for persuasion rather than force in the settlement of disputes and an understandable alarm at the havoc caused by aggressive nationalism since 1914.

SOCIALISM

Like the other major ideologies, Socialism emerged *in opposition to* a particular type of society and its ideological justification: nineteenth-century capitalism and *laissez-faire* Liberalism. Like the other ideologies too, Socialism has changed greatly through time, adapting itself to altered circumstances and different areas of the world and developing new theories. But its preoccupation with the defects of capitalism as a system of production and distribution of goods has remained, together with a concern with ways in which the market economy can be modified to bring about greater social justice.

Socialism as a world force

In the nineteenth century, Marx's Socialism had many rivals. There were, for example, the visions of ideal communities pictured by the early French Socialists, whom Marx dubbed 'Utopian'. An important body of anarchist thought, developed by Proudhon, Bakunin and Kropotkin, was libertarian in impulse and stressed the virtues of small cooperative self-governing communities. Later in the century, it was a strong influence upon anarcho-syndicalism – the idea that working-class emancipation was best achieved by industrial rather than political action. But as a systematic theory of the new class society generated by industrial capitalism, Marx's Socialism had no equals. The heart of his analysis is the notion of capitalism as exploitative of the working class. The precise way in which the capitalist exploited the worker, Marx explained through his theory of 'surplus value'. This theory is well described by Peter Singer in his book, *Marx* (1980), as follows:

> Suppose the cost of keeping a worker alive and reproducing for one day is £1, and suppose that a day's work consists of twelve hours. Then the exchange-value of twelve hours' labour will be £1 . . . Suppose, however, that the development of the forces of production means that a worker's labour-power can be used to add £1 to the value of some raw materials in only six hours. Then the worker effectively earns his wages in six hours. But the capitalist has bought twelve hours of labour-power for his £1, and can use the remaining six hours to extract surplus value from the workers (pp. 50–1).

Essentially, each worker's day, according to Marx, is divided into two parts: 'necessary labour time', during which the worker labours to produce goods whose exchange value is equal to the subsistence wage he receives; and 'surplus labour time', when he works to produce 'surplus value' for his employer.

A second point to make about Marx's theory is that this exploitation of one class by another is *systemic*, that is, it is structured into the capitalist mode of production. The implications of this are that what Marx saw as the harsh effects of capitalism cannot be removed by any change of heart by the capitalist or by government social or economic policy; nor can trade-union action gain workers their fair rewards. The system itself had to be over-thrown and Marx, impressed by the mass political action of the French Revolution and the Paris Commune (1871), thought that this would be achieved by an uprising of the workers themselves. Proletarian revolution would end class rule and destroy the oppressive State; after an interlude of worker dictatorship during which the last vestiges of the bourgeois regime would be rooted out, a communist society characterised by democracy and social equality would follow. By the early 1900s a fierce controversy had broken out among European Marxists over whether Marx's aims would inevitably have to be accomplished by violent revolution or whether, in circumstances of improved working-class living standards, a revolutionary social transformation could be attained by peaceful parliamentary methods. The outbreak of war in 1914 and the destruction of the tsarist autocracy in Russia soon provided an answer to this speculation.

The year 1917 was a major watershed in the history of Socialism. The triumph of the Bolshevik Party during the Russian Revolution led to its division into two major strands, Democratic Socialism (Western) and Communism (Eastern). With the victory of an anti-Liberal, revolutionary party, the USSR became a one-party State of which Marxist–Leninism was the official ideology. Lenin was the architect of the Bolshevik victory. His major theoretical addition to Marxism was the concept of the centralised party ('democratic centralism') which would serve as a vanguard in the attainment of the revolutionary aims of the working class and of their consolidation after the revolution. After Lenin's death, Stalin established Marxist–Leninism – a combination of the Marxist analysis of capitalism with Lenin's theory of the Party – as the official theory of the Bolshevik revolution and of the new Communist State. World Socialism thenceforth had a national base from which after 1945 it established itself in Eastern Europe and achieved considerable influence in the Third World. The success of the Chinese Communists under Mao after 1949 provided not only a further variant of Socialist ideology but also another – and, for the Russians, a rival – source of Communist support in the underdeveloped countries. The revival of Marxist theory which gathered strength after the 1960s in the West looked for inspiration to the libertarian writings of the early Marx, to the Italian Socialist of the 1920s, Antonio Gramsci and to the defeated and exiled Russian Bolshevik leader, Trotsky, whose reputation survived the moral discredit into which Russian Communism fell under Stalin.

Our analysis of the key concepts of Socialist thought which follows draws upon the British contribution to Western gradualist parliamentary socialism. Nonetheless, the British tradition itself is woven of many threads and fed from a diversity of sources. These links in the Socialist chain go back to the early nineteenth century and include Paine's radicalism, Owen's rationalist paternalism, Chartist democracy, the Nonconformist conscience, Fabianism and, in the twentieth century, the moral vision of R. H. Tawney. The central tenet of mainstream British Socialism is the idea of winning control of the State by democratic methods in order to eradicate poverty and create a more equal society.

Socialism is 'the ideology of the twentieth century' in the sense that Liberalism was the ideology of the nineteenth century and it has penetrated all the other ideologies – Conservatism, Liberalism, Nationalism and Fascism. In Britain, democratic socialism has joined forces politically with left (New) Liberalism since 1900 to use the resources of the State to modify the operation of the market economy in favour of the poorer sections of society. But it goes and has gone further than Liberals in the modification and elimination of market forces: for example, the post-1945 nationalisation of the mines, railways, gas, electricity and iron and steel industries and the establishment of the National Health Service (to include everyone and without any cash payment having to be made at the point of receipt of service by patients). Socialists argue that their political pressure has been a major factor in the social progress made in this century.

Human nature

In Socialist theory, human nature is inherently and potentially good but in capitalist economies human relationships are distorted and human goodness thwarted by an economic system which is geared to produce profits for the few rather than to satisfy the basic needs of the many. Capitalism makes people greedy, selfish and competitive rather than generous, altruistic and cooperative. It divides people from each other rather than uniting them, dehumanises them by constantly perceiving them in terms of the market economy – as 'units' of production, for example, or as 'consumers', rather than as individual human beings. Whilst not ignoring liberty, Socialists emphasize the need to bring about a form of society in which the values of equality and fraternity are more important than they are at present. They want a far more equal society in which differences of income, wealth, education and power are sharply reduced. They aspire to a society in which differences of reward are justified in terms of social function and in which differentials are allocated by a collective decision about the relative value of each job to the community. They think that such a society is also likely to be a fraternal one in which human relationships are characterised by affable cooperativeness rather than by suspicious and envious individualism.

Society

Socialists accord a positive role to society in the formation of individuals. Indeed, to the Socialist, individuals are inconceivable *apart* from their social relationships. Thus, language, knowledge, technology, capital are all *social* products. Whatever differences may spring up between people in the skills, capacities and knowledge they develop, the conditions under which they develop are set by society. To Socialists the most important of the relationships into which individuals are born are *economic* and, in particular, it is the character of the productive relationships existing at any given time which conditions the character of that society. Thus, in a capitalist system, the basic division is between the owners of productive resources (finance, factories and raw materials) and those who work for them – between the bourgeoisie and the working class. The relationship between these two classes is at best an unstable one, in which each seeks to increase its share of the product at the expense of the other. Only with the replacement of the private ownership of the means of production by public or collective ownership will the tension inherent in their relations be resolved. The goal of Socialism is therefore set by its social and economic analysis: the substitution of a classless society for a class-divided society.

Progress

Socialism is a progressive creed but one of the major differences between its various strains is over how its goal of a more equal society is to be achieved. One obvious one is between advocates of reform and proponents of revolution: the democratic socialist parties of English-speaking countries and of Western Europe fall into the first category; into the second fall Marxist–Leninists, Trotskyists, Maoists and many but not all Anarchists. Whilst parliamentary socialism has generally been the dominant form in Western European and Anglo-Saxon societies, small groups of revolutionary leftists have also been active in many of these countries, especially since the late 1960s. In Great Britain, for example, by 1975, the 28 000 Communists had been outflanked by 14 000 Trotskyists, 1500 supporters of pro-Chinese groupings and about the same number of anarchists organised in roughly a dozen groups (Peter Shipley, *Revolutionaries in Modern Britain*, pp. 16–17). Even the briefest examination of these extreme Left sects is enough to indicate that the line between peaceful and violent, evolutionary and revolutionary, paths to Socialism is in practice far less clear-cut than it may appear from the foregoing remarks. This is because many are prepared to use all means of influence available to bring about a Socialist society and in fact advocate the *tactical* use of peaceful and parliamentary methods to prepare the way for revolutionary transformation.

Another significant source of controversy amongst Socialists has been over the role of the State. In Britain in the inter-war period, the aim was to bring about a Socialist society by nationalisation and by a combination of direct State planning of the use of physical resources (manpower and supplies), as was to happen in fact during the Second World War. Post-war, however, the emphasis shifted to a combination of indirect control of the economy by Keynesian methods and public ownership; these went together with the establishment of 'universal' services in health, education and social security. By the late 1950s a debate was taking place within the Labour Party about the centrality of public ownership as a Socialist goal: fundamentalists thought it was essential that the Party retain its unequivocal commitment to nationalisation as an end; revisionists, reasonably satisfied with the existing blend of public and private ownership in the 'mixed economy', were keen to displace it as an essential objective of Socialism. In their view, it was simply one of many ways of achieving Socialist goals, and not necessarily the most important. By the 1970s, the debate had moved on again, fuelled by disappointment with the performance of the 'mixed economy' under success- ive Labour Governments and with that of the nationalised industries under the organisational form adopted after 1945, the public corporation. Amongst key sections on the left of the Party, control of the State bureaucracies together with the extension of worker control both in private and public enterprises had become major objectives.

Government

Socialist conceptions of class and social progress have led to a particular theory of parliamentary representation. To the democratic Socialist, it is *classes* rather than, as in the Liberal view, individuals, which are represented. Individuals at elections vote as members of classes for candidates as representatives of party. The role of a 'labour' or Socialist party, if elected to government, is primarily to translate its programme, for which it has received a 'mandate', into action. Politics, in parliament or anywhere else, is a matter of loyalty to class – 'solidarity' – rather than, as Liberals tend to conceive it, an affair of obligation to follow the dictates of conscience or to arrive at a reasoned conviction. Power, in the Labour Party, comes from below and the constant tendency of Socialist theory is to translate the Member of Parlia- ment into a delegate, a mere agent of *party*. Traditionally the Parliamentary Labour Party has subscribed to the norms of the British parliamentary system which accord the individual MP considerable independence of the party outside parliament. But, in the 1980s, the PLP came under fierce challenge from the Left to make intra-party democracy more of a reality (see further pp. 106, 108, 244–6).

Socialists generally have never lost their suspicion of the State as biased in the interests of the propertied classes. Nonetheless, in the dominant British (Fabian) Socialist tradition, it has never been seen as so hopelessly tainted by class interest that it must be destroyed. It can be captured by democratic means and used as an instrument to improve the lives of the vast majority. Marxists, however, continue to distrust it, and, as we shall see in Chapter 26, contest the view that the State can be used in its present form to create a more egalitarian society. It follows on this analysis that the Labour Party is wasting its time. Its objectives, as Ralph Miliband has argued in *Parliamentary Socialism* (1961), are always likely to be thwarted by the combined opposition of the capitalist classes, as expressed through the Conservative party, big business, the city, and the civil service.

SUMMARY

Ideologies are belief-systems which function as guides to action. Targeted at people as members of particular groups, they are of immense importance in shaping political behaviour and producing political change. Although retaining identifiable features, ideologies themselves alter through time, assuming revolutionary form in one epoch, a conservative guise in the next, being dominant in one century, displaced and under attack in the following one. They also contain within themselves different traditions and emphases. *Conservatism* combines pessimism about human nature, a preference for gradual change, support for leadership by an experienced, able élite, assertive nationalism, and a strong commitment to the preservation of order. The core doctrine of *nationalism* is that nations defined in cultural–linguistic terms should form States or possess considerable autonomy within multinational States. Contemporary nationalism takes four main forms: colonial liberation, State renewal and regeneration, nation-building in post-independence regimes and ethnic separatism. *Fascism* is an ideology of the extreme right: it is racist, élitist, authoritarian, and fiercely hostile both to Liberalism and Socialism. The key concept of *Liberalism* is individual freedom. Its thrust is individualist – towards the demarcation and protection of a sphere of activity in society against the claims of the State in which individuals may enjoy their rights and express their interests. The expanded State recommended by twentieth-century Liberals is carefully defined in terms of the minimum functions compatible with a decent life for all. *Socialism*, like Liberalism, is optimistic about human nature. Its leading tenets are that societies which are based on a more equal distribution of wealth, income and power and upon cooperation will be more humane, civilised and productive than societies founded upon hierarchy, inequality and competition. Gradual reform and modification of the free play of market forces has typified British Socialism.

FURTHER READING

Berki, R. N. (1975) *Socialism*, London, Dent.
Charvet, J. (1982) *Feminism*, London, Dent.
Eccleshall, R. (1986) *British Liberalism*, London, Longman.
Eccleshall, R., Geoghegan, V., Jay, R. and Wilford, R. (1984) *Political Ideologies*, London, Hutchinson.
Gellner, E. (1983) *Nations and Nationalism*, Oxford, Blackwell.
Lunn, K. and Thurlow, R. C. (1980) *British Fascism*, Beckenham, Croom Helm.
McLellan, D. (1971) *The Thought of Karl Marx*, London, Macmillan.
Nisbet, R. (1986) *Conservatism*, Milton Keynes, Open University.
O'Gorman, F. (1986) *British Conservatism*, London, Longman.
O'Sullivan, N. (1976) *Conservatism*, London, Dent.
O'Sullivan, N. (1983) *Fascism*, London, Dent.
Plamenatz, J. (1965) *Readings from Liberal Writers*, London, Allen & Unwin.
Rose, R. (1982) *Understanding the United Kingdom: The Territorial Dimension in Government*, London, Longman.
Ryan, A. (1974) *J. S. Mill*, London, Routledge & Kegan Paul.
Skidelsky, R. (1975) *Oswald Mosley*, London, Macmillan.
Smith, A. D. (1979) *Nationalism in the Twentieth Century*, Oxford, Martin Robertson.
Wright, A. (1983) *British Socialism*, London, Longman.

QUESTIONS

1. What do you understand by the concept of political ideology?
2. Can full Socialism be achieved by evolutionary as opposed to revolutionary methods?
3. What were the theoretical fundamentals of Fascism as an ideology?

ASSIGNMENT

Choose a political ideology (e.g. Socialism, Liberalism or Conservatism) and establish the different strands of thought within it, e.g. anarchism, syndicalism, Fabianism, Marxism, within Socialism. Describe the leading ideas of each strand and identify the particular features which enable it to be termed Socialist or Conservative or Liberal.

4

The Organisation of the State

The position reached so far may now be summarised. Politics is the sphere of life in which social conflicts are expressed and resolved. Conflict arises out of differences of material interest and out of intellectual disagreement. These differences and disagreements are channelled into a struggle by individuals and groups to gain power or to influence government. This struggle for power may be conducted by violent methods (by terrorism, *coup d'état* and revolution) or peacefully (by lobbying, campaigns and elections). Authoritative settlement of the most important social conflicts together with ultimate control over social priorities and values is the function of the State (Chapter 1). The prevalent norms, attitudes and values of the society into which people are born shape their political behaviour. Overall attitudes to government, the sense of political competence and willingness to undertake positions of responsibility are affected by the process of socialisation. In this process, family, school, peer group and, above all, class play important formative roles (Chapter 2). Ideology – which we defined as a system of belief which serves as a guide to action – is a vitally significant intellectual influence upon political behaviour. We explained the doctrines on man, society and government of the leading modern ideologies against a historical background (Chapter 3).

The theme of this chapter is also of central importance to politics: the distribution of power and authority within the State. We begin by proposing a threefold classification of forms of government which identifies the characteristic features of each type of regime and gives some leading examples. In doing so, we seek to establish some significant connections and interrelationships between forms of government and such matters as party systems, the nature and extent of political participation, economic development and types of economic system, class structure and ideology. We then turn to examine the formal organisation of the State, focusing on constitutions and examining how they are to be understood.

TYPES OF GOVERNMENT

Broadly speaking, systems of government fall into three categories: autocratic, communist, and liberal-democratic. However simplified, such a classification is necessary to enable sense to be made of what would otherwise be a

72

bewildering multiplicity of governments. The main criteria used in arriving at this typology are:

1. The extent and genuineness of political participation, taking into account not just the proportion of the adult population involved in politics but also and especially the degree of political choice which people have and their ability to influence and change their rulers by peaceful methods. This criterion enables distinctions to be drawn between countries according to whether or not they possess universal suffrage, an uncoerced and incorrupt system of elections and competing political parties.
2. The predominant method relied on by governments to secure popular obedience or compliance; these include force, deference, regimentation and persuasion. This criterion facilitates distinctions according to whether governments simply suppress all opinions other than their own; respond to the existence of intellectual diversity not only by repression but also by the *conversion* of dissenters to a single – often ideological – 'truth'; or try to achieve the amount of agreement all governments need in order to govern by methods of *persuasion*, relegating force to a last resort.
3. The aims of government, including their policy goals, which may be conservative, reformist or transformative. Regimes differ in the degree to which their policies merely preserve the privileged position of an élite or are of benefit to the whole population. They vary also in the extent to which they favour present as against future public welfare, in the extent to which they take into account the actual desires of the people in setting policy-goals and, finally, in the extent to which they seek to politicise the whole of life, ignoring and breaking down the boundary between public and private spheres.

Autocratic regimes

In *autocratic* regimes, a single person, party or group holds power, exercising it in an arbitrary manner. Political participation is generally low or heavily regimented. The autocratic type of government is a closed political system in which competition for power is strictly curtailed – often to a small élite – opinion is censored, opposition is suppressed and changes of government frequently take place by violence. This kind of political system is widespread throughout the Third World – Africa, Asia and Latin America.

Autocratic political systems further subdivide into *traditional* dynasties (e.g. Saudi Arabia), *military* regimes (e.g. General Zia in Pakistan, General Pinochet in Chile and the junta under General Galtieri in Argentina) and the *non-Communist one-party States* (especially common in Africa south of the Sahara, e.g. Dr Hastings Banda's Congress party in Malawi). The existence of more than one party is vital to the possibility of political choice: no second party, no choice. Neither traditional dynasties nor military regimes have parties and, in all, about one quarter of the countries in the world fall into the category of non-party regimes. In one-party regimes, choice is severely limited, normally to vanishing point, but may not be entirely absent because sometimes more than one party may be permitted by law, even if in practice a particular party is completely dominant (as, for instance, is the case in Mexico). Over one third of countries have single-party systems, although, of these, less than half fall into the category of *non-Communist* one-party States. Often, in such regimes, the party is the personal creation of a powerful leader (Nkrumah in Ghana in the 1950s; Kenyatta in Kenya) and, typically, it is used to mobilise the mass of the population behind modernising, nationalist goals. Characteristically, such regimes lack the resources to develop into totalitarian systems. The democratic institutions and procedures often established by law in such countries are usually reduced to a mere façade by restrictions on the freedom of the press, electoral intimidation and corruption and the closure of opposition parties.

Why are such regimes obeyed? What is the source of their authority? In traditional dynastic regimes, authority rests upon custom and religion. Customary obedience is unquestioned, and this uncritical acceptance receives powerful support from the mystery of religion. Certain families rule because God wills it so: government derives authority from being seen as part of the divine order of things. The rationale of military government, by contrast, is both pragmatic and nationalist: it is based on the two claims to be acting out of necessity and in the national interest. Military leaders only intervene, they say, when civilian regimes have broken down and lost their legitimacy. Certain reasons occur frequently in their self-justifications: the corruption and unconstitutionality of civilian governments; specific weaknesses in the economy – raging inflation or high unemployment; and the growth of public disorder and instability. Unlike traditional regimes, military systems of government often support their right to rule by appealing to popular sovereignty. The fact that they are authoritarian in essence, and lacking in both popular participation and political choice, does not prevent their invocation of the voice of the people, often by means of carefully-manipulated elections to approve their take-overs. Finally, the legitimacy of non-Communist single-party systems of government often depends upon the personality of an exceptional leader, a Kaunda, Nyerere or Bourguiba. The authority of their regimes may derive also from quasi-democratic institutions and processes and from the frequently-asserted claim to be serving the nation but it still depends most of all upon the special insights and moral attributes generally perceived in their leaders.

The bulk of autocratic regimes are to be found in Third World countries. These tend to have predominantly agrarian economies, low rates of adult literacy and low per capita incomes. Not only are they poor; they often have highly stratified social systems, in which a disproportionate amount of national income finds its way into the hands of a social élite. Many are ex-colonial States. Their economic backwardness is an important factor in their autocratic politics. Their poverty, relatively low urbanisation and generally inadequate provision with modern mass communications media are severe handicaps upon the development of democratic institutions. Often these disabilities are further worsened by the existence of tribal, ethnic and religious divisions. Together, these factors hold back the growth of an organised public opinion which could support the kind of consensus on procedural values which underpins democracy in the northern hemisphere. Lacking the secondary social associations – competitive multi-party systems and pressure groups, which enable government to change hands peacefully and be influenced by non-violent means – such countries are ill-fitted for anything other than autocracy, whether this is provided by hereditary ruler, military 'strong man' or charismatic leader in a populist style. Lacking social homogeneity, often composed not of one 'public' but of several based on tribes, ethnic groups or religions, they tend to be chronically unstable, characterised by numerous irregular and often violent transfers of power. Thus, S. E. Finer having noted that military interventions in politics is by no means confined to the Third World, citing pre-war Germany, Japan, Spain and Eastern Europe, continues:

> But for all that, the poorer, the newer and the extra-European states are the principal victims of military intervention in politics. The statistics are eloquent on this point. In the ... eleven years from January 1958 to November 1969, the military have made eighty-eight coups in fifty-two countries. By the end of this brief period twenty-two of the thirty-eight African states had been affected, fourteen of the twenty-six Asian states and eleven of the twenty-three Latin American and Caribbean ones ... And it is overwhelmingly the poorer that are affected. There were seventy-three states whose per capita income was less than 330 dollars (1963 figure): of these forty-five suffered military coups, that is to say, 62 per cent of the total (Finer, *Comparative Government*, pp. 532–3).

Communist regimes

A second group of States may be described as Communist regimes. These States in general terms are one-party regimes dominated by centralised Socialist parties. Notwithstanding their Socialist ideology, these countries do not form a single 'bloc', the main division being between the Marxist-Leninist USSR and the Chinese variant of communism based on Mao. The leading communist one-party States which may be grouped with the USSR are its East European satellites – Poland, East Germany, Czechoslovakia, Hungary, Bulgaria and Romania; China; a group of Asian Socialist countries – North Korea, North Vietnam, Laos, Kampuchea and Mongolia; Cuba; and two East European States which have demonstrated some independence of the Soviet Union – Albania and Yugoslavia. These countries range from the very poor (North Vietnam) to the relatively well-off, East

Germany (German Democratic Republic – GDR). They include the pre-industrial, the industrialised and those in the process of industrialisation. About one-third of the world's population (1.5 billion people) now live in communist one-party States. In recent decades many developing countries have adopted Marxist–Leninism as an ideology and they constitute 'the new Communist Third World'. These States are to be found mainly in Africa and include Benin, the Congo Republic, Guinea-Bissau, Mozambique and Madagascar. But they tend to resemble the autocratic States already discussed rather than the well-established communist States mentioned at the beginning of this section. Nor is the Marxist commitment of some of them more than superficial. Hence, they are not included in the examination of communist regimes in this section.

In terms of our initial criteria of types of government, communist single-party regimes are characterised by considerable but highly-regimented political participation; little or no political choice; and transformative policy goals which set the achievement of a fully Socialist society as their ultimate target.

1. Political participation is 'considerable' because (a) party membership figures are often high – in 1981, for example, membership of the Communist Party in the Soviet Union was 17.5 million; and (b) electoral turn-out is virtually total – 90 per cent (in Yugoslavia) is a low figure and in the USSR and some Eastern European States it tends to be higher still. But such participation is also 'highly regimented' in view of the absence of party competition and the limitation of political discussion to a single comprehensive official ideology.
2. The scant political choice occurs because party leaders are selected rather than elected: in the Soviet Union, they are chosen by the Politburo, the supreme policy-making body of the Communist Party, subject to final approval by the party's Central Committee. Leadership selection is thus a closed process limited to a very small group of top politicians. Second, elections to Communist legislatures are 'elections without choice': at the most, voters will be offered a very limited choice between candidates from the same party or between candidates of different groupings within a Communist-dominated coalition. Very often, there is not even a 'limited choice': the only alternative to voting for the official candidate is abstention. Moreover, as Roger Charlton points out in *Comparative Politics* (1986), it is also the case that even where there are elections in Communist States, they are confined to institutions of marginal importance: they do not affect policy or the leadership (p. 177).
3. Communist States are transformative regimes in the sense that they aim at bringing about a new type of society based on Marxist-Leninism or Maoism. The Communist Party itself in these societies is the repository and guardian of the official ideology and because truth is perceived as monolithic rather than diverse and pluralistic, it follows that it may take

what steps it sees as necessary to advance the truth and suppress dissident views. Discussion takes place therefore within strict confines and deviance from the 'party line' can be punished as dissent and 'corrected' by, for example, psychiatric treatment as 'error'. Through the party there is strict government control of the economy, culture and the communications media.

Unlike liberal-democracies which have predominantly market economies Communist States have command economies – that is, centrally-planned economic systems in which public ownership of enterprises is the rule. These transformative regimes are highly-organised, repressive States in which compulsory participation (in matters like voting) and, from time to time, explicit enthusiasm are required from the mass of the population. Fundamental freedoms of speech, association and movement are lacking in communist systems and individuals have no effective remedies against the actions of the State. In such regimes, the firm distinction to be found in Western liberal countries between the State as the sphere of compulsion and society as the sphere of uncoerced, voluntary activity disappears. Activities such as art, literature and earning one's living, which in liberal societies take place in the private sphere, in communist countries take place within the sphere regulated by the party in the name of the official ideology. Group activity operates under strict party supervision; there is no equivalent of Western-style pressure groups. Where dissident behaviour exists – as in attendance at churches and mosques – it does so in a shadowy way at the margins of society. Dissident writings likewise have no formal existence but are circulated secretly.

The physical agency through which this formidable type of power is exercised is the single disciplined party. Its principle of organisation – relation to the State and society – and its control of elections embody a massive concentration of power in the USSR. In Leninist theory, the Communist Party, from its 'seizure of power in 1917, has constituted a political élite, now officially called 'the vanguard of the people'. The supreme Party organ, the Politburo, that is, the Political Bureau of its Central Committee, is, in effect, the government of the Soviet Union. The Party is the State. The secretariat of the Central Committee provides the heads of the major government departments – they administer the police, the security service, the judiciary, agriculture, industry, transport, indeed, all the services and concerns of a major industrialised country.

Party control of society at large is achieved in two ways: first, through disciplined authority exercised over a wide party membership, amounting to about 20 per cent of the Soviet population; and, second, through the strategic location of party members in positions of power at all levels of society. The supreme principle with regard to the distribution of authority within the Party is 'democratic centralism', the essence of which is that the decisions of the higher party committees are unconditionally binding on the lower ones.

All members must obey the 'party line' and the usual penalty for not doing so is expulsion; there were 900 000 expulsions between 1951 and 1964. Second, the policy of the Party is to permeate society by forming party cadres in every institution and at every stage of political organisation. In so doing, it is seeking to ensure that a wide range of enterprises – industrial, agricultural, trading, cultural and education – conform to central policy directives. Finally, despite the fact that formal provision is made for elections to be contested, in practice they are also controlled by the Party which selects and approves all candidates.

Until quite recently, the term 'totalitarian' was widely employed to designate the Soviet and other communist dictatorships. The mobilisation of these societies behind a single official ideology, their centrally-directed 'command' economies, their obliteration of the distinction between State and society, the ruthless authoritarianism of their methods of government, the extermination of their opponents – all these features seemed to require them to be distinguished from traditional forms of autocracy. However, although useful to describe the Stalinist regime of the 1930s, the word is of diminished value today as a term of political science, first, because there is no agreement on its meaning and second, because the very idea of total power – as a practice rather than an aspiration – has been questioned.

Liberal–democratic systems

In the modern world, virtually all governments claim to be democratic including those already described as autocratic and communist. The reason for this apparently strange fact is not far to seek. The etymological origin of the word 'democracy' is the Greek word 'demos' (people) and the modern meaning of the term reflects its Greek origin – 'rule by the people'. Since 1918, 'democracy' has been the primary principle by which governments and governmental systems have sought to justify their existence. It is *the* contemporary method of legitimating power. Few political systems in the modern world do not claim to be operated by, with the consent or in the interests of the people. Thus, not only do the USA, France and the United Kingdom call themselves 'democracies', so also do Russia, China, North Vietnam and many other countries. There are three possible responses to this situation. One is to argue that the fact that the word can be employed to describe such widely-differing systems suggests that it has now lost all usefulness as a term of political classification; at best, it denotes a pre-condition of *all* modern government – that it needs to carry the mass of the population along with it if it is to accomplish its purposes. Accordingly, as Bernard Crick suggests, rather than continue to employ such a meaningless term, it would be preferable to abandon it completely and turn to a word such as 'republic' when a contrast with autocratic and Communist systems is sought (B. Crick, *Basic Forms of Government*, 1973, pp. 22–7). This seems a

mistaken approach, if only, but not only, because historically and concep-
tually 'republicanism' has very specific associations with *non-monarchical
government*. A second response is to maintain, as C. B. MacPherson does in
The Real World of Democracy (1966), that a wide variety of States may
legitimately call themselves 'democratic': for example, not only do China and
Egypt describe themselves as democracies, they are right to do so. Thus,
'democracy' has three variants, all equally valid, the Communist, the
Underdeveloped and the Western. The weakness of this approach is that it
seems to blur important distinctions between these three types of system. The
third response – the one adopted here – is to continue to employ the word
'democracy' as a useful term of political classification, but prefaced by the
adjective 'liberal'; thus, liberal-democracy. We decide to employ this expression as a way of characterising a form of government which institutiona-
lises both political *choice*, even if limited, and universal *participation*, even if
falling short of this ideal.

Joining the two terms enables us to express two basic features of this
political system. It is *liberal* in two senses: first, because it is a *pluralist regime*
in which there is open competition for power between individuals, groups
and parties; and second, because it is a *limited system of government* in which
the powers of rulers are curtailed by laws enforceable in the courts and the
scope of government is restricted by a combination of convention, ideology
and public opinion. It is *democratic* because government is both derived from
and accountable to public opinion; derived from it in the sense that
government owes its existence to regularly-held elections based on universal
franchise, and accountable to it in the sense that a legally-guaranteed
political opposition keeps government responsive to public opinion in the
intervals between elections.

The term 'liberal-democracy', then, expresses both a number of political
values and a set of constitutional mechanisms for putting them into practice.
It is the purpose of this section to explore further the values and institutions
of liberal-democratic systems of government.

Since 'democracy' must in a genuine way mean 'rule by the people', we
begin by asking how popular government can be achieved in geographically
extensive territories with large populations. Clearly, 'rule by the people' in its
most fundamental meaning of direct democracy – that is, participation in
decision-making by all citizens – is out of the question in any but the smallest
and most primitive face-to-face communities. In large, populous modern
States, democracy must be of the *representative* kind, in which popular
participation in politics is largely indirect through representatives whom 'the
people' defined in terms of the universal franchise elect to some kind of
representative institution, i.e. an assembly or parliament. However, the fact
that the only practicable system in the modern world is *representative
democracy* does not mean that the idea of direct democracy is without
influence. On the contrary, this concept has continued to infuse both the

values and the institutions of representative democracies.

It is clear that the degree of popular influence upon governmental decision-making in this political system may vary greatly. The minimal conditions of democracy may reasonably be said to include regular uncoerced elections – from which corruption and intimidation have been removed – universal voting rights, a party system based on two or more competing parties and free communications media. States exceed these criteria to differing degrees. In the spectrum of democracy, the USA appears in many ways to be a more democratic country than the United Kingdom. It goes to the polls more often, at local, State and Federal (i.e. national) levels, has an elective Upper House and a more egalitarian culture. As well as being a major element in a liberal-democratic political system, then, democracy is also an ideology. At the centre of democratic ideology is the doctrine that the more strongly the political system manages to incorporate popular influence, the better it is. This radical conception derives from the eighteenth-century European and American revolutions in general and from the theory of Jean-Jacques Rousseau in particular. It is the doctrine of the sovereignty of the people.

To a very considerable extent, representative democracy as a whole rests on this political principle. What legitimates the activities of governments in this type of political system is *popular consent*. This does not mean that individuals, groups and parties may be taken to endorse every single decision a government may make. It simply means that because citizens possess the means to effect peaceful and genuine changes of government, their support for the *system in general* can be assumed. Radical democrats, however, propound a strong version of the theory of popular sovereignty. They seek to make the promise of democracy into a reality. To close the gap between the public and its representatives, they favour a combination of constitutional devices, theories and institutions. In particular, they advocate frequent use of referendums, the delegate rather than the Burkean theory of the representative and the mandate theory of elections (see further below, pp. 81 and 82–83). It is enough to notice here that the model of direct democracy underlies radical theory. One example points up the contrast between what may be called the minimalist and maximalist versions of representative democracy. For the radical, the representative is an agent of the people, a mere instructed delegate; to the conservative, whilst the representative must at all times listen carefully to what his constituents say, his ultimate responsibility is to his own judgement.

In any case, it is clear that democracy in the modern world must be *representative*. But whom or what do the representatives represent? One obvious answer, implicit in the above discussion, is: their constituents or, more simply, their constituencies. The basis of representation in this sense is a particular unit of territory. Historically, both in the UK and the USA, this was the primary meaning of political representation, and, even after the right to vote became universal, it has remained of great importance. But territorial representation alone could not provide the basis of democratic government without the existence of another factor: that of *party*. Party systems developed in the age of the universal franchise as the sole practicable method of enabling voters *to choose their rulers*. To understand the significance of party, it is enough simply to imagine a representative system without them. Voters could certainly decide which individual they wished to represent them in parliament, congress or assembly, but, without party, that is all that they would decide. And the assembly would be an unstructured grouping of individuals. The only way a government could emerge in such circumstances would be by the actions of the representatives themselves. Again, in the absence of party, this too would be a difficult task, even though informal groupings might well exist. So far as the electorate were concerned, government would be both indirect, operating at one remove from popular influence, and also irresponsible. Modern representative democracy depends upon the existence of competing political parties.

In terms of the system as a whole, parties have two main functions:

1. They enable voters to elect *governments*. This is because, in seeking election in particular constituencies, candidates stand as party men or women, not just as individuals; and are voted for (and against) as such, that is, as the representatives of party. Parties, therefore, group candidates coherently so that votes in one constituency can be related to votes in another. They narrow down the alternatives at elections in such a way as to enable the verdicts of constituencies to be aggregated into the selection of a government. Democratic government is, above all, *party* government. By deciding the party composition of parliament, voters in the United Kingdom also determine the party complexion of the government; in the United States, they elect the President directly.

2. Party provides the primary source of political *opposition* to the government of the day. The role of the opposition or parties is twofold: to criticise and to win concessions from the executive; and to provide an alternative government. Sometimes, the practice of institutionalising opposition by means of party causes irritation, even in well-established democracies: half the cleverest people in the country uniting to prevent the other half governing, was how one nineteenth-century writer, Sir Henry Maine, put it. In fact, however, effective party opposition is essential in liberal-democratic theory because it makes governments accountable and provides genuine electoral choice as well as strengthening the system as a whole by enabling dissent to be openly expressed.

Indeed, it is possible to go even further and to argue that it is their legitimisation of the open expression of political dissent that constitutes the fundamental distinguishing mark between liberal-democracies, on the one hand, and autocratic and communist regimes, on the other. It reflects a particular conception of the basic nature of political activity. Because

TABLE 4.1

Autocratic

Major features Closed regime

No formal competition for power which is mono-polised by a single party, family or by military

Minimal public political participation

Political participation largely confined to social élite

Censorship of opinion

Suppression of opposition

Government legitimated by tradition, religion, the public interest as defined by the military, or the personality of a charismatic leader

Reliance on force, since strong foundations of public support are lacking

Often ended by violence

They are either without parties (traditional) or have authoritarian–populist parties, created by a dynamic leader, which often collapse after his fall from power.

Social and economic structure Predominantly poor and agrarian
Landowning élites appropriate surpluses
Large peasantries
Highly stratified social structure with large gulf between rich and poor (this applies even to oil-rich countries of North Africa and the Middle East)

Geographical distribution Largely Third World – Latin American, African and Asian countries

Communist

Major features Closed regime

Power concentrated in single disciplined party

Party becomes social and political élite monopolis-ing key jobs in State bureaucracy

Widespread public political participation, but this is regimented

Government legitimated by official ideology

No political opposition to this ideology is allowed; where it appears, it is suppressed

Ideology provides goal of egalitarian classlessness

Strict control over mass media; severe censorship and constant government propaganda

TABLE 4.1—*contd.*

Social and economic structures	May be largely agrarian (e.g. Asian Communist societies where peasants played a major part in revolution)
	Usually, industrialised and industrialising societies
	Public ownership
	Central planning of the economy
	Some of these countries, e.g. East Germany and Czechoslovakia, have significantly reduced material inequality, but the distribution of 'goods' by party membership introduces important distortions in social structure of Communist countries
Geographical distribution	USSR, and its Eastern European satellites, China, North Korea, North Vietnam, Laos, Kampuchea, Cuba

Liberal-democratic

Major features	Open regime
	High level of competition for power
	Two-or-more party system
	Variety of voluntary groups
	Universal suffrage
	Widespread popular political participation although for most people largely confined to elections
	Free mass media
	Legal and constitutional limitations on powers of office-holders
	Political opposition is both permitted and legally provided for
	System legitimated in terms of doctrine of popular sovereignty
	Adherence to liberal ideas and norms of behaviour is widely diffused
Social and economic structure	Mainly advanced industrialised capitalist societies
	Some poor market economies, such as India
	Most market economies are now 'mixed economies' in that they contain – as a result of political decision – significant public enterprise sectors
	Large and expanding middle classes
Geographical distribution	USA, UK, Australia, New Zealand, Canada, France, West Germany, Italy, Holland, Belgium, Scandnavian countries, Israel, Japan, India, Sri Lanka

disagreement is a basic feature of social life, it is considered wiser to make institutional provision for it – through free mass media and voluntary groups as well as through competing parties – than to attempt to suppress it. By these means, a minority may seek to transform itself into a majority and, above all, power may change hands peacefully. That liberal-democracy as a political system rests on rule by the ballot-box rather than by the bullet is undeniably a cliché yet one worth reiteration since it embodies an important truth. It does not mean, of course, that minorities *will* always 'play the political game' according to constitutional rules but it does put a high premium upon such behaviour. Nor is it intended to deny that force as an ultimate sanction lies behind the liberal-democratic State as it does other types of regime. What it does suggest is that liberal-democracies, in permitting a high degree of legitimate dissent, are also far more reluctant than other political systems to coerce recalcitrant minorities. Above all, it indicates that pluralist regimes regard compromise, conciliation and the willingness to negotiate as major political virtues and, in principle, consider political differences to be reconcilable.

Of the three broad kinds of political system we have considered, liberal-democracy is by far the most difficult to operate successfully. This is because its complex pattern of institutions – which include a system of competing parties, free mass media, a diverse range of voluntary groups and an independent judiciary – are not only inherently hard to achieve but also themselves depend for their effective working upon favourable social and cultural conditions. These include a politically-mature electorate and a political culture which is both tolerant of social diversity and respectful of legality. These circumstances have been virtually non-existent throughout the bulk of recorded history and remain comparatively uncommon at the present day. Only about forty countries – constituting less than one-third of the States of the world – can be described as liberal-democracies. They include the USA, Canada, Israel, the UK, France, Germany, Italy, Belgium, Holland, Switzerland, Iceland, India, Sri Lanka and the Irish Republic in the Northern hemisphere, and, in the Southern part of the globe Australia and New Zealand. It is no accident that this list contains most of the world's wealthy countries and is, in fact, largely composed of rich countries, the exceptions being India and Sri Lanka.

Considered in social and economic terms, these liberal-democratic States have three major characteristics. As Michael Kidron and Ronald Segal show, they are by world standards – with the exceptions we have noted – all rich or very rich; in most of them wealth tends to be – again by world criteria – relatively evenly-distributed; and they are all market economies (Kidron and Segal, *The State of the World Atlas*, 1981, Section 43). This argument does not imply economic determinism. East Germany and Libya both have high levels of income *per capita* but are respectively Socialist and military political systems. In East Germany and several other East European Communist regimes, the degree of material inequality is lower than in many industrialised democratic societies. The strongest correlation seems to be not between levels of wealth as such nor even between relatively even distribution of wealth and liberal democracy but between the market economy and a pluralist political regime. This is understandable since, historically, liberalism as a political system, and capitalism, have developed together over the past three hundred years, largely in the north-west corner of Europe and in North America. Indeed, in the present-day world, it is the liberalism rather than the 'democracy' of the liberal-democracies that stands out. The features which most distinguish them from the other types of regime considered earlier are their constitutionalism, their social and political freedom and the fact that they permit political opposition rather than the degree of participation they achieve.

Having described the predominant features of the three major types of government in the world (see Table 4.1 for a summary), we turn now to the second theme of this chapter – the formal organisation of a State, its constitution, taking as our particular theme the relationship between constitutional law and the realities of political power.

WHAT IS A CONSTITUTION AND HOW IS IT DISTINGUISHED FROM A 'POLITICAL' SYSTEM?

In discussing types of political system, we have made continual reference to such matters as how power is distributed throughout society, what arrangements exist for its transfer between one office-holder and another, the extent and nature of limitations on its exercise, and so on. Yet, in doing so, we have ignored up to this point one obvious source of such knowledge: the formal constitution of a State. Our reason for this omission is simple. Briefly, it is that formal constitutions are generally imperfect guides to political reality – to the *actual* as compared with the supposed distribution of power within a State. This point is easily demonstrated. Thus, many constitutions either omit or scarcely mention the roles in the political process of such important institutions as parties, pressure groups and civil services. Consider, by way of example, just one of these institutions, the party. So influential are the structure and number of parties upon the working of political systems that some leading political scientists follow Jean Blondel in *Comparing Political Systems* (1973) in seeing these factors as the major determinants of the nature of political regimes. Yet, vital as it is, the significance of party is by no means universally acknowledged in formal constitutions. The constitutions of the USSR and the Eastern European Socialist countries certainly refer to the all-powerful single party, but as Leslie Wolf-Phillips notes in *Constitutions of Modern States* (1968) the formal constitutions of at least two of the major liberal-democracies, the USA and the UK, omit or virtually ignore their role

(L. Wolf-Phillips, *Constitution of Modern States*, 1968, p. xxi). Swayed by the amount of actual political behaviour occurring outside the formal legal framework, one post-war school of political scientists nearly abandoned the study of constitutions altogether.

A second factor which has contributed to the neglect of formal constitutions has been the ease and frequency with which they are flouted and overthrown. The constant demolition of allegedly binding constitutions since 1918 appears to mock the nineteenth-century belief in the capacity of written codes of rules to mould political actions. The activities of dictators in destroying constitutions are merely dramatic examples of a familiar process. Slightly extending this category, two American students of politics, Charles L. Taylor and Michael C. Hudson in their *World Handbook of Political and Social Indicators* (1972), counted 147 of what they term 'irregular executive transfers' between 1947 and 1968. These were changes of ruling position from one leader or group to another which in their words are 'accomplished outside the conventional legal or customary procedures for transferring formal power in effect at the time of the event and accompanied by actual or directly threatened violence' (Taylor and Hudson, *World Handbook of Political and Social Indicators*, pp. 150–1). Clearly, charting the breaches of constitutional law which occur over the whole range of political activity purportedly covered by constitutions would be a task of awesome laboriousness and complexity.

Yet, powerful though these considerations undoubtedly are, they represent arguments for not expecting too much from the study of formal constitutions rather than for abandoning the exercise altogether. As S. E. Finer has pointed out, the fact that door locks are sometimes picked, or otherwise circumvented, does not mean that we can do without them. Nor is it a valid reason for neglecting their study that formal constitutions are invariably *incomplete* as guides to political practice. A moment's thought is enough to show that no document or set of documents could ever incorporate the whole of a country's political system in its vastly-complex entirety. Moreover, their lack of correspondence with political realities can be – and has been – exaggerated. To cite S. E. Finer again, few formal constitutions bear 'no relationship whatsoever to what goes on' in a political system and in some countries – for example, the USA, France and West Germany – 'the practice of politics does not widely diverge from the guidelines in the constitutional texts' (Finer, *Five Constitutions*, pp. 16; 13–14). 'Realistic' students of politics, it seems clear, need to distinguish between the formal and informal elements in a political system or State, between what may be termed the 'public' constitution, normally set out in a written document or documents, and the 'private' constitution, the unspecified activities of individuals, groups, parties and other institutions. Both components are necessary to any comprehensive description of the structure and operations of power and authority in a political community.

Formal, or 'public', constitutions matter for a number of reasons. First, they serve as revelations – and reminders – of the political principles which a particular people considers important, and wishes to live up to. For example, the Chinese Constitution in its Article 6 expresses that country's commitment to Socialism just as the US Constitution encapsulates American adherence to liberalism. Second, as sets of rules, they provide one means of restraint – alongside moral codes, cultural norms and the fear of exposure – upon politicians and civil servants. The American Constitution did not prevent the criminal behaviour of Richard Nixon but it did assist in bringing him to account. Third, although formal constitutions do not contain all the rules, practices and institutions that make up a political system, they are useful as indicators of many of the most important of them. The frequency of elections, the qualifications for voting, the composition and powers of representative assemblies, for instance, are all normally the subject of formal constitutional provision. Fourth, 'public' constitutions repay attention because, since human beings are generally rule-observing creatures and normally neither make nor break laws just for the fun of it, they enable political behaviour in certain circumstances to be effectively predicted. They make it possible for political practitioners and informed observers to forecast with some degree of accuracy in what circumstances, for example, an American President will use his veto or the Supreme Court be called upon to make a constitutional judgement.

What, then, is a formal constitution? The following definition by O. Hood-Phillips is a persuasive one. A formal constitution consists of 'the laws, customs and conventions which define the compositions and powers of organs of the state, and regulate the relations of the various state organs to one another, and to the private citizen (Hood-Phillips, *Constitutional and Administrative Law*, 6th edn., 1978, p. 5). In more general terms, as we saw in Chapter 1, a constitution allocates *authority* within a community. It makes provision for its government, formally laying down the roles of officers and agencies of government, their interrelationships and their relations with individuals in their public capacity as citizens. A constitution in this sense is the major way of giving *legitimacy* to a particular system of government – that is, to a particular pattern of offices, to a particular way of organising the distribution of power within a State.

Before considering the British Constitution, both formal and informal, 'public' and 'private', together with the historical, social, economic and cultural forces which have shaped it, we need to look briefly at the main ways in which formal constitutions have been distinguished. It is customary to classify formal constitutions according to whether they are 'unitary' or 'federal', 'written' or 'unwritten' and 'rigid' or 'flexible', and we deal with each set of terms in turn. It is enough to say at the outset that in recent years the value of the comparative study of political systems and constitutions has been powerfully underlined within the United Kingdom. To cite only a few of the numerous examples: entry into the European Common Market, the previously unprecedented referenda on joining the EEC and on Scottish and Welsh devolution, and the abolition of the Greater London Council have raised fundamental issues about the nature and integrity of the British Constitution and as a corollary the question of the extent to which the UK might profitably borrow from the constitutional practice of other countries.

Unitary and federal systems

Constitutions seek to create a viable order out of the diversity which confronts them – a diversity of classes, regions and ethnic groups. All these various subgroups demand from the makers of constitutions inclusion in the State in a manner which measures up to their sense of their own dignity and self-respect. Whilst the pressures that classes may exert should not be underestimated, the claims of regional and ethnic groupings are normally the hardest to accommodate constitutionally. Where the differing cultures and races in a State are not physically separate from the rest of the community, like Negroes in the United States or West Indians and Pakistanis in the United Kingdom, they have to seek protection of their civil rights by special constitutional guarantees and legislation. Where ethnic, cultural and national groups are located in geographically distinct areas, as with, for example, the Bretons, Basques, Walloons, Welsh and Scots, a classic problem of State-making exists: that of providing a single government for several territorial regions each with its own culture.

The two major forms of *political* Union are unitary and federal systems. Each recognises the territorial aspect of government – the need to provide for regional cultural diversity – in a different way.

In a *unitary State*, supreme authority remains in the hands of a single source; in a federal State, authority is constitutionally divided between several coordinate agencies. In a unitary State, where power, including the capacity to make rules, is exercised by agencies other than the supreme law-making body, it is always done under the supervision of the supreme body and always with the possibility that what is done may be revoked by the superior authority.

In *federal States*, on the other hand, supreme authority is shared between the central (or federal) government and the various provincial (or state) governments. The central government may have the more important responsibilities but the authority of the provincial governments is inviolable within their constitutionally-allocated sphere of responsibility against overturn by the central authority. Should a clash occur between the coordinate governments, the constitution normally provides a mechanism by which it can be resolved – for example, by a Supreme Court, or similar institution. In the contemporary world, the United Kingdom, France and Japan are unitary States; the USA, USSR and West Germany have federal constitutions.

Written and unwritten constitutions

All formal constitutions are selections of the most important legal and political practices. What is usually meant by referring to some constitutions as 'written' and others as 'unwritten' is the inclusion of the main body of the constitutional law of a country in a single, written document. In the States which do this – in fact, the great majority of the world's countries – the phrase 'the constitution' denotes a single document, however extensive and however amended it may be. States which do not incorporate their principal constitutional rules in a specific document have, on this conception, 'unwritten' constitutions. In recent years, however, the value of this classification has been questioned. At best, it enables only a relatively minor distinction to be made between a small number of countries and the rest of the world. For example, as Wolf-Phillips points out, only Britain, Israel and some Middle Eastern Kingdoms have allegedly 'unwritten' constitutions (p. xi). But the main criticism is that the constitutions of some of the countries even within this small group are not correctly described as 'unwritten', in view of the fact that they do have written laws. What they do not do is to *codify* their leading constitutional practices into a single document. Without jettisoning 'written' and 'unwritten' as constitutional terms, it would seem useful to deploy an additional set of terms such as 'codified' and 'uncodified' in order to distinguish between those countries which incorporate their major constitutional laws in a single document from those which do not.

'Flexible' and 'rigid' constitutions

However, the main purpose of the distinction between 'written' and 'unwritten' constitutions was, and still is, not primarily to classify but to draw attention to a matter which has always been vital to students of politics: the ease, or otherwise, with which constitutions may be altered. It is a major characteristic of 'written' – or, as we prefer to call them, 'codified' – constitutions that the constitutional law embodied in the form of a single document has the status of being fundamental or basic law. Consider, for instance, Article VI, Clause 2 of the US Constitution: 'This Constitution . . . shall be the supreme law of the land.' The point here is that codified constitutions are usually more difficult to change than uncodified ones, requiring special, more arduous procedures. Another pair of terms is often used to designate this further distinction between constitutions which are hard to change and those that are easily altered – the words 'rigid' and 'flexible'. A rigid constitution requires a special procedure for amendment; a flexible one does not, being amended by the same process as the ordinary law.

SUMMARY

Regimes are classifiable into three main types – autocratic, communist and liberal-democratic. The principal criteria used in arriving at this classification include the type of participation, the possibility and extent of electoral choice, the means by which power is transferred, the role of ideology and the existence and nature of ultimate policy goals. *Autocratic* regimes are subdivisible into traditional, military and charismatic leadership types: they are closed political systems characterised by minimal public participation, censorship of opinion and the suppression of opposition. *Communist* regimes are closed systems in which rule is by a single party: they are characterised by widespread but regimented participation and possess an official ideology in the name of which opposition is suppressed; they tend to be highly organised societies in which the population is mobilised by propaganda and other methods towards the goal of a completely Socialist country. *Liberal-democratic* regimes are open systems of government, with competing parties, a variety of voluntary groups, widespread unforced participation and an official opposition both permitted and formally provided for. In autocratic regimes, leaders often emerge by inheritance or forcible take-over, sometimes by limited élite competition and arrangements; in communist systems, they are selected by the top party institutions; in liberal-democracies, they gain and fall from power after regular free competitive elections involving normally the majority of the electorate.

Constitutions deserve study even though they form imperfect guides to political reality and are often overthrown. They need to be complemented by the study, in particular, of the actual working of parties and pressure groups and their interaction with governments (politicians and bureaucrats) in the political process and also by the study of political cultures. But constitutions are valuable as guides both to a country's political aspirations and, to a certain degree, its political practices. They are always important as sources of legitimacy (establishment of a moral right) for a particular distribution of power. The main broad classification of constitutions is as unitary and federal; codified and uncodified (which have largely replaced 'written' and 'unwritten'); and flexible and rigid.

FURTHER READING

Boyd, A. (1983) *An Atlas of World Affairs*, London, Methuen, 2nd edn.
Charlton, R. (1986) *Comparative Government*, London, Longman.
Crick, B. (1973) *Basic Forms of Government: A Sketch and a Model*, London, Macmillan.
Finer, S. E. (1974) *Comparative Government*, Harmondsworth, Penguin.
Finer, S. E. (1979) *Five Constitutions*, Harmondsworth, Penguin.
Hague, R. and Harrop, M. (1987) *Comparative Government and Politics: An Introduction*, London, Macmillan, 2nd edn.

Wolf-Phillips, L. (1968) *Constitutions of Modern States*, London, Pall Mall Press.
Handbook of World Development: The Guide to the Brandt Report, Longman, 1981.

QUESTIONS

1. To what extent and in what ways does a study of other regimes assist the understanding of British politics?
2. What are the most important differences between autocratic, communist and liberal-democratic regimes?

ASSIGNMENT

Conduct a case-study of a system of government which interests you. Collect information according to the criteria suggested on pp. 72–3. Be sure to examine the economic system of the country you are studying and try to relate it to the form of government.

Part II
Institutions and
Participation

5

The British Constitution

This chapter has four themes. It deals in turn with the main sources of the British constitution; its major principles, the working of the Constitution, and the most important recent pressures for constitutional change. We begin with the question

'WHAT MAKES CONSTITUTIONS POLITICAL?'

Sometimes textbooks on this subject have given the impression that constitutions are 'above politics', existing in a kind of free-floating limbo untouched by the daily affairs of the citizens whose lives they purportedly 'regulate'. Anyone who has read this far will realise of course that this is not the case. Constitutions are themselves both *about* politics and *in* politics. Before proceeding to consider the British Constitution, it is worth examining these two points further. First, constitutions are *about* politics because they provide the framework of rules which shape political behaviour. Constitutions provide 'the rules of the game'. No more than in football or cricket do you have to learn long lists of such rules in order to be able to play the political 'game'. But some broad description of the major features of 'the rules' is essential for an understanding of the 'play'. Second, constitutions are *in* politics because as bodies of rules they themselves are subject to pressure from the competing individuals, groups and classes whose activities they constrain. Constitutions at any given moment are always more or less advantageous to some groups and disadvantageous to others. A good current example is the single-member simple-majority system of representation which benefits the Conservative and Labour parties but operates against the Social and Liberal Democrats. As a set of rules, a constitution is something which politicians and political activists are always seeking either to change radically, modify, keep the same or, if they are revolutionaries, overthrow.

This second point is sufficiently important to develop further. Because the constitution is itself political it has to be seen in a dynamic rather than a static way. The British constitution, like other constitutions to a lesser extent, is a *historical* formation. This does not mean that we need a lengthy historical account here of how the constitution came to be what it is. It simply means that its provisions reflect a continually changing balance of social power between classes, groups and interests. It means also that this balance and those constitutional provisions have been changed as a result of *political* action by 'new' groups using such means as demonstrating, lobbying and marching in order to bring about concessions – primarily by legislation – from the established order. In this way, the aristocratic 'balanced' constitution of the eighteenth century became the middle-class liberal constitution of the nineteenth century which, in turn – as a consequence particularly of the franchise extensions of 1918 and 1928 – became the liberal-democratic constitution of the twentieth century. Major shifts of power between the leading national institutions have paralleled these broad constitutional changes. Thus by the mid-nineteenth century the monarchy and the House of Lords had been supplanted as dominative bodies by the House of Commons. One hundred years later, the House of Commons itself had been in part displaced from the centre of the constitutional scene by a large bureaucracy, itself only an aspect of the massive growth of the twentieth-century State, and by the emergence into the political limelight of a vast web of 'outside interests'. Clearly rules which have changed so often and so dramatically over the past two centuries will change again, and change considerably. Some of the current pressures upon the British Constitution to change will be considered later in this chapter.

One point is worth stressing about the *process* of constitutional change and about the *nature* of the constitutional 'settlement' which results from any period of intense constitutional activity. The process itself always consists of a kind of dialogue between (crudely) the forces of conservation and the forces of transformation and the upshot – *the* constitution at any particular moment – represents in essentials a compromise between them. In that sense, the constitution represents the terms, the arrangements, on which a country can be ruled. In this quite abstract but very important sense, constitution-making is about engineering popular consent to government. A simple example is sufficient to reinforce this point. Thus, agitation by the middle and working classes and by women broke the constitutional settlements prevailing respectively in the early nineteenth, late nineteenth and early twentieth centuries. At each time, public consent to the constitution was no longer possible on the old terms; change was a condition of political stability. In essence, the nature of constitutions is to express the conditions under which people will consent to be governed.

THE MAIN SOURCES OF THE BRITISH CONSTITUTION

Some people used to say that Britain altogether lacked a constitution. Later, when this view came to be seen as wrong in view of the large body of constitutional law that does exist, it became common to describe it as unwritten. It is now clear that this interpretation too is in error. Britain's formal constitution is not written down in a single document, but this does not mean that it does not exist. Rather than saying that the British Constitution is unwritten it is more accurate to describe it as *uncodified*, i.e. not set down in a single document like the Constitutions of the USA, USSR and most other modern countries. It is not codified because although often compelled to alter course, the country's political authorities have never in modern times been confronted by the kind of crisis which forced them to think the constitution through to first principles, and to set these down.

But, although uncodified, the British Constitution is *partly written*, as can readily be seen from a glance at its main sources. Philip Norton in *The Constitution in Flux* (1982) has described the formal constitution of the United Kingdom as deriving from four major sources. These are: statute; convention; common law; and works of authority. In what follows, we briefly describe and provide some examples of each type of source in turn.

Statute

Statute is easily the most significant source of British constitutional law. It is the largest single source and it contains the most important parts of the constitution. Statute law consists both of Acts of Parliament and of delegated (or subordinate) legislation made under the authority of the original Act. Its existence is the major reason for describing the constitution as part written. For example, the following matters are all regulated by statute: the composition of the electorate (*Representation of the People Acts*, 1832–1928); the relationships between the Crown and Parliament (*Bill of Rights*, 1689), between the two Houses of Parliament (*Parliament Act*, 1911), between the component parts of the United Kingdom (*Act of Union with Scotland*, 1707) and between the UK and the EEC (*European Communities Act*, 1972); and the rights of the individual against the State (*Habeas Corpus Act*, 1679, and the *Administration of Justice Act*, 1960). As sources of the constitution Statutes are superior to conventions and pronouncements of constitutional experts, are enforced by the State authorities and take precedence over any conflicting common law.

Conventions

Conventions are the least formal source of constitutional rules. Geoffrey Marshall and Graeme Moodie provide us with a persuasive definition. Conventions are 'certain rules of constitutional behaviour which are considered to be binding by and upon those who operate the Constitution, but which are not enforced by the law courts (although the courts may recognise their existence), nor by the presiding officers in the Houses of Parliament' (Marshall and Moodie, *Some Problems of the Constitution* (1967) p. 26).

There can be no doubt that, intangible though they are, conventions are absolutely essential to the working of the constitution. Thus, it is a convention of the constitution that the monarch must appoint as prime minister a person who has the confidence of the House of Commons; in normal circumstances, this person is the leader of the majority party. It is also a convention that the Sovereign must assent to measures passed by both Houses of Parliament. Conventions are a major means by which the constitution adapts to changing circumstances. Conventions develop gradually; the one whereby the Prime Minister should be chosen from the House of Commons is clearly one illustration of how an aristocratic constitution has accommodated itself to democratic reality. Conventions also disappear; formerly, the decision when to advise the monarch to dissolve parliament was taken by the Cabinet as a whole but from the early twentieth century, in keeping with the trend to exalt prime ministerial power, it has been taken by the PM alone, even though he or she may still choose to discuss it with colleagues. Conventions are observed largely because of the *political* difficulties which would follow if they were not – for example, for the Monarchy if it refused a request for a dissolution; for the Prime Minister if, in an age when the Commons is the superior House, he or she came from the Lords, or, again, for the Monarchy if it refused assent to a bill passed by both Houses of Parliament. Conventions are vaguer than laws and sometimes – when, for example, they are ambiguous or challenged – are replaced, or rather superseded, by rules of strict law. In 1911, a loose convention that the upper House should defer to the wishes of the lower House on matters of finance was threatened by the rejection of a budget by the House of Lords and the question of the relations between the two Houses was settled by legislation (*Parliament Act*, 1911).

Common law

Common law means case law and custom, the law which is made by the decisions of the courts or which has grown up as accepted practice over the years, as opposed to the law which is made by statute. As a source of constitutional law, it is now less important than statute, having declined markedly over the centuries. It remains of importance, however, in three main ways. First, the fundamental constitutional principle of *parliamentary sovereignty* derives from a small number of customary, common law rules. Second, what remains of the *royal prerogative* – for example, in the appointment of Ministers, the dissolution of Parliament, the power of pardon and the award of honours – derives from the common law. By convention, of course, these powers have now come to be predominantly exercised on the advice of Ministers, although circumstances are conceivable in which the Crown would have to act without such advice. Third, *judicial interpretation* is a significant source of constitutional law, especially in the field of civil liberties.

Works of authority

Its character as only part-written and as uncodified, together with the absence of any institution which can serve as a constitutional arbiter in cases of doubt such as exists in the USA in the Supreme Court, means that works of authority have on occasion to be invoked for purposes of guidance on the British Constitution. In the post-war period, for example, as S. A. de Smith points out, constitutional authorities have been turned to on such matters as peerage law, the law of treason and the jurisdiction of the English courts in British protectorates (de Smith, *Constitutional and Administrative Law*, 1983, p. 38). Authoritative sources include such works as A. V. Dicey's *An Introduction to the Study of the Law of the Constitution* (for the late nineteenth century), and, in more recent times, O. Hood Phillips's *Constitutional and Administrative Law* and Sir Ivor Jennings's *The Law and the Constitution*. On matters such as the law and custom of parliament, Sir Thomas Erskine May's treatise on the *Law, Privileges, Proceedings and Usage of Parliament* is regarded as definitive.

Before discussing the main principles of the Constitution, one other feature is worthy of comment. The British Constitution is a *flexible* constitution. Unlike those countries which lay down specific procedures for the amendment of the constitution – in other words, which make changing constitutional law more difficult than changing ordinary law, Britain has no such special procedures for altering its constitution. The British Constitution is a clear even extreme example of flexibility. Constitutional law does not possess any special status and may be changed by the same procedure as the ordinary law.

WHAT ARE THE MAIN PRINCIPLES OF THE BRITISH CONSTITUTION?

The British Constitution is *unitary* rather than federal in nature. It is based on the principle of *parliamentary sovereignty*. It is said to enshrine *the rule of law*.

In the first place, the United Kingdom is a political union of several countries each with a different constitutional status. Legally, it consists of the kingdoms of England and Scotland, the Principality of Wales and two-thirds of the province of Ulster (Northern Ireland) which chose to remain loyal to the British Crown in 1921, when the rest of Ireland split away to form what eventually became the Republic of Ireland (1949). However, although the national subdivisions of the British Isles lend themselves in theory to a federal constitution, the United Kingdom has remained a *unitary State*. Authority is not divided between coordinate governing institutions – for example, the Westminster parliament and (say) assemblies in Scotland, Wales and Northern Ireland – but rests solely in the United Kingdom parliament at Westminster. A major reason why Britain has become and remained a unitary State is the imbalance in population and resources between its component elements which greatly favour one nation, England. This, along with the strength of political will they displayed, enabled mediaeval and early modern English ruling groups successively to incorporate Wales (1536), Scotland (1707) and Ireland (1801) into a political Union on terms dictated by its most powerful member. The grounds that have been given for thinking that the UK is not a unitary State are not convincing. These are that Scotland retains its own legal system and, more significantly, that between 1921 and 1972 the status of Northern Ireland was more akin to that of a provincial unit in a federal system than to a constitutionally subordinate part of a unitary State. The constitutionally subordinate status of Scotland and Wales was revealed over the issue of devolution in the late 1970s when, having legislated devolved powers upon Scottish and Welsh assemblies in 1978, the Westminster parliament repealed them in the following year. The fundamentally subordinate position of Stormont, the Northern Ireland parliament, within the United Kingdom was starkly shown in 1972 when the Westminster government revoked its powers and reasserted direct rule over the province from Westminster. The Westminster parliament (in strict legal terms, the Crown-in-Parliament) remains the supreme constitutional authority in the United Kingdom.

A unitary State and *parliamentary sovereignty* go together. If there were not a single source of sovereignty, the State would not be a unitary one. In formal terms, parliamentary authority is unlimited; it can make or unmake law on any subject whatsoever; and it can do so retrospectively. The classic rule of its omnicompetence derives from William Blackstone the eighteenth-century jurist, who stated that parliament 'can do everything that is not naturally impossible'. No person may question its legislative competence and the courts must give effect to its legislation. If the United Kingdom had a codified constitution, the sovereignty of Parliament would be its foremost principle. However, the point we made at the beginning of this chapter about the essentially *political* context within which constitutions operate needs to be borne in mind here. First, it needs to be remembered that Parliament has liquidated its own authority as a result of political pressures over large areas of the globe this century and could do so again. It could do so nearer home, for example, by introducing a federal structure within the United Kingdom itself. As long as this fundamental structural change had the support of UK public opinion as well as a parliamentary majority, it is likely that it would be recognised by the courts. And from that moment, supreme power in the British State would be divided among several parliaments rather than, as now, residing wholly in one.

Second, we need to consider how far the sovereignty of the UK parliament has already been impaired by entry into the European Community. The *European Communities Act* (1972) has four main consequences. It gives EC law general and binding applicability in the United Kingdom; it gives the force of law in the United Kingdom to obligations arising under the EC treaties; it provides that directly applicable Community law should prevail over conflicting legislation by the British parliament; and it lays down that Community law in general should take precedence over all inconsistent national law. On the face of it, parliamentary sovereignty would seem to be seriously impaired, if not actually defunct. However, the position is by no means so clear-cut. First, membership of the EEC has not, it seems, broken the principle that parliament cannot bind its future action. There is general agreement amongst constitutional authorities that the European Communities Act is overturnable as, for example, the 1801 *Act of Union* with Ireland is overturnable. Had the referendum of 1975 on continuing membership of the EC gone the other way, the United Kingdom would probably have withdrawn from the Common Market. What about the matter of the primacy of EC law over all inconsistent British law? The *European Communities Act* is clear that British courts should give priority to EC law in circumstances of conflict. What if they do not? It is equally clear, as S. A. de Smith remarks, that the European Court cannot hold national legislation void because it is inconsistent with Community law (de Smith, *Constitutional and Administrative Law*, p. 90, and pp. 88–91). The European Community is not a genuine federation and, despite its general thrust towards becoming one, ultimate sovereignty remains with the member-States for the time being. However, even this is not the final word because, in practical terms, Britain's independence over a whole range of policy matters (see Chapter 24) has been limited by joining the Community. The British parliament cannot legislate on certain topics and, in those spheres in which it can legislate, it will have to do so in ways prescribed by the EC.

So parliament can liquidate its own sovereignty (where it grants a country independence) and it can reduce its freedom of action in such a way that its overall sovereignty must be said to be at least partly abdicated (as in the case of joining the EC). Finally, it is subject to *political* constraints on what it can actually – as opposed to what it may theoretically – do. Thus, the government of the day must constantly take into account a wide variety of pressures in drawing up its programme. Externally, it is inhibited by obligations assumed under treaties such as NATO or, as we have seen, by membership of the European Community. Its freedom of manoeuvre can even be limited by the terms of a foreign loan: in 1976, the Labour Government had to promise to introduce deflationary legislation into the UK as a condition of a loan from the IMF. Internally, although it may from time to time pass legislation which is genuinely unpopular, such as suspending capital punishment, overall it must govern in accordance with public opinion. This is largely what is meant by saying that whereas parliament is the legal sovereign (or possesses constitutional supremacy), the electorate is the *political* sovereign. This means in practice that government must pay some regard to the views of organised interest groups as well as keeping an eye on the opinion polls. Trade unions have wrecked legislation (e.g. the 1971 Trade Union Act); and the prohibition of alcoholic liquor, for example, would be as unpopular in Britain as it was for a brief spell in the USA.

The British Constitution is commonly said to be based on the principle of *the rule of law* but this principle has proved hard to define. It normally has two meanings:

1. The powers exercised by politicians and public servants must have a legitimate foundation, i.e. they must be exercised in accordance with authorised procedures.
2. It entails that redress–i.e. legal remedy for wrongs – is available to all citizens both against any other citizen, no matter how powerful, and against officers of the State.

Certain twentieth-century developments have given rise to anxiety about the contemporary validity of the principle of the rule of law. These include the wide range of discretionary powers assumed and exercised by public authorities; matters like the powers and accountability of the police and the security services; questions of the ability of the State to guarantee equality of civil rights to blacks and other minority groups; and, finally, concern about the impartiality of the courts especially in trade union and race relations cases. At the same time, the rule of law in the sense of observance by all groups of parliamentary methods came under threat increasingly from the 1970s from terrorists and groups prepared to resort to illegal methods in order to change the law. In response, the State was propelled into detention without trial and other abuses of legal procedure. Concern about the threat to the liberties of the individual have led some commentators to call for a Bill of Rights to protect, for example, such basic rights as freedom of expression, association and movement. All these issues will receive fuller discussion in Chapters 15 and 16. It is sufficient at this point to say that it is not merely problems of definition and protection that bedevil the rights inherent in the principle of the rule of law but questions of enforcement also. The minimum precondition for the enforcement of the rule of law has generally been taken to be the independence of the judiciary from the government, a situation regarded as achieved in Britain since 1701. But the constitutional theory that holds that judges are neither law-makers – since this is the role of parliament – nor in politics, has also taken some knocks recently. In the first place, judges 'make' law through the interpretation of statute law and the development of common law. Second, in their definition of the 'public interest' in such cases as that involving the trial of the civil servant, Clive Ponting, in 1985 under Section 2 of the *Official Secrets Act*, judges are clearly making political judgements. The trial judge in that case told the jury that Mr Ponting owed his primary duty to the policies of whichever government was in power, but the jury acquitted him.

THE WORKING OF THE CONSTITUTION

Parliamentary government under a constitutional monarchy

This phrase is the most apt description of the British liberal-democratic State. Its leading features are as follows. At least once every five years, everyone over 18 votes in a general election, the main purpose of which is to elect a government. In voting, electors vote for the party – either the one in government at the time or one of the opposition parties – which they consider to be best-equipped to govern the country. The party which gains a majority of seats in the House of Commons wins the election. By convention, the monarch then asks the leader of the majority party to form a government. The victorious party leader becomes the Prime Minister and forms first a Cabinet and then a government from his party colleagues. Names are submitted to the monarch who, by convention, assents to the Prime Minister's choice. The Cabinet is the committee which governs the country. Its major tasks are to prepare legislation, decide on policy and submit these decisions to parliament for its assent. It is also responsible for controlling and coordinating the major Departments of State. The Cabinet is collectively responsible to the House of Commons for its decision and, if defeated on a vote of confidence, must either request a dissolution of parliament – i.e. call a general election – or resign. This rarely happens because party discipline ensures that the party in government, which, as we have seen, normally commands a majority in the House of Commons, is secure against parliamentary defeat. All government ministers are formally responsible to the monarch and, by convention, through the doctrine of ministerial responsibility, to parliament.

The Cabinet is assisted in the making of decisions and the preparation of legislation by the Civil Service. Outside interests such as business, finance and the trade unions are normally consulted and in the twentieth century have become of increasing importance in the decision-making process. The House of Lords retains a significant, largely amending role in the parliamentary process but its powers diminished sharply after the Parliament Acts of 1911 and 1949 and it rarely rejects government measures. Once it has been passed by both Houses of Parliament, a bill goes to the monarch for assent which, by convention, is never refused. The bill is now an Act of Parliament (statute), has binding authority (it cannot be challenged in the courts) and is enforced by the agencies of State.

So far we have been dealing with the major agencies of central decision-making (Cabinet Ministers, other Ministers, Civil Service, Parliament). In one sense, this is fair enough. As we have seen, Britain is a unitary State, with the power of legislation for the entire UK centred in a Cabinet responsible to the Westminster parliament. Parliamentary sovereignty means that parliament can both give and remove powers from subordinate units of government. However, subordinate units of government have grown increasingly important since 1945 and warrant attention here as of undoubted constitutional significance. We deal first with these subordinate institutions at the national, UK level before going on to look at government at the local and regional levels.

At the national level, we need to examine two types of institution: the nationalised industries and, second, the non-departmental bodies known as 'quangos' (quasi-autonomous non-governmental organisations). As the twentieth-century State has taken on more and more functions – in such vital spheres as fuel and power, air, road and rail transport, communications and the manufacture of steel – it has chosen to legislate responsibilities for the management of these concerns to *public corporations* rather than administer them directly itself. Thus, although the Boards which run them are appointed by the appropriate Ministers, the nationalised industries are able to function in considerable independence from detailed day-to-day political control. (Some of these industries were returned to the private sector by the Conservatives after 1979.) '*Quangos*' likewise are public bodies established by governments to advise on or even administer particular matters of public concern which are not under the day-to-day control of a minister. By 1980, there were over 2000 of them. Good examples of these institutions are the Manpower Services Commission, the New Town Development Corporations, the Atomic Energy Authority and the University Grants Committee. The constitutional status of public corporations and 'quangos' is complex but taken together they employed about 2 million people in 1980 and were responsible for millions of pounds of public money. They are of great national importance (see chapters 8 and 14 for further discussion).

At the local and regional level, three kinds of public institution matter. At the highest sub-level, there are the government departments responsible for the administration of a wide range of functions in Northern Ireland, Scotland and Wales. In each of these countries, the respective Department or Office is given the responsibility for such matters as health, housing, education and environmental services within the territorial area. At an intermediate level non-elected quasi-governmental bodies operate at the regional level throughout England, Scotland and Wales for the administration of certain services. The best examples are the fourteen regional health authorities created under the 1973 Health Service Reorganisation Act and the ten regional water authorities. In addition, some government departments such as the Department of the Environment and the Department of Trade and Industry devolve authority to regional offices. Finally, the only elected form of government below national level on the British mainland (but not in Northern Ireland) exists in local government. The powers of local authorities are strictly curtailed: they can exercise only those functions authorised by law; they have to work within the framework set by national government; and three-fifths of their expenditure is provided by central

Exhibit 5.1   The British Constitution: the main concepts

These terms are often used to describe the British Constitution; this table contains a guide to their meanings.

1. *Constitutional government*
(a) government according to recognised rules, including rules about how the rules can be changed, these rules being both regular and well-known. To be legitimate, authority has to be exercised according to certain procedures so that where misuse or abuse of authority takes place, it is readily apparent; the citizen suffering misuse or abuse of authority may seek redress through the ordinary courts; and there are legal–procedural restraints on rulers, such as hear the other side, the rule against bias.
(b) constitutionalism is linked in liberal theory with the desire to avoid concentrations of power, for which purpose the doctrine of *the separation of powers* was developed in the eighteenth century: the idea that the institutions that make, carry out and adjudicate the laws should be both separate and in the hands of different persons. The only way in which the British system embodies this theory is in the independence of the judiciary; executive and legislature overlap in that the Government (Executive) is elected through the House of Commons (lower house of Legislature) not separately as in the USA, and Ministers are drawn from and remain within parliament. A related concept with the similar purpose of preventing the growth of absolute power is *checks and balances*, the idea of the division of authority between numerous governing institutions so that they provide curbs upon each other; such devices include judicial review and a bicameral legislature. Britain has a bicameral legislature (two houses of parliament), but not, as we have seen, judicial review or, except for an independent judiciary, separation of powers.
(c) two concepts which are negatively related to constitutionalism need examining here: unconstitutional and anti-constitutional. *Unconstitutional* means behaviour which breaks or threatens to break the constitution, or, more usually, a part of it; *anti-constitutional* refers to the effort to undermine the whole constitution out of a disbelief in the desirability of any constitutional restraints or a wish to produce a superior one more representative of the will of the people.

2. *Parliamentary government*
The British form of constitutional and representative government in which executive and legislative power is fused in and exercised through a single two-chamber assembly cf. their separation in the USA into two distinct institutions, the Presidency and Congress. Legislation and taxation originated by government are validated by the consent of parliament whose acceptance signifies and symbolises the consent of the nation. Parliament does not itself govern but the policies and activities of governments are criticised in parliament and, most importantly, all legislation emanates from parliament.

3. *Representative government*
A form of democratic rule in which government is by representatives (e.g. MPs or Congressmen) elected by popular votes; the exercise of authority is legitimated ultimately (although not solely, since it must be exercised also according to constitutional rules) by the popular election of power-holders. The idea of a representative in this system varies between two meanings:

continued

Exhibit ...   *– continued*

(a) *the Burkean view*, in which the representative, whilst having the duty to consult and take into account constituents' opinions, owes the primary duty to the national interest and to conscience. Parliament in this view is 'a deliberative assembly of one nation rather than a congress of ambassadors'; i.e. it should lead public opinion rather than simply reflect it. This idea of the representative has prevailed in the UK.

(b) *the delegate theory*, in which the elected representatives are considered to be the agent of and directly accountable to their constituents; the national assembly on this view is or should be a direct register or mirror of public opinion, rather than a director of it (always suspected as manipulation); this theory is part of the ideology of radical democracy and became increasingly influential in the late 1970s on the Labour Party (see below pp. 108).

4. *Responsible government*
This is the idea that government should be both strong – and therefore able when necessary to take unpopular decisions – *and* accountable for its actions to the elected representatives of the people. In the UK, the *collective* responsibility to parliament of Ministers for the policy of the Cabinet, and the *individual* responsibility to parliament of Ministers for the work of their Departments are the devices intended to achieve responsible government. It is often claimed that responsible government is more easily achieved by the UK parliamentary system than by the US system where President and Congress are separately elected and to a large extent function independently of each other.

5. *Party government*
Within liberal-democratic systems, competition between two or more cohesive parties for votes and their alternation in power is the method by which popular wishes are translated into public policy. So essential are parties to the successful working of democratic systems that some political commentators now prefer to describe them in terms of 'party government' rather than of 'representative' or 'parliamentary government'. They claim this not only because government and opposition are both by party but also because much of the behaviour of representatives suggests they owe their first loyalty to party rather than to their consciences, their constituents or the national interest.

government. Nonetheless, they are constituent parts of the British State. In the 1980s, as the Left gained control of some of the massive metropolitan counties such as West Midlands, South Yorkshire and the GLC created under the local government reorganisation of 1972, they became a formidable focus of political opposition to the government. In this context, it was argued by some that the abolition of the metropolitan counties and the GLC broke an important constitutional convention: that basic changes in the balance of central and local power should not be accomplished in haste but only after the considered reflection of a public inquiry (see Chapter 9 for further discussion of local government).

Three points are worth making about this deliberately brief summary of the principal features of the British system of parliamentary government:

1. It *is* only introductory and is intended to provide a succinct framework for the fuller discussions in the rest of the book. Such themes as the relationships between Prime Minister and Cabinet, between Ministers and Civil Servants, between parliment and outside interest abd between central and local government will receive closer attention later.
2. Although intentionally short, it is hoped that sufficient information has been provided to enable sense to be made of Exhibit 5.1 which relates certain key concepts habitually employed in the analysis of liberal-democratic systems to the British Constitution.
3. The survey has brought out the close interdependence between institutions like the Houses of Parliament, the Monarchy and the electorate with a formal constitutional role and those informal institutions like parties, without which the formal constitution could not work, and pressure groups, without which no realistic description of the contemporary system would be possible.

Ideological perceptions of the British Constitution

The political parties have differing perceptions of the British Constitution, both of how it works and of how – if at all – it should be changed.

Conservatism

Traditionally, Conservatives have seen authority as flowing from above. They emphasise government as the main agency in the system – governing, directing and initiating. Parliament has primarily a checking role and the electorate mainly a consenting one. Voters at elections choose between alternative teams of party leaders and may be taken to assent to whatever those leaders do in office. The main task of the party is to support government and to that end it must be united so that government is strong and stable; loyalty to the party and perhaps especially to the party leader is therefore a primary political virtue. Conservatives see the party as an integrative rather than a divisive force in society: it enables people of ability to draw support for the policies from all classes and groups in the community and so bind the nation together. In general terms, the Conservative party has not made constitutional reform a major plank of its platform in recent elections although it has defended the House of Lords and abolished the metropolitan counties. Two leading Conservatives, Lord Hailsham and Sir Ian Gilmour, concerned about the power which Britain's Constitution would allow an extremist left-wing party to wield, called respectively for a written constitution to limit the powers of parliament and for the introduction of proportional representation to strengthen the political centre.

Socialism

Within the many-roomed house of *Socialism*, three strands of constitutional thought are of particular importance. They are: the mainstream Labour Party, the Labour Party Left, and revolutionary Socialists. Traditionally, the *Labour Party* has accepted the idea of disciplined parties taking it in turns to govern. Socialism can be brought about by gradual instalments through parliamentary methods because the machinery of State – i.e. public servants at both central and local levels – is neutral and therefore bound to carry out the policies of whichever party is in power. Labour MPs owe their primary political allegiance to the party as the only sure way to produce social reforms of benefit to the working classes. Economic interests such as the trade unions are legitimately represented both in the party and via the party in parliament. For twenty-five years after 1945 when it alternated in power with the Conservatives, the Labour Party was little concerned with constitutional matters. But in the 1970s attitudes changed. The *Labour Left* dedicated itself to reforming the constitution, beginning with the Labour Party constitution, in the direction of radical democracy. Party reform aimed at making the leadership accountable to the rank and file and thereby preventing the 'betrayal' of Socialism by irresponsible parliamentarians as in the past. Hence, the Left advocated mandatory reselection of MPs, the extension of the right of electing the leader to the major elements in the party as a whole (both achieved in 1981) and giving the ultimate control over the party manifesto to the National Executive Committee which runs the party between Conferences (not achieved in 1981). Constitutional proposals included the removal of the remaining royal prerogative powers, the abolition of the House of Lords, curtailment of the powers of the Prime Minister and of the Civil Service, and restoration of parliamentary 'sovereignty' by withdrawing from the European Community. These proposals aim at eliminating all domestic and external checks upon the implementation of Socialist policies by a future Labour government. *Revolutionary Socialists* see a liberal-democratic system as a mere façade for capitalism. They believe that no real change can be achieved by electoral or parliamentary methods; on the contrary, by participating in liberal institutions, the Labour Party serves merely to perpetuate an economic system which 'exploits' the working class and, what is worse, conditions this class into acceptance of the rule of its bourgeois oppressors. Reform from within is impossible; what is required is a total change of the social system (see Chapter 26 for further discussion).

Liberal–SDP Alliance

Traditionally, *Liberals* are strong supporters of parliamentary government, individual liberties and minority rights. They have always placed especial emphasis on constitutionalism not only to protect political freedom but also to energise society. They see 'getting the constitution right' as the major precondition of the solution of social and economic problems. In the twentieth century, they consider that the role of parliament has been downgraded by the growth of Cabinet and Prime Ministerial power, the major contributory factors in this process being the development of programmatic parties with collectivist ethoses together with massive bureaucracy. Whilst the 'welfare State' has enhanced social and economic liberty, the 'warfare State' with its accompanying growth of police, secret service and military machines has eroded individual liberties. At the same time, the concentration of power at Westminster and the post-war emergence of a multicultural society have produced problems of the protection of national, regional and black minorities. The *Social Democratic Party* originated in dissatisfaction with the working of the two-party system and with the failure of the Labour Party at the time to move towards what the Social Democrat rebels perceived as a genuinely democratic constitution. The SDP put forward the 'adversary politics' thesis – the idea that two major parties were the prisoners both of their own extremists and also of the major economic interest groups, 'big business' and the trade unions. What was needed was to strengthen the forces of moderation in the political 'centre'. Social Democrats also believe that the British State is too centralised and accordingly wish to reinforce local and regional government. In its constitution, the SDP introduced a system of 'one member, one vote' by postal ballot for the election of its leader and president. Not surprisingly, the joint Liberal–SDP Alliance manifesto in the 1987 general election placed heavy stress on constitutional reform. Its main proposals were a new electoral system based on proportional representation; devolution of power to Scotland, Wales and the English regions; local government reform, including the introduction of a local income tax to reduce councils' dependence on central government; and a new Bill of Rights and a Commission of Human Rights to protect the rights and liberties of the citizen.

Regional Nationalism

Finally, the future constitutional role of Scotland, Wales and Northern Ireland within the United Kingdom became a matter of increasing and often bitter concern from the late 1960s. Scottish and Welsh Nationalists aim at ultimate independence with their countries enjoying 'Commonwealth' status similar to that of Canada, Australia and New Zealand. They regard devolution of power (home rule) to Scottish and Welsh assemblies as a first step. Labour supports devolution of power to Scotland, but only the Alliance supported devolution to Wales as well; the Liberals were prepared to go further than either SDP or Labour in advocating a federal system backed by a written constitution. None of the opposition parties except the Nationalists favours total independence for Scotland and Wales. The Conservatives oppose devolution altogether. On Northern Ireland, party and ideological divisions are even sharper. The Protestant Unionist parties support the maintenance of the Union with Britain; but the Catholic Social Democratic and Labour Party (SDLP) wants the ending of partition (the settlement in 1922 which created the present division) and the reunification of Ireland by political means and the Provisional IRA seeks reunification by violent methods. In the shorter term, Unionists support the ending of direct Westminster rule over the Province (which began in 1972) and the restoration of the pre-1972 Stormont government, but this proposition has no support from the Catholic parties. Slow progress towards a power-sharing assembly has been blocked in turn by Protestant groups (1974) and by Catholics (1982).

THE CONSTITUTION IN FLUX: PRESSURES FOR CHANGE IN THE 1970s AND 1980s

Having examined in some detail these sharply contrasting ideological perspectives on the British Constitution, we look finally in this chapter at the steadily mounting pressures for constitutional change in recent years. This topic will serve to underline the theme with which we began and to which we have constantly returned throughout the chapter: that constitutions are not sets of unchangeable rules but, on the contrary, subjects of often intense political controversy as rival parties and groups strive to gain, or to preserve, advantages in the 'game'. Consideration of the currently-changing parts of the Constitution will also serve to identify vital features which will form the subject of more detailed examination throughout the rest of the book.

The main constitutional innovations and pressures have come in the following areas in recent years: parliamentary sovereignty; the nature of parliamentary government; State centralisation; electoral reform; the use of the referendum; the role of the monarch in the eventuality of a 'hung' parliament; and the call for a written constitution and a Bill of Rights. There have been other trends and tendencies. A number of cases involving, for example, Ministers' powers and trade union rights have led to the courts extending their *interpretative* role. In the early 1970s, trade unions by *direct action* destroyed the parliamentary legislation (*Trade Union Act*, 1971) which aimed to curtail their privileges. But, although important, neither tendency seems to warrant the attention which the previously mentioned themes required.

As our earlier discussion showed, Britain's entry into the European Community has raised grave doubts about whether the doctrine of *parliamentary sovereignty* remains intact, and if so, to what extent. Our tentative conclusion was that parliamentary sovereignty had been partly surrendered but in any case this issue is unlikely to disappear since it is a major source of political division. Leading politicians on right and left such as Enoch Powell and Tony Benn continue to maintain that sovereignty has been extinguished; also cases involving conflict between domestic law and Community law will continue to arise for decision by the British courts

With reference to the nature and role of parliament in the system of *parliamentary government*, two issues are of concern:

1. The hereditary composition of the House of Lords disturbs Liberals and the Labour right, who call for reform, and enrages the Labour left, who advocate abolition. Proposals to mend or end the upper house tend to be most heard during or just after periods of Labour governments since its powers of delay are used more against Labour than against Conservative governments.
2. Constitutional reformers are anxious to find ways to increase the ability of the House of Commons to criticise government more effectively. Parliament's capacity to curb the Executive has waned in the twentieth century, but attempts to improve its restraining influence always encounter political difficulties since, in practice, it depends upon action by government and few governments are anxious to make their own task harder.

Centralisation of power in Whitehall and Westminster has also become a matter for growing political concern in the post-war period. It has coincided with, and in part been triggered by, an upsurge of political nationalism in Scotland and Wales and by a new phase of the question of Ireland after 1967, which involved the resumption of direct rule of Northern Ireland by the Westminster Government in 1972. The major problem of concentration of power at the centre, however, is raised by the habit of recent governments of setting up non-elective, appointive agencies of government rather than elective ones for the administration of services and, in addition, of exerting an ever-tighter grip on local government.

Electoral reform mattered to few outside the Liberal Party before the 1970s but became of wider concern as the major parties began to receive diminishing shares of the total vote. Political consensus disappeared as they shifted towards their extremes and the increasing proportion of the vote going to smaller parties was not reflected in parliamentary seats. Hence the demand for proportional representation arose – to enable governments to represent a majority rather than a minority of the electorate, to strengthen the allegedly 'moderate' political centre against the extremes, to create a House of Commons more representative of the wishes of the electorate and to make the system fairer to small parties. Also at this time, *the referendum*, hitherto regarded as an alien device of direct democracy unknown to, and undesirable in, the British system of representative democracy, was used twice – in 1975 to confirm membership of the European Community, and in 1979 to allow Scottish and Welsh voters to decide on devolution. Its employment took place against the more general tendency to make British politics more democratic by, for example, extending voting rights in parties and legislating for the use of strike and leadership ballots in trade unions.

During the 1980s, with the advent of electoral multi-partyism, the possibility of *a 'hung' parliament* arose. In a situation in which no party had an overall majority, what should the monarch do? To constitutional experts, there seemed to be three alternative courses of action for the Queen. These were:

(i)   to permit the leader of the previously largest party to continue;
(ii) to invite the leader of the largest party to attempt to form a government (assuming, of course, this were not the existing governing party);
(iii) to invite any individual from the House of Commons to try to constitute a government with a Commons majority.

What happened in this situation in February 1974 might be taken as a precedent.

On that occasion, when the Conservative Government failed to gain an overall majority at the general election, Edward Heath the existing Prime Minister, did remain in office for four days whilst he sought support from the Liberals to enable him to form a government. He failed and Harold Wilson, the leader of the largest party, formed a minority Labour government which he led for eight months until seeking a dissolution in order to obtain an overall parliamentary majority.

Opinions also differ about how soon and in what circumstances the Queen would grant a dissolution. Would she invite more than one party leader to make the attempt at forming a government or would she grant a dissolution to the first person to fail? Clearly much depends upon the view her advisers take about the extent of independent authority remaining to the monarch. Some constitutional experts argue that very little remains of the royal prerogative; others maintain that in such circumstances sufficient residual powers exist to justify the monarch playing a decisive role. Further, much depends also on the degree to which the monarch might be willing to be seen to be acting politically. One prominent view is that she would not wish her influence to be a crucial factor in resolving a crisis since this would impair her neutral stance 'above politics' and that consequently she would be likely to grant a quick dissolution to whoever requested it in order that the electorate should decide.

Finally, in view of the mounting uncertainties about British constitutional practice in the face of these waves of change, a written or, in the term we prefer, a *codified constitution* received some support. Advocates believed that it would not only make constitutional law on such matters as the composition of the Lords, the accountability of governments to parliament, devolution, the electoral system and the use of referenda more certain; above all, it would make individual rights more secure. After 1966, aggrieved Britons began to receive favourable judgements from the European Commission on

Human Rights on such varied matters as birching in the Isle of Man, the treatment of prisoners by the Ulster security forces and the rights of women, including the rights of British Asian women to be joined by their husbands. The frequency with which British laws and practices were found to be out of line with the European Convention of Human Rights which Britain signed in 1951 was not only a source of embarrassment to the British government but also prompted calls for a new British Bill of Rights. Such a demand was further fuelled by public disquiet over numerous well-publicised cases involving the treatment of suspects by the police, telephone 'tapping' and bureaucratic secrecy on matters of vital importance to citizens in a democracy.

SUMMARY

Constitutions are part of rather than above politics and are always subject both to change and to political pressures for change. The British Constitution, which can be categorised as partly written and uncodified, has four major sources – statute, conventions, Common law and authoritative works. It is unitary, not federal, and is based on the principle of parliamentary sovereignty. However, the sovereignty of the Westminster parliament operates within the constraints of voluntarily accepted treaty obligations, including EC membership. The rule of law is commonly said to be an underlying principle of the Constitution. It means that the powers of the authorities must be conferred by law and exercised according to authorised procedures; and, second, that redress of wrongs is available to all citizens against other citizens and against officers of the State. The orthodox liberal-democratic theory of the Constitution is outlined and the main concepts required for its political analysis are explored: these include constitutional, parliamentary, representative, responsible and party government. Perceptions of the Constitution and proposals for reform are shaped by ideological influences. Constitutional innovations and pressures for change intensified in the 1970s and 1980s.

FURTHER READING

Harden, I. and Lewis, N. (1987) *The Noble Lie: The British Constitution and the Rule of Law*, London, Hutchinson.
Jowell, J. and Oliver, D. (1986) *The Changing Constitution*, Oxford, Clarendon Press.
McAuslan, P. and McEldowney, J. (1985) *Law, Legitimacy and the Constitution*, London, Sweet & Maxwell.
Marshall, G. (1984) *Constitutional Conventions*, Oxford, Clarendon Press.
Norton, P. (1982) *The Constitution in Flux*, Oxford, Martin Robertson.
de Smith (1983) *Constitutional and Administrative Law*, edited by Harry Street and Rodney Brazier, Harmondsworth, Penguin, 4th edn.

QUESTIONS

1. What is 'a constitution'? To what extent are constitutions influenced by politics? Distinguish between written and unwritten, codified and uncodified constitutions and consider what type of constitution Britain has.
2. How democratic is the British Constitution?
3. List the main characteristics of the rule of law and discuss the extent to which the British Constitution is based on 'the rule of law.' (It would be helpful to read Chapters 15 and 16 before answering this question.)

ASSIGNMENT

Distinguish between parliamentary, representative, responsible, party and constitutional government and relate each concept to the British Constitution.

6

Prime Minister and Cabinet

In the next three chapters we consider the institutions which make up the Executive – the Prime Minister and Cabinet, the ministries (government departments) and civil service, and quasi-governmental bodies (QUANGOS). We begin in this chapter with a close examination of the two institutions at the pinnacle of the central decision-making process: the Prime Minister and the Cabinet. We consider their actual working before moving to the controversial question of whether the Cabinet system has been replaced by Prime Ministerial government. Finally, we examine two proposals for reform which are designed to make the office of Prime Minister more accountable and more effective.

THE PRIME MINISTER

The modern office of Prime Minister embodies a formidable concentration of powers. The Prime Minister has wide-ranging powers of patronage; directs and coordinates the work of the major governing institutions, Cabinet and its committees; and possesses overall responsibility for the operation of the civil service.

Prime ministerial patronage encompasses first and foremost the power to appoint the Cabinet and beyond that the range of Ministerial appointments which make up the government of the day. But the Prime Minister also exercises paramount influence in the selection of a wide variety of other leading posts in national life. This influence extends over the creation of peers (according to one calculation, 568 hereditary and life peers were created between 1945 and 1976 on the advice of seven Prime Ministers) as well as over the appointment of top civil servants at the Permanent Secretary level, the chairmen of nationalised industries, the heads of the security services and the chairmen of Royal Commissions. In addition, the Prime Minister has ultimate responsibility for recommendations of baronetcies, knighthoods, CBEs, MBEs and the like in the various New Year, Queen's Birthday and special honours lists.

The most important element of Prime Ministerial patronage, however, remains the power to select the one hundred or so politicians – drawn mainly from the House of Commons but also from the House of Lords – who at any given moment form the government itself. As Table 6.1 indicates, the Prime

TABLE 6.1

The Conservative Government after the 1987 General Election

	House of Commons	House of Lords	Total
Cabinet Ministers (excluding PM)	19	2	21
Ministers of State	21	5	26
Law officers	4	1	5
Under-Secretaries of State	25	5	30
Whips	14	7	21
Total	83	20	103

Minister appoints not just the Cabinet of normally 20–22 members but, in addition, Ministers of State, Under-Secretaries of State, Whips and Law officers such as Attorney-General and Solicitor-General.

Three points are worthy of note here. First, there is the sheer extent of this patronage. Between one-third and one-quarter (depending on the number of seats won) of the victorious party at a General Election can realistically expect office. By no means all politicians seek office but a great number, probably the majority, do. The first chapter of Gerald Kaufman's entertaining book *How to be a Minister* (1980) seeks to explain how to mark oneself out as a potentially effective Minister; it ends by advising aspirants to Ministerial office 'if you do get the offer from No 10, grasp it and make the most of it'. The knowledge that so many share this goal is a formidable source of control for the party leader both in Opposition and Government. Second, this particular Prime Ministerial responsibility is not a once-and-for-all affair but a continuing one, with Ministerial changes – by forced or deliberate 'reshuffle' – occurring at quite frequent intervals. By April 1986, for example, only half the Ministers appointed to Mrs Thatcher's Cabinet in June 1983 occupied the same Ministerial positions and as a result of demotion and resignation one-third of them were no longer in the Cabinet at all. This frequency of governmental changes keeps this aspect of Prime Ministerial power firmly in the forefront of public attention. Third, notwithstanding the constraints upon the Prime Minister's power of appointment (examined below pp. 131–3), it is a real power. First, it affords the means on occasion to exclude leading rivals who, if appointed, might be considered as likely to endanger the harmony of government. Thus, Edward Heath, who omitted Enoch Powell from his government in 1970, was himself omitted from that of Margaret Thatcher in 1979. Second, it provides the capacity to shape policy – again within the framework laid down by the manifesto and other policy documents – in the direction desired by the Prime Minister. Mrs Thatcher, in her first administration, ensured that the three key economic posts – Chancellor of the Exchequer, Chief Secretary to the Treasury, and the Secretaryship of State for Trade and Industry – were held by her supporters.

The Prime Minister is also responsible for the organisation of the whole work of government at the highest level. This is the other main area of responsibility attaching to the office. In the first place, it is the Prime Minister who decides upon the *structure* of government, involving in particular, the allocation of duties between the Departments of State. The fluctuations in the number of departments in recent times – thirty in 1951, twenty-one in 1983 – and the changes in their functions are evidence of considerable Prime Ministerial activity in this sphere. The recent history of the departments concerned with trade, industry and power provides a good example. Edward Heath brought the Board of Trade and the Ministries of Technology and Power together in 1970 to form a new 'super-ministry', the Department of Trade and Industry (DTI) only to hive off Power to form the Department of Energy after the oil crisis in 1973. On gaining office in 1974, Harold Wilson broke up the DTI into separate Ministries again – Trade, Industry and – a new creation – Prices and Consumer Affairs. Mrs Thatcher after 1979 merged Trade and Industry again, gave Prices and Consumer Affairs back to Trade and kept Energy separate.

Second, the Prime Minister is at the centre of the organisation of the *business* of government in terms of the work of the Cabinet and its committees. This is really the Prime Minister's most important area of responsibility. The Prime Minister is ultimately responsible for and normally personally involved in decisions about the agenda of Cabinet and the flow of information between the various offices. The Prime Minister's special status is evident particularly in the conduct of three areas of policy – defence and foreign relations, the economy, and national security. Clearly, a strong relationship exists between the importance of the issue and the degree of personal involvement and special responsibility of the Prime Minister. Thus, in the first two areas, post-war Prime Ministers have often taken decisions alone, usually after consultation with a small number of close advisers including Ministers; in times of national crisis such as the Falklands War, the small group of senior Ministers – often in normal times said to function as an 'inner Cabinet' – acquires more formal existence. The Prime Minister alone is responsible for matters of national security which never go before Cabinet. In addition, the Prime Minister may take a particular interest in any sphere of policy and this will necessarily involve a degree of intervention in the Department concerned; at various times during her premiership Mrs Thatcher has, for example, demonstrated a special interest in the Welfare State, education and the affairs of Northern Ireland. As well as deciding upon the nature and timing of the issues which reach the Cabinet for decision and upon the terms of reference and chairmanship of its committees, the Prime Minister also chairs Cabinet meetings. This chairmanship gives Prime Ministers the capacity to shape the direction and result of policy discussions

– for example, by making their views known beforehand, by the nature of their interventions and handling of the meeting (who is called upon to speak and in what order) and by their summing-up of 'the sense of the meeting' at the end. Votes are almost never taken in Cabinet. After the meeting, Cabinet conclusions are recorded – as a basis for action – by the Cabinet Secretary in consultation with the Prime Minister.

Finally, and more briefly, the Prime Minister is in charge of the work of the Civil Service. This power has three main aspects – appointments, organisation, and practices. Mrs Thatcher's premiership provides examples in all three areas. Whilst Prime Ministers are frequently willing simply to endorse the recommendations of the Senior Appointments Selection Committee on top bureaucratic appointments at Permanent Secretary and Deputy Secretary levels, Mrs Thatcher has taken a close personal interest in these appointments and, during her first three years of office when eleven of the leading twenty-three Permanent Secretaryships changed hands, sought to ensure that the new appointees possessed temperaments akin to her own. Second, Mrs Thatcher in 1981 abolished the Civil Service Department, handing over its functions first to the Treasury and Cabinet Office jointly and then to the Cabinet Office alone. Finally, she tried very hard to make the Civil Service more efficient by such methods as establishing an efficiency unit to recommend economies, reducing the size of the civil service and holding down civil service pay in relation to the private sector.

The emphasis in this chapter is on the specifically governing or executive functions of the Prime Minister. But other aspects of Prime Ministerial power also need to be considered, not least because they are often closely linked to the authority with which Prime Ministers are able to carry out their executive role. These other aspects involve the Prime Minister's relations with party, parliament, the media and the public and his or her role as national leader. It is as the leader of the party which has gained a majority in a general election that a Prime Minister comes to office in the first place; it is as a consequence of the regular support of that party in parliament that the Prime Minister can expect to govern and in particular to translate the party programme into legislation. Relationships with party, therefore, are of the greatest significance, and these are two-way. The Prime Minister seeks control of the party whilst the party strives for influence over the Prime Minister. The main weapons in the hands of the Premier are patronage (already examined), and the power of dissolution. The Prime Minister has the exclusive right to recommend to the Monarch the timing of the dissolution of parliament within a five-year span. This constitutional duty is of the utmost significance in party terms since misjudgements such as those of Edward Heath in calling a General Election in February 1974 and of James Callaghan in failing to call one in Autumn 1978 can contribute to a party's electoral defeat and, in doing so, lose many MPs their seats. The party can seek influence over the Leader by means of the Premier's meeting with backbench committees and through the Whips. Normally, the flow of influence is the other way. Mrs Thatcher is widely reported to have sought to establish good contacts with Conservative backbenchers in her first administration through personal appearances in her room in the House of Commons and in the Members' dining room, through her parliamentary private secretary and, more formally, through meetings with the 1922 Committee and, more frequently, its Chairman.

The parliamentary performance of the Prime Minister is always the subject of close scrutiny. Twice a week – for fifteen minutes – the Premier appears in the House of Commons to answer 'Prime Minister's Questions'. Prime Ministers can expect to answer about 1000 questions per session, a large proportion of them on foreign and economic affairs. Many of the questions appear as supplementaries for which no specific preparation is possible. Question Time is a testing ordeal, therefore, at which much is at stake, including personal reputation, command of party, and the authority of the government. Not surprisingly, Prime Ministers devote a great deal of their time to preparing for the occasion. Whilst parliament is sitting, Premiers may expect to be constantly preoccupied with it in other ways, too. Their concerns include the progress of government legislation, set-piece speeches in full-dress parliamentary debates, and, more generally, the state of party morale. 'Parliamentary business' is always an item on Cabinet agenda.

Contemporary Prime Ministers need to pay particular attention to the way they and their governments are presented in the media. Much of their lives are lived in public – being interviewed on television, making speeches at this or that public function, briefing lobby correspondents, responding impromptu in the street or airport lounge or on the doorsteps to queries about the latest crisis, scandal or leak. In order to ensure that a favourable impression is created, they need to be on their guard at all times. If they are successful in presenting a decisive image, they will be given credit for their handling – or, more pejoratively, for their 'manipulation' – of the media; if they are tripped up or fluff their lines, not only their own reputation but also that of the entire Government will suffer. In other words, self-presentation through newspapers, radio and television has become another vital Prime Ministerial concern. So has personal standing in the public opinion polls. The polling organisations – Mori, Gallup, Marplan and the like – repeatedly sound public opinion on such matters as the moral qualities (toughness, integrity, truthfulness and compassion), leadership style (dictatorial/consensual, right-wing/left-wing) and policy achievements of the Prime Minister. They compare the Premier's political standing with that of his or her main rivals (see Table 6.2) and then go on to compare these ratings with party support. Prime Ministers (and party leaders) whose personal popularity outruns that of their parties may be said to be electoral boons to their parties and gain greatly in authority as a result. These relative positions – Prime Ministers compared with other leaders; party leaders compared with their

TABLE 6.2

The political popularity of the party leaders during the 1987 General Election campaign

	8–12 May	21 May	28 May	8 June
Margaret Thatcher	40	37	40	40
Neil Kinnock	20	27	27	27
David Steel	9	12	10	8
David Owen	11	13	14	14
Don't know/None	20	11	9	11

Source: *Guardian*, 11 June, 1987 (Marplan Index)

parties – fluctuate continually during the lifetime of a parliament.

Finally, the Prime Minister occupies a special role which quite distinguishes the occupant of the office from other Cabinet-members – as national leader. This is always the case but becomes especially apparent at times of national tension. Thus, during such episodes as the US bombing raid upon Libya in April 1986, it was upon the Prime Minister that attention constantly focused during the crisis – as giving the final permission for the flight from British bases, as placing the whole country on alert against terrorist attack and as being required to justify Government action against criticisms.

The Prime Minister's Office

The Prime Minister has a relatively small personal staff of between 70 and 80 people. These may be divided into four groups: the Private Office; the Press Office; the Political Office; and the Policy Unit.

The task of the *Private Office* is to facilitate the efficient conduct of the Prime Minister's relationships as head of government with Whitehall, parliament and public. It has a small staff of six civil servants backed up by a number of secretaries, executive officers and duty clerks. It is headed by the Prime Minister's principal private secretary, who is particularly concerned with the machinery of government. Four private secretaries deal with overseas, economic, non-economic home affairs and parliamentary concerns whilst, under Mrs Thatcher, a fifth has acted as personal assistant to the Prime Minister.

As we have seen, media management is now considered an essential task of government and the role of the *Press Office* (1931) is to handle the Prime Minister's relations with the media. It briefs lobby correspondents 'off the record' on a daily basis and plans the Prime Minister's media appearances.

The specific task of the *Political Office* is primarily to deal with party political matters, especially liaison with party headquarters. In addition to a political secretary with a small staff whose main task is to deal with party affairs, recent Prime Ministers have also appointed a chief political adviser to act as a general confidante on current political matters.

Finally, there is a *Policy Unit* (1974) – again with a small staff – which was set up to provide policy analysis on a medium- and long-term basis. Another main purpose is to provide the Prime Minister with a source of opinion alternative to that emanating from the official party machine and the Whitehall departments which may criticise the advice which does come in from those sources. The Unit also maintains contact with the political and specialist staff appointed by Ministers in their departments. Mrs Thatcher – an interventionist Prime Minister – has not only expanded the size and scope of the Policy Unit, incorporating civil servants in it for the first time, but has also employed specialist policy advisers such as Professor Alan Walters (Economics), Sir Anthony Parsons (Foreign Affairs) and Roger Jackling, a civil servant (Defence).

THE CABINET

The Cabinet is the country's top executive committee. It normally consists of between 20 and 22 members. After the General Election of June 1987, the Conservative Cabinet contained 21 Ministers (see Table 6.3). Status within the Cabinet is not equal, and most Cabinets divide into a small circle, or 'inner Cabinet' who may expect to be frequently consulted by the Prime Minister on their own and other fields, and an outer circle of Ministers who count for less. The 'plum' jobs are the Chancellorship of the Exchequer and the Foreign and Home Secretaryships, which a party's leading few politicians may expect to occupy. The Cabinet meets at least once a week – on Thursdays between 10 a.m. and 1 p.m. – and sometimes also on Tuesdays. In times of national crisis, it will tend to meet more frequently and on other days of the week. Cabinet meetings have become more numerous throughout the century, an average of 90 meetings per annum in the 1970s comparing with about 60 per annum between the wars and 40 per annum before 1914.

Like the office of Prime Minister, the Cabinet lacks formal constitutional existence. Both institutions are creations of convention. The main convention influencing the operation of the Cabinet is the idea of *collective responsibility*. This doctrine holds that Ministers accept responsibility collectively for the decisions made in Cabinet. This means that, however strong the controversy surrounding a particular issue and however much they disagree with a decision, Ministers are expected to support it publicly, or, at the very least, not to express their lack of support for it. If they feel they must dissent publicly, they are expected to resign; if they fail to resign, it falls to the Prime Minister to require them to do so. The underlying purpose of the convention is to create and maintain the authority of the government which public squabbling between Ministers could be expected to damage. A precondition

TABLE 6.3

The Conservative Cabinet after the 1987 General Election

Prime Minister	Margaret Thatcher
Lord President of the Council	Lord Whitelaw
Lord Chancellor	Sir Michael Havers
Foreign Secretary	Sir Geoffrey Howe
Chancellor of the Exchequer	Nigel Lawson
Home Secretary	Douglas Hurd
Defence	George Younger
Trade and Industry	Lord Young
Energy	Cecil Parkinson
Education and Science	Kenneth Baker
Scotland	Malcolm Rifkind
Wales	Peter Walker
Northern Ireland	Tom King
Social Services	John Moore
Chancellor of the Duchy of Lancaster	Kenneth Clarke
Agriculture, Fisheries and Food	John MacGregor
Transport	Paul Channon
Employment	Norman Fowler
Environment	Nicholas Ridley
Leader of the House	John Wakeham
Chief Secretary to the Treasury	John Major

of the principle of collective responsibility is that Cabinet discussion is secret. Ministers need to feel free to speak their minds in the confidence that their views will not be divulged to the media. Ministers who are known to disagree with a policy can be expected to have little commitment to it, with potentially damaging consequences for public confidence in government.

In recent times, the convention of collective responsibility has been repeatedly broken in a number of ways: by deliberate suspension, by thinly veiled disagreements and 'leaks' and by publication of their memoirs by Cabinet ministers after leaving office. Thus, Labour Prime Ministers Harold Wilson in 1975 and James Callaghan in 1977 preferred to suspend the principle of collective responsibility on the issue of British membership of the European Community rather than risk the possibility of public squabbling by members of the Cabinet or of resignation by those known to oppose membership such as Tony Benn. The principle of secrecy upon which collective responsibility depends has been broken also by the practice of the deliberate leaking of information as a political 'weapon' by Cabinet Ministers. For example, during the Westland affair, involving rival bids to 'rescue' a British helicopter firm by an American Company and a European Consortium, Cabinet Ministers on both sides of the controversy transgressed a Cabinet decision to refrain from supporting either of the bids and to leave it to the shareholders of Westland to decide. Michael Heseltine, Defence Secretary, did so by continuing to campaign publicly on behalf of the European bid; in particular, in early January 1986 he published an exchange of letters with the Managing Director of Lloyds Merchant Bank, the advisers to the European consortium. Leon Brittan, Secretary of State for Trade and Industry, riposted by authorising the 'leak' of parts of a letter by Sir Patrick Mayhew, the Solicitor-General, to Michael Heseltine which suggested that the Defence Secretary should correct a 'material inaccuracy' in the letter he had written to Lloyds Merchant Bank in the previous week. It is clear that Ministers supporting each 'side' in the controversy used publicity selectively in their own cause as a weapon to win over public opinion. Finally, secrecy has also been breached in recent years by Cabinet ministers such as Richard Crossman and Barbara Castle who kept their own records of Cabinet discussions during the Labour Governments of the 1960s and mid-1970s and published diaries based on these soon after leaving office.

The convention of collective responsibility requires that the Cabinet should resign if defeated on a vote of confidence in the House of Commons. When the Labour Government elected in October 1974 was defeated in the House of Commons on a vote of confidence on 28 March 1979, the Prime Minister, James Callaghan, immediately requested a dissolution. This aspect of the convention clearly still operates unambiguously. But it should not be assumed on the basis of the last paragraph that the remaining evidence points unequivocally to the erosion of other aspects of the convention. The questions of the extent to which the doctrine survives in practice (thereby supporting the notion that Britain has a system of Cabinet Government) and whether collective responsibility has become one more device in the hands of the Prime Minister to control leading Ministerial colleagues (thereby supporting the idea that the country has moved towards prime ministerial government) are discussed later in the chapter. It is sufficient to note at this point that the implications of the Westland affair are by no means clear-cut. On the one hand, Cabinet secrecy was often breached. Moreover, Michael Heseltine's letter of resignation contained allegations that the Prime Minister had stifled Cabinet discussion of the matter. Because of the way in which the reconstruction of the Company had been handled, he asserted, the profound issues which it raised about defence procurement and Britain's future as a technologically advanced country had never been properly addressed by the Government. On the other hand, it could be argued that the outcome of the affair demonstrated that the principle of collective responsibility remains intact. The Defence Secretary resigned because he could not agree to clear all his future statements on Westland with the Cabinet Office and with all interested Departments, as the Prime Minister required him to do. This she did in accordance with the lengthy confidential memorandum entitled *Cabinet Practice: Questions of Procedure for Ministers* which lays down guidelines to Ministers and civil servants in the operation of Cabinet government. Continuing membership of the Cabinet, therefore, required both secrecy and the willingness to subscribe to a common viewpoint from Ministers. In the crucial few days before the Westland Board came to its decision, the Defence Secretary wanted to be free to speak his mind, could not do so *and* remain a loyal member of the Government and therefore resigned. On this line of reasoning the episode confirms rather than undermines the doctrine of collective responsibility.

Virtually all the major policy issues come before Cabinet in some form. Its business focuses especially on foreign affairs, forthcoming topics in parliament, and reviews of public expenditure. One of its most important functions is to act as the final arbiter of disputes between Ministers. Where agreements cannot be reached at a lower level, a Cabinet Minister's ultimate resort is to take – or to threaten to take – the matter to Cabinet. The entry in Richard Crossman's diary for 18 April 1965, mentions this example:

> The other big issue (as well as the Ombudsman) brought up to Cabinet was my housing programme. The reason it came to Cabinet was of course *because there was a disagreement between the Chancellor and myself*. I got the policy through as a result of the firm support of the PM and an alliance with George Brown. But even so we had some difficulty, because all the other departmental Ministers resented seeing Housing get more money at the cost of their own budgets (Richard Crossman, *Diaries of a Cabinet Minister*, 1979, p. 88) [our italics].

Of necessity, because of the sheer volume and complexity of modern governmental business, responsibility for the bulk of Cabinet decisions has been delegated to *Cabinet committees*. Their decisions have the authority of Cabinet decisions and only when they are unable to reach agreement does a matter falling within their terms of reference go to full Cabinet. The committee chairman must agree any decision to take a dispute to full Cabinet. The existence, composition and chairmanship of Cabinet committees are the responsibility of the Prime Minister and are supposed to be kept secret from the public. However, their structure is, in fact, known in some detail, partly as a result of revelations like that in 1979 by Mrs Thatcher, who announced that she had set up four standing committees – on economic strategy, defence and overseas policy, home and social affairs and legislation. Cabinet committees may be conveniently divided into two categories, Standing Committees – usually classified under a set of code letters – and *ad hoc* Committees, normally classified as MISC for 'miscellaneous', which come into existence to deal with a specific problem. The general structure of Cabinet committees in 1984 is outlined in Exhibit 6.1. A former leading civil servant, Sir Frank Cooper, who was Permanent Secretary at the Ministry of Defence, testified in 1986 that nowadays 'the great majority of issues are

Exhibit 6.1   The leading Cabinet Committees in 1984

A   *Economic and Industrial*

Committee initials	Chairman	Functions
EA	Prime Minister (Margaret Thatcher)	Economic strategy, energy policy, changes in labour law, leading EEC matters
E (EX)	Prime Minister	Exports policy
E (NI)	Prime Minister	Public sector strategy and oversight of nationalised industries
E (NF)	Chancellor of the Exchequer (Nigel Lawson)	Nationalised industry finance
NIP	Treasury official	Official committee on nationalised industry policy
E (PSP)	Chancellor of the Exchequer	Public sector and public service pay policy
E (DL)	Chancellor of the Exchequer	Disposal and privatisation of state assets
E (CS)	Chief Secretary to the Treasury (Peter Rees)	Civil service pay and contingency plans for civil service strikes
E (OCS)	Cabinet office official	Official committee for preparing contingency plans
PESC	Treasury official	Official committee of finance officers handling the annual public expenditure survey

B   *Overseas and defence*

OD ___	Prime Minister	Foreign affairs, defence and Northern Ireland
OD (O)	Cabinet secretary (Sir Robert Armstrong)	Permanent secretaries' group working to OD
OD (E)	Foreign secretary (Sir Geoffrey Howe)	EEC policy
EQ (S)	Cabinet office official	Committee of Deputy Secretaries steering OD (E)

C   *Home affairs, legislation and information*

L	Leader of the House (John Biffen)	Future legislation and Queen's speech
H	Lord Whitelaw (Lord President and Deputy Leader)	Home affairs and social policy, including education

continued

Exhibit . . .   *– continued*

C   *Home affairs, legislation and information (continued)*

Committee initials	Chairman	Functions
CCU	Lord Whitelaw	Cabinet office civil contingencies unit which plans to maintain essential services and supplies in industrial disputes
HD	Home Secretary (Leon Brittan)	Civil defence
HD (O)	Cabinet office official	Official committee shadowing HD
TWC	Cabinet secretary	Transition to War Committee for mobilisation of Whitehall and Armed Forces in period of international tension
MI0	No. 10 Press Secretary (Bernard Ingham)	Weekly meeting of chief information officers

D   *Intelligence and Security*

MIS	Prime Minister	Ministerial steering committee on intelligence, supervising MI5, MI6 and GCHQ
PSIS	Cabinet Secretary	Permanent secretaries' steering committee on intelligence working to MI5
Official committee on security	Cabinet secretary	Permanent secretaries' group on internal security
Personnel security committee	Cabinet secretary	Official committee supervising positive vetting

E   *Ad hoc*

MISC7	Prime Minister	Replacement of the Polaris force with Trident
MISC21	Lord Whitelaw	Ministerial committee which fixes local authorities' rate and transport support grant
MISC62	Lord Whitelaw	'Star Chamber' for forcing spending cuts on departmental Ministers
MISC79	Lord Whitelaw	Alternatives to domestic rates; rate capping

disposed of in Cabinet committees'. One critic, Richard Crossman, has contended that, because of the way Cabinet committees either take decisions on behalf of Cabinet or pre-package the issues which do go to Cabinet, they erode the authority of the full Cabinet. Against this argument, however, it may be said that by taking decisions below the highest level of importance in the name of the Cabinet and by preparing the vital ones, Cabinet committees make effective Cabinet government possible.

The Prime Minister and senior members of the Cabinet chair the main committees but as Exhibit 6.1 shows there is also a network of 'shadow' committees chaired by leading civil servants whose function is to clear away inter-departmental disputes before the ministerial committees meet. The most important committees are chaired by the Prime Minister: to designate them by their initials (see again, Exhibit 6.1 for their concerns) these are: the EA committee, the OD committee and the MIS committee. A key *ad hoc* committee is the so-called 'Star Chamber' (MISC 62) whose task is to arbitrate between the claims of the spending Departments, especially Defence, Social Services and the Environment, and the Treasury's demands for economy. Since the war, the number of Cabinet committees has been reduced considerably. There were 466 in the first post-war government but only 190 during the premiership of James Callaghan (1976–9) and Mrs Thatcher has reduced their number still further to 135 in 1987. Of these, 25 are standing committees and 110 *ad hoc*.

The second institution which enables the Cabinet to deal with the present-day volume of business is the *Cabinet Office*. Dating from 1916, the Cabinet secretariat is staffed by civil servants under the direction of the Cabinet Secretary. The main tasks of its 120 staff are to prepare the agenda for the Cabinet and its committees; to record their conclusions; and to supervise the carrying out of their decisions. Cabinet Office staff also prepare briefing papers for the Chairmen of Cabinet committees, themselves chair standing and *ad hoc* committees and serve on 'mixed' committees of politicians and civil servants. Documents relating to main items on the Cabinet's agenda are circulated two days in advance and, according to the 'Questions of Procedure for Ministers' rule-book, the Cabinet Office has to be given seven days' notice of any business a Minister wishes to raise in Cabinet and nothing may be raised orally in Cabinet without the Prime Minister's prior consent.

Finally, each Prime Minister approaches the business of chairing Cabinet discussions in a different style. Clement Attlee's manner was brusque and peremptory, designed to limit discussion to the absolute essentials necessary to extract a decision; he could be cutting with colleagues who talked too much or who had not briefed themselves adequately. From 1948, however, he presided over a seriously divided Cabinet, divisions which it was the object of the consensual style of Harold Wilson (1964–70 and 1974–6) to avoid. According to Harold Wilson, in his contribution to Anthony King (ed.) *The British Prime Minister* (1985), the aim of the Prime Minister should be 'to get the business through, with full consideration, and to reach a clear decision, with nothing fluffed or obscure – and, so far as possible, with the maximum emollient to wounded pride' (Harold Wilson in A. King (ed.) *The British Prime Minister*, 1985, p. 35). More than most Prime Ministers, Mrs Thatcher, a 'conviction' politician identified with clear policy objectives in a variety of fields, has tended to 'lead from the front', participating in Cabinet discussions rather than simply inviting contributions from Ministers and more concerned that a particular view should prevail than that consensus should be achieved. However different Prime Ministerial approaches to Cabinet management may be, accounts of its proceedings agree on three things at least: that, except on minor matters of procedure, it does not vote; the importance of the Prime Minister's summing-up; and the fact that its 'conclusions' are recorded but minutes are not taken. On the first point, Attlee stated 'You don't take a vote. No, never.' And the existence of this practice was corroborated by the testimony of Edward Heath about the premierships of Anthony Eden, Harold Macmillan and Sir Alec Douglas-Home and confirmed by Harold Wilson about his own. At the end of discussions, the Prime Minister sums up, usually in terms of the predominant view but sometimes in line with a view favoured personally whether this has majority support or not.

Recording the conclusions reached by Cabinet is the responsibility of the Secretary to the Cabinet, the head of the Cabinet Office. Here, however, opinions do vary considerably on the degree of Prime Ministerial involvement. In *The Castle Diaries, 1974–1976* (1980) Barbara Castle testified, on the basis of her experience as a Cabinet Minister: 'One of the hazards of Cabinet government is that one is at the mercy of the Minutes, *which often come out very differently from what one remembered.* Yet it is almost impossible to get them altered afterwards, particularly if the PM has a vested interest in the official version' (p. 252, our italics). In his *Diaries*, Richard Crossman also noted that the PM's hand in relation to the Cabinet was greatly strengthened by his 'being able to have the minutes written as he wants' (p. 626). Harold Wilson, however, maintained at the time (1970) that only 'very occasionally' did he see the 'minutes' and only 'very, very occasionally' was he consulted about them before issue. Later, Wilson stated that 'the writing of the conclusions is the unique responsibility of the secretary of the cabinet ... The conclusions are circulated very promptly after cabinet, and *up to that time no minister, certainly not the prime minister sees them asks to see them or conditions them in any way*' (cited in King (ed.) *The British Prime Minister*, 1985, p. 40; our italics).

A third version of the practice with regard to Cabinet ministers has been given by an MP, F. N. Forman, in his book *Mastering British Politics* (1985), 'It is open to the Prime Minister and, indeed, any Minister to see the minutes in draft, to point out errors and ask for suitable amendments' (p. 179).

PRIME MINISTERIAL OR CABINET GOVERNMENT

One of the major debates about the present-day British Constitution is whether, and, if so, to what extent, Prime Ministerial Government has superseded Cabinet Government. It should be stressed at the outset that we are not considering here the notion that the office of Prime Minister has become 'presidential' or 'quasi-presidential' as some commentators following Richard Crossman believe. To discuss the subject in these terms merely muddies the debate. Merely to list the differences between the two systems of government brings out the inappropriateness of the analogy. The US President is constitutionally separate from Congress, the British PM institutionally inseparable from parliament; the US President and Congress are each elected on a separate system, the British PM and the rest of the legislators on the same one; the US President has the support of a large personal Office, the British PM does not, and so on. If Prime Ministers have increased the powers of the office, they have done so in ways appropriate to a Parliamentary not a Presidential system; hence the term 'Prime Ministerial' is used to describe the phenomenon here.

Richard Crossman and Tony Benn have put forward the thesis of Prime Ministerial government. Crossman first propounded it in the introduction which he wrote in 1964 to a new edition of Walter Bagehot's Victorian classic, *The English Constitution*. He argued that power had slipped inexorably away from the Cabinet into the hands of the Prime Minister and later claimed that his experience as a Cabinet Minister in the Labour Governments of 1964–70 confirmed his views. Crossman maintained that the transition to Prime Ministerial government was already well under way in the third quarter of the nineteenth century when the Prime Minister's power to select Cabinets at will, to decide the agenda of Cabinet and announce decisions without taking a vote, and to control patronage gave the office 'near-presidential' status. This shift of power was completed in the period after 1945. The main factors in the process have been the centralisation of party machines which are directly under the control of the party leaders and the growth of a centralised bureaucracy so large that it cannot be managed by the Cabinet. Nowadays, therefore, all power is concentrated in the hands of the Prime Minister. Under this Prime Ministerial system, the Premier takes all the major decisions in consultation with whichever advisers are picked for the occasion; secondary decisions are taken by Cabinet committees and by the Departments. Cabinet meetings themselves no longer provide a forum for full debate of issues but exist merely to sanction decisions taken elsewhere. All that Ministers can do if they disagree is to protest but this is always within the context of a situation in which they owe their positions to the Prime Minister and not to the Cabinet and in which the Prime Minister may well have determined the policy of Departments. Collective Cabinet responsibility, however, is still maintained and enforced even though many decisions have been taken above the heads of Cabinet members and without their knowledge. The upshot of this process is that the Cabinet has now joined 'the dignified elements of the Constitution', although its decline has been concealed from the public eye. The reality of Prime Ministerial power in the post-war period is graphically illustrated by the major decisions – such as the manufacture of the A-bomb and the preparation of the attack on Port Said in the Suez affair 1956 – which were taken by the Prime Minister with the assistance only of his select advisers and without consulting the full Cabinet.

Benn, in an article entitled 'The Case for a Constitutional Premiership' (1985), put forward a similar argument with different emphases. He considers that, within the framework of public and parliamentary consent (both voters and, in the ultimate analysis, the House of Commons, still have the power to topple a Prime Minister and Government), a considerable centralisation of power in the premiership has occurred, amounting to 'a system of personal rule in the very heart of our parliamentary democracy'. Benn stresses certain powers in particular as elevating the position of the Prime Minister. First and foremost is the power of patronage which includes not only the capacity 'to appoint and dismiss Ministers without any constitutional need for approval by parliament or the party' but also the ability to create peers by advising the Crown, to nominate people for honours, to play a leading role in the appointment of the Chairman of the Nationalised Industries, to appoint the Chairmen of Royal Commissions, leading civil servants, ambassadors, chiefs of staff and the heads of the Security Services. Second is the complete personal control of a Prime Minister over the conduct of government business. The Prime Minister decides what Cabinet discusses and does not discuss, can set up and appoint to Cabinet committees without revealing their existence to the public or parliament, determines what papers are circulated within government and to whom, and can instruct the civil service on the conduct of its business. The Premier is thus able 'to use the government to bring forward the policies which he favours and to stop those to which he is opposed'. Under the Minute of Procedure for Government Ministers, the Prime Minister lays down extremely detailed regulations for the operation of the government as a whole, including everything from collective responsibility to the need for No 10 to authorise all broadcasts. The 1976 version 'ran to 27 printed pages, in 132 paragraphs, under 14 main sections and 51 subsections'. These rules are confidential to the government and unknown to party and public. In addition, the Premier can decide how much parliament and public are told about the activities of government through control of the publicity machine and of the system by which government papers are classified. The Prime Minister has personal responsibility for the Security Services, can use the royal prerogative to secure UK adherence to binding treaties without the need for formal ratification by parliament, and enjoys special responsibilities for the Armed Forces through the Secretary of State for Defence. Finally, the Premier has the power to terminate the Government's span of office either by requesting a dissolution from the monarch often before the end of its constitutional term or by offering his or her resignation to the sovereign, which automatically carries with it the resignation of the rest of the government. The Prime Minister's power of dissolution is a formidable threat by which to obtain the compliance of both government and party.

The views of Crossman and Benn have received some academic support from Martin Burch in an article in *Teaching Politics* (September 1985) entitled 'The demise of Cabinet Government?' He believes that 'the Cabinet has become a residual institution' and, moreover, that its 'erosion . . . seems to have accelerated in recent years'. In his view, what has made supreme control by the Cabinet impossible is the sheer volume of governmental business: in 1975 its legislation alone ran to 13 000 pages compared with a mere 450 pages in 1911. By gradual stage, he argues, institutions such as Cabinet committees and the Cabinet secretariat – developed to assist Cabinet decision-making – have either come to take decisions for it, or to shape decisions so as to predetermine their outcomes when they do reach Cabinet. Many major items, especially in the field of economic policy, never appear before Cabinet. The trend to decision-making in small informal groups around the Prime Minister, whether as an 'inner Cabinet', composed of senior Ministers, or as 'working parties' of Ministers, civil servants and political advisers, has increased in recent premierships. Under James C-allaghan (1976–9) many important decisions on monetary policy and international economics were taken by an informal 'seminar' of civil servants, political advisers and (mainly Treasury) Ministers which did not even have the status of a Cabinet committee. Such informal groups have become more common in the Administration of Mrs Thatcher. These considerations propel Burch to an inescapable conclusion: 'the idea that the Cabinet is in supreme control of decision-making must be judged untenable'. However, although, in Burch's view, the decline of the Cabinet has been accompanied by some shift of power towards the Prime Minister, the Premiership is not the only beneficiary of the weakening of the Cabinet, even though the Prime Minister has more opportunities and resources to wield influence than other parts of the Executive. Second, the organisational constraints which preclude total oversight of government by the Cabinet also preclude it for the Prime Minister. In short, the Premier is not the sole player nor does he or she always dominate the field. Burch's view therefore combines the idea that Cabinet Government no longer exists with the notion that the decline of the Cabinet has only partially benefited the Prime Minister. His view serves as a bridge therefore to the interpretations of those who are not only sceptical of the thesis of Prime Ministerial power but also doubt the decline of the Cabinet.

Prominent among those who are sceptical about the thesis of Prime

Ministerial power are an ex-Cabinet Minister, Patrick Gordon-Walker (see his book *The Cabinet*, 1973) and an academic, George Jones, whose essay, 'The Prime Minister's Power' (1965) (see A. King, *The British Prime Minister* (1985)) remains the most succinct expression of the sceptics' viewpoint. The doubters maintain that political, administrative and personal constraints prevent the Prime Minister from achieving the predominance suggested. *Political* constraints arise out of the need for the Prime Minister to take party considerations into account when making governmental appointments. Constitutionally, the Prime Minister may have a free hand; politically, however, such freedom is limited – by the need to satisfy the claims of leading colleagues (often to specific offices) and to ensure that the various sections of the party are represented in the Cabinet. Mrs Thatcher has gained a justified reputation for seeking to surround herself with subordinates of similar views. But what is equally true is that by early 1988 she had served longer in the office than any of her twentieth-century predecessors and that it was not until her third term of office that her Cabinet was shaped completely to her liking.

Each of the Prime Minister's colleagues is also a rival with personal ambitions which may include the party leadership; not infrequently also, they have a personal following in the party. Such people have to be consulted and bargained with, but not snubbed and certainly not humiliated. If they cannot be appointed at will neither can they be dismissed at the Prime Minister's pleasure. The PM may both demote and sack but must do both with caution. Macmillan in July 1962, in the so-called 'Night of the Long Knives' when he dismissed seven Cabinet Ministers and nine Ministers outside the Cabinet, is always said to have gone too far since the sackings caused resentment in the party and gave the appearance of panic to the country. No other modern Prime Minister has gone anything like so far. The point is that fellow-Ministers are political rivals as well as governing colleagues and Prime Ministers need to be constantly aware of that fact. The rapidity with which one circumstance can be transformed into the other was revealed by Michael Heseltine's resignation on 9 January 1986: one moment he was in the Cabinet Room as Secretary of State for Defence; a few hours later, after his resignation statement, the media was speculating – despite his denials – that he had just 'laid down a marker' for the leadership. At least one post-war Prime Minister faced an attempt by Cabinet colleagues to replace him: Clement Attlee when in 1947 Cripps and Dalton sought to make Bevin Premier. Another leading politician, Sir Alec Douglas-Home, who succeeded the ailing Macmillan as party leader in 1963, depended upon the support of his leading colleagues – Butler, Hailsham and Maudling – in order to be able to form a government. A Prime Minister, moreover, is constrained by party considerations not only in terms of personnel but also in terms of *policy*. The freedom of manoeuvre of Mrs Thatcher as Prime Minister, for example, was limited by party promises on tax cuts, control of public expenditure and privatisation. The Prime Minister keeps in touch with party opinion through the Whips' Office and relies upon the Chief Whip for information about government policies which are likely to cause trouble in the party.

There are also *administrative* constraints upon a Prime Minister. The Prime Minister's control of Cabinet agenda is less complete than has been contended. As the Heseltine affair revealed, a Prime Minister may keep an item off the agenda temporarily but only at the risk of a resignation will the Prime Minister attempt permanently to exclude a matter which a colleague strongly wishes to be discussed. Many external pressures shape the agenda, the great majority of which are quite outside the ability of the Prime Minister to control. A residual power remains in Cabinet – generally not asserted – to get any matter discussed. Again, in the handling of Cabinet meetings, a Prime Minister must listen to colleagues' arguments and has to sum up fairly within 'the sense of the meeting'; to do otherwise on more than the odd occasion is to court resistance. If a Prime Minister identifies with and drives for the acceptance of particular policies, he or she risks defeat on at least some of them. Anthony King stated in *The British Prime Minister* (2nd ed., 1985) that in the first phase of Mrs Thatcher's 1979–1983 Administration:

> the cabinet was deeply divided on almost every aspect of economic policy and . . . *the prime minister frequently failed to get her way.* She and her loyal group of economic ministers succeeded in controlling economic policy in the narrow sense – taxation and interest rates – *but they were defeated again and again over such matters as public spending and state subsidies to the nationalised industries; and the . . . Secretary of State for Employment, James Prior, thwarted her every attempt to persuade the cabinet to introduce measures to curb trade unions tougher than those envisaged in the party's manifesto* (p. 103, our italics).

Even on the Falklands, according to one minister, Mrs Thatcher had to carry the Cabinet on every major decision. In the view of reporter Peter Hennessy, the Task Force 'would never have sailed without Cabinet approval' (Peter Hennessy, 'Shades of a Home Counties Boadicea', *The Times*, 17 May 1983).

Finally, there are *personal* limits upon the power of the Prime Minister – the limits of any single individual's ability and energy. If it is difficult for a Minister ever to feel completely on top of the affairs of a single Department, then it might be surmised that detailed surveillance of the work of the entire government by a Prime Minister is a virtually impossible task. It can certainly be maintained that intervention in one area of government must always be at the cost of neglecting the remaining areas. In addition, given the support of only a relatively small personal Office, Prime Ministers lack the specific policy information and advice to enable them to intervene success-fully over the whole range of government policies. In practice, however much they may have interested themselves in certain spheres of policy, post-war Prime Ministers have not defined their role in interventionist terms. Rather, they have tended to perceive their task, in Harold Wilson's words, as 'conducting' the orchestra but not 'playing the instruments oneself'. Even under an interventionist Prime Minister such as Mrs Thatcher, there remain, according to Martin Burch, 'vast areas of government business which have not been subject to Prime Ministerial intervention'. Lastly, the significance of the personal element in the authority of a Prime Minister can be exaggerated. At certain times within the life-span of a government – after a General Election victory or a successful initiative in foreign policy, for example – the personal prestige of a Prime Minister will be very considerable, and may well exceed that of both party and government. Equally, at other times, Prime Ministerial popularity may run behind the party, or the public standing of the party may slump and the Prime Minister will be blamed: in this situation, the authority of the Prime Minister over the rest of the Cabinet is likely to be sharply reduced.

There are arguments on both sides of the debate about Prime Ministerial power, yet, in the final analysis, partly because of the lack of evidence caused by the convention of Cabinet secrecy, neither set of arguments is conclusive. Conclusions, therefore, must be largely negative. First, the verdict on the debate about Prime Ministerial power must be 'case unproven'. The Cabinet is directly involved in fewer decisions than formerly, and generally at a later stage; nor do all decisions come within its purview. Some issues which do come before it – especially those in which the Prime Minister takes an especial interest, e.g. economic, foreign and defence affairs – do not appear at a sufficiently early stage to enable the Cabinet to exercise a real influence. But although these considerations may suggest that Cabinet government has been weakened, they do not necessarily mean that it is dead. The bulk of major decisions still do go before Cabinet and the doctrine of collective responsibility is still applied, if anything more rigorously than before. Second, even if the Cabinet is making fewer governmental decisions than before, this does not mean that the Prime Minister is making all those which elude the Cabinet. Prime Ministerial power *has* increased but there remain too many areas in which involvement is sporadic and too many restraints upon it in general to accept the thesis of Prime Ministerial power unreservedly. What may be the case – such is the growth in the scale and complexity of governmental decision-making – is that ultimate growth control escapes *both* Prime Minister and Cabinet. As Martin Burch has argued, the consequence of the erosion of Cabinet combined with the failure of the office of Prime Minister to encompass what escapes Cabinet may be 'a less coordinated and responsible executive' in general. In the final section of this chapter, we deal briefly with recent proposals which are directed at making these institutions more responsible, effective and coherent.

PROPOSALS FOR REFORM

Tony Benn has made a case for a 'constitutional Premiership' (1980). He favours a strong executive to secure the country in the face of the threat from multinational corporations and the EEC but seeks to make it accountable, open and collective. His proposals for change are addressed to a situation when Labour is in government. He would restrict Prime Ministerial power by requiring that the whole Cabinet is subject to annual re-election by the Parliamentary Labour Party (PLP) and that the allocation of ministerial portfolios are approved by the PLP before being tendered to the Queen. The abolition of the House of Lords would also dispense with part of the Premier's patronage power by eliminating the need to create peers. A *Freedom of Information Act* would further curtail Prime Ministerial power by reducing secrecy in government which at present works to the Prime Minister's advantage. Finally, Benn would aim to tilt the balance of power away from the Executive towards parliament in general and the PLP in particular by according the PLP the role of final authority on all matters concerning the implementation of Labour policy. His objective is closer PLP surveillance and control of government policy. Benn's proposals may be criticised as one-sidedly applying only to when Labour is in office, as potentially a source of executive instability rather than strength and as likely to reinforce accountability to party at the expense of accountability to the whole electorate.

Whereas Benn's proposals are aimed at weakening the Premiership, Kenneth Berrill, a former head of the Central Policy Review Staff, has argued that the Premiership has insufficient resources at its disposal to enable its occupant to cope successfully with the job in the contemporary world (1980). He advocates a strengthening of the quality and depth – but not the amount – of advice available to the Prime Minister by the establishment of *a Prime Minister's Department*. In his view, a number of circumstances have combined to render it necessary for a modern Prime Minister to be well informed across the whole range of governmental activities. These are first, the need for the Prime Minister to be able to relate Departmental policies to the overall strategy of the government; second, to be able to answer in parliament and to the media for the policies of the government; and third, to be capable of dealing with detailed negotiations in face-to-face meetings with other heads of State. His conclusion is that 'Prime Ministers need and expect an advice system of their own to help in the work of cabinet and cabinet committees, in their reaction to issues raised in ministerial correspondence, in their relations with other heads of government – not least because of the time factor' (King, *The British Prime Minister*, p. 254). The work of a Prime Minister's Department would be a mixture of short-term advice on day-to-day issues and long-term in-depth studies. Its objective would not be to increase the Prime Minister's capacity to interfere in the daily running of Departments but to increase the strength of government 'at the centre' for the reasons specified. Other comparable industrial democracies – Australia for instance – have developed larger support staffs for their premiers than has the United Kingdom. Needless to say, there have been criticisms of this proposal, chief among which have been that the existence of such a Department would reinforce existing tendencies towards Prime Ministerial power, inhibit the Prime Minister's role of achieving a consensus by identifying a Premier with particular policies and, in general, increase the predisposition of Prime Ministers to meddle with the work of departments.

SUMMARY

The modern office of Prime Minister encompasses a formidable concentration of powers. Taken together, these make Prime Ministers far more than 'first among equals' in their relations with other Cabinet Ministers. However, the case that Prime Ministerial has replaced Cabinet Government is 'unproven'. In the twentieth century, with the growth in the scope and complexity of government, an elaborate committee system and a secretariat (Cabinet Office) have been developed to enable the Cabinet to deal with its vastly increased volume of business. Despite some weakening in the institution and with some qualifications, it remains possible to describe the British system as 'Cabinet Government'. Most major issues still appear before Cabinet in some form and the principle of collective responsibility is still applicable.

FURTHER READING

Burch, Martin (1985) 'The Demise of Cabinet Government?', *Teaching Politics*, 14, September.
Castle, B. (1984) *The Castle Diaries 1964–1970*, London, Weidenfeld & Nicolson.
Castle, B. (1980) *The Castle Diaries 1974–1976*, London, Weidenfeld & Nicolson.
Gordon-Walker, Patrick (1973) *The Cabinet*, London, Fontana.
Hennessy, Peter (1986) *Cabinet*, Oxford, Blackwell.
Howard, A. (ed.) (1979) *The Crossman Diaries*, London, Hamilton (Hamish).
King, Anthony (1985) *The British Prime Minister*, London, Macmillan, 2nd edn.
Mackintosh, John (1977) *The British Cabinet*, London, Stevens.
Norton, P. (1987) 'Prime Ministerial Power: A Framework for Analysis', *Teaching Politics*, 16, September.
Weller, Patrick (1985) *First Among Equals: Prime Ministers in Westminster Systems*, London, Allen & Unwin.

QUESTIONS

1. How appropriate is it to describe the modern British Prime Minister as 'virtually an elective dictator'?
2. Do you agree that 'Cabinet Government is dead'?

ASSIGNMENT

Imagine you occupy a particular post in the Cabinet. Explain the work of your Department at a Cabinet meeting and, over a period of at least several months, monitor developments within it as outlined in the daily press.

7

Ministers, Departments and Civil Servants

This chapter continues our examination of 'the Executive' by considering the major Departments of State. We begin by characterising them in terms of functions, size and organisation. We then turn to the two leading themes of the chapter – first, to a consideration of the roles of Ministers and civil servants, with special emphasis upon the nature of the relationship between them; and second to an analysis of the convention of Ministerial responsibility, which in traditional accounts has been held to describe the accountability of the heads of Departments of State to parliament. Our dual focus is, therefore, upon how decisions are made throughout the bulk of British Government and how those decisions are made accountable. We place particular emphasis on explaining these roles and relationships in the context of the major explanatory theories.

THE MAIN DEPARTMENTS OF STATE

In forming an administration, as we have already seen (Chapter 6, p. 115–17, especially Table 6.1), a Prime Minister makes scores of appointments. These include, in addition to government Whips, Ministers who head Departments – most of whom are of Cabinet rank, non-Departmental Ministers such as the Lord President of the Council, the Leader of the House of Commons and the Chancellor of the Duchy of Lancaster, and a large number of junior Ministers, i.e. Ministers of State and Under-Secretaries of State. As well as a Departmental head (Secretary of State) each Ministry normally contains at least one Minister of State and two or more Under-Secretaries of State: these junior ministerial appointments are an excellent way for aspiring politicians to gain experience of government and often but not invariably lead in time to promotion to full Ministerial rank. The Department of the Environment – a large ministry – has one Cabinet Minister at its head assisted by two Ministers of State and two Under-Secretaries of State. In the Treasury – a far smaller but key department – as well as the Chancellor of the Exchequer, there are a Chief Secretary of Cabinet rank, two Ministers of State and two Under-Secretaries of State; the Welsh Office – a very small Ministry – has one Cabinet Minister, one Minister of State and one Under-Secretary. Junior ministers normally assume responsibility for specific tasks: in the Treasury, for instance, there is a Financial Secretary, an Economic Secretary, a Minister of State (Civil Service) and Minister of State (Revenue).

Ministers are the political and constitutional heads of Departments. Departments, however, are largely composed of permanent officials. Below the ministerial 'team' there is a body of civil servants headed by the Permanent Secretary. Each Department is organised hierarchically: below the Permanent Secretaries, in order of rank, are the Deputy Secretaries, Assistant Secretaries, Senior Principals and Principals. Broadly speaking, each department is split up into a number of functional units (divisions) headed by an official of assistant secretary rank. The Department of Employment, for example, has the following divisions: Industrial Relations, Economic Policy (Manpower), Manpower (General), Economics and Social, Establishments, Finance, Solicitors, Statistics and Overseas. Figure 7.1 brings together the various points already made about Departmental structure in diagrammatic form.

There are eighteen major Whitehall Departments, including the three legal ones. Table 7.1 sets out their main responsibilities, together with the size of their staff and budgets, in 1985. Politically, the most coveted Departments are the three mentioned first – the Treasury, the Foreign Office and the Home Office. But of these 'plum' jobs only the Home Office confronts its head with

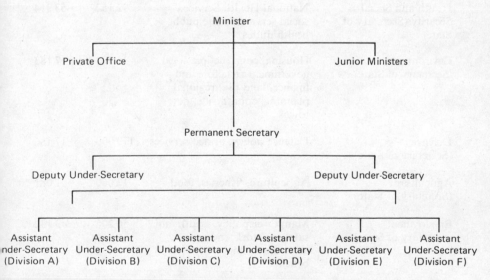

FIGURE 7.1 *Departmental structure*

This figure is of value so long as it is remembered that it does not describe an actual Department but rather draws attention to the kind of formal structure possessed by all Departments.

Source: Adapted from P. Norton, *The British Polity* (1984) pp. 188–9.

TABLE 7.1

The main Government Departments: responsibilities, size, budgets (1985)

Department	Responsibilities	Size–number of personnel	Budget (£)
The Treasury† (Chancellor of the Exchequer)	Economic policy, public spending and taxation, international currency policy	3 580	
Foreign and Commonwealth Office (Foreign Secretary)	Foreign policy (including relations with the EEC), defence of British interests overseas, some administrative duties in British dependencies	10 938	1 804
Home Office (Home Secretary)	Administration of justice, police, prison service, immigration, public morals, public safety, broadcasting policy	36 645	5 039
Trade and Industry (Secretary of State)	Industrial policy, overseas trade policy, aerospace, information technology	14 886	2 124
Health and Social Security (Secretary of State)	National Health Service, social services, some public health duties	92 152	53 914
Environment (Secretary of State)	Housing, construction, local government structure and finance, land use, regional planning, countryside, new towns	36 522	7 183
Defence (Secretary of State)	Defence policy, armed services	179 000	17 186
Agriculture (Secretary of State)	Agriculture, fisheries, food	12 060	2 081
Employment (Secretary of State)	Manpower policy, health and safety at work, industrial arbitration, unemployment benefits	56 206	3 132
Education and Science (Secretary of State)	Primary, secondary and higher education, encouragement of civil science	2 472	13 953

141

TABLE 7.1—*contd.*

Department	Responsibilities	Size-number of personnel	Budget (£)
Energy (Secretary of State)	Energy, nationalised industries, Atomic Energy Authority	1 106	2 591
Transport (Secretary of State)	Transport policy, movement of freight, railways, ports, inland waterways, road safety	14 528	4 583
Lord Chancellor's Department	Administration of the law and the courts	10 195	1 692
Scottish Office (Secretary of State)	Major governmental functions including economic planning, education, health, agriculture and development	9 909	7 032
Northern Ireland Office (Secretary of State)	Administration of UK policy in NI relating to finance, commerce, health and social services, education, housing, agriculture, manpower and community relations	196	4 000
Welsh Office (Secretary of State)	Agriculture (with Department of Agriculture), primary and secondary education, tourism, water, roads, forestry, town and country planning, new towns, urban grants	2 206	2 622
Law Officer's Department* (Attorney General)	Advice to government on legal matters; represents Crown in major court cases. Attorney General is responsible for enforcement of criminal law	22	
Lord Advocate's Department*	Has same function in Scotland as Law Officer's Department in England	22	

Source: Derived from Philip Norton: *The British Polity* (1984) pp. 186–71 and *The Guardian*, 16 January, 1986

Notes †The figure given here refers to the Treasury only; it does not include three financial and economic Departments with large staffs–Inland Revenue (70 200), Customs and Excise (25 350) and National Savings (8 025).

*Legal Departments

a major task of management. In terms of size, the Home Office can be counted a middle-rank Department along with Employment and the Environment but well behind large Departments such as the DHSS and giant ones such as Defence. Table 7.1, in fact, well brings out the disparity in size between Departments which range from Defence, at one extreme to 'minnows' such as Education, Energy, the Northern Ireland Office and the Law Officers' Department, at the other. Indeed, over three-quarters of the half-million non-industrial civil servants in 1985 worked in eight Departments only: Defence, the DHSS, Employment, Environment, the Home Office, Transport, and the Boards of Inland Revenue and of Customs and Excise. Another contrast is in terms of Departmental budgets: here, Health and Social Security is by far the largest spender of the three main spending Departments, the other two being Defence and Education.

Before examining the relations between Ministers and civil servants in depth, we look briefly at the nature of the Civil Service itself. A 'civil servant' has been defined as 'a servant of the Crown employed in a civil capacity who is paid wholly and directly from money voted by parliament' (Tomlin Commission, 1931). This definition covered about 608 000 individuals in 1985 who collectively constituted about 10 per cent of total public sector employment. Their numbers had declined from 730 000 in 1979 as a result of a deliberate policy designed to prune back the bureaucracy and carried out by Mrs Thatcher's Government, and were scheduled to fall still further to just over 592 000 by 1988. Within the Civil Service as a whole, it is useful to distinguish between the non-industrial and the industrial civil servants – i.e. those employed in ordnance factories, dockyards and workshops; as a proportion of the whole, the industrial civil servants declined from over 50 per cent in 1939 to under 25 per cent in the early 1980s. Of the non-industrial civil servants, only a relatively small proportion – about 17 per cent – work in Inner London; the rest work outside – 8 per cent in Greater London, 74 per cent in the provinces and a mere 1 per cent overseas. Within the London-based category, only about 4000 are in the highest Administrative grades of Principal and above. It is with this relatively small category of Administrative Group policy advisers that this chapter is concerned – the administrative élite. It is members of this group who, in cooperation with their Ministerial superiors, 'run the country'.

This Group is recruited from graduates by a system of open competitive examination followed by rigorous interviews. Nonetheless, in terms of social background and expertise, the bias of recruitment is towards middle-class – often public school – Oxbridge-educated Arts graduates. In 1982, fourteen of the twenty-four entrants into the Home Civil Service had gained Oxford degrees, three each had graduated from Cambridge and London, and one each from Bristol, Exeter, Keele and Sheffield. The preference is for a 'generalist' rather than for someone with specialist knowledge, scientific or otherwise: in 1981, thirty-five of the fifty-four entrants had arts degrees, sixteen had degrees in social science but only three had degrees in science or technology. The Civil Service Selection Board looks for a person with 'a good all-round intellect'; it likes its entrants to possess incisiveness, judgement, clarity and orderliness of expression, drive, determination, the ability to work with people, a sense of the way that bureaucratic decisions will affect ordinary people and, increasingly, numeracy. Once admitted, the training of a civil servant in the higher grades is predominantly whilst doing the job itself. The Fulton Report (1968) called for changes in civil service recruitment, promotion and training – specifically, for a movement towards more open recruitment and away from the 'generalist' towards a more specialist administrator possessing relevant expertise. By 1985, despite some attempt to introduce numeracy and psychological tests into selection procedure and some limited reforms elsewhere, the sway of the Humanities-educated 'generalist' with little scientific knowledge or training in management remained virtually undiminished. Once recruited, higher civil servants enjoy security of tenure in what is for most of them a life-long career with good pay and pensions. The remuneration of a Permanent Secretary from July 1986, for example, was £62 100 per annum.

DECISION-MAKING WITHIN DEPARTMENTS

The vast majority of governmental decisions nowadays are made in Departments. The proportion of Departmental decisions which are either sufficiently important or controversial to be taken to Cabinet has become very small indeed. As Secretary of State for Education and Science (1965–7) Tony Crosland took only two decisions to Cabinet in two-and-a-half years. An examination of decision-making in Departments, therefore, takes us to the centre of contemporary British Government. Not only do Departments take the bulk of decisions – from the relatively minor to the undeniably major, it is no accident that they do so. For whenever new responsibilities are created by legislation, parliament confers them squarely upon Departments. New powers developed by statute are given to Ministers, not to the Cabinet or the Prime Minister. The political and administrative importance of Departments stems directly from their legal–constitutional pre-eminence.

How decisions are taken within Departments is consequently of vital significance in British government. To what extent can Ministers be said to be the real decision-makers? How far, on the other hand, has their position been undermined so that the real power lies with civil servants? Patrick Dunleavy, in *Developments in British Politics* (1986) has suggested several different approaches to this issue, which we follow in modified form here. These are, first, the *traditional public administration* or *liberal–democratic* theory; second, the *new public administration* or *liberal–bureaucratic* model; and third, the *power-bloc* or *left-wing Socialist* approach. There is also a fourth approach often mentioned in the context of Minister–civil service relations but which is more centrally concerned with development *within* the Civil Service itself: this may be described as the *bureaucratic over-supply model* (pp. 360–3). It is worth mentioning and dealing with here, although in less detail than the other approaches, because it does in certain important ways touch upon and explain recent developments in Ministerial–civil servant relations, even if not directly involved in the explanation of them. This view is most closely associated with the New Right. In this section, we first briefly explain these models, then examine each in turn at greater length.

The traditional public administration model

This expresses the conventional perception of Minister–civil servant relations. According to this approach, the formal roles of Ministers and civil servants are clear, and politico-administrative reality approximates closely to constitutional theory. Briefly, the job of Ministers is to take policy decisions and to defend them in Westminster, Whitehall and in the country. The task of senior civil servants is to brief Ministers on all matters with which they have to deal; this involves processing information so that Ministers can choose between options in an informed way. This model assumes a clear dividing-line between political decision-making, which is what Ministers do, and administration, which is the job of civil servants in tendering advice and carrying out decisions. It is not only the traditional textbook view of Minister–civil-servant relations but also predominates today in the Civil Service itself as well as being held by several leading politicians. It is the liberal–democratic view and is well summed up by Sir Brian Hayes, the leading civil servant in the Ministry of Agriculture, in a radio discussion published in Hugo Young and Anne Sloman, *No, Minister* (1982):

> Civil Servants ought not to have power because we're not elected. Power stems from the people and flows through Parliament to the minister responsible to Parliament. The civil servant has no power of his own. He is there to help a minister and to be the minister's agent . . . I think the job of the civil servant is to make sure that his minister is informed; that he has all the facts; that he's made aware of all the options and that he is shown all the considerations bearing on those options. It is then for the minister to take the decision. That is how the system ought to operate and that is how I think, in the vast majority of cases, it does operate (pp. 20–1).

In recent years, the traditional approach has been strongly criticised. To many political observers, this model no longer accords with the realities of present-day Minister–civil servant relationships. In a number of different ways, Ministerial power has declined whilst the power of the permanent administrator has increased. The upshot has been to tilt the balance towards the civil servants. The phrase 'on tap but never on top' has traditionally been used to describe the role of the civil servant in relationship to Ministers, but how far is it now applicable?

Liberal–bureaucratic model

Many observers believe the 'traditional' description no longer applies. Critics continue to accept the traditional model as a norm but argue that Departmental decision-making in practice is better described in a manner which recognises the fact of Civil Service power. The theory which best expresses this approach consequently mixes liberal–democratic ideal with administrative reality – hence, the term for this model: *liberal–bureaucratic*. In recent times a number of academic commentators and practising politicians have moved towards it. Their worries are well summed up in the view of Sir Ian Gilmour that probably fewer than 'one Minister in three runs his department'. This approach does not exclude the possibility that a Minister can dominate a Department. But it does suggest that for most of the time the majority of Ministers are in the hands of their officials.

The power-bloc model

According to the *power-bloc* model, the Civil Service functions as an Establishment veto group. On this view, the Civil Service comprises an administrative cadre whose centrist–conservative bias reflects the interests of the privileged sections of society from which it is recruited. It deploys its administrative expertise and exploits its permanency of tenure to thwart radical departures in policy by Socialist governments. This is the Marxist view of the Civil Service prevalent on the far left. Important advocates are Ralph Miliband in *The State in Capitalist Society* (1969), Brian Sedgemore in *The Secret Constitution* (1980) and Tony Benn. Benn has well expressed this view of Minister–Civil Service relations in Hugo Young and Anne Sloman, *No, Minister* (1982), as follows:

> The deal that the civil service offers a minister is this: if you do what we want you to do, we will help you publicly to pretend that you're implementing the manifesto on which you were elected ... they are always trying to steer incoming governments back to the policy of the outgoing government, minus the mistakes that the civil service thought the outgoing government made (pp. 19–20).

The bureaucratic over-supply model

This suggests that the first concern of the Civil Service is generally its own interest rather than the public interest. This self-interested motivation is displayed in Civil Service behaviour with regard to pay, pensions, conditions of service and the size and status of the Whitehall bureaucracy itself. Disquiet about this aspect of the Civil Service came to the fore in the late 1970s. It is most closely linked with the ideas of the Conservative Right but is by no means confined to Mrs Thatcher and her immediate supporters. It also surfaced, for example, in works such as *The Politics of Power* (1977) by Joe

Haines, a former political adviser to Harold Wilson, and *Your Disobedient Servant* (1978) by Leslie Chapman, a former civil servant in the Department of Environment. The worries of this school of thought are well caught in Haines's second chapter entitled 'The Master Servants', which severely criticises Whitehall 'waste' and calls for sizeable cuts. He particularly condemns the way in which top civil servants (in 1974) pushed 'excessive' pay rises for civil servants against the wishes of the Employment Secretary, and singles out as a spectacular example of an overblown establishment the Ministry of Defence, with its 164 Press Officers (cf. the Home Office's forty and the Foreign Office's eleven) and the 200 cars at the disposal of senior MoD staff in 1976 (pp. 23–5). As already stated, the views of these critics do not bear directly on the Minister–civil servant relationship debate but require some discussion, first, because they underlie the determination of Mrs Thatcher's Government to 'cut the civil service down to size' and, second, because, if true, they affect Minister–civil servant relations indirectly since they reflect the self-confidence of the modern bureaucracy.

We focus first – and predominantly – upon the factors which have led significant numbers of political commentators to doubt the continuing validity of the *conventional public administration* approach. Factors which *can* tilt the balance of power away from Ministers and towards the Civil Service are the numbers, permanence, expertise, coordinating role, control of information and self-interested attitudes of the Civil Service in conjunction with the heavy workload, lack of alternative policy advice and sheer volume of decisions to be made on the part of Ministers.

Numbers

Two points are relevant here. First, the size of the Whitehall Establishment itself presents a formidable problem of management and control to the political heads of Departments: approximately 100 Ministers are confronted by about 4000 Administrative Group policy advisers of Principal level and above, a ratio of about 1:40. Second, this overall proportion may be of less importance ultimately than the particular context in which Ministers normally meet their Civil Servants, i.e. in circumstances also in which they are outnumbered, with a single politician habitually faced by a Permanent Secretary accompanied by two more civil servants of Assistant Secretary and principal rank.

Permanence

There is a sharp contrast between impermanent Ministers, who come and go with considerable frequency, and permanent civil servants who generally stay much longer in the same job and, even where they are newcomers in a Department, always have recourse to the accumulated expertise of the departmental files. In the post-1945 period, Ministerial reshuffles have resulted in an average tenure of Ministerial office of about two years; in certain Departments, the average stay of Ministers is even lower – there were, for example, twenty Ministers of Education between 1944 and 1979. Even in such a key post as the Chancellorship of the Exchequer, the turnover is little less rapid: there were fifteen Chancellors in the thirty-five years between 1945 and 1980. Clearly, these circumstances weight the scales in favour of the 'Departmental' view on matters of policy, especially when it is remembered that, on most realistic estimates, Ministers take anything from six months to a year to master the business of their Departments and, on entering their posts, have no access to their predecessor's files and hence are totally dependent upon briefing by their officials.

Expertise

Some Ministers, on taking office, are familiar with the concerns of their Departments, having 'shadowed' them in Opposition or having a strong interest in their business. Many, however, are in the position of Richard Crossman, who in 1964 became Minister of Housing having specialised in social security and 'shadowed Education' and who consequently had 'a complete lack of contact' with the subjects with which he was dealing. It is comparatively rare for Treasury Ministers, including Chancellors of the Exchequer, to have any knowledge of economics, at least at the beginning of their periods of office, a situation which is bound to make them ultra-dependent on their officials. Indeed, in the opinion of one Permanent Secretary at the Treasury, Chancellors uncritically accepted the advice they were given 75 per cent of the time. Nor is it simply the case that the weight of expertise is on the side of the officials. What has also become apparent in recent years is the difficulty – some would say, impossibility – of civil servants using their expertise in a neutral fashion when offering advice on policy to Ministers. Whilst the *party political* views of civil servants may not be obtrusive, their personal predispositions inevitably shape the assumptions underlying the policy options they present. Whether they are enthusiastic for a particular policy or, in the sceptical, somewhat world-weary vein often taken to characterise much civil service advice, unenthusiastic, their views *will* have an important *political* influence.

Coordinating role

Officials play an important role in coordinating Departmental policy with the policies of other Departments. Both formally through the system of official committees and through informal contacts with their opposite numbers in other Departments, top civil servants prepare and to a certain extent (some would say, a considerable one) predetermine the work of Ministers. As

Crossman says in his *Diaries*, 'very often the whole job is pre-cooked in the official committees to a point from which it is difficult to reach any other conclusion than that already determined by officials in advance' (p. 92). The official Whitehall committee system also provides civil servants with a further mechanism to delay and obstruct Ministerial wishes if that is what they decide to do. They can do so, for example, by contacting colleagues in other Departments (say B, C and D) to brief Ministers in those Departments to resist policies emanating from their own Minister (Department A) in Cabinet and elsewhere.

Control of information

Important aspects of the control on information by civil servants with regard to *content* have already been mentioned – initial briefings and the preparation of a constant stream of policy advice. It is worth underlining here the vital significance of officials' ability to decide what Ministers learn and, of equal significance, what they do *not* learn. Tony Benn as Energy Secretary, for example, was not told that a shipload of uranium had been hijacked in 1968, nor about leaks of toxic waste from Windscale. Their control of information also enables civil servants to undermine Ministers' positions if they wish by selective 'leaking' to the media. On the eve of the 1983 General Election, for instance, the Conservative Government was embarrassed by the leaking of three documents on public expenditure policy, one of which suggested that the government was considering the termination of direct State financing of education and the replacement of the NHS by private health insurance. In addition civil servants can influence policy by *the timing and manner* of the presentation of papers to Ministers – a second, sometimes neglected, aspect of control of information. As Philip Norton has written in *The British Polity* (1984): 'By submitting papers at the last minute and forcing a speedy decision, or by inserting the relevant documents in a mass of paperwork in the minister's file in order that their significance may not be obvious, officials may get the response they favour' (p. 191). Nor should it be forgotten that it is civil servants working in the Private Offices of Ministers who plan how Ministers spend their time, organising their daily diaries in ways which induced in Richard Crossman, at least, a feeling of unreality, of being divorced from the real world, a sense that 'one has to do absolutely nothing whatsoever in order to be floated forward on the stream' (*Diaries*, abridged, p. 25).

Self-interested attitudes

These have already been mentioned in *general* terms (see pp. 145–146 above). The best example of the consequences of official self-interest in the *political* sphere, however, is the way in which the Civil Service blocked and emasculated the major reform proposals of the Fulton Report (1968). Fulton thought 'generalists' were obsolete, but generalists remain. Fulton called for a unified structure assimilating the old Administrative Class to the rest of the Civil Service, but by and large the old Administrative Class (now called Group) is still there in all but name. Finally, Fulton made recommendations designed to bring about more efficient use of Department resources. In the opinion of Peter Kellner and Lord Crowther-Hunt, however, 'the cause of efficiency' did not 'appear to have greatly improved' by 1980 (Kellner and Crowther-Hunt, *The Civil Servants*, p. 94). The problem lies in the fact that the institution to be reformed was itself responsible for implementing that reform. Not surprisingly, perhaps, the reforms remain largely unmade, a classic instance of the capacity of the Civil Service to resist unwanted change.

Exhibit 7.1 A year in the life of the Secretary of State for Energy (1977)

During 1977 Tony Benn:
(a) Fulfilled fifty public engagements in his constituency, made twelve general speeches in Bristol, held sixteen constituency surgeries, and handled more than 1000 personal cases.
(b) Attended four General Management Committee meetings of the Bristol South-East Labour Party; attended twenty ward meetings, and five Labour Group meetings to discuss policy.
(c) Attended twelve meetings of the Parliamentary Labour Party, and made fourteen speeches to various subgroup meetings of MPs.
(d) Dealt in parliament with three Energy Bills, produced fifty-four statutory instruments; presented thirty-three explanatory memoranda to the House on European Energy matters; answered fifty-one oral questions and 171 written questions; had 154 meetings with non-governmental groups; produced 1821 Ministerial minutes on papers taken home in the official red box; made 133 appointments to various bodies, etc.
(e) Attended forty-two Cabinet meetings and 106 Cabinet Committee meetings; submitted four Cabinet papers and forty-five Cabinet Committee papers; received 1750 Cabinet papers covering the whole range of government policies.
(f) Made nineteen visits abroad, and received in his office thirty-two Foreign Ministers and Ambassadors.
(g) In the first half of 1977 presided over the Energy Council of the European Community. This involved taking the chair at six Council meetings and having sundry other official meetings on European Energy questions.
(h) Attended fifteen meetings of the Labour Party Executive and sixty committee meetings.
(i) Made eighty speeches up and down the country, gave eighty-three radio interviews, fifty-seven television interviews, gave thirty-four press conferences, wrote sixteen articles, had thirty interviews with individual journalists, and received or answered 1000 letters which did not involve constituency case-work or ministerial work.

Source: Peter Kellner and Lord Crowther-Hunt, *The Civil Servants* (London, MacDonald, 1980) pp. 215–16

Ministerial workload

The heavy workload of Ministers further weights the scales towards civil servants. Exhibit 7.1 provides details of a year in the life of a Cabinet Minister (Tony Benn) in the Labour Government of 1976–1979. It is a not untypical Ministerial routine and clearly reveals the variety and intensity of calls upon a Minister's time – by Cabinet, parliament, constituency and media in addition to the Department.

Few Ministers, perhaps, spend so much time as Benn on purely party matters. But it is quite normal for Ministers to spend most of their time on non-departmental business. An analysis by Bruce Headey of the working week of fifty Ministers between 1964 and 1974 revealed that they habitually worked a 60-hour week (excluding weekends), three-quarters of which was spent on affairs outside their department (cited in Kellner and Crowther-Hunt, *The Civil Servants* (1980) p. 216).

Lack of alternative policy advice

Until relatively recently, Ministers have lacked advice on policy alternative to that provided by civil servants. The habit of importing special political advisers into Departments to provide alternative viewpoints for Ministers began in 1964, was recommended by the Fulton Committee and became common but by no means universal practice in the 1970s. Denis Healey had a whole 'team' of such advisers in his years at the Ministry of Defence – a kind of Ministerial 'Cabinet'. Thirty-eight special advisers were brought into government by the incoming Labour Administration in 1974. But this development, which places a layer of 'political' advice between a Minister and his leading civil servants, has encountered opposition from top bureaucrats, who have numerous ways of neutralising them, including ignoring them, working round them and shunting them into administrative cul-de-sacs.

Volume of decisions

This point is simply made. No single Minister could possibly decide in person the massive volume of decisions which have to be resolved in any Department in a given year; in fact, even the most able and energetic person could deal with only a fraction of them. It follows that necessarily civil servants have to make the bulk of decisions in a Department, most of which in any case are lower level. The problem only arises when they are not.

Do all these considerations mean that the *liberal–bureaucratic model* must be preferred to the *liberal–democratic theory* as approximating more closely to the reality of modern government? The answer is: 'not necessarily'. What they do suggest is that the traditional model can no longer be automatically assumed. With strong Ministers in control of Departments, it remains relevant. Crossman's *Diaries*, in fact, testify to a series of 'victories' by the Minister in Departmental battles, as do the testimonies of other vigorous personalities such as Denis Healey and Michael Heseltine. Weak Ministers, on the other hand, do tend to be 'captured' by their officials. In other words, each departmental situation has to be considered on its merits. As Kellner and Crowther-Hunt aptly conclude: 'The exact balance between ministerial and civil service power will very much depend on what is being decided, the political circumstances surrounding it, and the relative abilities of civil servants and Ministers' (*The Civil Servants* (p. 234)). The value of the liberal–bureaucratic model consists simply in bringing out the fact that Minister–Civil Service relations are a matter of balance rather than automatically accepted authority (as the traditional theory holds) and also in pointing out the factors which *may* operate in various combinations to tilt the scales towards the bureaucrat.

With regard to the *power-bloc* model, it can certainly be agreed that the higher ranks of the civil service are largely recruited from socially privileged groups. But does it follow that (i) the higher Civil Service constitutes a monolithic bloc in terms of views and perceptions; (ii) that it will refuse to carry out the radical policies of Left or Right *Governments*; or (iii) that it invariably curbs the reformist impulses of radical *individuals*? We return to these questions in Chapter 26 but in this context the following considerations are relevant. If (i) *were* the case, the sharp *inter*-departmental struggles which are a frequent occurrence in Whitehall could hardly be expected to take place, e.g. especially, those which break out at Budget time between 'spending' Departments and the Treasury. Nor is it possible to give greater credence to the line of thought behind question (ii). Arguably, the two most radical Governments since 1945 have been the Labour Administrations of 1945–51 and the Conservative Administrations of 1979–87, yet the Civil Service can scarcely be said to have blocked either the Keynesian, Welfare and nationalisation policies of the one or the monetarist, anti-Welfare and privatisation policies of the other. Of course, the programmes of these Governments can be redefined as, in effect, 'moderate' and 'not truly radical', as Ralph Miliband does in his book, *Capitalist Democracy in Britain* (1982). Writing of Labour in power, he says: 'Civil servants in Britain have never had to confront a government with a "Socialist" programme or at least … a government determined to carry out such a programme' (p. 101). But this 'redefinition' effectively undermines the point by moving it away from an assertion which can be tested against the evidence to a hypothesis about what the Civil Service *would* do or would be *likely* to do *if* it were to be confronted by a radical government – which cannot be tested at all. Nor is it necessarily the case (iii) that the Civil Service is primarily to blame for the ineffectiveness of radical politicians. The key recent example around whose performance in office controversy has hinged is Tony Benn as Secretary of State for Industry in the Labour Government of February 1974. According to power-bloc theory Civil Service resistance must form the major explanation of Benn's failure to introduce sweeping measures of nationalisation (shipbuilding, aircraft and pharmaceuticals) and to effect planning agreements with companies. However, another view of the matter is that Benn failed (he was eventually transferred to Energy in June 1975) because he encountered political opposition from a different source entirely – the Prime Minister and other Labour Cabinet Ministers, i.e. *from his own colleagues in government.*

Finally, we turn to the *bureaucratic over-supply* model. As already stated, this theory achieved wide political credibility during the 1970s. Between 1960 and 1978, whilst 1 m jobs disappeared in the private sector, public sector employment (of which the Civil Service is a part) rose by $1\frac{1}{2}$ m. Considerations like this fuelled the drive by the Conservative Government of Mrs Thatcher after 1979 to reduce the power, prestige and privileges of the Civil Service. The considerable degree of success achieved by this policy by 1988 both created a climate in which Ministers could the more effectively assert control over their officials if they wished but also underlined the broader consideration that the Civil Service was not a species of self-propelling juggernaut but ultimately subject in its size, pay, honours, pensions and so on to democratic control. The Conservative Government sought to reassert control over the Whitehall establishment in a number of ways: (i) by policies of tight control over public expenditure through cash limits and other methods; (ii) by reducing civil service manpower directly by privatisation and by freezing recruitment. The Government made a 14 per cent cut in civil service numbers (730 000–630 000) between 1979 and 1984, and achieved further cuts of 32 000 by 1988; (iii) by introducing strategies to improve efficiency: for example, a special efficiency unit was brought in under Sir Derek Raynor (of Marks and Spencer) to review the whole field of government operations; this unit carried out 135 scrutinies and six inter-departmental reviews which produced immediate economies of £37 m and the possibility later of further, larger, savings; (iv) by working to inculcate a greater concern for the effective management of resources at the highest level of the civil service. The Conservatives, in fact, made improving civil service management a major political and administrative goal in the 1980s. Michael Heseltine, for instance, at Environment introduced a Management Information System which enabled him to reduce the size of his Department. Permanent Secretaries throughout the Civil Service became more conscious than before of the need to be efficient, deliver value for money and eliminate unnecessary costs; (v) by attempting to hold civil service pay down below rises in the private sector, as in 1986; and (vi) by abolishing the Civil Service Department, and dividing its work between the Treasury (thereby strengthening financial control over the Civil Service Establishment) and the Cabinet Office (thereby strengthening Prime Ministerial control).

In February 1988 the Prime Minister announced plans for the most radical reform of the Civil Service in its entire history. These were based on a 1987 report by Sir Robin Ibbs, head of the efficiency unit, and were strongly resisted by a number of Ministers, Permanent Secretaries and the Treasury. The scheme rested on a division of Departments into policy-makers and providers of services. In future, each Ministry would consist of only about 500 policy-makers; the remaining work of Departments would be hived off to independent agencies. The agencies would be run on business lines, the intention being to give them greater freedom and flexibility. A chief executive rather than a Permanent Secretary would be in charge and the agencies would report to a board of commissioners, not to a Minister. It was expected that the changes would be tried for an experimental period of one year before any decision about whether or not to go ahead on a permanent basis was made. During the trial period, staff who were transferred to the agencies would retain their status as civil servants.

THE CONVENTION OF MINISTERIAL RESPONSIBILITY

In traditional liberal constitutional theory, the convention of Ministerial responsibility governs relations between Ministers, civil servants and parliament. According to this theory, Ministers are accountable directly to parliament for activities within their Departments. When things go well, they take the credit; when things go badly, they take the blame, and resign. Civil servants are responsible to Ministers alone; they have no wider accountability to parliament or the general public. They are anonymous; their identities and the nature of the advice they offer to Ministers remain secret, and legitimately so. For they merely advise, simply assist in the implementation of government policy. Historically, the doctrine of individual Ministerial responsibility preceded that of collective responsibility. Originally, the method of making Ministers accountable to parliament for their conduct as royal servants was impeachment. By the early nineteenth century, however, the convention of individual ministerial responsibility had replaced impeachment as loss of office came to be seen as sufficient punishment of politicians for errors and misconduct in their Departments short of actual corruption. This section aims to test the contemporary validity of the convention. It examines the precise nature of the accountability of Ministers for the policy failures, mistaken judgements, maladministration and the improper conduct of themselves and their officials.

In general, it seems to be the case that Ministers still resign on occasion for *personal errors of commission or omission* but not vicariously for the mistakes of their officials. The most clear-cut examples occur in the case of personal misconduct. This is an elastic category but has most frequently involved mixing with unsavoury or shady associates. So defined, it would cover the resignations of Thomas Galbraith (1962), an Under-Secretary at the Scottish Office, for consorting with the spy, Vassall, during a former period at the Admiralty; John Profumo (1963), the Minister for War, for associating with a call-girl Christine Keeler, a former mistress of a Russian diplomat; Lords Jellicoe, Lord Privy Seal, and Lambton, Under-Secretary for the Air Force (1973), for entertaining call-girls; and Reginald Maudling (1972), then Home Secretary, who resigned after allegations that he had received money several years previously from an architect, John Poulson, who was the focus of a major corruption inquiry. Ministers, then, habitually resign after criticism for improper conduct or suspicion of it and at least four more cases occurring in the post-war period could be added to this list. These are John Belcher (1948), a junior minister, for accepting bribes for ministerial favours at the Board of Trade; Lord Brayley (1975), Under-Secretary for the Army, after financial inquiries had been made into a company with which he was formerly connected; and Ian Hervey (1958), an Under-Secretary at the Foreign Office, and Nicholas Fairbairn (1982), the Solicitor-General for Scotland, after adverse publicity about their respective private behaviour.

But although according to the theory Ministers ought to resign if closely associated with *a failed policy or with one which is severely criticised* in the House of Commons, they do not normally do so. In such circumstances, the Prime Minister and Cabinet usually come to the aid of a beleaguered Minister, expressing support in public, whatever may be said privately. In other words, individual Ministers in political difficulties over policy are shielded by the convention of *collective responsibility*. This was the case, for example, in the early 1960s when various spy scandals involving national security did not end in resignations. The then Prime Minister, Harold Macmillan, rejected the need for resignations on the grounds that it was the reputation of the government as a whole which was in question and this was better left to the judgement of voters at a General Election. Where policies have gone wrong, the eventual outcome for the individual Minister depends more upon relations with the Prime Minister and party than upon the gravity of the failure or upon relations with the House of Commons. No resignations followed directly as a result of spectacular fiascos such as the East African groundnuts scheme (1949) which, at a total cost to the taxpayer of £36½ m, failed to provide either margarine for Britain or jobs for Africans – a scheme with which, moreover, the Minister of Food, had closely associated himself, describing it as 'one of the most courageous, imaginative and well-judged acts of this Government for the sake of the world'. Nor were resignations the immediate consequence of discreditable failures such as Suez (1956) or the large-scale miscalculations over the final cost of the *Concorde* programme in the early 1960s. In both these cases, as with the spy scandals, the close involvement of the Prime Minister was probably conclusive in 'saving' the Ministers concerned. Sometimes, Ministers who have presided over unsuccessful policies are moved from their Departments in discreet reshuffles after the event: Emmanuel Shinwell was moved from Fuel and Power to the War Office eight months after the Fuel crisis of 1947 and James Callaghan agreed to switch to the Home Office rather than resign as Chancellor of the Exchequer in 1967 after the collapse of the attempt to avoid devaluation. Parliamentary criticism can certainly damage a Minister and can sometimes prompt changes of policy but cannot force resignation if the Minister has the support of Prime Minister and party.

In the light of these considerations, Lord Carrington as Foreign Secretary, his deputy, Humphrey Atkins, and junior minister, Richard Luce, behaved with a rare sense of constitutional obligation in 1982 in resigning their offices after the successful Argentinian invasion of the Falkland Islands. The reason Lord Carrington gave for his resignation was his failure to foresee and to take steps to prevent the invasion, which he later called 'a humiliating affront to this country'. But John Nott, the Defence Secretary, who was criticised at the time for the weakness of the Falkland Isles's defences and, more realistically, for signalling an apparently diminished British commitment to the retention of the Islands by a proposal to withdraw HMS *Endurance*, remained in office. On this occasion, it may well have been the case that, so grave was the situation, so intense the parliamentary and public disquiet, that collective responsibility could not save the Foreign Office ministerial team. A considerable sacrifice was called for but not so great a one that it rocked the government: hence Carrington and his subordinates went but Nott stayed.

It is even more unusual for Ministers to accept *vicarious responsibility for their officials* and resign after mistakes within their Departments have been brought to light. The assumption by Ministers of personal accountability for all that happens in their Departments has been undermined, it is often said, by the sheer size and complexity of modern Whitehall departments and the consequent impossibility for one person to keep informed about all that goes on therein. Numerous cases in the post-war period suggest the reluctance of Ministers to shoulder the blame for civil servants when things go wrong. This is not just the case where mistakes are made at *a relatively low level* as in 1982 when William Whitelaw did not resign as Home Secretary when security arrangements at Buckingham Palace were revealed to be deficient or when they are committed by low-ranking officials acting at a considerable distance from Westminster, as when the Colonial Secretary, Alan Lennox-Boyd, did not resign after eleven prisoners died and others received injuries from beatings meted out by colonial wardens at the Hola Camp in Kenya in 1959. By 1977, indeed, Sir John Hunt, then Secretary to the Cabinet, could maintain in evidence to the Commons Expenditure Committee that the idea of Ministers resigning over the mistakes of someone they had never heard of was 'out-of-date and rightly so'.

However, it is also true that ministerial resignations rarely follow the revelation of error by *high-ranking civil servants*. Thus, Sir Julian Amery did not resign as Minister of Aviation in 1964 after it had been revealed that the

Ferranti Company had made excess profits from Defence Ministry contracts to make the *Bloodhound* missile; John Davies, President of the Board of Trade, did not resign in 1971 after a Tribunal of Inquiry had exposed the failure of his Department to deal with the risk of the imminent insolvency of the Vehicle and General Insurance Company; and the doctrine of collective responsibility protected Tony Benn as Secretary of State for Industry, blamed by the Ombudsman in 1975 for giving misleading public assurances about the holiday operations of the Court Line travel company.

The only major example before 1986 of a Minister resigning for the mistakes of his officials was Sir Thomas Dugdale in the Crichel Down affair (1954). Dugdale as Minister of Agriculture accepted full responsibility for the negligence of his civil servants in dealings with a landowner who was anxious to buy back land which had been compulsorily acquired by the Government for use as a bombing range shortly before the Second World War. He did not resign immediately following the adverse findings of the Committee of Inquiry but some weeks later after considerable party pressure had built up. The Westland Affair (1986) provides a second example of a Minister accepting full constitutional responsibility for misconduct within his Department when Leon Brittan, the Secretary of State for Trade and Industry, took the blame by resigning for the 'improper act' – in the words of the Commons Defence Committee which investigated the affair – of the departmental Information Officer in 'leaking' to the press a select passage in a letter from the Solicitor-General to the then Defence Secretary, Michael Heseltine. The passage contained a criticism of Heseltine for issuing misleading information and formed one episode in the semi-public struggle between the Department of Defence and the Department of Trade and Industry over the destiny of Westland helicopters. Brittan may be said to have approved even if he did not directly authorise the 'leak' (some say he did authorise it) and resigned only after intense parliamentary pressure and after he had lost the confidence of his own party.

Does the small number of Ministerial resignations after strong criticisms in the House of Commons indicate that such resignations are in decline? Does it further suggest that the convention of Ministerial responsibility is a myth? The answer to both these questions is 'probably not'. Ministerial resignation in these circumstances has always been rare. S. E. Finer, writing in 1956, found none between 1805 and 1855 and only sixteen in the century after 1855; the nine or so clear-cut cases between 1955 and 1986 if anything slightly exceed the historical average of one resignation every six years. But in any case the rarity of Ministerial resignation does not mean that the convention of Ministerial responsibility is a myth. Ministers remain unanswerable to parliament for the work of their Departments. They must always be prepared to explain and defend departmental policy – at Question Time, during the Committee stage of government bills, before Select Committees and to MPs who raise matters privately with them. The possibility of being hounded into resignation remains an ultimate sanction upon them, nonetheless real for its infrequency. One reason for its rarity is the nature of parliament itself, which is legislative rather than judicial or quasi-judicial and therefore more appropriate to debating legislation than holding the executive to account. But in any case there are sanctions upon erring Ministers short of being forced to resign. The House of Commons can damage a Ministerial reputation or bring about demotion even if it can only seldom provoke resignation itself. Moreover, on policy matters, in view of the collective nature of the enterprise of government, it is arguably right that collective responsibility can on occasion prevent the resignation of an individual.

There is little doubt, however, that the anonymity of civil servants – an important corollary of the convention of individual Ministerial responsibility – has been seriously eroded in the post-war period. As ministerial willingness to assume responsibility for the mistakes of civil servants has declined, so the practice has grown of naming and blaming individual bureaucrats. The Crichel Down Inquiry (1954) announced sanctions against certain named officials in the Ministry of Agriculture; the Tribunal of Inquiry into the Vehicle and General collapse criticised the Under-Secretary and two Assistant Secretaries in the Board of Trade for negligent conduct; the Parliamentary Commissioner's investigation into the refusal of the Foreign Office to pay compensation to UK nationals who were victims of Nazi persecution revealed faults in the conduct of both Minister and officials. During consideration of this last-named case – the Sachsenhausen affair – by the Commons Select Committee on the Parliamentary Commissioner, Airey Neave named the official he considered to have the greatest responsibility. In its report on the Westland affair (1986), the Commons Defence Committee sharply criticised the behaviour of top civil servants including Sir Robert Armstrong, Cabinet Secretary and Head of the Home Civil Service, and Bernard Ingham, the Prime Minister's Press Secretary – the former for failing to provide clear leadership and the latter for conniving at the improper 'leaking' of a confidential letter whilst seeking to distance the Prime Minister from the act. It laid bare the constitutional obligation upon Ministers even if they themselves were not fully accountable when the conduct of their officials became a matter for public controversy. Ministers should either satisfy the House that their officials had behaved properly or ensure that disciplinary proceedings were taken against them. It is no accident that the general tendency towards the criticism of specific civil servants for misconduct and maladministration has occurred as alternative procedures for investigating the shortcomings of the administration outside the floor of the House of Commons have been developed in the post-war period. These are formal inquiries and tribunals of inquiry; the Parliamentary Commissioners (Ombudsman); and parliamentary Select Committees. Such procedures can give a sharper 'quasi-judicial' edge to inquiry into the executive, although few would maintain that they yet provide a wholly satisfactory answer to the problem of accountability, if only (but not only) because governments continue to adhere so firmly to the doctrine of ministerial responsibility.

SUMMARY

The bulk of governmental decisions are made in the Departments – hence, the importance of establishing (i) an appropriate model to understand how departmental decisions are made; and (ii) of analysing the contemporary validity of the convention which purports to explain departmental accountability. Under (i), it was suggested that both the traditional liberal–democratic theory of Minister–civil servant relations and the liberal–bureaucratic model have much to recommend them, depending on circumstances. Since 1979 Mrs Thatcher's Administrations have reasserted control of the Civil Service and the liberal–democratic model is currently most appropriate. With regard to (ii), although still normally invoked, the traditional doctrine of Ministerial responsibility does not mean that Ministers automatically resign after parliamentary criticism of the misconduct of their Departments. They normally resign only for personal misbehaviour, much more rarely for policy failures and almost never for the errors of their officials. Officials' anonymity, however, is in the process of erosion by the growing practice of naming and blaming civil servants. But, although its working is far from satisfactory, it is difficult to see that the principle of Ministerial responsibility has been dislodged, so central is it to understanding British constitutional practice. Ministers remain (at least) *answerable* for the conduct of their Departments, and the maximum sanction (resignation) still exists, even if its practice at any given moment is more a function of the political circumstances of the government, of relationships within it, and of relations between the erring politician and his own party, than of enforcement by parliament.

FURTHER READING

Burch, M. (1983) 'Ministers and Civil Servants', in B. Jones and D. Kavanagh (eds) *British Politics Today*, Manchester, University Press.
Forman, F. N. (1985) *Mastering British Politics*, London, Macmillan.
Fry, G. (1985) *The Changing Civil Service*, London, Allen & Unwin.
Judge, David (1983) 'Ministerial Responsibility and Select Committees', *Teaching Politics*, vol. 12, no 2, May.
Judge, D. (1984) *Ministerial Responsibility: Life in the Strawman Yet?*, Strathclyde Papers on Government and Politics, no 37.
Kellner, P. and Crowther-Hunt, Lord (1980) *The Civil Servants*, London, Macdonald.
Marshall, G. (1984) *Constitutional Conventions*, Oxford, Clarendon Press, ch. 4.
Norton, P. (1982) *The Constitution in Flux*, Oxford, Martin Robertson, chs 2, 4.
Norton, P. (1984) *The British Polity*, London, Longman, ch. 8.

Pyper, D. (1983) 'The FO Resignations: Individual Ministerial Responsibility Revived?', *Teaching Politics*, vol. 12, no 2, May.
Young, H. and Sloman, A. (1982) *No, Minister*, London, BBC.

QUESTIONS

1. To what extent does the phrase 'on tap but never on top' remain an apt description of the relationship of civil servants to ministers?
2. Critically examine the contemporary validity of the convention of individual ministerial responsibility.

ASSIGNMENT

State the doctrine of individual ministerial responsibility and analyse the implications of the Westland affair for the convention.

8

Quasi-government

This chapter examines the politics and organisation of quasi-government in Britain. The scope of government activity in society has increased considerably since 1945 and a great variety of bodies have been established to administer the expanded public sector. Such bodies, notably quangos and the nationalised industries, have been viewed with hostility by the political Right. There have been many practical reasons for nationalising specific industries or establishing certain quangos, but such measures have provoked ideologically-based opposition. Mrs Thatcher's Government has attempted to reduce the number of quangos in existence and to reduce the scope of the nationalised industries through pursuing a policy of privatisation. But will such policies bring the advantages that the Prime Minister and her colleagues envisage? We will examine the cases for and against nationalisation and privatisation. Others have criticised the world of quasi-government or 'government at arm's length', because there is too little accountability and public control. The chapter concludes with an examination of the measures which some have suggested will improve the powers of Parliamentary scrutiny over the nationalised industries, and will clarify the position of Ministers regarding the control of their commercial activities.

THE WORLD OF THE QUANGO

Two centuries ago the principal concerns of government lay in defending the realm against external threats and maintaining law and order in the face of possible disruption. During the nineteenth century government accepted wider responsibilities, such as providing education for the masses through the Education Acts 1870 and 1899, and during the twentieth century government has accepted responsibility for extending health provision into a fully fledged National Health Service, extending education to higher and further levels, and introducing a comprehensive social security system. In addition to providing welfare services which directly affect the majority of the population at one time or another, modern government is involved in controlling and regulating thousands of activities as diverse as sheep-dipping and house-building. In order to provide services and regulate activities government has developed a large public sector. Within the public sector is the Civil Service, but the Civil Service is not so involved in the total administration of the public sector as might be imagined. In fact less than 10 per cent of employees in the public sector are civil servants. The remainder work in local government, public utilities, nationalised industries, public corporations and the world of quasi-government. The position in the 1980s is that around 8 million of Britain's 25-million-strong labour force are employed in the public sector. This growth has led to anxiety in some circles about the power that the government now has over the individual. It has been argued that the political liberty of the individual is increasingly threatened by 'red tape', 'Big Government' or the 'mega-bureaucracy'.

Organisations in the public sector have been established as the need has arisen at different times to perform a variety of tasks. The result is a hotchpotch of bodies that frequently differ very much from one another and make it difficult to generalise about them or even to classify them into distinctive categories.

Indirect government

The world of quasi-government is inhabited by organisations referred to by political scientists as 'fringe bodies', 'non-departmental organisations', 'governmental bodies', 'semi-autonomous authorities' and 'quangos'. Even the latter name has been modified so that it may now refer to organisations which are 'quasi-non-governmental', 'quasi-autonomous-non-governmental' or 'quasi-autonomous-national-governmental'. *The Guardian*'s political correspondent, Michael White, suggested, rather tongue-in-cheek, that the House of Lords qualified as a quango, in which case the acronym stood for 'quaintly-archaic-near-gerontocratic-organisation'.

Quasi-government has been described as 'arm's length' or 'indirect' government. It is made up of organisations involved in government which is not done by (i) central government departments such as the Inland Revenue or the DHSS or (ii) local authorities. It consists of State-related organisations which may or may not have been created by government but which are influential in making or applying government policy.

The *Pliatzky Report on Non-Departmental Public Bodies* (1980) examined the world of quasi-government. It was reported that there were 489 non-departmental bodies which were 'executive' in nature and had a regulatory function; these employed 217 000 staff. Examples of executive-type quangos are the Arts Council, Agricultural Wages Board, Eggs Authority, United Kingdom Atomic Energy Authority, Countryside Commission, British Council, General Nursing Council and Commission for Racial Equality. In addition, there were 1561 'advisory' bodies which directly employed relatively few staff. Examples include the Food Hygiene Advisory Council, the Advisory Committee on the Supply and Education of Teachers, the Advisory Committee on the Safety of Nuclear Installations, the China Clay Council, the Police Advisory Board and the Parliamentary Boundary Commission for England. Finally, there were sixty-seven systems of tribunals which were often staffed by the department concerned. Examples include the Supplementary Benefits Appeal Tribunals, Pneumoconiosis Medical Panels, Vaccine Damage Tribunals, Rent Tribunals and Rent Assessment Committees, Agricultural Land Tribunals and the Independent Schools Tribunal. Sir Leo Pliatzky's report did not include the nationalised industries, public corporations or local government 'quangos'. Fifty-six of the latter were identified by Paul Cousins in his study of the London Borough of Bromley. Examples at the local level include the Bromley Library and Theatre Panel, Home Safety Committee, Bromley Savings Committee and the Kent Land Drainage Committee.

What are the reasons behind the growth of quasi-government? The answer frequently lies in the wishes of the government to have a function performed, and in not wanting this function to be the direct responsibility of a Minister. There are advantages for a Minister in establishing a quango to do a particular task rather than having that task done by civil servants in his department. It may be that the particular task is done more effectively by a single-purpose quango than by a department which is involved in a wide and complex area of administration. Establishing a quango also enables people from outside government to be involved in administration; this is particularly the case with advisory bodies which may enlist outsiders with expertise which is not available amongst civil servants. If the task to be done is a temporary one, there are advantages in having temporary organisations to do them. It may be easier to set up and then scrap a quango than to create a body inside the Civil Service which immediately gives some administrators a career or vested interest in its continuance. An example of a temporary quango is the Decimal Currency Board which was set up to effect the changeover of Britain's currency in 1971.

There may also be political advantages for a Minister in establishing a quango rather than in having his own civil servants perform certain tasks. Ministers may wish to distance themselves from sensitive or controversial issues such as race relations or arms sales. Quangos can monitor these issues without involving the Minister to any great extent in their day-to-day operations. This remoteness from certain sensitive issues can also be very useful to a Minister because it insulates him from Parliamentary attacks. He is seen as 'not responsible' for certain quango activities and therefore escapes criticism from both his own and opposition backbenches. Finally, having set up a quango which enables the participation of outside interests, the Minister is likely to find that the policy recommendations made by that quango will be publicly acceptable.

Is quasi-government democratic?

A considerable number of individuals remain unpersuaded by these administrative arguments which favour the growth of quasi-government. The main thrust of their case has been stated forcefully by Sir Norman Chester in his article 'Fringe Bodies, Quangos and All That', *Public Administration* (1979). He argues that:

> The growth of fringe bodies is a retreat from the simple democratic principle evolved in the nineteenth century that those who perform a public duty should be fully responsible to an electorate – by way either of a minister responsible to Parliament or of a locally elected council. The essence of a fringe body is that it is not so responsible for some or all of its actions (Chester, 'Fringe Bodies, Quangos and All That', *Public Administration*, 1979, p. 54).

In examining the issues raised by Sir Norman, Nevil Johnson comments that 'accountability and control are closely related terms. Accountability provides some assurance of control, whilst effective control is required if public office-holders are to be held accountable' (N. Johnson 'Accountability, Control and Complexity: Moving beyond Ministerial Accountability', in A. Barker (ed.) *Quangos in Britain*, 1982, p. 210). Political scientists have tended to make finely-balanced judgements about accountability and control in the light of their research into quasi-government. There is general agreement that little is known yet about the control of quasi-governmental bodies. Although quangos produce annual reports, these do not always provide much useful information on how the bodies actually operate. Reports can be written in very bland terms which reveal little or nothing of the policy disagreements, tactics or personality clashes which emerged during the year in question. Also the control of one quango may differ very much from that of another. For example, in some quangos the only full-time salaried member is the chairman and there is a tendency to see him as the most important influence. In others, there is a large full-time staff and it becomes far less easy to locate those who wield control.

In examining the accountability of quangos, some political scientists are cautious in giving full support to Sir Norman Chester's argument. This is because he uses the doctrine of individual Ministerial responsibility as a democratic principle. In reality, it is counter-argued, Ministers do not know all that is going on within their own departments and they are no longer held 'responsible' for the actions of their civil servants. In other words, the doctrine of individual Ministerial responsibility is a myth in modern administration and the position of a Minister in relation to his own department is not all that different from his position in relation to quasi-governmental bodies. Also it has to be noted that in the special case of the Advisory, Conciliation and Arbitration Service (ACAS) the Minister is obliged by statute to keep his distance from the world of this quango.

On the other hand, there is a feeling that quangos should be monitored more closely by Parliament. Since quangos receive public money, it is argued that in principle they should be made more accountable. Some believe that the system of Select Committees provides the best machinery for Parliament to scrutinise the work of quasi-government. Others doubt the practicability of this. Although Select Committees have scrutinised the nationalised industries and other bodies such as the BBC and Meteorological Office, they lack the resources needed for the mammoth task of reviewing quangos.

Quangocide?

The Conservatives came to office in 1979 determined to mount a purge on the quangos. It must be said that the image of quangos had become exaggerated into something of a bogey in the minds of many Tories. There was a popular feeling that quangos were created simply to provide 'jobs for the boys'. For example, in 1978 the Minister of the Environment made 313 salaried appointments and 856 appointments to fee-paid posts.

Since Parliament has little influence on who should be appointed to quasi-governmental bodies, it was suspected that Ministers used their patronage for dubious ends. At the same time, the scope of quasi-government was exaggerated by some critics. Estimates of the total number of quangos even included some public schools, with the result that quasi-government was seen as a process which had to be reversed.

After Sir Leo Pliatzky's Report, the Government announced that it intended to abolish thirty 'executive' bodies, 211 'advisory' bodies and six individual tribunals. Amongst the quango casualties were some unimportant bodies such as the Committee to Examine Standards of Lawn Tennis in Great Britain and the Hadrian's Wall Advisory Committee. Some bodies disappeared not through being axed, but through being merged. For example, the General Nursing Council for England and Wales, the Central Midwives Board, the Joint Board of Clinical Nursing Studies, the Panel of Assessors for District Nurse Training, and the Council for the Education and Training of Health Visitors were merged into a single organisation. In his contribution to C. Hood and M. Wright, *Big Government in Hard Times* (1981), Christopher Hood described these 'cuts' as no more than 'cosmetic surgery', since the scope of a quasi-government remained unaltered. He also pointed out that 'reincarnation' is not uncommon amongst quangos and observed:

> non-departmental bodies that have 'died' in the past have typically been 'reincar-
> nated' in the sense of being replaced or superseded by other forms of government
> activity. Their departure does not leave a complete vacuum ... the Physical
> Training and Recreation Councils and the Council for the Encouragement of
> Music and Arts – both long 'dead' in one sense, but living on in another sense in the
> form of the Sports Council and the Arts Council (p. 105).

The initial attempt to reduce quasi-government in Britain fell well short of total success. Some 250 posts disappeared from the 8 million that make up the public sector. No one could reasonably claim that killing off quangos was reducing 'Big Government'. Indeed to the embarrassment of some Conservatives the Government was undermining the modest economies that had been made. Within a very short period of eliminating thirty executive bodies, the Government actually created thirty new quangos. No doubt Mrs Thatcher's Administration had learnt the same lesson as previous governments; namely, that quangos were useful bodies. Whilst a modest number were axed in order to placate the political demands of the Tory backbenches and supporters in the constituencies, others were created to perform some of the many tasks necessary in the administration of a complex society. Although it is likely that there will be further attempts to reduce the number of quasi-governmental agencies, their numbers are likely to increase in the long run. Sometimes the implementation of government policies has the unintended effect of producing more quasi-government. For example, any future diminution in the responsibilities of local government would inevitably stimulate an expansion of quangos to levels that many Conservative critics would find it hard to accept.

THE NATIONALISED INDUSTRIES

The nationalised industries form part of the public sector and represent another example of arm's length government. In the same way as it proved difficult to define and classify non-departmental organisations, it is difficult to generalise about organisations concerned with public ownership. Even what is understood as existing under the umbrella term 'public ownership' varies from one political scientist to the next. For example, some argue that in the strictest sense schools, colleges, polytechnics, universities, roads, libraries, and recreation grounds are 'publicly owned'. Others accept that in practice 'public ownership' is a term used to cover business or commercial undertakings in which the State plays a major role.

What adds to the complexity of the terminology of public ownership is that the state can participate in business and commerce through different means. First, there is **nationalisation**, a situation in which the assets of an undertaking are owned nationally. British Rail, British Shipbuilders, the National Coal Board, and the British Steel Corporation are examples of nationalised industries. The nationalised industries do not include business undertakings owned by local government, such as council housing or the provision of leisure facilities. The term '**municipalisation**' is sometimes reserved for business and trading undertaken by local authorities. Some local authorities have become well known for certain business enterprises – notably Doncaster Racecourse, Luton Airport and the telephone system in

Hull. One political scientist argues that technically speaking Britain's hospitals were nationalised with the creation of the National Health Service, but his argument is not widely accepted. An odd custom that has become established is to consider electricity as a nationalised industry but not the water and sewerage industries. Most nationalised industries are now organised into the form of public corporations, but not all public corporations are publicly owned. The Independent Broadcasting Authority is a public corporation which is not in any sense publicly owned.

Finally, the State may own assets in certain business undertakings through holding shares. This gives the State a financial interest in a particular firm or company without giving the government total control over the way business is conducted. The State is simply another shareholder and has now more rights than the other shareholders. Even when the State owns the majority of shares in a company and therefore has the power to influence policy, governments in practice do not use this power and choose not to intervene in the running of the company's affairs. The State has a shareholding in companies such as the British Channel Tunnel Company, Harland and Wolff, the British Sugar Corporation and the Mersey Docks and Harbour Board.

Publicly owned bodies have been established at different times to meet a great variety of needs and to serve a wide range of purposes. It is this diversity which in part makes the tasks of definition and classification so controversial. Is the United Kingdom Atomic Energy Authority a nationalised industry or not? Are the Royal Mint and Her Majesty's Stationery Office public corporations or not? Where does agriculture fit into the scheme, being privately owned but publicly supported? These are typical of questions that political scientists have answered in different ways.

The State and the world of business

Not far below the surface of arguments about public ownership or the role that government should play in the economy are the ideological outlooks of the people concerned. The labels 'left-wing' and 'right-wing' really describe an individual's attitude towards property. Left-wing indicates sympathy towards the idea of public ownership: right-wing favours private ownership.

At its most simple, there are those who believe in the doctrine of *laissez-faire* and who believe that government involvement in the economy is undesirable. They believe that the market left to itself will solve economic or industrial problems. For example, they oppose attempts by the government to modernise industry, because, if the market mechanism is not disturbed, it will restructure industry with inefficient firms going out of business and efficient ones prospering. In other words, competition and the working of the free market always produce the best solutions.

In disagreement with this economic philosophy are those who wish to see an economy which is controlled by the government. They believe that the free market creates problems (such as poverty) that it cannot solve and that 'market-displacing' policies would provide a better economic climate. Such policies might include import controls, planning agreements with private firms, and nationalisation. Measures such as these would enable governments to achieve particular objectives such as a high rate of growth or low levels of unemployment. They have no faith in the ability of the market mechanism to modernise industry and expect the government to undertake this task through public corporations such as the Industrial Reorganisation Corporation or the National Enterprise Board.

Arguments for and against public ownership

When he was a leader of the TGWU, Frank Cousins commented that it was possible to have public ownership without having socialism but it was not possible to have socialism without having public ownership. His friends on the left wing of the Labour Party agreed with him and opposed those in the party who argued that 'modern' socialism did not require massive nationalisation. It was feared that if right-wing revisionists got their way, Labour would be turned into another capitalist party such as the Liberals or Conservatives. The Left pointed out that in 1918 Labour added Clause IV to its constitution and became a 'socialist' party, which committed it to securing:

> for the workers by hand or by brain the full fruits of their industry and the most equitable distribution thereof that may be possible upon the basis of the common ownership of the means of production, distribution and exchange, and the best obtainable system of popular administration and control of each industry or service.

Capitalism was seen as an evil system which produced extremes of wealth – that is, it led to 'poverty in the midst of plenty'. Capitalism also brought mankind's worst motives to the forefront of economic activity – greed and competitiveness. In capitalist language, 'profit' was a polite word for 'greed' and 'competition' stood for 'conflict'. Socialists wanted to build a new society to replace capitalism in which people would enjoy greater equality. Socialism would, therefore, be based on public ownership, not private ownership, and would promote cooperation between people rather than competition.

The first Labour Government with a majority in Parliament was elected in 1945. In a series of nine Acts of Parliament, major areas of the economy were brought into public ownership. The return of the Conservatives to power in 1951 did not lead to large-scale denationalisation of industries that Labour brought into public ownership. Only the road haulage and steel industries were returned to private ownership. Why did the Conservative Government

TABLE 8.1
The nationalised industries

	Royal Assent	Vesting Date
1. Bank of England	14 February 1946	1 March 1946
2. Civil Aviation	1 August 1946	1 August 1946
3. Coal	12 July 1946	1 January 1947
4. Cable and Wireless (entrusted to Post Office)	6 November 1946	1 January 1947
5. Transport	6 August 1976	1 January 1948
6. Land Development Rights (Town & Country Planning Act)	6 August 1947	1 July 1948
7. Electricity	13 August 1947	1 April 1948
8. Gas	30 July 1948	1 May 1949
9. Iron and Steel	24 November 1949	15 February 1951

Source: A. H. Hanson (ed.) *Nationalization: A Book of Readings*, London: Allen & Unwin (1963) p. 36.

retain so much of a socialist nationalisation programme? Frank Cousins's comment provides a clue to answering this question because many non-socialist, and even anti-socialist, governments have nationalised industries.

In Britain many concerns were 'publicly-owned' long before socialist ideas had become fully developed. For example, the General Post Office has been in public hands for over 300 years, Trinity House received its charter in 1514, and some municipal authorities were supplying domestic gas at the end of the eighteenth century. In 1908, a Liberal Government set up the Port of London Authority. Indeed, there were a considerable number of publicly-owned enterprises in Britain before the election of the Attlee Government in 1945.

These publicly-owned enterprises were established because they provided practical solutions to the problems faced at the time. The Conservative Government accepted most of Labour's nationalisation programme because it solved many economic problems. For example, after two world wars the coal mines were in a run-down state and in need of massive investment to help Britain's post-war recovery. Who else but the government would have been willing to provide the massive resources necessary for this vital but otherwise unattractive investment? Much the same could be said regarding the railways, which were also in a poor condition. Thus, for pragmatic reasons, the Conservative Government headed by Winston Churchill was content to see these and most of the other nationalised industries remain publicly owned.

Although Conservative instinct is to oppose nationalisation in principle, many Tories have accepted that it has a limited role to play in a modern economy. Edward Heath used the nationalisation of Rolls Royce in 1971 as a way of rescuing the company from financial collapse. In 1975, Labour mounted a similar rescue operation to save British Leyland. On the Right wing of the Labour party since the late 1950s have been MPs who feel that future nationalisation should be limited to such rescue operations as are needed from time to time, and that it should no longer have a central place in economic policy. Labour revisionists argue that modern socialism was more concerned with the distribution of wealth than whether that wealth happens to be produced in the private or the public sector. Attitudes towards nationalisation found in the SDP and Liberal Party until their merger in 1988 did not differ widely from this position. The Alliance partners favoured the mixed economy in which government intervention, which includes national-isation, is used to stimulate economic growth. In contrast, there is the 'alternative economic strategy' of the Labour Left, which is founded on the belief that large-scale nationalisation is the only policy that will bring about economic advance.

Opponents of public ownership have argued that nationalisation created monopolies, which could work against the interests of consumers. For example, all homes require energy for cooking, heating and lighting. The supply of electricity, gas and coal is each in the hands of a monopoly. Consumers cannot realistically escape being the customer of one or other of these monopolies. Others have argued that monopolies also exist in the private sector, and at least the nationalised monopolies are subject to public control. In addition, it is often the Government which insists on measures which are not in the consumers' interest, and not the Boards of the nationalised industries. For example, before privatisation Mrs Thatcher's Government – not the Board of the British Gas Corporation – set the levels of successive increases in the price of gas to the domestic user. Too often the nationalised industries have been blamed for decisions or policies made by the government.

A common argument is that nationalised industries tend to be inefficient because they are not spurred on by the need for profits. Both management and work-force adopt a leisurely attitude towards their business, knowing that they will be bailed out by public money if they turn in losses. This view is disputed by those who point out that many nationalised industries were making huge losses before they were nationalised. Nationalisation provided the opportunity for rationalisation and modernisation. Many firms, such as Ferranti, were rescued and put on the road to recovery by the National Enterprise Board. Also, publicly-owned concerns provide a social service as well as making a profit. A good example of this is the Post Office, which offers the same service at the same price to people no matter whether they live in John O'Groats or London. The Post Office could maximise profits by charging an 'economic' rate for people living in remote areas or by cutting out services to such areas altogether.

The Conservative privatisation programme

The Thatcher Administration moved in a new direction regarding public ownership. The Chancellor, Nigel Lawson, summed it up by saying 'The Conservative Party has never believed that the business of Government is the government of business.' Accordingly, the Conservatives launched a programme of privatisation which moved many public assets to private hands. For example, over half of British Aerospace was sold in 1981, the National Freight Corporation was sold to its employees in 1982, subsidiaries of British Leyland, British Rail and the British Steel Corporation were sold, and half the shares in Cable and Wireless were disposed of in 1981. At the same time, the monopolistic position of some nationalised industries was changed to allow competition. For example, private operators were allowed to compete against the National Bus Company, against British Telecom in supplying equipment, and against the Post Office in offering express mail services.

In their article 'Privatising Public Enterprise: An Analysis of the Government's Case', *Political Quarterly* (1982), David Steel and David Heald have questioned some Conservative assumptions about the effects of privatisation. They reveal some inconsistencies in the Conservative approach to free competition, wondering why an eight-month inquiry was necessary to consider a bid for Sealink from its major rival European Ferries when it should have been rejected in principle. In addition, they argue that competition can lower the quality of service, not improve upon it. For example, through cross-subsidisation, public bus operators have been able to serve remote areas as well as popular routes. Competition and price-cutting on popular routes removes much of the profit which was used to pay for rural services. Steel and Heald also point out that arguments about privatisation saving public money can be deceptive. The sale of interests in British Gas and the British National Oil Corporation has produced money which reduced the Government's need to borrow in the short-term, but it also loses the profits that those companies would have earned in the future.

Privatisation measures were promoted to be a major plank in the economic policies of the second Thatcher government. Major concerns such as British Telecom, British Gas, and British Airways were sold off, and massive council house sales also took place. By 1986, 3.5 per cent of the government's total spending came from privatisation revenues. Many other State assets such as electricity and water were officially selected for privatisation in the third Thatcher government, with the political Right pressing for many other concerns, such as British Rail, British Coal and the prison service, to be privatised.

The Government argued that privatisation would help to produce an 'enterprise culture' in Britain. More and more people would participate in capitalism through owning shares. Critics have argued that the benefits claimed for privatisation are rarely achieved. Privatisation, for example, does not always increase competitiveness and competition; critics cite the decline in British Telecom standards as a case in point. Also, it is argued that the industries privatised by the Government are the ones least likely to benefit from being put in the private sector because they were already successful in the public sector. It has been argued that the Government's main concern with privatisation has been the reduction of the Public Sector Borrowing Requirement (PSBR) and not with increasing quality or choice of services to consumers.

Control and accountability of the nationalised industries

Ideas about control and accountability of the nationalised industries have changed over time. Originally, it was felt that publicly-owned concerns should be directly under the control of the Minister who was responsible and answerable to Parliament for the actions of his department. Since Parliament provided the finance necessary for the public enterprise it was felt that the enterprise should be accountable to Parliament. In the last century, the main public concern was the Post Office, which was a government department staffed by civil servants. It was directly under the control of a Minister – the Postmaster-General. There are other trading bodies which have been administered as a part of central government; for example, the Ordnance Factories until their denationalisation in 1971.

During the 1920s and 1930s, the need was recognised for another form of organisation which combined business management with public accountability. Some organisations required greater freedom from political control in making day-to-day commercial decisions, whilst others dealt with sensitive areas and required greater distance from the partisan pressures of Parliamentary accountability. The *public corporation* was devised to meet these needs. The Port of London Authority, created in 1908, was the forerunner of the public corporation. The first fully-fledged public corporations were the BBC and Central Electricity Board established in 1926, and the London Passenger Transport Board set up in 1933.

William Thornhill has identified three main characteristics which distinguish a public corporation from a government department:

> First, it is free from *full and continuous responsibility* to Parliament through a Minister. Apart from matters specified in the statutes, a public corporation is legally and constitutionally free to carry out its business in its own way. In theory, if not always in practice, a Minister is answerable to Parliament for all the activities of his Department, and for its omissions; and he is the legal head of the department too. Secondly, the staff of the public corporation do not have the status and liabilities of civil servants; they have different conditions of tenure, remuneration, selection and management. Thirdly, the finances of a public corporation are not part of the finances of government (W. Thornhill, *The Nationalized Industries*, 1968, p. 22).

In short, public corporations were a compromise between the contradictory cultures found in the public and private sectors. They were publicly owned, yet independently managed. They were insulated from partisan political influences, yet responsible to the community at large.

Apart from Herbert Morrison, early Labour Party leaders were a little suspicious of public corporations. They were concerned about making publicly-owned bodies more like private enterprises, and were doubtful whether such bodies could create the economic and social change required by the goal of socialism. These early reservations about public corporations were dispelled during the 1930s and the Labour Party accepted that they could be used in planning the economy. Labour saw advantages in organisations which could carry out long-term politically-directed plans and which at the same time could still respond to short-term market forces. The Attlee Government used the public corporation structure to bring much of the economy into public ownership. In 1969, the Post Office finally became a public corporation. It joined other major public corporations such as the British Railways Board, the British Steel Corporation, the British Waterways Board, the National Bus Company and the National Coal Board.

The pre-war public corporations were subject to considerably less political control than the post-war creations. Leonard Tivey has made the point that contacts between government and contemporary public corporations exist at all levels. Civil Servants maintain contact with the staff of the corporations and discuss a wide range of matters. There is an elaborate system of consultation between government and the corporations which concerns four main types of issue:

(a) The general forward planning of the industry is clearly one such matter. The statutory powers of the Minister in relation to investment, finance, research and training are all focused in this direction.

(b) The central financial aspect of a corporation's business is the price at which it sells its products. It must be emphasised, however, that at all times appreciable changes in price levels in the nationalised industries have been, in one way or another, the concern of the Government.

(c) Wage negotiation is another subject of major Government interest. Negotiations take place between the corporations, as employers, and the trade unions representing the employees, and formally the Government takes no part. Yet in fact there is no doubt that the views of the Government are made known to the corporations, and their negotiators can hardly fail to take these into account.

(d) These three broad categories of Government influence should not obscure the wide range of topics actually discussed. In addition to plans, prices and wage settlements, a miscellany of particular topics is considered – the siting of power stations, land for opencast mining, air charter policy and so on (L. Tivey, *Nationalization in British Industry*, 1976, pp. 128–31).

The Role of the Minister

Each public corporation is controlled by a minister, and it conducts its affairs with government through his department which is sometimes described as the 'sponsoring' department. For example, the National Bus Company, the British Waterways Board and the British Railways Board related to central government through the Department of the Environment which took over from the Ministry of Transport. The Minister could appoint and remove members of each corporation's Board. Sometimes a disagreement between the sponsoring Minister and a Board Chairman would result in the latter's resignation. This occurred in 1970 when the Post Office Chairman, Lord Hall, was replaced after a dispute with the Minister. New appointments are usually people whose views are more in line with those of the Minister. The position of Ian McGregor as head of the British Steel Corporation, then National Coal Board, represented the appointment of someone of like mind not only to the Minister but also to the Prime Minister.

The powers that each sponsoring Minister has over a public corporation are set out in the enabling legislation. It is generally agreed that the powers which Ministers assume over corporations go far beyond their statutory powers. In plain language, Ministers interfere with the running of public corporations far more than anticipated. Ministers may even control the commercial decisions of the public corporations in a way which suits their other departmental or political interests. William Thornhill comments that:

> This has been seen throughout the post-war period in successive attempts by Governments to exercise control over prices: in the pressure on their aircraft corporations to buy aircraft different from that which they would have preferred to buy on commercial grounds; and in the special duty on oil used by the electricity industry to make coal financially more attractive (W. Thornhill, *The Modernization of a British Government*, 1975, p. 157).

Much of this pressuring and persuasion by the Minister goes on behind the scenes. It is rare for the Board of a public corporation to resist the wishes of the Minister. Corporations which are making a substantial loss and need bailing out are in no position to oppose Ministerial direction. Indeed, not only the sponsoring Minister but also the Treasury may effectively intervene in such a corporation's affairs.

The troublesome relationship between the Minister and the public corporation has been the topic of considerable debate. There are those who feel that Ministers should not be allowed to go beyond their statutory powers. If Ministers were prevented from exceeding their power, public corporations would gain a little more freedom from political control in making many of their day-to-day decisions, and much of the pressure 'behind the scenes' from their sponsoring departments would disappear. There are others who feel that the situation would be best clarified by the removal of all restrictions on

Ministers. The status of the public corporation would then be different from their own departments and Ministers would be free to intervene in affairs whenever and wherever they wished.

The Select Committee on Nationalised Industries (1968) examined this problematic relationship. The members of the Committee appeared to agree that Ministerial control experienced by some public corporations had been unsatisfactory. They felt that there were two fundamental purposes of Ministerial control; first 'to secure the wider public interest' and second 'to oversee, and if possible ensure, the efficiency of the industries'. The Committee believed that many problems could be laid at the door of the sponsoring departments. Therefore the sponsoring departments should be replaced by a new Ministry of Nationalised Industries. It was felt that this Ministry would develop expertise in coping with the particular types of problems experienced by nationalised industries. The Ministry of Nationalised Industries would be responsible for making appointments and ensuring that the nationalised industries were efficient. It would therefore be concerned with the price of industries' products, investment programmes and the achievement of financial goals. The task of ensuring that the public interest was being served by the nationalised industries would be undertaken by other appropriate departments.

The Government rejected the Select Committee's report. In a White Paper it was denied that 'the two responsibilities give rise to separable and distinct functions which would be best exercised by different departments'. The Government felt that the reforms proposed in the Select Committee's report would further complicate, and not simplify, administration of the nationalised industries.

Further reforms were proposed in the McIntosh Report, *A Study of UK Nationalised Industries* (1976), but once again the Government rejected the suggested measures. In this case it was proposed that each nationalised industry should have a 'policy council', which would distance the Minister from the Board. The policy council would be responsible for major appointments as well as for making plans for the industry and monitoring performance and efficiency. Ministers would no longer be able to intervene and effectively make these decisions although they would negotiate with the policy councils. Policy councils would consist of civil servants from the Treasury, representatives from the Board of the corporation concerned, unions and consumers. The chairmen would be 'independent'. Critics of the 'policy council' proposal felt that the problems concerned with too much Ministerial control could not be solved by creating more bureaucracy.

Control and accountability are not problems in cases where the Government is associated with a company through holding shares. The enterprise may be publicly owned but it retains characteristics of a company operating in the private sector. However, there is always the possibility of the company embarking on a policy which might embarrass the Government in a number of ways. For example, it was suspected that some companies in which the Government had an interest ignored sanctions that were imposed against Rhodesia after the declaration of UDI in 1965. In 1983, British Petroleum announced that it was going to sell part of its North Sea Forties Field. The Department of Energy was worried that its Ministers would be attacked for allowing a national asset to be sold off, possibly to a foreign buyer. The Department controlled all oil companies in respect of the transferring of licence interests in the North Sea, and could prevent the BP sale. On the other hand, the Treasury, which held nearly 40 per cent of BP shares at the time and could influence Board decisions, favoured the sale. It would give BP a tax advantage and the revenue gained from the sale would make a further sale of Government-owned BP shares more attractive. Thus, although BP is a private-sector company, it produced disagreement between government departments which had different interest in its policies. One Minister was accountable because of government policy which regulated licences, and he was vulnerable to criticism in the House of Commons. His Cabinet colleague, whose department had a substantial shareholding in BP, was less accountable and relatively secure from Parliamentary attack.

Parliament and the nationalised industries

There is a widespread feeling that the nationalised industries are not accountable to Parliament in a satisfactory manner. As we have seen, the position of Ministers in relation to the public corporations is controversial and far from being clearly understood. In Parliament Ministers are, in theory, answerable for those things over which they have power. Legislation gives them certain powers but inevitably Ministers exceed those powers in relation to the public corporations. So are Ministers answerable to Parliament only for those affairs over which they have formal responsibility, or for all the affairs in which they are influential, including those which are settled 'behind the scenes'? The answer to the question affects the powers of scrutiny available to backbenchers. There is, for example, a rule that Ministers should only be questioned about matters for which they are responsible. If this responsibility is contained in a statute then the position is clear and MPs can raise appropriate issues at Question Time. But where Ministers are believed to have intervened in a public corporation beyond this point, it is difficult to know whether or not the right of MPs to question them exists. In practice, Ministers are questioned beyond that for which they are formally responsible particularly if the issue concerned is thought to be important. At the same time, the ambiguity that surrounds the extent of Ministers' responsibilities might allow them to avoid giving a direct answer on potentially embarrassing or sensitive issues.

Backbenchers also have the opportunity to raise issues concerned with the nationalised industries during adjournment debates, debates on governments' public expenditure plans, debates on the annual reports and accounts submitted to Parliament by the public corporations, and Acts which introduce new nationalisation or privatisation measures.

The most detailed parliamentary scrutiny of the nationalised industries takes place in select committees. The Select Committee on the Nationalised Industries was first established in 1955, but its members found that the committee's terms of reference were too restricted for them to do anything worthwhile. As a consequence, a new committee was set up in 1957 with the following terms of reference:

> to examine the Reports and Accounts of the Nationalised Industries established by Statute whose controlling Boards are appointed by Ministers of the Crown and whose annual receipts are not wholly or mainly derived from moneys provided by Parliament or advanced from the Exchequer.

Later the Select Committee was to extend its investigations to include the Independent Television Authority, the Horserace Totalisator Board and the Bank of England. In reviewing the record of this select committee in questioning witnesses and calling for written statements, Leonard Tivey observed that it was 'generally considered to be a very successful body ... There is little doubt that the general understanding of Members has been improved by its reports, and that their debates are more enlightened as a result of the committee's influence' (L. Tivey, *Nationalization in British Industry*, 1973, p. 147). The reform of the House of Commons Select Committee system in 1979 led to the disappearance of the Select Committee on Nationalised Industries. Scrutiny of the nationalised industries is now shared by committees which investigate the five sponsoring departments – Energy, Environment, Industry and Trade, Transport, and the Civil Service. If the need arises, it is still possible to set up a joint committee to deal with matters affecting two or more nationalised industries. Despite this, the disappearance of the Select Committee on Nationalised Industries has left Parliament in a weaker position regarding accountability. Before the Select Committee system was reformed there were thirteen or fourteen backbench MPs with knowledge and expertise on the problems of running nationalised industries. The reforms encourage MPs to specialise in the affairs of sponsoring departments, only some of which will concern the nationalised industries. Therefore, the House of Commons is in danger of losing the expertise that enabled parliamentary scrutiny of the nationalised industries to be conducted so satisfactorily in the past.

The consumer

It might be felt that either the Government or Parliament is adequate to the task of representing the interests of the consumer in the running of the nationalised industries. But, as we have seen, the thinking of Ministers and their colleagues may be influenced by numerous political factors, only one of which is the protection of consumers' interests. Parliament may be ill-informed about consumers' interests or cross-pressured by conflicting consumer interests. In order to accurately represent customers, Nationalised Industry Consumer Councils have been established. One of the best known of these forty-four bodies is the Post Office Users' National Council.

Initially, it was generally agreed that the Consumer Councils added little to the inadequate protection found in Westminster and Whitehall. The existence of the Councils was not widely known and the number of complaints received was small when compared with the total number of customers. However, in recent years, the Councils have notched up a number of successes in modifying the policies of certain nationalised industries, particularly with regard to pricing.

SUMMARY

Indirect government is a useful, if undemocratic, way of making decisions and providing services. Although there have been attempts to reduce the size of quasi-government and the number of quangos in existence, some government policies such as the abolition of the GLC and Metropolitan authorities have led to a proliferation of quango-like bodies. Nationalised industries also represent a form of 'government at arm's length', and, as with other forms of quasi-government, problems of accountability and control have never been satisfactorily resolved. In Britain, nationalisation and privatisation are highly political issues. The Thatcher Governments have reduced the scope of public-sector activity through selling off assets and contracting-out, but the advantages promised have not always materialised once a concern has been privatised. The Thatcher Government believes that privatisation will help to create 'popular capitalism'.

FURTHER READING

Brittan, S. (1984) 'The Politics and Economics of Privatisation', *Political Quarterly*, 55, April.

Cox, Andrew (1987) 'The Politics of Privatisation', in L. Robins (ed.) *Politics and Policy-making in Britain*, London, Longman.

Hall, R. (1987) 'Privatisation and British Politics 1979–86', in L. Robins (ed.) *Topics in British Politics 2*, London, Political Education Press.

Hood, C. (1981) 'Axeperson, Spare that Quango . . .', in C. Hood and M. Wright, *Big Government in Hard Times*, Oxford, Martin Robertson.

Manser, W. A. P. (1982) 'Nationalization or Privatisation: The Case for Each', *Banker*, 132, December.

QUESTIONS

1. 'Quasi-government is undemocratic.' If so, can it be justified?
2. How might public corporations be made more accountable to the public?

ASSIGNMENT

Write an 800-word report which examines the case for and against the privatisation of local library services. Conclude with an appropriate recommendation.

9

Local Government

Local government is a controversial issue with arguments focusing on topics as diverse as its structure and accountability, the political activities of councils and their personnel, and even the need for local government at all. The role of local government has been questioned in recent years and some have argued that the services it performs could be best provided by other organisations. This chapter examines the organisation of local authorities together with the major problems of central–local relationships and the financing of local government which became acute in the 1980s.

LOCAL GOVERNMENT IN CRISIS?

Services can be delivered at a local level for people without providing them through local government. For example, there are post offices in every town and in thousands of small villages which provide not only for the payment of welfare, but also banking facilities as well as postal services. Local people use these services but they are centrally controlled and do not involve local political participation. The essence of local government is that those who provide services are accountable to the local electorate for their actions. Local government is based on the idea of representation. Advocates of local government argue that local people best understand the needs of their particular community and therefore decisions affecting their community should be made by representatives who can reflect those views. Centralised bodies, whether in Whitehall or the boardrooms of large corporations, cannot understand or meet local needs as effectively as local government.

It is not surprising, therefore, that the role of local government has been a topic of constant debate amongst administrators and politicians. But the direction of the local government debate has altered course over the years. During the 1960s and early 1970s, the main questions were about ways in which local government could be strengthened and made more autonomous. By the late 1970s there were warnings that local government had grown too much and was consuming too many resources. In the 1980s the debate has been about the way local government might be controlled by the centre, reduced in size and have its activities curtailed.

179

LOCAL GOVERNMENT STRUCTURE

Providing a system of local government that matches the demographic structure is a complex affair. Most of the population live in one of the great conurbations, but some live in small market towns, and others in the remote rural areas such as Dartmoor or East Anglia. Some areas are much more prosperous than others: unemployment is relatively low in the South and higher in the North. Some populations have a different age-structure from others: for example the 'dependency ratio' – calculated as the number of young children under 15 and people of pensionable age per 100 people of working age – is 0.99 in Worthing, 0.87 in Eastbourne but only 0.45 in Oxford and 0.20 in the City of London. Finally, some areas have relatively large ethnic communities which may have special needs. Thus, in terms of the diversity found amongst the population alone, organising one single pattern of local government that can be applied across the country seems an impossibility.

In addition, the services delivered by local government are diverse. They range from the provision of education, housing, fire services, local planning and social services to refuse collection and disposal, street cleaning, street lighting and recreation facilities. Some services might best be delivered by a large number of small administrative units whilst other services might be delivered most effectively through one local government unit which covers a much larger area. The problem of structural reform in local government is that different areas of the country require different structures in order to deliver effectively the particular mix of services required. Finding the optimum structure of local government in one period of time does not mean that the same structure would operate successfully in later years. This is because local populations change as a result of factors such as internal migration. In addition, the prosperity of areas can rise or fall with the development of motorways, ports, and airports and there can be changes in people's life styles, as a consequence of the increased use of private transport or the purchase of second homes. The problem of finding the most appropriate local government structure which responds to these and other changes can be complicated by political factors. A proposal for reform which has the support of administrators may not be welcomed by one political party or another because it undermines their power-base. For all these reasons, local government structure has been an issue which attracts a fairly constant stream of proposals for reform.

In 1966 a Royal Commission was set up under the chairmanship of Sir John (later Lord) Redcliffe-Maud 'to consider the structure of Local Government in England, outside Greater London, and to make recommendations for authorities and boundaries, and for functions and their division, having regard to the size and character of areas in which they can be most effectively exercised and the need to sustain a viable system of local democracy'. It was felt that to be effective in operation, local government should be efficient in looking after the well-being of people in different localities; be able to attract and hold the interest of its citizens; be strong enough to form a partnership with central government, and finally, be adaptable to change in the way people work and live. The local government system that existed then was criticised by Maud since it failed to meet these necessary criteria. England was divided into seventy-nine county boroughs and forty-five counties. The county boroughs provided services for the larger towns whilst the county councils and a lower tier of district councils served most other areas. This divided town from country and could fragment the administration of services which looked as if they could be run more efficiently by a single authority. For example, Southampton – a county borough – provided schools in the town whilst Totton, a suburb of Southampton, yet outside the town boundary, had its schools run by Hampshire County Council. The administrative structure made planning difficult, not just for education, but also for services such as planning and transportation.

Maud argued that the division of responsibility within each county between county councils and district councils also caused administrative problems, particularly with coordination, as well as being confusing to the electorate. Also, Maud found that many local authorities were too small in terms of size of their populations and the amount of revenues received. Both deficiencies prevented them from operating at an efficient level. Too often the services which should be in the hands of one authority were shared out amongst several. Overall, concluded Maud, the structure of local government no longer matched the pattern of life and work in contemporary Britain and was in need of reform.

Maud introduced an embryonic form of devolution into his proposals for reform by recommending the establishment of eight English provincial councils which would be indirectly elected and have responsibility for planning. Maud was attracted to the idea of unitary authorities, and recommended that England be divided into fifty-eight such authorities which would be based on towns and their rural and suburban hinterlands and which would have responsibility for all services. The large conurbations of Birmingham, Liverpool and Manchester should have their own metropolitan councils with a lower tier of metropolitan districts.

The Labour government responded positively to the Maud report although it shelved the idea of provincial councils until the concept of regional government had been more thoroughly considered. Labour, with its political support concentrated in urban areas, was attracted to the idea of local government reform based on all-purpose, single-tier city regions. The Conservative Party, however, was alarmed since its strength in the outer suburbs and rural areas of the region looked in danger of being submerged by the political weight of the city. The Conservatives rejected the Maud recommendations and, on winning the 1970 General Election, put their own proposals for reform in the Local Government Act, 1972. This Act came into operation in 1974 and abolished the county boroughs. It provided a two-tier structure throughout the country. The idea of metropolitan areas was retained with their number increased from three to six. In both metropolitan and non-metropolitan areas local government was divided between county and district councils. The Conservative government argued that the Act set up a new structure which provided a balance between efficiency, which needs large-scale units to provide the economies of scale, and democracy, which works best with smaller units of government (see Figure 9.1).

A White Paper from the second Thatcher government, *Streamlining the Cities*, argued there was no longer a real role for the metropolitan councils to play and proposed the abolition of the Greater London Council (GLC) and the six metropolitan councils (Tyne and Wear, Greater Manchester, West Yorkshire, South Yorkshire, Merseyside and the West Midlands). The government argued, with hindsight, that the creation of the metropolitan authorities ('mets') by a previous Tory government was a wrong decision. Abolition, it was argued, would save money and increase efficiency. Most of the functions exercised by the 'mets' would become the direct responsibility of the borough or district councils. For example, functions such as planning, highways, waste disposal, housing and trading standards would be handed over to them. Functions not passed to the boroughs or districts, such as fire, police and public transport, would be run by joint boards. It was proposed that these boards would be composed of members nominated by borough and district councils from amongst their elected members. The government argued that the GLC and the six metropolitan councils did too little and at the same time were too bureaucratic and too remote. Abolition would, therefore, strengthen local democracy. Some Tories feared that reforms might end up costing more rather than resulting in savings; they were worried that the creation of the new joint boards would mark a massive expansion of costly quango-like bodies; but most of all they were anxious about the abolition of the GLC which would leave London as the only major city in Europe without a directly elected city-wide authority. They were not reassured by an unofficial proposal, which found little support, that the interests of London could be safeguarded by a 'forum' of the eighty-four London MPs.

Other critics claimed that the metropolitan counties cost less, because of the economies of scale which are made when services are run regionally by metropolitan authorities, and not locally by the districts. It was also counter-argued that abolition of the 'mets' would not really get rid of a tier of government since many of the services would be transferred to new bodies, some to central government, and only some to the districts. The new system would be more complex, more remote, less accountable and therefore less democratic. In particular, critics of abolition were concerned about the

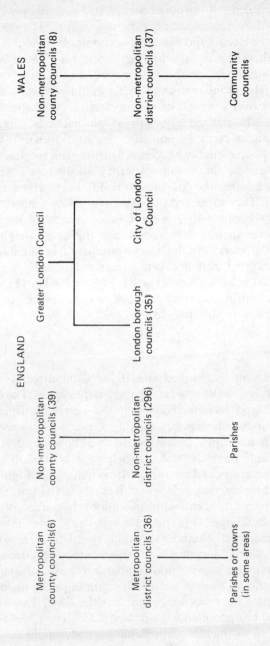

Source: L. Robins, T. Brennan and J. Sutton, *People and Politics in Britain* (1985)

FIGURE 9.1 *The structure of local government in England and Wales 1974–86*

membership of the joint boards which would control fire, transport and police. The special problems of the police joint board was that it would have magistrates appointed to sit alongside district councillors. The magistrates, naturally, would not be elected and would be accountable to no one. Finally, concern was voiced that the proposals in *Streamlining the Cities* would result in a less efficient system because the government was making unjustified assumptions that neighbouring district councils would cooperate with each other when they took over some of the metropolitan services. Indeed, some feared that there might not be goodwill at all between neighbouring Conservative and Labour councils, and that this would lead to a lack of cooperation, and to poorer quality and less efficiently-run services.

The GLC and six metropolitan counties were abolished on 1 April 1986. Many commentators felt that the government had failed to argue a convincing case for abolition. They suspected that the government wanted to get rid of the 'mets' simply because they were Labour-controlled and, in the government's eyes, 'over-spenders'. It was felt that there may well have been a case for scrapping the 'mets', but that the government had failed to work it out fully and the resulting abolition policy was a botched job. For this reason, there are some (including Conservatives) who would not be surprised to see local government structure being put back on the drawing board by the mid-1990s with a view to further reform.

Internal structure

In 1971, the government established the Bains Committee to consider preparations for introducing the new local government system. The Committee reported in 1972 and recommended that the new authorities should develop a corporate approach to policy-making. Central to this recommendation was that each authority should establish a Policy and Resources Committee which would have the tasks of helping a council to define its objectives, decide its priorities and coordinate its activities (see Figure 9.2). It was proposed that the powerful Policy and Resources Committee should have four subcommittees to deal with the major resources of finance, personnel, land and buildings. This structure was designed to increase the efficiency of management and planning functions through increased coordination and control. The old system was fragmented into departmental interests – which gave too many opportunities for wasteful duplication, unnecessary rivalry, and an overall lack of direction in policy-making.

The Bains Committee also recommended that the Chief Executive in a local authority should be appointed to lead the officers. The Chief Executive should be free from departmental responsibilities and should act as chief adviser to the council on general policy. Finally, he or she should lead a management team of Principal Chief Officers which would have the task of preparing plans to meet the long-term objectives of the council.

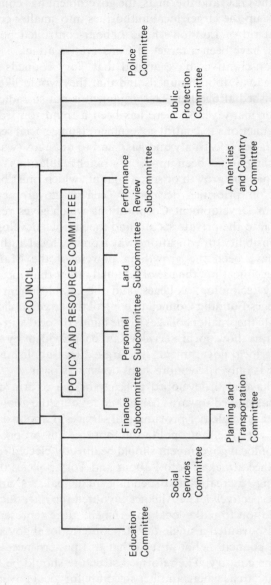

Source: L. Robins, T. Brennan and J. Sutton, *People and Politics in Britain* (1985)

FIGURE 9.2 *Committee structure for a non-metropolitan county recommended by the Bains Committee*

The future of local government structure

Since the abolition of the GLC and the 'mets' the government has considered a radical plan to break up the larger local authorities into smaller councils. This reform would get rid of London's huge Labour-controlled boroughs which, for many years, have been a target of Conservative attack.

In private, some Conservatives have argued that Tory councils can be almost as 'troublesome' as Labour councils and that they would like to see local government abolished altogether. This argument is not so radical as it might first appear. For many years, there has been a trend towards local government losing its functions to central government (some social services), to centralised bureaucracies (electricity and gas), and to quangos (water). In recent years, the government has been imposing stricter regulations on local government; for example, the growth of specific grants which must be spent by local government on priorities decided by central government, the establishment of Urban Development Corporations which gives responsibility for urban renewal to the private sector, and the various developments which are taking responsibility for education away from the local authorities. Amongst the latter have been the growth in powers of the Manpower Services Commission in education, the use of national rather than local funds to set up the new city technology colleges, and the establishment of the Polytechnics and Colleges Funding Council to control the large public sector institutions, leaving only the smaller colleges in the hands of local authorities. These examples illustrate how local services can be provided by central government by-passing local government. It is argued that abolishing local government altogether is only a few more steps down this path.

Opposition parties have also developed policies for the reform of local government. Labour has moved towards Maud and favours the abolition of most shire councils with a single tier providing all services. Labour does not have any plans to recreate the metropolitan authorities but proposes that above the unitary tier of local government should be directly-elected regional government. The Alliance attacked both Labour and Tory policies on local government for wanting to create 'high spending municipalisers' and 'low spending privatisers' respectively. The Alliance favoured the introduction of proportional representation to make local government more representative. Finally, the Alliance also wanted a single-tier structure for local government with a tier of regional councils – but argued that this pattern need not be imposed throughout the country. The reformed structure should be flexible enough to accommodate areas where another structure for local government would be more appropriate.

LOCAL GOVERNMENT PERSONNEL

Councillors

The increased politicisation of local government has resulted in a few councillors being as well known to the public as leading national politicians – Ken Livingstone and David Blunkett became media celebrities when they were councillors well in advance of their election to Parliament. But what sort of people comprise the many thousands of councillors who never enter the public spotlight, and what sort of duties do they perform?

Councillors are not typical of the population at large in terms of social class. For example, only a quarter of councillors have working-class jobs. Councillors tend to be better educated and to earn more than the average person in Britain. Councillors also come from the older sections of the population; only 8.5 per cent of councillors are aged between 21 and 34 years, yet 28.5 per cent of the total population is in this age group. In contrast, people between the ages of 55 and 74 years form 29.5 per cent of the total population, yet 47.5 per cent of councillors are in this age group. A significant difference of another kind is found in the 17 per cent of councillors that are female. Although this is far below the percentage of women in the general population, it is far ahead of the 6.3 per cent of women MPs in the new Parliament of 1987. Clearly, participation in local politics is easier for women than is participation in national politics, since the former political role is easier to combine with the domestic role of women.

It has been argued that paying a salary to councillors would attract more women to come forward as candidates, as well as more working-class and young candidates. This was considered by the Robinson Committee (1977) which recommended an annual payment of £1000 a year for councillors in addition to travelling and subsistence expenses. But Robinson fell well short of proposing that councillors should be paid a full-time salary. Some felt that paying councillors would attract the 'wrong sort of person' who would be encouraged to stand for office by thoughts of the salary rather than the idea of public service. Prior to reorganisation of local government, councillors received no payment as such, but simply a 'loss of earnings' allowance for attending meetings plus expenses. After reorganisation, councillors could also claim an 'attendance allowance' for undertaking their duties. One recent survey revealed that a growing minority amongst Labour councillors were giving up work and had become full-time councillors surviving on their attendance allowances. In this sense, full-time paid councillors are becoming a reality.

The role of the councillor is complex and, of course, the way it is interpreted varies to some extent from one councillor to another. In *Local Government in Britain* (1985) Tony Byrne has analysed expectations of councillors and argues that typically every councillor is a representative who is elected to represent a ward; an unofficial 'ombudsman' who has to deal with constituents' grievances; a manager who must oversee the work of the local government officers; a policy-maker who participates in shaping decisions in committee and council meetings; and finally a politician who seeks compromises through practising the art of persuasion.

In recent years, the focus of public attention has been on a relatively small number of Labour councillors which the tabloid press have dubbed 'the loony Left'. To some extent press exaggeration, moral panics and local over-reaction is to be expected in local government since it has become the battlefield between (local) left-wing socialism and (national) right-wing Thatcherism. From the Conservative government's point of view, some councillors, particularly in London, have abused their powers by spending public money on anti-racist, feminist and homosexual-awareness training. Many left-wing councillors were seen as having anti-police attitudes, reflected in the establishment of unofficial police monitoring committees, and pro-CND sympathies, reflected in the establishment of nuclear-free zones. Anxiety has also been expressed about the nature of employment of Labour councillors. A recent survey indicated that only 10 per cent of Labour councillors worked in the private sector compared with 40 per cent of Conservatives. Although there is nothing wrong or suspicious in this contrast, some concern was voiced regarding the number of councillors who worked in one authority but served in another. The law prevents an employee of a council sitting as a member of that council, but in some London boroughs two out of every five councillors had jobs with other councils. Potentially this smacked of 'jobs for the boys' as well as threatening the 'political impartiality' status of full-time officers. The Widdicombe Committee (1986) recommended, amongst other things (see below, p. 189), that senior local government officers should be barred from being politically active and serving as councillors in other authorities. This would bring them into line with civil servants who cannot stand as MPs or councillors.

Councillors at work

As Tony Byrne's analysis suggests, much of a councillor's time is spent on committee service. Some councils have implemented fully the Bains recommendations (see above, p. 184), whilst others have 'unscrambled' Bains and moved back towards the old committee and departmental structure. In the latter councils, the Policy and Resources Committee no longer has the role of coordinating policy but simply 'rubber stamps' decisions made in other committees. In all cases, the full council should approve the recommendations made by committees but, as we shall see, this situation does not appear to be the one which exists in practice.

Within the committee system, the role of committee chairman is critical in influencing how the system works. Commentators have noted that the system works rather differently in different authorities. For example, in one, the committee chairmen may act as the main policy-makers with the committees being of little importance save for giving habitual authority to their chairmen. In another, committee chairmen may play a different and far less individualistic role by simply overseeing the implementation of decisions made by their committees.

More important, however, has been the role of the party caucus in appearing to distort the working of the council system. In authorities where one political party has a ruling majority, the party caucus may become the dominant decision-making body. Although there may be nothing intrinsically wrong in this since it represents the reality of power, some voices have been alarmed by irregularities which have increased in custom and practice. In a number of authorities, including some London boroughs, those permitted at group meetings included not only the elected councillors but also members of constituency committees. Decisions arrived at by both elected and non-elected members of the party caucus would then be rubber-stamped in council meetings.

The Widdicombe Committee examined practices and procedures in local government and made a number of important recommendations. One proposal was that committees which take decisions for the council as a whole should reflect the political make-up of the whole council. It was felt that such committees take decisions on behalf of the whole council, not just part of it. Where a party group existed, this should be made clear to the public. Widdicombe recommended that decisions should be taken only by elected members.

Other Widdicombe recommendations included giving powers to the Audit Commission enabling them to stop councils from making unlawful expenditure; proposing that ratepayers should be able to question the auditor on matters concerning local government spending; and protecting the rights of electors by strengthening the local government ombudsmen system. It was argued that as well as receiving complaints direct from the public the ombudsmen should be able to investigate cases on their own initiative, and that remedies they recommended should be implemented by law.

Widdicombe not only recommended that senior local government officers at principal level or above should be banned from serving in other authorities, but also that there should be outside assessors to enforce rules which prevented political appointments being made. There had been considerable anxiety expressed about the employment in some authorities of 'political advisers' appointed in the guise of local government officers. Widdicombe argued that independent assessors were needed to ensure that all appointments made in an authority were on merit and not on political grounds. Finally, in an interim report, Widdicombe proposed a ban on party political advertising by councils, such as that mounted by the GLC against abolition. The report stated 'it is wrong for public funds to be spent on material that is strident, sloganised or partisan in style'. Widdicombe acknowledged that the problem of what became known as 'propaganda on the rates' was not widespread in local government. Most authorities at the time of Widdicombe were spending less than 0.1 per cent of their budgets on information and advertising with only the GLC spending as much as 1 per cent. The problem to which Widdicombe drew attention arose out of Section 137 of the *Local Government Act* 1972, which allows for discretionary spending by councillors in the interests of their areas. Some authorities, mostly metropolitan, had interpreted this section very widely and thus avoided the limits on spending for publicity contained in sections 142 and 111 of the Act.

Some reservations have been expressed about the Widdicombe recommendations, although it must be said that many politicians have welcomed all or part of Widdicombe. The main argument from the critics is that Widdicombe failed to strengthen local governments because it failed to understand that politics is part of local government. It was felt that many of the Widdicombe proposals were aimed to take politics out of local government and were trying to turn councils into an administrative service. For example, councils have a long history of being involved in political campaigns and it is not only the Labour-controlled GLC and the six 'mets' that have funded political campaigns against abolition but also Rutland and Fife. Critics argued against Widdicombe, saying that it was perfectly proper for any authority, Labour or Conservative, to use public funds in campaigning in the interests of their communities on issues such as nuclear dumping. They also criticised Widdicombe's proposals for the creation of 'assessors' on the grounds that 'assessors' could easily turn into 'snoopers' who were undemocratic in spirit and practice and who would report people for participating in local government. Likewise, it was felt that Widdicombe's proposed ban on the political activities of senior local government officers represented a significant withdrawal of their civil and democratic rights.

Local government officers

Local authorities employ administrators to assist them in carrying out their duties and in implementing their policies. The relationship between officers and councillors is frequently the focus of academic attention because it contains a number of inherent tensions. In the crudest sense, these tensions spring from the differences between professional administrators and amateur politicians. The former are selected for their qualities of expert knowledge, experience and professionalism. The latter are elected as candidates of political parties, often in elections with low turn-outs. Frequently, the electorate will have little personal knowledge of the candidates and vote for them solely on party political lines.

There may be occasions when officers recommend a policy which is rejected by members. Typically, the officers will feel that the policy formed on the basis of their professional expertise is superior. It will develop out of their specialised knowledge of the problems concerned and, in this sense, is politically neutral. Councillors may not perceive professional values as being political neutral and will prefer policies which are consistent with their own party's political philosophy. Also, councillors will be concerned with the political impact of policies on the electorate and may reject the 'best' policy if it is unattractive to local voters.

Some commentators have been concerned that officers wield too much influence in local government. This situation arises in part from the fact that the officers are permanent whereas councillors are essentially temporary, coming and going on the tides of electoral fortune. They feel that the contest between the permanent full-time professionals and the temporary part-time councillors is not evenly matched. This is why some support the case for full-time salaried councillors in the belief that this reform would allow councillors to build up their expertise and thereby become a match for the professionals.

In most authorities the senior officer is known as the Chief Executive, and the most important officer–member relationship is that between the Chief Executive and the Leader of the Council. It was sometimes alleged that this office–member link could develop into a powerful, cosy but essentially private relationship in which deals were 'sewn up', sometimes with scant regard for the wishes of other elected members. However, in May 1985 enormous changes swept through local government, leaving twenty-five of the forty-six counties with hung councils. The 'old rules' of local government had to be abandoned in these cases as all three major political groupings had to grapple with the realities of minority rule, balance of power bargaining and coalitions. Generally speaking, the arrival of hung councils ended many of the private agreements between committee chairmen and officers. Officers found that they became responsible to all political parties, and no longer to the ruling group. In other words, all councillors – not just the committee chairmen – became important in the eyes of officers since council meetings could no longer be relied upon to 'rubber-stamp' the deals previously made in private. Policy options could no longer be ruled out because they were politically unacceptable to the party in power; policies and options were discussed with all parties having greater access to information and decision-making.

In some hung councils, it was felt that the old private 'deals' between officers and chairmen had been swept aside and replaced by much more open and democratic local government. Some commentators, however, have voiced caution in drawing this general conclusion because in some cases the political situation has been so complicated that officers have been able to manipulate the resulting confusion and actually increase their powers.

Local Commissioner for Administration

The local government ombudsmen system was set up by the *Local Government Act*, 1972. The three local ombudsmen have long claimed that to work effectively they need greater powers. There are two basic problems which limit their effectiveness; first, there are still some councils which ignore recommendations from the ombudsmen and, second, ombudsmen learn of many cases of injustices resulting from maladministration which they are not allowed to investigate.

Neither the individual citizen concerned nor the ombudsmen can force a council to abide by the ombudsmen's verdict in a particular case. The most that can be done is that the ombudsmen issue a second report to the council and protest that nothing has been done. But, having done this, the ombudsmen are powerless if the council continues to ignore them. This problem is not a big one in terms of statistics – in one typical year, in only 92 of the 3000 cases referred were the ombudsmen not satisfied with the outcome of the council's responses. But, in human terms, it represents intense feelings of injustice for the citizens concerned, and Widdicombe proposed changes that would oblige councils to implement recommendations made by the ombudsmen.

The Audit Commission

The *Local Government Finance Act*, 1982 changed the way in which local authority accounts are examined. In the past, District Auditors – usually appointed by the authority – scrutinised local authority spending. The changes included the creation of an audit commission which is appointed by central government to ensure that local government spends its revenue economically. In keeping with the government's policy of 'contracting out', an increasing number of private auditors are being used.

CENTRAL–LOCAL GOVERNMENT RELATIONS

The relationship between central and local government is an extremely complex one to whose analysis political scientists have devoted considerable resources. There is agreement on the general trends but it is often the case that the complex detail uncovered in one particular case-study cannot be applied to all other cases. The relationship between central and local government is diverse, subject to changes in circumstance between one authority and another, and within one authority over time.

There has been a general trend in which central government has assumed more and more control over local government. Of course, in a democracy such as Britain where Parliament is sovereign, local government has never been autonomous. If an authority acts beyond the powers granted to it by Parliament, the doctrine of *ultra vires* will be invoked; the action of a local authority may be declared unlawful by the courts. Sometimes Acts of Parliament give Ministers great powers over local authorities. Indeed, many Acts give Ministers strong reserve powers over local authorities which fail to carry out their duties. In other words, if a local authority fails to perform a particular task, the Minister concerned may issue an order for it to do what is required. He or she may transfer the powers to another type of authority to get the task performed, or the Minister may take over the powers personally. An interesting case in this respect arose in Norwich in 1981. Under the *Housing Act* (1980), most local authority tenants were given 'the right to buy' their council homes. Many Labour-controlled authorities, including Norwich, appeared to the government to be very slow in selling their council houses. The Minister pounced on Norwich as an example to the others and announced that he would send commissioners to Norwich to oversee council-house sales unless the authority speeded up its programme of selling-off homes.

Recent years have seen a gathering momentum in the centralisation process which weakens the position of local government. As we have seen, many Labour-controlled authorities which challenged the government's policies on ideological lines were simply abolished. Many services once provided by local authorities such as education, are now run increasingly by central government or, like rubbish collection, street cleaning and office-cleaning, contracted out to private bodies. And, as we shall see, the financing and spending of local authorities has come under greater government control.

Supporters of local government argue that all these measures add up to the slow strangulation of local government and, more importantly, local democracy. The government challenged this line of argument in *Rates* (1983), a White Paper which stated 'we live in a unitary and not a federal state. Although local authorities are responsible to their electorates, they derive their powers from parliament.' In other words central government gave local government certain rights and just as easily it can limit or remove those rights. At its most extreme, central government created local government and retains the right to abolish it. Proponents of local democracy oppose the strict 'unitary state' argument by claiming that democracy in Britain involves as many people as possible participating in the decision-making process. Local government, therefore, is a vital part of democracy since local democracy is essential to national democracy. It is argued that 'new centralism' which seems a part of government policy results in the State gaining more and more power over people's lives. Strong local government is needed, it is contended, to provide the individual with some protection against central government.

It has been argued that increased centralised powers over local authorities had become necessary because local democracy was not working. Local mandates were often extremely weak because of the low turn-outs in local government elections. And surveys suggested that local issues did not feature in influencing the way people voted in local elections since they voted on national considerations. Counter-arguments to these points have been made with some vehemence. For example, although local government elections attract a lower turn-out than general elections, the former are held far more frequently. To this extent, it is argued, local authorities are much more subject to electoral pressure than is Parliament. Also, the fact that in some areas people tend to vote the same way in both local and general elections should not be surprising. The argument does not invalidate the local mandate; it just means that the local mandate favours one party because that party is strongest locally.

Some political scientists have explored ways in which central–local relationships might be understood in more theoretical terms. Basically, three models have been fashioned, each based upon a different type of relationship. These models are examined by D. E. Regan, 'Central–Local Relationships in Britain: Applying the Power–Dependence Model', in L. Robins (ed.) *Updating British Politics* (London, Politics Association (1984), pp. 161–170). The first portrays local government as an *agency* for central government. In this model, local government is simply the servant of central government, implementing the policies which central government lays down. In terms of power, local government is subordinate to central power. The second model portrays the central–local relationship in terms of a *partnership* with both sides working together for common ends. The two partners might not be equal in terms of power, but local government is not totally subordinate to central government. The third and most recently developed model sees central–local links in terms of a *power-dependence* relationship. It is argued that both central government departments and local authorities have a number of resources which each can use against the other. According to this model, central and local government are both independent of each other with neither having total control; their relationship is one of bargaining, exchange and negotiation. In terms of power this model suggests that the central–local relationship is more equal than the 'agency' model suggests, and more competitive than the 'partnership' model suggests. How might the 'power-dependence' relationship work in practice? Central government might supply (or refuse) financial resources to get a local authority to do (or not to do) something over which central government has no authority. R. A. W. Rhodes, who first applied this model to central–local relations, states that for both parties concerned 'their relative power potential is a product of their resources, the rules of the game and the process of exchange ... the process of exchange is influenced by the resources of the participants, strategies, personalities' (Rhodes, *Control and Power in Central–Local Government Relations*, 1981, Farnborough: Gower. See pp. 97–108).

The difficulties in applying these three models in an attempt to unravel the nature of central–local relations arise from a number of sources. The first is that relationships between central government departments and local authorities are not the same everywhere. They may vary from department to department, from authority to authority, as well as changing over time. The second is that the evidence at hand may be ambivalent or incomplete. What might be interpreted as the 'agency' relationship in action with an authority receiving a specific grant could just as easily be interpreted as 'power-dependency' at work if the political scientist perceived the use of the local press by councillors as part of a negotiation process. Finally, the models can be challenged because of the untested assumptions upon which they are constructed. For example, early interactionist theory in the USA was supported by sociological studies of mental homes when it was revealed that order, routines and life inside the homes were the product of negotiations between staff and inmates. In terms of the formal power structure, staff were in charge and inmates were powerless, but in practice it appeared that both parties had power and could negotiate what went on. But, of course, in reality some issues were never subject to negotiation and these were decided by the staff. Who locked whom in at night was a decision that was never arrived at through negotiation. The power-dependence model, drawn from this type of American theorising, is similarly limited in its usefulness. It appears to work only when the dominant party, central government, agrees that it can work. The abolition of the GLC and the metropolitan authorities as well as the diminishing role of local government suggests that those central–local negotiations that do occur are at the sufferance of central government.

LOCAL GOVERNMENT FINANCE

Local authorities are responsible for roughly a quarter of annual public expenditure. Since the government's economic policy has been aimed at controlling public expenditure, it has taken a great interest in local government finance. Local authorities may make a profit from commercial activities, such as from running leisure centres, but most of their income comes from (i) the domestic rate; (ii) the non-domestic rate which is paid by industry and commerce, and (iii) the grant from central government. In pursuit of its overall economic strategy, the government has taken measures to control local government income, and thereby spending. Proposals have been made to reform the rating system, and the proportion of total local government spending coming from central government has been steadily declining as

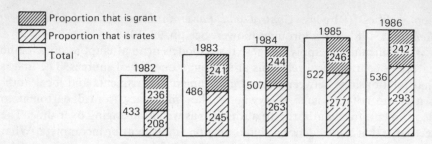

FIGURE 9.3   *Local government spending in England and Wales: Central government and rate contributions (£ per head of population)*

Figure 9.3 shows. In 1982, central government provided 53 per cent of local government revenue, but this figure had fallen to 45 per cent by 1986. But, as revenue from this source dropped, so local authorities made up the shortfall by raising the rates. The government came up with various voluntary spending targets for authorities, which some councils agreed with but subsequently ignored, before stricter penalty systems were devised.

The annual rate support grant settlement is the sum provided by central government and is agreed in Cabinet. It is usually a compromise between what the Treasury wants and what the Department of the Environment thinks is realistic. There is sometimes a conflict of departmental interests here since the Treasury wants to give the local authorities as little as possible, a position in line with the Chancellor's policy of limiting public expenditure. However, the Department of the Environment does not want too little from central government because this would mean local authorities having to find more money from rate rises. The government lets the local authorities know how much money they will be getting some time during the summer so that they can start planning their budgets for the year ahead.

From the government's point of view, local government has been guilty of 'overspending', with a relatively small number of 'high-spending' authorities contributing disproportionately to the problem. Throughout the 1980s the government has set up ever more stringent controls to limit local government spending. These have included voluntary spending targets based on previous spending patterns, and, in 1981, a new system of claw-back penalties was announced. For current account overspending, authorities lost a grant worth 3p in the £1 on the rates for each percentage point they spent over the government's target. However, initially there was a top limit to the penalty so that no council needed to put more than 15p on the rates to make up for the penalty grant losses.

Since most of the 'over-spending' was in sixteen 'high-spending' Labour-controlled authorities, there was a demand for specific controls to contain their spending and not general controls which sometimes penalised 'low-spending' Conservative authorities. Over-spending was calculated by how much an authority spent over and above what the government assessed it needed to spend, the Grant-Related Expenditure Assessment (GREA). Some low-spending Tory shires had been penalised for spending less than their GREA but more than their target. In 1986, spending targets for local authorities were scrapped, with the new system of central government control known as 'rate-capping' replacing them. Rate-capping enables central government to control the budgets of over-spending councils through setting upper limits on the amounts they can spend and the amounts they can raise in rates. An authority which ran into financial difficulties would no longer be able to get the money it needed to fund its spending from demanding higher rates because asking the public to pay 'excess' rates would be illegal.

Throughout this protracted debate over council financing and spending, there were those who challenged the government's semantics. It was argued that there was not a problem of over-spending which was particular to local government. Indeed, it was contended that local government spending was much closer to its target than was central government spending which far exceeded the Chancellor's target each year. The concept of 'over-spending' was also challenged in relation to particular authorities. The point was made that some authorities were high spenders because they faced severe problems which demanded high spending. 'High spending' was justified in such circumstances, it was argued, and should not be confused with 'wasteful spending'.

The debate on local government spending has not always divided straight down party lines. For example, about sixty Conservative MPs were reported as opposing rate-capping in principle because they saw it as an example of an unacceptable extension of State centralisation. They opposed the notion that central government could now interfere in the way an authority spends its money almost to the point of making the decisions that councillors once used to make. Even stronger Conservative opposition was expressed in 1981 to a proposal in a local government bill which would have forced local authorities into holding referenda before raising supplementary rates again, many Tory backbenchers objecting to what they saw as 'dictatorship from Whitehall'. The minister presented a new version of the Bill in which the referendum proposal was omitted. As a matter of interest, Coventry's Labour council voluntarily decided to ask its electors to choose between spending cuts amounting to £2 m or a one-third increase in the rates bill. Only a quarter of the electorate voted in the referendum (or 'public consultation process' as it was called in order to distance it from the Minister's proposal) and they supported the spending cuts by a majority of 7 to 1.

The ever-tightening controls on authority spending have led to some councils facing immediate or none-too-distant financial crises. In 1985, Liverpool City Council had enough resources to run its services for nine months but not for a full year. Councillors from the hard left wanted to 'shut up shop' for three months and make council employees redundant. They believed that this would force the government's hand into providing more money. As Liverpool neared bankruptcy a 'Blunkett' plan and a 'Stonefrost' plan independently devised rescue packages in which the council could avoid the collapse of services and mass redundancies. Liverpool councillors rejected both sets of plans but their position had been undermined since it was clear that alternative options did exist. The City Council withdrew from the brink by borrowing from Swiss banks in order to maintain services. Other authorities, particularly in London, were soon to follow Liverpool's example and escaped government controls through 'Deferred Purchase Agreements' which are basically a form of borrowing. But the problem with 'spend now, pay later' is that the money has to be paid back one day. Sooner or later the debts will catch up with these councils and they will face the danger of being plunged into even deeper financial crises.

Rate reform

Since the time when Mrs Thatcher was a shadow Environment Minister in the mid-1970s, she has championed the idea of abolishing the rating system and replacing it with a new method of raising local revenue. Rates are an ancient tax on property and are unpopular for a variety of reasons. They are a highly visible form of taxation unlike, for example, VAT which is 'hidden' within the price of goods. Rates are not directly related to the use made of local authority services; individuals in the 18–30 age group, for example, who make great use of services, pay disproportionately little in rates; improvements made to a property can lead to an increase in rates on that property; rates tend to hit poorer households hardest in the sense that they pay a higher proportion of their incomes in rates than more affluent households; and finally, rates are often based on the assumption that urban areas are wealthier than they actually are.

The advantages of rates tend to be procedural – they are easy to collect; they are cheap to administer; they are a form of tax which people understand and which it is difficult to avoid paying; and finally, there is great certainty about the amount of money rates will produce and they can be easily adjusted. Even if these advantages seem thin, and there is agreement that rates are an undesirable form of taxation, the real problem has been one of finding a superior replacement.

The government has considered reforms on a number of occasions and 'decided not to decide'. The principal alternatives include:

(i) *Local Sales Tax* This method of raising local revenue was opposed by many Conservatives because it was not consistent with the notion of the Tories being a tax-cutting party. The Treasury also disliked the idea of a local sales tax since it might limit the Chancellor's freedom to raise

VAT. Also, concern was expressed about the distorting effects this form of local tax would have if neighbouring authorities levied it at differing rates.

(ii) *Local Income Tax* This option was recommended by the Layfield Committee, 1976 and a decade later was supported strongly by the Alliance parties. But, as with local sales tax, it is contrary to the Tory party's tax-cutting image. Again the Treasury is opposed to this alternative because it would weaken the department's control over income tax in general.

(iii) *Poll Tax* This alternative was opposed by a former Environment secretary, Michael Heseltine, as well as by many others who did not want a tax based on the electoral register.

(iv) *A combination of two or more of these alternatives or a hybrid fashioned from a compromise between two or more* An example of the former would be a combination of a local sales tax together with a modified rating system; an example of the latter would be a 'variable poll tax' graduated according to income or the rateable value of the area lived in.

After intense deliberations during 1985–6, the government came down in favour of a 'community charge' to replace the rates. It is very similar to a poll tax although it is based on residence rather than on the electoral register. This proposal for reform was included in the Conservative's 1987 General Election manifesto although the Government ran into trouble with the party on the issue immediately on returning to office. Critics, including many Tories, argued that the community charge was regressive. In other words, individuals would pay the same despite differences in income. The community charge would be a 'bureaucratic nightmare' according to some Tories, who pointed out that it would cost £400 m a year to collect – twice as much as the old rating system. Some Tories considered that a poll tax was not consistent with 'family values' since it discriminates against wives and mothers who do not work outside the home.

The Thatcher Government's rejoinder to these criticisms included the point that no taxation system is going to be popular or perfect. The regressive nature of the community charge was no different from VAT where individuals pay the same rate regardless of whether they are rich or poor. The government believed that a flat rate is appropriate for the consumption of local authority services. It admitted that the community charge would be more costly to administer but pointed out that many more people would be paying it. A total of 35 million individuals would pay the new community charge including 17 million who had never previously paid rates. This was seen as the great advantage of the community charge, since it is likely to make all people who use local authority services take an interest in the affairs of local government. Under the old rating system, many people who used local authority services voted in the local elections yet did not pay rates. The community charge, argued the government, would restore the link between taxation and representation which had been absent in local government.

Finally, some Conservatives were anxious about the political impact of the community charge. If implemented, the new system was likely to come in just before the next general election. They believed that the Conservative electoral disaster in Scotland in 1987, which in part resulted from changes in the rating system, could be repeated to some extent in England.

The second ingredient of the government's rates reform package involved the 'nationalising' of the non-domestic rate. The government had been concerned for some time that a number of 'high-spending' Labour-controlled authorities were pushing up business rates and discouraging new investment and new jobs. The government's reform involved an initial revaluation of business properties with rates set nationally and rising only in line with inflation.

SUMMARY

Local government has been described as being in a 'policy mess' resulting from central government policy. Much of this 'mess' results from the contradiction present in two irreconcilable imperatives. First, central government believes that it has the right to control local authority activities through insisting on financial restraint. But, second, local authorities feel that they have a mandate from the local electorate to pursue their policies and spend as much money as is necessary. This conflict intensified when it became waged between Thatcher Governments and 'Socialist' authorities in the 1980s.

FURTHER READING

Alexander, A. (1982) *The Politics of Local Government in the United Kingdom*, London, Longman.

Bristow, Steve (1987) 'And After the Cities have been Streamlined?' in L. Robins (ed.) *Political Institutions in Britain: Development and Change*, London, Longman.

Byrne, T. (1985) *Local Government in Britain: Everyone's Guide to How it Works*, Harmondsworth, Penguin.

Henney, A. (1983) *Inside Local Government*, London, Sinclair Browne.

Jones, G. and Stewart, J. (eds) (1984) *The Case for Local Government*, London, Allen & Unwin.

QUESTIONS

1. Is there a case for local government in Britain?
2. To what extent can it be said that local government is 'alive and kicking' in Britain?
3. What is the case for further local government reorganisation?

ASSIGNMENT

Read the article which follows, then draft:

(i) a letter to a Labour MP urging him or her to support the introduction of the community charge to England and Wales,
(ii) a letter to a Conservative MP urging him or her to oppose a poll tax being introduced.

Exchange letters with your class colleagues and decide which are the most persuasively written.

The £4,000 early warning

Brian Wilson on some tough poll tax facts from Scotland

EVEN NORMAN TEBBIT at his most paranoid would have some difficulty in portraying the Chartered Institute of Public Finance and Accountancy as a hotbed of pinko subversion. But a two-volume publication which has recently emerged from that august body might come to be seen as a timebomb under the Conservative government.

The CIPFA's report on how the poll tax can operate was commissioned by the Scottish Office and is now regarded as 'the bible' by those hapless officials who have been told to make the thing work.

It sells at £4,000 for the two volumes, which scarcely suggests that a mass readership is intended. But Scottish local authorities have been provided with copies and both friends and foes of the poll tax have been startled by the contents, particularly on the matter of compiling a register.

While the report applies only to Scotland, it is essential that English and Welsh MPs should be aware of its contents. When the guinea-pig Scottish legislation was being pushed through suspicion could be voiced about the implications; now there is a much more authoritative source on which to base future interrogation of ministers.

The CIPFA's report takes a clinical approach to the fact that the potential exists for a huge level of poll-tax avoidance, thus pushing up the burden for those who do pay. That problem is unlikely to be resolved by the door-to-door canvass which is due to start in Scotland next April.

The CIPFA recognises that the unfortunates employed for the purpose 'may well face resentment and conceivably hostility and will need to be trained to cope with it.'

The consultants then addressed themselves to alternative sources of information for the compilation of the register once the more obvious ones – like the electoral and valuation rolls – had been exhausted. Other sources listed include the register of births, marriages and deaths and records of the education authority which 'will be useful for the registration of individuals once they reach the age of 18.'

The keepers of the poll-tax register are to scour health-board records and those of national utilities like gas, electricity and telephone companies. An eye can be kept on lists of users of local-authority services such as libraries and concessionary bus fares – a good one that for taxing out evading pensioners. Tabs will have to be kept on the local newspapers and estate agents' transactions.

Then, the CIPFA recognises, there are private trade organisations which provide information about individuals to members. Local authorities could subscribe to such lists in order to gain another cross check with the poll-tax register.

Only police records, it seems, will be immune from the researches of those – well over 1,000 in Strathclyde alone – who are to be charged with the massive task of maintaining a reasonably accurate register.

This unprecedented trawl to identify and trace each and every citizen – no parallel attempt has ever been contemplated in order to ensure that everyone has the right to vote – would stand a better chance of success if fewer people had the inconvenient habit of moving about the country, as well as turning 18 and dying.

All told, the CIPFA reckons there will be about 800,000 changes in the register each year – and that in Scotland alone.

In order to keep a month-by-month check on the mobile population, it is intended that each person should have 'a personal identifier' – individual codings similar to that which appears on driving licences. The Scottish Office has rushed to say that it does not mean the introduction of a national identity system, since the codings would be locally held. But that sounds more like a debating point than an argument.

The fact is that each individual would have a poll-tax identifier as part of the apparatus of minimising avoidance, and which the CIPFA says 'will be readily transportable between authorities.'

A country that has declined to go down the path of compelling its citizens to identify themselves to the state by means of name and number is now, it seems, to adopt that course of action as a by-product of the hare-brained poll tax.

Leaving aside the civil-liberty arguments, which are unlikely to impress the present Cabinet, the scale of bureaucracy which would be needed to administer such a system might cause some Tory MPs to think twice.

The extra cost of operating the poll tax in Scotland, compared to domestic rates, is put at £23 million a year – a figure which the Scottish Office accepts. Local-authority horror at what they are to be asked to do has transcended party differences.

To arrive at parallel statistics for England and Wales roughly multiply collection costs, would-be avoiders, register-compiling snoopers and annual register changes by 10. Then make special allowance for London, where constant monitoring of the mobile population could become Britain's second largest growth industry behind wine bars.

Are there 50 Tory MPs with the guts to say no to all of this dangerous nonsense, built on ideological obsessiveness? A glance at the Scottish election results should help to stiffen their backbones.

Brian Wilson is Labour MP for Cunninghame North (The Guardian 21 September 1987)

10

Parliament

The central concern of this chapter is the role of parliament in national politics. We examine the importance of party to the working of the House of Commons, the nature of the representativeness of the lower house of parliament, the constituency work of Members of Parliament, the functions of parliament in the political system, party organisation, recent changes in parliamentary behaviour and organisation, the role of the House of Lords and prospects for the future. The theme of party is the connecting link between these topics. It is argued that the role of parliament in the political system in general has to be understood primarily in terms of the working of the party system within the context of the choices of a democratic electorate channelled in a particular way by the electoral system (Chapter 12). We begin by explaining this key statement.

THE IMPORTANCE OF PARTY IN THE HOUSE OF COMMONS

The House of Commons is the nation's premier assembly. It consists of 650 MPs returned by that number of single-member consituencies, each elected on a simple majority by about 67 000 electors on average. MPs are elected as representatives of party, and party underpins their activities once in the House. Table 10.1 sets out the political composition of the House of Commons after the General Election of June 1987.

Table 10.1 shows how party determines the composition of the House of Commons, structuring it decisively into a party of Government (Conservative) and a party of official Opposition (Labour) flanked by a number of much smaller opposition parties. It also makes clear the very sizeable majority (101) enjoyed by the Conservatives over all the other parties after the 1987 General Election. Party underlies the activities of Government in the House of Commons in four ways – by providing it with a programme based on its election manifesto, which forms the basis of the legislation it puts before the Commons; by supplying a team of leading politicians to fill Ministerial posts (Chapter 7); by influencing backbenchers by its ethos, ideology and organisation to vote cohesively in support of the Government; and by providing a mass organisation to select candidates, campaign on their behalf, and, once they are elected, assist in keeping them up to the mark. Its overall majority taken in conjunction with the normally loyal support of its

TABLE 10.1

Party allegiance in the House of Commons after the 1987 General Election

Conservative	375	Governing party
Labour	229	Official Opposition party
Liberal	17	
Social Democrat (SDP)	5	
Ulster Unionist	14	
Scottish National Party	3	Combined opposition parties
Plaid Cymru	3	
Provisional Sinn Fein	1	
Social Democrat and Labour Party	2	
Conservative overall majority	101	

Note: This table does not include the Speaker of the House of Commons whose job is to ensure the observance of the rules of the House, and who takes no part in debates – unless the vote is tied. Total numbers therefore add up to 649, not 650

backbenchers generally ensures that the governing party can govern – that is, gain overall support for its executive activity and legislation from the House of Commons.

Party also underpins the activities of the official Opposition, providing it with an alternative programme and team of leaders with which to replace the government and sustaining it in its second constitutional function of systematic criticism of the government of the day. Equally, the minor political groupings are swayed by the imperatives of party to behave and vote cohesively behind a united policy.

Parliament, then, provides the major focus for the party battle between elections. Although not well reported in many sections of the press, the consequences of the struggle in the House of Commons between competing teams of party leaders to establish the authority of their respective cases and of new backbenchers to make names for themselves gradually filters down to the electorate via television, radio and the quality press.

FUNCTIONS

The House of Commons has five main functions: representation; legislation; scrutiny and influence of the executive (mainly Prime Minister, Cabinet and Departments); debate on the issues of the day; and recruitment of a government. By and large, these functions are shared with the House of Lords, although the Commons is easily the predominant partner in parliament as a whole and hence receives the bulk of attention here. The essence of parliament, its primary role in the political system, to which all these functions contribute, is *legitimation*. It serves as the fundamental agency whereby the actions of the rulers gain acceptance by the ruled. And it can fulfil this purpose because of its historic status, constantly renewed, as a unique forum for national representation, law-making, political criticism and debate.

Representation

The representative character of the House of Commons underpins its other roles. It is 'representative' in three senses: party, pressure group and constituency. These three kinds of representation combine in the person of the Member of Parliament, who is a representative of party (almost always), of interest (frequently) and of constituency (invariably). Representativeness in the context of *party* does not mean that the party composition of the Commons exactly reflects the distribution of party support in the country. The difference between the actual representation of parties in the Commons after the 1983 General Election and the distribution of party support there if proportional representation had been in operation is shown in Table 10.2. The Conservatives, with 120 fewer seats, would have lacked an overall majority over their main rivals, Labour, who would have had 29 fewer seats, and the Alliance, the major beneficiary of proportional representation, which would have had 143 seats more. What 'representativeness' in the context of party does mean is that MPs speak and vote as representatives of party.

Second, an MP may represent an *interest*. Representation of interests in the Commons can occur in three ways: by group sponsorship of candidates for election through the medium of one of the parties; by group payment of fees to existing Members to serve as parliamentary spokespersons; and by

TABLE 10.2

Consequences of proportional representation for party composition of the House of Commons after the General Election of June 1983

	Actual seats gained	Seats that would have been gained under proportional representation
Conservative	397	277
Labour	209	180
Lib/SDP Alliance	23	166
Scottish National Party	2	7
Plaid Cymru	2	3

Source: John Curtis and Michael Steed, Appendix 2 in D. Butler and D. Kavanagh, *British General Election of 1983*, London, Macmillan, p. 309

MPs who work in a particular occupation bringing their specialist knowledge of it to bear in debates. The most clear-cut example of the first category is the activity of the trade unions who at the 1987 General Election sponsored 164 Labour candidates, of whom 129 (over half of the parliamentary Labour party) were elected. Unions cannot, of course, instruct their MPs how to speak or vote in parliament – to do so would put them in breach of parliamentary privilege – but nonetheless obviously feel that sponsorship assists their cause. Many union-sponsored MPs were among Labour opponents of the Industrial Relations Bill in 1969 and some unions have lobbied for particular causes through the MPs they help to fund, the ASTMS lobby in the mid-1960s to force all employers to give redundancy pay being a case in point. Second, groups can pay MPs to represent their causes in parliament, providing them with (often sizeable) retainers to serve as consultants on a permanent basis. According to the *Observer*, the drugs and tobacco companies were paying their parliamentary consultants between £10 000 and £20 000 in 1984; much smaller sums – for example, £200 – were being paid for one-off services, such as putting down a written question, and 'considerably larger' sums for asking oral questions. Outside groups also gain the support of MPs by offering them honorary positions as directors or advisers, by recruiting them to executive positions and by simple lobbying of MPs known or thought to be sympathetic. Finally, MPs also represents particular interests by themselves pursuing outside occupations. Business, commercial and financial interests are well-represented in the Commons with the majority of Conservatives and a minority of Labour MPs having such an interest. As James Callaghan remarked in 1965: 'When I look at some Members discussing the Finance Bill I do not think of them as the Hon. Member for X, Y or Z. I look at them and say "investment trusts", "capital speculators" or "that is the fellow who is the Stock Exchange man who makes a profit on gilt-edged" '. Since 1975, parliament has kept a register of interests to strengthen the custom that MPs declare their interests at the beginning of any debate to which they contribute. However, there is still concern that these arrangements may be insufficient to safeguard the public interest in view of the facts first, that declarations of interest are often so vague as not to reveal the full extent of the interest and, second, that refusal to register an interest is merely a contempt of parliament and not a breach of the law.

Third, the House of Commons is representative of the United Kingdom in a geographical sense – that is, as divided up into territorial units called *constituencies*. Candidates for parliament may stand as party men or women but, once elected, each MP is expected to represent the interests of the constituency as a whole, and to be at the service of all constituents, irrespective of their party allegiances. In this way, as constituency representatives, MPs collectively may be said to represent the entire country, which would not be true of their roles as party and group representatives. This is the oldest meaning of 'representation' and formed the basis of the individualist liberal concept of parliamentary representation, which prevailed in the nineteenth century but was displaced in the twentieth century by the rise of the collectivist concept of party representation.

The idea of the MP as constituency man or woman and of parliament as an assembly of territorial representatives is a resilient one. It has undergone a resurgence in the third quarter of this century, primarily because people facing the complexities of local and national welfare bureaucracies have turned to MPs to assist them in understanding and asserting their rights. Most MPs now get very large post-bags from constituents; three-quarters of them in the early 1980s received between 25 and 74 letters per week, as the Labour MP Austin Mitchell reveals in *Westminster Man* (1982) p. 185. MPs take this case-work very seriously indeed, often setting aside two–three days each week as well as weekends to the task. MPs' constituency work falls into two main categories. First, they deal with a wide variety of problems on behalf of the individual citizen; the single most important of these is housing but other problems include matters such as jobs, pensions, planning applications, the allocation of children to schools, social security benefits and income tax. Second, MPs need to further the interests of the constituency as a whole by, for example, working to get orders for local industries, and industrial development certificates to encourage office and industrial building, to get roads built, to prevent factories, schools and hospitals closing, and to find solutions for local industrial disputes. A voluminous mail results with Ministers, Departments, local government and quasi-governmental agencies, to assist with which MPs in recent years have developed secretarial and research support. In a democratic society, this MP–constituency relationship is of profound practical and theoretical importance, serving as a barometer of public opinion for representatives and as both safety-valve and potential mechanism of grievance-resolution for citizens.

The House of Commons, then, can be seen as representative in these three distinct but overlapping ways. It is not a social microcosm of the nation, MPs being predominantly white, male, middle-aged and middle-class. Thus, there were only four black/Asian MPs in 1987 and only forty-one women MPs (twenty-one Labour, seventeen Conservative, one Liberal, one SDP and one SNP). 66 per cent of MPs in 1987 were aged between 40 and 59. Finally, all three main political groupings were largely middle class in educational and occupational background. About 70 per cent of Conservatives were educated at public school and university, whilst 66 per cent of Alliance MPs and just over 50 per cent of Labour MPs had received University education. Over 80 per cent of Conservatives and of Alliance representatives and well over 50 per cent of Labour MPs were drawn from business and the professions. Broad contrasts were readily discernible within these overall patterns: over one-third of Conservatives but under 20 per cent of Labour were drawn from business. Over 40 per cent of Conservative 'professionals' were lawyers;

about 60 per cent of Labour's 'professionals' came from teaching. Only Labour contained a significant proportion of manual workers – 29 per cent; the Conservatives had a mere 1 per cent (3 MPs) and the Alliance no MPs in this category.

Legislation

Parliament no longer makes policy either in the sense of initiating legislation or strongly influencing it. Most legislation originates with government and emerges from its passage through parliament more or less in the form intended by the government. The Government's majority backed by generally cohesive party voting normally ensures that this is so. Nevertheless, in order to become law, government measures must pass through both Houses of parliament in a series of stages with amendment and, very occasionally, even defeat of a Bill a possibility. Table 10.3 details these stages and it is worth noting particularly the points (see column 3) at which amendment is possible. Not only is the parliamentary legislative process a

TABLE 10.3
Legislative stages in parliament

Stage	Where taken	Comments
First Reading	Floor of the House of Commons	Formal introduction only, no debate
Second Reading	Floor of the House of Commons (non-contentious bills may be referred to a second reading committee)	Debate of the principle of the measure
Committee	Standing committee (Constitutionally important and certain other measures may be taken in committee of the whole House)	Considered clause by clause; amendments can be made
Report	Floor of the House of Commons (There is no report stage if the bill reported is unamended from Committee of the whole House)	Reported to the House by the committee; amendments can be made
Third Reading	Floor of the House of Commons (There is no debate unless six members submit a motion beforehand)	Final approval of the bill; debate confined to content of the bill
Lords Amendments	Floor of the House of Lords	Any amendments made by the House of Lords are considered usually on a motion to agree or disagree with them

Source: P. Norton, *The Commons in Perspective,* London, Longman (1981) p. 86

constitutional necessity, politically, owing to the possibility of amendment or even defeat of the Government's legislation, it is more than a formality or a foregone conclusion. Even if parliament no longer makes policy, its assent to government legislation is vital to the establishment of the legitimacy of that legislation.

Scrutiny and influence of the executive

Serving as an arena for constitutional opposition is another major function of parliament. It is in parliament (primarily the House of Commons) that the Government must explain and defend its actions. About 33 per cent of parliamentary time is given to debate on government legislation and under 5 per cent to private members' bills; the bulk of the remaining time is allocated to debate and scrutiny of government actions. Nowadays, the backbenchers of the majority party have as much to do with setting the limits of government action as do the opposition parties. Faced by a government with a sizeable majority, there is often little the Opposition can do except resort to delaying tactics. Nonetheless, the constitutional requirement embodied in specific parliamentary procedures that government must publicly subject its activities to appraisal is of paramount importance. Major scrutinising procedures and agencies of the House of Commons are Question Time, general, adjournment and emergency debates, Early Day Motions, Select Committees and correspondence with Ministers (see Table 10.4). Parliament's two other functions may be considered more briefly.

Forum for national debate

Critics in the second half of the twentieth century have repeatedly pointed out how the rise of party after 1880 has whittled away the power of parliament as a whole to legislate, authorise taxation and expenditure and control the executive. However, parliament remains able to command attention as the focus of national debate on all kinds of occasions in a manner denied to any other institution. It is not difficult to call to mind occasions when this is so: at Question Time and at the beginning and end of major debates in normal circumstances; at more heated moments such as the Westland affair (1986) when a Government's, a Prime Minister's or a leading Cabinet Minister's reputations are at stake with even a whiff of resignation in the air; and, lastly, at the great historic occasions such as the fall of the Chamberlain Government in May 1940, Suez in 1956 and the Falklands crisis in 1982. On such occasions, what may be termed the *theatrical* element in parliament is to the fore – an almost ritualistic rhetorical combat between rival teams of political gladiators urged on by a compact stage army of supporters.

TABLE 10.4

Main methods of Commons scrutiny of the executive

Procedure	Function
Question Time	Backbenchers submit questions to Ministers who appear daily to reply (Mon.–Thurs. at 2.35 p.m. for 45–55 min.) MPs are allowed one supplementary question; on Tuesdays and Thursdays, the Leader of the Opposition can tackle the PM directly at Prime Minister's Question Time
Debates	*General* – e.g. Debate on the Address on Government's programme at outset of each parliamentary session, but mainly on motions tabled by Government to discuss government policy or, on 19 Opposition Days, by the Opposition *Adjournment* – motion to adjourn can sound opinion on matters where government has no specific policy, or enable backbenchers to raise an issue of constituency interest and get a reply from (usually) a junior Minister *Emergency* – way for MPs to raise urgent matters for debate which lie within responsibility of the government and cannot be raised rapidly in another way; only about four per session granted
Early Day Motions	Much-used method of enabling MPs to express their views (hundreds are put down each session), although no debate follows on points raised
Select Committees	Able to scrutinise executive away from the floor of the Commons; have powers to send for 'persons, papers and records' and can interrogate civil servants and on occasion Ministers; 18 now exist, including Public Accounts Committee (traditionally chaired by an Opposition MP) which examines government expenditure
Correspondence with Ministers	Main way in which MPs pursue case-work on behalf of their constituents, the average MP being estimated to write anything up to about 25 letters per week following up constituency matters

Recruitment and training of the personnel of government

Parliament, of course, no longer selects Ministers but it remains 'a school of statesmanship' in the sense that Ministers are invariably drawn from parliament, predominantly from the House of Commons. Thus, whilst the electorate effectively elects the government directly, it is in the Commons that politicians serve as members of Shadow teams before receiving office or, as

Ministers, defend government policy. The skills of parliamentary debate are widely acknowledged to be no real preparation for running a Department nor are the two kinds of ability invariably present in the same person. Nevertheless, it is in the House of Commons that ambitious politicians first attempt to make, and then as Ministers try to sustain, their reputations.

PARTY ORGANISATION IN THE HOUSE OF COMMONS

There are three main elements in party organisation in the House of Commons: Whips, party meetings and party committees.

Whips

Since government and opposition are by party, it is vital for parties to remain united, especially in their formal activities such as voting in parliament. It is essential to avoid overt expressions of disagreement by significant numbers, and to minimise and counteract those which do occur. Failure to do so may at the least give encouragement to the rival party and at worst, for a Government, may jeopardise the passing of legislation and, for an Opposition, destroy any chance to embarrass or defeat a government. The worst eventuality is that a party will split and, as often happens, suffer electoral defeat – as Labour did in 1983 after splitting in 1981.

MPs are subject to three influences conducive to party loyalty before any formal mechanisms might begin to operate. These are, first, their natural sympathy for the causes and purposes their party represents; second, their desire (especially if they are ambitious) not to alienate the leadership; and, third, their concern to keep on good terms with their local parties which tend to dislike rebellions against party policy. MPs, then, vote with their parties for many reasons, other than the formal power of the Whips.

Whips nonetheless play a key part in the management of the parties in parliament. The Whips' main task is administrative: to keep their own MPs informed by producing and sending to them the documentary Whip. This is a weekly outline of parliamentary business which indicates the degree of importance attached by the party to the various items. Very important items are underlined three times, less important ones twice and minor ones only once. A member's attendance for items underlined three times is essential and defiance of a three-line Whip is a serious breach of political conduct. The written Whip also informs members of the forthcoming business of Standing, Select, party and other committees. If an MP wishes to be absent for a vote, he needs to find a member of the opposing party who also wishes to stay away. This arrangement is known as 'pairing' and requires the consent of the Chief Whips.

Whips also play a central role in the communication of views within parties, between the leadership and the backbenchers, and vice versa. It is the Whips who advise leaders on what the party will or will not stand; who offer ideas to leaders on how to head off backbench rebellion; and who indicate to disaffected backbenchers the likely consequences of their actions. Whips are persuaders rather than disciplinarians. Withdrawal of the party Whip from an MP – a matter for decision by the Chief Whip and Leader in the Conservative Party and by the PLP as a whole in the Labour Party – almost never happens. It may be an effective threat against one or two individuals but hardly constitutes a realistic possibility against twenty or thirty. The powers of the Whips are modest: they can deploy cajolery, threats and rebukes (the latter with caution since they must avoid causing offence) but most of the time they must simply try to persuade and, if they fail, just resign themselves to their failure. In the words of one former Chief Whip, in response to a question about what he did when someone voted against the party line: 'Well, first of all I get upset and then after that I have to live with it' (Bob Mellish, Labour Chief Whip in the 1960s). In the Conservative Party the Chief Whip is appointed by the Leader and in the Labour Party by the PLP.

Party meetings

The Conservative Party meets weekly as a body in the 1922 Committee. The Leader attends when the party is in Government although Ministers do not. The Leader does not attend when the party is in Opposition. No votes are taken at its meetings. When in opposition, the Labour Party meets as the PLP (Parliamentary Labour Party). When in government, the PLP elects a Liaison Committee consisting of Ministers and backbenchers (in a majority) to maintain contacts between the Cabinet and party backbenchers. The minor parties also meet weekly and, tiny as some of them are, appoint Whips.

Party committees

Each major party in opposition forms a Shadow Cabinet. In the Conservative Party, it is chosen by the Leader and usually referred to as the Consultative Committee. In the Labour Party, the Shadow Cabinet consists of the Parliamentary Committee (fifteen) together with several *ex officio* members – the Leader and his deputy, the elected chairman of the backbench MPs, the leader of the party in the House of Lords, the Chief Whip in the Lords and an elected representative of backbench peers. In addition, the Labour Leader appoints assistants to each Shadow Minister – a series of Shadow teams, in fact.

Each major party also forms a large number of specialist committees. In 1980, the Conservatives had twenty-four specialist committees and seven 'area' committees (where MPs from particular regions meet). When the party is in opposition, Conservative committees are chaired by the appropriate Shadow Minister; when it is in government, the committees elect their own chairpersons and Ministers are automatically excluded. In 1976, when it was in government, the Labour Party had nineteen subject groups (reduced to that figure from thirty-five on the recommendation of an internal party report in that year). As in the Conservative Party, Shadow Ministers chair the committees when the party is in opposition and backbenchers chair them when it is in government. Labour committees can make policy proposals which are referred to meetings of the PLP.

Consideration of party organisation in the House of Commons suggests two main conclusions: first, the extent to which already existing party loyalties are reinforced by party activities within the House, especially those of the Whips but also those of party meetings and committees as parties strive to govern or prepare themselves for government; and second, the considerable amount of important activity which takes place away from the floor of the House in backstage party gatherings.

RECENT CHANGES IN HOUSE OF COMMONS BEHAVIOUR

The Government controls parliament but cannot always rely on getting its way. In the sections which follow, this point is explained first with reference to the behaviour and structure of the House of Commons and then with reference to the House of Lords. We start with the mechanisms of governmental control before considering the ways in which the will of governments can be flouted.

Government control of the House of Commons rests on four main factors: its possession in normal circumstances of a majority, allied with the habit of loyal voting by its own supporters (in the next chapter Table 11.1, shows the size of Government majorities since 1945); its power to determine the parliamentary timetable; its ability to curtail debate; and its control over the drafting of legislation. Thus, first, two-thirds of elections since the war have produced governments with majorities ranging from the adequate (17) to the massive (over 100) and we have already looked at the forces constraining those majorities to vote cohesively. Second, it is true that parliamentary time is allocated to the Opposition which can initiate debate on 19 days per session and can also choose the subjects for debate in the reply to the Address from the Throne and on recess adjournment days and short evening adjournments. Also, about 22 days per session are given to private members' bills and motions. Nonetheless, government business occupies parliament for the bulk of time in each session. Third, three devices mainly enable the Government to restrict debate: the closure, selection of amendments, and the guillotine, this last-named weapon being used very sparingly each session. Finally, most Government legislation reaches the House of Commons in largely predetermined form on topics which, even if already aired in White Papers, have been rarely discussed in detail by the Commons. Many commentators would add that, in any case, MPs lack the resources to discuss government measures in a properly informed way. Although MPs now receive an allowance for secretarial assistance, in 1981 only three-fifths employed a full-time secretary, the remainder relying on part-timers. In addition, of those employing research assistants, about two-fifths employed part-time, a mere one-twentieth, full-time researchers.

The result of these factors is that it is virtually impossible in normal circumstances to bring a government down and, in practice, very difficult to engineer any defeat in the House of Commons. Of course, an Opposition can make life awkward for a Government in a number of ways, which include harassment of Ministers in debates and at Question Time and, principally, frequent use of delaying tactics. The Opposition can delay the passage of Government measures by putting down motions of censure (a tactic employed relatively infrequently – perhaps once or twice a session), by stalling ploys at the committee stage of bills and by calls for frequent divisions at the second and third reading stages. The maximum period for which any bill can be delayed is thirteen months. The Opposition can employ the tactics of delay or the threat of delay on politically uncontentious measures as well as on those to which it has serious objections on policy or principle, the aim being to force concessions on the last-named issues by disrupting the legislative timetable as a whole.

In fact, notwithstanding its adversarial context, much Government business is conducted by mutual agreement between Government and Opposition and the question of Opposition obstruction does not arise. This is first because much Government legislation *is* uncontentious, a fact which the Opposition acknowledges by not requesting a division. According to a calculation by Richard Rose, 78 per cent of government bills between 1970 and 1979 went through without a significant division against the Government (R. Rose, *Do Parties Make a Difference?*, 1984, p. 79). Second, the Opposition may have its own reasons for not pressing resistance too far. For example, in addition to recognising the difficulties of governing, it wants to avoid opposing popular legislation, being stigmatised as merely fractious and provoking similar treatment when the roles of Opposition and Government are reversed.

In practice, Governments may be defeated by a combination of their own backbenchers with MPs from the smaller parties and the Official Opposition. Between 1945 and 1970, no government was defeated in the House of Commons as a result of the dissenting votes of its own backbenchers. After 1970, however, the situation changed and cross-voting increased. In *Parliament in the 1980s* (1985) Philip Norton has described this increase in backbench rebelliousness (pp. 23–31). The Conservative Government of Edward Heath (1970–4; majority 30) was defeated six times, three of these defeats being on three-line whips. During this period, 20 per cent of all divisions in the House of Commons contained cross-votes and abstentions. Government defeats occurred even more frequently in the unusual circumstances prevailing after February 1974. Combinations of opposition parties were all that was required to defeat the minority Labour Government of February–October 1974 and such combinations brought about its defeat on seventeen occasions. The Labour Government of October 1974–June 1979 began with a tiny majority (3) but this had disappeared by April 1976; twenty-three of its forty-two defeats occurred as a result of its own backbenchers voting with the Opposition, whilst the other nineteen defeats were brought about by combinations of opposition parties. The Labour Government eventually surrendered office after its defeat on a Conservative 'no confidence' motion in late March 1979.

Between 1979 and 1983, backbench dissent continued, with ten or more Conservative backbenchers voting against the Government or abstaining on sixteen occasions and over forty doing so on four occasions. Even though this cross-voting on the floor of the House of Commons brought about the defeat of the Government only once (in December, 1982, on the immigration rules), the *threat* of cross-voting by its own backbenchers persuaded the Government to retreat on at least seven occasions; proposals withdrawn included charges for eye tests, reductions in the external services of the BBC and 'hotel' charges for patients in NHS hospitals. The Government was also forced to modify its policy on MPs' pay and student grants. During Mrs Thatcher's Second Administration (1983–1987), dissenting Conservative backbenchers were initially unable to defeat a Government which had a much larger majority (144) but the *threat* of rebellion forced the Government into concessions on such matters as a Rates Bill, housing benefits, the European Community milk production regulations, the Police and Criminal Evidence Bill and the rate support grant. On earlier occasions, the threat of defeat by their own backbenchers had forced the Labour Government of 1966–70 to withdraw its proposals for industrial relations legislation and House of Lords reform.

In April 1986 a combination of large numbers of dissident Conservative backbenchers with backbenchers from the opposition parties together with large-scale abstentions brought about the most significant Government defeat in seven years of Conservative rule on proposals to liberalise the Sunday shopping law. Table 10.5 reveals how this remarkable result was achieved. No single factor was decisive but it is worth pointing out:

1. the general cohesion of the anti-vote by the opposition parties – only three MPs (all Alliance) voted for the bill;
2. the scale of the Conservative backbench rebellion (72), with more than one in four of the rank-and-file defying the three-line whip;

TABLE 10.5
The defeat of the Conservative Government on the second reading of the Shops Bill, 1986

	For	Against	Did not vote	Total
Conservative	281	72	38	391
Labour	nil	188	20	208
Alliance	3	20	2	25
Nationalists	nil	4	nil	4
Others	nil	14	3	17
Total	284	298	63	645
	(plus Speaker and three deputies; 1 seat vacant – Ryedale)			649

Source: *The Guardian*, 16 April 1986

3. the fact that opposition abstentions (25) were more than offset by Conservative abstentions (38);
4. the impact of the return to Westminster of Ulster MPs ('others' in the Table) who had been boycotting the House after the Anglo-Irish agreement of 1985.

MPs' greater willingness to cross-vote after 1970, however, should not be exaggerated, either in itself – as reduced 'deference' to Whips and leaderships – or for its consequences – Government concessions. Statistics relating to the increased proportion of divisions in which cross-voting occurred also indicate that over three-quarters of Government legislation went through without dissent even in the more volatile parliamentary circumstances prevalent after 1970. Percentages of divisions with cross-voting are as follows:

	%
1970–4	20
1974	23
1974–9	28
1979–83	1
June 1983–July 1984	25

By contrast, cross-voting divisions rose above 10 per cent only once in the period 1945–70; this was in 1959–64, when it reached 13.5 per cent.

Contemporary trends in Commons voting behaviour can now be summarised. The Government controls Parliament, but needs to exercise more vigilance to get its way and can do so rather less than it could twenty years ago.

Finally, this section on behavioural change also needs to mention the greater impact of private members' legislation in recent times. In the 1960s private member legislation liberalised the law on capital punishment, homosexuality, divorce and abortion, and in the 1980s private members' bills have outlawed video 'nasties', compelled front-seat passengers to wear seat belts, and restricted advertising on cigarettes.

RECENT STRUCTURAL CHANGES IN THE HOUSE OF COMMONS

In this regard, the House of Commons has changed since the 1960s in its greater and more effective use of Select Committees and of specialised Standing Committees and in a number of procedural reforms. Parliamentary reformers since the 1960s had advocated the greater use of *Select Committees* to improve scrutiny of the executive and their case was reaffirmed in 1978 by the Select Committee on Procedure, which recommended the establishment of a wider range of Committees with enhanced powers. These proposals were implemented by Norman St John Stevas as Leader of the House in 1979. Some existing Select Committees (on the Nationalised Industries, Race Relations, Science and Technology, Overseas Development and Estimates) were abolished and others retained – Public Accounts, Statutory Instruments, European Legislation and the Parliamentary Commissioner. The new departure was the introduction of fourteen new Select Committees covering Agriculture, Defence, Education, Employment, Energy, the Environment, Foreign Affairs, Home Affairs, Industry and Trade, Social Services, Transport, Treasury and Civil Service, Welsh Affairs and Scottish Affairs (the latter could not be staffed by the government and was discontinued in 1988). The new committees are popular with MPs and have certainly been very active: in the 1979–83 parliament, they held 2140 meetings, took evidence from 1312 officials and 161 Ministers and issued 193 reports. But opinion is divided about their value. Supporters point to their wider coverage and more thorough scrutiny than the system they replaced; the way they have increased the accountability of government by requiring civil servants to defend their activities; and the notable contribution to the political education of the public made by their informative reports. Critics allege that they distract attention from the floor of the House; that they have insufficient powers – they cannot, for example, compel governments to attend to their recommendations and consequently their proposals are ignored by Departments; and that their effectiveness depends to a large extent on the willingness of members to subordinate the claims of party to an objective appraisal of the evidence, which may be neither possible nor even desirable in a partisan assembly such as the House of Commons.

The *Standing Committees* of the House of Commons were often criticised as ineffectual instruments for the scrutiny of government bills in the 1960s. This was largely a consequence of the fact that their composition reflects party representation in the Commons as a whole. After the 1987 General Election, for example, each Committee had a built-in Conservative majority of 6–8 MPs, reflecting the Government's overall majority of 101. Not surprisingly in the circumstances, Standing Committees nearly always approved Ministerial amendments whilst failing to get other amendments accepted. J. A. G. Griffith's research revealed that in three sample sessions between 1967 and 1971 under 5 per cent of Opposition amendments and only 10 per cent of amendments by government backbenchers at the committee and report stages of bills were successful. Present practice constitutes only a small improvement on this situation. In order to improve committee scrutiny of legislation, the Procedure Committee in 1978 recommended the establishment of Public Bill Committees, with only the House as a whole able to make exceptions to this procedure. However, although public bill committees or Special Standing Committees were established after 1979, their use (which has occurred only at Minister's request) has been limited, only five bills going before such committees between 1980 and 1984.

Other structural reforms include the establishment of the *House of Commons Commission* (1978). This has given the Commons more control of its own staff and finances and consequently more independence of government in this sphere. Second, there has been the creation of the *National Audit Office* (1983) which has meant that the audit of government Departments hitherto performed by a body dominated by the Treasury (the Exchequer Audit Department) is now done by an independent body which is ultimately accountable to parliament. Third, the role of the *Comptroller and Auditor-General* as an official independent of government has been strengthened. The Comptroller and Auditor-General uses the National Audit Office to examine the 'economy, efficiency and effectiveness' of Government Departments and other bodies; he is responsible to the *Public Accounts Commission* (not to be confused with the Public Accounts Committee), which consists of nine senior MPs and which began life in 1984. Finally, the House's ability to scrutinise public expenditure was improved by the introduction of three *Estimates' Days* (1982) when the House could debate and vote on the *details* of public expenditure. These are now held in addition to the thirty-two days when the whole of public expenditure is considered.

THE HOUSE OF LORDS

The powers of the House of Lords have been considerably reduced in the twentieth century yet it remains a significant if not major check on the House of Commons. It is because the Upper House retains its capacity to damage and delay if not destroy Commons (largely government) legislation that it remains the subject of proposals to reform and even abolish it. This section accordingly deals in turn with the powers, composition and recent behaviour of the Upper House, concluding with a consideration of proposals for its reform.

Powers

By convention, the House of Lords is part of the legislative sovereign – 'the Queen-in-parliament'. Constitutionally, therefore, despite its reduced powers, the Upper House remains an essential part of the legislative process. By the Parliament Act of 1911, the Lords completely lost its power to delay or amend money bills: these go for the Royal Assent one month after leaving the House of Commons, whether approved by the Lords or not. But it retained other powers which included the power to delay non-money bills for up to two successive sessions (reduced to **one** session only by the Parliament Act of 1949). The present powers and functions of the House of Lords may be conveniently summarised as follows:

1. to delay non-money bills for up to one parliamentary session/year;
2. to revise House of Commons legislation, giving Ministers an opportunity for second thoughts and allowing pressure-group points to be considered;
3. to veto (a) bills to prolong the life of parliament, (b) provisional order bills and (c) delegated legislation;
4. to initiate non-controversial legislation (in fact, about one quarter of all Government legislation since 1945 has been introduced in the House of Lords);
5. to exercise certain scrutiny functions on Private Bills, Statutory Instruments and the European Communities;
6. to carry out a judicial role, hearing appeals in the Appellate Committee and in the Judicial Committee of the Privy Council;
7. to conduct a deliberative role by holding debates on contemporary issues.

Composition

Membership of the Upper House is determined by birth, creation (by the Crown on the advice of the Prime Minister) or position. Most of its approximately 1200 members have been created in the twentieth century. About 800 are hereditary peers, 330 are life peers, and there are two archbishops and nineteen Law Lords (including the Lord Chancellor). Its composition has been affected by the Life Peerages Act 1958, which empowered the Crown to create life peers and peeresses and the Peerages Act 1963, which allowed hereditary peers to disclaim their titles and admitted hereditary peeresses into the House of Lords in their own right. About one-third of members of the Upper House attend rarely or not at all. Average daily attendance is low – about 302 in the 1983/4 session. But attendance in recent years has improved considerably compared with the immediate post-war period, average daily attendance being a mere 86 in 1950–1 and still only 142 in 1960–1.

Precise figures on political allegiance are difficult to calculate. According to the Information Office of the House of Lords, it was as follows in April 1984: Conservatives 418, Labour 136, Liberal 41, SDP 41, Cross-benchers 219. Unlike the position in the House of Commons, no overall Conservative majority exists in the Lords and there are very significant numbers of independents (cross-benchers). Nor are party loyalties as influential on voting habits in the Upper as in the Lower House. These three factors when combined with the low and irregular nature of attendance make for considerable uncertainty about the outcome of the vote on any particular issue in the House of Lords.

Recent behaviour

How does the Lords interpret its functions in relation to the House of Commons? The Lords accepts certain limitations on its own action. It rarely for example, uses its powers to press an amendment or delay a measure when it understands that what it proposes to do lacks the support of the Commons. But within these limits the Lords is able to amend legislation against the Government's wishes and, in recent times, has shown an increasing tendency to make life awkward for Governments. Philip Norton has described the difficulties faced by Governments in the Upper House. Between 1970 and 1974, there were 25 Government defeats in the House of Lords; in 1974, 15; between 1974 and 1979, 347 (this very large number of defeats is an indication of the hostility of a Conservative-dominated Upper House to a Labour Government); between 1979 and 1983, 45; and in 1983–4, 19 (Norton, *Parliament in the 1980s*, p. 14). The continuation into the 1980s of the rebelliousness shown towards Labour Governments in the 1970s has produced some significant changes in government legislation. Thus in the period 1979–85, the Upper House defeated a proposal to allow local authorities to impose charges for school transport, rejected a clause in a Housing Bill which would have enabled the sale of council houses built for old people, forced the government to pledge to introduce legislation to regulate telephone tapping, carried an amendment to the Police and Criminal Evidence Bill allowing only police officers in uniform to stop and search suspects and, in the Trade Union Bill, passed an amendment requiring trade union executives to be elected by postal ballot. The Lords regards itself as having a particular responsibility to uphold the Constitution. This concern was demonstrated in 1969 when it insisted on amendments to the House of Commons (Redistribution of Seats) no. 2 Bill which had been designed to eliminate the need for the Home Secretary to lay reports of the Boundary

Commissioners before parliament; the bill was lost. Perhaps the most important recent example of this concern, however, and, in addition, the most momentous defeat imposed by the Lords on the Conservative Governments of Mrs Thatcher up to that time, occurred in 1984 over the Government's plan to cancel elections for the GLC and the metropolitan counties, in preparation for the abolition of those authorities in 1985. The Lords disliked this proposal on several grounds:

1. it preceded the presentation of the abolition legislation to parliament, let alone its passing;
2. it replaced elected councillors by non-elected nominees from the second-tier borough councils;
3. it had the whiff of political trickery because its effect would be to replace Labour-elected representatives by Conservative appointees.

There are several reasons for the recent rebelliousness. First, the Upper House emerged unscathed from Labour's attempt to reform it in 1969. The failure of the Parliament (no. 2) Bill, which would have reduced the delaying power to six months and eliminated the voting rights of the hereditary peers, undoubtedly boosted the morale of the Lords by prompting the realisation that it had a valuable role to fulfil after all. Second, the advent of life-peers after 1958 has brought a broader range of experience into the House with peers drawn from a variety of occupations including business, journalism, education, the media, the trade unions and, especially, politics itself. The Upper House has gained considerably in authority as a consequence, with most debates attracting numerous expert contributions. Third, unlike the Commons, the Lords has accepted the TV cameras (in 1983) and the televising of debates has increased public interest in its proceedings and enhanced its prestige. The final reason relates to the political situation after the 1983 and 1987 General Elections when the size of the Government majorities (144 and 101 respectively) made it virtually secure against defeat in the House of Commons and encouraged the Lords to take an oppositional role upon itself to a greater extent. This disposition to resist the Government was further reinforced by the consideration that, even if the Upper House is not noticeably more accurately reflective of public opinion than the Lower House, at least in the Lords the Conservatives lack an overall majority, as they do both amongst voters and the electorate as a whole. Nor was the Alliance quite so badly under-represented as it was in the House of Commons (see Table 10.6). The ideological distrust of Thatcherism felt by traditional Tory peers together with the growing assertiveness of cross-benchers also contributed to this trend.

Three main attitudes may be discerned towards the House of Lords. These are:

1. Retain it with its present composition and powers.

TABLE 10.6
Party support in Lords and Commons and at 1983 General Election (%)

Party	Lords	Commons	Voters	Electorate
Conservative	48.9	61.6	42.4	30.8
Labour	15.9	32.2	27.6	20.1
Alliance	9.6	3.6	25.4	18.5
Other	25.6	3.2	4.6	3.3

Source: Peter G. Richards, 'The House of Lords: Recent Developments'. *Teaching Politics*, 14, 2, May 1985, p. 182.

2. Reform its composition whilst leaving it with broadly similar or slightly reduced powers.
3. Abolish it.

Conservatives in the 1980s have held a range of attitudes. Traditional and right-wing Conservatives wish to retain the House as it is at present. Other Conservatives, including Conservative leaders in the Lords, advocated moderate reform of its composition, the better to preserve its remaining constitutional powers against Labour proposals for their virtual or total abolition. The Alliance parties also favoured reform of its composition in order to make the Upper House more democratic whilst retaining its present powers. The Labour Left favoured abolition of the Lords and made the running in the late 1970s and early 1980s. The 1983 Labour Party manifesto promised to abolish the House of Lords, but not immediately; it would move straightaway to eliminate the Upper House's powers of delay and legislative veto, but its power to delay measures prolonging the life of a parliament would remain for the time being. None of these attitudes was able to gain the upper hand either among politicians or the general public. In the 1987 General Election the Alliance still advocated reform of the Lords, but the proposal to abolish it had disappeared from the Labour manifesto. The House of Lords remains the subject of inconclusive controversy.

The main arguments in favour of a Second Chamber with broadly the powers possessed by the Lords at present are threefold:

1. Its power of amendment and delay of non-financial legislation are a necessary remedy and check upon ill-considered and/or extreme legislation. These powers are given additional point in times when Governments lack overall majorities or have only small majorities.
2. The Lords takes some of the legislative burden from the Commons in that a significant proportion of government legislation (40 per cent between 1974 and 1979) is introduced in the Upper House.

3. The existence of a Second Chamber with a sizeable minority of experienced politicians able to conduct debates of high quality on the issues of the day unfettered by party and constituency pressures is of great value to the nation.

Other arguments include the usefulness of the House of Lords to the Prime Minister – to recruit Ministers or to 'reward' politicians who are no longer of use; the importance of the judicial functions of the Upper House; and the value of the hereditary principle itself.

Its opponents contend that a body based largely on a mixture of heredity and political appointments has no place in a democratic society. Some maintain further that an amending Second Chamber is unnecessary because it hinders the voice of the majority. But most critics wish to reform it, rather than abolish it.

However, an important stumbling-block to reform has been failure to agree on the composition and method of creation of a reformed institution. Recent proposals have included recommendations for a wholly elected body, and for one based one-third on appointment (by the Crown on the advice of the Prime Minister) and two-thirds on election (recommended by the Conservative Lawyers' Constitutional Reform Committee and Home Committee respectively, both 1978). Both these Conservative groups suggested election by proportional representation in large territorial constituencies. Other reformers would replace the existing body by representatives nominated by major economic interests such as business and the trade unions, a form of functional representation (this idea was put forward by a group of Conservative MPs in 1981 and by the Labour MP, John Mackintosh, in 1974). Others have advocated an Upper House composed of representing indirectly elected by regional assemblies (e.g. David Owen, SDP leader, in 1981). There are objections to all these alternatives. Appointment by Prime Ministerial patronage seems no more satisfactory than inheritance as the basis for membership. Election on the same basis as the House of Commons (simple majority) would merely duplicate the Lower House whilst election by a distinctive method (proportional representation) would run the risk of creating an over-powerful rival. Functional representation could increase the authority of sectional groupings which many consider to be adequately represented already, whilst regional representation might exacerbate regional rivalries without assuaging regional dissatisfaction (quite apart from the fact that regional assemblies do not at present exist and would therefore have to be created). Public opinion also is divided on the issue. In an NOP poll taken in November 1980, a mere 16 per cent favoured abolition of the Lords; a majority supported its retention; and just over one-third were sympathetic to reform. So, for all its apparent anomalies, the House of Lords stays, still performing useful functions to the general satisfaction of a majority and recently showing the capacity to evolve in perhaps surprising directions.

RETROSPECT AND PROSPECT

Both how we view developments within parliament over the 1970s and 1980s and how we evaluate prospects for the future are to a large extent shaped by the model of parliament we adopt. Here there are two models which recur continually in discussion: the *revived independent powerhouse* and the *Westminster model*. The former holds that parliament has been, retains the potential to be and may be in the process of becoming again a policy-making body in its own right. In the mid-nineteenth century, it is argued, parliament brought down governments, forced Ministerial resignations and initiated legislation. Although these capacities were seriously weakened before 1900 as a consequence of the emergence of the disciplined party system, the idea of a parliament substantially independent of the executive survived in the legal–constitutional concept of parliamentary sovereignty (the idea that the monarch-in-parliament makes law which the courts interpret). In this model, parliament possesses a strong corporate identity, a sense of its collective unity as a whole enabling it to rise above political divisions. According to the *Westminster model*, during the second half of the nineteenth century, parliament became subordinate to the government, and has remained so. Party discipline ensures that even in time of narrow majorities the bulk of government legislation goes through parliament as intended. Parliament's main function, therefore, has become to serve as a forum for Opposition criticism of government and for the party debate. Because it is so fractured by party divisions, parliament's sense of collective identity and purpose has been lost.

Since the 1960s Parliamentary reformers have maintained that parliament had become too subservient to the Government and have sought to increase its independence. They accepted the Westminster model as a broadly accurate depiction of political reality and the independent powerhouse as a desirable if never completely attainable ideal. The reforms they advocated had had a modest yet significant effect by the late-1980s. Behavioural changes such as the increased propensity of MPs to vote against the 'party line' and structural reforms like the introduction of a wide range of Select Committees strengthened the House of Commons in relation to the Government. The modest revival in the position of the House of Lords further contributed to this process in boosting the influence of parliament as a whole. Considerable weaknesses admittedly remained in parliament's powers of scrutiny: the Government could not be forced to attend to the reports of the Select Committees; moreover, such Committees could only request but not compel Ministers to attend. In addition, the procedure for scrutiny of government expenditure was still seriously inadequate, with the Public Accounts Committee able to examine only 60 per cent of Government finance and Commons scrutiny of the details of spending plans being insufficiently thorough. Also, no attempt had been made to improve procedure for the scrutiny of delegated legislation. However, despite these limitations, structural reforms and behavioural changes amongst MPs have extended the range of the House of Commons's activity, strengthened its position relative to the Departments and deepened the quality of debates. To reformers, therefore, it is both feasible and desirable to continue to work for changes on these lines in the future. The prospect of a general election producing a 'hung parliament' in which no party holds an overall majority further enhances the possibility of transforming parliamentary subordination into greater independence of the executive.

Sceptics argue that reformers exaggerate both the extent of change that has taken place and the desirability of such change. Despite the occasional defeat, the Government still gets by far the greater part of its legislation through in the form it wants. On the whole, moreover, it is right that it should. To call for an extension of the power of parliament is to advocate the defeat of policies on which governments have been elected, by shifting and ideologically incoherent coalitions of opposition and government backbenchers. The reformers' goal, if achieved, would work against the grain of the political system whose central principle is the production of a majority government secure enough to govern effectively by virtue of reliable party support. The present preferences of backbenchers reflect the distribution of power not in the ideal world of the reformers but in the real world of the Westminster model: most MPs would rather be Parliamentary Secretary to a Minister than the chairman of a Select Committee. The reforms have not been taken further because it is not in governments' interest to take them further. In the final analysis, only electoral reform could accomplish the shift of power towards parliament which reformers want.

SUMMARY

The Government of the day controls parliament through the exercise of its party majority but parliament remains important as a representative, legislative and scrutinising body, as a focus for political Opposition, as a forum for debate and as a training-ground for aspiring politicians. Over the past twenty years, for a variety of reasons, backbench independence has increased in the House of Commons and Government defeats have occurred more frequently although remaining relatively rare. The capacity of the House of Commons to scrutinise the activities of government has improved but important weaknesses still exist especially in relation to control of public expenditure; in general, the 'power of parliament' continues to fall short of the hopes of parliamentary reformers. The House of Lords retains its constitutional importance as primarily, but by no means exclusively, a checking and revising chamber. Gaining strength from modest reform of its composition (1958), from the failure of more drastic reform (especially 1969), and from various other developments, and adopting a

calculatedly self-imposed limitation on its own powers, the Upper House has inflicted some significant defeats on governments since 1970. Its predominantly hereditary composition makes it the subject of continuing political controversy. Political commentators' views on the current, possible and likely future role of parliament are shaped by the models they adopt, whether *revived independent powerhouse* or *Westminster*.

FURTHER READING

Critchley, Julian (1985) *Westminster Blues*, London, Elm Tree Books, Hamish Hamilton.
Drewry, Gavin (ed.) (1985) *The New Select Committees*, Oxford, University Press.
Englefield, D. (ed.) (1984) *Commons Select Committees*, London, Longman.
Forman, F. N. (1985) *Mastering British Politics*, London, Macmillan.
Jones, Bill and Kavanagh, Dennis (1983) *British Politics Today*, Manchester, University Press.
Mitchell, Austin (1982) *Westminster Man*, London, Methuen.
Norton, P. (ed.) (1985) *Parliament in the 1980s*, Oxford, Basil Blackwell.
Norton, P. (1986) 'Independence, Scrutiny and Rationalisation: A Decade of Changes in the House of Commons', *Teaching Politics*, 15, 1, January.

QUESTIONS

1. How far and by what means have backbenchers improved their control over the activities of Government in recent years?
2. Discuss the main arguments for and against reform of the House of Lords.

ASSIGNMENT

Examine some recent reports by Select Committees of the House of Commons. What are their leading conclusions and recommendations and how influential have they been?

11

Political Parties

Parties have already been encountered at several points in this book. In Chapter 4 we saw that democratic government was basically party government and in Chapter 5 it was noted that, although unknown to the British Constitution, these voluntary organisations were in fact essential to its working. In Chapter 6, we examined the role of party in government and, in Chapter 10, the functions and organisation of the parties in parliament, with special reference to their tasks in opposition. Chapter 12 will consider the role of parties in the electoral system and how they organise for general elections. This chapter focuses on the parties themselves, dealing with such important matters as their internal organisation, their financing and membership as well as recent trends in their support and some major interpretations of the changing party system. Before launching into these themes, however, we briefly summarise the major functions of party in the British political system. These are: first, to provide government and opposition; second, to serve as agencies of representation; and third, alongside other methods such as pressure groups, to enable popular participation in politics to take place.

THE FUNCTIONS OF PARTY IN BRITAIN

Government and opposition

Parties form governments – all parties do not have an equal chance of forming a government, but government is always by *some* party. It is true that party leaders when Prime Minister are expected to put the national interest before the interests of party (although they do so to varying degrees) and it is also the case that, for a number of reasons, the governing party does not always carry out its full programme. But government in the UK is still *party* government. Parties recruit the politicians by their selection of parliamentary candidates, develop the programmes expressed in manifestos on which government policy is based and run the major offices of State (approximately one-third of the party which wins an election may expect government posts).

Opposition, as we have seen, is also by party. The party with the second highest number of seats forms both the official opposition and the alternative government. All the non-governing parties in parliament, however, may collectively be said to be in opposition.

Representation

Parties are the single most important agency of political representation. They organise a mass electorate by enabling it to make meaningful choices. (The criticism that the degree of choice they offer has been exaggerated and could be increased is dealt with below, pp. 232–37.) Parties in the UK enable voters to elect governments by grouping parliamentary candidates together in a coherent way so that votes in one constituency can be related to votes in another: voters in other words vote for a party first and foremost, and for a particular candidate hardly at all. The elector has probably never heard of most if not all of the candidates on the ballot paper, but he has heard of the Conservative and Labour parties, the Social and Liberal Democrats, the SDP, the nationalist parties, the Communist party and the National Front. In voting, electors are (largely) expressing an opinion on which party they consider would form the most effective government and which party leader would make the most capable Prime Minister. (The qualification 'largely' is necessary because voters for most minor parties may not *primarily* be expressing a governmental but rather an ideological preference.) Parties are important instruments of communication between governments and governed. Parties shape the political ideas of other groups and individuals to their purposes and bring them into government. Conversely, through their conferences, their canvassing of voters at election time and in the meetings of MPs with party 'activists' and with constituents, parties use their machinery to take the concerns of government to their supporters and to the electorate at large.

Participation

Parties are the principal agencies of political participation. Participation can range from the fairly minimal – voting in elections – to the maximal – joining a party and working for it by canvassing, attending meetings and conferences and even eventually representing it in parliament and government. Parties enable individuals to assert their distinctive political identities; to register a commitment to what can be an important cause in their lives; ultimately, at the deepest level, to express an ideological preference for one kind of society rather than another. Parties have been losing ground to pressure groups as agencies of participation recently, and participation in elections has been declining. Parties, however, are *comprehensive* agencies; unlike pressure groups, they stand for election, proposing policy packages which enable voters to express their opinions over *a whole range* of issues. Because they offer the opportunity to participate in politics at every level from the highest to the most moderate and because they are the sole agencies of comprehensive choice at elections, parties deserve to be considered the leading agencies of political participation.

THE PARTY SYSTEM IN THE UK

Is UK politics best described as a two-party system, as a multiparty system, or as something between the two? If we think solely in terms of *government*, the answer seems straightforward. Between 1945 and 1987, the two major parties alternated in power: Labour, 1945–51; Conservative, 1951–64; Labour, 1964–70; Conservative, 1970–4; Labour, 1974–9; and after 1979, Conservative again. It became customary in the twenty-five years after the Second World War to think of a two-party system as a permanent feature of Britain's polity. Table 11.1 shows in detail the way in which the two major parties have dominated government since 1945.

But if we extend our historical perspective to cover the period before 1945, the situation is less clear-cut. There have been three phases of coalition government: 1915–22; 1931–2; and 1940–5, prompted respectively by war, economic emergency and by war again. Between 1932 and 1940, a National Government was in power, mainly Conservative but including representatives from two other parties. Moreover, there have been significant periods of minority government when the party in office lacked an overall majority in the House of Commons and was therefore dependent for its continuation in power upon the support of a third party. This was the case between 1910 and

TABLE 11.1

*Two-party government since the Second World War:
parliamentary majorities, 1945–87*

Election	Party returned to office	Size of overall majority
1945	Labour	146
1950	Labour	5
1951	Conservative	17
1955	Conservative	58
1959	Conservative	100
1964	Labour	4
1966	Labour	96
1970	Conservative	30
1974 (Feb.)	Labour	−33
1974 (Oct.)	Labour	3
1979	Conservative	43
1983	Conservative	144
1987	Conservative	101

1914, in 1924 and again between 1929 and 1931. In 1977 Labour lost its overall parliamentary majority and, in order to prevent continual defeats in the House of Commons, made a pact with the Liberal Party. This arrangement fell short of being a formal coalition as the Liberals did not enter the Government. However, it does represent a break, even if temporary (it lasted only until 1979) with the dominant post-war tradition in which two major parties have both taken it in turns to govern and, once in office, have ruled alone without assistance from any third party. In February 1974 also a period of minority government had occurred (see Table 11.1) but on that occasion Labour chose to rule alone before seeking enhanced support from the electorate.

In terms of *government*, then, the British system may still be considered predominantly a two-party system. But the very considerable exceptions to this generalisation before 1945 and the much slighter exceptions to it in recent history reveal the provisional nature of this situation. In other words, the system could change – either by legislation introducing proportional representation or by gradual increases in electoral support for minor parties – towards a multipartyism which would have a real effect upon government. At present, in terms of *electoral* choice, there is a multiparty system. Numerous minor parties coexist alongside the Conservatives and Labour – the Social and Liberal Democrats, the SDP, the Scottish and Welsh Nationalists, the Northern Ireland parties, the parties of the extreme right and extreme left. At the constituency level, the system is to a considerable extent regionalised, with differing patterns of parties confronting electors in each geographical area of the UK. Indeed, the Ulster parties, the Scottish National Party (SNP) and the Welsh Nationalists (Plaid Cymru) exist only in their particular regions. Alongside the other UK parties they serve to increase the range of electoral choice in Scotland and Wales. In Northern Ireland, where the other UK parties do not have a presence, the regional (Ulster) parties constitute the entire choice. But although a vote for these parties or for the parties of the political extremes expresses a political preference, it does not help to choose a government since none of them puts forward enough candidates to have any chance of gaining a UK majority. Nor would contesting more constituencies necessarily bring any electoral rewards: it is hard, for example, to see the SNP picking up many votes in SE England.

The British 'first past the post' electoral system exercises a remorseless 'squeeze' on third parties. The Alliance's reward for its high poll in 1987 was a mere 22 seats compared with Labour's 229 (see further pp. 279–281 below). However, although difficult, it is not impossible for a third party to gain rough parity with the two other main parties in terms of seats as well as of votes. This happened during the first half of the century as Labour rose to the position of alternative governing party while the Liberal party declined. For a time during this process, the three parties were 'neck and neck' and people even spoke and wrote of 'the naturalness' of the three-party system.

The answer to the question with which we began the section may be expressed as follows. Britain still has a two-party system at the Westminster level with one major party alternating with a second major party in government but at the constituency level the picture is much more varied with voters offered a wide range of electoral choice extending well beyond the two main parties to encompass a number of minor parties. Moreover, it is worth stressing that the system is at present in a state of flux and numerous important changes began in the 1970s.

The two major trends since 1970 have been a decline in support for the two major parties and an increase in the followings of the minor parties. In 1951, at the 'peak' of two-party dominance, the Conservative and Labour parties together received 96.8 per cent of the total vote and minor parties a negligible 3.2 per cent. By 1987, the situation was very different. The combined vote of the Conservative and Labour parties was just over 73 per cent of the total vote whereas support for the minor parties had risen dramatically to 26.9 per cent (see Tables 11.2 and 11.3). Over a period of just over one-third of a century, the two major parties lost the support of nearly one-quarter of voters. Until 1987, Labour suffered a much greater loss of support than did the Conservatives. As a glance at Table 11.2 shows, the Conservatives gained just under half the total vote in the three General Elections of the 1950s but were holding the support of only a little over two-fifths of voters in 1987. By contrast, voting support for Labour has declined much more considerably over this period, at first relatively slowly but then with gathering momentum in the 1970s and early 1980s.

TABLE 11.2

The major parties, 1945–87: seats, votes and share of the total vote

General Election	Seats		Votes		Percentage share of total vote	
	Lab.	Con.	Lab.	Con.	Lab.	Con.
1945	393	213	11.9	9.9	47.8	39.8
1950	315	298	13.2	12.5	46.1	43.5
1951	295	321	13.9	13.7	48.8	48.0
1955	277	344	12.4	13.2	46.4	49.7
1959	258	365	12.2	13.7	43.8	49.4
1964	317	304	12.2	12.0	44.1	43.4
1966	363	253	13.0	11.4	47.9	41.9
1970	287	330	12.1	13.1	43.0	46.4
1974 (Feb.)	301	297	11.6	11.8	37.1	37.9
1974 (Oct.)	319	277	11.4	10.4	39.2	35.8
1979	268	339	11.5	13.6	36.9	43.9
1983	209	397	8.4	13.0	27.6	42.4
1987	229	375	10.0	13.7	30.8	42.3

TABLE 11.3

The minor parties, 1945–87: seats, votes and share of the total vote

General Election	Seats	Votes (in millions)	Percentage of total vote
1945	34	3.1	11.8
1950	12	3.0	10.4
1951	9	0.9	5.8
1955	9	1.0	3.9
1959	7	1.7	6.8
1964	9	3.4	12.5
1966	14	2.7	9.7
1970	13	3.0	10.7
1974 Feb.)			
GB	25	7.1	22.7
NI	12	0.7	2.3
1974 (Oct.)			
GB	27	6.5	22.6
NI	12	0.7	2.4
1979			
GB	15	5.2	16.9
NI	12	0.6	2.2
1983			
GB	27	8.4	27.5
NI	17	0.7	2.5
1987			
GB	28	8.0	24.8
NI	17	0.7	2.3

Note: Before 1974 Ulster Unionists were affiliated to the Conservative Party but they broke this link in that year. From 1974, their results (together with those of smaller Ulster groupings) appear separately from the other British minor parties.

The main landmark in the break-up of major party dominance was the General Election of February 1974 when minor parties tripled their parliamentary representation and more than doubled their share of the vote (see Table 11.3). The leading elements in this change were the rapid increases in electoral support for the Liberals and the SNP and the rather more modest increase in the following of the Welsh Nationalists. Although there was some falling-off in 1979, the upward trend was resumed in 1983, gaining added momentum from the formation of the SDP and the establishment of the Liberal–SDP Alliance. A slight but very disappointing decrease in the Alliance vote and share of the vote occurred in 1987. This largely accounted for the 'dip' in minor party support.

Before considering the character of the parties in some detail, it is worth examining the degree of actual choice they offer voters at elections. This can best be done by comparing their manifestos in the 1987 General Election, an exercise which has the additional advantage of bringing out their differing ethoses. We focus on the three main political groupings, all of which had a nation-wide presence in 1987.

The Conservatives and Labour were sharply opposed on all the main policy areas – the economy, defence and welfare policy. The Alliance was somewhere in between, closer to Labour (whilst still significantly different) on economic and social policy, nearer to the Conservatives (although also in vital respects dissimilar) on defence. On the *economy*, party priorities differed, with the Conservatives stressing the eradication of inflation and more tax cuts and Labour and the Alliance emphasising the reduction of unemployment. On *inflation*, the Conservatives set a *nil* rate as their target; Labour's manifesto referred only to 'containing' it. The Conservatives clearly intended to seek to achieve their aim by continued curbs on public spending; Labour and the Alliance both preferred more consensual ways of controlling it. Labour placed its hopes on a national economic assessment which would identify the action to be taken by government, employers and trade unions to increase investment as well as contain inflation. The Alliance put its faith in a voluntary incomes policy backed by a reserve counter-inflation tax on companies. On *taxation*, the Conservatives promised further cuts (with a 25 per cent basic rate the eventual target) plus reform of the system: Labour intended to reverse tax cuts for the top 5 per cent and introduce a wealth tax on the richest 1 per cent. On *jobs*, the Conservatives promised to continue the assault on the 'intractable problem' of unemployment; to that end, they intended to expand the Community Programme, Job Clubs and Restart and to guarantee a Youth Training Scheme to every jobless school-leaver under 18. By contrast, Labour and the Alliance were both committed to tackling unemployment by large-scale public investment. Labour promised a £6 bn recovery programme, the Alliance, £1½ bn of capital investment. Both aimed to reduce unemployment swiftly by a considerable amount: Labour by 1 million over two years, the Alliance by 1 million over three years.

The two parties proposed getting unemployment down by a similar method: large-scale State intervention. To a significant extent, their detailed proposals were similar: institutional innovation at the top (a new Ministry of Science and Technology – Labour; a new Cabinet industrial policy commit- tee – the Alliance); increased investment in health and education, a reduction of employers' National Insurance contributions, early retirement for the over-60s, the encouragement of science and technology. Predictably, there were also differences: Labour promised capital repatriation, an industrial investment bank, regional development agencies and the encouragement of cooperatives; the Alliance proposed industrial investment bonds together with incentives to employers to encourage them to take on more workers.

Party policies also differed on *the balance between the public and the private sectors*. It was the Conservatives intention to sell off more public enterprises (with water and electricity specifically earmarked for privatisation) and to continue its programme of extending share ownership and increasing competition. The Alliance also promised to extend share-owning and privatisation; but it was more modest in its privatisation plans than the Conservatives, mentioning British Steel as a possibility if the industry's success were maintained. By contrast, Labour would extend 'social ownership', setting up British Enterprise to take a socially-owned stake in high-tech industries and other concerns, using the existing 49 per cent government stake in British Telecom to ensure 'proper influence' and converting private shares in British Telecom and British Gas into special new securities to be bought and sold in the market in the usual way.

The Conservatives' *trade union policy* stressed protection and improvement of the rights of members. They proposed to introduce a trade union ombudsman to help individuals to enforce their rights and there would also be measures enabling members to insist on a secret new ballot before a strike and safeguarding individuals who refused to join a strike against disciplinary action. They aimed to introduce postal ballots to elect union executives at least once every five years, to protect non-union employees against unfair dismissal and to abolish legal immunity for strikes in support of a closed shop. Both Labour and the Alliance promised to restore union recognition at GCHQ. But in other respects the Alliance was closer to the Conservatives: it advocated an extension of postal ballots and internal elections, was opposed to pre-entry closed shops and proposed independent arbitration before industrial action. Labour also favoured secret ballots on strikes and the election of union executives. The party's call for protection against unfair dismissal was for all workers, however, not just non-union employees and, in addition, it intended to extend employment protection to cover part-timers. It would legislate to protect trade union rights.

The parties' differences on *defence* were profound. The Conservative Party remained totally committed to a nuclear defence policy for Britain. It would go ahead with the plan to replace Polaris with Trident as the UK nuclear deterrent and would keep American nuclear missiles and bases subject to Superpower arms talks. It would maintain support for NATO and continue to increase the effectiveness of Britain's conventional forces. The climate of Superpower *détente* was reflected in the Conservatives' stated intention to strive for balanced, verifiable agreements to eliminate medium-range nuclear weapons, constrain shorter-range missiles, cut strategic nuclear missiles by half and ban chemical warfare world-wide. In complete contrast, Labour advocated a non-nuclear defence policy. It aimed to de-commission Polaris, cancel Trident and request the USA to remove its nuclear weapons from British soil. It would balance its policy of de-nuclearisation by improving conventional forces. The party remained committed to continuing membership of NATO. Like the Conservatives, the Alliance believed in a nuclear defence policy for Britain, but, unlike them, it preferred to rely upon a modernised Polaris and would cancel Trident. It would continue to accept American nuclear weapons and bases in Britain but on condition of a dual key (British veto) over US Cruise missiles. It would end cooperation with the American 'star wars' programme. The Alliance strongly supported multi-lateral disarmament and would maintain a minimum British nuclear deterrent until it could be negotiated away as part of a global arms deal. It promised to start negotiations for a nuclear test-ban treaty and a nuclear-free zone in central Europe.

In the wake of the Chernobyl disaster and in the light of the growing importance of environmental protection, the civil uses of nuclear power was an issue dividing the parties. Whereas the Conservatives intended to build the Sizewell nuclear power station, both Labour and the Alliance stated that they would not proceed with it. The Conservatives were committed to the deep disposal of nuclear waste; the Alliance proposed to store it on site while disposal research continued. Both Labour and the Alliance aimed to establish a Department of Environmental Protection, with Labour in addition committing itself to an environmental protection service; Conservatives simply promised an anti-pollution programme. All three parties aimed to protect the green belt, but Labour and the Alliance also promised energy conservation programmes.

Finally, *social policies* contrasted sharply, with party competition especially intense in this sphere. The Conservatives promised to build on the improvements in the *health service* introduced since 1979: they aimed to complete 125 hospital building programmes in three years, to extend computerised check systems for cervical cancer and to develop a national breast cancer screening programme. Labour claimed the NHS as its proudest achievement: it pledged itself to cut hospital waiting lists through computerised bed allocation, reverse increased prescription charges with the aim of eventually abolishing them and to introduce a computerised call and re-call screening service for women at risk of cervical and breast cancer. Nurses would get pay rises regularly and by right, not exceptionally as 'election sweeteners'. Pay-beds would be phased out and Labour would end both public subsidies to private health and privatisation in the NHS. The Alliance demonstrated the strength of its commitment to the NHS by undertaking to increase its budget by £1 m in five years. Like both other parties, it advocated more screening and, like Labour, more 'well-women clinics'. It recognised the right to private medicine but did not intend to allow the private use of NHS facilities at subsidised cost.

On *social security*, the Conservatives intended to maintain the value of State pensions; Labour and the Alliance both promised substantial increases (Labour by £5 per week single and £8 per week married; the Alliance by £2.30 and £3.65 respectively). This rise was part of Labour's anti-poverty programme which also included increases in child benefit by £3 per week for all children, the raising of the allowances for the first child by £7.36 and an increase of £2.20 in one-parent family benefit. The Alliance promised to raise child benefit by £1 per week in each of its first two years and to raise family credit, family premium and single-parent premium. Labour committed itself to restoring the State earnings-related pension scheme (SERPS); and to restoring and increasing the maternity grant and the death grant. Likewise, the Alliance would also increase the maternity grant (to £150 for the first child, £75 for subsequent children) and the death grant (to £400). Labour advocated a new Minister for the Disabled to be put in charge of a special programme for the disabled and a disability income scheme. The Alliance also promised measures to help the disabled. Labour would allocate a £5 winter premium to help to pay fuel bills for pensioners on supplementary benefit and for others on low incomes. The Conservatives' stress was very different – encouraging individuals to make their own pension plans and targeting public assistance on the most needy. Thus, they planned new tax incentives for personal pensions and a right for employees to make contributions to pension plans separate from their employers' scheme. They proposed family credit to help families with low income and thought extra help for the disabled might follow the current review.

On *housing*, the Conservatives had the threefold aim of encouraging ownership, extending the rights of council tenants and increasing the number of houses to let in the private rented sector. To these ends, they intended to keep the existing mortgage tax-relief system, enable council tenants to transfer their tenancies to housing associations or other independent landlords and create two new forms of tenancy to encourage private renting. Labour pledged itself to launch a major housebuilding programme and a public and private sector renovation drive. It intended to keep the right of tenants to buy council houses but aimed to use the proceeds to build more council homes. Both Labour and Alliance would retain mortgage tax relief but would limit it to standard rate tax payers.

On *education*, the Conservatives had very radical aims. They planned a massive shake-up of the system by imposing a national core curriculum; allowing State schools to opt out of local authority control; giving school heads and governors control over their budgets; establishing a new negotiating system for teachers' pay and conditions; and, in higher education, introducing new Funding Councils for Universities and Polytechnics. Both Labour and the Alliance emphasised increasing investment in education (i.e. more books and equipment); both would make nursery education available for all. Labour aimed to abolish the assisted places scheme (the Conservatives planned to expand it) and would eliminate all public subsidies to private schools. The Alliance promised to increase higher education places by 20 per cent in five years, the Conservatives by 50 000.

In short, the thrust of the party manifestos was markedly different. Each proposed changes within the context of its own ideology, interest and ethos. Thus the Conservative manifesto blended 'rolling back the frontiers of the State', popular capitalism and reduction of the power of trade union executives with plans to take educational institutions at all levels out of the hands of local authorities. But it continued to advocate a strong State with regard to defence and law and order (more police and more prisons). Labour's response was traditionally Statist to a crisis it defined in terms of unemployment and poverty: it aimed to attack the problem by a £6 bn public expenditure programme (£3 bn of it borrowed). Traditionally, again, it would restore union rights. Its radicalism lay in its defence policy: the abandonment of the British nuclear deterrent. The Alliance made a radical appeal to restore what it perceived as political moderation. Analysis of the party manifestos in terms of their specific statements on the economy, defence and welfare hardly does justice to Alliance proposals which focused on *constitutional* reform. Its major aim was proportional representation to end the period of minority governments but it also promised a Freedom of Information Act, repeal of Section 2 of the Official Secrets Act, devolution of power to the regions, reform of the House of Lords, enacting the European Convention on Human Rights into British law and a new Human Rights Commission to replace the Equal Opportunities and Racial Equality Commissions. Radical constitutional reform, it thought, would pave the way for a return to consensual policies on the economy, defence and welfare.

Enough has been said to show that British electors were offered genuine choices by the policy 'packages' of the political groupings which aspired to government. When the presence in many constituencies of candidates from parties which did not aspire to government is taken into account, that choice was wider still. The manifesto policies of all parties are, of course, the outcome of debates in which ideology, ethos, institutional interests, party groups, organisation and the factor of personality play a part. We now turn to examine more closely the character of the parties which make up the British party system.

THE CONSERVATIVE PARTY

The Conservative Party is the most successful modern party. Whether we take 1885 or 1918 as the point when Britain became a mass suffrage democracy, the Conservative Party has dominated its rivals, being in power, either singly, in coalition or in some looser form of alliance, for over two-thirds of the subsequent period. On the face of it, this fact requires some explanation. How has a party drawn predominantly from the upper and upper middle classes and whose political reason for existence is the defence of property and the Constitution consistently gained the electoral support of one-third of the working class? The answer lies in a combination of its own merits, political circumstances and the misfortunes of its rivals. The party's main electoral advantages have been, first, its own cohesiveness, adaptability, ethos and leadership.

1. *Cohesiveness*. The party puts a high premium on loyalty to the party and to the leader and on balance has been less subject to damaging faction fights than its rivals, or to splits, although it did split over tariff reform in the first quarter of the twentieth century. Being a party of 'tendencies' (i.e. differing strands of thought) rather than of 'factions' (groups organised to advance a particular set of ideas and policies) may have helped the party to avoid the worst effects of internal division but this theory should not be pressed too far in view of the intra-party groups which have sprung up in recent years (see below, pp. 239–40);

2. *Adaptability*. Conservatives are often said to value pragmatism, a non-doctrinaire approach to politics combined with an ability to adapt to changing circumstances, and this quality has served the party well in, for example, helping it to accept the post-1945 transition to a 'managed economy' and 'Welfare State', the loss of empire and British entry into Europe;

3. *Ethos*. The party's ethos blends nationalism ('putting Britain first'), individualism ('making the best of the talents you have') and the claim to good government (the country's 'natural' and most competent rulers) and consistently translates these elements into policies which sound like common sense in a political culture in which symbols and values of nation, individual striving and authority retain a strong hold;

4. *Leadership*. Conservatives have continually produced leaders able to dominate their political generations, in part by coining, or latching on to, phrases expressive of popular yearnings – thus, Baldwin ('Safety first') in a period of economic insecurity (the 1930s); Macmillan ('You've never had it so good') in an age of dawning affluence (the 1950s); and Mrs Thatcher ('Roll back the frontiers of the State') at a time of public anxiety about high levels of government spending and taxation (the 1970s).

Also, the party has benefited from political circumstances which favoured its appeal to nationalism. These have occurred quite frequently and include threats to the integrity of the British State either from within (Home Rule in the late nineteenth and early twentieth centuries) or from outside (the Kaiser's Germany in 1914–18, Hitler's Germany in 1939–45) or to its economy (the World Economic Depression of the 1930s). Finally, the Conservatives have derived indirect assistance from the misfortunes of their closest rivals. The Liberals, for instance, split in 1886 (over Home Rule for Ireland), in 1916–18 (over Lloyd-George's displacement of Asquith as war-time Prime Minister) and again in 1932 (over the abandonment of Free Trade). Nor could the party in general help but benefit from the long-drawn struggle between the Liberals and Labour to be the major force of social reform on the political left; this occupied most of the first half of the century but appeared to have been finally decided in the decades following 1945.

However, this situation recurred after 1979 when its electoral defeat led to turmoil in the Labour Party which produced the secession of the SDP, the formation of the Alliance and a chronically divided opposition in the elections of 1983 and 1987.

Conservative groups

The Conservative Party may be a party of 'tendencies' rather than factions but it still contains numerous groups formed to press for a particular set of policies.

The *Bow Group* (1951) is a London-based research group which aims to influence through its pamphlets and quarterly magazine, *Crossbow*. Open to all Conservatives (membership was 1000 in 1975), the group neither expresses a collective view nor organises meetings of MPs; rather it adopts an 'independent' freely critical standpoint. As a non-partisan 'think-tank' it is capable of airing ideas from both the 'one-nation' and libertarian sides of the party. In 1984, the group sought to keep Mrs Thatcher to her election promises, urging her to make tax cuts, reduce public spending and reform the tax and social security system.

The Monday Club (1961) is a right-wing group formed to organise grass-roots support of true Conservatism against what is perceived as a drift to the left under Macmillan especially on matters involving race. The Club has 'free market' opinions on economic and welfare policy but its major concern is the need to preserve Britain's material and moral defences against the internal and external threats of declining moral standards, rising crime, 'Socialism' (identified with bureaucratic controls and inefficiency) and Soviet expansionism. In the 1980s, it attacked the idea of a multiracial society, calling for the abolition of the Commission for Racial Equality, a ban on further immigration, and generous resettlement provisions for those prepared to leave the country. The Club had 2000 members in 1984, including eighteen MPs and fifteen peers. A policy paper in 1986 urged the Government to step up its privatisation programme, calling for the coal and electricity industries and the Post Office to be sold off.

The *Selsdon Group* (1973) supports 'free market' economic principles. It sees political freedom as wholly dependent upon economic freedom and strongly advocates reducing the public sector and expanding the private sector. Thus, nationalised industries should be privatised as far as practicable and, where this is not possible, they should be reintegrated into the private sector by, for example, being required to raise funds in the private market. Quangos also should be abolished or reduced in size and functions. Private initiatives in health, education and welfare should be encouraged. The Group has firmly 'monetarist' views on running the economy: thus, inflation should be curbed by keeping a tight grip on the money supply, public sector expenditure as a percentage of Gross National Product (GNP) reduced, and 'corporatist' bodies like the CBI and TUC excluded from economic policy-making. With Mrs Thatcher in power, the Group has seen its primary task as being to keep the government faithful to economic liberalism. In 1980, its membership of 250 included seven MPs.

Other 'free market' groups include the *Centre for Policy Studies* (CPS) which was originally established by Margaret Thatcher and Sir Keith Joseph in 1974 to examine the scope for introducing social market policies into Britain, and the *Institute for Economic Affairs* (IEA), which was founded in 1957 and became particularly influential during the Thatcher premiership. In the 1980s, the CPS has recommended legislation to prohibit strikes in essential services such as ambulance, fire, gas, water, electricity and hospital nursing. Workers forbidden to strike should enjoy statutory improvements in pay and conditions. There should be compulsory arbitration procedures for settling disputes and, where death or serious injury to members of the public resulted from their actions, strikers should receive substantial fines and imprisonment. A pamphlet published under IEA auspices in 1984 recommended massive privatisation (including railways, coal, hospitals and schools) and the abolition of the Manpower Services Commission and ACAS in order to clear the way for tax cuts, large increases in child benefits, the abolition of National Insurance contributions and reductions in VAT. Other New Right 'think-tanks' are the *Adam Smith Institute, the Social Affairs Unit*, and *Policy Search*.

The *Tory Reform Group* (1975) expresses 'moderate' Conservatism in the Disraelian 'one nation' tradition. In the 1980s, its major subject of concern was the social harm done by the government's rigid pursuit of monetarist policies and their divisive effects upon the country. The Group has a more favourable attitude to government intervention than that of free market Conservatives. In particular, it supports public investment which can assist economic modernisation (such as in coal, steel and aerospace) and the recovery of key industries (like Austin Rover). Peter Walker, its leading member, has proposed a large public investment programme to revitalise inner-city areas. The Group publishes a journal, *Reformer*, and had thirty-five backbench members in 1984.

The Conservative Party is hierarchically organised, with authority concentrated in the leadership. The leader appoints the Party Chairman, its 'Shadow' spokesmen (when the party is in opposition) and, in consultation with close colleagues, decides party policy. Electoral victory or the promise of it secures the position of the leader but defeat or the threat of it places it in immediate jeopardy. Defeat in October 1974 led to the swift deposition of Edward Heath and Mrs Thatcher became vulnerable in 1981 as a result of her own and the party's low ratings in the opinion polls.

Conservative leaders are elected by Conservative Members of Parliament. This system dates from 1965; before that, leaders 'emerged' after a process of secret soundings of party opinion. Under the present method, a candidate can succeed on the first ballot by gaining an absolute majority of the votes cast plus a 15 per cent lead over the nearest rival. Failure of any candidate to secure this winning margin means that nominations take place again and may include candidates who did not appear in the first ballot. In the second round, in order to win, an aspirant for the leadership has only to secure an absolute majority of the votes cast. If the second ballot should fail to produce a clear winner, a third and final ballot, restricted to the three leading candidates, is held. This time, the single alternative vote is used, enabling MPs to register their second preferences. If their first preferences still do not produce an overall winner, the candidate with the fewest first preferences is eliminated and the second preferences of those voting for this candidate are distributed between the two leading contenders; the one with the highest number of first and second choices combined is the winner. At the first election under the new rules (1965), one ballot was sufficient because although Edward Heath (150) lacked a 15 per cent majority over his rivals, Reginald Maudling (133) and Enoch Powell (15), they withdrew from the contest, leaving him as the winner. In 1975, on the first ballot, Margaret Thatcher (130) also failed to gain the required 15 per cent lead over her opponents, Edward Heath (119) and Hugh Fraser (16). Heath withdrew and, in the second round, Mrs Thatcher (146) achieved the necessary absolute majority over William Whitelaw (79), James Prior (19), Sir Geoffrey Howe (19) and John Peyton (11).

Conservative organisation outside Westminster reflects this 'top down' ethos, with power in general concentrated in the parliamentary party and, within that, in the leadership. The institution which represents all Conservative members is the National Union of Conservative and Constitutional Associations. It was formed in 1867 after the Second Reform Act, to spread Conservatism in the country by helping to form new associations and coordinating the existing ones. The main task of the National Union is to convene an Annual Conference which brings together leading Conservative politicians and ordinary members. Permanent staff, Young Conservatives, Conservative trade unionists and women's organisations are present at Conference but they are heavily outnumbered by representatives from the constituency associations. Conference enables the leadership to sound the opinion of grass-roots Conservatives, who are for the most part content to leave policy and strategy to the leaders. Conference debates tend to be carefully 'stage-managed' to avoid appearances of disunity and resolutions are often passed without a vote.

Conservative constituency associations are run by Executive Councils which contain representatives from the constituent elements of the party: Young Conservatives, Conservative Clubs and ward and district branches. They play an important role in the selection of parliamentary candidates under the overall supervision of the central party organisation, which maintains a list of approved candidates. Before 1981, the Vice-Chairman vetted candidates for this list but after that date candidates were encouraged to go before residential Parliamentary Selection Boards. Local Conservative associations are expected to consult the Vice-Chairman, who recommends some names from the list. But inclusion on the list is not essential to selection and constituency associations can consider other names too. Potential candidates apply personally, either directly to the local party or through Central Office. Their applications are considered by a small subcommittee of the Executive Council; this draws up short-lists of candidates who will go before a final selection conference, which usually consists of the full Executive Council. Its decision is normally final, subject to the formal approval (only very rarely refused) of a general meeting of the local membership. Readoption struggles were few between 1945 and 1975 (only 23), but the extensive boundary revisions in 1983 provoked some fierce re-selection battles and eight Conservative MPs failed to gain selection.

Central Office. Like other parties, the Conservatives have a party civil service. This is staffed by officials many of whom make their work a full-time career. They assist in such matters as the raising of money, organisation of election campaigns, selection of candidates, research and political education. A vital part of their work is liaison with the parliamentary party and the party outside Westminster. The Party Chairman has overall responsibility for party organisation but day-to-day administration is in the hands of the party Vice-Chairman. Central Office has three departments: Organisation, Research and Publicity. The largest single group at party headquarters are researchers. A vital function of Central Office is the training, certification and promotion of agents. Agents are the key professionals in the Conservative as in the Labour Party. Normally employed by the constituency parties, they play an important part in liaising between the party's central headquarters and its regional, area and local bodies; in fund-raising; and, most notably, in elections, especially in marginal seats. In the 1987 General Election, there were about 300 full-time Conservative agents covering all but two of the seventy-two seats identified as 'critical'. The party keeps in touch with constituencies through a network of Area Councils, which form the middle tier of the representative side of the party between the constituency associations and Central Office. Each of them has responsibility for about fifty constituencies and they are staffed by the senior area officials, who provide a link with Central Office.

The Conservative Party is the wealthiest party, its money being provided by business, the constituency membership and gifts from individuals. Just over 50 per cent of its income comes from business, but, as a proportion of party funds, this source has declined since the early 1970s when it constituted over 60 per cent. Moreover, there is always some uncertainty about its final amount since companies decide their contributions on a year-to-year basis. Over 20 per cent of party income comes from the local membership but this source also is a matter of concern in view of the declining membership, which fell from 2.75 m to 1.5 m between 1953 and 1976. In common with other parties, the Conservatives have found costs out-running income in the late 1970s and 1980s and have had to make economies. Nonetheless, their rivals are worse off and the Conservative expenditure (£11.8 m) in the 1987 General Election comfortably exceeded that of Labour (£6.7 m) and the Alliance (£3.9–4.2 m) put together.

THE LABOUR PARTY

The Labour Party originated in a decision of representatives of Socialist societies and trade unions in 1900 to press for independent working-class representation in Parliament. A Labour Representation Committee with five representatives from the Socialist societies and seven from the trade unions was established to guide this enterprise and gained its first major success in 1906, when 29 Labour MPs were elected. With the majority of the working class still lacking the right to vote, more significant political advance was not to be expected at this time. After the massive franchise extensions of 1918 and 1928, however, when the electorate trebled, Labour could be expected to forge ahead and the party did in fact gain ground steadily in the inter-war period, forming minority governments in 1924 and in 1929–31. However, although displacing the Liberals in the 1920s as the second largest party, Labour did not achieve an absolute majority over the other parties until its sweeping electoral victory of 1945. Between 1945 and 1985, it alternated in power with the Conservatives, ruling for seventeen out of the forty years. Its enduring strength has been its capacity to gain a majority of working-class votes.

In contrast to the Conservatives – middle class, hierarchical and capitalist – the ethos of the Labour Party is working class, egalitarian and, in a broad sense, Socialist. The party formally adopted its commitment to the common ownership of the means of production, distribution and exchange (clause 4 of its Constitution) after 1918, and this commitment has remained in its constitution despite efforts to abolish it by 'revisionists' in the 1950s. Its policies reflect both its working class or 'labourist' character and its commitment to Socialist ideals. Its bedrock sympathies and loyalties are clear. Thus, the Party's persisting commitments to greater social and economic equality, its traditional stress upon cooperation and collective endeavour and its preference for public enterprise were strongly evident in its 1987 manifesto commitments. So, too, were its sympathies for the underprivileged, including the unemployed, council tenants, families with children and disabled dependents, one-parent families, and, in more general terms, with women and ethnic minorities. The party believes in State education and in the National Health Service. Along with a ready identification with the 'underdogs' of society has gone an attack on privilege, and this strain appeared in Labour's manifesto promises to reverse tax cuts for the most wealthy and to introduce a wealth tax. Traditional loyalties were evidenced in the commitments to protect trade union rights generally and to restore trade union rights at GCHQ.

In practice, expression of the party's 'labourist' ethos and implementation of its Socialist ideals have been tempered by the need to win power in a society in which the traditional working class is shrinking and to administer a predominantly capitalist economy. Thus, the requirements of gaining power have forced it to make broad appeals to social groups which straddle the classes: to parents, pensioners and owner-occupiers. The demands of government, moreover, have often forced Labour to compromise with its fundamental instincts and principles: in office, it began, then was forced to abandon, an attempt to curb trade union powers (1969), on several occasions used compulsory incomes policies (in general disliked by the trade unions) and introduced cuts in public spending. Periods in government, with the compromises power entails, have almost always led to tensions within the party, most notably between Labour parliamentarians, on the one hand, and trade unionists and grass-roots activists, on the other.

The Labour Party contains numerous factional groupings expressing alternative varieties of Socialism. These encompass a spectrum of opinion ranging from the 'right' or 'centre-right' to the moderate or 'soft' left and the outside or 'hard' left. Leading right and centrist groups are *Solidarity* and the *Fabian Society*. The *Tribune Group*, one of the most important groups in the party, and the *Labour Coordinating Committee* are on the 'soft left' whilst the *Campaign for Labour Party Democracy* and the *Campaign Group* are on the 'hard left'. The *Militant Tendency* is a far-left Trotskyist organisation whose right to membership in the party came into serious question in the late 1970s. After Labour's electoral defeat in 1979, factional in-fighting within the party became very intense and the left gained an ascendancy which was reflected in the 1983 manifesto. The outcome of factional struggles, therefore, is of the utmost importance since it may determine the party programme, its manifesto and the policy of the government if the party wins office. Differences between the respective wings of the party covered the entire range of issues, including attitudes to nuclear weapons, the Common Market, incomes policy, nationalisation and intra-party democracy.

Solidarity (1981) originated in the opposition of Labour 'moderates' to the constitutional changes of 1981. They thought that the electoral college method of electing the leader and deputy leader gave too much influence to the trade unions and the constituency parties and too small a role to MPs. Solidarity – 'the gang of 150' – came into being after 150 Labour MPs had signed a statement opposing the new method. Roy Hattersley (who became Deputy-Leader in 1983) and Peter Shore took a leading part in forming the group which concentrated its immediate efforts on rallying support for Denis

Healey for the deputy-leadership against a left-winger, Tony Benn, and, post-1982, on excluding the Militant Tendency from the party.

The nearest origins of the contemporary Labour Right are in the *Manifesto Group* (1974) which opposed the influence of the Left in the Party, supporting continuing membership of the EEC and NATO, and the retention of nuclear weapons, and opposing further nationalisation. Those on the Right and Centre-right of the Party advocate 'one member, one vote' in the selection and reselection of parliamentary candidates. In policy terms, they support multilateral rather than unilateral disarmament and favour the mixed economy. They consider a strong private sector to be vital for economic efficiency and individual freedom, and have no principled objection to wider share-ownership and profit-sharing. But they also believe that selective public enterprise and public control are necessary to improve economic performance, especially to stimulate investment.

The *Fabian Society* (1884) has a sizeable local as well as parliamentary membership: it had nearly 9000 members in 1975 (there were fewer in 1985) and in 1984 about half the PLP belonged. It exists primarily to float ideas by pamphleteering and speaking; for instance, the idea of superannuation for workers not included in occupational pension schemes, which became law in 1975, owed much to a Fabian pamphlet. A Fabian Society publication in 1987 expressed concern about growing inequalities in British society and was followed by a Fabian Society call for a new Royal Commission to look into the distribution of income and wealth.

The *Tribune Group* is the leading 'soft left' faction. It takes its name from the weekly newspaper, *Tribune*, which dates back to 1937. It strongly opposed British membership of the European Community and, in economic policy, supports more nationalisation and a more vigorously interventionist approach by the government to the private sector (for example, by compulsory planning agreements with companies). It is against incomes policies. Aneurin Bevan (in the 1950s), Michael Foot (in the 1960s) and Neil Kinnock (in the 1970s) have all been prominent Tribunites. Tribune was the only Labour Left group in parliament until 1982.

The Labour Coordinating Committee (1978) and the Campaign for Labour Party Democracy (1973) both originated in the acute disappointment felt by many Labour activists at what were seen as the continual compromises of the Labour Governments of 1964 to 1970, and 1974 to 1979. There was an intense desire to secure a more resolute commitment in the Party to 'truly Socialist' objectives. The *Labour Coordinating Committee* (LCC) concentrated on securing such changes in party policy as a commitment to withdraw from the Common Market and the *Campaign for Labour Party Democracy* (CLPD) brought pressure for constitutional changes broadly aimed at giving more influence to grass-roots opinion and at making the parliamentary leadership more accountable to the rank and file. The LCC quickly achieved considerable grass-roots support and played a significant role in the general left-ward movement of the party after 1979 which culminated in the left-wing manifesto of 1983. After the election of 1983, the LCC moved towards a 'soft left' position, accepting the inevitability of a mixed economy although with a reduced private sector and backing Neil Kinnock for the leadership, having formerly supported Benn. The CLPD had three aims: to extend the right to elect the leader and his deputy from MPs to a wider constituency within the party; reselection of MPs; and final control over the manifesto by the National Executive Committee rather than the party leader. By 1981, the first two objectives had been achieved, and owed much to the success of the CLPD in winning support in Constituency Labour Parties and in the trade unions.

The Campaign Group is another far left group, a breakaway from the Tribune Group. A leading member is Tony Benn. As well as the objectives generally supported by the left such as large-scale public ownership, withdrawal from the EEC, unilateral disarmament, and an end to discrimination against women and blacks, it has particular constitutional goals. These include (nationally) the ending of all independently exercised Crown prerogatives, the abolition of the House of Lords, reduction of the life of parliaments from five to four years and the approval of all public appointments by the House of Commons and (for the party) the annual election of the Shadow Cabinet (or Cabinet) by an electoral college and teams of policy advisers elected by the specialist committees of backbenchers for all future Labour Ministers. By early 1988, as the party leadership sought to re-define the party programme in the wake of the 1987 election defeat, the Campaign Group was expressing alarm about the threatened departure from what it considered to be true Socialism and put forward Tony Benn and Eric Heffer to challenge Neil Kinnock and Roy Hattersley for the Leadership and Deputy Leadership.

The Militant Tendency is a far-left Trotskyist grouping which gained a foothold in the party after 1973 when Labour's list of proscribed organisations was abolished. It advocates massive nationalisation and public investment, workers' control of the banks, withdrawal from the EEC and nuclear disarmament. It is a powerful group with – in the mid-1980s – a membership of about 4500, an annual income of over £1 m and a staff of over 140. It produces a weekly newspaper which sells thousands of copies, although probably not the 40 000 it claims. Aware that the association with Militant was causing it considerable electoral damage, the Party decided to expel members of the Tendency, beginning with five members of the editorial board of its newspaper in 1983. Militant resisted strongly and despite the occasional spectacular purge such as that of the Liverpool Labour Party which included the expulsion of Derek Hatton, a relatively small number of its members had been expelled by 1987. However, in that year, the party intensified its efforts, setting up the National Constitutional Committee to accelerate the process. The Committee expelled thirteen Militants in its first year and, early in 1988, a further eighty-eight, including many leading organisers, were under consideration.

After the 1987 General Election, the Parliamentary Labour Party (PLP) was divided broadly into three groupings: the centre-right *Solidarity* group, with an estimated support of about 95; the soft-left *Tribune* Group, with an estimated support of about 90; and the hard left *Campaign* Group, with an estimated support of around 45. In general terms, both soft- and hard-left increased their representation in the PLP as a result of the election. But other groups on the left remained active: the Labour Coordinating Committee, for example, called for a rethinking of Party policies on council-house sales, share-ownership and tax cuts. It was the fragmentation of the Labour Left which continued to limit its influence despite the efforts of 'umbrella' groups such as *Labour Left Liaison* and *Campaign Forum* to produce united action. Again in 1987, as in the previous year, hard- and soft-left in the PLP failed to agree on a joint slate (common list) of candidates for the election to the Shadow Cabinet. But Tribunite ('soft-left') influence increased nonetheless, rising from four to nine members whereas Solidarity representation declined from ten to five. Leading Tribunites in 1987 were Bryan Gould, John Prescott, Michael Meacher, Gordon Brown and Jack Straw; prominent on the centre-right (Solidarity) wing of the party were Gerald Kaufman, Roy Hattersley, John Smith and John Cunningham; foremost far-left figures were Ken Livingstone, Dennis Skinner, Eric Heffer and Tony Benn.

Organisation

The organisation of the Labour Party reflects both its egalitarian ideals and – notably in the influence accorded to the trade unions – its 'labourist' ethos. Before 1981, the right to elect the party leader and his deputy was limited to Labour MPs, but a special constitutional conference in that year introduced a new system. Both left and right of the party wanted change, but whereas the right favoured 'one member, one vote' (excluding members affiliated by the trade unions) the left advocated an electoral college method in which each significant section of the party (PLP, CLPs and Trade Unions) received specific 'weightings'.

The system eventually adopted was in accord with left views both in the adoption of an electoral college and in a method of weighting which allocated more votes to the trade unions (40 per cent) than to the PLP and CLPs (each 30 per cent) and more influence in general to the party outside parliament (70 per cent) than to the parliamentary party (30 per cent). Voting is open, not secret as in the previous system, and if no overall winner emerges in the first ballot, a second ballot is held. The new system was first used in the deputy leadership election in 1981 when Denis Healey narrowly defeated Tony Benn. In 1983, after Michael Foot had resigned the leadership in the wake of Labour's electoral defeat, Neil Kinnock was elected leader and Roy

Hattersley deputy leader by the new system. Voting in the election of leader was: Neil Kinnock 71.3 per cent, Roy Hattersley 19.3 per cent, Eric Heffer 6.3 per cent, and Peter Shore 3.1 per cent. Neil Kinnock gained overwhelming support in the CLPs, almost three-quarters of the unions and nearly half of the PLP. Overall, in dispersing power to the constituent elements of the party rather than to its individual members, the changes reflected and intensified the federalistic structure of the party rather than democratising it.

Whereas Conservative Party organisation emphasises the role of the leader overall and gives prominence to the party at Westminster over the party in the country, the structure of the Labour Party reflects its origin in a mass movement. The trade unions took the lead in founding the party in 1900 and continue to be very influential. In the first place, they provide the bulk of the party's members and income. In 1978, for example, 5.9 m members were affiliated through the unions; individual membership which, according to the Houghton Committee (1976) was about 1 m in 1953, had declined to about 250 000 by that year. In 1988 it was slightly higher at 300 000, and the Party plans a vigorous campaign to increase individual membership. In 1983 the trade unions provided £5.1 m of the Party's total income of £6.1 m, with nearly 50 per cent of the union contribution being made by the four largest unions (TGWU, AUEW, GMWU and NUPE). Second, the unions play a predominant role at Conference which, by the constitution of 1918, is the ruling body of the Party. Unions are allocated votes at the Conference in proportion to the annual amount they pay in affiliation fees and cast their votes as a block vote without subdivision according to differences of opinion among the membership. Although delegates from the constituency parties generally outnumber union delegates at conference, the combined block votes of the five largest unions can usually gain an absolute majority.

Conference makes the decisions about policies which compose the party programme but of course would be too unwieldy to manage the party on a day-to-day basis. It annually elects the National Executive Committee (NEC) to do this. The composition of the NEC (twenty-eight) again reflects strong union influence, with twelve of its members elected by the unions; in addition, it contains seven constituency party members, five women's representatives and the single representatives from the Cooperative Movement, the Socialist societies and the Young Socialists; the leader and deputy leader are *ex officio* members. Constitutionally, any proposal receiving a two-thirds majority at Conference goes into the party programme, but the programme is not the manifesto, which is the joint responsibility of the Parliamentary committee of the PLP and the NEC, or – when the party is in government – of the Cabinet and the NEC.

Leadership of the Labour Party constitutes a more complex and delicate task than that of the Conservative Party. The Party outside parliament is powerful and constitutionally entrenched: the leader must balance the claims of parliamentarians, trade unionists and constituency activists. In addition, the voices of the Cooperatives, the Socialist societies, Young Socialists and women's groups demand a hearing; in the 1980s, a strong claim emerged for separate black sections. Even this grossly oversimplifies, for each element of the party contains its own divisions between left and right, with shades of opinion within and between, which have to be taken into account.

In conducting this balancing act and defusing actual and potential conflicts, Labour leaders command certain resources: personal prestige, the authority inherent in the position, a presence on both the Parliamentary Committee and the NEC, and above all perhaps, the desire of the Party for office, which has often provided a motive for compromise.

The leading official of the Party (General Secretary) and head of its permanent staff works from *Transport House*, the equivalent of Conservative Central Office. In 1988, the post was held by Larry Whitty. Transport House is organised into three main departments – Information, International and Research (the largest). A key position is that of the National Agent. The number of agents is declining and the party could afford only sixty-eight agents in 1987, although this was six more than in 1983. Contact with the constituencies is maintained through Regional Offices, where the senior official acts as secretary for the Regional Council which has responsibility for about fifty constituencies. Constituency Labour Parties consisting of delegates from a wide variety of labour organisations and societies are run by General Management Committees (GMCs) through Executive Committees. Selection of parliamentary candidates cannot begin without permission from the NEC which automatically forwards its two lists of approved candidates (list A is of union-sponsored, list B of all other potential candidates) to the constituency party concerned. Candidates have to be nominated to the Constituency Labour Party on invitation from its Executive Committee by affiliated organisations, such as trade union branches, socialist societies, and local cooperatives, which in this way perform an initial vetting process. Subcommittees of the GMCs shortlist candidates who then go before the entire GMC acting as a final selection conference. The NEC may, but only rarely does, refuse to endorse the selected candidate on such grounds as personal or political unacceptability or irregularities in the selection procedure. Mandatory reselection was adopted by the 1980 Labour Conference. This meant that all sitting Labour MPs had to face a reselection process no less than three years after the previous General Election. The 1987 Labour Party Conference voted for a new system of selecting candidates based on local electoral colleges in which the trade unions retained their influence. It wanted to expand the numbers involved in selection, but stopped short of 'one member, one vote'.

THE LIBERAL PARTY

Between the late 1860s and the First World War, the Liberal Party was one of the two major parties. Its primary cause was the liberty of the individual but it also stood for free trade, temperance, the rights of small nations inside the country and abroad and the settlement of international disputes by negotation rather than war. After 1914, it went into decline: its internal unity was destroyed by the fierce squabble between its two leaders, Asquith and Lloyd-George, and its ethos, which emphasised the value of voluntary action by individuals and a limited role for the State in social life, was undermined by the need for conscription and government regulation of the economy. In the inter-war period, it slumped into third-party status behind Labour, although continuing to return scores of MPs. Between 1945 and 1970, the Liberals were forced out into the margins of politics, their tally of MPs exceeding ten on only two occasions (1945 and 1966, when they had twelve representatives at Westminster). However, although weak, the party remained in existence. Indeed, apart from 1951 and 1955 when it received only $\frac{3}{4}$ m votes, it always attracted a sizeable electoral support of between 2 and 3 m. After 1970, its fortunes revived: in February 1974, its vote topped 6 m, 19.3 per cent of the total vote, and although its performance in subsequent elections in the 1970s did not quite match this achievement, electoral support never declined below 4 m. Liberals, moreover, began regularly to contest the majority of seats. In 1983, when the Liberals fought the election in concert with the SDP, this revival continued: the Liberal–SDP Alliance gained $7\frac{3}{4}$ m votes, 23 seats – of which 17 were Liberals – and 26 per cent of the total vote. *Parliamentary* breakthrough had not been attained, but nonetheless the Liberals together with their political ally had become a serious force again. Talk of their ability to hold the balance in a situation in which no party had an absolute majority became frequent. In 1985, many opinion polls not only showed the Alliance neck-and-neck with Labour and the Conservatives but also indicated growing public sympathy for the idea of coalition government.

　　Much of the credit for the Liberal revival went to the Party leader, David Steel. Steel's achievement was to transform the Party from being a mere generator of 'bright ideas' operating at the margins of British politics to a party with serious claims to play a part in government. Crucial stages in this transition were the Lib–Lab Pact of 1977–8 and the establishment of the Alliance with the SDP in 1981. The strategy was clear, although it would probably have to be effected in several stages: first to gain sufficient seats (if necessary in alliance with another party) to enable Liberals (and their allies) to hold the balance of power in parliament and then to negotiate for their own policies, especially proportional representation, as the 'price' for supporting either of the other two parties in government. Other important sections of the party, such as Young Liberals and Liberal Councillors, emphasised the need to make gains at the *local* level. Each played an important role in the revitalisation of the party. In the 1960s and 1970s, Young Liberals pioneered 'community politics', stressing hard compaigning on local issues and urging people to fight for improvements in their immediate environment. The influence of the Association of Liberal Councillors (ALC), another radical campaigning force, stemmed from its resources as well as its success in local elections: in 1983, it had an annual budget of £80 000, six full-time staff, an information bank, a sizeable library and three regular publications. In the autumn of that year, there were over 2000 Liberal councillors, and the Party controlled six councils and held the balance of power in twenty others.

The Liberal Party was the first party to allow ordinary members to participate in the election of the leader. By a change introduced in 1976, members voted by secret ballot in each constituency. Electoral votes were allocated to each constituency according to its length of affiliation to the party and the number of votes its candidate received at the previous General Election. David Steel (12 541 electoral votes) defeated John Pardoe (7032 electoral votes) for the leadership using this method in 1976, but in 1981 the complex formula was abandoned in favour of a simple 'one member, one vote' system.

Liberals saw political reform as a necessary condition of economic revival. By political reform they meant not only proportional representation but also a range of other measures including devolution of power to Scotland, Wales and the English regions and a Bill of Rights to protect civil liberties and to eliminate racial and other forms of discrimination. They were the first party to advocate British membership of the European Community. They attacked the two major parties as class-based, out-of-date and 'in hock' to business and the trade unions. In their turn, they called for incomes policy, industrial co-partnership involving employee profit-sharing and participation on boards of management, and radical reform of the tax and welfare systems to benefit the worst-off members of the community.

THE SOCIAL DEMOCRATIC PARTY

The SDP (1981) sought a realignment of the political 'centre', aiming to attact support from both dissident Labour and dissatisfied Conservative supporters and MPs. It considered that, ideologically, Labour had swung too far to the Left and the Conservatives too far to the Right. Like the Liberals, the SDP also felt that the two major parties had become too vulnerable to political pressures from their 'paymasters', the big economic interest groups. Its founders – the 'gang of four' (Roy Jenkins, Shirley Williams, Bill Rodgers and David Owen) – believed in a mixed economy with healthy public and private sectors and fewer boundary changes between the two. In addition, they were totally committed to Britain's continuing membership of the

European Community and to its practical success.

The party made rapid progress in its first year. Under its 'collective' leadership (Roy Jenkins, David Owen, Shirley Williams and William Rodgers) it recruited 70 000 members, attracted funds of £650 000 and won two significant by-election victories at Crosby and Glasgow Hillhead. It acquired a democratic constitution, by which a leader and president are elected by postal ballot of the membership and area groups select parliamentary candidates and elect representatives to the party's 'peak' institution, the Council for Social Democracy. The Council, meeting three or four times a year under the chairpersonship of the President, has the final say on policy but policy is developed by the Policy Committee (composed half of MPs, half of ordinary members) which decides the membership and terms of reference of twenty-five policy groups. In June 1981, the SDP forged an alliance with the Liberals and, by the end of the year, had a large lead in the opinion polls (with 46 per cent). Then came the Falklands War, with its boost to the Conservatives. By early 1983, Alliance support in the polls had slipped to 20–5 per cent. At such a level of support it could not expect outright victory nor could it expect to hold the balance between parties in a hung parliament; indeed, many of its MPs were likely to lose their seats. And so it proved. Despite polling strongly – $7\frac{3}{4}$ m (26 per cent of the total vote) compared with Labour's 8.4 m (28 per cent) – the Alliance won a mere twenty-three seats. Although Liberal representation increased (by five) to seventeen, SDP representation suffered a drastic decline from thirty to six. More hopefully, the Alliance gained a larger share of the total vote than any party other than Labour or the Conservatives since 1923; it showed that it was capable of gaining votes from all sections of society; and it won second place in 312 constituencies, a sound basis on which to build for the future.

The two Alliance parties between 1981 and 1987 were able to agree on a wide range of policies. In 1983, they jointly advocated electoral reform to strengthen the 'moderate' centre against the extremes and to end 'adversary' politics with its frequent reversals of policy on the management of the economy, control of prices and incomes and the trade unions. After the election, a further joint document recommended House of Lords reform, replacement of rates by a local income tax, a Bill of Rights, and a Freedom of Information Act as well as making the more familiar demands for proportional representation and devolution of power to the regions. Certain matters, however, proved more difficult to agree upon. These included defence policy; candidate selection; and the leadership of the Alliance. On defence, in 1983–4, the SDP supported the deployment of Cruise missiles in Britain, the Liberals opposed it; the only possible source of agreement was to propose no *further* deployment of Cruise. On candidate selection, the arrangement of 1983 favoured the Liberals, who were allocated the fifty seats in which Alliance candidates stood the best chance of being elected whereas the SDP received two-thirds of the hundred next best constituencies. In

1983–4, the two parties agreed a Pact on candidate selection whereby a joint national committee of the parties would be required to approve arrangements worked out by the parties at local level, a system which would tend to reduce the number of constituencies with joint selection procedures. However, the two parties could not agree upon who would be Prime Minister should the Alliance 'win' a General Election – the Liberal leader, David Steel, or David Owen, who had replaced Roy Jenkins as leader of the SDP soon after the 1983 election.

David Owen from the outset strongly opposed the full merger of the two parties. He believed that the SDP had a distinctive identity as a centre radical alternative to Labour. His speeches in the mid-1980s, with this aim in mind, dwelt on the theme of the 'social market economy', stressing both the role of the private sector in wealth-creation and the role of the State in management of the economy. On economic policy, he believed government should stimulate demand by increasing public investment and by industrial credit schemes and should actively encourage new technology. On social policy, the SDP would help the poorest groups by tax reforms which would rechannel the wealth of middle-income-earners; it opposed subsidies for private education and private medicine. On trade unions, the party thought that individual trade unionists should decide on an individual basis whether to contribute to the political levy ('contracting in') but it balanced this with the suggestion that shareholders should be able to ratify the political donations made by companies. Trade unions ought to ballot their members before calling strikes.

In 1986, the prospects for the SDP and for the Alliance were evenly poised. The task was a considerable one: the Alliance would need 37–9 per cent of the vote to become the largest single party and between 30 and 34 per cent to hold the balance. In three by-elections held in the first half of 1984, its support hovered at a creditable 34–5 per cent. The volatility of the electorate – between one third and two-fifths of voters changed their allegiances or moved into or out of abstentions between elections – also gave grounds for hope. Equally, the two major parties could regain lost ground.

In fact, the 1987 General Election proved a major disappointment to the Alliance. Although overall losses were relatively small (total vote down to 7.3 m, parliamentary seats to 22) the result was a severe blow in the light of its expectations. David Steel immediately called for the two parties to move quickly to a complete merger. This proposal split the SDP which in August 1987 voted by a 15 per cent majority to begin negotiations for a possible merger with the Liberals. Three of the SDP's five MPs (John Cartwright and Rosie Barnes as well as Dr Owen) opposed the merger. The full voting figures were 25 897 (47.4 per cent) for merger, with 19 228 (42.6 per cent) voting for a closer relationship with the Liberals, short of merger. David Owen resigned immediately and Robert MacLennan became the new leader of the Party. The vote to unite with the Liberals was confirmed by a rather larger majority at the SDP conference in September 1987 and the Liberal Party also supported the idea of merger at its conference.

THE DEMOCRATS

Despite some strains, the two parties' negotiating teams had agreed a constitution and a title (SLD) by January 1988. But the negotations were jeopardised at the last moment by a joint policy statement by the two leaders which caused intense alarm, especially amongst Liberals. The statement supported the Trident nuclear deterrent and also advocated the extension of VAT to food and children's clothing, the phasing-out of mortgage tax-relief and the abolition of universal child benefit. A new group of six led by Des Wilson for the Liberals and Edmund Dell for the SDP swiftly put together a less contentious document. Meeting later in the month, special Liberal and SDP assemblies endorsed the merger by large majorities, the Liberals by nearly 6:1 (2099:385, with 23 abstentions); the SDP by nearly 10:1 (273:28 with 49 abstentions). Pro-mergerites in both parties argued that fusion afforded the only remaining realistic opportunity of forging a viable third force in the centre of British politics. They maintained that the Alliance had failed, with electors in 1987 uncertain about its leadership (were they voting for David Owen or David Steel as potential Prime Minister?), strategy (was it aiming at total victory or merely at holding the balance of power?) and defence posture (how committed was it to nuclear weapons, with so many Liberals opposed to them?). Anti-mergerites in both parties feared the loss of their distinctive traditions. Radical Liberals were worried, for example, that their environmental and disarmament concerns would get little attention in the new party. The Owenites saw the Liberals as divided on crucial issues like defence. They would have preferred to continue the Alliance. Important minorities, therefore, held aloof from the merger. David Owen backed by two more of the five SDP MPs pledged to lead the 'continuing SDP' in the Campaign for Social Democracy. Michael Meadowcroft set up the Liberal Movement to promote radical Liberalism.

THE SCOTTISH AND WELSH NATIONALIST PARTIES

Support for nationalist parties in Scotland and Wales grew in the 1960s and 1970s for a variety of reasons. Some are specific to each country but many factors are common to both. These include the resurgence of cultural nationalism in both countries, their persistently higher rates of unemployment and lower levels of income per head, their growing resentment against what they perceived as remote bureaucratic government from London, the failure of the two major parties to produce acceptable rates of economic growth, and the consequences of class and party dealignment. Further common contributory factors were the diminished sense of UK national identity and purpose in an era which saw both the end of the British empire and the entry into the European Community – events which suggested the fluidity rather than the firmness of Britain's constitutional relationships. Factors specific to each nationalist movement were the discovery of offshore oil for Scotland and the renewed salience of the language issue for Wales. Oil undoubtedly acted as a triggering factor in the rise of the Scottish National Party (SNP), which made the phrase 'It's Scotland's oil' its rallying cry in the early 1970s. Wales had no equivalent issue despite the campaign to force English consumers of Welsh water to pay more for this natural resource ten years later. In Wales, where just under one-fifth of the community speak Welsh, the language issue is central to the nationalist cause in a way which it could never be in Scotland, where Gaelic-speakers form a tiny, geographically peripheral minority.

Both the *Scottish National Party* (1934) and *Plaid Cymru* (1925) the 'Party of Wales', aim at the establishment of elective assemblies as a first step towards the attainment of virtual independence or 'Commonwealth' status. Beyond this, Plaid Cymru presses for increasing use of Welsh in education, broadcasting and public administration, its ultimate aim being bilingualism in all Wales by AD 2000. Both act as pressure groups for their respective regions seeking to wring concessions for their countrymen out of Westminster governments over a wide range of cultural, economic and welfare matters. Popular support for each rose swiftly in the late 1960s and early 1970s, with the SNP gaining over 800 000 votes and 11 seats and Plaid Cymru 166 000 votes and 3 seats in October 1974. Both came in sight of attaining the first stage of their respective goals in 1978 with the Scotland and Wales Act providing for the establishment of assemblies in both countries. 1979 however brought a dramatic decline in the fortunes of both parties, largely as a consequence of the devolution referendum held in March 1979. In neither country did devolution achieve the 40 per cent support from the electorate which was required if the legislation was to remain on the statute book. In Scotland, only 32.5 per cent of the electorate (51.6 per cent of voters) endorsed the legislation; Wales, where a mere 11.8 per cent of electors voted for the proposals and 46.5 per cent voted against, overwhelmingly rejected it. The General Elections of 1979 and 1983 dealt the two nationalist parties further blows. In 1979, the SNP vote declined by 300 000 and nine of its MPs were defeated; the Plaid Cymru vote, from a much lower base, went down by 30 000 but, more seriously, the party's president, Gwynfor Evans, lost his seat in the House. In 1983 the two SNP and two Plaid Cymru MPs were re-elected, but the total vote of both parties continued to decline. In the 1987 election, however, each party slightly increased its representation at Westminster to three MPs. The SNP vote – at 416 873 – was significantly up; the Plaid Cymru vote – at 123 587 – slightly down.

Even at the height of their success, underlying weaknesses existed in the positions of both parties. First, they both operate within the context of a 'dual' system of allegiances in which an over-arching loyalty to Great Britain amongst Scottish and Welsh people offsets their cultural ties to their respective countries. Relatively small proportions of each population (smaller in Wales than in Scotland) sympathise with the major aim of the nationalist parties. In early 1987, for example, a MORI poll for Scottish Television showed only one-third of respondents in favour of independence. (A larger proportion – 47 per cent – supported a Scottish Assembly.) Second, both parties polled more strongly in the rural than in the more heavily industrialised areas such as Strathclyde and South Wales and both found it difficult to gain ground in the big cities. Third, both parties are internally divided between left-wing and conservative nationalists, divisions which were solidified in the formation of the *79 Group* committed to bringing about a 'Socialist and Republican Scotland' in the SNP, and the *National Left Group* (1980) in the Plaid Cymru which aimed at a 'decentralised Socialist' Wales. Despite these difficulties and their decline in support neither party should be underestimated in view of the strength of the national traditions in both countries.

After the 1987 election indeed there was much talk of a 'Doomsday scenario' with Scottish voters having sent fifty Labour MPs to Westminster (and only 10 Conservatives) confronted by a Conservative Government unsympathetic to devolution and the establishment of a Scottish Assembly. In these circumstances, it was suggested, Scotland might become increasingly difficult to govern.

THE NORTHERN IRELAND PARTIES

There is virtually no resemblance between parties and political issues in Northern Ireland and those in the rest of the UK. But Northern Ireland politics still deserve consideration because the province sends seventeen MPs to Westminster where they can bring pressure upon British governments not only upon Northern Ireland issues such as the Anglo-Irish Agreement (1985) but also over the whole range of UK affairs.

Northern Ireland parties divide over three main concerns: the constitutional position of Northern Ireland within the UK; the rights of Catholics, especially in such matters as internal security arrangements, representation in a devolved assembly and discrimination in jobs and housing; and relationships with the Irish Republic. The state of the parties after the 1983 General Election was: Unionist parties fifteen MPs, 57 per cent of the vote; nationalist parties two MPs, 31 per cent; and centre parties, no MPs, 12 per cent. In broad terms, then, the party system reflects a society polarised in sectarian fashion between Protestants (62.5 per cent) and Catholics (37.5 per cent).

The 1987 General Election saw gains for the moderate nationalists at the expense of the Unionists, with the Social and Democratic Labour Party (SDLP) triumphing at the expense of Enoch Powell in South Down and the party doubling its majority in Newry and South Armagh which it won in a by-election in 1986. After the election the Unionists sent thirteen MPs to the Westminster parliament, the nationalists four MPs. The reduction in the vote for the two Unionist leaders and the increase in the vote for the Alliance were widely interpreted as representing a shift of Unionist opinion in favour of the Anglo-Irish agreement.

The primary aim of the Unionists is to maintain the constitutional link with the UK. They regard the Union as a guarantor of Protestant ascendancy and a barrier against a united Ireland ruled from Dublin. Since the British government resumed direct rule of the province in 1972, Unionists have disagreed with Westminster Governments over the terms on which the link should be continued. British policy has been to extend civil rights to Catholics and to devolve power only to an assembly in which the Catholic community is represented. But Unionists wish to retain the 'British connection' on their terms, which means no major extension of political, social and economic opportunities to Catholics, no power-sharing with the nationalist (Catholic) parties, and continuation of policing responsibilities in the hands of the Protestant-dominated Royal Ulster Constabulary (RUC) and Ulster Defence Regiment (UDR). In many ways, Northern Ireland Unionism, which is itself internally divided mainly between the more middle class *Official Unionists* led by James Molyneaux, and the smaller more working-class *Democratic Unionist Party* led in populist style by the Rev. Ian Paisley, is just the political expression of the fiercely intolerant Protestant Orange Order. The *Social Democratic and Labour Party* (SDLP, 1970) is a Socialist party whose main objectives are the abolition of discrimination against Roman Catholics and, in the longer term, the achievement of a united Ireland based on the consent of the majority. It held only one seat after 1983, won by its leader, John Hume, but increased its representation to two in 1986, and then three in 1987. In the 1980s, the position of the SDLP as the leading Catholic anti-Partition party came under increasing challenge from *Provisional Sinn Fein*. This extremist party won a 13.4 per cent share of the total Northern Ireland vote in 1983 against the SDLP's 17.9 per cent, and its leader, Gerry Adams, ousted the former SDLP leader, Gerry Fitt, from West Belfast. But Adams's majority was sharply reduced in 1987. The relatively insignificant 'middle ground' of politics in Northern Ireland is occupied by the non-sectarian Alliance party (8 per cent) and the Workers' Party (4 per cent) although as we have seen, the Alliance vote increased in 1987.

Attempts by the British Government to devolve power back upon Stormont after 1972 broke down on the intransigence of the sectarian groupings; on the unwillingness of the Protestant Unionist Parties to share power with parties representing the Catholic community and on the refusal of the nationalist parties to enter any assembly which did not contain an Irish dimension.

THE EXTREME RIGHT

The *National Front* (1967) is the leading party on the extreme right. It makes an openly racialist appeal, calling for the repatriation of all coloured immigrants and blaming high unemployment, poor housing conditions and inadequacies in the education and welfare services on the 'black and brown aliens'. Internationally, it calls for closer ties with South Africa, realignment of British foreign policy away from Israel towards the Arab States and withdrawal from the European Community. It opposes the United Nations and is violently anti-Communist. It contests elections in the same way as liberal-democratic parties but also maintains secret links with neo-Nazi groups both at home and abroad, notably with the *British Movement* (BM), a virulently anti-Semitic group led by a prominent post-war Nazi, Colin Jordan. It has had little success in national elections (in 1979, it polled just over 190 000, a mere 0.6 per cent of the total vote) but has done better in local government elections in some inner-city areas with sizeable coloured populations, such as the London boroughs of Hackney, Newham and Tower Hamlets where it gained over 10 per cent of the vote in 1977. Its activities also include 'demos' and marches by youthful militant supporters which are intended to demonstrate its determination and physical effectiveness. By the 1983 election, internal splits had further undermined its political appeal and the two extreme right parties, the *National Front* (NF) (led by Martin Webster) and the *British National Party* (BNP) (led by the former NF leader John Tyndall) gained only just over 40 000 votes between them. Meanwhile, the street challenge of British fascism continued with violent anti-black and anti-Jewish propaganda and racist attacks on Asians and their property. In July 1986, the BNP chairman, John Tyndall, and the editor of the party newspaper, Andrew Morse, were both gaoled for one year, having been found guilty of conspiracy to incite racial hatred.

LEFTIST GROUPS

The *Communist Party of Great Britain* (CPGB, 1920) remains an important Left group. Its ideology is Marxist–Leninist, but it has pursued its goal of a Socialist Britain in recent years through a comparatively moderate 'parliamentary' strategy. It is not prepared to 'write off' the Labour Party as the party of the working class, but seeks to draw it closer to 'true' Socialism by effective propaganda, electoral activity and work within the trade unions. It advocates withdrawal from the EEC and NATO, abolition of the House of

Lords, nationalisation of land, banks, insurance companies and all productive enterprises, and free collective bargaining. It opposes workers' representation on boards of management as 'class collaboration'. Its most successful period occurred in the 1940s but it has declined since then. In 1945, it polled over 100 000 votes and returned two MPs but since 1950 it has not elected another MP and in 1983 its vote was down to a mere 11 606; membership fell from 56 000 (1942) to 13 500 (1984); and the circulation of the party newspaper declined from 122 000 (*Daily Worker*, 1947) to 28 250 (*Morning Star*, 1985).

In the 1980s a severe internal struggle between a traditionalist pro-Soviet faction and the more 'liberal' Eurocommunists culminated in the expulsion of the conservative hard-liners, including Ken Gill, the general secretary of the white collar engineering union, TASS, and subsequently Chairman of the TUC.

Eurocommunists depart from the more traditional 'class struggle' emphasis by advocating a broad left alliance of feminists, gays, blacks, environmentalists and nuclear disarmers and criticise the Soviet Union over its record on Poland, Afghanistan and human rights. Under a Eurocommunist editor, the party's journal *Marxism Today*, was an undoubted success, providing a forum for informed Left debate and opening its columns to non-Marxists. However, violent dissension broke out again at the 1983 party congress, with the Eurocommunist leadership once again under fire from the pro-Soviet traditionalists led by the industrial correspondent of the *Morning Star*, Mick Costello. The critics condemned the leadership for abandoning the class struggle in industry in favour of a broad radical alliance and for disapproving of Soviet actions in Afghanistan and Poland. The pro-Soviet faction was heavily defeated and defeat was followed by an immediate purge of seven critics of the leadership from the Executive Committee: these included the editor of the *Morning Star*, his deputy and Costello himself. Large-scale expulsions of dissentient members followed. But the Eurocommunist leadership failed to gain control of the *Morning Star* in 1984; it went on to found another newspaper, *7 Days*. Those expelled from the party formed a *Communist Campaign Group* to recapture the party for Leninism. Granted the Eurocommunists' commitment to the validity of parliamentary reformism, the struggle between them and the pro-Soviet faction seemed likely to continue.

Other far-Left groups grew in importance after the late 1960s. The most significant are the *Socialist Workers' Party* (SWP) and the three Trotskyist groupings, the *Workers' Revolutionary Party* (WRP), the *Socialist League* (SL), which was formerly the international Marxist Group (IMG), and the *Militant Tendency*. These groups reject and aim to destroy the parliamentary system even if they do give the appearance of accepting it by running candidates at elections.

The deeper origins of the *Socialist Workers' Party* can be traced back to

1947 when the Revolutionary Communist Party broke up and to the activities of the International Socialists (IS) in the 1960s. The IS became the SWP in 1976 and adopted a tactic of 'electoral interventionism'. In practice, however, its parliamentary candidates gained minimal success and the greatest impact of the SWP has always been on the industrial front. Its membership increased significantly – to about 5000 in 1980 – as a result of the SWP's aggressive involvement in right to work and anti-racism campaigns in the late 1970s.

The *Workers' Revolutionary Party* supports the IRA, the Libyan leader Colonel Gadaffi, and the Palestine Liberation Organisation (PLO). Led (until 1985) by Gerry Healy it is probably the most fundamentalist Trotskyist group, periodically attacking not only the Labour Party (for class treachery) but also its fellow-Trotskyist groups (for reformism and revisionism). It promotes its industrial activities through the *All Trade Union Alliance* movement. Its membership in 1980 was estimated at about 3000. Already notorious for its apocalyptic pronouncements and internal authoritarianism the group was riven by a series of splits in the mid-1980s (beginning in 1985 with the expulsion of the 74-year old Healy), a process of fractionalisation from which four groups emerged.

The *Socialist League* which, as the IMG in the 1960s, contained a number of leading Marxist intellectuals such as Tariq Ali, Robin Blackburn and Ernest Mandel, is the most respected for its theorising. It is the British section of the United Secretariat of the Fourth International, which was established by Trotsky in 1938 to organise the opposition to Fascism more effectively than the Third International had done. The IMG was formed in 1965 but renamed itself the Socialist League (SL) in the early 1980s. It forged very close relations with the Campaign for Nuclear Disarmament (CND) and resumed the tactic of 'entryism' into the Labour Party which had been abandoned in 1969.

By far the most effective group politically is Militant Tendency. It is the most successful practitioner of 'entryism' – a classic tactic of the revolutionary Left, which involves infiltration of the mainstream Labour Party in order to push it into more hard-line Socialism, win converts to its cause and provoke division and possibly splits from which it might benefit. Its leader, Ted Grant, was formerly a member of the Revolutionary Communist Party with Gerry Healy (subsequently WRP) and Tony Cliff (late SWP). Militant Tendency ran five candidates in Labour colours at the 1983 General Election and is influential in a number of trade unions including the Civil and Public Servants Union (CPSA), the Post Office Engineering Union (POEU), the Bakers' Union and the Fire Brigades Union. In the early- and mid-1980s it was the dominant faction on the Labour council in Merseyside. Extreme Left activities include propaganda by newspapers such as *Socialist Worker* (SWP), *Newsline* (WRP), *Socialist Action* (SL) and *Militant*; industrial work within the trade unions; and anti-racism campaigns like the Anti-Nazi League in the late 1970s.

THE GREEN PARTY

The *Green Party*, which began as the Ecology Party in 1973, rejects the industrial and agricultural practices which pollute and destroy the environment. Specifically, it protests against acid rain which results from the dirty burning of coal, lead in petrol, and the dumping of nuclear waste. The Party is part of the wider 'green' movement which includes such groups as *Friends of the Earth* and *Greenpeace* as well as the very considerable numbers in conservation societies. Its main success prior to 1985, when it had 5500 members, was in the education of public opinion. Its electoral record was disappointing with its 108 candidates in 1983 gaining only 54 299 votes, a mere 1 per cent of the poll in the seats it contested. Its single-cause basis and lack of credibility as a party (as distinct from a pressure group) together with the adoption of environmentalist policies by other parties, limited its appeal. Its adoption of a new name in 1985 brought it into line with its European counterparts. Supporters of the name-change believed the move would assist the Party in resisting the efforts of mainstream parties to steal their environmental policies. The Green Party's best hope of national influence – apart from that via the other parties, an influence which in its view was unacceptably diluted – was through the adoption of proportional representation. This became its immediate political objective in 1985. In that year its influence was limited to about sixty seats on parish and community councils.

Its 1987 manifesto called for unilateral disarmament; the phasing-out of nuclear power for domestic energy needs; the reduction of pollution to a minimum; the encouragement of socially useful products not just commercially viable ones; a fresh approach to the organisation of work, including more job-sharing and part-time arrangements; and help to the Third World in ways which would include encouraging countries to restructure their economies on sustainable lines.

The Green Party put forward 133 candidates in the 1987 Election and gained a total vote of 89 753, a sizeable improvement on 1983. By 1988 membership had increased to about 7000, and it had four District Councillors.

SUMMARY

Parties fulfil three main functions in the British political system. First, they provide governments and oppositions: the Government is composed of members of the majority party (about one-third can expect government posts) and the second most successful party form the official Opposition. The British system therefore is accurately described as *party* government. Second, parties serve as agencies of representation, organising a mass electorate in a way which enables genuine choices to be made by voters. Third, parties are the principal agencies of participation: they provide the means by which citizens register commitment

to political causes by voting and by political activity. In terms of *government*, Britain still has a two-party system – since 1945 the Conservative and Labour parties have alternated in power. *Electorally*, the rise of minor parties in the 1970s and 1980s has produced a situation of multi-partyism at constituency level. There are important differences of ideology, policy and organisation between the two major parties; within each, groups and tendencies representing differing strands of opinion compete for influence. Of the minor parties, the Liberal–SDP Alliance failed to 'break the mould' of British politics in the two elections of 1983 and 1987 and the challenge of the mainland nationalist parties faded without disappearing after 1979. In 1988, the Liberals and SDP merged as the Social and Liberal Democratic Party, with significant minorities in each party opposing fusion. The Green Party raised public awareness of environmental issues and influenced the policies of other parties, but gained representation only at local, not national, level. The activity of groupings on the extreme right and far left increased but their main impact was felt in industry and on the streets. Militant Tendency 'entryism' posed severe problems for Labour and two members of the Tendency became MPs; parliamentary candidates of other extreme groups usually lost their deposits.

FURTHER READING

Arthur, P. (1983) *The Government and Politics of Northern Ireland*, London, Longman.
Beer, S. H. (1969) *Modern British Politics*, London, Faber, 2nd edn.
Bogdanor, V. (1983) *Liberal Party Politics*, Oxford, University Press.
Bradley, I. (1981) *Breaking the Mould? The Birth and Prospects of the SDP*, Oxford, Martin Robertson.
Callaghan, J. (1987) *The Far Left in English Politics*, Oxford, Blackwell.
Drucker, H. and Brown, G. (1980) *The Politics of Nationalism and Devolution*, London, Longman.
Finer, S. E. (1980) *The Changing Party System, 1945–1979*, Washington DC, American Enterprise Institute.
Kavanagh, D. (ed.) (1982) *The Politics of the Labour Party*, London, Allen & Unwin.
Norton, P. and Aughey, A. (1981) *Conservatives and Conservatism*, Hounslow, Temple Smith.
Rose, R. (1974) *The Problem of Party Government*, London, Macmillan.
Rose, R. (1980) *Do Parties Make a Difference?*, London, Macmillan.
Taylor, S. (1982) *The National Front in English Politics*, London, Macmillan.

QUESTIONS

1. Critically examine the relationships between the Conservative Party and business interests, and between the Labour Party and the trade unions. How far, and in what way, do these relationships influence the two parties?
2. Compare the two major parties in leadership (style and method of election), organisation in the country, ideology, policy and ethos.

ASSIGNMENT

Conduct a study of the ways in which the parties organised for the election campaign of 1987. Be sure to include in your coverage a consideration of the following features: party manifestos (both contents and how the contents were selected); campaign teams; strategies; number of candidates for each party; role of the media (TV, radio and the newspapers); finances; attention to marginals; use of advertising agencies; role of opinion polls. Give careful consideration to the result, analysing it at the national and regional levels. Attempt to identify the factors mainly responsible for the particular outcome, and place them in order of importance.

12

Voting Behaviour and Elections

In the late 1960s a political scientist could observe with considerable justification that in Britain 'class is the basis of party politics; all else is embellishment and detail'. Twenty years later social class appears to explain much less about variations in political behaviour and today political scientists talk of 'class dealignment' as having taken place. But, as we shall see, there is much disagreement about the extent to which dealignment has occurred. Political scientists have developed various models to help explain the changes which have taken place in voting behaviour. Each model is useful in that it explains some aspect or other of voting, but none explains voting patterns entirely. The political scientist can be frustrated by trends such as tactical voting, which change the meaning of the voting act and which can distort the significance of correlations between party allegiance and social characteristics. Would the patterns of voting change if a different, and some would say fairer, electoral system were introduced? The chapter concludes with an examination of alternative situations in terms of systems and behaviours.

Casting a vote is one of the simplest forms of political participation; it takes little time, requires only minimal skill and knowledge, and is performed infrequently, yet is is part of the political process that has attracted a great deal of attention from political scientists. The television pundit forecasting electoral fortunes with the assistance of a 'swingometer' forms the popular image of the political scientist. Is the concentration of research into voting behaviour justified because it forms an essential part of democracy and the outcome of elections has considerable impact on our lives? Or does it occur, as some cynics have suggested, because voting in elections is one of the few areas in political science that generates a steady flow of statistics and an opportunity for endless speculation?

Voting studies conducted by political scientists frequently include quantification that is produced by sophisticated research techniques. Such statistics may have a quality, intimidating to some and seductive to others, resulting in the rows of figures being granted an authority they do not really deserve. There is a tendency for statistics spewed from a computer to be seen as the unchallengeable truth, whereas arguments in written or literate form often seem 'softer' and more vulnerable to intellectual challenge. But some would

264

argue that statistical 'facts' should be treated just as warily as written arguments. Questions should be asked about the origins of the statistics, the means by which they were produced, as well as whether the way in which they have been interpreted is plausible. There have been occasions when a political scientist has discovered a 'fact' about voting, but on closer analysis the origins of this new piece of information are not located in the world of politics but are the product of a methodological fault or error.

THE DECLINE OF THE TWO-PARTY SYSTEM

The electorate is not an unchanging entity, nor is it stable. Some changes will occur because its composition is changing as young people attain voting age and become included, whilst others die. Other changes will occur because of movements in attitudes, values and behaviour from one election to the next. Figure 12.1 shows the steady decline in the percentage of the total vote won by the Labour and Conservative parties. In 1951 96.8 per cent of voters supported either Labour or Conservative. These figures touched a low point in the 1983 election, but the overall downward trend remained visible in 1987 when 73.1 per cent of people who actually voted did so for either Labour or Conservative. When the whole electorate was considered, which includes every individual eligible to vote, then only 55.1 per cent voted Labour or Conservative.

One of the major causes for this decline is weakening levels of *partisan attachment*. In other words, the links between voters and parties have grown weaker as fewer and fewer voters identified with one particular political party. This trend has been recorded by political scientists in election surveys; in 1964 eight out of ten electors thought of themselves as being Labour or Conservative whilst only seven out of ten did so in 1983. Perhaps more significant, for every fifty Labour or Conservative supporters who described their partisan loyalty as being 'very strong' in 1964, only thirty-five did so in 1983. As party loyalties weakened, so electoral volatility has increased. Because an increasing number of voters do not have such strong emotional ties to particular parties, they find it easier to switch their vote to another party or to decide not to vote at all.

What processes have been at work to cause the weakening of the voter–party link and the consequent decay of the two-party system? As might be expected of such a complex topic, no one single theory can explain adequately all the changes that have occurred in recent decades. Figure 12.2 portrays some of the difficulties of explaining patterns of voting behaviour in diagrammatic form. Some aspects of changing behaviour may be best explained by developments within wider society, such as changes in the class structure or changes in gender, ethnic or regional consciousness that are reflected in changes in political behaviour. Other aspects of changing voting

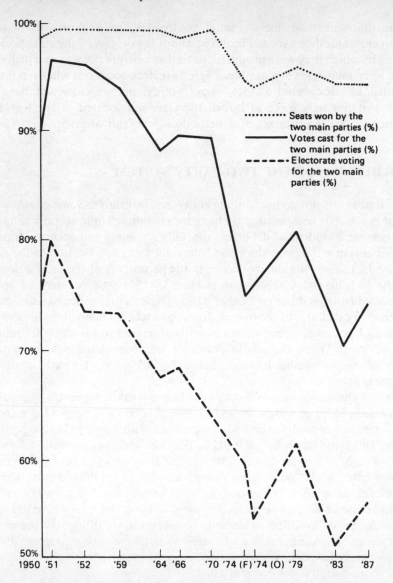

FIGURE   12.1   *The decay of the two-party system, 1950-87*
Source: Adapted from Martin Harrop, 'The Changing Electorate', *Teaching Politics*,
September 1983.

behaviour may be explained more usefully by changes in the political system,
such as the arrival of new issues on the political agenda or the growth of new
political parties. But whatever theories or models political scientists have
devised to explain how some of the changes have come about, it must not be
forgotten that we are examining the behaviour of a collection of individual

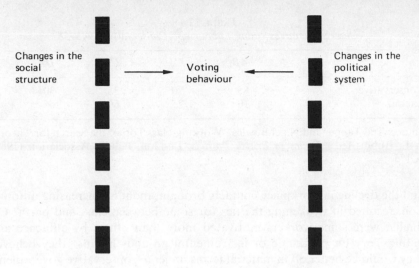

FIGURE 12.2   *Social and political change and voting behaviour*

humans and not a mass of automata. This can be frustrating in some ways because, no matter how attractive or persuasive a particular theory is, it will not be perfect in explaining fully all aspects of the topic being considered. Individuals do not respond in identical ways to similar events in their political, social and economic environments; they interpret them in different ways and accordingly act upon them in different ways.

THE SOCIAL BASIS OF VOTING BEHAVIOUR

Social class and voting behaviour

Of all the social divisions – such as age, gender, ethnicity, and the urban–rural split – it is social class that has preoccupied political scientists. As Table 12.1 indicates, in the early post-war years there was a fairly positive relationship between social class membership and voting behaviour. Political scientists of the time were more interested in the 'class defectors' – the middle-class socialists and the working-class Tories – than they were in the majorities of voters who supported their 'natural' class party. Most research focused on the working-class Tories since this was the most extensive of the deviant behaviour. Did a third of the working class vote Tory because they were deferential and preferred being governed by their social superiors? Was society – in the form of the mass media and education – undermining working-class consciousness and thereby confusing a minority of working people as to which political party they ought to support? Had other social processes, such as slum clearance, the decline of occupational communities

TABLE 12.1
Class percentages voting Labour and Conservative 1945–58

	AB	C1	C2	DE
Conservative	85	70	35	30
Labour	10	25	60	65

Source: Ted Tapper and Nigel Bowles, 'Working-class Tories: the Search for Theory' in L. Robins (ed.) *Topics in British Politics*, London, Politics Association (1982) p. 175.

and the decline in workplace contacts brought about by increasing automation, resulted in weakening the ties for some between class and party? Or, finally, were some workers motivated more than others by affluence and voting Tory on pragmatic or instrumental grounds because they believed they would be better off in material terms under a Conservative government? These were the sort of questions that political scientists posed and set about answering.

During the 1960s and particularly during the 1970s the relationship between class and party weakened. This process of *class dealignment* was reflected in a reduction in Conservative support from the professional and managerial classes and a reduction in Labour support from the working classes. Table 12.2 indicates the voting behaviour of social classes in the 1987 General Election.

As one political scientist commented, by the General Election of 1979, knowing which social class an individual was from was about as reliable as tossing a coin in predicting which way he or she would vote. The questions being asked by political scientists changed dramatically – no longer did they ask why some of the working class voted Tory, by the 1980s they were asking why so few voted Labour. In the early post-war years, support for the major political parties was rooted firmly in the social structure, so what happened to weaken the links between class and party?

In exploring causes of class dealignment some researchers focused on changes that had taken place within the social structure: how far were

TABLE 12.2
Class voting in the 1987 General Election

	AB	C1	C2	DE
Conservative	54	47	42	31
Labour	13	24	35	46
Lib/SDP	30	26	21	20

Source: ITN/Harris poll, *The Independent*, 13 June 1987.

changes in voting behaviour influenced by changes in the class structure? Some social scientists such as Erik Olin Wright had argued that since the Second World War a 'new' middle class had come into existence alongside the 'old' middle class. This new middle class was one which was largely based on people employed in the public sector – such as health authority staff, social workers, teachers and civil servants. It was argued that, unlike the old middle class, the new one was in what is termed 'a contradictory class location' insofar as there was a divergence between the security of class members in the social structure and their ideological orientation. The contradictory class location of this group can be illustrated with the example of college lecturers. They work in the public sector and the overwhelming majority are middle class or bourgeois in outlook. Yet, as recent cutbacks in some authorities have shown, lecturers are not much safer from the threat of redundancy than factory workers. Although lecturers may be bourgeois in outlook they do not have traditional bourgeois security as does the old middle class. At its simplest, a contradiction exists between the political views of lecturers (which are middle class) and their job security (which is similar to working-class conditions). For this new middle class, then, their contradictory location would appear to present a barrier to their support for the traditional party of the middle class, the Conservatives.

Changes have also occurred amongst the working classes. According to one theory, an increased number of individuals whom social scientists would describe as being working class actually see themselves as being middle class. This subjective form of class membership frees them from any loyalties that in the past would have resulted in their support of Labour. This misidentification of class is an extreme example of how the working class has fragmented during the post-war years. The work of K. Roberts *et al.* has revealed the nature of these changes. It is possible to split the working class into union and non-union, affluent and poor, public sector employed/private sector employed, and so on, with each division having distinct political implications. Ivor Crewe has drawn some of these divisions together in compiling what he terms the 'new' and 'traditional' working classes. His data for the 1987 election, contained in Table 12.3, reinforced his earlier conclusion that whilst Labour remained largely working class, the working class was no longer largely Labour. Labour had come to represent the declining fragment of the traditional working class whilst failing to attract the more affluent and expanding working class of the high-tech and service economy.

Three political scientists, Anthony Heath, Roger Jowell and John Curtice, conducted a survey which led them to conclude that class dealignment had not taken place on such a large scale as previously thought. Their findings are given in *How Britain Votes* (1985). They argue that social class is still an important factor in determining the way people vote; hence, Labour's electoral problems sprang from the shrinking size of the working class, not from weakening class-loyalties. Their study utilised a number of new

TABLE 12.3

The fragmentation of the working-class vote

The new working class

	Lives in South	Owner-occupier	Non-union	Works in private sector
Conservative	46	44	40	38
Labour	28	32	38	39
Lib/SDP	26	24	22	23

The traditional working class

	Lives in Scotland/ North	Council tenant	Union member	Works in public sector
Conservative	29	25	30	32
Labour	57	57	48	49
Lib/SDP	15	18	22	19

Source: Ivor Crewe: *The Guardian*, 15 June 1987.

techniques, including a new definition of class categories and the assigning of women in work to class categories according to their own jobs rather than according to their husbands' jobs. In most previous surveys, two women working side by side in an office would have been put into social classes according to their husbands' occupations. For example, if one was married to a teacher, she would have been placed in class B; if the other was married to a skilled mechanic, she would have been placed in class C2. But under the system followed by Heath, Jowell and Curtice, both women would be placed in the same 'routine non-manual' class. The earlier system would only classify a working woman according to her job if she was single and lived on her own. The analysis of class and voting in the 1983 general election using these new research methods is shown in Table 12.4. The group revealed as providing the Conservatives with strongest support are the self-employed rather than the wider professional and managerial AB class. Also, Labour's 49 per cent of the working class vote is considerably greater than the 35 per cent of C2 and 44 per cent of DE which earlier studies showed it winning in 1983. However, it must be stated that Heath, Jowell and Curtice's study came under much criticism from other political scientists who argued that, amongst other things, their new social class definitions were inadequate in embracing the whole of society.

TABLE 12.4
Class voting in the 1983 General election

	Conservative	Labour	Lib/SDP
Petty bourgeoisie (self-employed)	71	12	17
Salariat (managers, professionals)	54	14	31
Foreman/technician (supervisors)	48	26	25
Routine non-manual (clerks)	46	25	27
Working class (supervised at work)	30	49	20

Source: A. Heath, R. Jowell and J. Curtice: *How Britain Votes*, Oxford, Pergamon (1985) p. 20.

Gender and voting behaviour

It has been argued that political scientists have portrayed an inaccurate image of women in the political system. With regard to voting there has been a tendency to assume that many wives were influenced by their husbands in the way that they voted. It was generally believed that women were less informed and interested in politics than men, that they were less likely to vote than men, and that they were more right-wing in their beliefs than men.

Feminist political scientists have challenged these assumptions and argued that on occasions where the political participation pattern of women does differ from that of men, it is because women have to carry an additional domestic burden which necessarily restricts their behaviour. If men carried those burdens, it would similiarly restrict their opportunities to participate. Any variations in political behaviour are not, then, the result of any innate differences between men and women. Table 12.5 analyses the 1987 election result in terms of the way in which men and women voted. It can be seen that the poll results for both men and women are very close to the popular vote for each major party. But, on the face of it, women do appear marginally more right-wing than men, with 2 per cent more voting for the Conservatives and 2 per cent fewer voting for Labour. However, a more thorough

TABLE 12.5
Voting by gender in the 1987 General Election

	Conservative	Labour	Lib/SDP
Men	41	33	23
Women	43	31	23
All	43.3	31.6	23.1

Source: ITN/Harris poll, *The Independent*, 13 June 1987

consideration raises doubts as to whether the figures really do 'speak for themselves'. Since women live on average about six years longer than men, the female sample is likely to include more elderly as a proportion than the male sample. For both men and women, there is an overall increase in Conservative support with increasing age. Thus, the apparently stronger Tory support amongst women may just reflect a more aged female population.

Explaining voting behaviour

In the 1960s political scientists generally agreed that individuals identified with a political party as a result of the political socialisation process. A child, it was argued, is born to a family which is located at a particular position in the social structure. Political loyalties are transmitted from parent to child, and later reinforced by friends and neighbours who are located at the same position in the social structure. The monopoly of influence wielded by parents over their young and the pressures on young people to conform which are exerted by others in their social environment result in individuals absorbing class values and class allegiances. During the 1970s, however, the concept of political socialisation fell out of favour with political scientists and was largely discarded as an analytical tool. The usefulness of political socialisation was questioned because (i) there was no substantial evidence that the values of young people stayed with them through the life cycle and (ii) there was no evidence that a person's political values and attitudes guided his or her behaviour.

Some political scientists were attracted to models of voting in which new cleavages cut across the old class divisions. Since the Second World War the growth of government had resulted in divisions between those employed in either the public or private sectors, and between those who used the services produced by the public and the private sectors. Dunleavy and Husbands have argued that 'The most important implication of the growth of the public services for the social structure has been the emergence of sectoral cleavages in consumption processes, by which we may understand social cleavages created by the existence of public and private . . . modes of consumption' (P. Dunleavy and C. Husbands, *Democracy at the Crossroads*, 1985, pp. 21–5). A consumption cleavage would divide those who use public services (for example, Council housing, State-maintained schools, public transport, and the NHS) from those who use private services (for example, owner-occupation, independent schools, private transport, and private health care). It is argued that an individual's voting choice is influenced by the various party policies on his or her pattern of consumption; for example, an owner-occupier might find it impossible to support a party proposing to end tax relief on mortgage repayments. These cleavages are not necessarily in line with the divisions of the class system. As we have seen, an increasing number of middle-class people are employed in the public sector, with the great majority of them relying on State-maintained schools to educate their children and the NHS to tend their sick. On the other hand, there has been an increasing number of working-class people employed in the private sector, who are owner-occupiers and who use only private transport.

To what extent do the interests associated with different sectors explain voting behaviour? Table 12.3 appears to provide some evidence to support the consumption cleavage model since the Conservatives are by far the most popular party amongst working-class owner-occupiers, and the Labour Party is by far the most popular amongst working-class Council tenants. However, it is not possible to argue that these consumption patterns by themselves explain the degree of support for the different parties. As Martin Harrop has asked, 'Do home-owners vote Conservative because they are home-owners or because they are affluent, middle-aged and living in pre-dominantly Conservative environments in the Midlands and the South?' (Harrop, 'The changing electorate' in L. Robins (ed.) *Political Institutions in Britain* (1987) p. 170). He continued by arguing that people who bought their Council houses did not defect heavily to the Conservatives, they were already a relatively Conservative group.

Cleavages within the middle class provide similarly ambiguous data; Table 12.6 contains voting statistics based on employment sector. The Conservatives have the overwhelming support of private sector employees in the middle class; amongst public-sector employees, although the Tories are the single most popular party, non-Tories are in the majority. Clearly, there is a superficial association between the sector of employment and voting preference, but is the link one of 'cause' or 'effect'? Do middle-class people move to the left and support Labour or the Alliance because they are employed in the public sector, or are they attracted to public sector occupations in the first place because of their radicalism? Harrop argues that for middle-class radicals 'the public sector provides a favourable environment for strengthening their political values but does not create them' (Harrop, 'The changing electorate', p. 171).

TABLE 12.6
Divisions in middle-class voting behaviour

	Public Sector	Private Sector
	%	%
Conservative	44	65
Labour	24	13
Lib/SDP	32	22

Source: Ivor Crewe, *The Guardian*, 15 June, 1987

POLITICAL DEVELOPMENTS AND VOTING BEHAVIOUR

The weakened bonds between voters and parties are also the result of a complex process sometimes referred to as *partisan dealignment*. Partisan identification has declined as voters have taken a greater personal interest in political issues rather than granting almost automatic support to their 'class' party regardless of its policy commitments. One issue that concerns some voters is their perception of the party's ability to govern. A party which is internally divided, presents policies which are not fully worked out or consistent and has leaders who appear incompetent on the media will not strike the electorate as being 'fit to govern'. The party image, including the personal images of its leaders, becomes influential in deciding how the electorate votes. It is widely agreed that in the 1983 General Election Labour's poor showing in the polls resulted from the party's lack of credibility as an alternative government. Labour's Left-wing manifesto was described by one of its own leaders as 'the longest suicide note in history'. The election campaign was run in all but the last nine days by a relatively open committee of up to forty members. The resulting campaign was by common consent unsophisticated and uncoordinated by comparison with the Conservatives. W. Miller commented 'The issues were not inherently against Labour. Instead, disunity and incompetence in the Labour leadership destroyed Labour's credibility on its own natural issues and allowed its opponents to put their issues on the agenda ... Labour was not ready for government in 1983 and the electorate knew it' (Miller, 'There Was No Alternative: the British General Election of 1983', *Parliamentary Affairs*, 4, 1984, pp. 379, 383).

The impact of issues on political perceptions

New issues can arise on the political agenda which do not fit into the traditional class interests of the parties, and can therefore blur the lines linking party and voter. For example, advocates and opponents of nuclear power development cross party lines causing divisions amongst trade unionists in particular. The miners have an interest in actually closing existing nuclear power stations, whilst workers in the nuclear power industry support its expansion. Moral issues, such as the abortion issue or health education, can become salient issues which have little relation to party positions and are better understood in terms of authoritarian or liberal orientations. For example, there are Conservatives and Socialists who support an education campaign advising the public about precautions which will reduce the risks of catching and spreading AIDS. But within each party are those who take a stricter line arguing that chastity before marriage and fidelity afterwards are the only lessons that need to be taught.

The emergence of the EEC as an important political issue, considered again later, is an interesting case-study of how traditional divisions between and within parties provided little guide to politicians' attitudes. On the left-wing of the Labour party were both strong supporters and hostile enemies of the EEC. Applying socialist principles, some saw the EEC as a first step in the creation of a 'third force' socialist Europe which would eventually stretch from Ireland to the Urals. The concentration of political power and removal of national boundaries were welcomed as creating the necessary precondi-tions for third-force Europe. Others on Labour's left-wing, also applying Socialist principles, opposed the EEC, which they saw as a capitalist economic underpinning to NATO. They thought the European Community would perpetuate the cold war and generally frustrate the development of socialism. The right wing of Labour was similarly split into pro- and anti-EEC factions. The right-wingers applied revisionist values to the issue, in which prospects for economic growth to underpin increased welfare were central. Some believed that the EEC presented Britain with the best available opportunity to increase economic growth, whilst others saw the EEC as a threat to growth with better prospects available through joining other international trading organisations. Thus, Labour members found them-selves sharing similar EEC platforms with colleagues who had reached the same decision for completely different reasons. At the same time, the Conservatives were divided in an equally complex way on the issue and even the Liberals, the most pro-EEC party of the 1960s, contained its anti-EEC faction. Given these difficulties in understanding the EEC issue along lines which gave meaning to already existing issues, it is not surprising that the electorate were unstable in their views. According to opinion polls conducted throughout the 1960s, views on British membership of the EEC vacillated as the electorate assimilated the issue. Over 50 per cent favoured entry in 1961 but only 36 per cent in 1962; in 1966 71 per cent approved entry but only 43 per cent did so in 1967.

Can issue preferences explain voting behaviour?

With the weakening of class influences on voting and the emergence of new issues which did not fit traditional partisan splits, some political scientists argued that an increasing number of the electorate were voting on the basis of issue preferences. Mark Franklin found, for example, that the effect of voters deciding which party to vote for according to issue preferences more than doubled between 1964 and 1983 (Franklin, *The Decline of Class Voting in Britain*, 1985). Some political scientists argued that Labour's electoral defeats since 1979 were accounted for in part because its policies were no longer popular, even with its long-standing supporters. For example, Ivor Crewe considers that trends in public opinion reveal a quite exceptional movement of opinion away from Labour's traditional positions amongst Labour supporters over the past twenty or thirty years. There has been a spectacular decline in support for the 'collectivist trinity' of public owner-ship, trade union power and social welfare. By contrast, the policy positions of the Conservative party and its supporters have remained strong and stable.

A 'consumer model' of voting behaviour has been constructed by H. Himmelweit and colleagues which is derived from an issue-based theory of voting (Himmelweit, Humphreys and Jaeger, *How Voters Decide*). Voters 'shop around' to find the party with a programme of policies which offers the closest fit to their own policy preferences. Of course, voters may not have perfect information about various parties' policies and, even when they do have the relevant information, they may suspect that a party, if elected to office, would not implement its manifesto proposals. Although past studies showed that party support could be predicted with 80 per cent accuracy from consumer preferences, the 1987 General Election raises some doubts about seeing voters as analogous to shoppers in the political market-place.

A survey of *British Social Attitudes* (1986) challenged the view that seven years of Thatcherism had moved the political consensus of the electorate to the right. Poll results showed that Conservative supporters opposed reduced taxation almost as much as Alliance and Labour supporters did, if it meant reduced social spending. A majority favoured an increase in taxation if increased revenue was spent on health, education and social benefits. On defence, those in favour of Britain giving up nuclear weapons had increased from 19 per cent to 27 per cent in the three years up to 1986. During the election campaign of the following year, when asked by pollsters which were the most important issues facing the country, voters consistently mentioned the NHS, education, unemployment and defences as the top issues. Despite attempts to present a more 'caring' image to the electorate, the Conservatives did better than Labour only on the defence issue. As Ivor Crewe commented regarding the 1987 General Election result in an article in *The Guardian*, 'Labour's poor performance remains a puzzle because its campaign did succeed in placing its favourable issues much further up the agenda than in 1983 ... Had electors voted solely on the main issues Labour would have won. It was considered the more capable party on three of the four leading issues – jobs, health and education – among those for whom the issue was important ... On all three social issues there was widespread agreement even among Conservatives, that matters had deteriorated' (*The Guardian*, 16 June 1987).

Thus, in social surveys conducted in the year prior to the 1987 General Election and in polls taken during the campaign, there is evidence that when 'shopping around' the electorate was attracted most of all by Labour's issues. If the election had been decided by issue-based voting, then Labour should have emerged the winner. The consumer model fails in the main to explain voting behaviour in 1987 because it appears that despite many voters sympathising with Labour's social policies they actually felt personally better-off under the Conservatives and voted accordingly. In other words, feelings of individual prosperity outweighed issue preference in deciding which way a vote would be cast.

Multi-party politics

It is difficult to argue whether the increase in voting for third parties is a cause or effect of the traditional links between the electorate and the two main parties becoming weaker. Figure 12.1 shows the declining proportion of votes cast for the Labour and Conservative parties over four decades. Nationalist parties – Plaid Cymru and the Scottish Nationalist Party – have enjoyed periodic surges of support as did the Liberals (later the Liberal/ Social Democratic Party Alliance in the 1970s and 1980s). The Alliance parties 'bridged' the left–right divide that separated the two main parties whilst others such as the Nationalists and the Green Party fell outside the traditional left–right spectrum. This proliferation of parties together with declining levels of party attachment has resulted in increased electoral volatility. The increased presence of credible third parties make it psycho-logically easier for voters to switch from one party to another, to support one party in local elections and another in general elections, or to vote tactically in order to keep out their 'most disliked' party.

The increasing volatility of the British electorate began in the by-elections of the late 1950s. The Liberals enjoyed huge surges of support, particularly, as it turned out, when Conservatives were in government. The share of the popular vote won by Liberals also increased during the 1970s reaching a peak of 26 per cent in partnership with the SDP in the 1983 General Election. Table 12.7 shows the popular vote and by-election averages in one of the best periods in the Liberal/SDP Alliance's performance of attracting support for a third party.

Electoral fortunes fluctuated, with the Conservative government winning back in 1983 many of the votes lost in previous by-elections. Psephologists

TABLE 12.7
By-elections, 1981–3, and the 1983 General Election

	% of vote in by-elections 1982–3	% of vote in 1983 General Election
Conservative	27.5	43.5
Labour	34.7	28.3
Alliance	31.2	26.0

Source: Donley T. Studlar, 'By-elections and the Liberal-SDP Alliance', in L. Robins (ed.) *Updating British Politics*, London, Politics Association (1984) p. 117

have pointed out that one of the reasons that by-elections are not necessarily a good guide to general election results is the difference in levels of turnout. Voters are not only volatile in switching support from one party to another but also fluctuate in terms of voting and abstaining. Although the Alliance's by-election share of the vote rose to an average of 31.2 per cent in the 1981–3 by-elections, turnout in those elections was down by 12.5 per cent on 1979 figures. What sometimes, then, looks like a massive shift in opinion from supporting one party to another on the part of voters may in fact be a reflection of the movement of voters to abstainers and abstainers to voters. Also, as mentioned earlier, the electorate is subject to demographic trends and what might look like a change in political views may be in large part the result of some previous voters dying and migrating as well as new voters joining the electorate. Although swings may increase still further, the element caused by vote-switching has remained relatively constant since 1974.

The phenomenon of tactical voting can obscure the meaning of election statistics, since a tactical vote is particularly superficial in that the voter concerned is in no way a convert to the party he or she supports. A tactical vote is essentially negative and based on a calculation that the most preferred party cannot win: support is therefore given to another party which is seen as in a better position to block the advance of the least preferred party. In the 1987 General Election, a tactical vote was essentially an anti-Tory vote, and tactical voting appeared to reach considerable proportions. The run-up to the election contained much journalistic speculation about a hung or 'balanced' parliament as well as press advertisements from TV87 Campaign. Pippa Norris commented

> on the basis of the aggregate results we can conclude that there was some evidence of limited tactical voting, benefiting both Labour and the Alliance vote in marginal Tory seats where they were clearly established in second place, although the impact was too limited to lead to dramatic gains. Further support for this can be found in the election surveys particularly the Harris/ITN exit poll: when asked whether they had voted for the party of their first choice, 17% said they were tactical voters. Over 36% of those who switched to Labour or the Alliance from 1983 to 1987 identified themselves as tactical voters (Norris, 'The 1987 British General Election: The Hidden Agenda', *Teaching Politics*, September 1987).

The geography of voting

In the 1950s, the swing from one party to another in a general election was remarkably uniform throughout most constituencies. This pattern of consistent swing has broken up as different parts of the country show relatively wide variations in movement of support. For example, in the 1987 General Election, the two-party swing from the Conservatives to Labour was 1.8 per cent, but in the North it ran at 4.3 per cent and at 5.9 per cent in Scotland. But in London, the South-east and East Anglia the biggest swing was to the Conservatives, mainly at the expense of the Alliance.

The geographical polarisation of British politics has been developing since the mid-1950s. Labour's support is concentrated in the industrial towns of the North and Scotland, whilst the Conservatives' strength lies in the South, suburbs and rural areas. Whilst talk of a North–South divide is somewhat oversimplified, it provides a useful summary of major electoral outcomes. For example, the Conservatives suffered a disastrous defeat in Scotland in 1987 when their already small contingent of twenty-two MPs was reduced to eleven. Many large northern industrial towns – such as Newcastle, Bradford, Manchester and Liverpool – are without any Conservative MPs. In some Scottish and northern constituencies, Labour was the choice of nearly three-quarters of the voters. In contrast, the South outside London is marked by an almost total absence of Labour MPs. The qualifications to the argument of a North–South divide are that there are Tory MPs in Scotland and in Northern 'pockets of affluence' such as Batley and Spen and rural seats such as Ryedale; and there are Labour MPs in the South outside London, namely in Bristol, Norwich and Oxford. Also, the North–South split was cross-cut by an East–West divide. In Wales and the South-west the swing was 1.5 per cent and 0.8 per cent respectively away from the Conservatives whereas in the South-east the swing was 2.6 per cent to the Tories. In the North-west, the swing away from the Conservatives was 2.0 per cent whilst in Yorkshire and Humberside it was only 1.2 per cent; also, Labour failed to win several north-eastern target seats such as Batley and Spen, Keighley and York.

One effect of the regional concentration of support for the Labour and Conservative parties has been a reduction in the number of marginal seats. In 1983, there were three seats in which Labour had an 'ultra-safe' majority of over 50 per cent; by 1987, the number had increased to twenty-two. Conservatives increased their 'ultra-safe' seats from twenty-four in 1983 to forty-four in 1987. The result of this trend has been to reduce by more than half the number of highly marginal seats. This has worked to the disadvantage of the Alliance parties. Their share of the popular vote declined by 2.9 per cent in 1987 with only limited gains being made in Argyll and Bute, Fife North-east and Southport whilst Alliance losses included some of their best known personalities.

THE ELECTORAL SYSTEM EFFECT

Britain's first-past-the-post electoral system is not neutral in converting the share of votes received by a party into the share of seats won. It causes a distortion in the relation between the share of votes and the share of seats and, in many ways, can be thought of as a system of 'unproportional representation'. Figure 12.1 shows that the two-party system still dominates the House of Commons although it has declined steadily in the country. Britain's electoral system rewards parties which can concentrate their political support in specific areas and punishes parties which have their support more evenly spread. This was most evident in the 1983 General Election when the Alliance received only 2.3 per cent less of the popular vote than Labour, but whereas Labour's 28.3 per cent of the votes won it 209 MPs, the Alliance's 26.0 per cent won it only twenty-three MPs. Putting it another way, for every 40 000 votes cast for it, Labour won an MP and, for every 33 000 votes cast for it, the Conservative party won an MP. But it took the Alliance a massive 338 000 votes for every MP elected. Even in 1987, when the Alliance did less well, if each party's share of the vote had been reflected in the number of seats won, there would have been a hung parliament with the Alliance holding the balance of power.

The introduction of a proportional representation system of voting (the Single Transferable Vote) has long been amongst the constitutional reforms supported by the Alliance, but PR has supporters amongst members of all parties. In 1983, an all-party Campaign for Fair Votes was set up to join the long-established Electoral Reform Society. The Campaign for Fair Votes was deliberately vague about exactly what form of PR it favoured but it argued that PR 'gives the voters more choice and better representation and it offers more stable and effective government'. Opponents of first-past-the-post have long argued that as a system it failed to produce a parliament which reflected the main trends of political opinion within the electorate; that it therefore failed to produce a government which acted according to the wishes of the majority; and that it did not guarantee the existence of strong and stable government. Within recent times the Labour government of 1964 was kept in power by a very narrow margin, and Britain had a hung parliament after the February 1974 General Election with a Labour minority government and later in 1977–8 a coalition-flavoured Lib–Lab pact to support a minority Labour government. Opponents of the present voting system point out that it was condemned by an earlier generation of politicians and survived until now only because of deadlock between the Commons and Lords on which system should replace it.

Supporters of first-past-the-post argue that the coalition politics which PR produces is far from democratic because the electorate does not know in advance what sort of deals or bargains are going to be made in order to form a government. Therefore, the electorate will not have voted for the policies which are finally implemented. It is almost customary for opponents of PR to point out the complexity and potentially confusing nature of PR (despite STV having been used successfully on several occasions in Northern Ireland) and to blame PR for the forty Italian governments established in thirty-four years and the twenty-five French governments that came and went between 1945 and 1958. Some opponents point to the danger of PR giving extremist parties a foothold, claiming that PR assisted the rise of the Nazi party in Weimar Germany by enabling them to win seats in the Reichstag while still representing a small number of voters.

Since the prospects for electoral reform being introduced to Britain are exceedingly slim in the foreseeable future, some individuals have been rethinking electoral tactics. They argued that the 1987 General Election result was predictable in 1983 as indeed are all the general elections to the end of the century at least. They believe that a string of Conservative victories is inevitable because of the processes discussed earlier and because of the way in which the electoral system works. It is argued that the Conservatives could lose almost a quarter of their popular vote in a future election and yet, because of factors such as electoral geography and the way the opposition is divided, they could still be returned to government. The example of Labour in 1987 is cited because, despite its professional campaign, the party still polled its lowest share of the vote since 1923, with the exception of the disastrous performance in 1983. Thus, it is argued, the task facing the opposition parties is an extremely daunting one.

Confronted with this situation some anti-Tories have proposed ways in which the present electoral system could be 'bent' to their advantage. The tactical voting campaign, TV87, was such an example; it was based on the idea that the Conservatives' position could be undermined by tactical voting in marginal seats. Earlier ideas included the formation of a 'popular front' or 'Rainbow alliance' in order to re-create a two-party system with voters. The proposal involved all parties to the left of the Conservatives combining forces in order to defeat Thatcherism. It was argued that Labour and the Alliance parties should form an electoral pact with candidates standing down in each others' favour in appropriate constituencies. This would forge a double two-party system where the electoral contest in the North and Scotland would be between Labour and Conservative, and in the south between Alliance and Conservative. Although individual members of the parties concerned expressed enthusiasm for the creation of a wide Rainbow alliance, respective party leaders have expressed no interest in the concept. Some even doubt its feasibility since it is built on the unproven assumptions that Alliance voters prefer Labour to Conservative and Labour voters prefer Alliance to Conservative.

SUMMARY

During the post-war years, there has been a declining attachment of voters to parties, and a subsequent increase in the volatility of voting behaviour. There has been a decline in the class basis of voting, but the extent to which that decline has taken place is not agreed upon by political scientists. Models of socialisation, sectoral cleavage and issue-based consumerism add to our understanding of voting behaviour although each explanation has weaknesses which limit its explanatory power. The geography of voting suggests that a simple split between the north and south of Britain is modified by an east–west split. However, the basic situation of Labour being strong in the north and the Conservatives strong in the south has drawn some non-Tory politicians towards the idea of parties making electoral bargains with each other in an attempt to dislodge the Conservatives from office.

FURTHER READING

Butler, D. and Stokes, D. (1974) *Political Change in Britain: The Evolution of Electoral Choice*, London, Macmillan.

Butler, D. and Kavanagh, D. (1988) *The British General Election of 1987*, London, Macmillan.

Heath, A., Jowell, J. M. and Curtice, J. K. (1985) *How Britain Votes*, Oxford, Pergamon.

Himmelweit, H., Humphreys, P. and Jaeger, M. (1984) *How Voters Decide*, Milton Keynes, Open University Press.

Sarlvik, B. and Crewe, I. (1983) *Decade of Dealignment*, Cambridge, University Press.

QUESTIONS

1. Assess the extent to which Britain retains a two-party system.
2. Describe and account for the changing relationship between class and voting.
3. 'Talk of a North–South divide in Britain's electoral geography is misleading.' Comment on this view.
4. How accurately does it describe the dilemma of third parties in Britain to say that they need proportional representation to enter government, but need to be in government to get proportional representation?

ASSIGNMENT

Many young voters are ill-informed about voting. What might go into a 20-minute video designed to explain the different methods by which an individual can cast a vote, how votes are counted, how the result is announced, who the various personnel involved are, and so on, in a general election. Sketch a plan for such a 'user's guide to election day' bearing in mind how you would present the information whilst retaining the interest and attention of the viewer. Draw up a list of the objectives you would try to achieve with your video, making it clear how you would hope to achieve each one.

13

Pressure Groups

Pressure groups, like parties, are informal political institutions which seek to influence decision-making. But, unlike parties, pressure groups do not stand for office; they do not aim to become the government. Also, they differ from parties in not being 'purely' political. For example, churches may enter the political arena by making reports on the condition of the inner cities, universities may do so by protesting against cuts in their budgets, trade unions by lobbying against legislation they see as hostile, but no one doubts that the primary purposes of these institutions are respectively religious, educational and industrial. They are 'partial' organisations which are only to a certain degree concerned with politics. Although not aiming to exercise power directly, however, pressure groups do share some characteristics with parties. In particular, they are agencies of *representation* and *participation*. They are mechanisms for the expression of interest and opinion and they facilitate popular involvement in politics. In both these ways, alongside parties, they contribute to the successful working of liberal democracy. They may also, even though they do not seek election, play a significant role in government, exercising power through hundreds of regulatory and supervisory bodies which depend on their cooperation to function at all. Finally, whilst the distinction between parties and pressure groups on the grounds of office-seeking is an essential one, it is not absolutely watertight. For, if the two types of organisation are theoretically separable, in political practice (which is usually messier) they overlap. Pressure groups are to be found operating inside parties, contributing to their funds, trying to 'capture' their policies and, in the case of the trade unions within the Labour Party, being embedded in their constitutions.

This chapter focuses on the role of these important institutions in British Politics. Starting with a definition of pressure groups, it then explores some leading examples by means of case-studies, and finally examines their targets for influence, the strategies they employ, and the resources they command.

PRESSURE GROUPS DEFINED

There are two main types of pressure group – (i) interest, and (ii) promotional.

Interest groups arise out of the performance of an economic function in

283

society: they exist to represent people as engaged in certain professions, trades and occupations – as, for example, teachers, shopkeepers, miners and company directors. Their main task is to defend and advance the interests of their members. They are also referred to as sectional groups because they represent particular sections of society. The primary purpose of such groups is not generally speaking political: rather, they aim to provide a range of advice and services and to establish standards for their respective occupations. However, granted the politicisation of modern life, they find that, in order to look after their members' interests effectively, they need to enter politics – in which circumstances, they are operating as pressure groups.

In contrast, *promotional* groups exist to further particular causes. People join them because they believe in certain values or hold a particular set of attitudes. Promotional groups are also referred to as cause, attitude, ideological and preference groups. Examples are Shelter, the Disablement Income Group and the Campaign for Nuclear Disarmament (CND). Whereas membership of an interest group is largely involuntary (even if one does not pay one's dues, one 'belongs' merely by virtue of engaging in a particular occupation), the main characteristic of promotional groups is their voluntary nature. Although it contains a large amount of truth, even this distinction does not hold completely. Conscience as well as self-interest may impel people to join unions. Equally a decision to become a member of the AA may be said to contain a large element of prudent calculation of interest, especially for people who need to drive for a living. Also, whereas promotional groups such as the National Trust or a large charity like OXFAM are predominantly preference groups in terms of the nature of their membership, they also hold property and hence have material interests to defend. These qualifications should be borne in mind when discussing the various kinds of pressure group, but it still makes sense to subdivide them into two main categories, interest and promotional.

The term 'pressure group' can also describe a type of *activity* as well as a kind of organisation. All institutions whatever their purpose are subject to attempts at influencing their policies and behaviour by groups of individuals. We have already noticed the existence of such groupings within the political parties. Pressure groups themselves are not immune: witness the divisions on strategy between rival groupings on the miners' union executive or within CND, or the attempts by radicals to inject more militancy into the RSPCA on animal experiments and the fur trade. All this activity may be accurately termed 'pressure group' politics, even if the groups in question generally lack permanency and are, on the contrary, extremely fluctuating in membership and relatively transient. From time to time, divisions within pressure groups (in the organisational sense) harden, splits occur and pressure groups (in the activity sense) develop a permanent character as separate organisations. The emergence of an independent Union of Democratic Mineworkers out of the National Union of Mineworkers in 1985 is a case in point. The way the SDP was formed in a breakaway from the Labour Party in 1981 reveals the same process at work in an overtly political institution. This chapter focuses on pressure groups as organisations, but pressure as a form of activity in all institutions is of great importance and recurs frequently throughout the book.

HISTORY AND RECENT TRENDS

There is nothing new about pressure groups. They have existed for a very long time. In the nineteenth century, pressure groups campaigned for the abolition of the slave trade, the extension of the franchise to the working class and to women, the disestablishment of the Church of England and the abolition of the Corn Laws. Politics was also continually swayed by the large economic interests – landowning, commercial, manufacturing, professional, ecclesiastical. However, the twentieth century has seen a transformation of the role of groups in the political system. There have been two major phases: (i) 1920s–1960s; (ii) 1960s–1980s. In the first phase, two significant developments occurred. First, a large number of permanent, well-organised sectional groups emerged, making demands on government. Second, it became recognised practice for governments to consult the groups before making decisions affecting their interests and also a widely-accepted norm that they should do so. The practice came about because government added to the regulative functions it already possessed both extensive new responsibilities and spending commitments on a considerable scale. Much of this change occurred after 1945 as governments took on the task of management of the economy and of maintaining large welfare and defence establishments. The system of functional (i.e. sectional) representation developed against this context as a result of the mutual needs of government and of groups. Government needed to consult interest groups in order to be able to carry out its policies effectively; groups had to lobby government to ensure that their members' interests were considered when decisions affecting them were made. A second reason why functional representation developed on such a scale alongside the more traditional system of parliamentary representation is that it fitted in with the ethos of each major party during this period. Both the Labour and the Conservative Parties had collectivist rather than individualist theories of representation: both saw it as legitimate for particular social interests (e.g. business or the unions) to seek influence not only within the parties themselves but also directly at the level of government.

If the first period saw the institutionalisation of the influence of sectional groups on a large scale, the second phase (1960s–1980s) has witnessed a very considerable growth in the numbers and memberships of promotional groups. Joining a 'cause' or protest group became for large numbers of people a more effective way of achieving a desired political end than joining a political party. As party membership declined, pressure-group membership increased. People were attracted to a wide range of causes: feminism, anti-nuclear protest, environmental campaigns, animal rights. Much of this upsurge of activity took place at the local level. Some groups such as tenants' associations, neighbourhood councils and environmental protesters had a naturally local context. But, in addition, some 'national' movements such as CND and women's liberation have a participant ethos and a decentralised structure which encourages local membership.

Why has 'cause' group activity increased so dramatically? Explanations include the spread of affluence; increases in educational standards; the emergence of individualist and libertarian philosophies; the intensified build-up of nuclear arms; the failure to eliminate poverty; the development of a multicultural society; and the decline of class. None of these explanations is more than partial; together they shed some light. A relatively wealthy society in which the majority are reasonably well-off can afford to take non-materialist issues such as the environment seriously. A better-educated society, especially one with over 10 per cent of the age-group in higher education, is likely to be more sensitive to issues involving the rights of minorities. As Superpower strategies moved towards the 'winnability' of a nuclear war, so peace and disarmament movements spread. Because poverty has not been eliminated, pressure groups are necessary to represent the deprived – for example, children of poor families, the mentally and physically handicapped, the homeless, the old. Because society is still disfigured by racism, ethnic minorities have to organise for self protection. Finally, the weakening force of social class in structuring political attitudes and loyalties means that people are more open than before to the influence of other factors, such as gender, race, intellectual conviction, personal tastes and morality, as guides in their political behaviour.

SOME LEADING INTEREST AND PROMOTIONAL GROUPS

Interest groups

The leading sectional groups may be divided into groups representing capital and groups representing labour. Groups representative of capital display a considerable variety. All sectors of the economy – finance, manufacturing industry, commerce and retailing, and the professions – have representative organisations (see Table 13.1). In addition, *within* each sector, individual institutions – big companies like ICI for example, or leading insurance companies – may lobby governments on their own behalf. Down to the 1970s, most of the contacts between the financial sector and government took place through the Bank of England. In recent years, however, contacts between government and the various financial institutions in the City of

TABLE 13.1

The main sectional groups (1): industrial, financial, commercial and professional

Industry	Finance	Commerce	Professional
Confederation of British Industry	The Bank of England	Retail Consortium	British Medical Association
Smaller Businesses Association	Committee of London Clearing Banks	Association of British Chambers of Commerce	The Law Society
British Institute of Management	British Bankers' Association	National Chamber of Trade	Institute of Chartered Accountants
Institute of Directors	Accepting Houses Committee (Merchant Banks)	Motor Agents' Association	Royal Institute of British Architects
Aims of Industry	Investment Protection Committee (Pension Funds)	Road Haulage Association	Royal Institution of Chartered Surveyors
Economic League	City Liaison Committee	National Food and Drink Federation	Institution of Mechanical Engineers
Engineering Employers Federation	Institution Shareholders Committee	National Grocers' Federation	Institution of Electrical Engineers
National Federation of Building Trades Employers	Council for the Securities Industry (Stock Exchange)	National Federation of Wholesale Grocers and Provision Merchants	Royal Town Planning Association
United Kingdom Textile Manufacturers	The British Insurance Association (Joint Stock Insurance Companies)		British Dental Association
National Association of Master Bakers, Confectioners and Caterers	Building Societies Association		Association of University Teachers
British Footwear Manufacturers Federation			
Society of Motor Manufacturers and Traders			
National Farmers Union			

London (including the banks, the Stock Exchange and the insurance companies) have become more formal and, with this development, these institutions have formed representative organisations. Thus, the *Committee of London Clearing Banks* (CLCB, 1971) and the *British Bankers' Association* (BBA, 1972) emerged in banking, and the *Council for the Securities Industry* (1977) for the Stock Exchange. Unlike other sectors of the economy, the City lacks a 'peak' organisation, probably because its interests are so various. Attempts to found one in the Institution Shareholders Committee (1973) failed and the other potential 'peak' organisation, the City Liaison Committee, looks towards Brussels (and the EEC) rather than towards Westminster (and the British government). Within industry, there are employers' organisations (e.g. the Engineering Employers' Federation) which normally handle negotiations with trade unions over conditions and wages and trade associations which consult with government at local as well as national level and serve as dispensers of information to members about such matters as changes in the law affecting them. A particularly strong trade association is the *Society of Motor Manufacturers and Traders* (SMMT) which had a staff of 118 and an income of £1.7 m in 1978.

The *Confederation of British Industry* (CBI) formed in 1965 by a merger of three earlier employers' groups is the 'peak' employers' organisation. It is well-resourced, having an annual income of £4.6 m, and employing a staff of 440 to serve its 15 000 members in 1978. Although small firms employing under 200 constitute the bulk of its membership, large companies really dominate the organisation. Three-quarters of the top 100 companies are members and big companies with over 1000 employees provide over half its income. Despite the efforts of the CBI to represent them more effectively, many small firms withdrew in 1971 to form the Society of Independent Manufacturers, later the *Smaller Businesses Association*. The larger firms tend to value the CBI particularly for its ability to represent the needs of industry to government whereas the small firms tend to join for the services it provides, which include advice, information and assistance on a wide range of matters and a means by which new contacts can be made. It faces two handicaps in its role as lobbyist for business interests. The first is a consequence of the diversity of its membership: divisions of interest occur between large and small firms; between firms in sectors which would benefit from import controls (e.g. textiles) and firms which fear the retaliatory results of such a policy; and between private sector members and the nationalised industries. These divisions make it difficult to speak with one voice. Second – again partly because of the variety of its membership, which makes it hard to mobilise industrial opinion in a concerted way – the CBI lacks political 'clout' in its dealings with government. However, despite its failure to wield effective sanctions, the organisation has won concessions on prices policy and corporation tax (1974), lobbied successfully to destroy Labour's proposed compulsory planning agreements (1975) and successfully undermined the Bullock Report's recommendation of worker representatives on Boards of Directors (1977). The CBI has no formal links with any political party and departures from this tradition of neutrality – as in 1983, when its President appeared to endorse the Conservative Party – are criticised by the opposition parties. But although it has no formal links with the party, in practice, the CBI is closely associated with the Conservatives. It does not contribute to Conservative funds but many of its members do; and when its Director-General criticised the party in 1981, a number of firms withdrew or suspended their membership. Like the TUC, its influence in government appeared to wane after 1979, as a consequence of the 'arm's length' policy pursued by Mrs Thatcher towards the 'peak' organisations representing capital and labour.

The *Retail Consortium* (1967), which includes the Multiple Shops Federation, the National Chamber of Trade, the Retail Distributors' Association and the Cooperative Union, speaks for retailing interests. But its lack of resources and internal cohesion have so far prevented it from developing into such an effective 'peak' organisation as the CBI. However, despite the fact that the CBI includes some major retailers (such as W. H. Smith, Sainsburys and Boots), the formation of the Retail Consortium did arise out of the clear perception that retailing needed representation separately from that of manufacturing. Agriculture has a particularly effective organisation in the *National Farmers' Union* (NFU). Its strength as the lobbyist of the farming community is a function of a number of factors: its size – it represents the bulk (78 per cent) of its 'industry'; its wealth – it had an income of almost £5 m in 1979; its long-established contacts at the highest levels of business, finance and politics; and the fact that it negotiates almost entirely with a single government department, the Ministry of Agriculture, Fisheries and Food.

In the 1980s, lobbying by professional lobbyists on behalf of private firms became a huge growth industry itself with an estimated income of £10 m a year. As the *Guardian* reported on 8 January 1988,

> The Government has been lobbied intensely on virtually every recent occasion when it has made difficult decisions involving business. The lobbyists were busy in the contested bid for Westland, the Guinness take-over of Distillers, the race between Boeing's, AWac's, and GEC's Nimrod for the £1 bn airborne radar contract, and the contest between the Scandinavian SAS and British Airways for British Caledonian.

The *Trades Union Congress* (TUC, 1868) is the 'peak' organisation of labour. In 1982, it contained over 100 affiliated unions with a combined membership of 11.6 m representing about 48 per cent of the total workforce. Its membership does include very small unions (e.g. the Spring Trap Makers' Society, which has ninety members), but the majority of Britain's 407 unions (1985) are small (under 50 000) and a large proportion of these are not members of the TUC. In practice, however, most trade unionists are in large unions (of over 200 000), and it is these unions which dominate the TUC (Table 13.2).

Its political role increased between 1945 and the late 1970s against a context of government intervention in the economy. Its broad aims are to defend and extend the legal freedoms of unions and to influence government economic policy. Since 1967, it has published a detailed economic analysis in an annual *Economic Review*. Its refusal to cooperate thwarted the industrial relations legislation of successive Labour and Conservative governments in 1969 and 1971 but it had little success against a series of Conservative Acts aimed at limiting the powers of the unions after 1979. Responsibility for the formation of policy lies with its annual conference but the General Council (48) and General Secretary (Norman Willis in 1988) have considerable policy influence as well as executive powers. It is a difficult organisation to 'manage' for several reasons. Unions retain their powers of independent action when they affiliate to the TUC; the larger unions, in particular, normally develop their own separate relations with government and their leaders wield considerable authority in their own right. Compared with the top unions, moreover, the TUC is not well resourced: its annual income of £2 m and total staff of 130 (1977) may be contrasted (to its disadvantage) with the incomes and staffs of the leading half-dozen unions (in particular cf. TGWU and GMWU which had annual incomes of £18.8 m and £10.7 m and staffs of 483

TABLE 13.2
The main sectional organisations (II): the trade unions

	1983 Membership in 000s
Transport and General Workers (TGWU)	1547
Amalgamated Union of Engineering Workers (AUEW)	943
General, Municipal, Boilermakers' and Allied Trades Union (GMBTU)	875
National and Local Government Officers' Association (NALGO)	689
Union of Shop, Distributive and Allied Workers (USDAW)	403
Electrical, Electronic, Telecommunications and Plumbing Union (EETPU)	365
Union of Construction, Allied Trades and Technicians (UCATT)	260
Confederation of Health Service Employees (COHSE)	222
White collar engineering (AUEW-TASS)	215
Society of Graphical and Allied Trades (SOGAT)	213
National Union of Teachers (NUT)	210
National Union of Mineworkers (NUM)	208
Union of Post Office Workers (UPW)	196
National Union of Railwaymen (NUR)	156
Association of Scientific, Technical and Managerial Staffs (ASTMS)	30

Source: Derived from D. Marsh and J. King, 'The Unions under Thatcher', *Teaching Politics*, 14, 3, September, 1985, p. 399.

and 282 respectively in 1976). Expulsion is the ultimate sanction against a recalcitrant union but is almost never used. In 1985, for example, the TUC withdrew its threat to expel the electricians' union (EETPU) for defying TUC policy on taking State cash for union ballots, fearing a split in the movement but it did at last very reluctantly expel the union in 1988. Finally, like the other 'peak' organisations, the TUC is hampered by internal divisions: left and right struggle for control of unions and the balance of forces on the General Council at any given time reflects the upshot of these contests. In 1986, for example, a left-winger controlled the TGWU (Ron Todd) whilst right-wingers led the AUEW (Gavin Laird) and the EETPU (Eric Hammond). Differences over policy occurred during the 1970s over incomes policy and Britain's membership of the EEC and in the 1980s over backing for the NUM in the miner's strike and over acceptance of government finance for union ballots.

In recent times, the TUC has presided over a movement in which important changes are taking place, and it has come under pressure to reflect these changes. The first change of significance is the considerable growth, then even more rapid decline, in membership of trade unions between the early 1960s and mid-1980s. After a decade of stagnation, union membership accelerated after 1960 and from a mere 8.2 m had reached 12.1 m in 1979; thereafter, hit by rising unemployment, it declined to a mere 9.8 m at the end of 1985. TUC effectiveness – from brokers of power in the late 1960s and 1970s to humiliating exclusion in the 1980s – reflects the buoyancy (or otherwise) of union membership as well as the profound change in the political climate. It is not easy to develop strong policies towards government in such contexts of decline as were suffered between 1979 and 1985 by, for example, the transport workers (down 30 per cent), the construction workers (down 28 per cent), the railwaymen (down 25 per cent) and the engineering workers (down 20 per cent). Second, the composition of the movement has shifted away from the manual towards the white-collar unions, a move which itself reflected a decline in employment in manufacturing industry and strong growth in service and public sector jobs. In 1960, only 16 per cent of TUC members were in white-collar occupations; in 1979, over one-third of all trade unionists were white-collar. One of the main changes affecting trade unionism since 1945 has been the rising influence of white-collar unions such as the local government officers (NALGO), public employees (NUPE), civil servants (CPSA), technicians and managers (ASTMS), teachers (NUT) and health service workers (COHSE). In 1983, a change in the rules governing membership of the TUC General Council came about as a result of pressure from the white-collar unions which felt themselves to be underrepresented; the change resulted in an increase in their representation and a decrease in that of the manual unions. Third, within unions themselves, there has been a post-war trend towards decentralisation of decision-making. This has occurred in two main ways: first, in a move away from nationally negotiated agreements towards shop-floor bargaining over pay and conditions (a TUC estimate suggested there were just under 300 000 work-place representatives in 1975). Second, there has been an increase in the use of ballots on such matters as the election of union officials, strikes and the existence of political funds, largely as a consequence of legislation in the 1980s. This was another development which made unions somewhat unpredictable and contributed to the problems of their management in this period.

Some leading promotional groups

'Cause' pressure groups were active over the whole range of policy in the 1980s – hence, selection is inevitable and this brief introduction concentrates on five prominent areas of their activity: international affairs, the environment, welfare, civil liberties and animal rights (see Table 13.3 for some leading welfare and environmental groups).

TABLE 13.3
The main promotional groups: welfare and environmental

Welfare	Environmental
Shelter	Greenpeace
Child Poverty Action Group (CPAG)	Friends of the Earth (FOE)
Age Concern	The Conservation Society
Disablement Income Group	World Wildlife Fund UK
National Association for Mental Health	The Woodland Trust
Disablement Alliance	Council for the Protection of
Abortion Law Reform Association	Rural England
Society for the Protection of the Unborn	Society for the Protection of
Child (SPUC)	Ancient Buildings
National Council for One-Parent Families	Ramblers' Association
Action on Smoking and Health (ASH)	Royal Society for the Protection
Voluntary Euthanasia Society	of Birds (RSPB)
National Society for the Prevention of	Campaign for Lead-Free Air
Cruelty to Children (NSPCC)	(CLEAR)
	National Trust
	Civic Trust

International lobbyists

In this sphere, three leading causes are expressed by the Campaign for Nuclear Disarmament (CND), Amnesty International and the Aid Lobby.

CND is the foremost organisation in the peace movement (see Chapter 24 for discussion of disarmament as an issue). It maintains that Britain should unilaterally renounce nuclear weapons, withdraw from NATO and adopt a neutralist stance. As public anxiety about the accelerating East–West nuclear arms race mounted in the early 1980s, its support increased dramatically; by 1984, it had 100 000 national and 400 000 local members and its leaders, Mrs Joan Ruddock and Monsignor Bruce Kent, were better-known than most politicians.

Amnesty International (1960) campaigns to free prisoners of conscience throughout the world; to get fair and prompt trials for political prisoners; and is against torture and the use of the death penalty. In 1985, it was working for the release of over 5000 prisoners of conscience. Its membership worldwide was half a million and had increased substantially over the previous two years. It employed a full-time staff of 200 and operated on an annual budget of £5 m. A controversial issue within the organisation was its policy of not campaigning for the release of prisoners such as the black South African nationalist leader, Nelson Mandela, who had used or advocated violence. The purpose of the *Aid Lobby* is to raise and distribute aid to the underdeveloped countries in general and, increasingly in the mid-1980s, to the famine-torn countries of Africa. Table 13.4 provides some information about the five leading aid agencies. The aid agencies rely considerably on advertising and were greatly assisted in 1984–5 by media coverage of the Ethiopian famine which vastly extended their appeal and brought an unprecedented influx of funds. Their own success gave additional weight to the aid agencies' criticisms of the British Government, the United Nations and the European Community for the inadequacy and slowness of their responses to world famine.

TABLE 13.4
The five leading aid agencies

Agency	Full-time staff	Supporters	Income (1984) in £m
Oxfam	about 700	20 000	23.9
Save the Children	860 (including part-time)	818 branches	16.5 (about two-thirds goes overseas)
Christian Aid	about 160	3000 committees	11.2
Catholic Fund for Overseas Development	36	700 support groups	6.0
War on Want	16	6000	1.7

Source: *The Guardian*, 22 March 1985

Campaigners for the environment

By 1980, when it had between two-and-a-half and three million supporters, the environmentalist movement had become, in the words of P. Lowe and J. Goyder, 'a major social phenonemon' (Lowe and Goyder, *Environmental Groups in Politics*). Its support had doubled every decade since 1960 and there were estimated to be nearly 100 national groups and several thousand local ones. Most of these groups, various as they were, shared a common concern or rather a number of closely-related concerns – about pollution, about the destruction of the natural and man-made environment and about the depletion of the planet's resources. Table 13.3 gives a clear idea of their range: a broad gulf separates such long-established organisations as the *Royal Society for the Protection of Birds* (RSPB), with its 300 000 members (many of them youthful) from contemporary campaigning groups like the American-inspired *Friends of the Earth* and *Greenpeace*. It is also useful to distinguish between 'emphasis' groups such as the *National Trust*, whose aims might command wide assent, from genuine promotional groups such as *Transport 2000* (the champion of public transport on social and environmental grounds) or the *Anti-Nuclear Campaign*, which seeks to change public values. In many respects, it is the strong campaigning groups which are most typical of the contemporary environmentalist movement – at international, national and local levels. Thus, in the first two categories, Greenpeace's world-wide and Friends of the Earth's national campaigns against nuclear testing, the dumping of toxic waste, seal culls, and the extermination of the whale by excessive hunting were constantly in the headlines in the 1970s and 1980s. Even more typical of environmental protest in many ways are the local pressure groups of the 'I don't want it passing at the end of my garden or flying over my house type'. Thus, when, in the late 1960s, the decision was taken to site London's third airport at Cublington, a North Bucks village, the *Wing Airport Resistance Association* emerged to oppose it (successfully); when in 1985, the government decided to locate the third airport at Stansted, the *North-West Essex and East Hertfordshire Preservation Association*, which thought it had won its battle to keep the airport away from Stansted twenty years before, had to be mobilised again.

Welfare groups

Welfare groups, sometimes referred to as 'the poverty lobby', have emerged since the Second World War to represent and to mobilise the clientele of the Welfare State: pensioners, parents of dependent children, single-parent families, the mentally and physically-handicapped and the poor. Two leading ones are the *Child Poverty Action Group* and *Shelter*. The *Child Poverty Action Group* (1966) originated as the Advisory Council for the Alleviation of Poverty and was established primarily to redirect government policy in favour of low-income earners. During the 1970s, however, it came to focus especially on the needs of families, campaigning for higher child benefits and leaving the *Low Pay Unit* (which developed out of it) to lobby for more pay. It points out that the tax system has moved against the parents of dependent children since 1945; in 1985, it was campaigning for the retention of child benefit as the most effective way of helping poor children. *Shelter*, the National Campaign for the Homeless (1966) aims to raise funds to house the homeless and to gain a higher priority for housing in government policy. It argues that local councils should be compelled by legislation to house the homeless. In 1985, with the decline in expenditure on public housing under the Conservatives, *Shelter* was predicting a major housing crisis in the late 1980s.

Civil liberties campaigners

The *National Council for Civil Liberties* (1934) is the principal civil liberties group. In recent years, it has campaigned for the abolition of the Official Secrets Act, new 'freedom of information' legislation and an increase in local police accountability. Its major problem is to maintain political balance within a democratically structured organisation. In 1985, an internal battle erupted over its interim report on the miners' strike which contained an acknowledgement of the right to work as well as the right to strike. Left-wingers within the organisation gained a majority vote for its rejection by the AGM and the General Secretary, Larry Gostin, a Fabian left-winger who believed that the Council could not afford to be seen to be politically-biased, resigned. He believed that the NCCL had to be prepared to defend the civil liberties of all and not merely the liberties popular on the Left and he was criticised within the organisation for advising individual members of the National Front.

Animal rights group

During the 1970s and 1980s, militant direct action groups emerged alongside moderate traditional groups such as the *RSPCA* and the *League against Cruel Sports* (1926). These groups included the *Animal Liberation Front*, *Animal Liberation League*, *Animal Aid*, the *National Anti-vivisection Society*, the *Animal Rights Militia*, the *Hunt Saboteurs* and the *Hunt Retribution Squad*. Some older organisations like the *British Union for the Abolition of Vivisection* (1894), whose membership jumped from a mere 2000 to 23 000 in four years after 1980, were radicalised by a new generation prepared to resort to illegal methods to promote their cause and the new militancy even led to a struggle between radicals and traditionalists within the RSPCA. The main targets of animal liberationists are blood sports, factory farming and experiments on animals, and their methods include raiding laboratories, publishing photographs of animals used in experiments for publicity, releasing animals on fur farms, spraying researchers and their property with abusive slogans, disrupting hunts and sending letter-bombs to leading politicians.

Channels of influence

This section explores the various ways – pressure on the government and parliament and appeals to public opinion – in which groups seek influence. The channels of influence are shaped by the character of the political system and the political culture. The mode of influence chosen in a particular instance reflects the nature of the group.

Pressure groups and government

A well-established system of formal and informal contacts links sectional groups with government. Increasingly, formal contacts have become institutionalised through interest-group membership of a variety of government-established committees. These include advisory committees (both *ad hoc* and permanent, of which there were over 1560 in 1978), executive committees (able to make regulations and dispense money; nearly 500 in 1978), Committees of Inquiry (over 1000 this century) and Royal Commissions (twenty-nine between 1945 and 1974). More in the public eye are meetings between government and the 'peak' business and labour organisations on such institutions as the *National Economic Development Council* and CBI and TUC involvement in training and job-creation schemes on the *Manpower Services Commission* and in finding solutions to industrial disputes through the *Arbitration and Conciliation Service* (ACAS). The great majority of contacts, however, occur at a lower level and indeed much business is done informally by telephone and face-to-face discussion between civil servants and representatives of the groups.

Three features of the relationship of regular consultation and negotiation between pressure groups and government Departments invite comment. These are first, the extent to which groups in their linkages with specific Departments form 'issue communities' for the making of policy; second, the degree to which Departments and their officials identify with the lobby; and third, the extent to which group representatives are 'captured' by the Departmental 'line'. The first point draws attention to the way in which policy-making is done in compartments – education, the environment, industrial relations and so on. In each area, policy emerges out of a continuous process of consultation between civil servants and group spokesmen, and this constitutes a 'policy community'. In transport, for example, the policy community is made up of the full-time officials of the Department of Transport together with representatives of such groups as the British

Road Federation, the Society of Motor Manufacturers and Traders, the Freight Transport Association, the Road Haulage Association, Transport 2000 and the motoring organisations. The second point is that, in a system in which Departments of State compete for resources, groups can act or be used as departmental allies. A Department may sympathise with a group's case to the point of itself lobbying for the case *within* government; or, to strengthen its own hand against other Departments, it may encourage groups to exert strong pressures from outside. This whole relationship in which government Departments come to identify closely with group viewpoints has been called *clientelism*. This term describes a situation in which politicians, permanent official and group spokesmen share an interest in increasing the resources devoted to a given policy area. The final point brings out the 'price' paid by groups for consultation on a regular basis. In return for being taken into the government's confidence and for the opportunity to state their case and conceivably gain concessions, groups are expected to 'sell' the ultimate 'decision-package' to their members. They are expected at all times to be discreet about discussions in Whitehall and to refrain, even where they may feel aggrieved, from 'going public' and, especially, from criticising Ministers.

The *advantages* to both government and groups of this system of functional representation have often been described. Groups get a hearing for their case, a chance to influence policy (including legislation) at its formative stage and often an executive role alongside government. Governments get up-to-date, often technical and highly specialised, advice, 'market' information in various sectors, acquiescence in – even positive assent to – their policies, and sometimes assistance in the administration of schemes. The overall benefits to the public interest of smooth, dissension-free administration are also clear. But so are the *disadvantages*. The system of 'bureaucratic accommodation' has been criticised for shutting out parliament; for leading to delays as groups are appeased and persuaded; for making new policy initiatives and departures from previous policy too difficult and sometimes impossible; and for leading to a far from optimum use of national resources, which are distributed more in terms of the 'muscle' of lobbyists and departments than according to any more apparently rational calculations.

Pressure groups and parliament

Parliament is a less important channel for pressure group influence than are government departments but contacts with MPs are still worth making for both sectional and promotional groups. Such contacts can be of value in three main ways: to sponsor legislation; to influence legislation; and to gain additional publicity for an issue first raised outside the House. In the first case, groups wishing to change the law have need of elected representatives as sponsors for their legislation: for example, in the 1960s, groups campaigning to abolish capital punishment and to liberalise the abortion law found parliamentary sponsors for their bills, in Sidney Silverman and David Steel respectively. Second, groups may use sympathetic MPs to influence the legislative process in a number of ways – for instance, to persuade Ministers to back down on a controversial detail, to clarify an ambiguous point or to win a Ministerial assurance favourable to themselves on the interpretation of a particular clause. Occasionally, they may force retreats on entire proposals; for example, the trade unions mustered parliamentary opposition to Labour's industrial relations legislation in 1969 and the Wing Airport Resistance Association (WARA) won all-party support in the House against an inland site for the third London airport in 1970–1. Third, groups may seek to use MPs to help to create a favourable climate of opinion for their cause, as a source of useful publicity. The Conservation Society in combination with MPs gained the kind of intense publicity on the dumping of cyanide waste which pushed a reluctant government into action in 1971–2 on an issue which had hung fire for several years. In the late 1960s, backbench pressure on the controversy over heavy lorries led to environmental groups (the Civic Trust and the CPRE) being included on the Ministry of Transport's 'consultation list' for the future (Richardson and Jordan, *Governing Under Pressure*, p. 127).

Groups are linked with MPs in a variety of ways. Some offer MPs honorary positions as directors or advisers, others recruit them to their executives; others again give one of their officials responsibility for maintaining contact with MPs. The most direct link is sponsorship of MPs by trade unions. Since 1945, approximately one-third of Labour MPs in every parliament have been trade-union sponsored. In 1987, 129 Labour MPs were sponsored by trade unions and they constituted just over half of the Party in the new House of Commons. It is customary to play down trade-union sponsorship as bringing little direct benefit. It would constitute a breach of parliamentary privilege if unions, or any other outside group, were to instruct MPs how to speak or vote. However, it is hard to believe the trade-union movement gained no advantage in their resistance to proposed industrial relations legislation in 1969 through the existence of a bloc of trade union MPs. The main recent trends are towards increased sponsorship by white-collar unions (e.g. ASTMS, NUPE and COHSE), declining numbers sponsored by the NUM and NUR and a general tendency to sponsorship of more highly educated professionals rather than rank-and-file officials. Finally, a majority of Conservative MPs and a minority of Labour MPs have business, commercial and financial interests – as, for example, chairman, executives, partners, directors and major shareholders of companies.

Traditionally, the possession of outside interests by a Member of Parliament has been considered acceptable so long as MPs declare their interest at the beginning of debates and so long as the rules of parliamentary privilege are observed. However, after growing public concern had been expressed about the influence of outside interests, parliament decided in 1975 to publish a *register of interests* (revised three or four times a year) in which MPs would disclose the sources of their personal incomes and other interests but not the amount. However, the disclosure of interests is still not a legal obligation – disclosure is required only by resolution of the House, not by legislation – and some MPs, such as Enoch Powell, have refused to enter their outside interests in the register. In the face of these weaknesses (lack of legal requirement to disclose, statement of the amount of outside financial interests not required), public concern has continued. A House of Commons *Select Committee of Inquiry*, which investigated dealings between certain MPs and the architect, John Poulson, in 1977, criticised three MPs for conduct 'inconsistent with the standards which the House is entitled to expect from its members'; in fact, Poulson paid large sums of money to MPs to advance his interests. In 1984, *The Observer* publicised the amount of the sums which can be involved; £10 000–£20 000 may be paid to parliamentary consultants and smaller, but not inconsiderable, sums (£200) may be paid to MPs for putting down written questions and 'considerably more' for asking oral questions.

Basically, pressure groups run two types of public campaign. These are *long-term educational and propaganda campaigns* designed to produce signifi- cant shifts in public opinion and *short-term 'fire brigade' campaigns* aimed at warning public opinion about a specific threat and averting it. The cam- paigns of CND, Shelter and Child Poverty Action fall into the first category. Wide publicity can be used to get an issue on to the political agenda, to accelerate action where government is uninterested or complacent, to delay or prevent undesired change and to achieve recognition and even as we have seen inclusion on government's list of groups to be consulted. Some groups aim to persuade 'informed' rather than 'mass' opinion, the campaigns of the National Society for Clean Air for 'smokeless zones' in the 1950s and of the Abortion Law Reform Association and the Homosexual Law Reform Society in the 1960s being cases in point. Typical of campaigns in the second category in 1985 were the anti-juggernaut protesters whose aim (not sucess- ful) was to halt the construction of the M40 link between Oxford and Birmingham; the campaign of environmental groups against the proposed nuclear reprocessing plant at Dounreay; and the lobby by environmentalist groups against proposals to route the Okehampton bypass through common land on the edge of Dartmoor.

Strategies

There is broad agreement amongst political commentators that the strategies used by pressure groups reflect the nature of the political system. Thus, pressure groups focus their attention predominantly upon Whitehall because that is where the bulk of political decisions are made; they devote a considerably smaller amount of their time to parliament and less still to public opinion. This prioritisation of targets is especially true of sectional groups but also, to a lesser extent, of promotional groups. However, this should not be taken to mean or to imply that sectional groups go for the executive, whereas promotional groups incline towards parliament and public campaigns. In fact, the way in which groups allocate their efforts between government departments, parliament, and public (including media) campaigns depends also upon the nature of the group and its cause. It is not difficult to show, for example, that whilst the major biases of the strategies of sectional and promotional groups are as described above, each is able to deploy other than its predominant strategy or strategies where necessary.

The main focus in the study of sectional groups is their relationships with the bureaucracy and many of these relations are institutionalised. The close cooperation between the Ministry of Agriculture, Food and Fisheries and the National Farmers' Union is often taken as typical of such relationships. It is made possible by the willingness of the State and the farming community to develop such links and, above all, by their capacity, each working through a single institution (MAFF and the NFU respectively) to do so. Unlike other economic groupings, the NFU represents a very high proportion of a generally cohesive community. However, two of the most effective sectional group actions of recent years were the blocking of industrial relations legislation (in 1969 and post-1971) and the disruption of incomes policies by the trade union movement, each of which depended more upon rank-and-file resistance away from Whitehall than it did upon any persuasiveness of TUC 'barons' with permanent officials. Sectional groups may, then, on occasion 'go public', calling for national days of action, protest marches and demonstrations of membership solidarity against policies and legislation perceived as against their interests.

Equally, certain promotional groups all the time and other promotional groups for some of the time may go for Whitehall. Thus, the *Howard League for Penal Reform* has secured semi-permanent 'insider' status in its relations with the Home Office largely because it directs its efforts for liberal reforms within an acceptance of the legitimacy of the criminal law; in the 1960s, it was unwilling to 'go public' and organise a mass campaign for fear of disrupting this well-established relationship with Whitehall. Very different are two other groups in the penal lobby, as M. Ryan shows. Both the Marxist-inspired *Radical Alternative to Prison* (RAP) and the *Preservation of the Rights of Prisoners* (PROP), the prisoners' pressure group, have little chance of achieving 'insider' status. RAP calls for the abolition of prison, and PROP aims to spread the idea that the penal system simply reflects and reinforces the class system amongst prisoners (M. Ryan, 'The Penal Lobby: Influencing Ideology', in D. Marsh (ed.) *Pressure Politics*, pp. 176–9).

The *Child Poverty Action Group* has pursued a 'mixed' or double strategy aiming at both the executive and public opinion, a blend of 'insider' and 'outsider' strategies. Just as RAP and PROP seek to attain ideological shifts in perceptions of prison and prisoners' rights, the CPAG, as well as getting poverty on to the political agenda, has also sought to change public conceptions of what constitutes poverty. It has departed from more historical 'absolute' ideas of poverty in terms of inadequate means of subsistence to a relative definition in terms of lack of access to the goods and amenities enjoyed by the average. At the same time, it has lobbied the government in traditional 'cause' group style for increases in child benefit and at times achieved some success; child benefit went up from £2.35 in 1978 to £4.75 in 1980. However, its abrasive style and radical demand for sweeping reforms in its 'ideological' campaigning and, also, its lack of obvious usefulness as a provider of information or policy-implementer have handicapped its relationship with the Department of Health and Social Security.

In resisting Cublington as the site for London's third airport between 1968 and 1971, and in trying to block the various attempts to reduce access to legal abortion by amending the 1967 Abortion Act, both the Wing Airport Resistance Association and the Abortion Law Reform Association (ALRA) respectively, had no alternative but to run public campaigns. WARA recruited 60 000 members in the first few months, drenching North Buckinghamshire with its publicity. ALRA, itself only a small organisation targeted on 'élite' opinion, played a key role in creating a mass-membership umbrella organisation for the pro-abortion lobby, the *National Abortion Campaign* (1975) when the 1967 Act came under major attack for the first time.

However, both WARA and ALRA also made effective use of parliament, as they had to do if their efforts were to succeed. Thus, after failing to win its case at the Roskill Commission (appointed to consider the remaining four alternatives when Stansted was ruled out in 1968), WARA used parliamentary contacts skilfully – first, to establish an All-Party Committee of Backbenchers and then to launch an early-day motion with an eventual 219 signatures and to 'manage' the Commons debates on the Roskill Report. WARA's public and parliamentary campaign succeeded (Foulness was chosen as the site for the third airport at that stage) because, as J. J. Richardson and A. G. Jordan indicate in *Governing under Pressure* (1979), it had demonstrated the sheer volume of opposition that existed to the choice of that particular inland site (Richardson and Jordan, *Governing Under Pressure*, p. 125).

The pro-abortion lobby gained considerably from the change in attitude of the *British Medical Association* (from being against, to being in favour of the 1967 Act) between 1967 and 1975. But a major reason for its effectiveness in opposing the campaign by anti-abortion groups such as the *Society for the Protection of the Unborn Child* (SPUC) and *LIFE* was its ability at decisive moments to call upon knowledge of parliamentary procedure. This it was able to do through having previously established valuable contacts with and gained the support of the Labour Party women's organisations as D. Marsh and J. Chambers show in 'The Abortion Lobby: Pluralism at Work' (in D. Marsh (ed.) *Pressure Politics*, 1983, pp. 148–9).

Resources

A group's effectiveness depends not only upon the choice of an appropriate strategy but also upon its *resources*. Resources include public acceptability, sanctions, finances, expertise and leadership, and the character of the membership. A high degree of *public acceptance* is clearly an advantage for professional groups such as the British Medical Association and the Law Society as opposed to lower status professional groups such as the teacher organisations and, even more, as opposed to manual worker unions. With regard to *sanctions*, sectional groups are generally considered more powerful than promotional groups because they possess stronger weapons. The withdrawal or the threat of withdrawal of cooperation, where cooperation in the formation and implementation of policies is required, can be a powerful source of pressure. Proposals for the compulsory fitting of seat-belts were held up for some considerable time because the Ministry of Transport was reluctant to override the objections of the Society of Motor Manufacturers and Traders, and simply impose them upon the motor industry. Resistance by the CBI blocked the implementation of the Bullock Report's proposal for worker-directors. Similarly, the strike or the threat of it can be a potent political weapon especially when government is closely involved with industry both as employer (public corporations and services) and manager of the economy. In the hands of the National Union of Mineworkers a strike helped to bring down the Heath Government in 1974 and forced the Conservative Government to back down on pit closures in 1981 – Mrs Thatcher's only significant defeat by a trade union. But even this weapon should not be exaggerated in view of the defeat of the NUM in 1984–5 after a bitter year-long struggle, although at massive cost.

The superior *finances* of sectional groups are usually – and rightly – considered to give them more political 'muscle' than promotional groups. Yet here adequacy of income for its purpose is also important. The very considerable resources of the mineworkers' union were insufficient in 1984–5; the TUC is often considered to be under-financed as a leading 'peak' organisation; and the very expensive anti-nationalisation campaigns run by business between 1945 and 1979 were failures. By contrast, the much more modest sums available to 'cause' groups if backed by *expertise* can be sufficient to enable them to make their cases – the £44 000 raised by the Wing Airport Resistance Association enabled it to present a skilful case to the Roskill Commission even though it did not win that phase of its protest. On the other hand, lack of resources has undoubtedly been one of the factors hampering the anti-nuclear lobby in its protest against the extensive nuclear energy programme of the Conservative Government after 1979. As Ward shows well, in this sector, the struggle between environmentalists and their opponents is an extremely unequal one since the forces on the side of the development of nuclear power (pressurised water reactors) as the major source of national energy needs include not only the government but also the Central Electricity Generating Board (which supervises the largest integrated grid outside the USSR), the Atomic Energy Authority, big national firms such as GEC, Northern Engineering Industries and the construction company Taylor Woodrow and large multinationals like Westinghouse and Rio Tinto Zinc (H. Ward, 'The Anti-Nuclear Lobby: An Unequal Struggle', in D. Marsh (ed.) *Pressure Politics*, p. 195).

Finally, the size, density, solidarity and quality of a pressure group's *membership* have to be considered. In terms of *size*, sectional groups (frequently numbered in hundreds of thousands) normally have the advantage over promotional groups (usually numbered in thousands), although not invariably. The very large memberships attracted by CND and by the environmental movement have already been noticed (above, pp. 293–94). It also needs to be remembered that whereas there is a 'given' element in sectional group membership, promotional groups have to build up their membership from nothing. *Density* also matters. The idea of *primary density* with regard to a sectional group refers to its member-potential/member ratio – that is, the proportion of those eligible to join who actually do join. This concept is important because failure to recruit and retain a high proportion of potential members may be regarded as a source of weakness, of lack of full representativeness in a group. Thus, trade unionism is less powerful to the degree that only about half the workforce are members of trade unions and the CBI's authority as a spokesman for industry is undermined by its failure to persuade small businesses to join it. The *solidarity* of its membership clearly reinforces a group's case, especially if it can be demonstrated by ballot or opinion poll; just as clearly, divisions within its membership weaken it. It was a source of weakness to the NUM in its fight against pit closures in 1984 that it failed to hold the ballot which might have demonstrated majority backing for the strike; without a ballot, the media could engage in damaging speculation about divisions within the union both at leadership (Left versus Right) and grass-roots levels, and differences were allowed to harden into a split which after the end of the strike led to the formation of a new union, the *Union of Democratic Mineworkers*. Finally, *quality* of membership matters, especially for small cause groups. As D. Marsh and J. Chambers have pointed out, the Abortion Law Reform Association relied for its effectiveness in the mid-1960s 'on the dedicated efforts of a handful of people who had a detailed knowledge of the issue, rather than on a mass membership or sophisticated organisation' ('The Abortion Lobby: Pluralism at Work', p. 146).

SUMMARY

The chapter began by identifying the two major types of pressure group. Interest groups represent people as members of occupations; promotional groups press the case for particular causes. Two significant developments have taken place since the 1920s: (i) the institutionalisation of consultation between groups and government, an arrangement seen as advantageous by both sides; and (ii) a rapid upsurge in promotional group activity since the 1960s; in the contemporary period, participation in groups has come to rival membership of parties as a means of expressing people's commitment and political ideas. The major channels of influence for groups are the executive (Ministers and civil servants), parliament and public opinion. Groups make strategic decisions on which targets to seek to influence and by what methods. Their resources include public acceptability, sanctions, the amount of money they have, their expertise and the nature of their membership. Large size, substantial finances and the availability of powerful sanctions are normally advantages. But their presence does not automatically bring success and their absence does not necessarily spell failure.

FURTHER READING

Alderman, G. (1984) *Pressure Groups and British Government*, London, Longman.
Cawson, A. (1978) 'Pluralism, Corporation and the Role of the State', *Government and Opposition*, 13, 2.
Grant, W. (1984) 'The Role and Power of Pressure Groups', in R. Borthwick and J. Spence, *British Politics Perspective*, Leicester, University Press.
Grant, W. and Marsh, D. (1977) *The CBI*, London, Hodder & Stoughton.
Holmes, M. (1983) 'Trade Unions and Governments', in H. Drucker *et al.*, *Developments in British Politics*, London, Macmillan.
King, R. (ed.) (1982) *Capital and Politics*, London, Routledge & Kegan Paul.
Kirby, S. (1983) 'Peace by Piece: The Revival of Anti-Nuclear Protest in Britain', *Teaching Politics*, 12, 3, September.
Lowe, P. and Goyder, J. (1983) *Environmental Groups in Politics*, London, Allen & Unwin.
Marsh, D. (ed.) (1983) *Pressure Politics*, London: Junction Books.
Moran, M. (1985) 'The Changing World of British Pressure Groups', *Teaching Politics*, 14, 3, September.
Moran, M. (1986) 'Industrial Relations', in H. Drucker *et al.*, *Developments in British Politics, 2*, London, Macmillan.
Richardson, J. J. and Jordan, A. G. (1979) *Governing under Pressure*, Oxford, Martin Robertson.
Taylor, R. (1980) *The Fifth Estate*, London, Pan.

QUESTIONS

1. Justify and criticise the role of pressure groups in democratic politics today.

2. To what extent and in what ways did the political influence of business and the trade unions change in the 1980s?

ASSIGNMENT

Select a pressure group (interest or promotional) and compile a dossier on its activities. Concentrate especially on establishing its membership, financing, leadership and strategy, and consider the relationship between these factors and its eventual success or failure.

14

The Mass Media

The communication of political information is an important process in the political system, and the mass media play a central role in this activity. Some political scientists believe that the mass media in Britain help democracy work through allowing a wide variety of views to be expressed. Others believe that the media are anti-democratic because of their power to manipulate the way people think about politics at home and abroad. The media, in other words, are politically biased. This bias, it is argued, results from the fact that much of the media is privately owned and controlled. Added to this, most professional journalists and news managers have a middle-class outlook which they inject into their interpretation of the news and current affairs.

Other critics have accused the mass media of trivialising politics. Because different television channels and newspapers find that they are competing for a limited number of viewers and readers, there is the tendency to make the news more attractive by treating it as entertainment rather than as a serious business. Social psychologists have speculated that the mass media, television in particular, have the capacity to bewilder rather than inform. Faced by repeated periods of crisis and calm, viewers become dependent on their political leaders and are easily controlled and manipulated by them. The chapter concludes by considering the impact of election television and the possible effects of televising Parliament.

THE MASS MEDIA AND SOCIETY

Only a small proportion of Britain's population is actively engaged in politics and therefore learns about political affairs from first-hand experience. What the majority 'know' about politics is made up principally from what they learn from the mass media. In other words, for those individuals who do not participate directly in politics the mass media define their 'real world' of politics. Peter Golding has argued that 'The media are central in the provision of ideas and images which people use to interpret and understand a great deal of their everyday experience' (Golding, *The Mass Media*, 1974, p. 178). This, of course, gives the mass media enormous power since they can either set people's minds against the political system or help to generate popular support for it.

The 'media as part of democracy' viewpoint

There are two basic viewpoints concerning the relationship between the mass media and society. First, there is the view that *the media are part of democracy* since they are themselves a 'free' institution. The media assist the working of a democratic system through facilitating free speech and unrestricted public debate. In Britain, there is no State control of either the press or broadcasting, although the latter is regulated so that it always serves the interests of the community as a whole. This results in a great variety of political opinions being given an airing, and many of them are hostile to the government of the day.

Broadcasting is bound by law to be 'impartial'. For example the Independent Broadcasting Authority is legally required to ensure that all news is presented with due accuracy and impartiality and that 'due impartiality is preserved on the part of persons providing the programmes as respects matters of political or industrial controversy or relating to current public policy'. During times of national emergency the government may extend greater control over broadcasting as part of its strategy for coping. John Whale has pointed out that the laws relating to both the BBC and ITA make it clear that ministers could instruct them to broadcast or withhold whatever government wanted. He added 'That particular cannon has seldom been fired. It is not much use to party politicians: it was meant to guard the interests of the State (especially in Wartime), not of any one political party' (J. Whale, *The Politics of the Media*, p. 12). Direct intervention in broadcasting by the government is rare but we shall see governments can be extremely sensitive about what is broadcast.

The government has no substantial role in the newspaper business. There is no censorship apart from D (Defence) Notices. It is true that British government attempts to operate in a climate of greater secrecy than some other Western governments, notably the US administration. But does this secrecy mean that the Press is ineffective in reporting the affairs of State? It can be argued that despite the government's and Civil Service's attachment to the idea of secrecy, a system of 'open government' exists in reality. This is because of the lobby system in which politicians, including Cabinet members, give confidential briefings to journalists. Their stories, which may involve details of Cabinet meetings, will be published without mentioning the name of the Minister or politician who provided the information. Also, Cabinet papers may be 'leaked' to the press, as was the case with a Labour government in 1975. Labour policy planned to introduce a new child benefit but the Cabinet agreed that such a scheme was too costly. The Cabinet papers recording the decision that the new scheme would not be implemented were leaked to *The Observer*. From time to time there has been 'whistle blowing' by employees or ex-employees who have felt that certain confidential decisions being made within the broad sweep of government should be known to the public. For example, a retired secret service officer, Peter Wright, published some serious allegations of misconduct in his memoirs, *Spycatcher*. The Government argued that Wright had a life-long obligation to keep confidential his knowledge of MI5 and successfully blocked publication in the UK although the book became a best-seller in the USA (see also Chapter 16). Finally, many secret reports written by official bodies have been leaked to the Press. For example, a year before its abolition the CPRS ('Think Tank') drafted a report on the implications for the Welfare State of a low-growth economy. The report envisaged the need for radical cuts in health and education, and was 'leaked' at a time which ensured that it would be discussed by the autumn round of party conferences. This flow of confidential information, from all levels of government – Cabinet Ministers to clerical employees – together with the skills of investigative journalists, results in there being relatively few secrets in Westminster or Whitehall.

The fact that newspapers and commercial broadcasters rely on advertising revenue has not restricted freedom of expression. Some people have expressed fears about newspapers only printing news that will not upset their advertisers. But there have been many cases which should allay such fears. For example, *The Sunday Times* campaigned against Distillers over the treatment of Thalidomide victims, and independent television exposed the faults of timber-framed houses at the very time when Barratts, the builders, were running a substantial television advertising campaign.

In a democracy, it is to be expected that the mass media will often take the initiative when acting out their 'watchdog' role. But in terms of political values and attitudes, the media simply reflect what exists already in society rather than try to create new opinions. John Whale argued that 'the media do more towards corroborating opinion than creating it'. If newspapers present a consensus view of society, it is because that is what readers want. He noted:

> It is readers who determine the character of newspapers. The *Sun* illustrates the point in its simplest and saddest form. Until 1964 the *Daily Herald*, and between 1964 and 1969 the broadsheet *Sun*, had struggled to interest working people principally through their intellect. The paper had declined inexorably. Murdoch gave up the attempt and went for baser instincts. Sales soared. It was an owner's decision, certainly: but it would have meant nothing without the enthusiastic ratification of the readers (Whale, *Politics of the Media*, p. 84).

John Whale continued to argue that the British Press is predominantly conservative in tone because its readers are. The *Morning Star*, founded as the *Daily Worker*, is an anti-capitalist paper, but it has a low circulation. Whale commented 'if any substantial number of people seriously wanted the structure of society rebuilt from the bottom, the *Morning Star* would sell more copies than it does' (ibid, p. 85).

The bias in the Press towards the Conservative Party is also inevitable; this is because the newspaper industry remains almost exclusively in private hands; and for as long as the tussle between private and public ownership is taken to be one of the central disputes in politics, and the private side is espoused mainly by the Conservatives, then there is a case for supposing that the press must be predominantly Conservative in its sympathies' (ibid, p. 75). Having said this, the Press has never shied away from criticising the Conservative Party or a Conservative government. And not all the papers support the Conservatives. The *Daily Mirror*, a mass circulation tabloid, supports Labour whilst *The Guardian* takes an independent line which is rarely pro-Conservative. The consequences of an overwhelmingly Conservative Press must not be exaggerated. Even when the majority of newspapers give their support to the Conservatives, Labour can still win as they did, for example, in the two General Elections of 1974.

The 'media as a tool of the ruling class' viewpoint

An alternative view of the mass media in relation to society sees *the media playing a much more creative role in shaping people's ideas, attitudes, beliefs and actions*. In other words, the mass media do not simply reflect public opinion so much as help to mould it in the first place.

The mass media structure the complexities of the social world and make it understandable to readers, viewers and listeners. For example, journalists invariably use a consensus view of society as a framework which is imposed on their reporting in order to explain or make sense out of events. In doing this, the media tend to give authority to certain institutions – such as Parliament – whilst making those who advocate non-parliamentary or direct political action appear as extremists or irresponsible fanatics. Journalists frequently consult or interview 'experts' for their opinions on issues; and these experts are invariably powerful people in society and naturally support the system which gives them power. Although experts may be seen to disagree with each other on specific issues, they are unlikely ever to challenge the consensus view of society in a fundamental way.

This adds up to a situation where the variety of opinion found in the mass media is far more limited than the variety of opinion found in society at large. The Press do not reflect working-class views on political issues. From time to time the TUC examines the feasibility of setting up a replacement to the *Daily Herald* as a newspaper for the labour movement because existing papers fail to reflect union views. Broadcasting rarely wanders outside the 'liberal consensus'. An interesting fate befell a news programme, *The Friday Alternative*, on Channel 4. This was based on the ideas of the Glasgow University Media Group. However, the ITA brought pressure on Channel 4 to take the programme off the air because it fell below normal journalistic standards. The TV journalists concerned were reported as saying that the programme was stopped because 'we've upset too many important people on sensitive issues'.

The mass media in Britain, even television and radio, cannot be neutral or impartial. This is because the media are a product of Britain's culture, a culture which is biased like any other culture, with assumptions and prejudices of its own. The imposition of this cultural framework is seen in what is referred to as the 'social manufacture' or 'social production' of the news. News does not 'just happen', rather 'it is made'. This process is described by Stuart Hall in Exhibit 14.1. News programmes and newspapers have a number of predefined categories to be filled by 'the news' – e.g. sport, human interest, politics, economics, and so on. Visually interesting material is more likely to become 'news' than are abstract developments. The selection process of what will become news is known as 'agenda setting'.

Agenda setting is important politically because of the consequences of an issue being placed on the agenda. If industrial strikes are put on the agenda rather than industrial accidents, it will lead to demands for tighter trade union legislation rather than stricter factory regulations. News about 'social security scroungers' will stir up different feelings about society than news about 'tax evaders'. Sometimes there is an over-reaction to what is seen as a threat to society and this is referred to as a 'moral panic'. During the 1970s there was a feeling that mugging was a new, violent and increasingly common street crime. The reaction was out of all proportion to the threat, which was not new, but nevertheless demands for more policing and tougher penalties were fed into the political system.

The language of news reporting also gives a clue to the one-sided nature of the mass media. The following headline appeared in the *Morning Star*: 'Wildcat Tory peers carried their wrecking tactics to new extremes last night'. Its mocking appearance is a reminder of how strong the custom is to refer to trade unionists in this sort of language. Any group of workers in conflict with their employers are likely to be labelled as 'wreckers', 'bully boys', 'reds' or 'extremists'.

Journalistic conventions also convey hidden, but nevertheless biased, messages. For example, if a strike is being reported on TV the management will usually be interviewed in the quiet surroundings of an office. The surroundings confer authority on the manager, who is sitting behind a desk. He is able to speak in a calm and reasonable way. In contrast, the workers are frequently interviewed outside the factory gate, and have to compete with the passing traffic in order to be heard. Their surroundings suggest that they are an unreasonable rabble.

A common hidden message in news reports is that dominant groups or individuals in society are to be given favourable treatment. This may be clearly evident in the style of questioning. For example, in a TV interview concerning a hospital consultants work-to-rule in 1975, the Minister concerned was asked 'Mrs Castle, on the face of it this seems a terrible indictment of you as an employer that the very top people in the medical profession should be forced for the first time in history to take this action.' A

Exhibit 14.1   Making the news

The media do not simply and transparently report events which are 'naturally' newsworthy *in themselves*. 'News' is the end-product of a complex process which begins with a systematic sorting and selecting of events and topics according to a socially constructed set of categories. As MacDougall puts it:

At any given moment billions of simultaneous events occur throughout the world ... All of these occurences are potentially news. They do not become so until some purveyor of news gives an account of them. The news, in other words, is the account of the event, not something intrinsic in the event itself.

One aspect of the structure of selection can be seen in the routine organisation of newspapers with respect to regular types or areas of news. Since newspapers are committed to the regular production of news, these organisational factors will, in turn, affect what is selected. For example, newspapers become pre-directed to certain types of event and topic in terms of the organisation of their own work-force (e.g. specialist correspondents and departments, the fostering of institutional contacts, etc.) and the structure of the papers themselves (e.g. home news, foreign, political, sport, etc.).

Given that the organisation and staffing of a paper regularly direct it to certain categories of items, there is still the problem of selecting, from the many contending items within any one category, those that are felt will be of interest to the reader. This is where the *professional ideology* of what constitutes 'good news' – the newsman's sense of *news values* – begins to structure the process. At the most general level this involves an orientation to items which are 'out of the ordinary', which in some way breach our 'normal' expectations about social life, the sudden earthquake or the moon-landing, for example. We might call this the *primary* or *cardinal news value*. Yet, clearly 'extraordinariness' does not exhaust the list, as a glance at any newspaper will reveal: events which concern élite persons or nations; events which are dramatic; events which can be personalised so as to point up the essentially human characteristics of humour, sadness, sentimentality, etc.; events which have negative consequences, and events which are part of, or can be made made to appear part of, an existing newsworthy theme, are all possible news stories. Disasters, dramas, the everyday antics – funny and tragic – of ordinary folk, the lives of the rich and the powerful, and such perennial themes as football (in winter) and cricket (in summer), all find a regular place within the pages of a newspaper. Two things follow from this: the first is that journalists will tend to *play up* the extra-ordinary, dramatic, tragic, etc., elements in a story in order to enhance its newsworthiness; the second is that events which score high on a number of these news values will have greater news potential than ones that do not. And events which score high on *all* dimensions, such as the Kennedy assassinations (i.e. which are *unexpected* and *dramatic*, with *negative* consequences, as well as *human tragedies* involving *élite persons* who were heads of an extremely *powerful nation*, which possesses the status of a *recurrent theme* in the British press), will become *so* newsworthy that programmes will be interrupted – as in the radio or television news-flash – so that these items can be communicated immediately.

(Stuart Hall *et al.*, *Policing the Crisis*, London, Macmillan (1978) pp. 53–4).

group of manual workers working to rule for the first time could not expect this sort of favourable reporting. Sometimes the hidden messages are conveyed in a more subtle form. In *More Bad News*, the Glasgow University Media Group show that the use of super-captions can reflect status. Two types of individuals were often interviewed without the use of super-captions indicating names; the low-status person who is informally interviewed or the high-status person who is so well-known that showing a name is unnecessary. However, there were cases in which high-status but less familiar individuals had their names shown in capital letters and low-status individuals had their names shown in lower-case letters.

OWNERSHIP AND THE MASS MEDIA

The mass media are big business. Six leading newspaper publishers – Reed International, News International, Beaverbrook, Associated Newspapers, Thomson, and S. Pearson and Son – account for some 80 per cent of all daily, Sunday and local newspaper sales. Most of these concerns are conglomerations which have financial interests in other sectors of the communication industry. For example, S. Pearson and Son publish *The Financial Times* but also have interests in Longman, Ladybird books and Penguin books. Some concerns, such as Thomson, have considerable interests in independent television and commercial radio. Other conglomerations have an even wider base in industry and commerce. Trafalgar House, which owns the *Daily Express*, and Lonrho, which owns *The Observer*, have investments in areas as diverse as mining and shipping. Graham Murdock and Peter Golding argue that this pattern of ownership represents a threat to democracy:

> First, concentration limits the range and diversity of views and opinions which are able to find public expression. More significantly, it is those views and opinions representing the least powerful social groups which are systematically excluded by the process of concentration . . . Second, concentration of control over the media into the hands of large conglomerates emphasises production for maximum profit at the necessary expense of other social goals that should be a vital aspect of communication media. Third, such concentration is undemocratic in two senses. It removes the media from public surveillance and accountability, that is, it renders them externally undemocratic. In addition the concentration of control further away from the point of production reduces internal democracy within the media organisations themselves (Murdock and Golding, in P. Beharrell and G. Philo (eds) *Trade Unions and the Media*, pp. 105–6).

John Whale was considerably less worried about the effects of ownership on communication. For, at the time he was writing, the 'Press baron' who owned papers and who personally dictated editorial policy had disappeared. There were no proprietors like Lord Beaverbrook or Lord Northcliffe, who used to instruct their editors what to put in the *Daily Express* and *Daily Mail* respectively. Contents and policy were determined by professional staff journalists who decide what items to cover, and what items to comment about. However, events were to overtake this argument with the emergence of a new generation of Press barons such as Rupert Murdoch and Robert Maxwell. There was concern that not only were these new proprietors so powerful that they could intervene in the same ways as the old Press barons but also that they did not usually have to intervene since editorial staff anticipated and wrote what they know would find the approval of their respective proprietors. In addition John Whale saw the pattern of ownership as something which was inevitable in the modern communications newspapers. He acknowledged that 'such an arrangement imposes its own restraints, certainly. In the nature of things, the *Financial Times* cannot report on Pearson Longman's interests in book-publishing so unselfconsciously as it would the affairs of any other publisher' (Whale, p. 79). He added that 'a newspaper owned by a commercial group writes inhibitedly about a handful of concerns at most: a paper owned by the State, the effective alternative, would be guarded in its outlook on whole areas of the national life' (Whale, *Politics of the Media*, p. 80).

Although commercial broadcasting is privately owned, John Whale argued that 'the influence of individual shareholders is fragmented and haphazard. Ownership is no more a dominant force in commercial broadcasting than it is at the BBC. If it mattered, programmes from the two sources would differ more than they do' (ibid, p. 71).

Commercial broadcasting is regulated by the State and some franchises change hands at the end of a fixed term. For example, in January 1982 'Television South' replaced 'Southern TV' and 'Central' replaced 'ATV'. Also, the IBA may alter shareholdings in television companies in order to avoid one group dominating. In 1964, the Thomson Organisation owned 80 per cent of voting shares in Scottish Television. This was reduced to 55 per cent, and later to 25 per cent.

Television viewing

Most people rely on television as their main source of information. As long ago as 1962 a BBC survey showed that 58 per cent of the sample learned the news primarily from TV whereas only 33 per cent learned it mainly from newspapers. Another study ten years later revealed that 85 per cent named television as their main source of information. There is a tendency for people to believe what they 'see' on TV but to be sceptical about what they read in the Press. Nearly 70 per cent think that television is the 'most trustworthy' news source whilst only 6 per cent are prepared to rank newspapers so highly.

The Broadcasters' Audience Research Board showed that in 1982 the average viewing time per person was 20.3 hours a week. A year before the figure was 23.1 hours a week, the decline being accounted for by

314   *Institutions and Participation*

the increased viewing of videos rather than transmitted programmes. But the fact remains that around 60 per cent of the adult population hear or see at least one news bulletin a day, and by the time young people leave school they will have watched TV screens for many thousands of hours.

There is differentiation amongst television audiences. This is reflected in the audiences of various TV news programmes (see Table 14.1). BBC news is watched by a considerably larger proportion of the small top socio-economic group than ITN news. To a lesser extent, this is also the case with the white-collar and skilled workers category. A larger proportion of the lowest socio-economic group watched ITN.

These statistics were collected before Channel 4 was launched in 1983. Early indications were that it was watched by an average of only 5 per cent of the viewing audience, but that this included a larger proportion of affluent and young people than did the ITN audience generally.

Research by the Glasgow University Media Group revealed that between 20 and 25 per cent of news-time was devoted to reporting Parliament, pressure group activity and news concerning political figures (see Table 14.2). But, when added to coverage of other current affairs items which had political implications, over half the news was 'about politics'. The time spent on each item varied, but never lasted for more than two minutes.

Only a crisis, such as the Falklands War, received extensive coverage. Sceptics have said that if Moses had come down from Mount Sinai in the age of television, the event would have been condensed into a 90-second news item: 'Today at Mount Sinai, Moses came down with the Ten Commandments, the most important three of which are . . .'.

TABLE 14.1

Estimated audience composition for television news (Wednesdays January–March 1974)

| | | Socio-economic group of persons aged 15 and over | | |
		A %	B %	C %
ITN	12.40	1	2	3
BBC1	12.55	1	1	1
BBC1	17.50	18	19	15
ITN	17.50	6	9	17
BBC2	19.30	1	1	—
BBC1	21.00	21	21	15
ITN	22.00	12	13	19

A = the 'top' 6 per cent in professional and managerial positions
B = the next 24 per cent, mainly white-collar and skilled manual workers, and
C = the remaining 70 per cent

Source: Annual Review of BBC Audience Research Findings, 1973–4; extracted from Glasgow University Media Group: *Bad News* (Routledge & Kegan Paul, 1976) p. 3.

TABLE 14.2

Distribution of items by bulletin (weekdays), showing percentage of items in each category

	BBC1			BBC2		ITN		
	Lunch-time	Early	Nine O'Clock News	Newsday	News Extra	First Report	Early	News at Ten
Political	21.1	22.0	21.6	23.6	25.4	23.6	22.3	21.1
Industrial	17.9	16.6	16.6	18.6	15.3	14.3	16.6	13.1
Foreign	24.7	21.9	21.1	20.7	25.7	27.3	24.3	25.9
Economic	5.2	8.3	9.8	9.7	6.9	7.1	7.7	7.6
Crime	4.3	4.8	4.5	5.5	2.8	4.3	5.2	5.1
Home Affairs	5.2	6.6	6.9	5.8	6.9	5.6	5.4	7.2
Sport	7.1	7.6	7.5	5.0	4.1	6.5	6.0	7.4
Human Interest	4.6	5.3	5.4	4.2	5.1	3.2	4.7	6.6
Disasters	9.9	6.1	5.1	6.3	5.8	6.7	5.9	4.4
Science	—	0.7	1.5	0.5	2.0	1.3	1.8	1.6
Total	100.0	99.9	100.0	99.9	100.0	99.9	99.9	100.0
n =	324	685	826	381	393	462	613	942

Source: Derived from Glasgow University Media Group: *Bad News* (1976) p. 98.

The time constraint on news items is not the only factor which results in the trivialisation of events. Some have argued that because BBC's *Nine O'Clock News* competes with ITN's *News at Ten* for audience ratings, this leads to efforts on both sides to make the news more attractive, even more entertaining. Producers are tempted to exclude complex or technical issues in preference for the simple and dramatic. Politicians have long complained that the mass media exaggerate the importance of personalities whilst tending to ignore the impact of issues. Conflict is portrayed, for example, as a personality clash between Mrs Thatcher and Edward Heath or between Tony Benn and Roy Hattersley rather than as differences in policy preferences.

Newspaper readership

Newspapers have experienced fluctuating fortunes. Since the end of the last war a number of national newspapers have disappeared. A number of these, such as the *Sketch* or *Reynolds News* had low circulation figures. Others, such as the Liberal-supporting *News Chronicle* and Labour-supporting *Daily Herald*, ran into financial difficulties despite relatively large circulations. Newspapers have been launched despite the unfavourable economic climate; these include the *Sun*, the *Star*, *Today* and the *Mail on Sunday*.

The rack of papers seen outside any newsagents symbolises the British class system. The quality press is read overwhelmingly by the higher socio-economic groups whilst the mass circulation *Sun*, *Mirror* and *Star* have predominantly working-class readers. Between the 'haughties' and the 'naughties' are the *Mail* and *Express* which, reflecting their lower middle class pitch, are read across the social spectrum (see Table 14.3).

Treatment of the news varies enormously between papers. The quality papers contain much more of what might be described as 'news' in addition to comment and editorial. The mass circulation papers more closely resemble adult comics and are designed for 'looking at' rather than 'reading'. Much space is taken up with photographs and large-print headlines. Where the quality press focuses on international events and city news, the mass circulation papers rarely fail to devote considerable space to 'scandal' of one sort or another.

The political weeklies have suffered a 40 per cent decline in circulation since 1970. The most successful amongst them is *The Economist* with a circulation of 202 000 of which over a third is sold overseas. Other circulation

TABLE 14.3

Readership of national newspapers: by social class, 1982

	Percentage of adults in each social class reading each paper in 1982						Readership (millions) 1982	Average circulation (millions) 1982
	A	B	C1	C2	D	E		
Daily newspapers								
The Sun	7	11	23	37	41	28	12.6	4.1
Daily Mirror	6	10	19	32	33	19	10.4	3.3
Daily Express	15	16	17	13	11	8	5.8	2.0
Daily Mail	17	18	18	10	8	7	5.4	1.9
Daily Star	1	3	6	15	16	10	4.6	1.3
The Daily Telegraph	34	22	11	3	2	1	3.4	1.3
The Guardian	9	10	4	1	1	—	1.4	0.4
The Times	14	6	2	1	1	—	0.9	0.3
Financial Times	10	4	2	1	—	—	0.7	0.2
Any daily newspaper	77	71	72	76	76	62	31.6	
Sunday newspapers								
News of the World	8	11	18	33	38	29	11.5	4.2
Sunday Mirror	6	12	21	31	31	17	10.3	3.6
Sunday People	6	11	18	29	30	21	9.9	3.4
Sunday Express	33	28	23	14	10	9	7.4	2.9
The Sunday Times	31	22	12	4	2	2	3.7	1.3
The Mail on Sunday	9	9	9	5	4	2	2.7	1.0
The Observer	18	15	8	3	2	2	2.6	0.8
Sunday Telegraph	20	13	7	2	2	2	2.3	0.8
Any Sunday newspaper	79	75	73	79	77	64	32.5	

Source: *Social Trends*, 14 (1984) p. 144.

figures are *The Listener*, 30 000; the *New Statesman*, 39 000; the *Spectator*, 18 000; *New Society*, 28 000 and *Tribune*, 10 000.

Finally there is the 'fringe' or 'underground' press. The anti-establishment *Private Eye* has made important political disclosures from time to time, and underground papers such as the now-defunct *OZ* have occasionally played a political role.

THE POLITICAL IMPACT OF THE MASS MEDIA

There is a view that the mass media can actually create news by 'setting up' newsworthy events that otherwise could not have taken place. Some think that the mere presence of TV cameras at a demonstration increases the risks that it will develop into a riot. If such a riot is shown on the TV news some people think that this creates 'copycat' riots in other areas. There is another view that the mass media may enhance or reduce the importance of events, but those events cannot be created by the media. For example, Colin Seymour-Ure argues that the media were influential in making Enoch Powell into a major political figure in 1968 'as the result of intense, sustained publicity for his views on immigration' (Seymour-Ure, *The Political Impact of the Mass Media*, 1974, p. 21). Yet 'that status depended also on the distinctive character of his views and the existence of a political crisis that gave them point' (ibid, p. 21). He continues to argue that the political impact of any communication will be influenced by its timing, frequency and intensity.

Timing

One of the most interesting examples of political impact resulting from the timing of news took place during the General Election campaign of 1924 with the publication of the Zinoviev letter. The letter, commonly believed to be a fake, was marked 'Very Secret' and was sent from the Third Communist International in Moscow to the Central Committee of the British Communist Party. It urged the need to stir the British working class into revolutionary action and form them into a British Red Army. The letter was published in the Press on 25 October and dominated the campaign until polling day on 29 October. The *Daily Mail* gave the letter the most sensational treatment and amongst the remaining papers only the *Herald* declared it to be a forgery. Some argue that the 'Red Scare' resulting from the Zinoviev letter lost Labour the election. In other words, had the news of this letter which had been known for some considerable period been released at a different time, then Labour would have won the General Election.

Frequency

The constant repetition of messages over a period of time may make an impact on the political climate. As we shall see, radical critics of the media argue that there is a constant anti-union bias in the media and that this type of exposure has a long-term effect on people's perceptions. Colin Seymour-Ure argues that the habit of the mass media in presenting a 'Westminster' view of British politics can mislead the public:

> The construction regularly put upon the nature of British politics by the mass media stresses heavily the 'Westminster' as opposed to the 'Whitehall' elements. The power of Parliament, and the extent to which it figures in political processes at all, are arguably emphasised more than they should be if an accurate impression of events is to be given. If that is so, the frequency of media coverage has much to do with it (Seymour-Ure, *The Political Impact of the Mass Media*, p. 36).

He also points out that there is a political impact for issues which are *neglected* by the mass media. For example, during the 1950s and 1960s the population of mainland Britain remained unconcerned about developments in Northern Ireland as a consequence of Irish affairs not appearing in the news.

Intensity

When one story dominates all others, it is said to be communicated more intensely. Seymour-Ure cites general elections as events which are communicated with high intensity in the media with the consequence of focusing public attention on them. He calculated that 61 per cent of lead-stories in the national press in the three weeks before Polling Day in 1970 were about the election.

An unexpected or urgent event can be turned into a crisis by the intensity of media coverage. The Falklands War of 1982 is an interesting example of a high-intensity media event. But because lives were at risk, there was a conflict of interests between the Government and the mass media. The essence of successful warfare is secrecy whereas the essence of successful journalism is publicity and disclosure. Despite the intensity of communication, there was relatively little raw information to transmit. It seems likely, also, that the British Government were bearing in mind that TV coverage of the war in Vietnam had undermined public support amongst Americans for the conflict to be pursued. Thus, whilst there was the technical capacity to send Falklands War pictures back to Britain from the South Atlantic, these facilities were denied to journalists. In the absence of 'live' coverage, news and current affairs programmes relied on military 'experts' to speculate on events with the aid of cartoons and models.

There was also considerable disagreement about the role of the mass media during the crisis. On the one hand the Prime Minister was extremely angry about the 'neutral' tone of a BBC *Panorama* programme. On the other hand, journalists did not believe that national security was at stake and did not expect to be part of the State's propaganda machine. Nevertheless, the Press was unwittingly used by the Ministry of Defence in order to spread disinformation and confuse the enemy. An example of this occurred when newspapers carried reports that the nuclear submarine *Superb* had been sent to the Falklands. Later this was found not to have been the case. In a Parliamentary enquiry the Ministry of Defence denied that its officials had lied to the mass media, but confessed to 'news management'. Sir Frank Cooper, Permanent Under-Secretary of State, put it nicely: 'We did not tell lies, but we did not tell the whole story.' He agreed that when HMS *Superb* left Gibraltar there was a speculation that she was going to the Falklands, and that the Ministry 'did nothing to correct' this rumour.

It is not unusual for there to be tensions between politicians and the media, particularly television. For example, Anthony Eden fell out with the BBC for not giving strong support to the Suez invasion; Harold Wilson complained that the BBC refused to treat the government's National Economic Plan as non-controversial, and Edward Heath argued with the BBC over a documentary programme on Northern Ireland (*A Question of Ulster*). A Conservative Home Secretary, Leon Brittan, attempted to ban another programme on Northern Ireland (*Real Lives*), and the Chairman of the Conservative Party, Norman Tebbit, announced that he was setting up a 'bias monitoring unit' to scrutinise broadcasting. For some time, Conservatives had been complaining about anti-Tory bias in BBC radio and television. The first report of the monitoring unit focused on coverage of the American bombing of Libya. The report concluded that, compared with ITN news coverage, the BBC was anti-American. The accusations of bias were refuted with an ease which embarrassed many Conservatives. The BBC admitted that, along with ITN and the newspapers, it did make an error in associating the Hindawi bomb plot with the American raid. In fact, the BBC has a code of practice known as the 'yellow book' for presenting news and current affairs. On bias, editors are 'required to maintain within their respective programmes political balance over a period'. Balance is defined in practice as coverage which 'should reflect the support obtained by parties in the preceding election'. Predictably, the Alliance parties argued that 'support' should be interpreted as the share of the vote obtained, not the number of seats won in the Commons.

The BBC has a very difficult path to tread insofar as it does not wish to fall out with the Government at a time when the future of broadcasting is being discussed. If it so wished, the Government could reorganise broadcasting in a way which would destroy the BBC. At the same time, if the BBC allows itself to become a tool of government, it will lose its integrity and not be worthy of maintaining.

Trade unions and the mass media

Although television news usually appears to be 'neutral' in its approach to current events, radical critics have argued that a subtle ideology is possibly at its most visible in the reporting of trade unions. This is because society is divided into fundamentally antagonistic groups, and those who control the mass media sympathise with the management side of industry and are hostile to trade unions. The systematic management bias and routine news practices inevitably lead to the production of 'bad news' about trade unions.

In what has become an important piece of media research by the Glasgow University Media Group, published as *Bad News* (1976), all television reports of a month-long strike at the Cowley plant of British Leyland were monitored. Coverage began with the reporting of a speech delivered in Huyton by the then Prime Minister, Harold Wilson. The researchers observed that:

> This speech covered many areas notably government policy on industry and investment, but the section of it which received most attention from the television news was a reference made by Mr Wilson to 'manifestly avoidable stoppages of production' in the car industry. This reference was interpreted by all three channels in such a way that they presented strikes as the main problem facing the car industry in general and British Leyland Motor Corporation in particular (Glasgow University Media Group, *Bad News*, 1976, pp. 256–7).

Initially the BBC reported that 'The Prime Minister, in a major speech tonight on the economy, appealed to *Management and Unions* in the car industry to cut down on what he called "manifestly avoidable stoppages".' However, within the space of two hours the BBC had changed the report to say that 'The Prime Minister has appealed *to workers* in the car industry to cut down on avoidable stoppages.' From the outset, ITN reports presented Harold Wilson's speech as applying only to the workforce: 'The Prime Minister tonight defended the government policy of stepping in to help companies where jobs were threatened but he also gave *workers* a blunt warning' (ibid, pp. 257–9).

It could be argued that there were many possible weaknesses which had caused problems at British Leyland; poor quality management, too little investment in the past, unreliable delivery of components from outside suppliers, and so on. But the dominant theme of the television news was overwhelmingly that strikes and the workforce were the source of Leyland's problems. The Glasgow University Media Group felt that this was consistent with the wider picture of society drawn by the media in which the blame for most industrial problems is laid at the door of the workforce. Contradictory evidence is either ignored, smothered or reinterpreted so that it supports the views of the journalists. In *Bad News* it was pointed out that an MP who disagreed with the Prime Minister's speech as reported received only 15 seconds in which to put his point of view, and the answers of the Cowley shop steward convenor which offered alternative explanations for Leyland's problems were ignored by the interviewer who kept returning to questions about strikes.

The Annan Report on Broadcasting (1977) went some way towards agreeing that trade unions were poorly reported, but it was felt that distortion of union affairs resulted from technical considerations rather than political bias. The Report stated that 'the broadcasters were not guilty of deliberate and calculated bias. But that coverage of industrial affairs is in some respects inadequate and unsatisfactory is not in doubt.' It continued:

> They too-often forget that to represent the management at their desks, apparently the calm and collected representatives of order, and to represent shop stewards and picket lines stopping production, apparently the agents of disruption, gives a false picture of what strikes are about. The broadcasters have fallen into the professional error of putting compelling camera work before news.

Television reporters felt that they had reported Harold Wilson's speech and the Cowley dispute fairly. They argued that when politicians make public speeches they often run through several themes before coming to the major one which they know will get reported in the news. In the case of Harold Wilson's Huyton speech, it was argued, he did make a wide-ranging speech on the economy but the section of it which was emphasised in the news was clearly the section that he wanted them to report.

Other critics of the *Bad News* studies have argued that the Glasgow Group expect journalists to act like sociologists in the way that they report society. This ignores the fact that journalists are guided by a different set of professional values. Another criticism of *Bad News* is that its authors do not allow for the fact that the audience may be critical of what they watch. The audience may use considerable judgement when assessing the news and dismiss an item as being 'just another TV story'. In other words, the audience do not absorb news in an uncritical way. On hearing Harold Wilson's speech, some might suspect that only half the story is being told whilst others may dismiss his message because 'he has never worked in a car factory and doesn't know what he's talking about'. Although some in the audience will believe all that they see on TV, many will resist manipulation by the media.

In his book, *The Media and Political Violence* (1981), Richard Clutterbuck argued that newspapers and broadcasts tended to reflect their respective audiences' dislike of strikes rather than setting out with a strong bias against the unions. One of his case-studies is the series of strikes by low-paid public service workers during the winter of 1978 9, which journalists called the 'Winter of Discontent'. The mass media did try to answer genuine questions raised by the public, although newspaper headlines such as 'Famine Threat – Food Stores Empty in Ten Days' (*Sun*); 'Cancer Ward Torment' (*Express*), and 'Target for Today – Sick Children' (*Mail*) capitalised on such anxiety and alarm as there was. In this sense they were biased, as too were some current affairs programmes on television. But Richard Clutterbuck argued that survey findings showed that the overwhelming majority of viewers did not feel that coverage of these strikes on BBC and ITN news was biased in favour of management or the unions. He continued:

> The chief problem, however, is not one of bias but of time and space. A two-minute TV news item can show only the highlights of a day's picketing and these give neither a true nor a fair picture. Like the quality papers, the current affairs and documentary programmes which do have time to give the background are seen only by a small minority – consisting mainly of people least likely to be personally involved in a confrontation on a picket line, but who are likely to be adversely affected by a strike. It is, however, in the interest of everyone, strikers included, to understand the background, including the cost of the dispute to the strikers themselves (e.g. if it will take three years to make up the lost pay) and to the community, both in the short term and the long term. The problem of background needs urgent study by the media (Clutterbuck, *Media and Political Violence*, p. 48).

Television and politics as a spectator sport

Some American political scientists, notably Murray Edelman have explored the social psychology of relationships between political leaders and their wider public. The mass media, particularly television, play a vital role in this relationship:

> For most men most of the time politics is a series of pictures in the mind, placed there by television news, newspapers, magazines and discussions. The pictures create a moving panorama taking place in a world the mass public never quite touches, yet one of its members come to fear or cheer, often with passion and sometimes with action (Murray Edelman, *The Symbolic Uses of Politics*, 1964, p. 5).

In other words, only a few people are actually in touch with the situations reported in the news; most understand these situations through the symbols that engage them: 'Politics is for most of us a passing parade of abstract symbols' (ibid, p. 5). These symbols help the public to understand what is happening around them, such as unemployment statistics or crime rates or, like the symbol of the Royal Family, may generate emotions of patriotism and loyalty. Edelman explains: 'Every symbol stands for something other than itself, and it also evokes an attitude, a set of impressions or a pattern of events associated through time, through space, through logic, or through imagination with the symbol' (ibid, p. 6). For example, the words 'Soviet Union' make up a neutral geographical term which is the name of a large country. But, for many in Britain, it is a political symbol which stands for danger and creates feelings of fear and distrust: for a minority, it is a symbol which generates feelings of warmth.

The relationship between leaders and the public is complex, because 'the nature of man and the functioning of the system are part of a single transaction'. Leaders and followers provide each other with psychological benefits. The leader can respond to *threats* against the country, which create mass anxiety, with *reassurances* that the dangers can be overcome. The leader may do this through giving their impression of resolution, will and strength, in which case he is likely to receive public support.

Some political symbols will tend to mobilise people into action, whereas others will induce passive behaviour. Edelman comments, however, that if a person's experience as far back as he can remember 'consists of emergencies, crises, and hazards following temporary periods of relief and hope, followed by new crises, what influence will this have on his behaviour? It may well induce helplessness, confusion, insecurity, and great susceptibility to manipulation by others' (ibid, p. 14).

East–West relations are characterised by periods of crises and *détente* of the type Edelman describes. There is a view that political leaders in both the liberal democracies of the West and the Communist countries of the East use 'Cold War' symbols to induce feelings of helplessness in their peoples and thereby increase their reliance on their respective leaders. In other words, without the use of Cold War symbols, the people in Britain, but much more so the people in the Soviet Union, would be more difficult to govern. In a typical news programme, the British viewer may be angered by rising unemployment figures; be anxious about an economic forecast that inflation will be worse next year; be saddened by the closure of a hospital ward because of health service cuts; be worried by an aggressive speech made by President Andropov; and support the Minister of Defence's decision to purchase more advanced nuclear warheads from the USA. He may well feel insecure, helpless and confused by 'politics'. But the most important impact, according to Edelman, is that he will remain politically docile.

Election Television

The Television Research Unit monitored the impact of the 1959 General Election programmes on voting intentions. In their study *Television and the Political Image* (1961), the researchers, J. Trenaman and Denis McQuail, reported that television had an educational function insofar as the more individuals watched campaign programmes the more accurately they became informed on issues. But television exposure did not appear to affect the voting or attitudes of electors to the Labour or Conservative parties. Although attitudes towards the Conservatives improved during the campaign, there was no evidence that the mass media played any role in this change of attitude.

A study of the 1964 General Election by Jay Blumler and Denis McQuail, showed that 9 per cent of their sample switched votes during the campaign, and that the Liberals benefited from this. Both Labour and Conservative got fewer votes than they were 'promised' at the outset of the campaign, but the Liberals actually received 70 per cent more votes than they were promised. It was observed that:

> . the upsurge of Liberal support at the polls in 1964 was powerfully assisted by exposure to the preceding campaign. Election television was centrally involved in this development, and the greatest contribution was apparently made by the party election broadcasts – especially those which the Liberal Party originated (Jay Blumler and Denis McQuail, *Television in Politics: Its Uses and Influence*, 1968).

Almost twenty years after this investigation the Alliance, particularly the SDP, appeared to be gaining support through media exposure. Indeed, many opponents of the SDP felt that the party was created by the media. In an article in *Political Quarterly* (1982) Colin Seymour-Ure explored reasons why the Social Democrats received so much publicity. Some argued that the Alliance partners got 'disproportionate representation' in the mass media considering they were both minority parties. In the 1979 General Election, there were 110 minor parties; many were eccentric (Dog-lovers' Party, Silly Party) but others were serious (Ecology Party, Workers' Revolutionary Party, Communist Party, National Front). None of them received the blaze of free publicity in the media enjoyed by the SDP and Liberals during and since 1981. Seymour-Ure believed that the SDP fitted in with news values:

> It is oriented to personalities more than policies. Its leaders are already elite politicians, focusing on Parliament, an elite institution. The party is 'negative', in the sense that it reacts or deviates from the old parties – and 'bad news is good news'. It is 'culturally proximate', readily comprehensible to the media audience (unlike many 'extremists') and located firmly in that middle ground towards which national news media – especially the broadcasters – tend to gravitate. It involves the unexpected and unpredictable ('Who'll be the next to join?') within a familiar and predictable frame of reference. It is a good running story, with a progressive dribble of MPs defecting to it, of by-election challenges and so on (Colin Seymour-Ure, 'The SDP and the Media', *Political Quarterly*, 53, 4, 1982, pp. 433–4).

Although media coverage alone cannot 'break the mould' for the SDP and Liberals, it can affect the electorate's views on what the key issues are in an election campaign.

Party political programmes are possibly the least popular element of election television. As long ago as 1964 a survey revealed that 55 per cent thought that there were 'too many' party political programmes and only 1 per cent thought that there were 'too few'. A survey conducted in 1983 revealed that over 50 per cent of those questioned thought television coverage of politics was excessive whilst 40 per cent thought it was about right.

Televising Parliament

Proposals that Parliament should be televised have always been greeted with controversy. This may be because Parliament and television are rival institutions with certain questions about their relationship as yet unanswered. Colin Seymour-Ure drew attention to one sensitive aspect of relations between these institutions:

> Put briefly, which is 'bigger' – Parliament or television? Parliament, constitutionally, is the representative body of the electorate, to which the Cabinet is responsible; a deeply entrenched institution claiming sovereignty in the law. Voting in a parliamentary election is the only political action most people ever perform. For most people too television is the main source of political information; a pervasive medium, powerful in that it communicates fast, wide and directly and involves the senses both of sight and sound. Is Parliament bound to be changed by the development of television: or can it shape and limit the medium to its own ends? (Seymour-Ure, *Political Impact of the Mass Media*, 1974, pp. 137–8).

The broadcasting of edited parliamentary debates, together with occasional select committee hearings, has taken place on the radio since 1975. This move was hailed as a radical departure at the time but is now considered to have been a rather modest development. Recordings of parliamentary proceedings are contained in short programmes, *Today in Parliament* and *Yesterday in Parliament* which are broadcast late at night before being repeated early the following morning. A digest, *The Week in Westminster*, is broadcast on Saturday mornings. From time to time proceedings of various select committees are broadcast on Sunday evenings. Important debates are broadcast 'live' during the afternoon and evening but these are relatively rare. Occasionally sound recordings of Parliament are used in television news programmes, usually accompanied by a still photograph of the politician whose voice is being heard.

There were a number of attempts – mainly by Jack Ashley and Austin Mitchell – before 1988, to introduce television cameras into the Commons, but they met with no success. On one occasion the Commons came within a single vote of agreement to televise proceedings privately as an experiment. In February 1988, however, the Commons voted by an unexpectedly large majority (318:264) to allow the televising of its proceedings for an experimental period of six months.

Those who favour the idea argue that Parliament should be televised because most people now learn about politics from television. In the past, programmes on important issues, such as Britain's entry to the EEC, have been based on 'mock' debates in Parliament and have attracted large viewing audiences. Advocates argue that the public should not have to watch imitations of Parliament when the real thing is available. Also, the presence of television cameras in the Commons would ensure that members of the

Government, including the Prime Minister, fully respected the status of the Chamber. There have been numerous occasions in the past when an important announcement has been made first on television and then in the Commons. Naturally, this greatly annoys backbenchers. Ministers would not be tempted first to announce new measures on programmes such as *Panorama* if the Commons announcement was also televised.

Critics of televising Parliament argue that there is no substantial audience for such programmes, as is shown by the small numbers who listen to the radio programmes. But, more importantly, television would mislead the public about the nature of Parliament. Front-bench 'super-stars' would dominate programmes and backbenchers would find themselves having to explain to their constituents why they were never seen on the screen. Ministers would 'play to the cameras' and not address the House. Even in the budget speech which is broadcast live on radio the Chancellor is tempted to speak to the mass audience rather than the House. Also, the wrong impression of Parliament would be gained by seeing an almost empty Chamber for many debates. Viewers might conclude that their MPs are neglecting their duties rather than appreciate that many of them are engaged elsewhere on committees or constituency matters.

Finally, opponents of televising Parliament fear that the presence of cameras would encourage outrageous behaviour by MPs in the knowledge that it would make 'good television'. Even without cameras there are occasional brawls and other undignified events. Television would trivialise Parliament by featuring telegenic MPs with interesting personalities or styles at the expense of the visually unattractive MP and the analysis of issues. The presence of cameras would also encourage MPs themselves to trivialise proceedings, as in the case of an Australian MP who used a parliamentary broadcast to pass a message on to his dentist. However, the limited experiment in televising the Lords saw no such abuses and those commentators who believed that it was just a matter of time before the Commons allowed the cameras in for broadcasting to the public were proved correct.

SUMMARY

The mass media are amongst the most powerful political institutions in society although it is difficult to be precise about the extent of their influence. Some academics see the mass media as free institutions which are part of democracy, whilst others see them as manipulators of public opinion in the interests of the ruling class. The general population seem to be sceptical about the political content in newspapers but to trust what they see on television. Perhaps as a result of this, many leading politicians from Anthony Eden onwards have at one time or another been very sensitive about the way in which television reported their activities. Television cameras have entered the Lords but until early 1988 the Commons resisted such a move, although many always thought that the Commons would eventually concede and agree to be televised.

FURTHER READING

Beharrell, P. and Philo, G. (eds) (1977) *Trade Unions and the Media*, London, Macmillan.
Clutterbuck, R. (1981) *The Media and Political Violence*, London, Macmillan.
Curran, J. and Seaton, J. (1985) *Power Without Responsibility: The Press and Broadcasting in Britain*, London, Fontana/Methuen.
Glasgow Media Group (1980) *More Bad News*, London, Routledge & Kegan Paul.
Whale, J. (1977) *The Politics of the Media*, London, Fontana.

QUESTIONS

1. 'The mass media are persistently biased against the working class.' Evaluate this statement.

2. Outline the arguments for and against televising the House of Commons. State which arguments you find persuasive, and why.

ASSIGNMENT

Select a current issue in politics – either British or global. The extract below from *The Guardian* is an example of reporting of one major contemporary issue. Note the ways in which it is reported on radio, BBC and ITV television, and in the Press. Assess whether there are differences in political bias in the way the issue is reported. How can such political bias be explained? Attempt to construct a brief written account of some aspect of the issue in question which is bias-free. Finally, consider the moral implications. Are there some issues which should be applauded or condemned in media reports?

BBC 'OBSESSIVE AND BIASED' ON SOUTH AFRICA

Apartheid

The BBC was accused in the Commons yesterday of biased, 'boring' and anti-Thatcher coverage of the South Africa crisis.

Mr Tony Marlow (C. Northampton N), demanding an emergency debate, accused the BBC of an 'obsessive and, therefore, possibly misleading view' of South Africa, leaning towards the pro-sanctions lobby.

'Is there, outrageously, a corporation point of view?' he asked. 'Or is their approach motivated merely by an institutional megasulk, part of it a vindictive crusade against any policy advocated by the Prime Minister – in particular her positive and courageous stand on South Africa.'

People were giving no sign to MPs in letters of concern on the South Africa issue, said Mr Marlow. 'But day-in and day-out the BBC has been boring on about little else.'

South Africa concerned the 'demonstrating and posturing classes', but was 'not a topic of constant concern on the Northampton omnibus', said Mr Marlow.

Bishop Tutu, urging sanctions, and Winnie Mandela, the 'promoter of the unique barbarism of dangling burning tyres around the necks of living victims', appeared on the BBC, he told MPs. But the Zulu leader, Chief Buthelezi, and leading white South African opposition member, Mrs Helen Suzman, did not. It was 'virtually censorship', he claimed.

The Speaker, **Mr Bernard Weatherill**, however, rejected the call for an emergency debate.

The Guardian, 1 July 1986.

15

Politics, Police, the Courts and Redress

This chapter has three main themes all concerned with the broad question of the relationship between law and politics. It deals in turn with the general functions of law in our society, including types of law and the courts system; the issue of citizens' rights and redress, with special reference to the procedures and institutions which exist to protect these rights; and the role, operation and accountability of the police – the main law-enforcing agency.

THE LAW AND POLITICS

Law and politics are closely related. Three key connections exist:

1. at the level of *principle*, the 'language of the law' and its accompanying norms and practices inform political discourse in virtually all its guises;
2. at the level of *personnel*, lawyers are to be found occupying important positions in politics and government;
3. at the level of *practice*, the courts system provides an orderly method of settling disputes between individuals and between citizens and government.

We examine each of these links in turn.

Principle

First, politics is consistently discussed in terms of law, notably in terms of *rights, obligations and remedies* – for example, of the right of the citizen to a fair trial, of the obligation of the government to provide an education service under a particular Act of Parliament and of the remedies available to citizens in cases where their rights are infringed. Above all, politics is constantly discussed in terms of the *principle* of the rule of law. We last encountered this concept in Chapter 5, where its two meanings were briefly noted: (i) in order to have a legitimate basis, the powers exercised by 'the authorities' – politicians, civil servants, the police – must be conferred by law and exercised according to the procedures laid down by law; and, (ii) that redress, i.e. legal remedies for wrongs is available to all citizens both against any other citizen, no matter how influential, and against officers of the State. We shall return to this principle shortly. There has been a massive enlargement of the province of law in social and political life after the Second World War under the aegis of the Welfare State. This occurred first in a burst of legislation immediately after the war when a variety of 'welfare' entitlements were conferred – for example, to unemployment, pension and housing benefits. Second, it happened under the impetus of the 'radical law' movement of the 1970s, when legislation pushed the law more deeply into protecting the rights of tenants, workers, welfare claimants and towards the prohibition of discrimination on grounds of race and sex.

Personnel

Legal personnel are strongly represented *in* politics. Lawyers formed one-sixth of the House of Commons in the second Thatcher Administration and seven of the twenty-three members of the 1985 Cabinet had legal qualifications. The *Lord Chancellor* is a Cabinet Minister; heads an important office of State; presides over the House of Lords in its legislative and deliberative capacities; can sit as a judge; and appoints other judges. In other words, he is a practising politician as well as being the nation's senior judge and head of the legal profession. His Department has a £500m budget. The *Attorney-General* and the *Solicitor-General* as well as the Scottish law officers are also members of the government. Conversely, the legal profession itself is regulated by the State. The government from time to time pronounces on the practices of the legal profession in terms of who is allowed to practise law, how legal education is organised and the internal rules of solicitors. An example is the 1985 legislation which permitted licensed conveyancers to compete with solicitors in a field of the law where formerly solicitors had a monopoly. There are other important instances of overlap between political and legal personnel. Judges – generally considered to be politically impartial – are often used to head inquiries into politically sensitive events, e.g. the inquiry headed by Lord Scarman into the Brixton riots in 1981. Finally, politics and the law mingle in the institution of the House of Lords, which draws a number of its members from the law (the Law lords) and which combines the major constitutional roles of upper House of Parliament and supreme court of appeal.

Practice

The role of the legal system is to provide an orderly method of settling disputes between citizens and between citizens and the State. Broadly speaking, the *criminal law* provides standards of conduct as well as machinery (police, courts system) for dealing with those who commit crimes.

Crimes are normally classified as (i) against the State (treason, public order), (ii) against the person (murder, assault, rape) and (iii) against property (robbery, malicious damage). *Civil law* is concerned with the legal relations between persons. Normally, proceedings in a civil court depend upon a plaintiff pursuing an action against a defendant and they generally result in some 'remedy', such as damages, specific performance (where the defendant has to keep his side of the bargain), or a 'declaration' of the plaintiff's legal rights. Cases in criminal law have to be proved 'beyond reasonable doubt'; actions in civil law are decided on the 'balance of probabilities'. In general, and for the most part, a clear-cut distinction exists between civil and criminal law, but they may on occasion overlap, as, for example, where a private person initiates criminal proceedings, or the State takes action in the civil courts, or where someone is sued privately for damages and also prosecuted in the criminal courts, or, where a court has jurisdiction (as magistrates' courts have) in both civil and criminal matters.

Administrative law, as H. W. R. Wade has stated, is 'the body of general principles which govern the exercise of powers and duties by public authorities' (Wade, *Administrative Law*, 1979, 4th edn, pp. 5–6). This is the sphere of law which has undergone prodigious expansion in the twentieth century as the State through legislation has intervened in aspects of social life hitherto untouched. Administrative law is concerned with the legal restraints which surround the activities of those who apply policy decisions. It is a key example of the inter-connectedness of politics and law, with a variety of judicial and quasi-judicial institutions (the ordinary courts, tribunals, the ombudsman) supplying and applying a framework of rules within which public authorities act. It is centrally involved in the question of citizen rights and redress of grievances.

CIVIL RIGHTS AND THE REDRESS OF GRIEVANCES

The hallmark of a liberal-democratic State, it is often said, is the effectiveness with which a range of basic citizen rights or civil liberties are guaranteed. These rights or liberties have long been enthusiastically extolled by British people and it is vital, therefore, to examine to what extent this confidence in the security of such rights is justified. Three points provide a context for this discussion:

1. Virtually all British civil liberties stem from a fundamental principle: that people may do what they like so long as no law prevents them.
2. Legal protections against infringements of this fundamental freedom in specific instances (e.g. freedom of expression, meeting, association and so on) have been established gradually throughout history and are not enshrined in any particular statute (whether they *should be* is considered later in the chapter).

3. The question of citizen rights or liberties has both a positive and a negative aspect: the right to do certain things *and* the right *not* to have certain things done to you.

Exhibit 15.1 is concerned with the civil rights enshrined in the principle of classical liberal theory, rights which have achieved gradual realisation, largely over the past two centuries.

Exhibit 15.1   Civil liberties in the United Kingdom

Freedoms/Rights	*Comments*
1. *Political rights*	
Include right to vote in periodic elections, at local and national level (peers, prisoners, aliens and mental patients excluded)	Guaranteed by *Representation of the People Acts* (1918, 1928, 1948 and, the most recent, 1969), which lowered the franchise to 18
2. *Freedom of movement*	
Includes right to move freely within one's own country, to leave it; and not to be deprived of one's nationality	Home Secretary has power to detain suspected terrorists under *Prevention of Terrorism Act* (1984) and confine them to British mainland or Northern Ireland
3. *Personal freedom*	
Includes freedom from police detention without charge, i.e. right to be brought promptly before a judge or court; freedom from police searches of home without warrant; right to a fair trial including assumption of innocence until proved guilty; freedom from torture or coercion by the State	Protection against wrongful detention first enshrined in *Magna Carta* (thirteenth century) and *Habeas Corpus* legislation (seventeenth century). No person may be detained for more than 24 hours without charge or, if a 'serious arrestable offence', for more than 36 hours without charge (*Police and Criminal Evidence Act*, 1984). *Exceptions* in Northern Ireland, where police abuse of emergency powers has led to unlawful detention and local security forces have committed abuses against detained terrorists; also, in wartime when Defence Secretary (under *Defence Regulation 18B*) could detain any person he believed hostile to the State.

continued

Exhibit . . .   *– continued*

Freedoms/Rights	*Comments*
	Freedom from police searches of house without a warrant *not* applicable if arrested at one's premises or arrested elsewhere for an arrestable offence.
4. *Freedom of conscience* Includes right to practise any religion (freedom of worship); to marry a person of another religion; to withdraw one's children from an Established religion in school; and not to be compelled to undergo military service	Religious assemblies enjoy legal protection from disturbance
5. *Freedom of expression* Includes individual freedom to seek information and communicate ideas; freedom of the press, publishing houses and the broadcasting media from political censorship; and the absence of State policy and machinery to direct artistic work (theatre, cinema, literature) in accordance with a particular ideology	Free expression limited by law on treason, sedition, blasphemy, obscenity, libel, insulting words or behaviour, incitement to racial hatred, defamation, contempt of court and parliament and *Official Secrets Act*; 'D Notice' system imposes constraints on press. No censorship of theatre (since 1968) but some of TV and cinema
6. *Freedom of association and meeting* Includes the right to meet, process and protest freely; and to associate for political and other purposes	Again no absolute freedom exists; public meetings are limited by laws on trespass, nuisance, obstruction, and local authority bye-laws; also, by discretion of police (who can re-route or ban a march they consider likely to provoke disorder) and of Home Secretary (who imposed a temporary ban on all marches in 1980). Whilst there are few restrictions on setting up or joining a trade union, picketing in furtherance of a trade dispute is confined to one's place of work or that of 'first customers'/'first suppliers' (*Employment Act*, 1980)

continued

Exhibit . . .   *– continued*

Freedoms/Rights	*Comments*
7. *Right to property* Includes right to hold property, to use it as one will and not to be deprived of it without due process	Frequently invaded by parliament in twentieth century in name of nationalisation, compulsory purchase for slum clearance and safeguarding of public health. Right to use as one will also qualified by, e.g., legislation preventing certain forms of transfer or imposing taxation
8. *Right to privacy* This 'right' not recognised in British law although as a moral norm it is invoked with increasing frequency against what are taken to be State intrusions on the individual by political surveillance, 'bugging', telephone tapping, and so on; also, on behalf of public figures (e.g. Royalty) against harassment by the media	Since no general right exists, privacy has to be protected in practice by specific laws, e.g. against trespass, nuisance, and breach of trust and confidence
9. *Rights at work* These include protection from unfair dismissal, the right to a satisfactory environment at work and freedom from racial and sexual discrimination in employment	These rights have been the subject of recent legislation e.g. the *Employment Protection Act* (1978), which lays down the criteria for fair dismissal; workers may appeal to tribunals against unfair dismissal. The *Race Relations Act* (1976), the *Equal Pay Act* (1970) and the *Sex Discrimination Act* (1975) legislate against various kinds of racial and sexual discrimination, including at work
10. *Social freedoms* These include the rights to marry and divorce (for men and women equally), to use contraceptive methods, to early abortion and to practise homosexual relations between consenting adults	Divorce (1969), early abortion on broad social and medical grounds (1967) and homosexuality (1967) have all been the subject of post-war legislation

How are the rights and freedoms set out in Exhibit 15.1 protected? Six distinct areas of judicial and political support may be identified:

 (i) an independent judiciary allied with the principle of judicial review of executive actions;
 (ii) a political culture and a public opinion in which the principle of the rule of law is widely understood and zealously guarded;
 (iii) the vigilance of Members of Parliament in defence of civil liberties;
 (iv) the effectiveness of administrative law, and, in particular, the system of administrative tribunals and inquiries;
 (v) the capacity of the ombudsman to investigate and provide remedies for cases of administrative injustice;
 (vi) the role of the European Court of Human Rights in assisting British citizens to obtain their rights.

We deal with each in turn, concluding this section with a consideration of the arguments for and against a British Bill of Rights.

The independence of the judiciary and judicial review

The independence of the judiciary from political control or influence is a fundamental safeguard of civil freedoms. It is achieved in the UK by a combination of statute, common law, parliamentary rules and the self-restraint of governments – that is, their acceptance of the rule-of-law principle that they should not interfere with the conduct of the courts. The practice of senior judges holding office 'during good behaviour', in fact, dates back to the *Act of Settlement*, 1701. Since then their conduct has been the subject of complaint in Parliament on less than a score of occasions and only one judge has been dismissed (in 1830). Their salaries are fixed by statute so that annual parliamentary debate is avoided; since 1971 their salaries have been kept under review by the Top Salaries Review Body.

The highest judges are appointed by the Queen on the advice of the Prime Minister (normally after consultation with the Lord Chancellor); judges at High Court level and below are appointed by the Lord Chancellor. Although they are appointed and promoted by or on the advice of politicians, professional rather than political grounds are paramount in their appointment. Judges have a statutory retiring age of 75. They enjoy immunity from civil proceedings for anything said or done while acting in a judicial capacity. It is sometimes said that because judicial independence in the UK is in large part secured by statute, it is illusory. What Parliament has given, Parliament can with equal ease take away. But this is almost certainly to go too far. Whilst the independence – from political pressures – of politically appointed judges sounds paradoxical and is not enshrined in a single written constitutional settlement, it nonetheless possesses a certain validity. Considerable political difficulties would follow any attempt to tamper with judicial independence.

Because Parliament is sovereign and judges work within this context, they cannot strike down legislation as unconstitutional. Nor can they pronounce on its *merits* – that is, they are not justified in substituting what they would have done for what parliament enacted on a given occasion. But by virtue of the doctrine of *ultra vires*, judges do have the power of *statutory interpretation*; they can declare the action of a public servant under a particular Act invalid as exceeding the discretion conferred by the Act or they can void an action because the power does not exist. In general, in their work of interpretation, judges must have regard to what is reasonable; that is, what reasonable people might justly be held to consider reasonable conduct by a public authority. In reviewing the activities of administrators, judges may also invoke the common law principles of *natural justice*. These are twofold – first, the rule against bias (no one to be a judge in his own cause); and second, the right to a fair hearing (hear the other side). Under the first rule, administrators must not have any direct (including financial) interest in the outcome of the proceedings; nor must they be reasonably suspected of being biased or of being likely to be biased. The right to a fair hearing requires that no one should be penalised in any way without receiving notice of the case to be met and a fair chance to answer that case and to put one's own case.

Judges of the higher courts also possess the authority to *review* the outcome of disputes decided in all inferior tribunals. These include courts, special tribunals, professional disciplinary bodies and ordinary clubs, unions and associations. They may also review the decisions of public authorities charged to act fairly with regard to the rights, legitimate interest or expectations of citizens. Specific legal remedies are available. Thus, it is possible to quash the decision of a body outside its jurisdiction (*certiorari*); to prevent a tribunal considering a matter which is outside its authority (prohibition); to compel the performance of a public duty (*mandamus*); to restrain the commission or continuance of unlawful conduct (an injunction); and simply to clarify the legal position (a declaration). Needless to say, important as these principles (*ultra vires*, natural justice) and remedies are, they only come into play after a plaintiff has initiated proceedings. Judges' capacity to control executive encroachment on individual liberties depends, at least in the first instance, upon individuals' willingness to act in their own causes.

Powers of judicial review were rarely asserted before the 1960s but the past twenty years have seen a significant increase in review of administrative acts by the courts. Recent cases in which the courts have checked executive action – for the most part because it was *ultra vires* or failed to take into account the principles of natural justice – are set out in Exhibit 15.2. The cases are explained in sufficient detail to bring out what was involved in each instance. The table is not intended to be comprehensive but rather indicative of the new judicial interventionism and its consequences.

Exhibit 15.2   Review of administrative action by the courts

1. *Laker Airways Ltd* v. *Department of Trade* (1977)

At issue   Freddie Laker obtained a license from the Civil Aviation
Authority in 1972 to operate his Skytrain on the transatlantic route.
However, in 1975 the Secretary of State for Trade directed the CAA that
British Airways were to retain a monopoly on scheduled transatlantic routes
and Skytrain's licence was withdrawn. Laker appealed.

The decision   The High Court found that the Secretary of State's action was
ultra vires (a) because he was statutorily authorised (by the *Civil Aviation
Act* 1971) only to guide and not to direct the Civil Aviation Authority; and
(b) because his advice was contrary to the criteria laid down in the Act for
the licensing of air services by the CAA, which included the principle that
British Airways should not have a monopoly on any route.

Result   The court held that the Secretary of State had acted unlawfully.
Laker Airways accordingly won their action and hence the right to compete
on the transatlantic route.

2. *R.* v. *Leicestershire Fire Authority* ex parte *Thompson* (1978)

At issue   The Leicestershire Fire Authority reduced one of its fire officers to
the ranks on the evidence of its Chief Fire Officer, who had brought the
disciplinary charge.

The decision   The Divisional Court quashed the decision on the grounds
that the Chief Fire Officer had spent several minutes with the committee
concerned after its members had retired to consider the matter. The court
considered that the suspicion of bias would inevitably arise as a consequence
of the Chief Fire Officer's behaviour and *natural justice* (the rule against
bias) therefore applied.

Result   The demoted fire officer was reinstated. Reveals courts' greater
willingness to apply natural justice to administrative authorities after *Ridge*
v. *Baldwin* (below, next)

3. *Ridge* v. *Baldwin* (1964)

At issue   The Chief Constable of Brighton, who by statute could only be
removed on the grounds of neglect of duty or inability, was dismissed by the
Watch Committee without a hearing.

The decision   The House of Lords held that the Watch Committee's act was
invalid. In dismissing the Chief Constable (a) without prior notification of
the charge and (b) without giving him the opportunity to put his case, it had
failed to observe *natural justice* (hear the other side). It had not given the
Chief Constable a fair hearing.

continued

Exhibit . . .   *– continued*

Results   A very important decision: hitherto, the courts had limited the application of the rules of natural justice to authorities acting in a *judicial* or *quasi-judicial* capacity; thereafter, the courts were prepared to extend the application of the rules of natural justice to any *administrative* authority whose decisions affected people's rights or legitimate expectations.

4. *Conway* v. *Rimmer* (1968)

At issue   After being cleared of a charge of theft, a probationary police constable was dismissed soon afterwards. He brought a charge of malicious prosecution against his former Superintendent, during which case the Home Secretary objected to the disclosure of reports relating to the ex-Constable's probationary period, claiming that their publication would be against the public interest.

The decision   The House of Lords held that the courts had the power to inspect the documents in private in order to decide whether it was against the public interest to disclose them and, having examined the papers, ordered disclosure.

Result   An exceptionally important case; hitherto, the courts had generally followed the ruling in a war-time case, *Duncan* v. *Cammell, Laird and Co.* (1942), where the Minister's conclusive right to pronounce disclosure of documents against the public interest had been upheld. The implication of *Conway* v. *Rimmer* was that it was the courts rather than the executive which should decide whether such confidential documents should be produced in future.

5. *Padfield* v. *Minister of Agriculture* (1968)

At issue   South-east milk producers complained to the Minister of Agriculture that the prices paid by the Milk Marketing Board were too low and requested him to refer the question to a committee of investigation. The Minister refused to do so, giving his reasons, which included the political difficulties which would ensue if the committee found against him and he were forced to implement its report.

The decision   The House of Lords held that the Minister had allowed irrelevant considerations to weigh with him and had failed to promote the purposes of the Act establishing the milk marketing scheme. An order of *mandamus* was issued directing the Minister to consider the complainants' case. The Minister was held to have *misused his discretion*.

Result   The Minister appointed a committee, whose report in favour of the south-east milk producers was subsequently rejected by the Minister.

continued

Exhibit . . .   *– continued*

However, the important principle established was the subjection of executive discretion to review by the courts and their identification and remedy of misuse of administrative power.

6. *Congreve* v. *Home Office* (1976)

At issue In order to avoid paying an increase in his television licence fee, a TV licence-holder, Mr Congreve, bought a new licence at the existing rate before his old licence had expired. The Home Secretary, who possessed a statutory discretion to revoke TV licences, revoked the new licence after Mr Congreve had refused to pay an additional sum to cover the increase.

The decision The Court of Appeal held that the Minister's reasons were inadequate. The Minister had pleaded loss of revenue and unfairness to those license-holders who had not anticipated the increased licence fee in the manner of Mr Congreve. Consequently, the Minister's behaviour was unlawful.

Results Another important case in which the courts demonstrated a willingness to consider and pronounce adversely upon the soundness of reasons given for executive decisions. (The Home Secretary riposted by taking power to raise licence fees in future without giving advance warning.)

7. *Secretary of State for Education and Science* v. *Tameside MBC* (1977)

At issue The newly-elected Conservative council in Tameside proposed to reintroduce selection and not to go ahead with plans for comprehensive schooling as directed by the Secretary of State. The case came before the courts after the Secretary of State had applied for an order of *mandamus* to enforce his directions.

The decision The Divisional Court ordered the Council to carry out the Secretary of State's direction but the Court of Appeal overturned the decision and was upheld by the House of Lords. The case hinged on the meaning of 'reasonable' behaviour by the local authority. The Secretary of State contended that the council was acting 'unreasonably' but the House of Lords disagreed, holding that behaviour could only be described as 'unreasonable' if it could be considered that no reasonable authority would have acted in the way Tameside did. Since it could not be held that Tameside had acted 'unreasonably', the Minister had exceeded his powers.

Result Judicial review could not be excluded by conferring a discretion on a Minister in subjective terms. In this instance, the Minister was empowered to direct a local authority if satisfied that it had acted or was proposing to act unreasonably (Section 68, 1944 Education Act). His ability to direct a local authority depended only upon his being satisfied that it was acting unreasonably – a subjective matter.

continued

Exhibit . . .   *– continued*

8. R. v. *The Greater London Council*, ex parte *Bromley* (1981)

At issue   The GLC introduced a supplementary rate to pay for fare
reductions on London's bus and underground services, as promised in the
election manifesto of the Labour group in the capital. The London Borough
of Bromley challenged its legal right to do so.

The decision   The High Court found against Bromley but the Appeal Court
reversed the judgement, holding that the GLC had abused its powers and
that its action was *ultra vires*. The GLC had failed to balance the interests of
travellers and ratepayers in a reasonable way. The GLC appealed against the
judgement but the House of Lords upheld the decision of the Appeal Court.

Result   This case brought the higher judiciary firmly into the political arena
with the verdict being criticised by Labour politicians for undermining the
policies of an elected authority and Bromley's initiative in bringing the
action being commended by Conservatives.

Support for the rule of law in political culture and public opinion

A second main support for civil liberties is well-established public support for
the rule of law. It is important as a norm constraining the behaviour of
authorities and guiding the expectations of citizens. To a considerable extent,
it is institutionalised in the procedures and practices of the legal, political and
constitutional systems. The modern principle of the rule of law owes much to
the nineteenth century lawyer, A. V. Dicey, but also needs to go beyond his
formulation, as de Smith suggests in his *Constitutional and Administrative
Law* (1983, p. 30). Dicey remains important because he stated well two of its
cardinal principles (indicated below). A modern definition, however, needs to
go further than Dicey for a number of reasons. First, Dicey saw the judge-
made common law as the foundation of individual liberties: the twentieth
century has revealed the extent to which these can be undermined by a
sovereign Parliament which has conferred arbitrary powers on governments
in war-time and in emergencies. Second, Dicey distrusted what he called
'administrative law' as savouring of Continental systems of law which gave a
privileged position to State officials; however, under the aegis of the Welfare
State, vast new empires of administrative power have been established. The
modern problem is neither to dismiss, ignore nor keep administrative law at
arm's length but rather, to infuse into 'the administrative powers of the State
. . . the legal ideals of fair procedure and just decision' (H. W. R. Wade,
Administrative Law, 1977). Even though the rule of law guidelines need to be
more extensive than in Dicey's day, however, and their coverage wider, the

point of producing such a list remains the same: to provide a constant witness of legal ideals for both public and practitioners.

These are the main principles, then (Dicey's formulations indicated):

1. *All persons are equal before the law*; in more detail, people of any class, race or gender are universally subject to one law administered in the ordinary courts and there is no distinction in law between ordinary citizens and servants of the State (Dicey).
2. *No one is punishable except for a breach of the law*; the laws are published and publicly accessible – that is, they are known or can be discovered (Dicey); and they are enforced through independent courts.
3. *The powers held by the authorities must be conferred by law (i.e. by Parliament) and exercised according to authorised procedures;* in particular, powers conferred by Parliament must be defined and exercised within strict limits – by a combination of administrators' self-restraint and the vigilance of the courts.
4. *Certain basic standards of justice should permeate the law*; natural justice (the right to a fair hearing, the rule against bias) should inform procedures wherever people's rights and legitimate expectations are under consideration; since rights depend upon remedies, remedies should be available against those who exceed and abuse discretionary authority.

Members of Parliament as defenders of civil liberties

According to traditional constitutional theory, MPs occupy a prominent role in the defence of civil liberties. The rights of citizens, so the theory goes, are protected in two ways: first, by means of Ministerial accountability to Parliament; second, through the case-work of Members on behalf of their constituents. Few now consider this theory to be valid. For whilst Parliament remains the central forum for scrutiny of the actions of the executive (see Chapter 10), it is equally clearly no longer the mechanism (if indeed it ever was) through which aggrieved individuals can pursue remedies for perceived injustices. Basically, this is because the limit of an MP's influence on behalf of a constituent is the limit of the power of public opinion – or the threat of it – to compel. Whilst effective on occasion, this system is unsound as a *general* enforcer of executive respect for civil rights simply because, faced by an obstinate Minister, an MP lacks the capacity either to insist on a revelation of the facts or to compel any form of restitution if it can be shown that a constituent has suffered an injustice. The system is arbitrary in its dependence on the investigative skill and persistence of MPs and on the voluntary willingness of Departments or other executive agencies to make amends where faults have occurred. In short, even though parliamentarians may play a valuable role in first airing an individual problem or grievance, this method of defending civil liberties lacks both universal reliability and certain remedies.

Administrative law

Administrative tribunals

Tribunals are a very important part of the British system of administrative justice. They are normally established by legislation and cover a wide range of functions, many of them in the field of welfare. Thus, there are tribunals for national insurance, pensions, housing, education, the National Health Service and immigration. Claims arising out of injuries at work, industrial disputes, unfair dismissal and redundancy are dealt with by industrial tribunals. Tribunals are usually composed of a chairman with legal qualifications (often a solicitor) and two lay-members representing interests related to the concerns of the particular tribunal. They are independent and not subject to political or administrative interference from the Departments under whose aegis they usually work. Their functions may be described as quasi-judicial: to hear appeals against initial decisions of government agencies or, sometimes, disputes between individuals and organisations. Their role is to establish the facts of each case and then apply the relevant legal rules to it, i.e. in the majority of instances to decide what the statutory rights and entitlements of the aggrieved actually are. Except where the parties request privacy, tribunals hear cases in public. They provide simpler, cheaper, speedier, more expert and more accessible justice than the ordinary courts in their specific sphere of responsibility. It is possible to appeal against their decisions – normally to a superior court, tribunal or a Minister. For a small number of tribunals, however, including the National Health Service Tribunal, the Social Security Commissioners and the Immigration Appeal Tribunal, no appeal is available.

The mode of operation of tribunals is determined by the *Tribunals and Inquiries Act*, 1971. Under this Act, a *Council on Tribunals* has the functions of reporting on the tribunals under its supervision (to the Lord Chancellor and Secretary of State for Scotland, and ultimately to parliament); of hearing and investigating complaints against tribunals from members of the public; and of being consulted by the responsible Minister before procedural rules for tribunals and inquiries are made. A second important provision of the Act concerns the giving of reasons for tribunals' decisions, another matter supervised by the Council on Tribunals. Most of the tribunals listed in the first schedule of the Act are required to supply oral or written reasons for their decisions (unless exempted by order of the Chancellor after consultation with the Council). But tribunals are only required to give reasons if requested and are not obliged to inform the parties of their right to request them.

The general trend of the last quarter of a century has been towards making the procedure of tribunals more judicial, but without forfeiting the advantages of tribunals over ordinary courts. These are greater informality, specialisation, capacity to conduct their own investigations and flexibility in terms of the formulation of reasonable standards in their own spheres. The *Franks Committee on Administrative Tribunals and Inquiries*, 1957 recommended that tribunals move towards 'greater openness, fairness and impartiality'. Proceedings should be held in public and reasons for decisions should be given; the parties before tribunals should know in advance the case they had to meet, should have the chance to put their own case either personally or through representatives, and should be able to appeal against decisions; finally, proceedings should not only be impartial, through stronger safeguards regulating their composition, but also be seen to be impartial by no longer being held on the premises of Government Departments. Under the supervision (since 1958) of the Council of Tribunals, the procedures of administrative tribunals have become both more uniform and more fair in many of the ways recommended by Franks, such as proper notice of hearings and of the case to be answered, rights of appeal and legal representation at hearings. Outstanding problems in the system relate primarily, although not solely, to the lack of appeal from certain tribunals (already noted); its limited extension (not all tribunals are included); and the particular condition (on request only) of the obligation to give reasons even if, in practice, tribunals do provide reasons.

Statutory inquiries

The standard method for giving a hearing to objectors to a Government proposal is the *statutory inquiry*. Virtually all legislation concerned with planning and land use makes provision for holding an inquiry. Most often, inquiries arise about new towns, housing, town and country planning, road, aviation and other transport developments, agriculture and health. Inquiries are usually held, then, within the context of Government policy: notable examples are individual appeals against a compulsory purchase order for the acquisition of land for a specific purpose or against the refusal of planning permission by a local authority. Procedure before, during and after the inquiry is regulated by rules laid down by the *Tribunals and Inquiries Act*, 1971. Decisions of inquiries may be challenged either on the grounds of procedure or the substance of the decision in the High Court within six weeks of the decision. Whilst affected third parties in land-use cases do not have legally enforceable rights, legislation governing planning usually protects their interests to a certain degree. Proposals have to be adequately publicised, for instance, and third parties have to be afforded the opportunity to state their cases before decisions are taken.

Whilst realising the need not to impose unnecessary delays on inquiry procedure, the courts in hearing appeals from inquiry decisions have sought to safeguard the rights of the public. For example, they have ruled that objectors at an inquiry should be able to take 'an active, intelligent and informed part in the decision-making process' (1977) and that they must be given 'a fair crack of the whip' (1976) in putting their case. The courts have received important support in this regard from the *Council on Tribunals* which not only raises specific questions relating to inquiries with the Chancellor, but also (as with tribunals) reports on their working, has the right to be consulted before procedural rules are made for them, and receives public complaints about them. How successful the courts and Council had been in bolstering the inquiry system as a bastion of democracy became a matter of increasing controversy, however, during the 1980s mainly as a result of disquiet about government handling of issues arising out of its proposals for the management of nuclear waste. Keen to avoid the delays and furore surrounding the 340-day *Inquiry into the Sizewell-B Nuclear Reactor* (1985), the Government in late 1985 proposed to limit the terms of reference of the Inquiry relating to the Dounreay Fast-Breeder Reactor to the question of where to dump the waste rather than to allow the Inquiry to enter the debate about whether to dump or, as its critics preferred, store it. As a result, protest groups proposed to boycott the inquiry and the *Commons Select Committee on the Environment* proposed to make the inquiry system the subject of its next investigation.

The ombudsman

As well as legal rights, citizens have a more general right to a good standard of administration. Despite difficulties of precise definition, this right is still a significant element in administrative justice. In 1967, after rising public concern that traditional parliamentary channels were inadequate to protect the citizen against administrative abuse by government departments and agencies, the *Parliamentary Commissioner for Administration* (ombudsman) was established by Act of Parliament. His brief is to investigate and, if possible, remedy complaints by individuals and corporate bodies who feel that they have experienced 'injustice in consequence of maladministration' at the hands of central government.

Appointed by the Crown on the advice of the Lord Chancellor, the ombudsman enjoys an independent status similar to that of a high court judge. His salary is fixed by statute and charged on the Consolidated Fund; he holds office 'during good behaviour' and can be removed on addresses from both Houses of Parliament. He has a staff of about fifty-five, largely drawn from the civil service. During his investigations, which are conducted in private, he can call for the relevant files of the Department concerned; as a matter of course, he informs the Head of Department and any civil servant involved, of his investigation. He possesses the powers to investigate a matter thoroughly: he can administer oaths and compel the attendance of witnesses as well as the presence of documents. Where he finds maladministration, he invites the Department to correct it; if the Department refuses, the ombudsman can lay a special report before parliament. The *Select Committee on the Parliamentary Commissioner for Administration* of the House of Commons has the task of examining his special and annual reports; its support is a way of ensuring that his reports will be taken seriously. The ombudsman actually investigates between 700 and 800 cases a year and injustice through maladministration is found in about 10 per cent. As he himself commented in 1979:

> The complaints which I have had to consider scarcely attained a national dimension . . . But to the complainants the grievance of each was important: and it is the mark of a great civilisation that it believes in the importance of the individual and finds time for his concerns (cited by de Smith, in *Constitutional and Administrative Law*, p. 631).

It seems clear that up to a point the Parliament Commissioner has proved a cheap and reasonably effective way of achieving administrative justice.

Nonetheless, the limitations on his scope and powers have been the subject of criticism. His jurisdiction, initially limited to Departments of State, was extended by the appointment of ombudsmen for local government, the NHS and nationalised industries during the 1970s, but still excludes the police. Nor has the Parliamentary Commissioner any power to initiate investigations: complaints are referred to him through Members of Parliament; those sent straight to him, he redirects to MPs, indicating his willingness to investigate. His brief covers maladministration which can embrace a wide variety of faults: as de Smith puts it 'corruption, bias, unfair discrimination, harshness, misleading a member of the public as to his rights, failing to notify him properly as to his rights or to explain the reasons for a decision, general high-handedness, using powers for a wrong purpose, failing to consider relevant materials, taking irrelevant material into account, losing or failing to reply to correspondence, delaying unreasonably before making a tax refund or dealing with an application for a grant or licence, and so on' (de Smith, *Constitutional and Administrative Law*, p. 629). There is some overlap here with the courts' review of the discretionary powers of government departments, the ombudsman having been established before the post-1970s wave of judicial activism. Thus, in *Congreve* v. *Home Office* (1976) (see Exhibit 15.2), the ombudsman had already found maladministration on the grounds of the Home Secretary's failure to make policy clear to the public. Critics, however, allege that the concern of the ombudsman should go beyond failure to follow established rules and procedures to the quality of the policies themselves, i.e. the scope of the office should include matters of substances as well as of procedure. They point to the broader scope of the role of the ombudsman in other countries (Sweden and New Zealand, for example). Finally, the ombudsman has no executive powers: he cannot alter or rescind decisions. However, it undoubtedly is the case that his reports have often brought response from Departments. One of his best-known successes occurred over the famous *Sachsenhausen case* (1967) when the Foreign Office was found responsible for procedural maladministration in its handling of an application by former prisoners-of-war for their sufferings in a Nazi concentration camp, and paid compensation. More usually, it is the Inland Revenue and DHSS which are involved in making restitution to an aggrieved member of the public after a report by the ombudsman.

The European Court of Human Rights

The European Court of Human Rights has played an important part in upholding and enlarging civil liberties in Britain since 1965. It does so in a somewhat roundabout way which nonetheless deserves careful attention. The United Kingdom ratified the European Convention on Human Rights in 1951 (see Exhibit 15.3). Although these are not legal rights in Britain and therefore not enforceable in British law, they have turned out to be an important influence on civil rights.

Exhibit 15.3   Rights under the European Convention

To be protected against torture and inhuman or degrading punishments

To freedom of expression, thought, conscience and religion

To education and teaching to conform to one's parents' religious and philosophical opinions

To a fair and public trial

To form and join a trades union

To peaceful enjoyment of possessions

To respect for private and family life without interference from a public authority

---

These rights are not enforceable in British law because, although Britain renews its ratification of the Convention every year, unlike the other countries who have signed the document, *it has never incorporated the Convention into British law*. Hence, British citizens cannot use the Convention to appeal to British courts when their rights are infringed. They can appeal to the European Court, but only after they have tried and failed to find remedies in the British courts. Complaints go to the *European Commission* at Strasbourg in the first instance. The Commission then decides whether the case is 'admissible' to the European Court; normally cases go before the Court only after the Commission has first failed to achieve a friendly settlement between the parties concerned. Every year the Commission opens about 800 provisional files on complaints by British citizens –

more than from any other country. Of these, a small number are declared 'admissible'. If 'admissible', cases are registered and in 1986, about one-quarter (140 out of 533) of registered cases were from the UK. In all, the Court pronounced on ninety-six cases between 1955 and 1985; fourteen of these were from the UK, and of these judgements all except two went against the British Government. The other seventeen member-States which permit individual petitions had had thirty-nine violations recorded against them (*The Guardian*, 29 May 1985). Exhibit 15.4 gives some major examples of cases in which the 'rights' of British citizens have been upheld by the European Court. No other signatory-State has lost so many cases before the European Court as the United Kingdom. The decisions of the European Court are not, strictly speaking, enforceable in the United Kingdom. But the UK Government, like other countries which have signed the Convention, has agreed to respect the decisions made by the Court and, in practice, its verdicts are observed, normally by changing British law accordingly.

Exhibit 15.4 *European Court* **decisions bearing on the rights of British citizens**

The European Court:

- has criticised treatment of suspected terrorists interned in Northern Ireland by the UK Government;
- allowed prisoners their right to correspond with their lawyers, MPs and the newspapers;
- condemned corporal punishment in schools;
- ruled against inhuman conditions in solitary confinement;
- criticised undue interference with a free press in the *Sunday Times* thalidomide case against Distillers;
- upheld the rights of workers against closed shops;
- condemned as inadequate the review procedure for life-sentence prisoners recalled after release;
- declared British immigration rules to be unlawful because they discriminated against women; the rules allowed foreign men with full residency rights in the UK to bring in their wives or fiancées, but did not allow women with residency rights to bring in their husbands;
- criticised the ineffective judicial protection of a detained mental patient; it ruled that *habeas corpus* provided inadequate redress against wrongful confinement in this instance;
- condemned the legal ban obtained by the government on press disclosure of documents used in evidence in court;
- ruled that a group of shareholders in shipbuilding and aircraft companies nationalised in 1977 had been inadequately compensated.

The situation is by no means ideal. The Strasbourg Court will hear a case only if domestic attempts to find a settlement are exhausted; no legal aid is available; and the Court takes a long time to reach its judgements – both the immigration and nationalisation compensation cases shown in Exhibit 15.4 took about five years. Nonetheless, the Court has bolstered the rights of prisoners, immigrants, women, mental patients, journalists, expropriated shareholders and workers who may not want to join a union in as effective a way as circumstances allow. It is in order to render such protection even more effective that many concerned about the state of civil liberties in the UK call for a British Bill of Rights.

A BILL OF RIGHTS FOR BRITAIN?

No single document enumerating the rights of the citizen exists in the United Kingdom. This absence of a single written code does not mean that the individual lacks civil rights. These rights and the way they are secured – in general by a mixture of common and statute law – are set out in Exhibit 15.1. However, over the past two decades many have come to doubt whether civil liberties in Britain are sufficiently secure. These doubts have surfaced for a number of reasons. The primary reason is the growth of concern about the capacity of *parliament* to protect individual liberties either positively by espousing the causes of aggrieved citizens or negatively by not actually invading individual rights. How many MPs see one of their major roles as that of serving as a one-person ombudsman or, assuming they do, have the time, energy, capacity and resources for such a role? Again, parliament – by means of regislation pushed through by the governing party with the aid of its majority – may invade civil liberties as much as protect them. The clamour for a Bill of Rights first surfaced in the 1970s, being raised by Conservatives who saw Labour legislation as a threat, especially legislation on trade unions and nationalisation. However, Labour could with equal legitimacy point to the Conservatives' use of the Official Secrets Act in the 1980s in a number of instances as invasions of individual rights. Again, *judicial review* of administrators' discretionary powers and the work of the *Ombudsman* are only encouraging up to a point. Gaps in the protection of civil liberties include:

(i) the difficulty of challenging Ministerial discretionary powers in the courts on the grounds of *ultra vires* because of the broad subjective way in which such powers are framed;

(ii) the difficulty of protecting certain kinds of rights (e.g. to supplementary benefits) in the courts because of problems over interpreting individual need;

(iii) the fact that challenge of administrative decisions depends on reasons being given yet the statutory obligation upon administrators to give reasons is far from universal;

Exhibit 15.5   A British Bill of Rights: for and against

For	*Against*
1. Greater clarity: a code would make clear governmental responsibilities, enable citizens to know their rights more easily and provide courts with a well-defined set of freedoms to protect.	1. Difficulty of defining rights (a) Socialists and most Liberals would include social and economic rights, Conservatives seek to limit to civil and political rights; (b) If social and economic rights are included, these are likely to fluctuate, e.g. Labour in 1970s legislated in favour of closed shop, Conservatives in 1980s against it.
2. Courts superior to parliament at protecting civil rights: (a) courts are independent of the Government not aspiring to be part of it, like MPs; (b) a Bill of Rights would make available to British citizens civil rights which at present have to be sought at the European Court, but more speedily and cheaply; (c) A Code of rights would have a moral force lacking in present law, and thereby be harder to flout by, for example, government or big interest groups.	2. Courts *not* better than parliament at protecting civil rights: (a) unlike MPs, judges unelected and unaccountable, and have undeclared rather than explicit political biases; (b) certain issues – e.g. race relations, industrial relations, press freedoms, privacy, police powers and national security – *are* inherently political and therefore need to be decided openly by politicians, not covertly by judges; (c) Judges might interpret rights narrowly, whittle them down rather than guarantee them; anyway, unwise to *politicize* judges.
3. Bill of Rights backed by courts works well in other countries, e.g. USA, where Supreme Court judgement against racial segregation (1954) played key part in eventually gaining civil rights for the black minority.	3. Institutions do not necessarily transplant well, e.g. US Bill of Rights works in context of very different separation of powers system. British system is based on parliamentary sovereignty – better to reform rather than transform it, e.g. by extending powers of Ombudsman, restricting coverage of Official Secrets Act, increasing investigative powers of MPs, introducing Freedom of information.
4. Educational value of Bill of Rights; great need in Britain is for understanding of rights to be well-grounded in political culture, and this would be facilitated by a specific code.	4. Nothing in present situation regarding rights to prevent spread of understanding of them.

(iv) the failure of the courts to develop damages as a remedy for unlawful administrative action.

One critic, Lord Scarman, has pointed to the inability of the common law – i.e. the ordinary courts – to guarantee rights and liberties in four key areas: (i) welfare; (ii) the environment; (iii) industrial relations; and (iv) Britain's international obligations under the European Convention.

There are three ways of enacting a Bill of Rights:

1. By drawing up a list of individual rights and providing for their constitutional entrenchment by an Act of Parliament. The courts would have the authority to strike down any subsequent Act of Parliament or administrative action which conflicted with it. This way of proceeding would destroy parliamentary sovereignty since, once enacted, the Bill of Rights would take precedence over all subsequent legislation and would in all cases have to be upheld by the courts.

2. (A modified form of 1, preserving, parliamentary sovereignty.) Legislation could enact a Bill of Rights which the courts would uphold unless otherwise directed by parliament, and which would remain in place until amended or even superseded by subsequent rights legislation.

The first has the merit of greater security for rights at the expense of parliamentary sovereignty as well as a certain rigidity; with the second, rights are rather less secure but parliamentary sovereignty as well as a greater flexibility remains.

3. By incorporating the European Convention on Human Rights into British law. This would give Britons the right to seek redress in British courts against infringements of their liberties as set out in that code.

Two attempts in the mid-1980s to legislate a British Bill of Rights both took this form, Lord Broxbourne's Human Rights and Fundamental Freedoms Bill in 1985; and Sir Edward Gardner's bill in 1987. The latter failed by only six votes to secure a second reading in the House of Commons, support coming from sixty Conservatives, eighteen Alliance, fourteen Labour and Plaid Cymru, and one SDLP.

THE ROLE OF THE POLICE

The broader context for the discussion which follows is twofold: first, the monopoly of the legitimate use of violence held by the State and second, its obligation in a liberal democracy to control the law-enforcement agencies and ensure that they operate according to certain rules. Two public needs have to be balanced – (i) the need to protect society from the activities of criminals, especially violent criminals; and (ii) the need to ensure that the process of bringing suspects to justice takes place within the law, with the officers of the law fully accountable to elected representatives.

Police organisation, accountability and complaints

There is no single national police force in Britain; the police are locally organised in England and Wales in forty-three separate forces. This number itself represents a rapid and very considerable reduction from the 117 local forces in 1963. The sole exceptions to local control of the force are the Metropolitan Police and (since 1973) the Royal Ulster Constabulary, which are responsible to the Home Secretary. Since the 1960s the idea of a local force serving the needs of the local community has been undermined by trends which seem to point to the emergence of a more national force. This erosion has been the consequence of at least four developments:

(i) the growing use of modern technology in support of police activity, the major example of this being the Police National Computer (PNC), on which is recorded national information such as missing persons, stolen vehicles, vehicle owners, names of criminals, fingerprints, and so on. Its main significance in this context is that it facilitates both central coordination and the capacity of forces to work across force boundaries;

(ii) the centrally coordinated policing of the Miners' Strike in 1984–5 through the National Reporting Centre at Scotland Yard in a manner which, to critics on the Left, deliberately employed the police as a weapon of Government political policy;

(iii) motorised patrols have been increasingly used in place of the traditional pedestrian policeman 'on the beat', a policy which seems to render the force more remote from the community;

(iv) the force has become not only larger, with the smallest provincial force being at least 800 and the largest over 4000, but also more professional and increasingly specialised, as a result of the formation of special groups and squads to deal with drugs, serious crime, terrorism and riots.

Taken together, these developments have made it more difficult for the ordinary councillor and lay magistrate to acquire sufficient understanding of modern policing to criticise it from an informed basis. In these circumstances, it is perhaps not surprising that police accountability became increasingly prominent in public debate in the 1980s.

Police accountability has three aspects – political, legal and internal disciplinary:

(1) The Force is *politically accountable* to local police committees, Chief Constables and the Home Secretary.

The *police authorities*, or 'committees' on which elected councillors are in a majority (two-thirds councillors, one-third magistrates), are responsible for the maintenance of their forces – i.e. ensuring that they have sufficient resources such as adequate premises, equipment and so on, and for determining the 'establishment' (number of each person of each rank) of their forces. They are also empowered to appoint Chief Constables, Deputy and Assistant Chief Constables; to require senior officers to retire in the interests of efficiency (subject to the approval of the Home Secretary); to receive an annual report from the Chief Constable on the policing of the area; and to request reports on specific issues.

Operational decisions are in the hands of *Chief Constables*, who are accountable only to the law, not to any political authority: they cannot be ordered to do anything regarding policing policy and operations; in the control and direction of their forces they are independent. However, this operational independence should not be taken to mean political unaccountability: the police authority which appoints, can also dismiss; and – rather more remotely – Chief Constables must have some regard for public opinion.

The final factor is the *Home Secretary*, who has wide powers to influence the nature of policing. His authority covers pay, conditions of service, and approval of the Police Authorities' decisions regarding the appointment and dismissal of Chief Constables, and their decisions in relation to resources. He provides an annual grant equal to approximately half of each Force's budget. The Home Secretary supervises the efficiency of the police service through his control of Her Majesty's Inspectors of Constabulary, who carry out inspections of each Force. As police authority for the large (20 000 +) Metropolitan Police Force, the Home Secretary can encourage policing practices for other authorities to follow.

  (ii) *Legal accountability.* The police have to keep within the law of the land. They can be prosecuted in the criminal courts for offences such as assault and can be made the subject of civil actions for damages or wrongful arrest.

 (iii) *The Force's own internal disciplinary procedures.* Since the *Police and Criminal Evidence Act* 1984 non-policemen have been involved in internal investigations into complaints against the police. For serious complaints an investigation is conducted by a senior officer from another Force whose appointment has to have the approval of the *Police Complaints Authority* (PCA), whose members are appointed by the Prime Minister, and which is completely independent of the Police. It regards itself as the impartial representative of the public.

The investigation is itself supervised by a member of the PCA who is in continuous contact with the *investigating officer*. The investigating officer reports to the PCA, sending a copy to the Chief Constable, who must then decide what action to take. (Normally, the Assistant Chief Constable is in charge of internal discipline.) The decision usually amounts to a choice between (a) a recommendation that the case go forward for consideration by the *Director of Public Prosecutions* (DPP), who initiates all prosecutions of particular officers; (b) internal disciplinary procedure; or (c) no further action.

After considering the investigating officer's report, the PCA submits a Statement to the Chief Constable, saying whether or not the investigation was conducted to its satisfaction and possibly commenting on other matters which it feels should be brought to the attention of the parties concerned. If dissatisfied by the outcome of this procedure, aggrieved individuals can complain to the PCA.

Public disquiet about the issue of police accountability and about the independence and effectiveness of complaints procedure remained in the mid-1980s. Two 1979 attempts by private members' bills to legislate greater powers for police authorities in relation to Chief Constables had failed. The unsuccessful bills included provisions to give police authorities power to determine 'general policing', i.e. to get involved in matters of policing strategy; to extract information from Chief Constables; to reject their recommendations; to create all-elective police authorities; and to end the anomalous position of the Metropolitan Police. The real problem was the degree of consultation of police authorities by Chief Constables. Certain police authorities – most notably, Merseyside, over the 1981 riots; South Yorkshire and Derbyshire, over the Miners' Strike, 1984; and Manchester, over the conduct of the Deputy Chief Constable, John Stalker, 1986 – engaged in public disputes with the Chief Constables. Moderate critics considered that the way forward here might be more in the direction of developing a relationship of 'explanatory accountability' between police authorities and their chief constables rather than in the direction of legislative tightening of 'controls' through directives and sanctions. The concept of 'explanatory accountability' is thoroughly discussed in Geoffrey Marshall, *Constitutional Conventions* (1984) pp. 146 *et seq*. Many critics believe that an attempt to tighten police authority control over 'strategy' would encounter political difficulties from police officers zealously guarding their independence as 'officers of the Crown', not as instruments of government. This obstacle would exist over and above problems of deciding what matters belong to general strategy and what to day-to-day operations. The concept of 'explanatory accountability' involves a more thorough use of existing provisions for the debate on policing at local level as well as the more energetic pursuit of Lord Scarman's recommendation for the establishment of local consultative committees, composed of members of the police force and of the communities for which they are responsible. The advantage of setting up and working within a framework of 'explanatory accountability' is that discussion between the police and locals might well extend to operational matters as well as general strategy; and could result in greater public cooperation with police operations. The Metropolitan area presents a special problem of accountability, because there is no direct democratic accountability to the local community. The Greater London Council finances the Metropolitan Police but the Metropolitan Police Commissioner is responsible to the Home Secretary who is in turn responsible to parliament for the policing of London.

There was also a widely-shared concern that complaints procedure was still insufficiently independent and lacked 'teeth'. In 1986, the Police Complaints Authority dealt with 15 865 complaints against the police and by the end of the year, proceedings had been brought against forty-eight officers; 116 officers left the Force before completion of investigation of complaints against them; and 1212 officers were criticised for behaviour which had been the subject of complaint. In the vast majority of cases (12 505) evidence was either conflicting or insufficient and the PCA decided that no disciplinary charges could be brought. In its 1986 Report the Authority itself commented on the difficulty of removing unsuitable officers; other than on medical grounds, this could only be done after a case had been proved against an officer at a disciplinary hearing.

But it was the apparent lack of real independence of the PCA and its apparent inability to pursue its investigations to a conclusion that worried the public. Three investigations in particular caused deep disquiet – its reports in 1987 on its inquiries into scenes between police and students outside Manchester University and between police and the hippy convoy at Stonehenge (both events in 1985) and its 1986 report on alleged assaults on boys in the Holloway Road by officers from a police patrol van (August 1983). In the Manchester University case (thirty-three individual complaints, seventy-one general complaints, with the overall total including forty-four about the use of excessive force) three police officers were prosecuted – two for perjury, one for assault; in the hippy convoy case, where the allegation was that some of 1363 officers involved in making 537 arrests used excessive force, no prosecutions or disciplinary proceedings resulted; and in the Holloway Road case, the PCA reported that the internal inquiry into the incident had made little progress and that a prosecution appeared unlikely because of a cover-up by the officers involved. Eventually the Holloway Road case culminated in the gaoling of three officers for assault, and two for conspiracy to pervert the course of justice – but only, critics said, after a public outcry at the cover-up. In each case problems arose in identifying culpable officers in incidents in which there had clearly been transgressions of the law. Second, there was concern because, however independent members of the PCA might be, the actual detailed work of investigating complaints continued to be done by the police themselves.

It was suggested after the Holloway Road case that the PCA ought to be given its own staff – in the way Customs and Inland Revenue already had – to enable it to conduct properly independent investigations. The PCA itself commented in its 1986 Report that, although police officers did the groundwork for its inquiries, this did not prevent the Authority from 'exercising an entirely independent judgement and close control over the course of events', an opinion echoed by the Home Office Under-Secretary ('a most effective investigating body') during a parliamentary debate on the Holloway Road case.

Law and order as a political issue

The problem of 'law and order' became a major political issue in the 1970s and 1980s. This catch-all phrase hid three major concerns:

(i) Rising crime figures alarmed public opinion.
(ii) There was an apparent deterioration in police–community relations. This involved police relations with black people, police procedures in questioning suspects and treatment of people in custody, and allegations of corruption in the police, especially the Metropolitan and City of London Forces and the Criminal Investigation Department (CID).
(iii) Public concern arose about sentencing policy and over-crowding in prisons.

Rising crime figures

The crime figures showed a constantly upward trend, with the number of recorded offences in England and Wales rising from 797 000 in 1960 to 1.6m in 1971, 2.96m in 1981 and a record 3.8m in 1986. Approximately 95 per cent of crime was against property, the two largest categories being theft and burglary. At the same time, the clear-up rate fell (by 4 per cent) to less than one-third of all crime at 31.6 per cent. Within this average, clear-up rates varied considerably according to the offence: thus, the clear-up rate for theft of a bicycle was 11 per cent, for criminal damage 20 per cent, for burglary 25 per cent, for rape 62 per cent, for assault 80 per cent, and for reported attempted murders 96 per cent.

The figures need to be taken seriously but also handled with caution. The statistics cannot be explained away but their context needs to be borne in mind. The media's continual harping on 'rising crime' can be misleading. For example, domestic burglaries doubled between 1979 and 1986, from $\frac{1}{4}$m to $\frac{1}{2}$m, but it is likely that much of the recorded increase was the result of higher reporting rates by householders intent on claiming their insurance. The crucial point to notice is the difference between all crime, and 'recorded crime', which is the crime reported to the police and recorded by them. Only a proportion of the former appears in the statistics of the latter category.

Much crime simply goes undiscovered, hence unreported and unrecorded – e.g. street and pub brawls, incidents on the terraces at football matches and petty theft. The extent to which a particular crime is reported – and recorded – can vary according to a number of circumstances. The increase in recorded rapes, for instance, in the late 1970s and 1980s was largely attributable to changes in court procedure enabling victims to remain anonymous, and to greater sensitivity in police treatment of victims. Other factors influencing the reporting of crimes include, changes in the law, the requirements of insurance policies (police notification necessary before a claim) and access to a telephone or police station. The recording of crimes by the police can vary according to the preoccupations of the Chief Constable, discretions of individual officers, and so on. In the circumstances, it is certainly possible to say that recorded crime is rising and to perceive this as a matter for some concern. But it is not possible to say what proportion recorded crime forms of all crime, and whether this is rising or falling.

Police–community relations

Police relations with certain sections of the community deteriorated in the 1980s. The traditional view of the police has been as neutral upholders of the law but the force became distrusted by blacks in the inner cities, as evidenced by the 1981 riots at Toxteth, Brixton, Moss Side, Handsworth and Bristol, and by miners, after being used to contain the picket lines during the 1984–5 Miners' Strike. The police were already facing heavy criticism for lack of sympathy towards blacks as a result of their heavy-handed treatment of black suspects, detention of blacks under the 'sus' law and predominantly white recruitment when the riot occurred on the Broadwater Farm estate in Tottenham (6 October 1985) which ended in the murder of a police-constable, a tragedy which itself followed the tragic deaths of two black women during police searches of their homes. An independent report by the *Policy Studies Institute* commissioned by Scotland Yard in 1983 concluded that one-third of all stops made by the Metropolitan Police under the 'sus' law, and observed by researchers were illegal because the police lacked any 'reasonable suspicion' for stopping people; on the other hand, although about 1.5m stops were made every year, only about one in twelve led to the detection of an offence. Racist language was pervasive in the 'Met' but was not normally carried over into action; police relations with black people were often friendly and West Indians were just as likely as white people to call the police when victims of crime. Reviewing police–community relations in London in 1987, Sir Kenneth Newman, the retiring Metropolitan Police Commissioner, drew attention to two different categories of causes of disorder:

(i) a deeper level of predisposing social causes, such as discrimination, underprivilege, unemployment and poor housing;
(ii) a second level of precipitative causes which could include – and in the case of the 1985 Tottenham riot, had included – inept police action.

In his view, the underlying causes were still present in London, although he considered that community policing should help to reduce the chance of another riot. He also thought that the police were better prepared to handle riots, with support groups better trained and disciplined, and under a strict structure of command. The 'Met' now had 356 black officers – just over 1 per cent of the Force, compared with up to 40 per cent in some US cities – but had to learn to use them more effectively. He did not favour positive action to increase this proportion.

In 1988 the debate was still in progress. On the one hand the Metropolitan Police pointed out that responsibility for the urban deprivation and racial prejudice that underlay much inner-city crime was not at root theirs. They felt that serious efforts were being made to improve police relations with the black community by community policing, the encouragement of *Neighbourhood Watch* schemes and the issue in 1985 of the *Police Code of Behaviour*, which included reference to the need to treat people of all races with courtesy and understanding. On the other hand critics referred to the inadequacy of the efforts to investigate racial attacks in East London and the dissatisfaction of members of the Asian community with that response.

Two other more general concerns about police behaviour went beyond relations with a particular part of the community. These were (i) apparent malpractices in questioning suspects and in care of people whilst in custody and (ii) worries about police corruption, especially in the Metropolitan police. Public concern that the judges' rules in questioning suspects were being flouted had existed for some time before being dramatically highlighted during the Blakelock trial (1987). (The *'judges' rules'* exist for the guidance of police in the questioning of suspects and are designed to ensure that interrogation is not intimidatory, statements are voluntary and police advise about the 'right to be silent'.) The judge in the Blakelock trial accepted that the police confronted massive difficulties in the conduct of their investigation, first, because they faced a community which lacked trust in them and which therefore 'closed ranks' and second, because there was an almost complete absence of forensic evidence. But he criticised the police for oppressive behaviour (removing one suspect's clothes); for interrogation without a relative or solicitor present; and, in the case of two 15-year-old suspects, for illegal conduct (locking them up in a cell overnight, a clear breach of the *Children and Young Persons Act*). The police argument on the exclusion of solicitors was that this course of action was acceptable since solicitors might pervert justice by wittingly or unwittingly passing messages which could lead to the destruction of evidence or the disappearance of suspects or witnesses. The police in this case were criticised for 'oppressive behaviour'. More worrying were examples – which came to light disturbingly often – of physical intimidation and maltreatment: between 1970 and mid-1979, 143 out of 245 deaths in police custody were not from 'natural causes'. The All-Party Commons Home Affairs Select Committee found no evidence to support general complaints of police brutality when it reported in 1980 but accusations and cases of police brutality continued during the 1980s. Finally, numerous accusations of police corruption surfaced in the 1970s, mainly involving the Metropolitan and City of London forces and the Criminal Investigation Department. Between 1972 and 1977, over 450 officers were removed from the Metropolitan Police and a Specialist Department was established to handle complaints. But the investigation specially commissioned by the Home Secretary ('Operation Countryman') to inquire into corruption in the London police resulted in few convictions. It was allegedly hampered by an inability to obtain adequate evidence and by obstruction from senior London officers.

Sentencing policy and overcrowding in prisons

Britain's prison system was in crisis by the second half of the 1980s. The prison population had risen steadily from the mid-1960s: it was at about 32 500 in 1966 but rose gradually through the 1970s and much more rapidly in the 1980s, reaching 51 000 in July 1987. At this point, prison population exceeded prison capacity by about 9600 places (Home Office figures). The situation had come about as a result of a combination of two factors. First, the percentage of the convicted being sent to prison (under 10 per cent) remained the same throughout the 1970s as the crime rate increased. Second, prison building under the Conservatives fell a long way short of the really dramatic rise in the prison population which took place in the 1980s; about 4500 new places were provided by the Conservative Governments by July 1987, whereas in the period from winter 1984 to late summer 1985 alone, the number of people in gaol in England and Wales rose by 5400. Critics considered that British penal policy made too much use of imprisonment; the UK imprisoned one in every thousand of its population, a higher proportion than any other EEC country. For lesser crimes, they argued that not enough use was made of alternatives to prison, such as community service, and that, in any case, sentences for minor crimes tended to be too long.

In July 1987 the Government faced intensifying pressure both from the police, who objected to having to divert their resources to supervise the overflow of prisoners into police cells, and from representatives of prison officers, who were concerned at the deterioration of conditions in the gaols and feared the possibility of riots if overcrowding were to continue. In response, the Government announced a package of emergency measures. The main proposal was the early release of non-violent offenders, who would include the 18 000 offenders estimated to be serving sentences of eighteenth months or less. Critics maintained that the proposal was merely a short-term expedient and that the Government should explore more radical steps, such as keeping petty and juvenile offenders out of prison altogether and abolishing imprisonment for non-payers of fines.

Parties' approaches and policies towards 'law and order'

There are sharp divisions on 'law and order' between the parties. Policy differences flow inexorably from contrasting ideological perspectives. The Conservative approach is readier to sympathise with the victims of crime than to search for explanations of crime or ways of reforming criminals. To Conservatives, crime is rather the result of inborn psychological factors such as envy, greed, malice and hatred than of social factors like poverty, unemployment and bad housing. Hence, it is remediable, if at all, more by changes in moral attitudes produced, for example, by more care and discipline in the home, than by improvements in the physical environment. The Conservatives emphasise individual responsibility: the criminal could have chosen otherwise; nothing is inevitable or predetermined. They believe in deterrence; and their policing and penal policy focuses on enhancing the likelihood of capturing wrongdoers by raising police pay and numbers; on increasing the chances that, once caught, suspects will be found guilty; on deterring wrongdoers by tougher sentences; and on protecting society by using imprisonment as the predominant form of punishment. Whilst also sympathising with the victims and condemning crime, especially violent crime, Labour and the Alliance laid their emphasis on the social roots of crime in material deprivation and racist attitudes and look for remedies in policies which tackle these evils. Their policing policy stresses crime prevention whilst their penal policies lay importance on rehabilitation and the investigation of alternatives to imprisonment; the Alliance wanted to keep minor offenders out of prison altogether. The thinking of Labour and the Alliance also converged on the imperative need to establish an independent police complaints procedure and to devise ways of making the police more accountable whereas the Conservatives would maintain police independence. Exhibit 15.6 compares in detail the parties' 1987 manifestos.

Exhibit 15.6   Party manifestos on law and order in the 1987 General Election

Conservative	*Labour*	*Alliance*
1. *Fighting crime*		
Increase police numbers	Get more police on the beat	Strengthen police by increasing numbers in places with high crime rates
Strengthen special constabulary	Remove uniformed officers from duties not connected with law and order, so they can concentrate on crime prevention	4000 extra police overall
Tighten law on offensive weapons		
2. *Penal policy*		
Increase criminal penalties	Abolish cuts in numbers able to claim injuries compensation	Introduce minimum standards for prisons to reduce recidivism
Confiscate criminals' assets	Allocate extra staff to deal with current waiting list of 64 000 claimants	Keep minor offenders out of prison
Improve extradition procedure		Wider use of police cautions and warnings
Raise compensation for victims		More community service orders as alternative to prison
Review parole system		Uniform youth custody sentence to replace 'short sharp shock' treatment which is a failure
		Offenders to recompense their victims
		Curbing of widely obtainable offensive weapons (e.g. catapults)
3. *Courts and judicial procedure*		
Abolition of defendants' right to challenge jurors without reason		New Ministry of Justice to improve legal aid and court procedures
Permit use of video in court for child-witnesses		Maximum period of remand to be 100 days; if no prosecution then prisoner to be released
		Reinforced sentencing guidelines

continued

Exhibit . . .   *– continued*

Conservative	Labour	Alliance
4. *Crime prevention*		
Build on Neighbourhood Watch scheme	Crime prevention grants for householders Safer streets policy for local authorities i.e. more street-lighting, park-keepers and other public employees as deterrent 'Safe Estates' policy, i.e. stouter doors, stronger locks, vandal-proof windows Stronger laws to protect women	Local authorities to set up Crime Prevention Units to coordinate with expanded Neighbourhood Watch Police telephone posts Grants to householders for entry phones of locks Better street-lighting More caretakers Legal obligation on British Telecom to keep phone boxes in working order Anti-crime planning on new housing estates Insurance schemes as part of council-house tenancy Royal Commission to analyse effects of violence portrayed on media
5. *Police accountability and complaints system*		
Maintain police independence	Ombudsman for complaints against police Reform of police accountability	Immediate establishment of fully independent complaints authority Royal Commission to study accountability Increased accountability to local communities

In a public opinion poll taken during the 1987 General Election campaign by the Harris Research Centre for *The Observer*, law and order appeared as the Conservatives' second-best election issue (defence rated highest). 46 per cent of the respondents in the sample trusted the Conservatives most on law and order, with Labour and the Alliance trailing well behind at 22 per cent and 14 per cent respectively.

Conservative policy on law and order since 1979

The main themes of Conservative policy on law and order since 1979 have been threefold:

(i) *strengthening the police force* by expanding its numbers (which rose from 110 500 to 121 800 between 1979 and June 1987, with an increase of 2000 planned for 1988) by raising its pay (which increased 30 per cent between 1979 and 1983) and by creating special units to control riots;

(ii) introducing a tougher sentencing policy for violent crimes and young offenders;

(iii) bringing in changes in police interrogation and judicial procedure in ways which will assist the police and the prosecution.

The main Conservative policies were embodied in the *Criminal Justice Act* 1982, the *Police and Criminal Evidence Act* 1984, and the proposed Criminal Justice Bill 1987. Policy on the maintenance of public order, the prevention of terrorism and capital punishment also warrant consideration.

The *Criminal Justice Act* 1982 represented a reaction against the 1970s 'welfare' approach to young offenders based on the *Children and Young Persons Act* 1969. That legislation had seen juvenile delinquents as 'deprived' rather than 'depraved' and sought to compensate for family and social deprivation by community programmes, by treatment rather than punishment. By contrast, the Conservative measure brought in a 'short, sharp shock' regime for juveniles aged 14 and over and increased the punitive and deterrent elements in the juvenile custody system. Four new detention centres with tough military-style discipline were established to carry out the 'short, sharp shock' policy. Critics of the policy argued it was more likely to alienate than cure young offenders, and would probably assist in 'criminalising' them even more. Their argument received some support from the high 'recidivism' rate to centres of detention (70 per cent) i.e. the proportion of offenders returning to centres. The Government could reply to its liberal critics by pointing out that the Act also extended rights of legal representation at hearings and made the sentence of community service order available for 16-year-olds as well as for adult offenders.

The *Police and Criminal Evidence Act* 1984:

(i) Made the power to stop and search available throughout England and Wales (it already existed in London and some other areas); police officers have to have reasonable suspicion that the person is carrying stolen goods, offensive weapons or housebreaking or similar implements.

(ii) It also enlarged the category of arrestable offence not only to include people suspected of indecent assault, kidnapping and attempt to pervert the course of justice but also to include people who refuse to give their names and addresses, people suspected of giving false or unsatisfactory addresses for the service of a summons, and people who might injure themselves or others or damage property or obstruct the highway.

(iii) On detention, the general principle that an arrested person be brought to court as soon as practicable is replaced by the power to detain for 24 hours without charge on non-serious offences and for a maximum of 96 hours without charge on serious offences; police have to apply to a magistrate for permission to detain a person beyond 36 hours, at which point the suspect is entitled to legal representation.

(iv) There are new powers of search of premises, including the right to look for murder weapons and to obtain evidence of commercial or financial fraud; body searches, for weapons and category A drugs like heroin; and seizure of evidence.

(v) An independent prosecuting service – the Crown Prosecution Service – replaced the existing system under which prosecution as well as arrest was undertaken by the police;

(vi) All police authorities were required to establish consultative machinery between police and community as recommended by the Scarman Report.

The Government retreated on its plan to give police access to personal materials and files, including the correspondence between lawyers and their clients, and the confidential notes of journalists.

To the allegations by its critics that the Act constituted a substantial infringement of civil liberties the Government riposted

(i) that the new police powers were vital to the fight against crime;

(ii) that the Act contained major new safeguards for individual rights. These included a new Police Code of Practice, the tape recording of interviews of suspects, police recording of stops and searches and periods of detention, and the Duty Solicitor Scheme, with all suspects having a statutory right to free legal advice (delayable for 36 hours for serious arrestable offences only) which could if required, be provided by the new duty solicitors.

Two other pieces of legislation in the Conservatives' second term of office increased police powers – the *Prevention of Terrorism Act* 1984 and the *Public Order Act* 1986. The *Prevention of Terrorism Act* extended police powers in relation to detention of suspected Irish terrorists to cover all suspected terrorists. The new Act, like the previous anti-terrorism legislation of 1974 (renewed in 1976), allows suspects to be detained without charge for up to seven days, to be excluded from the country without hearing evidence and to be charged with belonging to a proscribed organisation.

The Public Order Act created a new offence of disorderly conduct, a new sentence for football hooligans (the exclusion order) and gave the police new powers to control pickets, demonstrations and hostile assemblies. Under the new power of exclusion, the courts can order any person convicted of an offence at a football match, or of a violent offence whilst travelling to a match, to be excluded from future matches for an unlimited period. The Act also widened the existing powers of the police to impose conditions on marches to prevent serious public disorder. The new grounds were 'where there would be serious disruption to the life of the community' and 'where the purpose of the march was coercion or intimidation'; on these grounds, the police could also intervene in demonstrations, pickets and assemblies involving more than three people. The Act sought to provide more protection for people threatened by racial hatred by creating a new offence of possessing racially inflammatory material and giving police a new power to search for and seize racially inflammatory material.

On the restoration of capital punishment Mrs Thatcher had promised a free vote and the House of Commons in fact voted twice on the issue during the 1983–7 administration, twice rejecting it, 368 votes to 223 in 1983 and, on a proposal to restore it for 'particularly evil' murders, by 342 votes to 230 in 1987. Advocates of restoration argued for it as a deterrent (because most people feared death more than imprisonment); to increase public security from released or escaped killers; and to bring the law into line with public opinion. Opponents maintained that restoration would militate against civilised standards, would eliminate the possibility of correcting sentencing mistakes and would place an unacceptable burden on jurors and, ultimately, the Home Secretary, as guardian of the prerogative of mercy. They also considered that it was unlikely to prove more effective as a deterrent than the certainty of life imprisonment (minimum 20 years), that public support would soon wane if it were restored and that it would play into the hands of political terrorists by making martyrs of them.

Finally, the Criminal Justice Bill, which was suspended by the 1987 General Election and whose main proposals figured in the Conservative manifesto, was reintroduced after the election. Its proposals included life sentences for carrying firearms to commit a crime; more powers for courts to confiscate the assets of criminals; wide powers for courts to order offenders to compensate victims; the abolition of defendants' right in criminal trials to challenge three jurors without giving reasons; the removal of the option of a Crown Court jury trial for certain offences (including common assault, taking and driving away a vehicle and criminal damage under £2000), and reform in the extradition law to make it easier for other countries to get back their fugitives from Britain.

Critics of the Bill concentrated particularly on the abolition of a defendants' right of peremptory challenge: they pointed out that traditionally this right had been used to adjust the composition of a jury in terms of age, race and sex in a way thought to secure the defendant a better chance of a fair hearing. Its removal represented a serious undermining of the jury system and would particularly threaten the right of black defendants to obtain a racially-mixed jury. Critics felt that the Government was over-reacting against recent 'not guilty' verdicts returned by juries (including the Clive Ponting acquittal), that it was hypocritical because the prosecution's right of peremptory challenge was being retained and that it was acting in bad faith because its own study into the use of jury challenges failed to support its case and yet it was pressing ahead with the change all the same.

SUMMARY

Law underpins politics in various ways, two very important ones being the provision of guiding principles such as the rule of law and of a courts system for the orderly settlement of disputes, including disputes between the citizen and the State. Administrative law regulates the behaviour of public authorities and is of central concern in considering citizen rights and redress of grievances. Civil liberties, which are extensive in Britain, derive from, and are limited by a complex variety of procedures and laws largely emanating from statute and common law, but not from a single written document. Protected by a number of political and judicial methods with varying degrees of adequacy, civil rights came to seem less secure in the 1970s and 1980s than formerly. In circumstances in which British citizens often and successfully appealed to the European Court of Human Rights, a significant body of opinion advocated a Bill of Rights for Britain; however, there are difficulties as well as potential benefits in this course.

The police force (except in London and Ulster) is still organised on a local basis but in the 1980s there were some trends towards a more national force. Problems arose in police accountability and complaints procedure. 'Law and order' became a major political issue in recent decades because of mounting public concern about steady increases in the recorded crime figures accompanied by decreases in the clear-up rate, deteriorations in police–community relations and the emergence of grave problems in the prisons. The political parties presented sharply-contrasting approaches to the issue of law and order. The Conservatives emphasised the capture and punishment of offenders whereas Labour and the Alliance stressed the prevention of crime by attacking its social roots, and by precautions. Finally, Conservative Governments under Mrs Thatcher pursued policies and passed legislation which were controversial on police powers, judicial procedures, public order, the prisons and terrorism.

FURTHER READING

Drewry, G. (1981) *Law, Justice and Politics*, London, Longman, 2nd edn.
Griffith, J. A. G. (1985) *The Politics of the Judiciary*, London, Fontana, 3rd edn.
Jones, B. (1985) *Political Issues in Britain Today*, Manchester, Manchester University Press, ch. 17.

Marshall, Geoffrey (1984) *Constitutional Conventions*, Oxford, Clarendon.

Norton, P. (1982) *The Constitution in Flux*, Oxford, Martin Robertson.

Savage, S. (1984) 'Politics and Accountability in the British Police Force', *Teaching Politics*, 13, 1, January.

Savage, S. (1986) 'Fighting the Enemy Within: Law and Order under the Tories', *Teaching Politics*, 15, 1, January.

Reiner, R. (1985) *The Politics of the Police*, Brighton, Wheatsheaf.

Smith, S. A. de (1983) *Constitutional and Administrative Law*, Harmondsworth, Penguin, Parts 4 and 5 especially.

QUESTIONS

1. How are the rights of citizens protected in Britain? What improvements could be made?

2. Why did policing become such a contentious issue in the 1980s? Should the present system of police accountability and complaints procedure be modified and if so, why?

ASSIGNMENT

Draw up a detailed comparison of Conservative, Labour and Alliance proposals on 'law and order' in their 1987 General Election manifestos, making sure to show in what ways the parties' policies differ and in what they are similar.

16

National Security and Defence

During the 1980s, issues of national security and defence attained considerable prominence in British politics. Government prosecutions of two civil servants, Sarah Tisdall and Clive Ponting, under the Official Secrets Acts for revealing State secrets; its banning of trade union membership at GCHQ; the revelation that Anthony Blunt, the distinguished art historian, spied for Russia in the Second World War; the sentencing of a middle-ranking member of MI5, Michael Bettaney, for 23 years imprisonment on espionage charges; the Government's sustained campaign in the courts to prevent the publication of *Spycatcher*, the memoirs of a former MI5 man, Peter Wright; together with a series of other episodes kept State security firmly in the public arena. This chapter deals with some central questions arising out of these episodes, focusing particularly upon the nature and accountability of the security services, the character of State secrets and the controversy over reform of the Official Secrets Acts. The constitutional and institutional background of these concerns has already been provided – in the discussions of the theory and practice of liberal democracy (Chapter 5), of Prime Minister, Cabinet, Civil Service and Parliament (Chapters 6, 7, 10), of the press (Chapter 14) and of civil liberties (Chapter 15). For the concepts of a liberal State, of ministerial responsibility to, and the control of the executive by, Parliament and of the freedom of the press provide the essential context for this chapter. In broad terms, its concern is with what has been described as the 'secret State', by which is meant both non-elected institutions which exercise considerable power in substantial freedom from democratic control and the legislation and practices by which the State precludes public discussion of purportedly secret matters.

THE SECURITY SERVICES

The main Security Services are *MI5*, the domestic counter-intelligence or anti-spying agency; *MI6*, the overseas intelligence service; *Special Branch*, the internal political police; and *Signals Intelligence* (SIGINT), the international radio surveillance service. The security services as a whole had a combined annual budget of £1000m and a total manpower of 10 000 in 1986.

MI5, which was established in 1909 by the Committee for Imperial Defence, has a staff of about 2000 working from Curzon Street House, its

Mayfair headquarters. During the 1970s and 1980s, its role changed and expanded. Its earlier preoccupation with the threat from the Communist Party of Great Britain diminished, because of the decreasing numbers and increasing disillusionment of Communist Party members and possibly also because of MI5's successful neutralisation of the organisation in the 1960s. Instead, its concern shifted to the proliferating small groups on the extreme left and, to a lesser extent, on the extreme right. It is internally organised into branches with specialist functions:

'A' Branch – charge of field operations, burglary, planting bugs and the like;
'B' Branch – mainly the recruitment and vetting of personnel;
'C' Branch – the safety of Government buildings and secrets and the vetting service for the civil service, the armed forces and the police (this Branch has a special responsibility for plans to counter terrorism and sabotage);
'K' Branch – the monitoring of the Russians at their embassy, trade delegation and so on;
'S' Branch – the running of the Joint Computer Bureau, which is linked to MI6 and MI5's registry, which holds dossiers on half a million people;
'F' Branch – the handling of domestic political surveillance.

The range of 'F' Branch's own subdivisions indicates the breadth of its concerns, which, in addition to the Communist Party, include trade unions, Irish terrorism, terrorism in general, left-wing and right-wing groups, and – through a sub-section named FX – the infiltration of trade unions, political parties and other organisations. Its competence, methods, breadth of surveillance and lack of parliamentary accountability became of acute concern in the 1980s.

MI6 is a spying agency primarily concerned with the collection of intelligence and the organisation of espionage outside Britain. Its headquarters is at Century House near Lambeth North Tube Station. Its reputation in the post-war period was affected by a series of revelations of penetration by Soviet agents culminating in defections to the USSR, the defection of Kim Philby being especially damaging as Kilby was the head of the anti-Soviet section.

Special Branch is a political police which functions virtually as an extension of the domestic security service, making the arrests and searches for MI5. Established in 1883 to deal with the Irish Fenians, its primary focus is still countering IRA terrorism on the British mainland. Like MI5, the organisation expanded rapidly in recent decades from about 350 nation-wide in the late 1960s to roughly 1750 in 1984. As well as working closely with MI5 on domestic subversion, and on its own initiative on Irish Republican terrorism, Special Branch is also concerned with the protection of VIPs (the Royal Family, leading domestic and visiting politicians and diplomats), watching ports and airports, vetting naturalisation applicants and enforcing the *Official Secrets* and *Prevention of Terrorism Acts*.

SIGINT is a major source of international intelligence for the government. Its employees are drawn from the Royal Signals Corps and the Foreign Office and it operates by international radio eavesdropping. The organisation is under the control of the Foreign Office and Ministry of Defence but SIGINT reports to the Cabinet Secretariat, where a Deputy-Secretary always has an unacknowledged responsibility for security and defence coordination. It operates under the secret *UKUSA Pact* (1947), under which international radio monitoring is carried out by the USA, the UK, Canada and Australia. The British part of the system works from the *Government Communications Headquarters (GCHQ)* at Cheltenham, which has a staff of 4000. The US part of the system, the *National Security Agency* (NSA), has bases on the British mainland in Scotland, Cornwall, Yorkshire and Bedfordshire.

In 1985, a major political storm broke out over trade union membership at GCHQ, when the Government announced that GCHQ staff must either give up their union membership or seek employment elsewhere. Major industrial action by the civil service in 1981 involving GCHQ workers had led to the USA expressing anxieties about the tightness of British security. This coincided with the Government's own concern about the security aspect of GCHQ staff having access to industrial tribunals and resulted in the ban. A battle in the courts ensued. The civil service unions sought and successfully obtained an injunction restraining the Government from altering the terms of employment at Cheltenham. The initial decision in the High Court went against the Government because the court considered its lack of prior consultation with the unions constituted a breach of natural justice. However, the Court of Appeal overturned the decision on the ground that national security was involved and, on that matter, the Government had the sole right to make decisions. The House of Lords upheld this decision and the ban on trade union activity at GCHQ, Cheltenham, remained.

THE CONTROL, SCOPE AND ACCOUNTABILITY OF THE SECURITY SERVICES

In the 1980s, a series of allegations about the security services together with a major spy scandal led to virtually continuous public debate about their control, competence, breadth of surveillance and accountability. The constitutional position of the security services is by no means clear-cut. The Home Secretary and the Prime Minister are the Ministers most closely concerned. MI5 is departmentally responsible to the Home Secretary whilst Special Branch is also answerable to the Home Secretary in his capacity as Police Authority for the Metropolitan Police. But the precise constitutional position is muddied by the occasional statements by Prime Ministers that the Prime Minister is formally responsible for national security. This is also the position with regard to MI6. The Foreign Secretary is formally responsible but, as with MI5, the Director of MI6 has direct access to the Prime Minister and it is the Prime Minister who carries the ultimate responsibility. The role of Parliament is minimal. Only the Prime Minister sees the true security services budget – a 'doctored' version allegedly going before Parliament – whose scrutiny of this item of public expenditure is, therefore, virtually non-existent. The Liaison Committee of the House of Commons proposed a review of the security services budget by a select committee in 1982–3, but this had not happened by 1988. Mrs Thatcher refused to allow any member of the security services to appear before a select committee in 1985. The *Security Commission* (Chairman in 1988, Lord Bridge) has the responsibility of general supervision of the security services, but reviews its operation only after specific cases have become public. It has seven members, three of whom are deployed to investigate and report upon suspected breaches of security or any other matters, when required.

The rules regulating the domestic security service (MI5) derive primarily from a series of governmental directives, not from statute. Its Charter (1948) lays down the principal task of MI5 – gathering information on subversives of both left and right – but the key document is the 1952 directive to the Director-General. In the context of the controversy surrounding the operations of MI5 in the 1980s, the significant passages are those delimiting its work to actions related to espionage, sabotage and subversion of the State and directing it to maintain its freedom from political bias and influence. The meaning of 'subversion' received more precise definition from the Home Office in 1975: it involved those activities which are intended 'to overthrow parliamentary democracy by political, industrial or violent means'. Trade-union militancy, it was thought, is 'not necessarily subversive'. Other directives relate to the terms under which warrants may be authorised for telephone-tapping and the interception of mail. The *Burkett Report* (1957) laid down the principle that warrants for such purposes be issued only where, first, there was major subversive or espionage activity likely to injure the national interest and, second, the material likely to be obtained by such methods was of direct use to the Security Service in carrying out its specific tasks. Warrants could be issued only where there was 'reasonable cause' to believe subversive activities were already being carried on. The 1980 *White Paper on Interceptions* reiterated these two conditions and added a third – namely, that normal methods of investigation must have been tried and failed or be judged unlikely to succeed. Finally, Lord Diplock's 1981 Report further laid down that warrants should be issued only where the information likely to result from interception is of sufficient importance to justify the step and where the interception applied for offers a reasonable prospect of providing the information sought. The 1952 Directive also touched upon ministerial accountability for the Security Services. There was a well-established convention, it said, whereby Ministers 'do not concern them-selves with the detailed information which may be obtained by the Security

Service in particular cases but are furnished with such information only as may be necessary for the determination of any issue on which guidance is sought'.

The domestic security services came under intense public scrutiny in the 1980s. In 1984, Michael Bettaney, a middle-ranking MI5 officer, was sentenced to 23 years imprisonment on spying charges. His case raised worrying questions about the quality of 'positive vetting' within the service since his heavy drinking suggested he was a high security risk and indeed ought to have lost his security clearance at an earlier date. A report by Lord Bridges on the service was followed by a Government decision (1985) to introduce a large-scale reorganisation of MI5, which would include improvement of procedures for recruiting and vetting officers. However, public disquiet about the case focused upon the accountability of the security service as much as its management and this aspect was not considered in the Government's proposals for reform. Internal vetting procedures as well as overall accountability once again became the subject of a furore in 1987 when the Prime Minister disclosed to the House of Commons that Sir Maurice Oldfield, the head of MI6 between 1972 and 1978, had in 1980 admitted to concealing his homosexuality during vetting and as a result had had his internal security clearance withdrawn. At the time of his confession, he had been recalled from retirement to oversee security in Northern Ireland because of severe problems in the relationship between the police, the army and the undercover forces. This episode led to renewed calls for tighter control and accountability of the security services.

During 1985, the breadth of MI5 political surveillance and the methods employed by the organisation provided further public controversy. A Channel 4 documentary entitled 'MI5's Official Secrets' contained allegations by a former MI5 officer, Cathy Massiter, that MI5 had broken its own rules. It had done so, first, by vastly expanding its political surveillance to include 'soft' targets like members of the peace movement and of certain professions and, second, by tapping their telephones. Once again, the Government ordered an inquiry by the Chairman of the Security Commission but annoyed the Opposition and other critics by restricting its terms of reference to whether Ministers since 1970 had operated under official guidelines in authorising telephone tapping. *Lord Bridge's Report* cleared governments after the 1970s of issuing warrants for interceptions outside accepted guidelines. However, the Shadow Home Secretary maintained that the most serious questions had not been answered because of the restricted terms of reference. These questions were:

(i)   had individuals been falsely classified as subversive to give legitimacy to the issue of a warrant?
(ii) had material obtained by MI5 been used for party political purposes?
(iii) had interception taken place without Minister's knowledge?

(iv) had investigations taken place into the politics and personal lives of members of non-subversive organisations?

The Liberal leader, David Steel, was concerned about the failure of the inquiry to deal with complaints about surveillance without ministerial warrant. But, in addition, he referred to anxieties about blanket surveillance of a whole organisation under a single warrant and interception of transatlantic calls not subject to ministerial warrant. Mrs Thatcher continued to resist calls for a wider inquiry into political surveillance. She argued that what could be said in the House of Commons was very limited for security reasons; that her prime ministerial predecessors had said very little on the subject either (in fact, she considered she had said rather more than they had done); and that, when she had been Leader of the Opposition, she had supported the Labour Government in such matters.

Legislation on this matter was already in the pipeline as the political row broke out. The *Interception of Communications Act* 1985 placed the already-existing criteria for the issue of warrants on the statute book. These are:

  (i) national security;
 (ii) preventing or detecting a serious crime;
(iii) protection of the country's economic well-being.

The Act also established a tribunal of five legally qualified members to hear complaints from those aggrieved by what they consider to be illegal interception of communications. The tribunal has power to quash improperly-issued warrants, to order the destruction of material obtained in an improper manner and to require the Secretary of State to pay compensation. Two developments in 1984 had compelled Government to legislate on telephone-tapping. The first was an amendment by Opposition peers to the Telecommunications Bill. The second was a ruling by the Court of European Rights that the British Government was in breach of the European Convention because of the lack of legal controls over Government telephone-tapping. This last judgement arose out of the case of Roger Malone, a former antiques dealer, who discovered – during a hearing in which he was acquitted of handling stolen goods – that the police had tapped his telephone.

At the same time as the legislation was under parliamentary consideration the Home Secretary, Leon Brittan, sought to allay anxieties by informing the Commons that he had undertaken a personal investigation of MI5 practices and was satisfied that there had been no breach of its guidelines covering surveillance, investigation or action against any individual. In 1986, the Campaign for Nuclear Disarmament lost its case in the High Court that a telephone-tap on its vice-president, John Cox, in 1983 was unlawful. The judge refused to rule that the Home Secretary's authorisation of the tap was unlawful. He considered that the then Home Secretary, Leon Brittan, might have had other evidence (of which Cathy Massiter was unaware) which had led him to decide to issue the warrant. Request for the warrant by MI5 was not, on the surface, unreasonable. Although no longer 'communist-dominated' as in the 1970s, CND was still in 1983 'communist-penetrated' and Mr Cox was a communist who had twice served on the executive committee of the Communist Party of Great Britain. However, the judge did rule that the courts were entitled to review allegations of illegal activity in the security service. He took issue on this point with the Home Secretary who, in line with traditional practice, had maintained his right not to disclose taps authorised in the interests of national security. In 1987 CND was reported as having decided to drop its intended legal action against MI5 for unlawful telephone-tapping for fear that the principle of judicial review of alleged illegal activity in the security service established in the Cox case might be overturned. Instead, it proposed to pursue the issue through the tribunal set up by the *Interception of Communications Act* and, if not satisfied there, possibly at the European Commission.

The question of the control and accountability of the security services is not easy to solve. Critics in the late 1980s maintained that the existing system was unsatisfactory and continued to call for reform. The issue constitutes a classic case of 'who guards the guardians?' Proposals for reform included the establishment of a House of Commons all-party security and intelligence committee composed of senior MPs, together with an independent inspector-general with authority to investigate all the intelligence agencies. This would be on similar lines to the system established in Australia in 1986. It would be accompanied by a more rigorous – and limited – definition of what constitutes 'subversion'. In 1986 the Labour Shadow Home Secretary, Gerald Kaufman, called for a Parliamentary Commissioner of Civil Rights responsible to a House of Commons Select Committee. Such an officer would have the power to scrutinise the security services and would be the person to whom those who believed their telephones were being tapped would appeal. Also, the Commissioner could be consulted by public servants worried that ministers or higher officials were taking unlawful or unprincipled decisions. The Government continued to maintain that national security was inherently a matter on which the strictest secrecy had to be upheld. To open up the activities of the Security Services to public inspection – as the setting up of a more rigorous system of parliamentary scrutiny would do – would be more damaging than the disease it was intended to cure.

THE OFFICIAL SECRETS ACTS

The vital legislation under which the State can defend itself against unauthorised disclosure of its secrets consists of the *Official Secrets Acts* of 1911, 1920 and 1939.

Section 1 – the 'spying clause' – makes it an offence punishable with fourteen years imprisonment to collect or disclose information which might be directly or indirectly useful to an enemy or to engage in conduct 'prejudicial to the safety or interests of the State'.

Much more controversially, *Section 2* makes it a criminal offence for public servants to retain without permission or to communicate without authorisation information obtained in the course of their employment or for a person to receive such information knowing or having reasonable cause to believe it has been disclosed in breach of the Act. This catch-all clause, which, it has been suggested, created 2324 separate offences, has provided twentieth-century governments with a potent but arbitrary weapon to guard the secrecy of their operations. Under Section 2 of the Act, the Government can if it wishes prosecute someone for revealing such a trivial matter as the number of coups of tea drunk in a particular Government Department. The key word here is *authorisation*. For Government as a matter of course routinely divulges large quantities of information through Ministers who are self-authorising in the matter and through civil servants whose authorisation, more vaguely, is implied. Within Whitehall, information is normally classified, on an ascending scale of sensitivity, as 'restricted', 'confidential', 'secret' and 'top secret'. The 'restricted' category contains much routine material including instruction manuals and telephone directories. But the point is that, no matter how information is classified, and no matter how much 'leaks' of classified information have become part of the system by which the media acquire news, government can choose to make the *unauthorised* disclosure of *any* piece of information an offence. The very wide coverage of the Acts means that civil servants and journalists may be in technical breach of the law frequently.

The *Franks Committee* (1972) criticised Section 2 of the Officials Secrets Acts as a 'catch-all' and 'a mess'. It recommended the repeal of this section and its replacement by a new Official Information Act. Under this Act, *only matters of major importance* would be protected against disclosure by the criminal law. This would involve information classified as 'top secret' and 'secret' in the fields of defence, security, foreign relations, currency and the reserves; Cabinet documents; and information facilitating criminal activity or breaking the confidentiality of information supplied to government by or about individuals. Before a prosecution could be brought, the Minister would have to certify that the information was correctly classified at the time it was divulged. The Committee recommended the establishment of an advisory committee on matters relating to classification with a similar role to the Defence, Press and Broadcasting ('D' Notice) Committee. A 'D' Notice is a confidential letter sent by a Government Department to editors working in the mass media, and sometimes also to publishers, requesting that information be not published because publication would damage national defence or security. Widely employed to inhibit publication on defence and security matters in the 1960s and 1970s, the system was still being used in the 1980s.

Reform of the Official Secrets Acts on the lines recommended by Franks did not prove straightforward and had not occurred by 1988. Since the late 1970s, however, 'freedom of information' legislation has been a much-debated topic. A White Paper issued in 1978 by the Labour Government proposed legislation on the most restrictive aspects of the Official Secrets Acts. When Labour was defeated in 1979, the in-coming Conservative Government immediately introduced a Protection of Official Information Bill, 1979. However, this legislation would have been even more restrictive than the existing Acts, especially with regard to the coverage of the security services. It was very unpopular and when the revelations about the spy, Anthony Blunt, appeared just as the bill was under parliamentary consideration, the Government decided to drop it. During the following years, the Conservative Government was to have substantial recourse to the Official Secrets Acts and to other means in order to exert control over the civil service and to inhibit publication of material which, in its judgement, endangered the national interest.

Trials under the Official Secrets Acts in the 1970s and 1980s

During the 1970s, the Officials Secrets Acts were invoked first to prosecute the *Daily Telegraph*, a journalist (Jonathan Aitken) and a military officer, for the publication of a confidential report on the Nigerian civil war situation which upset the Nigerian Government. The defendants were acquitted and the judge suggested that Section 2 of the Acts might be abandoned (1970). The so-called *'ABC' Trial* (1977) took its name from the first letters of the surnames of the three defendants, Crispin Aubrey, John Berry and Duncan Campbell. They were arrested by Special Branch officers while journalists Aubrey and Campbell were interviewing Berry, a former corporal in Signals Intelligence, about his work. They were initially charged under Section 2; charges under Section 1 were added later but then dropped after the judge had condemned an espionage prosecution as 'oppressive'. The defendants were convicted under Section 2 but given only minor non-custodial sentences.

The Conservative Government after 1979 undertook two further prosecutions under the Acts which received wide publicity. Both involved the leaking of defence-related documents against the wishes of the Government. But, although the context was similar – a Government determined to enforce its will on matters which it perceived as relating to national security backed by a judiciary in an 'executive-minded' phase – the outcome of the trials was very different. In the *Sarah Tisdall* case (1984), the defendant, a junior Foreign Office clerk, was convicted and gaoled for six months. In the case of *Clive Ponting* (1985), the defendant, an Assistant Secretary in the Ministry of Defence, was acquitted, a severe blow not only to the Government but also to the Acts themselves. It led to a renewed campaign for their repeal. But first we examine the issues involved in these important judgements in more detail, beginning with a case-study of the Sarah Tisdall prosecution

The Tisdall case

On Friday, 23 March 1984, Sarah Tisdall, a 23-year-old clerk at the Foreign Office, was gaoled for six months for 'leaking' secret Ministry of Defence documents to *The Guardian* newspaper in the previous October. She was tried and sentenced for committing an offence under Section 2 of the *Official Secrets Act*, to which charge she pleaded guilty. Ms Tisdall was a grade 10 diplomatic service officer, one of the staff of ten, consisting of a principal private secretary, two first secretaries, four clerical officers and three typists, who composed the 'private office' of Britain's Foreign Secretary. Her job was routine but very important: it consisted of logging papers in and out, copying correspondence and distributing documents to other departments. The position was one of trust, involving the handling of highly sensitive classified material. Sarah Tisdall was competent at her job and well aware of it as a position of trust: during her induction course in July 1980, she had signed a declaration indicating that she understood the import of the Official Secrets Act. This Act (pp. 373–4, above) was designed to stop leaks of documents prejudicial to the interests or safety of the State; specifically, it made it an offence to communicate to an unauthorised person information likely to help an enemy.

On 20 October 1983, a Ministry of Defence memorandum marked 'Secret – UK eyes only' and entitled 'Deliveries of Cruise Missiles to RAF Greenham Common – Parliamentary and Public Statements' arrived in the private office of the Foreign Secretary on its way to the registry of the defence department of the Foreign Office. Written by the Secretary of State for Defence, Michael Heseltine, and addressed to the Prime Minister, it dealt with plans to handle the parliamentary and public response to the arrival of Cruise missiles; it also contained a second document relating to security preparations for the Greenham base. Required to photocopy the former document as part of her routine duties, Sarah Tisdall read it and was shocked. Although far from being a 'Greenham woman' (she was not even against nuclear weapons) she found its contents 'indecent' and 'immoral'. What seems to have upset her was its revelation of political calculation on the part of the government in its handling of the Cruise issue. Her conscience outraged, she made extra copies of the two documents, and took them to *The Guardian*. They arrived in the office of the newspaper about 8 p.m. on Friday, 21 October, when the early edition of the next day's paper was almost complete.

Having checked the first document for authenticity, the editor published a front-page story based on its contents in the later editions the following day under the headline 'Whitehall sets November 1 Cruise arrival'. The paper published the first document in full on 31 October but decided not to publish the second one because, in the view of the editor, it contained parts which, if they became public knowledge, might be used by an unbalanced individual to impede the police. Meanwhile, the government began an urgent inquiry aimed at tracing the source of the leak, which culminated in a letter dated 11 November requesting *The Guardian* to return the published document. The newspaper considered destroying the document but in the end, acting on the advice of its lawyers, decided not to destroy it but to resist its return. The editor believed that the convention of journalism which allowed him to refuse to divulge his sources had received statutory protection by the *Contempt of Court Act* 1981. He did, however, offer to return the document with the various pen markings on it excised, which would have made it impossible to use it for the purpose of identifying the internal 'mole'. The Government turned down this offer and issued a writ for the return of the unmutilated document. In the High Court on 14 December, Mr Justice Scott ruled against *The Guardian*, holding that the *Contempt of Court Act* did not apply; in his view, it was simply a matter of the ownership of the document, and since it belonged to the Government, the newspaper must return it. *The Guardian* appealed against this judgement, but lost the appeal too. Sir John Donaldson, whilst accepting that the document in question contained no information that would be of use to enemies of the country, took the view that the real issue was the question of betrayal of trust by an employee of the Crown. He stated: 'The maintenance of national security requires that untrustworthy servants in a position to mishandle highly classified documents passing from the Secretary of State for Defence to other Ministers shall be identified at the earliest possible moment and removed from their positions.'

The editor of *The Guardian* and his closest colleagues, now faced an agonising choice. To return the leaked document intact would almost certainly incriminate their unknown informant; to retain it without destroying it would lead to the financial ruin of the paper since it would be fined increasingly large sums daily by the court until it either did so or went out of existence; to destroy it (an option considered seriously by the editor) would lead to a once-only fine for contempt of court, together with some action against the individual responsible. A major reason for the newspaper's decision to hand over the document which led to the immediate arrest and eventual sentence of Sarah Tisdall was its desire to uphold its integrity as 'a law-abiding newspaper'. As a regular advocate of the rule of law, it could not practise selective law-breaking when this suited it, and still retain its liberal reputation.

The trial proceeded and culminated in the six-months prison sentence imposed on Sarah Tisdall after the judge, Mr Justice Cantley, had spoken of the need for a custodial sentence 'in these days'. His words reflected the judge's sympathy for the Government's position on this occasion, a sympathy even more fully symbolised in the statement of Sir John Donaldson, the head of the Appeal Court:

> The responsibility for deciding what should or should not be published is that of the government of the day and not that of individual civil servants or editors.

The case raises questions central to the practice of the rule of law in a liberal-democracy. The responsibilities of governments (for national security), editors (for informing the public about matters of national importance), judges (for interpreting the law on key issues) and individuals (to their consciences, on serious public issues) were all involved. To the Left, the decision to try Sarah Tisdall at the Old Bailey rather than in a magistrates' court for an isolated and misguided action was politically partisan. To the Left also, and to many liberally-minded people generally, the sentence on Sarah Tisdall was a harsh one, the more especially because national security was not, in fact, endangered by her action. The Left stressed that the Official Secrets legislation under which the prosecution was brought is discredited, amongst other things by the wide drafting that prevents the publication of many items quite unconnected with national security. To that side of the political spectrum, the case raised questions of press freedom and was widely seen as further justification for a 'Freedom of Information' Act. The editor of *The Guardian* was criticised by many for releasing the documents which led to Sarah Tisdall's sentence, the National Union of Journalists in particular castigating his action as a betrayal of journalistic ethics. On the other hand, Sarah Tisdall got little sympathy from the political Right, who considered she deserved her punishment for abusing her position of trust.

The Ponting case

The immediate issue upon which *the Ponting case* came to public attention was that of the circumstances surrounding the sinking of the Argentine ship, the *General Belgrano*, with heavy loss of life at the beginning of the Falklands War on 2 May, 1982. Nearly two years later, the account of the event which had been given by the Government at the time became the subject of parliamentary concern after the publication of descriptions of the sinking which appeared to contradict it. Confronted by what he perceived as Ministerial attempts to mislead the House of Commons over information which was neither classified nor, in his view, involved national security, Clive Ponting sent the information to Tam Dalyell, a Labour MP with a strong interest in the matter. Ponting believed that the Government was simply seeking to save itself from political embarrassment. He also felt that his action in releasing unauthorised information was covered by a Treasury Note of 1978, which held that officials could give information without breaching the Official Secrets Acts so long as the material only went to

Parliament. However, the Government did decide to prosecute Ponting under Section 2 of the Official Secrets Acts. Ponting's defence was that he had acted in accordance with the national interest, which was to know the truth about the sinking of the Argentine ship. His broader duty as a citizen overrode his narrower duty as a public official. The prosecution case, upheld by the judge in his instruction to the jury, was that the national interest was the same as the policy of the government of the day. The Government had decided that *Belgrano* information was to be withheld from Tam Dalyell and, accordingly, it was the duty of Ponting to follow that policy. His duty was simply and solely his duty as a civil servant to do what he was told by his political 'masters'. To general surprise, and government consternation, however, Ponting was acquitted.

In the immediate aftermath of the case, heated exchanges took place in the House of Commons over the process by which the Attorney-General had decided to prosecute. To what extent had he been influenced by other members of the Government, Opposition leaders wanted to know? Constitutionally, while the Attorney-General may *consult* his colleagues, he cannot be directed by them. The office of Attorney-General is a political appointment and its holder is a member of the Government like other ministers. But he is also a law officer of the Crown and is therefore required not to be influenced by partisan considerations. The first result of the Ponting case was that the independence and discretion of the Attorney-General became a political issue. The line of questioning pursued by the Leader of the Opposition suggested that the Attorney-General had been unduly influenced by other members of the Government. Mrs Thatcher denied the accusation, stating that ministers were not involved in the decision to prosecute. This reply left it open for critics to allege that the Attorney-General had misused his discretion in making such a reckless prosecution.

Second, the Government responded to the issues raised by the trial by publishing a stern set of guidelines for civil servants – *Notes of Guidance on the Duties and Responsiblities of Civil Servants to Ministers*. The document was presented by Sir Robert Armstrong, the Cabinet Secretary, who stressed that civil servants were servants of the Crown and were therefore expected to support the policies of the Crown's Ministers. Civil servants confronted by the dilemma faced by Ponting should either accompany their advice to ministers with a memorandum of dissent or speak privately to the Cabinet Secretary about the problem.

A third consequence of the Ponting case was the renewal of calls for the abolition of the *Official Secrets Acts* and their replacement by less all-embracing legislation. All opposition parties – Labour, Liberal and SDP – expressed support for the repeal of the Acts and the introduction of a 'Freedom of Information' Act with strictly defined exemptions. By 1987, the campaign for repeal – first begun in 1984 by the National Campaign for Civil Liberties in the wake of the Tisdall case – had broadened out to include leading former civil servants and judges as well as Conservative back-benchers. Des Wilson was co-chairman of a campaign which had also gained considerable public support and some legislative success by that date. A poll conducted by MORI in July 1986, for the Campaign for Freedom of Information showed that nearly two-thirds of respondents were in favour of a Freedom of Information Act, subject to exemptions for national security, crime prevention and personal privacy.

The Campaign for Freedom of Information was in fact pursuing a step-by-step campaign which would culminate in a Freedom of Information Act. In 1986 the *Local Government (Access to Information) Act* became law, unopposed by the Government. The second move of the step-by-step campaign came with the introduction of the Access to Personal Files Bill early in 1987. This had the support of 146 MPs (72 Labour, 54 Conservatives, 20 Alliance) and 85 national organisations. The Bill would cover medical, education and employment records and had widespread public support (the MORI poll in July 1986 showed that nearly three-quarters of those polled were in favour of access to personal files).

The Government's *Data Protection Act*, 1984 already allowed people access to records, including medical and educational ones, held on computer; but it opposed the extension of rights of personal access to information held on manual files. Whilst accepting that Section 2 of the Official Secrets Acts was no longer defensible, it was not in favour of a Freedom of Information Act, even with exemptions for national security and other highly sensitive information. It took its stand on the principle of ministerial responsibility. Where a grievance was felt against refusal to disclose, appeal would be to the courts or an ombudsman, and this would bypass ministerial accountability to Parliament. However, the Government's preferred solution – legislation on the lines of its tough 1979 bill – was unlikely to be acceptable either.

During 1987, three more cases involving national security occurred. In two of these the Government invoked the *Official Secrets Acts* to prosecute those in unauthorised possession of secret information or to restrain its publication. *Peter Galvin*, an arms dealer, was sentenced to six months imprisonment in 1986 for an official secrets offence. His decision to appeal was the first in the history of the Acts. At his trial, he was accused of being in unlawful possession of a manual for a Rolls-Royce Olympus engine, although it had been sent, officially, to fourteen countries and had also been given to the Midlands Air Museum and two other individuals. His defence counsel argued that the manual could no longer be a secret document because it was already in the public domain. The prosecution countered that the limited disclosures of the manual was in no way inconsistent with the Ministry of Defence requiring its employees and contractors to observe the Official Secrets Act. His defence – that the manual could be rightly seen as neither 'official' nor 'secret' – was accepted by Warwick magistrates. But the prosecution circumvented their decision by taking the case to the Crown

Court, which convicted Galvin. This case caused little public stir.

But the so-called *'Zircon affair'* aroused considerable controversy. When the BBC proposed a series of programmes entitled *Secret Society* to be screened in March 1987, Special Branch raided its Glasgow office with a warrant issued under the *Official Secrets Acts* and seized all materials relating to the programmes. Its real target was a programme on Britain's proposed spy satellite, *Zircon*, researched by the journalist, Duncan Campbell. On protest by the BBC, five films were returned but the Zircon film was retained by the police. Once again, there was public disquiet over an apparent infringement of media freedom. Opposition leaders complained that the raid had eroded the integrity and independence of the Board of Governors of the BBC. The Government's case was that the proposed disclosures about Zircon would alert the Soviet Union to the existence of the satellite and encourage it to take counter-measures; transmission of the film would also endanger cooperation with the USA in gathering intelligence. Critics of the government riposted that the existence of the proposed satellite was more widely known than the Government suggested and that, in any case, once launched, the position of the satellite would be easily detected by the USSR. One reason for the Government's wish to stifle discussion, it was suggested, was its political embarrassment that the project was likely to be delayed. The Government was successful in getting a High Court injunction against disclosures about *Zircon* by Duncan Campbell. But, again, critics argued that public debate would have been valuable in assessing the worth of a project whose considerable cost would have to be assessed against the benefits of making Britain less dependent upon the USA for intelligence information.

Spycatcher

During 1986–7, the Government also sought and obtained injunctions against newspapers in Britain reporting or repeating what they had already reported of the revelations about the Security Services of a retired MI5 agent, *Peter Wright*, in his book *Spycatcher*. In this long-drawn-out, complicated affair, the Government took its stand not on the *Official Secrets Acts*, but on the fact of breach of duty by a servant of the Crown. The first duty of any public servant, it argued, is one of trust and confidentiality; and this duty is of special importance for an employee of the Security Services. The publication of the memoirs, it further maintained, would cause 'unquantifiable damage' by leading other friendly foreign intelligence services to lose confidence in the Government's ability to protect classified information. To allow publication in the case of Wright would serve as a bad example to others in positions of confidence and trust by encouraging them to publish their memoirs, so turning MI5 into 'a laughing stock'. The Government agreed with its critics that it was in the public interest that allegations of wrongdoing in the security service should be investigated and, if necessary, punished but differed from them in arguing that this was an internal matter, not one for wide public exposure.

The Government's critics, who included quality newspapers and the three main opposition parties, focused in the first place on the illogicality of the Government position. By late July 1987, when the Government appealed successfully to the House of Lords to prevent *The Guardian* and two other newspapers from reporting allegations about MI5 in *Spycatcher* and gained a High Court injunction preventing further serialisation of the Wright book in the *Sunday Times*, the substance of the book was in the public domain. It had already been widely reported in the UK and actually published in the USA, whence copies were arriving in Britain as the Government had failed to place an import restriction on the book. Second, they stressed the inconsistency of the Government position. Many of the allegations about MI5 made by Wright had already appeared in earlier works and a Granada TV programme before his book was written, and the Government had not sought to ban them. Third, they maintained that the allegations made by Wright, who had been personal assistant to Sir Maurice Hanley, the Director-General of MI5, were so serious that they warranted an immediate top-level inquiry. Wright alleged among other things that a right-wing faction within MI5 plotted to destabilise the Labour Government of Harold Wilson in the 1970s and that the organisation committed numerous illegal and treasonable acts, including the faking and forging of documents, smear campaigns and illicit 'bugging' and burglaries. Not to hold an inquiry into such grave revelations, critics held, is more damaging to confidence in the security services than to establish which ones are true and which can be discounted, and to introduce reforms where necessary. The real needs are twofold: proper contracts of service with members of the security services which provide clear guidelines about what may and may not be publicly revealed and a proper system of democratic accountability for the security service, such as exists in the USA and Australia. Critics were unable to accept the argument of the Government against holding an inquiry – that refusal to do so was in line with the traditional practice that an Administration does not investigate the conduct of its predecessors.

In retrospect it can be seen that many of the problems bedevilling national security in Britain in the 1980s had a specific historical origin:

1. The security services had a non-statutory beginning as the Secret Service Bureau in 1909; this gave them their essential character as a highly secret organisation in whose establishment the wishes of the Foreign Office were everything and those of Parliament nothing. Not surprisingly – even in ostensibly more democratic times – Parliament has had difficulty in establishing the proper *accountability* of the services.
2. The security services were established deliberately in such a manner as would enable their existence to be disowned if necessary. Britain was given

an intelligence service which had no official existence. Hence, *management* of the services has been a problem. The Liberal Government which founded them – and subsequent governments also – have been willing to give up their obligation to supervise the operation of the services in return for effective results. Hence governments have lacked real authority when faced by the betrayals and leaks of the post-war period.

3. Having set up a secret service which was secret not only in the vitally necessary sense that its operations were covert but also in the unnecessary sense that the Government could deny its existence, the Government needed a way of protecting this secret organisation and relationship.

This arrived in the form of the *Official Secrets Act*, 1911 backed by the *'D'* *Notice* system (originated 1913), which was initially accompanied by a disavowal of any intent to use the new legislation against the Press. The legislation was very widely drawn to preclude divulgence not only of matters which would genuinely imperil national security but also much information that would not, including matter whose revelation would merely embarrass the government. The context of its specific Clause 1 was the intensifying military rivalry with Germany. The context of its very broad Clause 2 was more complex: the habits born of a still aristocratic form of government, for whose members secrets were traditionally an aspect of power limited to the few; the growth of a professional civil service which had come to view official information as government property; and, finally, the development of a national press devoted to casting light on the processes of government, against which the Government sought to strengthen its powers of conceal-ment.

SUMMARY

The chapter briefly surveyed the main intelligence-gathering agencies – MI5, MI6, Special Branch and Signals Intelligence (GCHQ) – before discussing problems of their management and accountability. Ministers including the Prime Minister, who has a general overall responsibility for security, do answer questions about the security services in parliament but try to give as little away as possible – to be 'uniformly uninformative' in the words of a former PM, Harold Wilson. Disquieting queries about the politicisation, illegal methods and possible treason of the internal counter-espionage service were raised in the 1980s by the allegations of former MI5 officers (Massiter, Wright and others) and the Bettaney spy case was not the only episode to suggest grave weaknesses in internal vetting procedures. The Government introduced a large-scale reorganisation of the security service (1985) which included recruitment and vetting but did not tackle its accountability; calls for an inquiry into its operations were rejected. The *Official Secrets Acts* 1911, 1920 and 1939 allied with the 'D' Notice system are the methods by which the Government controls media publication of sensitive information, including matters involving national security. Section 1 relates solely to espionage, and there is widespread agreement on the need for severe restrictions with regard to genuine national security matters. Section 2, however, is widely drawn. It can be and has been used (Tisdall, Ponting) to prosecute public servants who pass unauthorised information to the press and to Parliament. Prosecutions were successful in the former case, unsuccessful in the latter. There is some political agreement between Left, centre and Right opinion about the unsatisfactory nature of the Official Secrets Acts, but none on how to replace them. Labour and the Liberals favour a Freedom of Information Act with certain restrictions; Conservatives – on the evidence of their 1979 proposed bill – support much more restrictive legislation. Left and Right, in general, are far apart on secrecy, as the assumptions made by the Government and its critics on the Wright and other cases reveal.

FURTHER READING

Hooper, D. (1987) *Official Secrets: The Use and Abuse of the Act*, London, Secker & Warburg.
Leigh, D. (1980) *The Frontiers of Secrecy*, London, Junction Books.
Marshall, G. (1984) *Constitutional Conventions*, Oxford, Clarendon, ch. 7.
Norton-Taylor, R. (1985) *The Ponting Affair*, London, Cecil Woolf.
Peele, G. (1986) 'The State and Civil Liberties' in H. Drucker *et al.*, *Developments in British Politics, II*, London, Macmillan.
Ponting, C. (1985) *The Right to Know*, London, Sphere.
Smith, S. A. de (1983) *Constitutional and Administrative Law*, edited by H. Street and R. Brazier, Harmondsworth, Penguin, ch. 23.
Wallington, P. (ed.) (1984) *Civil Liberties 1984*, Oxford, Martin Robertson.

QUESTIONS

1. What are the main public concerns about the operation of the security services and how may these anxieties be allayed?

2. Critically review the character and working of the Official Secrets Acts and discuss the arguments relating to proposals for their abolition and replacement.

3. What can be said for and against the Government decision to prosecute Sarah Tisdall and Clive Ponting?

ASSIGNMENT

Imagine yourself in the situation facing a civil servant like Sarah Tisdall. What would you do and for what reasons?

Part III
Issues and the Policy Process

17

Government, the Economy and Public Spending

A considerable share of Britain's wealth is spent by central and local government, and the question of whether more or less money should be spent by government has become a major political issue in recent years. Public expenditure – or government spending – is the money spent on providing things such as social security, defence, education, the National Health Service and all the other services and payments which come from the State. Money to pay for these services comes from a great variety of taxes, incomes and, in recent years, from revenues obtained by the sale of state assets. If the Chancellor does not have enough money collected in a year to pay for the public spending bill he borrows money, and the amount borrowed is known as the public sector borrowing requirement (PSBR). Reducing the PSBR was a major goal of the Chancellor during the 1980s. This chapter explores the arguments surrounding economic policy and paying for the welfare state.

PHILOSOPHICAL APPROACHES OF THE MAJOR PARTIES

From the late 1940s to the mid 1970s, there was a consensus between the major political parties that government should be deeply involved in the provision of welfare services and should play an active role in the economy. Since the mid-1970s, however, there has been fundamental disagreement on the scope of public spending, the nature and purpose of welfare provision and the extent of economic intervention. The difference in views has not, however, been simply between parties but also within them.

The liberal-minded 'One Nation' tendency within the Conservative Party contains individuals who believe that government should assume key responsibilities in providing welfare and regulating the economy. Sometimes labelled as the 'Tory wets', these Conservatives believe that the State should be the partner of industry and that the Conservative Party should be concerned with achieving social justice for all, with the Welfare State providing the best means to achieve this aim.

The radical Right of the Conservative Party expounds a very different philosophy which aims, in the words of Mrs Thatcher, to 'push back the frontiers of the State and set the people free'. This would involve the government both in spending less on welfare and in collecting less in taxes. The radical Right argues that high levels of state expenditure have sapped resources from the economy, led to high levels of taxation, and by molly-coddling people has reduced people's sense of responsibility. In other words, the Welfare State and associated high levels of government spending have resulted in economic decline and a spiritual malaise amongst Britain's population. The radical Right maintains that the economic burden of the Welfare State should be reduced, releasing resources which would foster an 'enterprise culture' which would work towards increasing the wealth, freedom of choice and sense of responsibility amongst the population. The radical Right draws much of its philosophy from the classical theory of political economy expounded by Adam Smith in which the State is seen as a potential tool of coercion which limits the freedom of the individual. It considers that individual freedom is protected by the workings of the free market, and thus the radical Right supports the introduction of free market forces into areas of the public sector in general and within the Welfare State in particular. Proposals for education and health voucher schemes have been canvassed periodically and, as we shall see, many services once operated by the public sector have become privatised.

The Labour Party is customarily associated with support for high government spending in general and for a large Welfare State in particular. In fact, Labour exhibits two discernible approaches. The Right-wing, or revisionist, wing of the Party espouses a social democratic ideology in which the development of the Welfare State is a prime objective. Indeed, it can be argued that, within revisionist minds, the development of a full Welfare State is equated with the creation of a socialist society. Although the rhetoric differs, Liberal and SDP philosophies down to 1987 were very close to revisionist Labour views. In his influential book, *The Future of Socialism* (1956), Labour revisionist Anthony Crosland argued that after 1945 nineteenth century capitalism had been transformed out of all recognition into the modern mixed economy. Britain's major problems, he argued, were no longer economic in nature, but social. The establishment and development of the Welfare State would redistribute income within society and solve these social problems.

Labour's Left wing, sometimes referred to as fundamentalist Socialists, never shared Crosland's belief that the economic problems within the capitalist system had been solved. Consequently, the Left did not believe that the only remaining problems were social in nature. Since Britain still had major economic problems, the Left believed that the Welfare State could only 'tinker' with them rather than 'solve' them. The Left believes that the mixed economy is essentially a capitalist economy which can be manipulated by powerful private forces. The Left still sees ownership as a major problem in the economy and believes that government should play a large role through greater public ownership. Socialism is viewed as an economic philosophy and the Left believes that most social problems will be solved once the economy is organised along Socialist lines. The Left supports the Welfare State, but does not equate it with the arrival of Socialism.

MANAGEMENT OF THE ECONOMY

Conservative Chancellors, in the 1980s, Sir Geoffrey Howe and Nigel Lawson, have been committed to implementing policies which have their origins in the thinking of the Conservative radical Right. Such policies are described as being 'monetarist' in nature. What is monetarism and how has it worked?

In the British context monetarism has three important ingredients:

(i) Reductions in the supply of money in the economy must be made each year. Monetarists believe that reducing the money supply will eradicate inflation and create the conditions for Britain's economic revival. Planned reductions in the money supply, measured as sterling M3, were built into the Treasury's 'medium-term financial strategy'.

(ii) Reductions in the amount of money spent by the government must be made each year. This is seen as having the effect of reducing the amount of money that the government has to borrow each year to help pay for public spending. A large PSBR is seen as one of the main causes of growth in the money supply.

(iii) Increased emphasis on the working of the free market in society. This should include greater privatisation and lower taxation.

The money supply

Conservative Chancellors experienced great difficulty in controlling the money supply. Figure 17.1 shows how rarely the published targets set by the Chancellors in their Medium Term Financial Strategy have been met. The government has tried to overcome its difficulties in meeting its monetary targets by periodically raising the targets. But this failed since M3 grew faster still. Faced with this, the Treasury abandoned M3 as a measure of money supply and adopted the more narrow measure of MO. Most financial experts dismissed MO as an irrelevant measure of money supply in today's relatively cashless society.

According to monetarist theory, there is a time-lag of about two years between reducing the money supply and seeing a reduction in the inflation rate. Yet the money supply has soared out of control and inflation has fallen. Likewise, monetarist theory predicted an inflation rate of around 15–20 per cent based on a growth of 19 per cent in M3 in 1985. The actual rate of

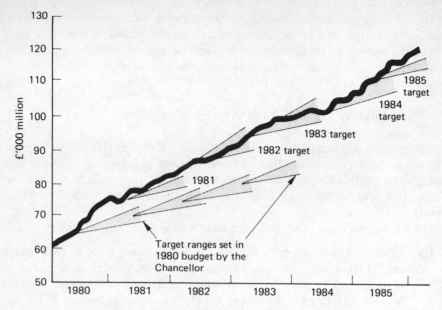

Source: Adapted from *The Guardian*, 24 October 1985

FIGURE 17.1   *Monetary targets, 1980–5*

inflation for that year of around 3–5 per cent severely dented the credibility of monetarist thinking. In other words, the inflation rate came down but not, it seemed, as a result of monetarist methods.

Public spending

Mrs Thatcher's first election manifesto argued that 'the State takes too much of the nation's income. Its share must steadily be reduced.' One of Nigel Lawson's first acts as Chancellor was to get an emergency £5000m in revenue from selling off government assets. The 'big spending' government departments suffered most since cuts were made in defence, education and health. The new Chancellor made it clear that he would soon be demanding bigger cuts to a total of £2500m. Negotiations to reduce public spending in bilateral talks between the Treasury and individual spending departments and within the 'Star Chamber' proved a complicated and controversial affair. In the end, the Chancellor won his cuts through creative accounting techniques. This included forecasting greater revenue from North Sea Oil than previously expected, the use of the government's contingency fund for normal spending uses, and the use of privatisation revenue to reduce public spending. This latter move meant that public spending could actually increase yet stay within strict targets because the money from privatisation is counted as 'negative spending'.

In reality, the Chancellor has replaced his battle to *reduce* public expenditure with the aim of limiting the *growth* in public spending. In other words, the government claims to have 'brought public spending under control' but it cannot claim to have reduced it. There is confusion over public spending because some items have been cut whilst others have had more money spent on them. Sir Leo Pliatzky's study, *Paying and Choosing* (1985), examined the changes between 1978–9 and 1983–4. Government spending on agriculture rose by 50 per cent, on law and order by 34 per cent, on social security by 25 per cent and on education by 0.7 per cent. On the other hand, government spending on housing fell by 55 per cent, on overseas aid by 15 per cent, and on assistance to industry by 11 per cent.

Table 17.1 contains revised estimates of public expenditure revealed by the Chancellor in his Autumn statement of 1986. Public spending, particularly in the areas of education, health and social services, was planned to rise by an extra 2 per cent in real terms for the following year. Presented with 'new' plans which were so much greater than the 'old' ones laid only a year earlier, Tory monetarists complained bitterly that the Star Chamber had turned into the school tuck shop!

The Conservative government has spent more in every year since it took office in 1979. This is mainly because of a massive increase in unemployment benefits and social security payments created by the severe economic recession of 1980–1. High unemployment, which is associated by many with the pursuit of monetarist economic policy, presents the government with higher bills for unemployment benefit, supplementary and housing benefit, and redundancy fund payments in addition to 'hidden costs' resulting from the greater use of the NHS by unemployed people. At the same time, the government receives less in income tax (around £6000m), less in national insurance contributions (around £5000m) and less in indirect taxes (around £1500m) because of the high numbers of unemployed people who no longer pay them.

Some economists have argued that in reality any Chancellor has very little scope to make savings in public spending. They calculate that around 21 per cent of the government's spending is fixed because of firm long-term commitments (e.g. payments to the EEC, defence). Another 67 per cent or so

TABLE 17.1
Public expenditure plans (£ billion)

	Old	New	Change
1986/7	139.1	140.4	+ 1.3
1987/8	143.9	148.6	+ 4.7
1988/9	148.7	154.2	+ 5.5

Source: *The Guardian*, 7 November 1986

is determined by demand (e.g. the number of unemployed who need social security, the number of sick who need treatment). This leaves only 12 per cent where the government can make real cuts and save money. But even here cuts would bring hardship to some, possibly damage some aspect of the country's future development, and would certainly raise fierce opposition from those who would be affected.

Privatisation and the free market

Privatisation is the other side of the coin to public spending cuts. If the Chancellor cannot save as much as he wants through public spending cuts, he can still solve his problems by collecting in more money. But a monetarist-minded Chancellor would not want to collect more money through higher taxation or government borrowing, because these measures would *increase* the scope of government involvement in the economy. However, a monetarist Chancellor would favour getting in more money through privatisation because this would *reduce* the scope of government activity.

In many ways, privatisation is one of the hallmarks of the Conservative government's approach to economic policies in the 1980s. Some privatisation has been accomplished through 'liberalisation' or 'de-regulation', which involves relaxing government monopoly and opening up areas to competition. But the main thrust of privatisation has come in the form of 'denationalisation' or the sale of State-owned assets. The list of companies sold by the government includes household names such as British Petroleum, Ferranti, British Aerospace, Britoil, Jaguar, Sealink, British Telecom, British Gas, the National Bus Company, Rolls Royce, and British Rail Hotels. The Treasury forecast that in the ten years up to 1989 the privatisation programme will have raised over £22 billion.

Some monetarists have criticised the government for being too cautious in its privatisation policy and urge that prisons, motorways, school and hospital buildings, British Coal and the Bank of England be sold off. Critics of privatisation argue that in terms of monetarist philosophy alone, privatisation has failed. According to monetarists, the central arguments for privatisation are based on private sector companies being more efficient than public sector ones and on privatisation freeing markets and increasing consumer choice. Critics argue that the benefits claimed for privatisation are often far from evident:

1. Privatisation does not always free the market because the market is not attractive to competitors. To some extent, this has happened with the deregulation of local bus services, where only 3 per cent of route miles has more than one company offering a service. The privatisation of British Telecom also failed to free the market and witnessed the transformation of a public monopoly into a private monopoly.

2. Standards of service do not necessarily improve. Indeed a MORI survey conducted for the National Consumer Council revealed that customers felt that BT standards had declined since privatisation. Around half of those interviewed thought that charges were too high and a quarter felt that BT was offering an inferior service since privatisation. These findings were partially confirmed by Oftel, the watchdog body set up the government, which received 56 per cent more complaints in the second year of privatisation than in the first, revealing the declining public image of BT.
3. The critics of privatisation have pointed out that the companies privatised so far have been the ones least likely to benefit from being put in the private sector because they were already very successful in the public sector. In other words, the central criterion for deciding which companies would be privatised was simply their value on the stock market and little to do with the potential benefits of increased efficiency and greater consumer choice.

PAYING FOR THE WELFARE STATE

The use of private health care outside the NHS and private education have grown considerably under the Conservative government since 1979. This may be based on public fears that the NHS and State education have deteriorated through economic cutbacks rather than on intrinsic merits being seen to exist in the private sector. Although the general public may not be supporters of government intervention in the form of nationalisation of industry, they do believe in government intervention in the shape of the Welfare State. Numerous academic studies of public opinion show that only a very small minority want reduced welfare services whilst a majority want more public spending to combat poverty.

Conservative 'wets' have argued that the Welfare State is a thoroughly Conservative institution and, in response to public anxiety over government policies, the radical Right in 1983 seemed to have abandoned the aggressive approach which it was adopting towards the Welfare State in 1979. Indeed, the government was embarrassed when a Central Policy Review Staff report was leaked to the Press prior to the 1983 General Election. The Think-Tank's report concluded that if the economy failed to grow in the years ahead, then Britain could no longer afford a Welfare State. In other words, the Welfare State as we know it would have to be dismantled. The report included examples of how individuals and families might have to pay directly for their welfare services – it was calculated that a family of four would have to pay £600 a year in health insurance and £950 a year for each child's school fees.

The political problems in reducing welfare were revealed in the area of social security. The Secretary of State for Social Services presented what he believed would be 'the most sweeping social security reforms in the forty years since Beveridge'. Yet the White Paper (1985) was far less radical than the controversial Green Paper which preceded it. For example, the Green Paper contained proposals to scrap the State earnings-related pension scheme (SERPS) which provides increased pensions for people, generally the less well-off, who are not in occupational pension schemes. In the face of much opposition, the government retained SERPS in a slimmed-down version which saved a relatively small sum by the far distant year 2033. This was done by linking SERPS benefits to 'all-life earnings' and not the 'best twenty years' earnings as previously. This sort of compromise flavoured the Fowler Review, with payments to clients being rationalised and small savings being made, particularly in the area of housing benefits. In spite of the Minister's initial bold claim that he was intending to implement sweeping reforms, the Fowler Review eventually resulted in modest changes. Certainly the Fowler Review was a far cry from the radical thinking of the Think-Tank.

The relationship between Britain's economic performance and social policy has been the subject of a study by Treasury economists, which was leaked in 1983. The dilemma for the Chancellor is that monetarist-related policies may be appropriate for reducing inflation but they are not the policies which immediately stimulate high levels of economic growth.

Figure 17.2 shows that Britain's economy requires at least consistent moderate growth in order to support a viable Welfare State. The Treasury's first scenario was based on steady economic growth of 2.5 per cent a year until 1990. Unemployment would then fall to around 2 million, which would reduce social security costs and increase revenue from taxation. Public spending would fall to take up 39.3 per cent of total national output. The second scenario shown in the graph is the pessimistic one based on the

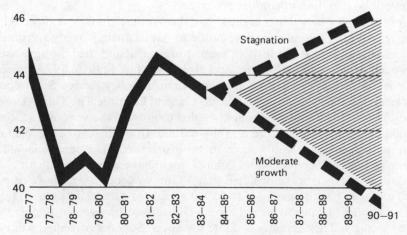

FIGURE 17.2   *Public spending as a percentage of national output*

assumption that there will be very little economic growth and that the economy will stagnate until 1990. Under these circumstances, public spending would rise to take up 46.8 per cent of the national wealth. This would mean that either taxes would have to rise sharply in order to pay for the higher public spending or politically difficult decisions would have to be made about substantial cuts in the Welfare State.

In fact, the performance of the British economy improved after the recession between 1979 and 1981 during which national output had fallen sharply. The economy began to pick up in 1982 and sustained a promising growth rate thereafter, faltering slightly in 1986. Within the economy, the manufacturing sector recovered only slowly and did not exceed its 1979 peak level until 1987.

Many economists argue that the economy as a whole improved because the Chancellor did a U-turn and abandoned monetarist policies. Indeed, the Chancellor was castigated by members of the Treasury Select Committee in 1985 because, in their view, economic policy had 'obviously changed' and they argued that he should admit to this. There were clear indications that the Chancellor had abandoned control of the money supply and had increased considerably the total public spending bill. These measures helped to fuel a huge consumer boom. Retail spending in shops increased by nearly 25 per cent in real terms between 1979 and 1986, and in 1986 was growing twice as fast as the economy as a whole. The growth of credit and higher social spending, it was argued, marked the end of the monetarist experiment in Britain. Furthermore, it was argued that improvements in the economy stemmed from the abandonment of monetarist policies.

Economists point to numerous dangers – many of them in the world economy and beyond British influence – which could still throw economic growth off course and cause problems in financing the Welfare State. Amongst the greatest of these is declining revenue from North Sea oil. Earnings received as royalties from North Sea oil are an important source of revenue for the government. If the price of oil drops on the world market, or if oil reserves are depleted faster than anticipated, then a number of complex economic consequences may be triggered off. In addition to the government losing revenue, Britain could experience balance-of-payments problems and be forced into adopting the deflationary policies characteristic of the 1960s.

ALTERNATIVE STRATEGIES

According to Conservative rhetoric, public spending gobbles up resources which would otherwise be invested in the private sector of the economy. Many Conservatives argue that if the Chancellor could reduce public spending he would release money which would help the private sector to expand and prosper. The opposition parties do not accept this view of public spending 'crowding out' private investment. In fact, Labour believes that public money spent on new jobs, new buildings and new school books actually helps the private sector to prosper. For example, a new school built with public money will increase the demand for bricks, cement and glass, and so will mean more work and prosperity for the men who produce building materials. Unemployed building workers will leave the dole queues to construct the school. They will now take home more money which they will spend buying more goods which, in turn, will give more people work manufacturing them.

Labour has dismissed the government's huge privatisation policy as irrelevant to the problems facing a de-industrialising economy. It is true that Britain has experienced problems with its manufacturing industries. These can be conveyed in a number of simple statistics. In 1980 Britain exported £5.5bn more manufactured goods than were imported; by 1984, Britain was importing £4bn more manufactured goods than were being exported. The quantity of goods being manufactured, rather than their value, shows the extent of de-industrialisation in a dramatic way. In 1973, Britain made 1 747 000 cars; in 1984, Britain made 908 000 cars. In 1973, Britain manufactured 7183m bricks a month; in 1984, 4008m a month. In 1973, Britain manufactured 731 000 tonnes of man-made fibre; in 1984, 383 000 tonnes. The *House of Lords Select Committee on Overseas Trade* published a highly controversial report in 1985 which concluded that Britain's poor industrial prospects posed 'a grave threat to the standard of living and to the economic and political stability of the nation'.

The Report argued that unless policies were changed, even more manufacturing industries would disappear in the future. In addition it was argued that national output would get smaller since no other non-manufacturing indus-

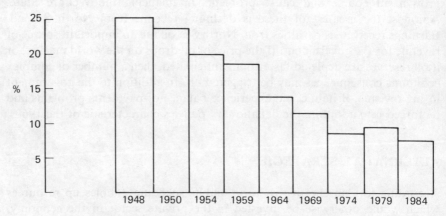

Source: Adapted from data given in House of Lords Select Committee *Report on Overseas Trade*, London, HMSO, 1985

FIGURE 17.3   *Britain's declining share of world manufacturing exports*

tries such as banking or entertainment would expand to fill the gap in the nation's wealth caused by the collapse of manufacturing; that very high levels of unemployment would become a permanent feature of the British economy; that fewer firms and fewer people in jobs would result in the government collecting less tax so that drastic real cuts would have to be made in public spending; and that as the economy stagnated and North Sea oil ran out, so the value of sterling would fall, causing the cost of imported raw materials to rise, with consequent high inflation.

Labour's solution to Britain's 'de-developing' economy, in which the value of new investment each year is less than the depreciation of the old investment it is replacing, lies with its policies of social ownership. Labour has rethought the role of nationalisation in the economy and replaced it with the more flexible concept of social ownership. The most important ingredients of Labour's social ownership proposals are the creation of British Enterprise, a body similar to the last Labour government's National Enterprise Board, and the setting-up of a National Investment Bank. Labour would no longer rely on nationalisation as a way of sustaining jobs in 'lame duck' industries, but would use the National Investment Bank to invest directly in the creation of new jobs. The National Investment Bank would offer long-term investment to industry, but would be funded by private financial institutions, not by the Treasury. A Labour government would require the pension funds, insurance companies and investment trusts to invest at least 10 per cent of their assets in Britain, rather than invest abroad and thereby 'export' jobs. The institutions would receive the current rate of interest on their investments in the National Investment Bank. Labour would also reduce the outflow of investment funds from Britain which has been taking place since currency regulations were abolished in 1979, and would require the financial institutions to repatriate much of the foreign investment made since that year.

Labour leaders argue that social ownership policies would regenerate Britain's economy, particularly the ailing manufacturing sector, and make considerable inroads on unemployment. From this improved economic base, Labour would increase the provision of welfare services with particular attention being given to improvements within pensions, housing and the NHS.

SUMMARY

The ideology behind the government's thinking on economic policy is one which favours individual responsibility for welfare above collectivist provision by the State. Although strict monetarism has been abandoned by the government, there still remain policies in which the Chancellor gives tax-cuts a higher priority than increases in public spending. Alongside this, the government has

encouraged privatisation in its many forms including the contracting-out of previously State-funded services as well as greater use of private welfare services. Economists disagree on the exact state of health of the British economy, but if those who argue that de-industrialisation has rendered it weak are correct, then the Welfare State is vulnerable to yet more financial cuts.

FURTHER READING

Congdon, T. (1978) *Monetarism*, London, Centre for Policy Studies.
Gamble, A. (1985) *Britain in Decline: Economic Policy, Political Strategy and the British State*, London, Macmillan, 2nd edn.
Keegan, W. (1984) *Mrs Thatcher's Economic Experiment*, Harmondsworth, Penguin.
Kirby, S. (1987) 'The Politics of the Mixed Economy', in L. Robins (ed.) *Politics and Policy Making in Britain*, London, Longman.
Stewart, M: (1977) *The Jekyll and Hyde Years: Politics and Economic Policy since 1964*, London, Dent.

QUESTIONS

1. Explain the different ideological approaches which exist within the different parties towards the provision of welfare.

2. 'Monetarism is dead in Britain.' Can this statement be justified?

3. 'It's an irony that the very time when a country needs a Welfare State most it cannot afford to provide one.' How true is this statement regarding Britain?

ASSIGNMENT

Study the following newspaper article, in conjunction with the section dealing with health in Chapter 17. Write a short speech attacking the 'decline of NHS treatment' and another defending the 'outstanding record' of the NHS in terms of resources which are devoted to health care.

CANCER CHILDREN MAY DIE 'BECAUSE OF SLIMLINE NHS'

By Nicholas Timmins
Health Services Correspondent

Rapid advances in treatment for childhood heart defects, kidney disease, cystic fibrosis, childhood cancer and others are threatened by the new 'slimline' National Health Service.

Child cancer specialists said yesterday that the NHS does not have the cash to pick up services as they move from the research stage to standard treatments.

'There are many specialities growing like topsy, which started out as research programmes and were quite properly funded by research monies,' Cliff Bailey, consultant child cancer specialist at St James's Hospital, Leeds, said.

'In the old days there was enough fat in the system to allow them to be absorbed as they moved from research to service. But in the new slimline health service there is no fat in the system. They can no longer be absorbed because the service no longer has the money to pick up the bill.'

If the NHS ignored such developments 'we are going to get a progressively inferior service, not just for children with cancer but right across the board'.

Dr Bailey was speaking at the launch of a report warning that advances in treatment have outstripped resources to the point where some children who could be cured may soon die.

The report, from all 19 UK centres specialising in childhood cancer, calls for the Department of Health to recognise and fund the service as a regional speciality. It gives a warning that treatment for children with other illnesses is being compromised by the demands childhood cancer, which can now be cured in 60 per cent of cases, is putting on paediatric wards.

The report has been endorsed by the Royal College of Physicians, and the Department of Health said yesterday that it would be considered by the Government's Standing Medical Advisory Committee next month.

Lack of day care and outpatient facilities in Newcastle meant children with cancer were having to sit on bean bags for blood transfusions, or others had to give up their bed for the day to allow cytotoxic drugs or transfusions to be given, Alan Craft, consultant paediatrician at the Royal Victoria Infirmary, said.

In Leeds, the services for children with less serious illnesses, such as asthma, diabetes and chest infections, were suffering because of the pressure the child cancer service put on beds, Dr Bailey said.

Many junior doctor posts, some senior posts, and 22 out of 28 social workers specialising in child cancer were existing on charitable and research monies, the doctors said.

But the research charities were becoming understandably reluctant to fund NHS service work, according to Dr Judith Chessells, chairman of the UK Children's Cancer Study Group.

In Newcastle, Dr Craft said, three out of his four junior doctors were on charitable money. 'It makes it very difficult to run the service not knowing whether you are going to get funding, and senior doctors spend considerable time raising money locally.'

Any further expansion at local level now had to be at the expense of something else. At about £1000 for each year of life saved, allowing children to become wage-earning adults, treatment was not only successful but cost-effective, he said.

Source: *The Independent*, 22 September 1987.

18

Education, Health and Housing

The Welfare State is an extremely complex set of organisations and structures providing services from 'the cradle to the grave'. Its very success can cause problems regarding its future development. Improved services can increase demand for those services and so drain resources. On the other hand, those who have benefited from opportunities provided by the Welfare State in the past may, with greater affluence, look at the private sector for future provision. This chapter considers the problems which became apparent in the 1970s and 1980s together with proposed remedies. It also examines how centralism and free market forces impinge upon decision-making in each issue-area.

HISTORICAL BACKGROUND

The Beveridge Report, published in 1942, identified 'five giant evils' which plagued British society but which could be eradicated by social and economic policies – want, squalor, disease, ignorance and idleness. After 1945, a fundamental consensus emerged between the major political parties on the pursuit of Keynesian economic policies and the construction of a Welfare State to combat these social evils. Central to this endeavour were education policy, the National Health Service and housing policy. As a consequence of the 1944 Education Act which was implemented by labour after 1947, schools were reorganised into an expanded national system which replaced elementary education with secondary education for all up to the age of 15. It was widely believed that giving all pupils equal educational opportunity would make it possible for everyone to fulfil his or her latent talents and, in benefiting individuals, society as a whole would also benefit. Whilst these developments were taking place in the education system, enormous changes were occurring in the areas of health care and housing. The world's first comprehensive national medical service was created in a far-reaching social experiment. The National Health Service which began in 1948 was formed to bring a uniform standard of health care to all citizens according to their needs and no matter what their income. In the area of housing, vast slum clearance programmes were completed and the once-overcrowded cities were rehoused in the course of the post-war house building boom. The rehoused population lived under circumstances of tenure which were very different from those existing at the end of the Second World War. For example, in 1945 only 12 per cent of households lived in council houses, with 62 per cent living in privately rented accommodation. By 1969 30 per cent of households lived in council houses with only 21 per cent remaining in the privately rented sector. During those years, owner-occupation also enjoyed a boom; the percentage of people living in 'homes of their own' rose from 26 per cent in 1945 to 49 per cent in 1969.

By the 1980s the optimism of the early post-war years had all but gone, with education, health and housing all facing severe crises. The political consensus had become shattered with the major political parties championing policies which were in the interests of distinct groups within the electorate. Labour is particularly concerned with the most deprived and disadvantaged sections of society and supports government intervention aimed at increasing individual freedom through creating a more equal society. Conservatives are concerned with increasing the liberty of as many individuals as possible and therefore they support the extension of market forces into more areas of life so as to widen freedom of choice. Of course 'liberty' has a very different meaning within Labour and Conservative philosophies, and it is this contested value that explains many of the policy differences which now separate them.

EDUCATION, POWER AND CHOICE

The twenty years after the late 1960s witnessed the disintegration of the post-war consensus on education. Right-wing critics attacked progressive education because they believed that it led to a reduction in standards. The Socialist and feminist Left attacked progressive education because under the surface it was seen as being conservative in nature and purpose, changing nothing. The political centre also attacked education with the most damning blow coming in 1976 when the Prime Minister, James Callaghan, suggested that educational standards were falling and that schools were failing to serve Britain as well as they might. The education system, which had enjoyed many years of public confidence, was now the subject of doubts and reservations in many minds. During the 1980s these feelings crystallised into real concern as the public-spending limits reduced the money available for teachers' salaries and the maintenance of school buildings and equipment. Prolonged industrial action by demoralised teachers during the mid-1980s over pay and the removal of the Burnham pay negotiating machinery caused considerable disruption in schools. A report from Her Majesty's Inspectors of schools in 1986 added to public concern over the state of education in England and Wales. The HMIs found that poor-quality teaching adversely affected the standard of work in 30 per cent of the lessons they observed but, almost as significant, poor classrooms and a lack of resources such as books badly affected 20 per cent of the lessons they saw. The bi-partisan consensus on comprehensive schools declined with the government's encouragement of market forces and parental choice as factors that should shape educational provision.

Increased centralised control

The Education Act 1944 established the informal partnership that would be responsible for major decisions about teaching and schools. The three power-blocs were:

(i)   central government in the shape of the Department of Education and Science (DES);
(ii) the local education authorities (LEAs);
(iii) the teachers' unions, especially the NUT.

The working of this partnership during the post-war decades has often been described as the 'mystique of English education'. Within this decision-making structure, the DES played a rather limited role. To a considerable extent, teachers were independent within their classrooms, being subject only to minimal external interference, and head teachers were free to run their schools as they saw fit. Classroom teachers and head teachers enjoyed professional autonomy. Ted Tapper and Brian Salter observe that

> Whole areas of the process of schooling were considered to be the special, almost the sole, responsibility of the teachers. This is particularly true of the curriculum that one Minister of Education was moved to describe as a 'secret garden' (Tapper and Salter, 'The Politics of Secondary Education', *Teaching Politics*, May, 1986, p. 207).

Agreement from all three power blocs in this relationship was necessary before any major development could take place. Control of education policy was essentially decentralised and the DES played a role which frequently seemed to build less influence than the other parties.

After 1970 the DES flexed its political muscles and moved from a position of relative marginality to one of considerable dominance. Throughout the 1970s the DES effectively redrew the tripartite partnership of the post-war years and weakened the position of the LEAs and teaching unions. The criticism that education had not met the needs of industry and had failed to generate economic growth led to demands for increased vocational education in schools. Reshaping educational goals in a vocational direction resulted in the Manpower Services Commission directly influencing the school curriculum. The MSC comes under the sponsorship of the Department of Trade and Industry, not the DES, but nevertheless the expanding influence of the MSC also represents a considerable centralisation of power within educational policy-making.

The growing power of the DES was seen in the debate concerning the *core curriculum* and *subject criteria*. The concept of a core curriculum necessarily involves powers to decide on what is to be taught being taken away from teachers and decided centrally. Indeed, some educationalists believe that the core curriculum together with national attainment testing will ultimately develop into a national centralised curriculum which will control what is taught in schools, how it is taught, and when it is taught. The weakening influence of the LEAs is evident in a number of areas. These include the establishment of city technology colleges by the DES, by-passing the LEAs, and the promise during the 1987 election campaign that schools could opt out from LEA control if the governors so wished. If implemented, this radical measure could lead to the break-up of the present education system and the end of local authority influence. The weakening in the position of teachers is seen in the increase of parental influence in the running of schools through increased representation on school governing bodies. Teachers have also been on the losing side in conflicts over negotiating rights; contracts will define teaching duties more precisely, with the possibility of further control being exercised over them in the shape of 'no strike' agreements. In short, the old triumvirate of DES, LEAs and NUT which marked the post-war decades has now passed into history and been replaced by a more centralised concentration of power in the educational decision-making system.

The growth of free market forces?

On the face of it, there appears to be a contradiction in arguing that there has been a centralisation of decision-making power within the educational system whilst at the same time saying that there has been an attempt to introduce market forces to education. In some ways it is the contradiction locked into Mrs Thatcher's once-stated priorities of 'less taxation: more law and order' which is also found in the Whitehall-controlled yet privatised area of local government. Within education the contradiction has been resolved to some extent through pursuing the different goals at distinct 'operational' and 'aspiration' levels. In other words, actual policy has involved centralisation whilst rhetoric and speeches have focused on free market intentions.

The most obvious working of the free market is found in the existence of the private sector in education. Table 18.1 shows the class background of pupils in independent (i.e. private) and maintained (i.e. public sector) schools. Private schools have increased in popularity during the years of the Thatcher governments, with a greater share (about 7 per cent in 1988) of the overall school population being taught in independent schools. This increase is disguised by the fact that there has been a large decline in the school population, but while there was a 13.8 per cent drop in the total of all school-age children between 1976 and 1984, independent schools lost only 4.3 per cent of their pupils.

TABLE 18.1
Class background of pupils based on fathers' occupations

Social class	Independent schools %	Maintained schools %
Upper middle/middle	72	23
Lower middle	9	11
Skilled/unskilled manual	17	65
Unclassified	2	1

Source: T. Tapper, 'Legitimating Independent Schooling', *Teaching Politics*, vol. 13, no. 1, 1984.

Many Conservatives, particularly on the right of the party, are attracted by schemes and changes which make the education system 'a market' through increasing the element of choice available. The assisted places scheme is seen as providing parents of academically able children with a choice of remaining in the maintained sector or transferring to the independent sector. More choice has been given to parents – in the form of parent-governors – in deciding how schools should be run. Through representation parents have more say in what is taught and who is appointed to the schools attended by their children. It is assumed by educationists that increased parental power and choice will exert a conservative influence on schools, particularly in controversial areas such as race education, peace education and sex education.

From time to time the idea of a voucher scheme is raised as a method which would increase parental choice and introduce free market forces to the school system. The idea involves every child receiving education vouchers which parents would be able to 'spend' by sending children to schools of their choice in either the maintained or independent sector. If the latter was chosen, then parents might have to add private money to the voucher in order to meet school fees. But the essence of the scheme is that popular schools would prosper, with unpopular schools having either to improve their reputations or to face the prospect of withering away.

Many Conservatives see individual freedom as best promoted by the expansion of the market, which guarantees liberty to the individual to choose as he or she wants. In other words, they believe that competition maximises the freedom of each individual to satisfy his or her needs. Thus, the more parental choice there is within and between schools, the greater is individual freedom within education.

Labour's philosophy does not accept that individual freedom is guaranteed by the free market at work because not everyone has sufficient money to exercise choice. It is argued that when a 'freedom' is confined to a restricted number of people it becomes a 'privilege'. Freedom is indivisible and not something that can meaningfully be exercised by minorities. For example, everyone is free to buy a Rolls Royce in the sense that there are no restrictions on purchasing one if you have enough money. But, Labour would argue, since most people will never have the huge sums of money necessary, they are not in any real sense free to buy one. Labour contends that the freedom to buy a Rolls, like other Conservative freedoms, only applies to the better-off in society. Labour's concept of freedom is based on redistributing wealth and creating a more equal society which gives more people the opportunity to exercise more choices.

Stemming from this view that a fairer society maximises freedom, Labour supports higher government spending on comprehensive forms of education. Thus the party is not sympathetic to education in independent schools outside the maintained sector, nor does it support selection within the maintained school sector. Labour believes that selection is divisive in education and a Labour Education Minister, Anthony Crossland, issued the now famous Circular 10/65 which invited LEAs to submit plans for reorganising secondary schools into a comprehensive system. Twenty years later, of those pupils in maintained secondary schools, only 10.5 per cent were not in comprehensives.

HEALTH CARE

Rival political claims about the state of the NHS are often less contradictory than they first appear. On the positive side, the NHS employs more staff than at any previous time, with a 10 per cent increase in doctors, nurses, midwives and dentists; a 22 per cent increase in technical staff, and a 6 per cent increase in administrative staff between 1975 and 1984 alone. The NHS now employs over 1 million people, and, in Europe, is second only to the Red Army as an employer. Between 1974 and 1986 the number of patients treated by the NHS rose by a quarter, yet the NHS is said to be in a state of crisis. This is because, on the negative side, Britain gets its comprehensive medical service 'on the cheap' spending less of its GDP on health care, including private medicine, than any other Western country (See Figures 18.1 and 18.2). Between 1975 and 1985, many hospital wards were closed with a consequent loss of 66 000 hospital beds and waiting lists that grew by 20 per cent. How can it be that the devotion of more and more resources to the NHS has gone hand-in-hand with a mounting crisis (see Figure 18.2)?

Some of the reasons for the NHS's problems lie in its enormous success. For example, improved treatment has resulted in an increasing number of old people surviving illnesses that once would have proved fatal, and care for older people costs more; care for a patient aged 75 or over costs more than six times as much as that for a patient of working age. Because Britain has an ageing population, the NHS needs an extra 2 per cent a year in resources just

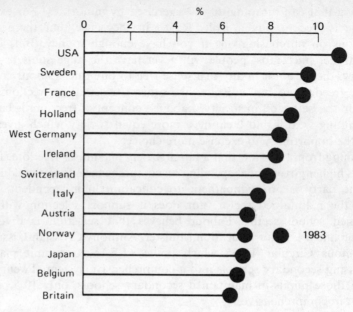

Source: *The Economist*, 31 May 1986

FIGURE 18.1   *Total health-care spending as percentage of GDP*

to keep pace with the growing demand from the elderly. Also, advances in medical technology now provide expensive cures which keep alive patients who would at one time have died. Furthermore, new technology and treatments have actually stimulated consumer demand and are now sought by people who once would have endured illness without expecting to be cured because either the services were restricted or the technology was not available.

The major political parties adopt rather different approaches to the 'big spending' National Health Service which is funded overwhelmingly by the Treasury. Labour's solution to the NHS crisis lies in devoting more resources to health care, viewing it as a form of investment in people. Conservatives have been trapped on health care, with monetarist instincts calling for less to be spent on the NHS but political instincts realising that the NHS is popular and hence reassurances being given that 'the NHS is safe with the Tories'. As a result, the Conservative approach has been to strive for greater managerial efficiency, increased privatisation and private health care, and savings on the NHS's drugs bill.

The NHS was reorganised in 1974 in a way which was designed to bring the service under greater centralised control but which, in the event, was counter-productive and created greater bureaucracy. A further reorganisation took place in 1982 when Area Health Authorities were replaced by more

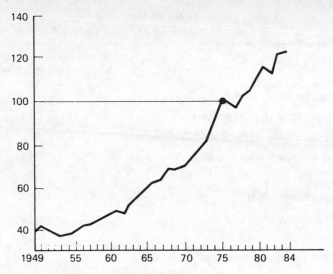

Source: *The Economist*, 31 May 1986.

FIGURE 18.2 *Spending on the NHS (per head, in real terms: 1975 = 100)*

numerous District Health Authorities, with the aim of increasing managerial efficiency through matching the services provided more closely to local needs. Consistent with the view of private sector efficiency many back-up services in the NHS such as catering, laundry and cleaning have been contracted out, resulting in a 14 per cent drop in the number of ancillary workers between 1979 and 1986. Since 1979 Conservative governments have encouraged the expansion of private health care as a means of taking the strain off the NHS. In 1984 private care accounted for 7 per cent of all hospital-based treatment. Finally, savings were planned by allowing doctors to prescribe mainly generic drugs from a restricted list rather than the same drug sold more expensively under a brand name.

Inequalities in health care

Health and illness are linked to occupational class. Table 18.2 shows the relationship between different occupations and death rates, and it can be seen that certain groups of unskilled workers are two-and-a-half times as likely to die between the ages of 15 and 64 as some groups of professional workers. In 1986 official statistics revealed that the class-linked health gap had widened since 1979 with death and disease continuing to rise along with poverty and unemployment. The report, *Occupational Mortality*, revealed that women married to men in social classes IV and V are up to 70 per cent more likely to die young than are wives of men in classes I and II. There are no straightforward or simple explanations for this relationship; obviously

TABLE 18.2
Death Rate: Men aged 15–64 – by Occupation

	Direct age-standardised death rate per 100 000
University teachers	287
Managers in building and contracting	319
Ministers of the Crown, MPs, Senior Civil Servants	371
Primary and secondary school teachers	396
Postmen	484
Coal miners (underground)	822
Coal miners (above ground)	972
Fishermen	1028
Labourers and unskilled workers, all industries	1247
Bricklayers' labourers	1644
Electrical engineers	1904

Source: Adapted from Judy Allsop, *Health Policy and the National Health Service* (1984), p. 161.

poorer people may be more susceptible to disease because of low incomes and poorer diets or because many working-class jobs are more dangerous. But when health care services exist why do lower classes use them less? It seems that the cost of using the NHS varies according to social class; for example, many manual workers have their pay docked for the time they are absent from work receiving medical treatment whilst for middle-class occupations this is rarely the case. Thus manual workers are discouraged from seeking treatment in a way that professional employees are not.

On an individual basis the poor, who need health care most, use the NHS less than the affluent, who need health care least. This unequal distribution of NHS resources amongst the different social classes has been described as an 'inverse care law'. It is reflected in regional inequalities between the 'affluent South' and 'poor North' with, for example, one doctor for every 2198 people in the North and one for every 1934 in South West Thames and every 1825 in North West Thames.

Political influence in the NHS

A number of studies have analysed the NHS as an organisation in order to establish how decisions are made at a variety of levels. Is the NHS a pluralist organisation, in which power is distributed amongst doctors, consultants, nurses, health service administrators, ancillary staff, the public, not to mention the Minister and the DHSS, with no single group having sufficient power to dominate the rest? Or does the NHS have an élitist power structure in which one powerful group dominates all others?

The National Health Service Act became law in 1946 and the NHS came into existence in 1948. From the very outset it was clear that senior doctors had to be 'bought off' by the Minister of Health, Aneurin Bevan, with the consultants, in particular, entering the health service on their own terms. It was agreed from the outset, for example, that private 'pay-beds' could exist in NHS hospitals. In 1976 the trade unions representing low-paid ancillary workers challenged this situation, and argued that pay-beds represented private privilege and had no place within an egalitarian health service. The Labour government agreed to phase out pay-beds, but met strong opposition from the doctors. Doctors were able to block government intentions until 1979 when the newly-elected Conservative government made it clear that it favoured closer cooperation between the NHS and the private sector, including the continued existence of pay-beds.

The élitist model, then, in which the interests of a powerful body of doctors are served to the near exclusion of other groups presents what is probably a more plausible account than the pluralist view of the NHS. This is so if only because the other major group which might wield influence on size alone – the nurses – is split between membership of ideologically differing bodies such as the Royal College of Nursing, and trade unions such as the Confederation of Health Service Employees and the National Union of Public Employees. The élitist model may also help to explain other aspects of NHS operation, such as the concentration of resources in high-prestige areas of medical care at the expense of the low-prestige 'Cinderella' services of geriatric care and mental illness.

HOUSING POLICY

The quality of housing is frequently linked with other aspects of social behaviour, such as educability or social stability. For example, in education it has long been noted that those children who do least well at school tend to come from families housed in substandard dwellings. Thus an improvement in educational attainment would appear to depend in part on an improvement in housing standards. Yet, far from housing standards going up, Britain appears to be in the middle of a housing crisis. In 1986, 14 000 families were in temporary council accommodation; twenty years before, the comparable figure was 2500 in temporary accommodation. In 1986, over 100 000 families were officially homeless at some time during the year, with an incalculable number of individuals sleeping rough, literally without a roof over their heads.

Why are there not enough homes to house Britain's population? Figures

18.3 and 18.4 show that, although there are over 20 million dwellings in Britain, the rate of new house buildings has slowed down dramatically. For example, during the 1950s, around 300 000 new houses a year were built, and 400 000 a year during the 1960s; but the 1980s have averaged less than 200 000 a year. The housing situation is worsened by two other aspects of housing decay amongst the existing stock. Many of the council houses built during the 1920s and 1930s have deteriorated and are in need of modernisation. At the same time, much of the council housing of the 1960s, particularly high-rise blocks of flats and experimental system-built houses, is in need of major structural repair resulting from poor design, poor workmanship and the use of low-quality building materials. A report from the Department of the Environment in 1985 revealed that it would cost £19 bn to repair council housing alone. If all substandard dwellings in both public and private sectors were repaired, the Institute of Housing calculated (also in 1985) that the total bill would be an enormous £40 bn.

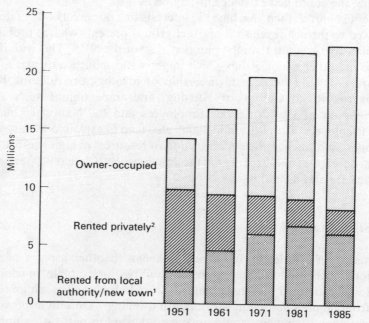

1　Estimates of stock in England are based on the 1971 and 1981 Censuses. Estimates for Wales and Scotland prior to 1981 are based on the 1971 and earlier Censuses. Estimates for Northern Ireland are largely based on rates returns and are subject to revision.
2　Includes housing associations and dwellings rented with farm or business premises, and those occupied by virtue of employment.

Source: *Department of the Environment*, reprinted in *Social Trends*, 17, 1987.

FIGURE 18.3　*Stock of dwellings: by tenure.*

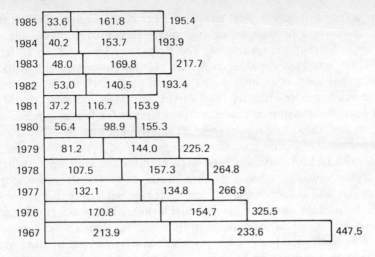

1985	33.6	161.8	195.4
1984	40.2	153.7	193.9
1983	48.0	169.8	217.7
1982	53.0	140.5	193.4
1981	37.2	116.7	153.9
1980	56.4	98.9	155.3
1979	81.2	144.0	225.2
1978	107.5	157.3	264.8
1977	132.1	134.8	266.9
1976	170.8	154.7	325.5
1967	213.9	233.6	447.5

Source: Adapted from C. Smallwood, 'Why We Need a Building Boom', *Sunday Times*, 10 August 1986

FIGURE 18.4 *Numbers of houses built per year 1976–85 compared with 1967.*

In the mid-1960s, a BBC docu-drama *Cathy Come Home* recounted in a harrowing way the break-up of a family because of homelessness. The programme provoked great public indignation that such harsh realities could exist for British citizens. But in many ways the situation became far worse in the 1980s, and yet no public outcry about the housing crisis occurred. The answer to this probably lies in the fact that the crisis was 'hidden' because attention had been diverted to other housing issues such as council-house sales, property prices in London and the South, and mortgage interest rates. Also, there tends to be a lack of public sympathy for the poor and the homeless, until people are confronted directly with the human consequences as in *Cathy Come Home*. In abstract terms, there is wide public recourse to an image of 'scroungers' who are too lazy to find work and who are subsidised by the State in their welfare and housing. As they are frequently encouraged by the tabloid press to think like this, it is of little wonder that people are inclined to see the homeless as undeserving. Finally, the housing crisis remains hidden because the victims, in circumstances of poverty or homelessness, lack the very resources necessary for them to take effective political action.

Peter Malpass and Alan Murie, in *Housing Policy and Practice* (1982) have pointed out that, despite being part of welfare provision, housing policy is different from other aspects of social policy such as education or health. This is because nearly all the population (93 per cent) turn first to the state-run National Health Service when they are sick, and nearly all parents (93 per cent) send their children to State-maintained schools for their education. Yet when it comes to housing most people (62 per cent in England) turn to the private sector and become owner-occupiers. Ray Forrest has made some interesting observations on this in 'The Politics of Housing', in L. Robins (ed.) *Politics and Policy-making in Britain* (1987). He urges some caution in assuming that there is an intrinsic or natural preference for owner-occupation. He acknowledges that by 1984 survey responses indicated that 77 per cent of households sampled expressed a preference for home-ownership, but he argues that these findings have to be interpreted against a backcloth of social, political and economic factors prevailing at a particular time. For example, the lack of private rented accommodation, long waiting-lists for public sector housing, or being allocated a run-down property or unpopular high-rise flat will influence the preference for owner-occupation. If it were possible to present an alternative of highly available, good condition and attractively-designed houses in the public sector, then owner-occupation would in all likelihood become less popular. Also, owner-occupation may be made more or less attractive by government policy regarding tax concessions on mortgage relief or discounts on the price of council houses. The sums involved are substantial and provide an attractive incentive to home-ownership. For example, in 1985–6 the estimated cost of the mortgage relief tax concession was £4.7 bn. Council tenants were also encouraged to buy their homes which were offered at a discount on market value, rising to 60 per cent for long-term tenants.

Privatising the public sector

Council housing is an area of government activity which has felt the full impact of monetarist-inspired policies. Whilst other areas of public spending such as health, education, social security, law and order and defence have increased in real terms during the Thatcher years, housing has experienced a massive cut-back in spending. Housing has moved from being a major spending programme in 1979 to a minor one a decade later. Expenditure has fallen in real terms from £6.6 bn in 1979/80 to £3 bn in 1983–4 with a further planned reduction to £2.4 bn in 1988–9, representing an overall reduction of 64 per cent in ten years. There is, however, an element of illusion in these statistics since some money previously in the housing budget has been transferred across to the social security budget. But despite this change in government accounting, the net result is a downward movement in spending.

   The sale of council houses has represented one of the most ambitious privatisation measures undertaken by the Conservatives. Forrest states that 'for the Conservative Party it was seen as a route to a more equitable distribution of wealth, a means of producing a "better" social mix on council estates and the most significant and effective contribution towards a property-owning democracy . . . The sale of British Telecom or British Gas may have made headline news but it is the sale of council houses which has been the single most important sale of public assets carried out since 1979' (R. Forrest, *The Politics of Housing*, p. 77). The market value of council houses sold between 1979 and 1984 was over £11 bn. After allowing for the discounts to be deducted, the sales netted £6.4 bn.

The revenue received from the sale of council houses has been used to finance new house-building and other housing benefits such as rehabilitation grants for private owners. But councils are only allowed to reinvest a proportion (initially 50 per cent but later reduced to 20 per cent) of their receipts from house sales in new building. Thus, much of the money made from council house sales is locked up by Treasury controls on capital spending. From the government's point of view, the sales have made council-house building substantially self-financing and thus reduced demands on the PSBR. It is probably valid to argue that without the receipts from council-house sales new council-house building would have been even harder hit. The problem could still become acute if the sales of council houses were to slow down in the future, thereby causing a reduction in revenue. New initiatives from the government to maintain the momentum of council house privatisa-tion include a change of emphasis from selling single houses to individual tenants to the large-scale transfer of entire estates to new private landlords. Tenants – already the 'losers' in the housing situation – are likely to find themselves further disadvantaged insofar as councils have been given the power to evict tenants so that their homes may be sold. There is no evidence to show that council tenants support the sale of the roofs above their heads which makes them into private tenants.

Labour responses

Part of Labour's vision of a fairer society is the right of all citizens to a decent home, and Labour sees the local authorities playing a major role in providing this. Labour has opposed the cut-back in the housing programme, particu-larly the slow-down in new building. But to some extent Labour is the victim of an unpopular image in the area of council housing, despite being its champion. To many people, Labour is associated with the repression of tenants' individuality, resulting in drab and uniform estates. Compared with the Conservatives who appear to want to give tenants choice, Labour is seen as the party of petty restrictions, not allowing people to do this or that.

Labour was caught off-guard by the popularity of selling council houses to sitting tenants. Although council houses have been sold off since the 1920s, Labour was unprepared for the massive acceleration in sales and the immediate response of the party was to oppose privatisation. After delibe-ration, Labour changed its policy to one of supporting the right of council tenants to buy their homes (with the exception of some inner-city tenants who would be offered grants to buy from the private sector rather than have the right-to-buy in the public sector). In presenting this major change in housing policy, Jeff Rooker argued that 'there is nothing particularly socialist about public landlordism on a grand scale . . . Socialism comes from letting people choose'. With hindsight, Labour leaders agreed that the party's initial opposition to council house sales was wrong and simply reinforced Labour's repressive image in many people's minds. It was agreed that from the outset Labour's policy should have been directed towards making it easier for all tenants to buy houses in both the public and the private sectors, and not towards making it harder for council tenants to buy.

An interesting problem for social administrators is that middle-class clientele use welfare provision more successfully than do working-class clients. The growth of free-market forces which has occurred over recent years may threaten the already disadvantaged with yet more disadvantage – educationalists are worried that market forces in schooling will result in the development of inferior inner-city 'sink' schools; in health, market forces could turn the NHS into a second-rate service for the poor; and in housing, market forces could result in the poorest members of society being herded into the most undesirable properties which have very low resale values.

SUMMARY

The post-war Welfare State based on the principle of state provision of health and educational services 'free' at the point of receipt came under increasing strain after 1970. The strains were perceived in terms both of excessive claims on public resources as the economy faltered and of inadequate quality of service. To some extent, problems arose as a consequence of success – of the NHS, for example, in keeping people alive longer and in developing new technologies and remedies. The responses of Conservative Administrations in the 1980s focused on tight control of public expenditure; the encouragement of private provision in schooling and health care; council-house sales; more effective management of services; and a national curriculum. Conservative unleashing of market forces in some areas was strongly criticised by experts and the opposition parties.

FURTHER READING

Allsop, J. (1984) *Health Policy and the National Health Service*, London, Longman.
Fraser, D. (1984) *The Evolution of the British Welfare State*, London, Macmillan.
Klein, R. (1983) *The Politics of the National Health Service*, London, Longman.
Malpass, P. and Murie, A. (1987) *Housing Policy and Practice*, London, Macmillan, 2nd edn.
Robins, L. (ed.) (1987) *Politics and Policy Making in Britain*, London, Longman.
Salter, B. and Tapper, T. (1981) *Education, Politics and the State*, London, Grant McIntyre.
Short, J. (1982) *Housing in Britain*, London, Methuen.

Simon, B. and Taylor, W. (eds) (1981) *Education in the 1980s: The Central Issues*, London, Batsford.

QUESTIONS

1. Socialism comes from letting people choose.' If this is the case how does socialism differ from Thatcherism?
2. 'Analyse recent changes in the power structure of educational decision-making and describe the impact of such changes.
3. Assess the impact of privatisation policies on either (i) health care, or (ii) housing.

ASSIGNMENT

How schools make the selection

MORE than 5,500 places are available each year on the assisted places scheme. The normal entry age is 11 or 13, but there are places at sixth-form level. Sixty per cent of places have to go to pupils previously state-educated, but the rest are open to privately educated children. In practice, many schools offer a majority of places to state school pupils.

The selection of pupils is made by schools and most expect applicants to take an entrance test, and probably attend interviews. Selection arrangements and closing dates vary with each school. A list of participating schools is available from the Department of Education and Science, Room 3/65, Elizabeth House, York Road, London SE1 7PH. Telephone 01-934 9211/9. Assistance with tuition fees is available on a sliding scale. Some families will be eligible for other expenses. Relevant income is the total of all income before tax from both parents and any unearned income of dependent children, less an allowance of £950 for each dependent child other than the assisted placeholder. Assistance is reviewed annually.

Relevant income 1986-87 tax year (after allowances) for dependants) £	Parents' Contribution to fees: 1987-88 school year	
	One assisted place holder £	For each of two assisted place holders £
6,973	15	9
8,000	123	93
9,000	273	204
10,000	471	354
11,000	681	510
12,000	921	690
13,000	1,161	870
14,000	1,449	1,086
15,000	1,779	1,335
16,000	2,109*	1,581

* The maximum relevant income at which pupils will be eligible for assistance will vary in relation to schools' fees. In many schools the fees will not be as high as this and where this is so parents at this level of income will be ineligible for assistance.

Source: *The Independent*, 10 September 1987

The government's assisted places scheme is designed to help bright children from lower-income families to attend independent schools. The extract above shows the parental contribution at various income levels. Consider the political principles involved and attempt to:

(i)   draft a letter to the Labour Shadow Minister of Education urging that Labour should support the assisted places scheme,

(ii)   draft a letter to the Conservative Secretary of State for Education urging that the scheme should be wound up since it contradicts certain Tory ideas.

Circulate your draft letters and attempt to assess which are the most persuasive in their arguments. Discuss how far it is possible to use the same political principles either to support or oppose a particular policy.

19

Wealth and Poverty

Some critics of capitalism argue that it is an economic system which creates problems that it cannot solve. The central problem according to them is that capitalism generates huge differences in wealth between the richest and poorest members of society. Should the state 'humanise' capitalism and redistribute wealth from the rich to the poor? Or should enterprise be rewarded, with very large incomes acting as incentives for successful entrepreneurial effort?

THE DISTRIBUTION OF INCOME AND WEALTH

Inequality exists in all societies and politics has been described as the process by which it is decided 'who gets what, when and how'. The distribution of wealth and income amongst the population of Britain shows that a minority of individuals receive much more than the others. In terms of personal *wealth*, for example, the richest 1 per cent of the population own a quarter of all personal wealth, with the richest 5 per cent owning nearly a half of all personal wealth. In stark contrast, the poorer half of the country's population own only 5 per cent of all personal wealth. The pattern of inequality is repeated in the distribution of *income* of Britain; the richest 20 per cent of the population receive 38.8 per cent of all incomes, with the poorest 20 per cent receiving only 6.8 per cent. Inequality in income is not confined to the private sector, where private enterprise and the profit motive generates difference in reward. Table 19.1 contains details of annual increases and pay calculated on a weekly basis for individuals employed within the public sector following the controversial recommendations of the *Top Salaries Review Body* in 1985. What the head of the Civil Service received as a weekly *rise* is seven times the *total* weekly wage received by the lowest-paid council labourer.

Statistics sometimes fail to convey the meaning and consequences of income distribution as it affects Britain's population. Almost any edition of a newspaper will carry gossip stories of glamorous celebrities alongside news items about people who are suffering from numerous economic and social disadvantages. The *Sunday Times* (20 October 1985) carried a number of sober stories to illustrate the point. The business news supplement reported the results of a survey conducted by P. A. Personnel Services, which revealed that chairmen and chief executives of large companies were earning an

417

TABLE 19.1
Public sector pay awards 1985

Post	Rise p.a. %	Weekly rise £	Weekly pay £	Numbers
Head of Civil Service, Permanent Secretary to Treasury	46.3	457	1442	2
Admiral of the Fleet	46.3	457	1442	1
Lord Chief Justice	17.2	212	1442	1
Permanent Secretaries	31.2	279	1154	22
General, Admiral, etc.	31.2	279	1154	20
High Court Judge	17.1	168	1154	102
Under-Secretaries	5.1	29	596	490
Police	7.5	10–16	139–231	150 000
Teachers	7.0–10.5	11–13	114–195	500 000
Nurses	8.5–14.5	8–24	101–192	400 000
Town Hall staff	5.5–9.75	6–7	66–130	500 000
Council manuals	5.6–5.7	4	78–80	1 000 000

average annual income of £40 750. Once fringe benefits such as a car, petrol, pension, medical assurance and telephone were included, their incomes were worth an average of £54 447 a year. The gossip column carried more details on a Minister – a celebrated gourmet – who had resigned from office announcing that his £33 000 parliamentary salary was not sufficient to support his life-style. Finally, a feature article contributed by an American focused on the consequences of gradual economic decline in Britain. Against the backcloth of increasing shabbiness, mounting incidents of street violence and urban rioting, greater squalor and more drug-taking, a new unemployed 'underclass' had been created which is 'deprived, ill-educated, unhealthy, without hope'. Chairmen of big companies and members of the new underclass share citizenship in Britain, yet in terms of wealth, power and status they inhabit different worlds.

POVERTY IN BRITAIN

Despite taxes on wealth and progressive taxation on incomes, the late 1970s and 1980s saw a trend towards polarisation in which the rich were getting richer and the poor becoming poorer. For example, in the years between 1976 and 1980 the richest 20 per cent of the population received an extra 3.5 per cent in their share of income whereas the poorest 20 per cent became 10.5

per cent worse off in terms of their income share. The gap between rich and poor widened still further in the 1980s. One of the main reasons behind this trend is that unemployment has risen to an extremely high level; apart from the effect that this has on poverty as such, it also reduces the bargaining power of trade unions in wage negotiations.

Economic inequality, however, is not just a question of *relative* proportions of wealth and income divided amongst the population. In *absolute* terms, Britain's population is better off than it used to be. Poverty still exists in society, but the poor are better off than they were in the past. If ownership of consumer durables is taken as an indicator of affluence then many in Britain are well-off: over three-quarters of all households have telephones, over 60 per cent are centrally heated and over 96 per cent have fridges and televisions.

A paradox exists in Britain, for alongside this pattern of affluence is found considerable poverty. Currently, some 6m people are on, or below, the poverty line. Yet how do we calculate quality of life and decide on what 'poverty' is? The supplementary benefit level is usually taken as the official poverty line. Some disagree on this definition of poverty and argue that the official poverty line is set too low. If the yardstick for poverty is taken as having an income 50 per cent above the supplementary benefit level, then 18m people in Britain suffer from poverty.

The groups most vulnerable to poverty are pensioners, the unemployed, disabled people and one-parent families. A recent study showed that almost 90 per cent of one-parent families are headed by women, and that incomes to single-parent families were on average 45 per cent of those received by two-parent families. Pensioners experience a different set of problems; many suffer hardship in connection with the cost of heating and fuel.

However, some people in Britain who do not fit into any of these categories experience poverty; they are young, in work and frequently part of a two-parent family. Their economic hardship is caused because they earn low pay. Low pay is usually defined as two-thirds of average male earnings, and is broadly equivalent to supplementary benefit payments to a two-child family. The Low Pay Unit calculated in 1982 that over 30 per cent of the full-time adult work force could be deemed 'low paid' in terms of their basic wage; this included 1.9m men and 2.4m women. In 1984, the Low Pay Unit estimated that the number of full-time employed individuals receiving low pay had risen to 4.7m. Added to this were another 3.6m part-timers whose hourly earnings rate was two-thirds or less of average hourly rates. Of this total of 8.3m in the 'low-paid' category, 5.7m were women.

Many low-paid workers get caught in the poverty trap and find it very difficult to improve living standards. It is frequently the case that if a low-paid worker does overtime or receives a pay rise, his family ends up worse off. This occurs because some of the extra wage goes back to the Inland Revenue in the form of income tax, but, more critically, the increase in income might take the worker's wage above the level at which benefits are paid. When the wage increase is worth less than the total benefits which are lost, such as free school dinners, the worker's family is worse off.

There is also a geographical aspect to poverty since some parts of Britain experience much higher levels of economic hardship than others. Regional inequalities have become particularly obvious in the current recession with Scotland and the North suffering much worse than the 'rich' South-east. The most glaring example of regional inequality however, is provided by Northern Ireland.

GOVERNMENT AND THE REDISTRIBUTION OF WEALTH

Governments have a wide range of options and strategies open to them which redistribute income more evenly amongst the population. If unemployment is among the principal causes of poverty, the government is able to manage the economy in order to increase employment. Keynesian economics involves what is termed 'demand management' to stimulate the economy and cause it to grow. The economy is managed by the government so that the total demand is sufficient to utilise all the resources of the country including manpower. The government must be careful not to stimulate too much demand in the economy since that can cause inflation and attract too many goods into the country as imports. The government is able to use public spending as a tool to create demand; money spent on new roads, schools and housing can create new jobs throughout the economy. The mechanisms by which additional public expenditure works to increase employment are explained in Chapter 17.

Keynesian economic methods seemed unable to cope with the inflation of the mid-1970s which resulted from the energy crisis and the quadrupling of the price of oil. 'Stagflation' hit the economy as the rates of inflation and unemployment rose together. Control of inflation became the government's top priority and this was tackled by the Labour Government of 1974–9 by means of control of the money supply and an incomes policy. Monetarist discipline involved 'cash limits' being applied to government spending.

The Conservative Government which came to power in 1979 was much more committed to supply-side economics. This monetarist strategy involved strict control of the money supply, high interest rates and a reduction in public spending. Inflation fell sharply after 1981 but the deflationary effects of monetarism quickly pushed Britain into a severe recession. Unemployment soared to reach new record levels.

Governments can use the taxation system as a method for redistributing income. A progressive system results in wealthier people paying back in tax a higher proportion of their incomes than do the less wealthy. It can be accompanied by expenditure taxes (like VAT) which can be applied to luxury goods, such as alcohol and jewellery, but not to essentials, such as food and rent. However, even a progressive system of taxation has failed to redistribute income to the point of eliminating poverty. As the *Survey of Personal Incomes* published by the Inland Revenue in 1984 demonstrated, the variety of tax allowances and reliefs effectively benefited the higher-paid more than the lower-paid. Indeed, the tax cuts introduced by the incoming Conservative Government in 1979 helped to widen the gap between high- and low-paid earners.

Governments can also intervene with *regional policy* to help the economics of depressed areas in Britain. The foundation of post-war regional policy until 1960 was the *Distribution of Industry Act* 1945. This Act created 'Development Areas' in which the Board of Trade could build factories and make loans in order to attract industry. Regional policy was given a greater emphasis in the 1960s. The *Local Employment Act* 1960 replaced the 1945 legislation as the basis of policy. The *Industry Acts* of 1972 and 1975 were used by the governments led by Edward Heath and Harold Wilson respectively in attempts to mitigate the effects of industrial decline and high unemployment. This was accomplished in the main by the use of regional development grants and by temporary employment policies supervised by the Manpower Services Commission. By early 1979 it was calculated that some form of regional aid was being given to 40 per cent of the workforce. The Conservative Governments led by Mrs Thatcher have laid greater emphasis on the importance of market forces and reductions have been made in regional aid.

INCOMES POLICIES

At various times, governments have attempted to control wage increases as part of the wider goal of controlling inflation in order to keep Britain competitive and thereby save jobs. The first major post-war incomes policy was implemented by the Chancellor, Selwyn-Lloyd, in 1961 when he introduced a nine-month 'pay pause'. Labour pursued a prices and incomes policy between 1965 and 1969, creating a National Board for Prices and Incomes which monitored developments. A Conservative Government attempted an informal control of public sector incomes from 1970 to 1972, and a full-scale statutory policy on all incomes between 1972 and 1974. The next period of incomes policy, after 1974 was known at various times as the 'social compact' or 'social contract', and took the form of an agreement on a variety of issues between a Labour Government and the trade union movement. However, first and foremost, the social contract had the function of restricting pay rises. The policy collapsed in the 'winter of discontent' of 1978–9 as union rank-and-file withdrew their cooperation from the social contract. Widespread and prolonged strikes in the public sector paved the way to Labour's defeat in the 1979 General Election.

The Conservative Government led by Mrs Thatcher rejected the use of a formal incomes policy as a means of curbing inflation. Yet curbing the money supply and the imposition of 'cash limits' restrained wage increases, particularly of workers in the public sector. Although Mrs Thatcher had no 'incomes policy', there was a 'policy for incomes'.

The failure of the social contract has taken the Labour Party and trade unions back to the drawing-board in search of a mutually acceptable policy for incomes. Labour's preference is for an incomes policy which will prevent the wages of the most powerful section of the workforce surging ahead at the expense of the least powerful. However, the preference of most trade unions is for 'free collective bargaining' which is not controlled by guidelines or norms. An agreement has emerged that a future Labour Government will make a 'national economical assessment' which will include a strategy for wages but nothing in the form of government-imposed wage restraint. Critics have accused Labour of fudging this sensitive issue, since the Party and the unions have not made explicit how wages, and hence inflation, would be controlled.

SUMMARY

Society contains contradictory trends in terms of wealth and poverty. At the same time as levels of affluence are increasing for many families, others are being propelled downwards into poverty. Poverty is a difficult concept to define, but one which invariably embraces vulnerable groups such as one-parent families, the sick and the old. To date, government policies have succeeded neither in eliminating poverty nor in significantly closing the gap between rich and poor.

FURTHER READING

Donnison, D. (1982) *The Politics of Poverty*, Oxford, Martin Robertson.
Fagin, L. and Little, M. (1984) *The Forsaken Families: The Effects of Unemployment on Family Life*, Harmondsworth, Penguin.
Field, F. (1981) *Inequality in Britain: Freedom, Welfare and the State*, London, Fontana.
Mack, J. and Lausley, S. (1985) *Poor Britain*, London, Allen & Unwin.
Townsend, P. (1970) *Poverty in the United Kingdom*, Harmondsworth, Penguin.

QUESTIONS

1. Can large differences in wealth be justified in Britain?
2. In what ways can government redistribute income?

ASSIGNMENT

Regional profile I

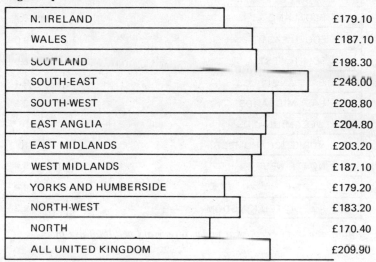

N. IRELAND	£179.10
WALES	£187.10
SCOTLAND	£198.30
SOUTH-EAST	£248.00
SOUTH-WEST	£208.80
EAST ANGLIA	£204.80
EAST MIDLANDS	£203.20
WEST MIDLANDS	£187.10
YORKS AND HUMBERSIDE	£179.20
NORTH-WEST	£183.20
NORTH	£170.40
ALL UNITED KINGDOM	£209.90

Average weekly household income

Regional profile II

NORTH	Unavailable
N. IRELAND	31.1
WALES	25.5
SCOTLAND	30.6
SOUTH-EAST	33.4
SOUTH-WEST	29.4
EAST ANGLIA	26.2
EAST MIDLANDS	27.9
WEST MIDLANDS	23.4
YORKS AND HUMBERSIDE	28.3
NORTH-WEST	21.7
ALL UNITED KINGDOM	28.3

Percentage of school-leavers going into further education

Regional profile III

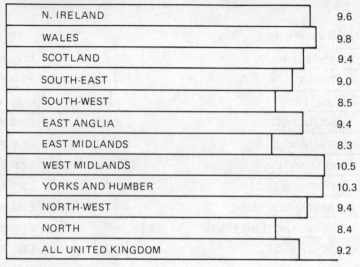

N. IRELAND	9.6
WALES	9.8
SCOTLAND	9.4
SOUTH-EAST	9.0
SOUTH-WEST	8.5
EAST ANGLIA	9.4
EAST MIDLANDS	8.3
WEST MIDLANDS	10.5
YORKS AND HUMBER	10.3
NORTH-WEST	9.4
NORTH	8.4
ALL UNITED KINGDOM	9.2

Infant mortality (deaths at under 1-year-old per 1000 live births)

Regional profile IV

N. IRELAND	18.0
WALES	14.6
SCOTLAND	14.0
SOUTH-EAST	8.6
SOUTH-WEST	10.2
EAST ANGLIA	8.8
EAST MIDLANDS	11.3
WEST MIDLANDS	14.1
YORKS AND HUMBER	13.3
NORTH-WEST	14.6
NORTH	17.3
ALL UNITED KINGDOM	11.3

Percentage unemployed

Regional Profile V

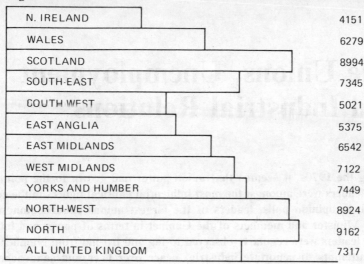

N. IRELAND	4151
WALES	6279
SCOTLAND	8994
SOUTH-EAST	7345
SOUTH WEST	5021
EAST ANGLIA	5375
EAST MIDLANDS	6542
WEST MIDLANDS	7122
YORKS AND HUMBER	7449
NORTH-WEST	8924
NORTH	9162
ALL UNITED KINGDOM	7317

Notifiable offences recorded by police, per 1000 population

Regional profile VI

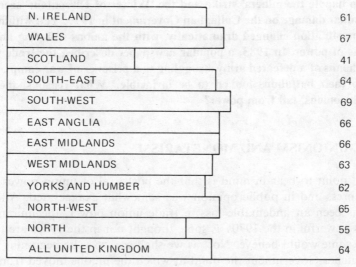

N. IRELAND	61
WALES	67
SCOTLAND	41
SOUTH–EAST	64
SOUTH-WEST	69
EAST ANGLIA	66
EAST MIDLANDS	66
WEST MIDLANDS	63
YORKS AND HUMBER	62
NORTH-WEST	65
NORTH	55
ALL UNITED KINGDOM	64

Percentage of owner-occupiers

Source: All six Regional profiles adapted from *The Guardian*, 2 July 1987.

Study the Regional profiles shown above. To what extent do the data support the argument that there is a North–South divide in terms of economic and social factors? Do some factors have a different profile from others? Put your assessment into a 400–500-word summary.

20

The Unions, Unemployment and Industrial Relations

During the 1970s, it seemed that union power had grown to the point where union leaders were amongst the most influential political figures in the country. Indeed, in opinion polls, leaders of the largest unions ranked alongside the Prime Minister and members of the Cabinet in terms of power and influence. Union leaders were regularly observed to-ing and fro-ing from Number Ten in their attempts to negotiate industrial peace over beer and sandwiches. The Governments of the 1970s led by Wilson, Heath and Callaghan all lost public support to some extent because they did not appear to be able to cope with the unions. Some blamed Heath's electoral defeat in 1974 on his Government's failure to handle the miners' strike and the 'Winter of Discontent' seemed to inflict similar damage on the Callaghan Government in 1979. Yet, within a few years, the situation changed dramatically, with the unions suffering an enormous loss of power. In 1983, a popular newspaper described the trade unions 'Like columns of a defeated army struggling to a prisoner of war camp ... Not long ago their battalions looked to be invincible.' What reasons, then, lay behind the unions' fall from power?

TRADE-UNIONISM AND MONETARISM

The first point to bear in mind is that the portrayal of union power in the tabloid press and in public opinion was somewhat exaggerated. Although there has been an undeniable loss in trade union power, the unions were never as powerful in the 1970s as some thought nor in the 1980s are they as weak as some would believe. Nor, as we shall see, was the beginning of the first Thatcher Government the point at which the unions moved from their position of relative strength to one of relative weakness. Although the influence of the unions has declined during the Thatcher Governments, the process of decline began years before in a Labour Government.

Part of the Butskellite post-war consensus in British politics was the commitment by governments to full or high levels of employment. This was part of a bargain struck between the unions and governments which relied on interventionist techniques to manage the economy; the Government would maintain high levels of employment in exchange for the unions delivering their part of the bargaining such as pay restraint. But too often it appeared that the unions were not able to deliver their side of the bargain, not even to Labour Governments. Whilst union leaders made agreements with the Government of the day, they could not make their mass memberships keep to those agreements. In the eyes of the public, the unions became more and more unpopular as they 'had their cake and ate it'. The most remarkable feature of Mrs Thatcher's Governments in this respect was that they did not need any agreements or bargains with the unions in order to implement economic policy. Unlike all previous post-war Governments, Mrs Thatcher could ignore the trade unions. This was possible in the main because her monetarist policies had no role for the unions to play. The Governments' prime economic goal of squeezing inflation out of the system no longer relied on winning agreements from the unions on limiting pay demands, but on the control of interest rates, reductions in public spending and control of the money supply. And none of these techniques relied on union support or cooperation. But far worse for the trade union movement, monetarist policies added to the unemployment which was already resulting from a world economic recession so that within the first four years of Thatcherism the unions lost 2 million members. With the unions now weakened by unemployment, or the threat of it, the Government further reduced their political and industrial roles through confining them within a legal framework.

THE IMPACT OF UNEMPLOYMENT

The Conservatives fought the 1979 General Election with the campaign slogan 'Labour isn't working' on the now-famous dole-queue poster, yet, by the time of the next election in 1983, the rate of unemployment had risen from 5 per cent to 13 per cent. After peaking at a total of 3.3m, the unemployment total levelled off in 1986 and by the end of the year began to fall. The Government had long argued that the unemployment statistics disguised the underlying strength of its economic policies. Between 1983 and 1986, for example, over 1m new jobs were created, giving Britain more jobs than had ever previously existed with unemployment rising simply because an even greater number of young people were entering the labour market (see Figure 20.1).

The Chancellor argued in 1984 that Britain did not have an 'unemployment' problem so much as a 'high wages' problem and claimed that a free labour market would reduce unemployment. He argued that there was a link between wages and jobs: the cheaper jobs are in terms of wages, the more will be demanded by employers. The Chancellor stated: 'I see little prospect of reversing the trend in unemployment unless we can decisively moderate the

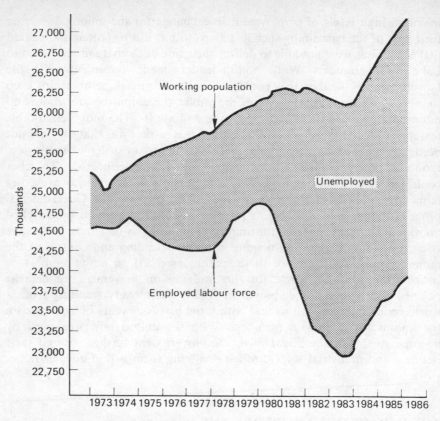

Source: *Employment Gazette*, July 1986.

FIGURE 20.1   *Working population and employed labour force: Great Britain (seasonally adjusted)*

growth in real wages'. He told Parliament that 200 000 new jobs would be created for every 1 per cent cut in real earnings and, if wages only kept pace with inflation, 1½m new jobs could be created in three years. The job market was seen as being distorted by high social security payments, wages councils which set minimum pay rates, and trade unions which pushed wages up to unrealistic levels.

Others on the right of the political spectrum, such as the former Chairman of British Leyland, Michael Edwardes, were arguing that the real level of unemployment was much lower than the official statistics indicated. They felt that unemployment was overestimated by the Government because the impact of the 'black' or 'hidden' economy was not being taken into account. Some firms understated their profits and provided more employment than was being declared; some 'moonlight' workers only declared one of the several jobs they did whilst 'ghost' workers did not declare the fact that they were employed at all and still drew unemployment benefit. Some calculated that the unemployment statistics included about 2m people who actually had jobs in the black economy.

Not surprisingly, all these views were challenged by the trade union movement and the political left. Labour's Shadow Employment Minister argued that the real number of unemployed people was around 5m. He accused the Chancellor of having a policy for unemployment statistics rather than a policy for employment, and argued that the official statistics were being massaged to give a favourable impression of the situation. The basis on which unemployment is calculated had been changed nineteen times between 1979 and 1987. Amongst what Labour saw as 'fiddles' were:

1. a change in the method of counting the unemployed from the number registered at Job Centres to the number registered at Benefit Offices;
2. the decision to take unemployed men over 60 out of the figures on the grounds that they were no longer seeking work;
3. the inclusion of people on temporary employment schemes as 'employed';
4. the exclusion of married women seeking work from the 'unemployed'.

Use of these four techniques alone, argued Labour, artificially reduced the unemployment total by over a million.

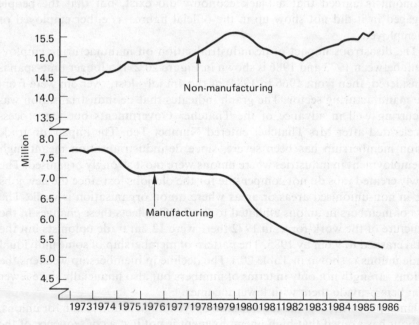

Source: *Employment Gazette*, July 1986.

FIGURE 20.2 *Manufacturing and non-manufacturing employees in employment. Great Britain (seasonally adjusted)*

The Chancellor's critics argued that the new jobs created after 1983 were quite different from the ones lost in the years before. Most of the jobs lost were in manufacturing (see Figure 20.2) whereas most of the new jobs were in service industries and frequently part-time. For example, of the 250 000 new jobs created in 1984, most were taken by part-time female workers in service areas such as retailing, hotels and catering. Only 6000 of the jobs were taken by full-time male employees. It was argued that once a factory had closed down the jobs it provided were permanently lost. Although low-skill 'no-tech' jobs in the service economy reduced unemployment in the short run, they did not provide the 'high-tech' manufacturing skills which brought benefit in the long term.

The unions also challenged the Government's view that high wages were 'hiding' jobs and claimed that any link between wages and jobs was unproven. For example, wages in Britain doubled in real terms between 1964 and 1970 yet the rate of unemployment was similar in both years. It was also argued that low pay actually created more unemployment since workers on low pay do not have the purchasing power necessary to spend on goods which other workers make. In short, low wages would lead to further de-industrialisation and job losses. Finally, the notion that the black economy made the unemployment statistics meaningless was challenged widely. Economists agreed that a black economy did exist, but that the people engaged in it did not show up in the official figures as either employed or unemployed.

The disastrous impact of de-industrialisation on manufacturing employment between 1973 and 1986 is shown in Figure 20.2. If a longer time-span is considered, then from 1966 to 1984, of the 4m jobs lost, over 3m were from the manufacturing sector. The graph indicates that de-industrialisation was occurring well in advance of the Thatcher Governments but the process accelerated after Mrs Thatcher entered Number Ten. The impact on trade union membership has been severe, since de-industrialisation meant high unemployment in industries where unions were most strongly organised. The newly created jobs do not compensate for the old jobs lost since the new jobs are in non-unionised areas or areas where union organisation is weak. The loss of members in unions affiliated to the TUC reflects these changes in the structure of the work-force; in 1972 there were 12.2m trade unionists but the total crashed to 9.6m by 1985. The pattern of membership of some individual trade unions is shown in Table 20.1 The decline in membership weakens the unions' strength not only in terms of numbers but also financially since fewer members provide them with lower incomes.

Unemployment also has a debilitating psychological dimension for unions. Labour has argued that high unemployment is not just a consequence of the Government's economic policy, it is a tool used to carry out economic policy. The party's deputy leader has stated 'the Government both anticipates and

TABLE 20.1
The decline in trade union membership (in thousands)

	31 December 1979	31 December 1983	% Change 1979–83
TGWU	2086	1547	− 25.4
GMWU	967	875	− 9.9
NUPE	692	689	− 3.3
USDAW	470	403	− 12.8
UCATT	348	260	− 19.1
NUM	253	208	− 28.6
NUR	180	156	− 13.4
BIFU	132	143	+ 3.0

Source: Adapted from D. Marsh and J. King, "The Unions under Thatcher" 1985 in L. Robins (ed.) *Political Institutions in Britain* (1987) p. 225.

plans for a permanent reservoir of three million unemployed, to use that pool of unemployment as a sort of incomes policy to hold down wage demands and to use it to emasculate the trade unions'. The fear of unemployment can undermine union solidarity, as Dave Marsh and Jeff King have suggested:

> The effect of the threat of unemployment was well illustrated during the miners' strike with the collapse of the Triple Alliance between the miners, the rail unions and the steelworkers. The steelworkers union felt unable to support the miners by halting the production of steel because despite the large scale capacity cuts since the mid-1970s further closures and job losses were expected and threatened. The steel mills at Ravenscraig and Llanwern were particularly threatened so when the NUM called for a total shutdown of these two mills, as well as other plant, the steelworkers saw jobs as taking precedence over solidarity. (Marsh and King, 'The Unions Under Thatcher' (1987) p. 223)

UNIONS AND GOVERNMENT

In the years following the Second World War, the unions maintained the close links that they had developed when cooperating with Government during the war. The unions had, as it were, become 'respectable' with their influence no longer stemming from mass rallies in Trafalgar Square but from the quiet persuasion exercised in the corridors of Whitehall. Unions were invited to serve on important committees by both Labour and Conservative Governments, and political scientists during the 1960s talked of a corporate state developing in Britain. It seemed as if policy was forged from a consensus amongst ministers, employers and union leaders on how the economy should develop. In exchange for participating in government through bodies such as the National Economic Development Council ('Neddy') and influencing policy, union leaders were expected to deliver their members' agreement and cooperation. However, with considerable publicity being given to a rash of 'wildcat' strikes, particularly in the car industry, it seemed that union leaders wielded little control over their members. In short, the lesson to be learnt from Britain's industrial relations front was that union leaders 'could not deliver'.

A Labour Government headed by Harold Wilson attempted to introduce legislation which would have changed the power structure of unions to the advantage of union leaders. The White paper, *In Place of Strife*, was introduced by Barbara Castle in January 1969 and initially received a fairly favourable response from the TUC. However, opposition to the proposals developed during the year, resulting in the PLP threatening to oppose the Government if it proceeded with *In Place of Strife*. The Government capitulated, withdrew legislation based on the White paper and accepted a face-saving 'Solemn and Binding Agreement' from the TUC as an alternative. The first attempt to take union power from the 'militant' rank-and-file and place it in the hands of 'moderate' leaders ended in sound defeat.

A TUC–Labour-party Liaison Committee was set up in 1970 to repair the bad feelings that existed between the industrial and political wings of the Labour movement following the '*In Place of Strife*' bill. Initially, the Liaison Committee spent much of its energy opposing the trade union legislation of the Conservative Government led by Edward Heath. But in due course, the Liaison Committee considered issues beyond industrial relations, such as economic policy and the possibility of a 'social contract' between the unions and a further Labour Government. During the years of Opposition, the Liaison Committee was frequently described as the most important committee in the Labour party – even more important than the NEC. However, after Labour returned to Government in 1974 the Liaison Committee came to be seen as less important since union leaders preferred direct contact with ministers rather than consultation via the Liaison Committee.

Included in the Conservative manifesto of 1970 was a proposal to 'put unions on a legal footing', and in 1971 the Heath Government passed its *Industrial Relations Act*. The Act represented an all-out assault on union privileges and generated vigorous opposition from 'moderate' and 'militant' unionists alike. In practice the Act was clumsy and soon abandoned as unworkable. Thus the second attempt to reform the unions through the use of legislation came to grief and was formally repealed by a subsequent Labour government in 1974.

The period from 1974 to 1979 is seen by some political scientists as the time when union leaders exercised great influence, almost control, over the Labour Governments. The Labour Government and unions had drawn up a

Social Contract which represented a bargain with commitments on both sides. Other political scientists, however, see the period 1974–9 in a more qualified light. At first, the TUC was influential and in 1974–5 the Social Contract did appear to work in favour of the unions. In particular, a string of legislation – the *Trade Union and Labour Relations Act 1974*, the *Employment Protection Act 1975*, and the *Health and Safety at Work Act 1975* – improved the position of trade unionists. However, from 1975 onwards, the advantage of the Social Contract ran in favour of the Government, since it was implemented to work in the same manner as an incomes policy. In 1976 the unions were not only accepting pay restraint but were also having their opposition to public spending cuts dismissed by the Government. Thus for most of its life the Social Contract was mainly an incomes policy and, as Marsh and King commented, 'based first on the active cooperation, and subsequently on the acquiescence, of the unions. In the end it collapsed in the 'Winter of Discontent' of 1978–9 as the TUC could no longer deliver the support of its member unions and union leaders could no longer deliver the support of their members' (*Marsh and King*, 'Unions under Thatcher', p. 216). Initially, then, the Labour Government had pursued a corporatist strategy which involved a close relation between Government and unions but this gave way to a mild form of monetarism and the distancing of Government from the unions.

The 'Winter of Discontent' provided the mass media with a long-running, frequently exaggerated story which nevertheless included workers placing the poor, the sick and the elderly at risk. To many who had not thought so beforehand, the unions now deserved to be disciplined by the government. The Conservatives came to power in 1979 pledged to reform the unions, and the stage was set for a political struggle. But union leaders found the fight against the Thatcher Government more difficult to organise than their successful campaigns against Wilson and Heath. The new trade union legislation was unlike previous attempts in that it did not consist of one major attempt to restrict union activity, but rather it was a step-by-step approach that gradually eroded union power.

The first major piece of legislation was the *Employment Act 1980*, which curbed picketing, secondary picketing and the use of the closed shop. Picketing was restricted to a person's own workplace with changes outlawing mass picketing but allowing picket-lines of six. The Act also made it easier for workers to avoid joining closed shops on grounds of conscience. The *Employment Act 1982* introduced further restrictions on closed-shop agreements, as well as making unions liable for members' actions and outlawing strikes which were political in nature. As Marsh and King observe:

> The resurrection of the spirit of Taff Vale renders the unions no longer the beneficiaries of immunities they have enjoyed since 1906. The Act makes them liable to claims of damages of up to £250 000 from any person whose business is

damaged by 'unlawful means', within the new, narrower, concept of a trade dispute. The autonomy of shop stewards and full-time union officials is thus circumscribed by an Act which makes the unions responsible for those actions (Marsh and King, 'Unions Under Thatcher', p. 219).

The *Trade Union Act 1984* focused on the internal workings of unions; it required secret ballots of all members for strikes and elections both for union executives and for the existence of political funds. The latter provision was designed to reduce unions' political influence by cutting links with the Labour Party but in the event no union membership voted against the existence of a political fund. A fourth major piece of trade union legislation was prepared by the Conservative Government returned in 1987 in which it was proposed to increase the protection of individual worker's rights. Even where a majority of trade union members had voted to strike in a secret ballot, it was proposed that the right to work of the minority should be granted. The Government was also considering the establishment of a 'commissioner for trade unions', a new legal officer who would make it easier to institute cases against unions through the courts.

At the same time the Government had taken other measures which undermined the position and strength of the unions. Social security payments to families of striking workers were reduced through 'deeming' them to have received strike pay from the union. Trade unions were banned at GCHQ without prior consultation. An agreement was offered by the unions which gave the Government everything it was ostensibly seeking – no strikes, no disruptions, and no outside union officials at GCHG – but it was rejected flatly by the Government. And finally at both national and local levels privatisation was weakening the position of unions. This was particularly the case with low-paid employees in the public sector where services were now being subcontracted out by local authorities and health authorities.

The trade unions were unable to challenge and reverse government policy as they had during the 1960s and 1970s. The TUC organised official 'days of action' and 'mass rallies' but these were not always as successful as hoped for and they petered out. However, a struggle of gargantuan proportions began in March 1984 with the outbreak of the miners' strike in protest at the National Coal Board's plan to reduce the size of the coal industry. Led by Arthur Scargill, the NUM's resistance to the NCB assumed an ideological dimension as the threatened workers engaged in what was seen by some on the Left as a class war against the whole apparatus of the State, the NCB, the police, the courts and the mass media, which represented capitalist interests. Some argued that Arthur Scargill was driven by ambition not just to defeat the NCB but to bring down the Government in the wake of the miners' action, after the manner of Heath's defeat in 1974. Others believed that the strike was deliberately provoked by the Government because Mrs Thatcher wanted a confrontation with the miners which would end in their defeat. It was reported that Mrs Thatcher saw militant unionists in terms of 'the enemy within' and believed that victory over the miners would be symbolic of the defeat of Left-wing forces in wider society.

After the defeat of Edward Heath in February 1974, many Conservatives considered that public sector unionism posed a grave threat to a future Conservative Government. A number of working parties inside the Conservative party explored the problems concerned and made appropriate recommendations. A group under the chairmanship of Lord Carrington examined the confrontation between the Heath Government and the NUM and proposed that a future Conservative Government should prepare for this sort of crisis and that special attention should be devoted to conditioning public opinion. Another group, chaired by Nicholas Ridley, considered how a challenge from the NUM could be defeated through such means as

  (i) countering mass flying-pickets with mass mobile police;
 (ii) cutting supplementary benefits to strikers and their families;
(iii) avoiding disruption of electricity supplies by amassing coal stocks at power stations;
(iv) ensuring that any confrontation with the miners should be on the grounds of the Government's choosing.

Andrew Taylor observed that the two Conservative groups 'complement each other in that the *Ridley Report* showed how the problems identified by the *Carrington Report* could be overcome' (A. Taylor in his article "Terrible Nemesis? The Miners, the NUM and Thatcherism" in *Teaching Politics*, May 1986, p. 295). Government strategy proved successful in overpowering the NUM. Although the miners were on strike for a full year, outlasting the great lock-out of 1926, the action was not solid from the start since some areas such as Nottinghamshire refused to strike and the steady drift back to work of other miners undermined the credibility of the union's leadership.

THE NEW REALISM

In 1983, the unions pinned their hopes on a Labour election victory which would be followed by an improvement in their position. Defeat for Labour in 1983 and again in 1987, with a future Labour victory seeming a distant prospect, forced union leaders to reappraise their role on the more realistic basis that Thatcherism was here to stay. Union leaders also had to square up to the evidence that many of the Conservatives' union reforms were popular with their trade union members. But individual trade unions responded to these changed circumstances in different ways. Some unionists did not like the new laws but accepted that they had to come to terms with a Government which would be in power until the next general election, and perhaps beyond. These were the views of leaders often described as 'moderates' or 'new realists'. Opposed to them were unionists who so opposed the new laws that they were prepared to ignore them and thereby challenge the Government. These were the views of leaders sometimes described as 'militants' or 'old fundamentalists'.

The defeat of the NUM came as a blow to the old fundamentalists who had argued that they could not learn to live with Thatcherism, whilst the birth of a new pit union, the UDM, represented the new realists amongst mineworkers, who argued that union values had to adapt to new circumstances. These divisions caused tensions within the TUC and conflict between individual unions. The most notable split emerged in the newspaper industry between the electricians (EETPU) and the printworkers (NGA) as production utilised new technologies. In a controversial move, News International changed from old printing methods in Fleet Street to new production methods at Wapping. The old craft union, the NGA, appeared to the public to be almost Luddite as it refused to enter realistic negotiations whereas the EETPU which took over News International printing projected an image of being progressive and forward-looking. Some of the old guard in the trade unions accused the new realists in unions such as the EETPU of forming right-wing 'bosses' unions' in which the rank-and-file were more like clients and participating members. The new realists rejected this sort of accusation and replied that whilst they rejected class as the basis for union action, the real difference was one of attitudes towards new technology and competition.

The response of the trade union movement to Thatcherism has caused fundamental disagreements on policies and divisions and break-aways within unions. From time to time there has also been speculation that under certain circumstances the new realists might withdraw or be expelled from the TUC and form a rival organisation. At other times, there has been talk that the Labour–union link is in need of modernising, since, as it stands, the unpopularity of the unions has damaged Labour's support and Labour's repeated electoral defeats have prevented the return of a government sympathetic to the unions. No matter how these, and any future debates, are resolved the future of the trade union movement in the late 1980s looks bleaker than at any time since 1945.

SUMMARY

Monetarist policies contained no positive role for the trade unions to play and when implemented in tandem with a world recession further weakened the position of unions through creating mass unemployment. Conservative Governments in the 1980s imposed a legal framework on the organisation and conduct of trade union activities. Much of the new legislation stressed individual rights over and above the collectivist tradition of unions. Trade unions disagree on how to cope with the prospect of Conservative government for the foreseeable future. Some favour continued opposition and are prepared to struggle against

Thatcherism, whilst others argue that the only future for trade unionism lies in complying with the new laws.

FURTHER READING

Dorfman, G. A. (1979) *Government and Trade Unions in Britain Politics since 1968*, London, Macmillan.
Marsh, D. and King, J. (1987) 'The Unions Under Thatcher', in L. Robins (ed.) *Political Institutions in Britain*, London, Longman.
Panitch, L. (1976) *Social Democracy and Industrial Militancy: The Labour Party, the Trade Unions and Incomes Policy, 1954–74*, Cambridge, University Press.
Taylor, R. (1984) *The Crisis of British Labour*, Harmondsworth, Penguin.

QUESTIONS

1. In what ways did the Thatcher governments' approach to trade unions differ from that of previous governments?

2. Analyse the effects of unemployment on trade union activity.

3. How far have the new realists in trade unions departed from traditional union values?

ASSIGNMENT

Strikes: Working days lost

1976	3 284 000	1981	4 266 000
1977	10 142 000	1982	5 313 000
1978	9 405 000	1983	3 754 000
1979	29 474 000	1984	27 135 000
1980	11 964 000	1985	6 402 000

Tasks

(i) Investigate reasons for and explain the high figures for 1979 and 1984.

(ii) Locate and retrieve information from publications such as the *Employment Gazette* which enables you to bring the table up to date. Attempt to explain any patterns which emerge.

(iii) Discuss whether it is necessary to take other trends into account, such as rising levels of unemployment, when interpreting the statistical data above.

21

Ethnic Minority Politics

Black people tend to be portrayed as a 'problem' in British politics – the problems of controlling immigration numbers, and of maintaining law and order in the black populated inner cities, and the problems posed by the disadvantages of black people in areas such as housing, education and employment. How justified is this problem image of Britain's black population? Could the real problem be white racism, explicitly and implicitly present in the mainstream culture, rather than in black shortcomings? And how have politics and the political system worked to resolve or exacerbate the situation? This chapter explores these questions.

BLACK AND BRITISH

Britain has experienced considerable demographic change in terms of immigration and emigration. Numerous groups have settled in Britain –Irish, Jewish, Polish, Chinese, among others – whilst British-born people have set up new homes in countries such as Canada, Australia, New Zealand, South Africa and Rhodesia. Britain has a long history of immigration and emigration but a new pattern of immigration was established after the Second World War. The *British Nationality Act* 1948 allowed citizens of the Commonwealth to settle in Britain and this facilitated a new era in which most of those people who made new homes in Britain were black. In 1982 an official estimate put Britain's population originating from the new Commonwealth at 2.2m, a figure which represented 4 per cent of the total population.

New Commonwealth immigrants formed numerous ethnic communities based on common language, religion and race. But, unlike previous immigrants from countries such as Ireland or Poland who could 'blend in' with the way of life, immigrants from Pakistan, India and the West Indies remained visibly distinctive through skin colour. In other words, they were visible as 'strangers' and because of this many British people formed hostile attitudes towards them which, in turn, made it more difficult still for the new black immigrants to adapt to Britain's traditional culture. It was hoped that in the course of time, British-born blacks would not experience the isolation of their immigrant parents but a survey conducted by the Runnymede Trust in 1986 found this was not the case. It was reported that fewer than 5 per cent of black schoolchildren had been invited into a white home and, although over 40 per cent said they had white friends at school, most felt that British society at large did not like them (see further on the survey, p. 441 below).

The use of 'black' as a shorthand term in both everyday language and the social sciences can be misleading. At the immediate level, it is obvious that 'blacks' are no more black than 'whites' are white. But just as the term white can embrace widely differing cultures, so the term black disguises the diversity that exists amongst people from a relatively small number of countries in the new Commonwealth. Although general distinctions are made between the Afro-Caribbean and Asian communities, far greater diversity exists than is implied by this simple two-fold categorisation with some ethnic communities having surprisingly little in common. In Leicester, for example, one resident in five is a member of what is popularly known as the 'Asian community'. Yet this community is actually made up of numerous groups based on seven main languages further divided into numerous dialects. Some groups have to resort to a second language, such as English, in order to communicate at anything more than the most basic level with other groups. The Asian community is further fragmented by different religions, values, cultural practices and castes, as well as by the political tensions found in the politics of the Indian subcontinent. For our purposes, then, 'black' is a general label or political colour which covers members of all ethnic communities who are located in a broadly similar position in society.

RACE RELATIONS

It is a sad fact that many individuals have negative attitudes towards others purely on the grounds of racial difference. Racial prejudice can be expressed by whites against blacks, blacks against whites or, indeed, between ethnic groups, as in the case of Asian prejudice against West Indians. Clearly, the most politically significant prejudice is that expressed by the white majority against the black minority. On occasions in the past that prejudice could be activated lawfully into racial discrimination for example, with lodging houses displaying 'No Blacks' signs in their front windows. There is little doubt that deliberate acts of racial discrimination still take place in British society which are beyond the remit of law. Sometimes, however, racial discrimination has been unintentionally practised by organisations in the public and private sectors which have operated policies which contain a hidden bias against black people. Many bodies now practise race-monitoring in specific areas as a check against unintentional discrimination.

In the late 1950s Britain experienced its only major race riots – as opposed to gang skirmishes – when whites attacked blacks in Notting Hill and Nottingham. These riots came as an unexpected shock and the government adopted both a tough and tender response. The former represented a response to public anxiety about black immigration to Britain whilst the latter was an attempt to promote racial harmony within Britain.

The Commonwealth Immigrants Act 1962 was the first of a number of Acts which restricted the entry of black first-time immigrants and their families to Britain. A second *Commonwealth Immigrants Act* was rushed through Parliament in 1968 to tighten up the 1962 Act, which did not apply to East African Asians. The *Immigration Act* 1971 tightened controls still further, although its restrictions were waived on humanitarian grounds to allow Asians expelled from Uganda to enter Britain freely. A new *Nationality Act* in 1981 represented even tighter restrictions. All this legislation, passed by both Conservative and Labour governments, has been criticised for being founded on racist principles. The prime goal has been not the restriction of immigrants who have claims to be British, but the restriction of *black* immigrants who have claims to British status.

Illiberal immigration policies towards blacks living outside Britain have been accompanied by liberal policies towards those already resident within Britain. The *Race Relations Acts* of 1965, 1968 and 1976 outlawed direct and indirect discrimination in widening areas of public life and provision such as housing, employment and education. What is sometimes called the 'race relations industry' was established with complaints taken to the Race Relations Board, later replaced by the Commission for Racial Equality, with Community Relations Councils operating at local level. The view expressed by many liberal-minded individuals of the time was that the 'race' problem would eventually wither away. It was felt that the children of immigrants would not suffer from the cultural problems and disadvantages of being newcomers and, given time, economic growth would provide benefits to all Britain's citizens. The blacks, at the end of the queue for property, would be served in due course. How far have these early beliefs been justified by subsequent developments and trends?

EMPLOYMENT, EDUCATION AND HOUSING

Sociologists are divided over the question of where Britain's black population is located in the social class structure. Some believe that the overwhelming majority of blacks belong to the same working class shared by many of Britain's white population. They have argued that data held up by some sociologists as proof of racial discrimination is no more than evidence of class discrimination which also affects whites. Other sociologists disagree with this view and see the effects of additional racial discrimination in areas such as employment, education and housing pushing blacks into a separate underclass located beneath the traditional working class. As we shall see, the statistical evidence is sometimes ambivalent but there are reasons for believing that an underclass embracing the black population has not yet formed in Britain.

Studies of employment during the 1970s when unemployment was relatively low revealed that, compared with white workers, black workers were found disproportionately in lower-status jobs. Whilst this resulted from discrimination by whites, and from blacks being less-well-qualified and often having a poor command of English, the black 'skew' in the labour market was not as marked as many expected. The argument that black families formed an underclass seemed difficult to sustain in the light of these studies. The situation found in the 1980s, when there was relatively high unemployment, still supported the argument that a separate underclass had not been formed despite black disadvantage in the labour market. A study by the Runnymede Trust, *Employment, Unemployment and Black People* (1986), revealed that the black population earned less than the white and suffered disproportionately from unemployment. These findings were confirmed by a government survey, *The West Indian School Leaver* (1986), which showed that West Indians in particular were hard hit by the recession. Those West Indians resident in Britain before the age of 5 took twice as long to get work as did white school-leavers; those who arrived in Britain after the age of 11 took three times as long. Some accused the Youth Training Scheme of practising unintentional discrimination in placing young people into differing programme modes of its vocational training scheme. During 1984–5, nearly 400 000 young people entered YTS, but it was revealed that black school-leavers were overrepresented in the lower-status-mode programmes which held fewer prospects of leading to a full-time job.

An interesting academic controversy has developed over the progress of black pupils in Britain's schools. The conventional view is that white and Asian pupils perform far better at school than do West Indian pupils. The Rampton Report (1981) identified racism as a key factor which explained the relatively low educational achievement of West Indians. This racism was often unintentional and occurred through teaching an Anglo-centric curriculum where the approach to school subjects stresses the values of white, Christian and English society. Teachers could also slip into racial stereotyping without being fully aware of the fact, expecting West Indian pupils to be good at sport and music whilst at the same time not expecting them to do well academically. The Swann Report *Education for All* (1985), accepted these findings and argued that schools should incorporate multicultural and anti-racist approaches to the curriculum. The report did not favour separate schooling for minority groups but advocated supplementary education as a means of preserving ethnic heritages and traditions. Swann found that Bangladeshi pupils did less well at school than other Asian groups, but once again the performance of West Indian pupils was singled out as a cause for concern.

This orthodox view has, however, been challenged by other contemporary research. Since black pupils are concentrated in schools where the attainment of all pupils is below average, it is not valid to compare whites in 'good' and 'poor' schools with blacks in 'poor' schools only. If the effect of factors such as social class is taken into account when comparisons are made, then a completely different picture appears to emerge. With the effects of social class held constant, it is argued that under-achievement by West Indian pupils disappears. Indeed, West Indian girls 'over-achieve' and actually do better than their white counterparts.

In terms of housing, early immigrants tended to live in rather decrepit inner-city dwellings which resulted in the popular association between black people and overcrowding and squalor. The development of 'ghetto' neighbourhoods seemed to support the notion that a separate black underclass which was structurally distinct from the traditional working class had been formed. But, surprisingly, the pattern of housing tenure that has developed does not lend immediate support to the underclass thesis (see Table 21.1). Asian families are much more likely than the general population to be owner-occupiers whilst the tenure pattern of West Indian families closely follows that of the general population. But tenure of housing may be less important than the quality of housing. A Policy Studies Institute (PSI) report, *Black and White in Britain* (1982) argued that the

> quality of the housing of black people is much worse than the quality of housing in general in this country. Blacks are more often at higher floor levels, and those with houses are less likely to have detached or semi-detached property; black families have smaller property on average, and, with larger household size, their density of occupation is much higher; black households more often share rooms or amenities with other households; the properties black families own or rent are older; and they are less likely to have a garden (PSI Report, *Black and White in Britain*, 1982).

Thus, the original housing disadvantage of early post-war black immigrants had persisted through the years of high economic growth and affluence and was still present to be recorded by the PSI survey in 1982. But whether this disadvantage equates with the existence of an underclass remains open to debate. The majority view is that it does not.

TABLE 21.1

Housing tenure of minorities and general population

Heads of household	Asians %	West Indians %	General population %
Owner-occupied	76	50	50
Rented from council	4	26	28
Privately rented	19	24	22

Surce: D. Smith, *Racial Disadvantage in Britain* (Penguin, 1977), p. 210

LAW AND ORDER

The frustrations of under-privileged young people have been expressed from time to time in 'street politics'. In 1980 there was rioting in St Pauls (Bristol); in 1981, rioting in Brixton (London), Toxteth (Liverpool) and Moss Side (Manchester); in 1985, rioting took place in Handsworth (Birmingham), and again in Brixton and Tottenham. Although it is difficult to comment with any certainty on the nature of specific riots, since they are hardly appropriate situations in which to conduct interviews or questionnaire surveys, it does seem that the earlier riots were essentially multiracial protests with black and white youths taking to the streets. The later disturbances, however, did have a more definite racial overtone since both were sparked off by the injury and death of black women during police raids on their homes. During the Broadwater Farm riot in Tottenham a police officer was hacked to death.

The rioting was perceived in different ways with consequent disagreement on the best response to it. Some argued that the cause of the rioting was rooted in social deprivation and aggravated by oppressive police tactics. In terms of personal affluence, reflected in the quality of housing and value of possessions, and in terms of individual opportunity, reflected in educational provision and employment prospects, society was seen as having become polarised between the 'haves' and the 'have notes'. The riots were seen as resulting from the frustrations of the 'have nots'.

The *Scarman Report* on the inner-city rioting in Brixton in 1981 maintained that crime could not be understood if it was separate from its social background. Liberal-minded individuals argued that the solution lay in implementing new government policies to improve the inner cities through increasing employment, raising standards of living and improving education, as well as through the introduction of more sensitive policing methods.

Others did not accept that poor conditions cause either riots or crime since individuals were seen as being responsible for their own behaviours. For example, Lord Hailsham, then the Lord Chancellor, believed that 'individual wickedness' rather than urban deprivation resulted in crime. Some Conservatives believed that the value shift that took place during the 'swinging sixties' had resulted in many young people showing less respect for authority. Norman Tebbit shared this view and argued that 'the permissive society in turn generated the violent society'. Whatever particular cause for the inner-city rioting is identified, there is a tendency for individuals on the political Right to see the participants as criminal riff-raff and therefore to believe that the solution lies in tougher police methods and heavier punishment.

Consideration of the riots focused attention on the poor relations which existed between the police and many black communities. There were a variety of explanations as to why young blacks had so little confidence in the police. Some research suggested that black hostility to the police was, for the most part, an expression of a more general disaffection with Britain's white society and its widespread discrimination against blacks. In other words, it was argued that young blacks were anti-police simply because the police were symbols of an unfair white society. Other research suggested that blacks were hostile towards the police because low-ranking officers on the beat tended to harass and victimise them. But one study of 'negative contacts' between police officers and young blacks and whites found that black experience with the police was only marginally worse that that of white youths. The researchers concerned argued that black hostility to the police was part of the shared beliefs of young blacks, even amongst those who had not had direct personal experience with the police. The stereotypes of the unpleasant and aggressive policeman, they argued, was part of the 'folk history' of young blacks.

The police too seem to have their stereotype of the young black male. Studies of the way of life of policemen have revealed the existence of a 'cop culture' which is conservative and based firmly on a cult of masculinity. A PSI report, *Police and People in London* (1983) stated that although 9 per cent of officers in the Metropolitan Police are women 'the dominant values of the Force are still in many ways those of an all-man institution such as a rugby-club or boy's school'. The report explored the 'cop culture' and stated: 'Certain themes tend to be emphasised in conversation in an exaggerated way: the prime examples are male dominance (combined with the denigration of women), the glamour (but not the reality) of violence, and racial prejudice.' Although the PSI report found that racism was part of the cop culture, it did not find that racist attitudes were reflected in actual police behaviour when dealing with black people. Other studies have contested this conclusion and argued that racism is carried into policing by low-ranking officers.

In 1983 the Metropolitan Police Force's crime statistics included a controversial breakdown of certain offences into racial categories. The figures indicated that 57 per cent of all assailants in street crimes were black, but since less than 14 per cent of London's population is black the conclusion waiting to be drawn was that mugging was a black crime. Critics of the way in which this information was presented and thus likely to be understood by the public pointed out that the statistics were based on the victims' perception of their attackers which can be both biased and unreliable. Also, it was argued that street crime accounts for only 3 per cent of all serious crime, and yet it was the only type of crime for which race statistics were collected. The remaining 97 per cent would almost certainly include many criminal activities which are white-dominated.

Some of the tabloid newspapers sensationalised the Metropolitan Police crime statistics without conveying any need for caution when interpreting the 'facts'. The association between violence, mugging and young West Indian males presents the danger of a self-fulfilling prophecy if, in response to political pressure, the policing of ethnic neighbourhoods is intensified, thereby leading to the 'discovery' of yet more black crime. The Press Council has expressed anxiety that certain popular tabloid newspapers are in danger of encouraging, or pandering to, racial prejudice. It was noted that when a crime is committed by a white person there tends to be no mention of race, but where the criminal is black then his or her race tends to be included. For example, Liverpool Football Club is noted for not having black support yet when fans rampaged in the Heysel Stadium causing havoc which resulted in many deaths, there was no media mention of 'white' Liverpool supporters. Can we imagine a similar rampage by West Indian cricket supporters being reported without inclusion of the adjective 'black'?

THE POLITICAL RESPONSE

Some commentators feared that what they saw as the emergence of a new right-wing form of populism in Britain would be accompanied by a new racism. Whilst the new Right expressed relatively little sympathy towards the poor and disadvantaged in society, which includes many of the ethnic communities, there has been no significant embrace of racist causes. Racist ideology has remained the preserve of the National Front and British Movement although a report from the Young Conservatives expressed concern in 1983 that members of these organisations were infiltrating the Party at constituency level. The report also criticised a small number of Conservative MPs for having links with extreme Right-wing groups such as WISE (Welsh, Irish, Scottish, English) and the London Swinton Circle as well as condemning some Monday Club MPs for the racist attitudes expressed at the group's meetings. But, for the main part, the 'enemies within' identified by the new Right included militant trade unionists and left-wing councillors rather than ethnic minorities.

The most controversial contribution from the Conservative Right came in a speech made by Enoch Powell in 1968 when he called for a halt to black immigration and moves to repatriate blacks already settled in Britain. In a widely publicised section of his speech he stated: 'As I look ahead I am filled with foreboding. Like the Roman I seem to see the River Tiber foaming with much blood.' He was immediately sacked from his post in the Shadow Cabinet by the Tory leader, Edward Heath. Conservative nationalism, such as that expressed by Powell, stressed the continuity of Britain's institutions and culture. The nation is seen as being founded on the race, so, by definition, black newcomers to Britain who are excluded from its history cannot be included in its present or future. There is an unwillingness to accept Britain as a multiracial society since that is seen as breaking with the past and Britain's strengths lie in its continuity with the past. Only once in public has Mrs Thatcher appeared to be influenced by this sort of national-ism when in 1978 as new Conservative leader she told a radio audience that she understood fears that the British character might be swamped by people of a different culture. As Prime Minister, Mrs Thatcher has distanced herself from those on the Tory Right who support repatriation and call for the dismantling of the 'race relations industry'.

Labour's political image is one of being 'soft' on immigration but this does not conform to Labour's tough policy when in government. For example, Labour severely restricted new Commonwealth immigrants in the 1968 Act and its alternative to the Conservative *Nationality Act* 1981, whilst sounding more liberal, would have worked in much the same way.

Labour in the 1980s has been posed the politically interesting problem of how to accommodate increasing demands for black influence within the party. Whilst recent general elections have revealed that Labour has been losing working-class support, the black vote has remained largely loyal. A Labour subcommittee investigated the issue of black participation and recommended the establishment of black sections, but the NEC and conference rejected this proposal. The leadership argued that black sections were unnecessary because black candidates had been selected as parliamentary candidates and returned to Westminster. Also, it was argued that having black sections was unacceptable because it would segregate people according to their racial origin, an action which had more in common with apartheid than with socialism. Members from the unofficial black sections that already existed at constituency level argued that the establishment of black sections was vital because they provided a way in which the ethnic communities could participate in the Labour Party.

SUMMARY

Many white British people have found it hard to accommodate to the reality that new black ethnic communities now exist in Britain. Governments have found it necessary to pass legislation outlawing racial discrimination internally whilst operating racially biased immigration policies towards people external to the United Kingdom. There is disagreement amongst social researchers about both the scope and nature of such disadvantages. There is, however, a commonly accepted stereotype existing amongst the population at large which associates ethnicity with criminality. Unfortunately, the way in which the tabloid press sometimes presents news reinforces this misleading impression. Although there are now some black MPs, the role of the political parties is not particularly successful in terms of channelling and responding to black aspirations.

FURTHER READING

Anwar, M. (1985) *Race and Politics*, London, Methuen/Tavistock.
Brown, C. (1984) *Black and White Britain*, London, Heinemann/PSI.
Cashmore, E. E. and Troyna, B. (1983) *Introduction to Race Relations*, London, Routledge.
Layton-Henry, Z. (1984) *The Politics of Race in Britain*, London, Allen & Unwin.
Layton-Henry, Z. and Rich, P. B. (eds) (1986) *Race, Government and Politics in Britain*, London, Macmillan.
Scarman, Lord (1981) *The Scarman Report*, London, HMSO, Cmnd 8427.

QUESTIONS

1. In what ways are some ethnic minorities disadvantaged in Britain?

2. To what extent can rioting mobs be thought of as 'pressure groups of the poor'?

3. Consider the case for and against major political parties having constitutions which guarantee black representation on policy-making committees.

ASSIGNMENT

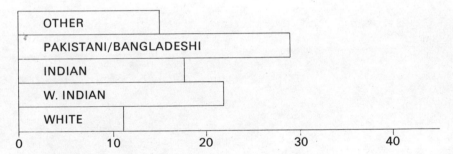

Unemployment amongst ethnic minorities, males, aged 16–64
Source: Adapted from *Employment Gazette*, January 1987

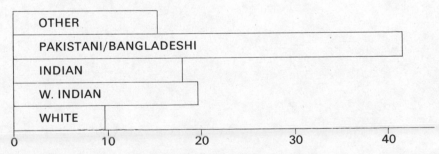

Unemployment amongst ethnic minorities, females, aged 16–59
Source: Adapted from *Employment Gazette*, January 1987

Using the bar charts above together with any other data to which you have access, write a commentary on unemployment amongst Britain's ethnic minorities. Discuss whether all employers should operate equal opportunities policies and how such policies might be monitored. Should the number of black employees be (i) near the proportion of blacks in Britain or (ii) near the proportion of blacks living in the area local to the place of employment? Should either the proportion of blacks employed, or the grade of job at which they are employed be monitored?

22

Women, Inequality and Politics

In the past, an understanding of women's role in political life was gained from the research of male political scientists. Recently female political scientists have challenged the familiar portrayal of women and successfully modified the way in which women are seen to act politically. This chapter examines the new portrayal of 'political woman' and considers the women's movement as a force for change in society. We shall see that women do occupy many political roles, but the pattern is uneven. Why is this so?

In the past many assumed that the rough-and-tumble world of politics was more suited to men than women. This was because men alone were seen as having the personal qualities –ambition and aggression – needed to survive in political life. Political scientists, who are mostly men, were influenced by this view. Their research often reinforced the biased belief that women were unsuited for political careers or public service. Political scientists were blind to the contribution that women made to politics in the past, not recognising, for example, their part in the food riots of the seventeenth and eighteenth centuries and the anti-Poor Law demonstrations of the nineteenth century. It was argued by political scientists that boys were socialised into behaving like men and therefore would take an interest in politics, whereas girls were socialised into behaving like women and as a consequence would be much less interested in politics. In modern voting studies, where daughters and fathers or wives and husbands were found voting for the same party, it was inevitably assumed that the female's vote in each case was a reflection of the male's. Few researchers even considered the possibility of daughters influencing the way their fathers voted or wives influencing the way their husbands voted.

This unflattering portrait of women's role in politics has been challenged. For example, the argument that women are less interested in politics than men and less likely to vote in an election is hard to sustain. Recent studies have shown that there is only a different of 1 per cent in the turnout rate between men and women in general elections. The orthodox portrayal of women being more conservative than men can be misleading. This image of women may be no more than a reflection of the fact that people become more conservative as they grow older and women live longer than men. Female political conservatism, then, is more likely to be related to demographic factors than it is to attitudes towards politics. Certainly, support for the Conservative Party in recent elections does not give much support to the idea that conservatism is more likely to be found amongst women than amongst men.

Today, the study of political science is much more conscious of its male bias and the false assumptions that were made about women and politics in the past. This new awareness to the role of women has been triggered by the explosion of feminist literature and by the activity of women in the real world of politics. Political science and politics in society are still, as we shall see, 'a man's world' but far less so now than even twenty years ago.

THE WOMEN'S MOVEMENT

All contemporary societies are to varying degrees male-dominated. In Britain, as in other Western countries, prestige is attached to 'men's work', be it the glamour of a professional career or the *machismo* of manual labour, whilst women's place of work is seen as in the home. The difference is reflected in rewards; men's work earns a salary or wage whilst women's domestic labour is unpaid. When women enter paid employment, their average incomes are lower than men's. Part-time, unskilled and low-paid jobs are filled overwhelmingly by women. Despite the fact that women account for approximately 40 per cent of Britain's total labour force, women receive far less promotion and career advancement than men. Also, the very nature of women's jobs makes them most vulnerable to automation, and it is women's jobs that are most likely to be lost first as a direct result of the introduction of new technologies.

Why do women experience these inequalities? The most obvious explanation lies in the physical differences between male and female, the male being both bigger and stronger than the female. In addition women, being child-bearers, are particularly vulnerable during pregnancy and require the support of others. These biological differences, and their associated inequalities, have been challenged by Ann Oakley in *Sex, Gender and Society* (1972). It has been argued that within each sex, size and strength varies. Many large or athletic women are stronger than small and puny men. Also, the fact that women bear children need not result in women relying on male protection and support. In some non-Western societies, childbirth only causes a small interruption in a woman's working life and the tasks of child-rearing are as much male as female occupations. In short, it is argued that the biological sex-based differences between men and women are not the cause of female inequality. Rather, it is the cultural differences and differing role-expectations between men and women – described as 'gender' – that determine differences in status and power. For example, the fact that there are few female lorry-drivers is based on *gender* (what is understood in society about what is 'men's work' and what is 'women's work') and not on *sex* (since there is nothing in physical terms to prevent women driving lorries).

Given these gender-based inequalities, it is not surprising that some women have campaigned to improve the status of women in society. What is termed the 'first wave' of the women's movement involved the struggle of women to win the vote in the early decades of this century. The 'second wave' began in the mid-1960s, made considerable progress during the 1970s, but is experiencing mixed fortunes at the present time.

The women's movement is not a formal political organisation in the sense that it has a national, regional and local structure which recruits members who, in turn, elect officials. It is informally organised and highy factionalised. The women's movement is made up of a network of small localised groups, some of which work within established organisations such as trade unions or political parties. At the beginning of the century, the first wave of the movement exhibited 'moderate' and 'radical' wings and these survive today. The struggle to obtain the vote was waged by the 'respectable' suffragists and the 'militant' suffragettes. The Housewives' League, led by Irene Lovelock, was an example of a 'moderate' post-war protest against 'women's lot', which was made up of rationing, queueing and austerity.

The contemporary women's movement has been studied by Vicky Randall and in *Women and Politics* (1982) she has identified at least three major strands or factions:

1. *Radical feminists* are the most militant within the women's movement and include extremists such as the political lesbians. Generally speaking, radical feminists emphasise the extent to which women are physically oppressed and dominated by men. They point to wife-battering, rape and pornography as manifestations of male oppression.
2. *Marxist feminists* also have a conflict view of society, but believe that the struggle of the working class and the struggle of women are not necessarily one and the same. The class struggle is recognised as the more significant of the two, but it is also believed that female inequality will still exist after the overthrow of the capitalist system and that a separate struggle will still lie ahead for female emancipation. Marxist feminists do not shun collaboration with men, as does the radical element, and they work with Left-wing and trade union organisations in order to improve the lot of women. The second-wave radical and Marxist feminists are often lumped together by the mass media and described as 'Women's Lib'.
3. *Reformist feminists*, the heirs of the constitutionally minded suffragists, form the third strand. It is probably true to say that most people, male and female, would accept the arguments of reformist feminists as constituting the 'reasonable face of feminism'. Reformists argue that generally speaking women suffer from a series of handicaps and disadvantages in

society, and that all of these can be eliminated over time by equal rights legislation.

Reformist feminists argue that much of the battle against female inequality has been won. The *Equal Pay Act* 1970 stipulated equal pay for equal work and the *Sex Discrimination Act* 1975 ended discrimination against women in employment, education, housing, as well as in other service areas. The Act also established the *Equal Opportunities Commission*, a body to investigate infringements of the Equal Pay and Sex Discrimination Acts. Residual inequalities – in areas such as retirement and taxation – can be eliminated by future legislation.

The women's movement has also made legislative advances in the area of abortion reform. The abortion issue is of great importance to feminists since it symbolises a woman's reproductive self-determination. As a result, some feminists have taken an extremely hard line on abortion and have been accused of displaying a fascist disregard for human life. On the other hand, many women, including Roman Catholics, put the 'right to life' above 'the woman's right to choose'. Regardless of the moral arguments, the number of legal abortions has increased steadily throughout the 1970s, with over 160 000 operations being carried out in 1981.

The women's movement is not without its critics. Some of them point out that, despite feminist claims that sex is the fundamental division in society and causes inequalities above and beyond those caused by social class or race, the women's movement itself it a very middle-class political phenomenon. It has failed to appeal or to mobilise those women who suffer greatest social disadvantage, namely those found in the working class. It is argued that this prove that social class *is* a greater cause of inequality in society than is sex. In addition, critics contend that the women's movement has failed to win the support of all middle-class women.

It might also be argued that feminists have *not* made any substantial improvements in women's place in society. For example, attempts to reduce or eliminate the inequalities facing women at work have hardly been successful. As the Equal Opportunities Commission has acknowledged, attempts to do this using the Equal Pay and Sex Discrimination Acts have been largely unsuccessful. There were only 150 actions brought under the latter Act in 1982. Perhaps surprisingly, 26 per cent of the applicants were male. 63 per cent of all applications were 'cleared' without a tribunal hearing. Those applications that arrived at a tribunal hearing (56 out of 150 in 1982) led to a dismissal of the application in thirty-two cases, compensation in seventeen cases and a 'recommended course of action' in seven cases. Success using the Equal Pay Act is even less. In 1982, there were only thirty-nine applications; thirteen were brought to tribunal, and a mere two actions were successful. It is widely accepted that the poor success rate of actions has resulted in many women being unwilling to try to use the Act to remedy the inequalities they experience at work.

Some critics of the women's movement argue that feminists undervalue the traditional role of women in society and underestimate the political influence already wielded by women. For example, it is argued that feminists neither recognise the responsibilities involved in child-rearing nor do they understand the extent to which mothers shape the personalities and views of their children, be they boys or girls.

WOMEN IN POLITICAL OFFICE

Women form 52 per cent of the electorate in Britain yet under 7 per cent of MPs are female. It is, perhaps, a little misleading to focus on Britain's longest-serving modern Prime Minister since for long periods Mrs Thatcher was the only woman in her Cabinet. Of course MPs are elected to represent their constituencies and not a particular social group. Whilst the composition of MPs in Parliament is not expected to reflect the composition of society at large, on commonsense grounds alone it is clear that women are underrepresented. The position is somewhat better in local government; in 1977, 17 per cent of local councillors were women.

The Labour Party, but not the Conservative Party, is the focus of much feminist political activity. Although five of the twenty-seven places on Labour's National Executive Committee (NEC) are reserved for women, this has not satisfied demands that women should play a larger role in the movement. The existence of the Women's Section on the NEC is somewhat misleading as an instrument for female representation since the whole of Labour's Conference takes part in the voting. This means that the result of elections to the Women's Section is decided by the large block votes cast by a small number of powerful – but more significantly, male – trade union leaders. Often, union leaders make bargains with each other in order to fix support for their candidates in the elections to Labour's NEC and TUC's General Council: 'I'll support your candidate for the Women's Section of the NEC if you'll support my candidate for a place on the General Council.' The voice of female representation in the Labour Party can become very faint when such power politics operate within the wider movement. Many women believe that the five places on the NEC should be elected by Labour's National Organisation of Women Conference and not by the male-dominated Annual Conference.

Labour women also complain that not enough women are selected as prospective parliamentary candidates. This is partly a reflection of the fact that trade unions sponsor many Labour candidates, and women tend to play a very small role inside the unions. The SDP went further than the other major political parties in facilitating the participation of women. According to the Party's constitution, at least two women must be included in the final panel of candidates from which an SPD prospective parliamentary candidate will be selected. Women play a significant role in the selection of Conservative candidates but not one that feminists find palatable. In the selection of prospective MPs, candidates' wives are also 'vetted' in order to check on their suitability. There is a strong tradition in the Conservative Party which views women as merely an adjunct to the political male.

The House of Commons has been described as 'the best gentlemen's club in the world'. The working of the Westminster system is certainly designed to meet the comfort and convenience of its male members. The daily routines of an MP in the House – including late-night sittings – are not organised in a way to help female MPs who have young children. In a study of the 1974 Parliament, it was revealed that only two of the twenty-seven female MPs had children under the age of 10. There is a tendency for women MPs to be either single or divorced. The higher proportion of women in local government reflects greater opportunity to combine the domestic role with the public role than is available in national government. Some women have campaigned for reforms in retiming and relocating meetings so that more women would be able to play an active role in politics, but so far their demands for change have gone unheeded.

It has been argued that the biggest barrier to women holding political office lies in the belief held by many that they will not be successful. In other words, because many women feel that they stand little chance of being selected, they do not allow themselves to be put forward as candidates. In addition, even if a woman is selected as a candidate, there is a view that 'the electorate don't like voting for a woman'. If a potential woman candidate expects there to be a slim chance of being selected by the party in the first place to fight an election, and then sees her sex as an electoral liability if the candidates put forward by rival parties are men, we cannot be surprised that there are so few women in Parliament and in local councils.

WOMEN IN PUBLIC OFFICE

Ministers have powers to appoint members to serve on numerous public bodies, such as nationalised industry consumer councils or quangos. In 1977 the Equal Opportunities Commission conducted a survey to monitor the number of women appointed to such bodies. By 1981, it had found that 23 per cent of all appointments went to women. Women were found in greatest numbers on 'caring' bodies and consumer affairs bodies, and in fewest numbers on bodies responsible for trade, industry and the police. For example, it was found that women made up 30 per cent of the appointments made by the Home Office but only 1.9 per cent of those made by the Department of Industry.

The world of trade unions has experienced a dramatic increase in the number of women members, but little else has changed in this male-dominated movement. About a third of all union members are women, and the Equal Opportunities Commission found that between 1970 and 1979 membership growth for women was 41.7 per cent compared with 6.1 per cent for men. At the same time, more than half of all female workers were not members of a trade union. Although the position is changing slowly, most women are passive union members with only a very small number taking

TABLE 22.1

Representation of women in trade unions, as members

Union	Membership		
	Total	Women	% Women
APEX	95 049	50 594	53.2
ASTMS	390 000	87 750	22.2
BIFU	154 579	78 765	50.9
CPSA	190 347	137 369	72.2
GMBATU	766 744	258 739	33.7
NALGO	766 390	390 859	51.0
NUPE	680 000	455 600	67.0
NUT	250 499	180 179	71.9
NUTGW	76 509	69 319	90.6
TGWU	1 490 555	228 750	15.3
USDAW	392 307	239 170	61.0

Source: *The Guardian*, 2 September 1985.

TABLE 22.2

Representation of women as active officers in trade unions

	Executive members		Full-time officials		TUC delegates	
	Total	Women	Total	Women	Total	Women
APEX	15	3 (8)	47	2 (25)	13	5 (7)
ASTMS	22	2 (5)	95	6 (21)	28	3 (6)
BIFU	32	4 (16)	37	7 (19)	19	4 (10)
CPSA	29	4 (21)	14	3 (10)	30	9 (22)
GMBATU	38	1 (13)	287	12 (97)	86	4 (29)
NALGO	71	20 (36)	191	20 (97)	72	23 (37)
NUPE	26	10 (17)	180	12 (120)	34	10 (23)
NUT	41	8 (29)	27	2 (19)	37	10 (27)
NUTGW	15	8 (14)	38	4 (34)	13	10 (12)
TGWU	42	1 (6)	500	9 (76)	92	9 (16)
USDAW	18	1 (11)	122	10 (74)	35	5 (21)

(Figures in brackets show how many women there would be if represented according to their share of membership)
Source: *The Guardian*, 2 September 1985.

active roles in the form of positions on executive committees or full-time officials. Britain's first woman general secretary of a trade union was Brenda Dean, leader of SOGAT 82. But as Table 22.1 indicates the general picture of the trade union is one of female underrepresentation. For example, in the shopworkers' union, USDAW, women form 61 per cent of the membership. Yet only one member of its executive is a woman and only ten of its 122 full-time officials are women. Also GMBATU and the TGWU represent nearly half a million women yet have only two female executive members between them. Tables 22.1 and 22.2 show the representation of women in trade unions, as members and as active office-holders.

WOMEN'S 'INVISIBLE' POLITICAL ACTIVITY

It has been argued that women make a contribution to political life through informal, less conventional means and, furthermore, that this contribution goes largely unrecorded by political scientists and journalists. For example, women have campaigned on numerous moral issues which have failed to attract sustained media attention. In the past, women were highly influencial in the Temperance movement; during the 1970s, the 'Mothers of Peace' movement lit a brief glimmer of hope in Northern Ireland, and today women play a large role in the Peace Movement.

What all these campaigns have in common is a loosely structured organisation. Their activities are only 'newsworthy' when dramatic newsreel can be filmed; otherwise, their activities go unnoticed. Frequently, women organise 'protest politics' at local or community level regarding the provision of facilities, and this too tends to be ignored by the media. Women are prominent in tenants' groups, child-care campaigns, health campaigns, and anti-poverty lobbies. Women combine self-help projects – such as meeting the needs of the single-parent family – with pressure-group activity. A most important development of self-help was the welfare and political activity undertaken by miners' wives during the 1984–5 coal dispute.

Furthermore, some women's groups which are often defined as apolitical in nature do, in fact, attempt to influence government policies. Women's Institutes, Townswomen's Guilds, the Mothers' Union and the WRVS have an estimated membership of 3m. They have participated in campaigns and lobbying on issues such as the payment of Child Benefit, taxation policy, local planning decisions, closure of local schools and the provision of public transport in rural areas.

It is possible, therefore, to conclude that women still play a minor role in the formal institutions of Britain – Parliament, local councils, political parties, public bodies and established interest groups. If, however, female political activity is explored in informal political settings – community groups, moral campaigns, the women's movement network, and the political activities of organisations such as the Women's Institute, a very different picture emerges. In areas which are free from male prejudices and arbitrary constraints which discourage women, and which allow them to combine domestic roles with public roles, there is a great deal of female political activity. There is enough, certainly, to question the commonly held assumption that 'politics is a man's world'.

SUMMARY

The political role of women is being increasingly appreciated although it is still largely absent from many formal political limitations, with the House of Commons as the most important example. The women's movement provides an interesting case-study of an informally structured political organisation with mainly middle-class participation. Frequently, female participation in politics takes unorthodox forms since this allows women to reconcile their traditional domestic roles with practical roles.

FURTHER READING

Culley, L. (1985) *Women and Power*, Leicester, Hyperion Press.
Hunt, K. (1987) 'Women and Politics', in B. Jones (ed.) *Political Issues in Britain Today*, Manchester, University Press.
Oakley, A. (1972) *Sex, Gender and Society*, Hounslow, Temple Smith.
Randall, V. (1987) *Women and Politics*, London, Macmillan, 2nd edn.
Vallance, E. (1979) *Women in the House*, London, Athlone Press.

QUESTIONS

1. 'Where power is, woman is not.' Is this an accurate reflection of women's role in British politics?

2. Comment upon the success and failures of the women's movement.

ASSIGNMENT

Using the tables as a resource, write a short study which examines male and female patterns of qualification and graduate employment. What patterns, if any, are still 'typically male' and which 'typically female'? What measures can a government take to ensure equality of opportunity for both sexes to enter all types of careers?

Intended destination of school leavers: by sex, 1984/85

England & Wales	Percentages and thousands	
	Boys	Girls
Leavers intending to enter full-time further or higher education as a percentage of all school leavers – by type of course		
Degree	8.5	6.3
Teacher training	0.1	0.7
HND/HNC	0.5	0.4
OND/OND	0.2	0.1
BTEC	1.7	1.7
GCE 'A' level	3.8	4.6
GCE 'O' level	1.9	2.1
Catering	0.7	1.5
Nursing	—	1.7
Secretarial	—	3.7
Other full-time	6.7	10.0
Total leavers intending to enter full-time further or higher education		
(percentages)	24.2	32.9
(thousands)	96.1	126.4
Leavers available for employment[1]		
(percentages)	75.8	67.1
(thousands)	300.9	257.3
Total school leavers (=100%)		
(thousands)	397.0	383.6

1 Includes leavers going into temporary employment pending entry into full-time further or higher education or whose destination was not known.

Source: *Department of Education and Science: Welsh Office;* reprinted in *Social Trends,* 17, 1987.

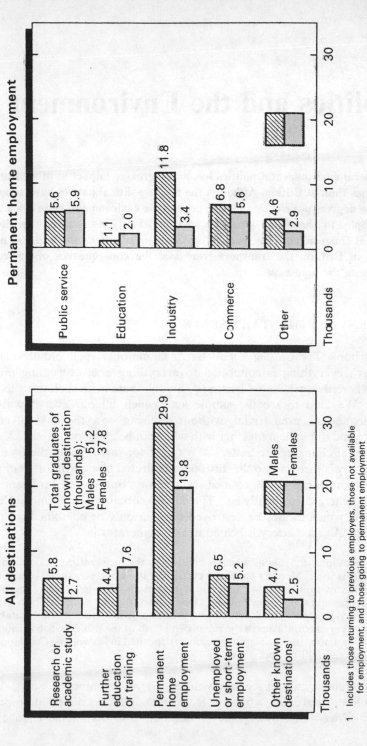

Destination of first degree graduates: by sex, 1984/85
United Kingdom

All destinations

Permanent home employment

1 Includes those returning to previous employers, those not available for employment, and those going to permanent employment overseas.

Source: *Department of Education and Science* reprinted in *Social Trends*, 17, 1987.

23

Politics and the Environment

In general environmental politics has made greater impact in other European countries than in Britain. Although the major political parties have adopted to varying degrees policies designed to protect the environment, none has a 'green' philosophy to shape and structure such policies. This chapter considers the political dimension of three current environmental issues – the future of nuclear power in Britain, the transport issue and the consequences of agricultural decline on the landscape.

THE ENVIRONMENTAL DEBATE

In his book *The Closing Circle* Barry Commoner spelt out the 'laws of ecology': everything is connected to everything else; everything must go somewhere; Nature knows best; and, finally, there is no such thing as a free lunch. We tend to see the simple acts which fill our everyday lives as inconsequential, even trivial, without realising how the laws of ecology operate and draw them together with what can be awesome impact. A simple example of changing the battery of a transistor radio makes the point. The old battery is thrown into the dustbin, is collected along with other domestic rubbish and taken to the council incinerator. 'But', asked Professor Commoner, 'where does it really go?' The battery contains a heavy metal element, mercury, which cannot be destroyed but can only be combined with other elements. As the battery is heated in the incinerator it

> produces mercury vapour which is emitted by the incinerator stack, and mercury vapour is toxic. Mercury vapour is carried by the wind, eventually brought down to earth in rain or snow. Entering a mountain lake, let us say, the mercury condenses and sinks to the bottom. Here it is acted on by bacteria which convert it to methyl mercury. This is soluble and taken up by fish; since it is not metabolised, the mercury accumulates in the organs and flesh of the fish. The fish is caught and eaten by a man and the mercury becomes deposited in his organs (Commoner, *The Closing Circle*, 1971, pp. 33–46).

The interconnection of seemingly unrelated yet commonplace acts – changing a battery and eating a fish; the fact that the mercury did not disappear but simply moved from one place to another; that man-made changes were detrimental to the environment; and that the benefits of a battery-operated radio are gained at the cost of pollution and possible ill-health – together illustrate the working of ecological laws. These laws are working across such a wide range of behaviours with such adverse effects that some scientists talk of there being an 'ecological crisis'. They believe that great damage has already been done to the thin skin of earth, water and air that clothes 'Planet Earth' with yet greater damage in store. The air is polluted by carbon dioxide resulting from the burning of coal and oil, and this is producing the 'greenhouse effect' as the atmosphere slowly heats up because excessive carbon dioxide absorbs heat that previously would have been radiated away. Some believe that this will result in climatic changes which will melt the polar ice-caps and transform the world's most fertile areas into deserts. Burning coal and oil also produces large quantities of sulphur dioxide in the atmosphere resulting in acid rain which kills forests and water life. Nitrogen fertilisers used in increasing quantities by farmers have now been washed from the land and have found their way into drinking water causing a major health hazard for young children. Nuclear testing has put radioactive substances into the bones of children for the first time in human history. Exposure to another heavy metal – lead – put into the atmosphere by car exhausts has resulted in the impaired mental development of many urban children. Cancers have been caused through exposure to asbestos. The thinning in the ozone layer which surrounds the Earth has concerned the scientific community. This layer of gas acts as a vital filter which protects animals and plants from the Sun's ultraviolet rays and it has almost disappeared altogether over Antarctica. Scientists do not know the precise cause of this; some blame the action of chlorofluorocarbons from aerosol sprays on the ozone layer whilst others believe the damage may be inflicted by supersonic aircraft. This list of potential disasters seems endless, so why is global society not in a state of panic?

Environmentalists argue that many of the major ecological threats are recent, and their effects have not yet been fully understood or felt. They sometimes use the analogy of a pond which is gradually being covered by a weed. The area covered by the week doubles each day, so that by the twelfth day half the pond is covered. Suddenly, on the thirteenth day, the pond will be totally covered by weed. Environmentalists see a crisis creeping up on mankind and taking governments by surprise in a similar way. How has the political system responded to the relatively new environmental lobby and with what results?

THE NUCLEAR POWER DEBATE

Many environmental problems are caused by our ignorance about what impact a new substance will have on the environment until it is produced and its effects become evident. Sometimes it appears that 'technology' is well ahead of 'scientific knowledge' in terms of wider developments. For example, American civil defence films made during the early years of the Cold War advised on ways in which to survive a nuclear attack. 'Duck and cover' was the advice which ran over scenes of a relaxed family on a picnic outing in the countryside. They smiled at each other with serene confidence and sheltered under a tablecloth as mushroom clouds rose from mock nuclear explosions in the surrounding fields. The nuclear industry is in its infancy and there is still as much possibility of a similar naivety existing in the 1980s regarding the risks involved as there is of environmentalists exaggerating the potential dangers.

The nuclear industry has argued that it can safely produce increasingly cheaper energy. These claims have been challenged at various enquiries by groups such as *Friends of the Earth* (FoE), who have pointed to issues such as nuclear power stations facilitating nuclear proliferation as well as their vulnerability to terrorist attacks. Concern has also been expressed about health risks. Evidence regarding the incidence of childhood leukaemia is interpreted in quite different ways by epidemiologists. For example, in the Seascale community close to Sellafield, leukaemia in people aged 25 and under is ten times higher than the national average. Similar concentrations are found near to other nuclear installations in Britain. Some experts have found this correlation compelling evidence that nuclear plants cause child-hood leukaemia, but others have been more cautious and have pointed to concentrations of leukaemia cases in areas such as Dane End in Hertford-shire, Slough and Lytham St Anne's which are distant from sources of nuclear radiation. They have argued that rare diseases frequently appear as uneven outbreaks. They have also pointed out that cancer cases amongst Sellafield workers are lower than national rates. The controversy was not settled by the official report from Sir Douglas Black in which a qualified reassurance was given to people living near Sellafield. It was subsequently revealed that actual radiation levels around Sellafield were up to five times higher than the nuclear industry had informed the Black inquiry.

The safety of reactors from serious accidents is an issue which concerns the nuclear lobby and environmentalists alike. The US Atomic Energy Commis-sion calculated that the chances of an accident big enough to kill seventy people was one in a million. That remote chance cropped up very early in the life of the Chernobyl reactor in Russia. Fallout from the Chernobyl nuclear accident fell over the norther hemisphere with many countries, including Britain, placing restrictions on the movement of livestock and agricultural produce. It appears that the Soviet plant was of inferior design and poorly managed, giving superficial credibility to the British nuclear industry's claim that 'it couldn't happen here'. But although Britain has not experienced a Chernobyl-type disaster, neither has the industry been accident-free. For example, Windscale (now Sellafield) had a fire in the plutonium reactor in

1951 and the government ordered the destruction of 2m gallons of local milk which had become contaminated. Since then over 300 small accidents have occurred at Sellafield, a record which has brought some criticism from official quarters on the plant's management.

Sellafield has tended to be at the centre of the civil nuclear debate in Britain because the plant deals with the 'dirtiest' part of the industry in recycling waste. In the memorable words of the *Daily Mirror*, it is 'the world's first nuclear dustbin'. The European Parliament and the Manx Tynwald have called for its closure and as recently as 1983 Greenpeace activists revealed that the Sellafield discharge pipe has released radioactive waste which contaminated the local sea and beaches. Getting rid of low-level nuclear waste has posed the nuclear industry a problem which has raised domestic and foreign opposition to its proposals. The Nuclear Industry Radioactive Waste Executive (Nirex) proposed test drilling at possible sites for dumping low-level waste in Humberside, Lincolnshire and Bedfordshire but met with active opposition from community-based groups before eventually abandoning the exercise. Another Nirex proposal was that waste should be buried in boreholes thousands of feet below the North Sea. Norwegian and Danish governments expressed anxieties over the potential hazards of such a method of waste disposal and criticised the British nuclear industry for not solving the problem of waste removal before embarking on a nuclear energy programme.

How has the civil nuclear debate been approached by the major political parties? The most sustained opposition in the 1970s and 1980s came from Liberals; the greatest support is found in the Conservative Party. Labour and the unions are split on the issue, for Sellafield employs 15 500 workers in an area of high unemployment. Engineering unions support nuclear power development, whilst it is in the interests of miners to oppose it. Labour's official policy represents a traditional compromise which reconciles the conflicting interests within the party. The party is committed to withdrawing from nuclear power, but at the same time it recognises that implementation would necessarily be slow and take the lifetime of several Labour governments to accomplish.

What can the nuclear power debate tell us about the nature of British politics? An élitist interpretation would stress the cult of secrecy that restricts the flow of information to the public. If 'knowledge is power' then the nuclear debate is confined to a small élite of experts. It would also be argued that the great public inquiries regarding Windscale in the 1970s and Sizewell in the 1980s were sham insofar as they only had the appearance of pluralism in operation. The reality was of two sides unmatched in resources, with FoE having only a fraction of the wealth that was deployed by the nuclear industry, and in each inquiry the result in favour of the nuclear industry was a foregone conclusion. In other words, regardless of the relative quality of the cases presented to the inquiries by the environmentalists and nuclear industry, it was never anticipated that the environmentalists might win.

A pluralist interpretation of Britain's nuclear debate would stress that what could have been merely local planning inquiries were 'opened up' to provide a forum for a national debate and public participation to consider all the issues involved. In 1975 there was departmental opposition from the Treasury, Ministry of Defence, Department of Trade and Industry, and the Foreign and Commonwealth Office to Windscale being the subject of a local inquiry, but the Cabinet overruled their objections. Pluralists would emphasise the influence of specific groups in the decision-making progress, such as the community action groups which contested Nirex's proposals. The development of nuclear power in Britain is seen as inevitable not because it is in the vital interests of the capitalist system, but because a professional civil nuclear lobby has convinced governments that 'what is good for the nuclear industry is good for Britain'. To date, the other lobbies, such as the environmentalists, have been less persuasive and less skilful in capturing the ear of government but this need not remain the case. Pluralists argue that new circumstances, such as a major disaster, would make the arguments of rival lobbies more salient. Some anticipate that the privatisation of the electricity supply will create such a change of circumstances; since the nuclear power industry was created 'artificially' by government, so it has been argued that the free market will eventually cause its demise. For an example of what could happen in Britain, pluralists look to the USA where an unexpected alliance between Right-wing conservative politicians and the environmental lobby has successfully opposed nuclear developments.

THE TRANSPORT DEBATE

An assessment of the impact of the manufacture and use of cars has been made by M. Gibbons and R. Voyer. Their useful article entitled 'Technological Assessment: bias-free analysis' was first published in *New Scientist* (25 May 1974) and is cited in F. Sandbach, *Environment, Ideology and Policy* (1980). In addition to the more obvious benefits, such as bringing geographic mobility and expanding personal freedom, and obvious disadvantages, such as increasing levels of pollution and congestion, the arrival of the car has made an impact which is felt throughout society. Indeed, much of society has been shaped around the car. For example, mass car ownership has brought changes in patterns of courtship, socialisation and training of children, work habits, use of leisure time and family patterns; it has caused changes in the patterns of crime; it has created a new class of semi-skilled industrial workers; it has resulted in a shift of population to the suburbs; it has led to an expansion of industries such as tourism and insurance as well as being the life-blood of many other dependent industries; it has increased government income through a variety of taxes; and it has led to the decline in public transport.

In short, much of the way in which we live and the quality of life is based on car-ownership. Yet not everybody drives or has access to a private car, so the advantages are not evenly spread. Thus, the politics of 'who gets what' characterises the transport debate, with the nation divided into car-owners and non-owners. Who benefits and who loses? In 1984 61 per cent of Britain's households had the use of a private car. In the south-east of England, there were 340 cars per thousand population with a considerably lower figure of 204 cars per thousand in the North. Car-ownership is associated with two basic factors – need and affluence. Ownership is higher in rural areas, where cars are needed to travel to amenities, and amongst the wealthier in society. For example, in the richest 10 per cent of households, 90 per cent have cars whereas in the poorest 10 per cent of households only 10 per cent have cars. Those who depend upon public transport facilities include not only the less wealthy but also women, children and pensioners. Even on car-based housing estates, there are many women who do not drive the family car.

Not only are those without cars denied the benefits of car-ownership, they are also disadvantaged by the decline in public transport caused by increased car use. Between 1971 and 1981 bus services in Britain were cut by a quarter, and between 1963 and 1983 rail routes were cut by a third with the total number of railway stations cut by almost half. For both bus and rail, having fewer passengers resulted in higher fares and reduced services. This situation – in which the already disadvantaged were to be disadvantaged still further – was repeated in areas of wider social organisation referred to by Gibbons and Voyer.

The increase in car use has led to the development of hypermarket shopping facilities with plentiful parking space at the edges of towns. There is an increasing trend for massive developments to be located near motorway access points. These developments are very convenient for private car users, but they put at risk the viability of inner-city supermarkets which are used by non-car-users. The increase in car use has also led to demands for more roads to be provided. In urban areas the policy has been to carry out road-building on the cheapest land, which is inevitably found in the poorer neighbourhoods. Thus, the very people who will suffer from the increased pollution brought by new roads will include those least likely to own a car and least likely to benefit from new roads.

Environmentalists think that the increase in road traffic is partly to blame for Britain's high levels of respiratory illnesses and heart disease, as well as ecological damage. They argue that the odds are loaded against public transport in the way decisions are made. For example, between 1980 and 1987 40 000 people died on Britain's roads, yet this loss to the nation is not part of any calculation regarding transport policy. If 40 000 people died as a result of street crime over a similar period it would be a national scandal, yet as a total for road deaths it is an acceptable price for car use and road haulage. In the same period, only thirty-two British Rail passengers died in accidents yet this is not recognised as a positive benefit in the manner environmentalists would wish. They have argued that British Rail is unpopular with government because it receives a subsidy to operate. They have also argued that road transport, which led to the decline in rail transport, receives a hidden subsidy from the wider public. The licence fee from private car-users subsidises heavy vehicles which pay a disproportionately low licence fee in relation to the costs they bring about in road maintenance. Private car use is subsidised insofar as many firms supply their employees with 'company cars', the cost of which is passed on to the consumer in higher prices.

There are two basic philosophies which have shaped transport policy and these are represented in Labour and Conservative approaches. Labour tends to view public transport as a social service which can extend the opportunities of less well-off communities, and so the party supports subsidising public transport. An interesting case arose when the Labour-controlled Greater London Council (as it then was) lowered public transport fares and intended to raise a supplementary rate in order to provide an increased subsidy. It was argued by the GLC that its 'Fares Fair' policy attracted many additional passengers who had previously travelled by car and therefore the capital's roads were being less polluted and less congested. However, some ratepayers' associations argued that car-users did not benefit from lower fares although they had to pay the supplementary rate. Bromley Council challenged the GLC, with the case eventually going to the House of Lords which ruled in favour of Bromley.

The Conservative approach relied much more on the laws of supply and demand to shape public transport provision. The working of the free market was seen as more efficient than subsidies in meeting customer needs. Consistent with this approach to public transport, the National Bus Company was broken up and privatised with many routes deregulated, and British Rail's subsidy was cut by a third over a seven-year period in pursuit of commercial viability. Critics have argued that the outcome of market forces has been mixed, with urban bus services improving but rural ones being decimated, and with BR meeting its financial targets only by making counter-productive economies such as scrapping rolling stock and reducing services.

The Department of Transport is frequently accused of having a pro-private/anti-public transport bias. It is argued that this is reflected in, for example, the Department refusing to acknowledge rail safety as a factor when assessing the relative advantages of investing public resources in road and rail developments. Critics have argued that the Department's staff include many road engineers who identify closely with the interests of the highly organised road lobby. Although many groups such as FoE, the Ramblers' Association, Women's Institutes and numerous civic bodies, express an interest in transport issues, they are no match for the British Road

Federation (BRF). The BRF acts as an umbrella organisation for groups such as the Road Haulage Association, the AA and RAC, the Freight Transport Association, the Society of Motor Manufacturers and Traders and British Aggregate Construction Materials Industries. In addition to this, the general business lobby, including hypermarket traders and oil companies, attempts to influence government to favour road investment. Although community groups and environmental groups may win isolated victories on specific localised proposals, business interests appear to be winning the contest to influence policies at the national level.

THE COUNTRYSIDE DEBATE

Holding a romantic view of the countryside is said to be part of the British culture which values the timeless pace of life, the small village community, and visions of stout farmers doing honest toil in their fields. But the rural landscape of contemporary Britain is very different from the Utopian vision. Indeed, it is very different from the agricultural landscape of Britain only forty years ago. Large agricultural undertakings in the hands of employed farm managers have taken away much of the countryside from the yeoman farmer. Since the end of the Second World War, England has lost 80 per cent of its old woodlands, 90 per cent of its ponds and 95 per cent of its hay meadows. A patchwork of small fields has been turned into a landscape of large fields, with the process of 'prairification' being accomplished by the removal of enough hedgerow to encircle the earth six times. Many of the old village communities are now lifeless during the daytime since the original inhabitants can no longer afford to live there. A new class of long-distance commuter and second-home owner now populates the real Ambridges.

Rachel Carson's book *Silent Spring* (1962) drew attention to the harmful effects of pesticides on wildlife. The production of agrochemicals – fertilisers, pesticides and herbicides – is big business, as farmers push up their output through the application of more and more chemicals to the land. From 1953 to 1976, for example, the use of chemical fertilisers increased eightfold and between 1944 and 1975 the number of pesticides available to farmers increased twelvefold. But what facilitated the green revolution of rapidly rising yields also damaged the environment. In the 1950s it was discovered that widespread use of organochlorine pesticides, such as DDT, was killing off species of bird life and use of herbicides was reducing the variety of wild flowers previously found in the countryside. Fertilisers were also causing problems since many phosphates and nitrogenous treatments were being washed into streams where they stimulated excessive growth of algae. Such growth gradually excluded light from the previously clear water, resulting in fresh water fouling up.

The 1960s and 1970s were characterised by political conflict between environmental and conservationist groups on the one hand, and farmers on the other. Conservationists argued that in the space of a few decades farmers had destroyed the rich and beautiful rural landscapes depicted by Constable, and replaced them with ugly and lifeless prairies. Farmers argued that they were in the business of producing food and not concerned with the romantic fantasies of those whose idea of the countryside was derived from pictures on chocolate boxes. The latter interest predominated and in referring to the influences of pressure groups on government, the National Farmers Union was frequently cited as an example of a powerful, perhaps *the* most powerful, group. Its influence, along with that of the Country Landowners Association, was brought to bear in the passing of the wide-ranging *Wildlife and Countryside Act* 1981. FoE and other environmental groups were dismayed by the Act which was very much in line with the wishes of the NFU with, for instance, provisions in Part II of the Act giving only minimal protection to Sites of Special Scientific Interest. However, by the late 1980s a new crisis in the countryside resulted in a realignment of interests, with farmers and conservationist coming together in an alliance against government.

High levels of subsidy for the production and storage of food along with high-technology farming methods have resulted in the accumulation of vast food surpluses. Within the European Community as a whole, millions of acres of farmland are no longer needed to grow food. In Britain alone, the highest estimate was that 85 per cent of farmland was surplus to requirements. Even the lower estimates put the proportion of redundant farmland at between an eighth and a third of the total acreage. The immediate political problems involve what to do with the farmers and what to do with their land.

The first problem poses government with the task of reducing agricultural output and thereby cutting farm incomes. This is a difficult task since many farmers borrowed heavily from the banks at a time when high land prices provided security. In 1985 the total farming debt was £9bn, a sum four times larger than current farm income. If farm incomes are reduced, then many farmers will be placed in positions of financial difficulty and even face bankruptcy. The government can reduce the quantity of produce or the level of income by establishing quotas (as in the case of milk production) or lower intervention prices (as in the case of grain). Such moves, together with falling land prices, have marked the start of a process of declining farm prosperity.

The second problem involves evolving a policy on what to do with unwanted farmland. It is expected that there will be enormous pressure to build on the low-fertility land in the south, such as Hampshire and Berkshire, with some fearing that the low-fertility land in the north will simply be abandoned to form huge tracts of wasteland. In 1987, the government set up a departmental working party code-named ALURE (Alternative Land Use and the Rural Economy). This drew up proposals which lifted building restrictions on less fertile land, encouraged conifer afforestation and encouraged land to be 'set aside' for non-agricultural uses, such as riding schools or golf courses. These proposals were accepted and put forward by the government to the dismay of both conservationists and the farming community.

Whilst the large cereal-growers looked to yet more intensive methods as a strategy for survival, some small farmers and environmentalists joined forces in advocating low-intensity farming methods. The environmental lobby argued that farmers should continue to receive subsidies but that these should be based on stewardship of the countryside rather than on maximising output, as in the past. Low input, using far fewer chemicals, would result in the now acceptable result of lower output coupled with environmentally acceptable farming methods. The new coalition of environmentalists and farmers was based on the preference of stepping backwards to adopt traditional arable and grazing techniques rather than on the proposals to abandon agriculture envisaged by ALURE.

CONCLUSION

Is a government's attitude towards the environment in any way related to the nature of the political system of which it is part? Are governments in capitalist countries influenced more by short-term profit motives which may put some aspect of the environment at risk, whilst communist governments are able to take environmental factors into account in their long-term planning? The immediate answer is that such a simple division between the East and West cannot be applied, for both systems are striving to increase economic growth and both systems share responsibility for pollution. Indeed, the industrial pollution from Eastern Europe in amongst the worst in the world and the Soviet nuclear disaster at Chernobyl caused more damage than the American near-accident at Three Mile Island. If any country or system wins credit in the estimation of environmentalists, it is China. It is argued that unlike the Americans, the Europeans or the Soviets, China does not measure economic progress by increases in the GNP. Chinese priorities are reflected in the wider goals of restricting urbanisation, encouraging local self-sufficiency and the careful use of scarce resources and recycling. Such goals are achieved in a manner which is not particularly damaging to the environment.

In terms of governmental organisation and legislation, Britain gives the impression of being an environment-conscious country. In 1970 the large Department of the Environment was created from the former Ministries of Housing and Local Government, Public Building and Works, and Transport. The functions of the new 'super-ministry' were to include 'the preservation of amenity, the protection of the coast and countryside and the control of air, water and noise pollution'. There are numerous Acts of Parliament designed to protect the environment; recent examples are the *Control of*

Pollution Act 1974, which superseded earlier Acts and covered wide areas of waste disposal and water, noise and atmospheric pollution, and the *Conservation of Wild Creatures and Wild Plants Act* 1975.

Nevertheless, the environmental lobby has criticised governments for being too slow in recognising the existence of problems and, in legislative terms, 'closing the stable doors after the horse has bolted'. It is also argued that what is on the Statute Book is frequently more impressive than policy implementation. The *Control of Pollution Act* 1974 is cited as an example of a well-intentioned Act which, because of financial cutbacks, is enforced minimally. In addition, environmentalists have argued that whilst nuclear power and motorway development public enquiries have given opportunities for wider participation, some Acts of Parliament have restricted public participation. For example, the *Opencast Coal Act* 1975, the *Community Land Act* 1976 and the *Offshore Petroleum (Scotland) Act* 1976 included provisions which curtailed a right to inquiry.

Environmentalism is represented in British politics by numerous groups and parties, and in political terms is a 'broad church movement'. The Green Party in Britain resulted from the Ecology Party changing its name in 1985, and the Ecology Party grew out of the People's Party which was founded in 1974. Green Party candidates attracted only minimal support in the 1987 General Election although in some previous local elections candidates won up to 30 per cent of the vote and have been represented on some parish councils. Some political scientists in the 1980s drew a contrast between the media coverage devoted to the 'new politics' of the SDP which received intensive news reporting, and the 'new politics' of the Green/Ecology Party which has gone unnoticed. It was felt that this differential treatment resulted to some extent from the fact that the SDP could be understood in terms of the already existing party political framework with Conservatives on the right and Labour on the left, but the radicalism of the Greens fell outside the traditional Left/Right dichotomy. Since their message could not be conveyed in an easily understandable form, they were discarded as unimportant 'eco-freaks'.

The 1980s has also seen the 'greening' of all major political parties. The Conservatives found that green issues such as the Channel Tunnel development, the M25 orbital motorway development and the Nirex test-drilling for nuclear waste dumps concerned MPs in Conservative-held constituencies. The 'new politics' of the Alliance's early years embraced environmentalism and Labour's *Charter for The Environment* included traditional green proposals such as greater public involvement in planning. The Green Party was not impressed by this new-found interest by the major parties in environmentalism and argued that it simply represented cosmetic vote-catching rather than an acceptance of the green philosophy.

Why do environmental issues play only a minor role in politics? If the environmental crisis is as serious as ecologists say it is, then it seems reasonable to ask why elections are not fought between parties offering less economic growth, less pollution, less road traffic, more of the nation's energy to come from wind and wave power and more organic agriculture. It is possible to interpret events in different ways in an attempt to answer this political riddle. First, it can be argued that environmental crises come and go, and that public interest in them builds up as a particular crisis emerges, and fades away as it is solved through the application of new technologies or procedures. The energy crisis of the mid-1970s stimulated by OPEC and the nuclear disaster at Chernobyl are examples of such crises. The second argument interprets these events as steps taken towards some ultimate ecological crisis. The energy crisis was an early glimpse of a world in which non-renewable resources have become depleted, and Chernobyl was the first act of global contamination springing from a civil and military reliance on nuclear power. More and bigger disasters will, it is argued, result in environmental concern eventually becoming the most important of political issues.

SUMMARY

All political parties and governments want to be seen as having a responsible attitude towards protecting the environment. But frequently there is a gap between words and deeds, with the environment suffering damage in some way as a consequence of governments' failure to act or to act in time. If environmentalists are correct in their prediction of a sudden deterioration in the conditions necessary to sustain life on earth, then green politics may yet become the most important issue in world politics.

FURTHER READING

Johnson, B. (1983) *An Overview – Resourceful Britain*, London, Kogan Page.
Levitt, R. (1980) *Implementing Public Policy*, Beckenham, Croom Helm.
Sandbach, F. (1980) *Environment, Ideology, and Policy*, Oxford, Basil Blackwell.
Wilson, D. (ed.) (1984) *The Environmental Crisis: A Handbook for all Friends of the Earth*, London, Heinemann.

QUESTIONS

1. Why has environmentalism not become a major issue in British politics?
2. Does the élitist or pluralist model best explain decision-making on the environment?
3. Evaluate the roles played by parties and pressure groups in environmental politics?
4. To what extent can it be argued that environmental concern is 'non-political' since everyone suffers from the consequences of environmental deterioration?

ASSIGNMENT

Aerosol carbon blamed for hole in ozone layer

By John Ardill,
Environment Correspondent

British scientists are calling for an immediate 85 per cent cut in the use of chloro fluoro carbons (CFCs) used as aerosol propellants and foam-blowing agents after establishing that the chemicals are responsible for a big hole in the stratospheric ozone layer over antarctica.

The demand for the British Antarctic Survey will put extra pressure on the UK and EEC governments at an international protocol in Montreal next month to control CFCs. The ozone layer is critical in filtering ultra violet rays which cause skin cancer.

Latest research by the survey which discovered the hole, hardens a cautious stance by an official Stratospheric Ozone Review Group in its first report, published yesterday by the Department of the Environment. Dr Joe Farman, a member of both groups, who is reporting his latest findings and a call for action in a forthcoming issue of Nature, said that the ozone group report which was written months ago was already out of date.

He may not be supported by all members of the group. Met Office scientists said yesterday that the new findings would not necessarily change their view that the cause of the hole is not yet known.

Dr Farman said: "I was far too lax in agreeing to the consensus that is put forward. We should have stressed much more strongly that although there was little conclusive evidence in favour of the CFC theory at that time, really there was no evidence for anything else.

"Now I think we can safely say that the recent work does show pretty clearly that all the other suggestions really aren't on. It really is a 99.9 per cent probability that the CFCs are responsible.

"The situation is such that we shouldn't let the CFCs grow any more, which means in effect that we have to make an 85 per cent cut pretty sharply, because at the moment we are putting them in six times as fast as nature is removing them."

The DoE said that the review group report showed that use of CFCs at present-day levels was unlikely to lead to a reduction of the ozone layer. The report says the cause of the Antarctic hole is unknown.

Stratospheric Ozone, Stationery Office, 9.95.

Source: The Guardian, 7 August 1987

You have read the press cutting above together with other reports that the risk of developing skin cancer is likely to rise by a third over the next forty years as a result of the depletion of the ozone in the atmosphere. How might you set about organising your friends and colleagues into a small group which lobbies for policies to protect the ozone layer?

   (i)   What might be a realistic programme for a local group in terms of the policies you would campaign for?

  (ii)   How would you attract publicity towards the issues?

 (iii)   If other like-minded local groups were to spring up, how might their activities be coordinated?

 (iv)   What politicians and other pressure groups would you expect to contact in the course of your campaign, and why?

24

Devolution, Integration and British Sovereignty

England . . . Britain . . . the United Kingdom . . . Great Britain . . . or the British Isles? It is quite understandable that some citizens are not quite sure about the name of the country in which they live and use the examples above as if they were interchangeable. This situation arises from the complex constitutional structure and history of the United Kingdom. This chapter considers the implications of nationalist sentiment on the State structure and also examines Britain's role in relation to other nation-states. Britain's imperial role is now all but over. Has entry to the European Community resulted in citizens feeling that they are 'European' as well as 'British'?

FROM GLOBAL TO REGIONAL POWER

The boundary of a country and the territory which it claims to control are frequently issues which concern political leaders. The location of borders which separate States has often been the source of conflict. This is because borders mark the territorial recognition of political power and sovereignty. When States argue about where a particular border should be drawn between them, they are arguing about who has the power to control the lives of people who live in the contested area.

As Britain has retreated from global responsibilities, so the number of conflicts involving Britain has diminished. Throughout the 1950s and 1960s, British troops were involved in numerous conflicts in Africa and Asia. The only significant 'defeat' came in 1956 with the humiliating withdrawal of British forces from Suez, when the British Government came under great pressure from the White House to pull out. As the Empire was transformed into the Commonwealth, and as the Commonwealth became less deferential towards Britain, so British forces played a smaller role overseas. Britain, for example, did not counter the Rhodesian rebellion with military force, nor did troops from Britain fight alongside the Americans in Vietnam. It came as something of a surprise in 1982 when the discarded imperial role was

474

resumed and Britain sent a naval task force to win back the Falkland Islands after they had been occupied by Argentina. Britain seems unlikely to face this sort of problem again. The handover of Hong Kong to China has been negotiated successfully, and, although British rule over Gibraltar remains a sensitive issue for Spain, it is not expected that the two countries would ever go to war in order to resolve differences.

As Britain has changed from being a global into a regional power, so the nature of its territorial problems have altered. With the afore-mentioned exceptions of the Falklands and Gibraltar, Britain's territorial debate has been less about sovereignty abroad than about the constitution at home. Contemporary Britain is marked by a constitutional crisis over the existence of the United Kingdom. Individuals and groups in Northern Ireland, Scotland and Wales argue that the established links with England should be reviewed and changed, with some English voices calling for the English regions to be given powers at present enjoyed by Westminster. At the same time, Britain is a member of a supranational organisation, the European Community, which is also experiencing a serious and prolonged crisis.

It is ironic that the British State is under strain from the forces of national devolution and international integration simultaneously. But the two seemingly separate issues are connected. Whilst Britain enjoyed the prestige of being a global world power, the constituent parts of the United Kingdom were relatively contented to share Britain's international status. Whilst Britain – alone at first, later with America – acted as a world policeman patrolling the Atlantic, Indian and Pacific oceans, there was no interest in joining the six countries of Europe which were beginning to cooperate with each other in a supranational context. These countries, after all, had all been defeated or occupied during the Second World War and many believed that Britain had no place in 'the losers' club' which was to become the European Community. Devolution and integration are also linked on a more immediate political level. Community resources are consumed in Britain, but many nationalists feel that Scotland and Wales would benefit more from membership if they sent their own MEPs to represent a separate Scotland and Wales.

THE DISUNITED KINGDOM

Nationalism in Scotland

The 1983 General Election was not a good one for the Conservative Party in Scotland, with only twenty-one of Scotland's seventy-two MPs being Conservatives. However, support for the Conservatives in Scotland collapsed yet further in the 1987 General Election when only ten Scottish Conservative MPs were returned. What was described as the 'Doomsday Scenario' had arrived in Scotland. Nationalists argued that the Conservatives had enjoyed a massive victory in England but had been soundly defeated in Scotland, a situation which legitimised their demand for Scottish home rule. From the nationalists' point of view, Scotland is now governed by a small minority which has no mandate in Scotland.

Nationalists argue that Scotland is a nation which is very different from England – it has a separate legal system, a different education system, different newspapers, and its own church. Nationalists see Mrs Thatcher as an 'English nationalist' who is far more concerned about London and the south of England than about Scotland. They argue that Mrs Thatcher sees Scotland as a 'problem area' and not as a country with a strong national identity. Many blame the Government for the economic decline which has hit Scottish industry, particularly steel-making and shipbuilding. Nationalists argue that if Scotland had its own parliament these industries and jobs could be saved. The Government has replied that Scottish nationalists are wrong in thinking that independence will improve the economic situation. Scotland has done no worse than many regions in England, such as Merseyside. Indeed, public spending per head of population is 25 per cent higher in Scotland than in England. In other words, taxpayers in England and Wales, along with Scottish taxpayers, are helping to support industries in Scotland. Furthermore, Conservatives argue that despite their poor showing in the 1987 General Election they still polled many more votes than the Scottish Nationalist Party (SNP).

In March 1979, a referendum was held in Scotland on whether or not there should be a separate Scottish Assembly. It was decided that at least 40 per cent of the Scottish electorate must vote 'yes' before the devolved assembly could be set up. More Scottish voters said 'yes' than 'no' in the referendum, but only 32.5 per cent of the *total* electorate said 'yes' and this was not enough support for the constitutional change to take place.

The situation looks rather different a decade later. First, the 'Doomsday Scenario' has arrived with some nationalists arguing that Scotland is now under colonial rule from London. Second, a pressure group – the *Campaign for a Scottish Assembly*, with all-party support – has a greater level of activist support than any Scottish political party. Third, recent opinion polls show that up to 80 per cent of Scots want some form of devolution for Scotland. Of course, poll results are open to different interpretations. The SNP maintains that support for independence has doubled since the Conservatives were elected in 1979. Conservatives have counter-argued that, despite all the economic problems of Scotland, around 80 per cent of Scots do not want to break away from England.

Some nationalists see devolution as a step towards a separate and independent Scotland; other nationalists see it as a half-way compromise which would block total independence. In the 1987 campaign, the Conservatives were the only party in Scotland not supporting a new constitutional position for Scotland. Devolution was part of the Alliance's wider policy for constitutional reform. Labour's policy included the establishment of a Scottish assembly which would have responsibilities for health, social welfare, education, housing, local government, transport, agriculture, forestry, fishing, tourism, law and aspects of the economy. In contrast, the Conservatives, and Mrs Thatcher in particular, considered themselves to be 'unionists' and thus opposed any constitutional changes that would threaten the union that brings Scotland, Northern Ireland and Wales together with England. However, the shock fate of Conservatives in Scotland may lead to a reappraisal of this position since some form of constitutional compromise is now clearly needed to strengthen or perhaps even to save that union. Exhibit 24.1 provides a summary comparison of the demands of devolutionists and nationalists for Scotland.

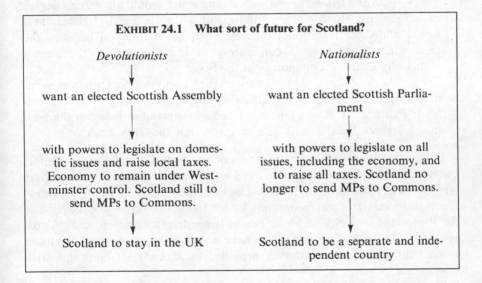

EXHIBIT 24.1   What sort of future for Scotland?

Devolutionists	*Nationalists*
↓	↓
want an elected Scottish Assembly	want an elected Scottish Parliament
↓	↓
with powers to legislate on domestic issues and raise local taxes. Economy to remain under Westminster control. Scotland still to send MPs to Commons.	with powers to legislate on all issues, including the economy, and to raise all taxes. Scotland no longer to send MPs to Commons.
↓	↓
Scotland to stay in the UK	Scotland to be a separate and independent country

Ulster's loyalists in revolt

The links between Britain and Northern Ireland (Ulster) have been under great strain. Indeed, at times it has looked as if this part of the United Kingdom has been on the verge of open rebellion. Widespread political strikes, massive demonstrations, the formation of the 'Ulster Resistance' citizens' army alongside the terrorism of the IRA have contributed towards the politics of protest in Northern Ireland. The history of Northern Ireland has developed into a situation which some commentators describe as being a political puzzle with no solution. The path to peace in Northern Ireland is littered with constitutional experiments – such as the power-sharing Executive in 1974, the Constitutional Convention in 1976 and the now-dissolved Northern Ireland Assembly which was set up in 1982 – which have proved to be disastrous failures.

In 1983 a *New Ireland Forum* was established by John Hume, leader of the Social Democratic and Labour Party to seek a way in which 'lasting peace and stability could be achieved in a New Ireland through the democratic process'. A report was published in 1984 which explored three possible options for the future of Northern Ireland:

1. *The creation of a unitary state formed from Northern Ireland and Eire.* There would be special protection for the Unionist minority within 'all Ireland' through a guaranteed level of representation in a Senate which would have sufficient power to block changes of major importance being made.
2. *The creation of a federal or confederal state* which would allow for a degree of self-government for Northern Ireland within a united Ireland. This would allow for traditional differences to be maintained between the predominantly Protestant community in the North and the almost exclusively Catholic community in the South.
3. *The establishment of joint authority* so that London and Dublin governments would have equal responsibility for administering Northern Ireland. This option, it was felt, would be a compromise between the view that Northern Ireland is 'British' and the view that it is 'Irish'.

Following closely on the publication of the New Ireland Forum Report but not in any way a consequence of it, Mrs Thatcher signed the *Anglo-Irish Agreement* at Hillsborough in 1985. The agreement between the two governments included (i) formal recognition by the Irish Government of the right of the Protestant majority to block moves towards reunification and (ii) provision for the Irish Government to have a say in the running of Northern Ireland through a joint authority provided by a newly set up Anglo-Irish Conference.

The British Government hoped that the Agreement would undermine the IRA by removing its support in the Catholic areas and by closer cross-border cooperation between the police on both sides. But the Ulster Unionists saw the Agreement as an act of betrayal by the British Government. They saw it as the first step on a path that would lead eventually to the reunification of Ireland under the control of the Dublin Government in the South. Unionists were furious with Mrs Thatcher because they had not been consulted about the Agreement. They contrasted their fate of being British citizens, yet betrayed by Mrs Thatcher, with that of the Falkland Islanders, who were not British citizens, and yet who were defended at great cost from enduring a future they did not want. It has to be said that Mrs Thatcher signed the Anglo-Irish Agreement in an attempt to preserve the Union but her arguments have appeared weak because the Dublin Government more than the British Government has interpreted the Agreement as being about Britain relinquishing sovereignty. Unionist MPs stood down and caused a mini-general election to be held in Northern Ireland which was interpreted by them as a referendum which recorded opposition to the agreement.

The Ulster Unionists, then, have said 'no' to the Anglo-Irish Agreement, but to what have they said 'yes'? There is no simple or straightforward answer since the Unionists are themselves divided over the future of Northern Ireland. However, three basic options have been discussed:

1. *Independence for Northern Ireland* in the shape of an Ulster Free State. This would be set up along lines similar to the Irish Free State in the South in 1921. A minority of Unionists who have come to feel very detached from and disillusioned with Britain support this option. If an independent Ulster cannot be negotiated, then, in certain circumstances, some hard-line Unionists are prepared to make a Unilateral Declaration of Independence in the same way as Rhodesia in 1965.
2. *The full integration of Northern Ireland into Britain.* The Unionists are not interested in either independence or devolution for Northern Ireland since both are 'disloyal' to Britain. They want the counties of Northern Ireland to have the same constitutional status as, say, Sussex or Leicestershire.
3. *Devolution for Northern Ireland.* This is favoured by successive British governments as well as by some Unionists. However, the dissolution of the Northern Ireland Assembly in 1986 represented a blow to the policy of devolution since the Assembly was set up to consider how devolution might proceed. But the Assembly was undermined by protest from the start; for example, SDLP Assemblymen decided not to take their seats. This meant that the Assembly was not representative and quickly turned into a Unionist-dominated forum. Devolution for Northern Ireland remains a long-term goal, although it has experienced a temporary setback.

Welsh Nationalism

The position of nationalism in Wales forms a sharp contrast with the rising nationalist sentiment in Scotland and the increasing Loyalist backlash in Northern Ireland. Welsh nationalism is not attracting wide popular support. In the 1987 General Election only 7.3 per cent of Welsh voters supported Plaid Cymru. How can this situation be explained? Part of the answer is found in the character of Welsh nationalism which, unlike Scottish nationalism, is not fundamentally political in nature. In some ways Welsh nationalism is more about preserving the Welsh culture and less about 'home rule for Wales'. As a consequence of this, non-Welsh-speaking voters in Wales are not likely to be attracted to Plaid Cymru. A Welsh nationalist has summed up the problem of Plaid Cymru as being 'how to expand its appeal without watering the pure milk of Welshness'.

BRITAIN IN EUROPE

Britain did not participate fully in the establishment of the forerunner of the European Community – the European Coal and Steel Community (ECSC, 1951). For a variety of reasons, Britain remained rather aloof from developments in Europe during the early post-war years. Regarding the ECSC in particular, the Labour Government led by Clement Attlee welcomed the Schuman Plan which proposed the pooling of the coal and steel resources of France and Germany, but felt unable to join in and kept only tenuous associational links with this new initiative. Britain was in the throes of nationalising its own great coal and steel industries and it was felt that further supranational schemes were not appropriate. The ECSC Treaty was signed by 'the six' (France, Germany, Italy and the three Benelux countries).

The integration of the coal and steel industries was seen as the first step that would lead to far more fundamental European integration. The next experiment was the 'Pleven plan' which involved the concept of establishing a European Defence Community. However, for a variety of reasons this idea was too ambitious and in 1954 it failed. The British Government assumed that the failure of the Pleven plan meant that 'Europeanism' was now dead. But HMG was mistaken. In 1955 the six countries of the ECSC decided to persist with their efforts towards greater European unity. A committee chaired by the Belgian Foreign Minister, Paul-Henri Spaak, recommended the establishment of the European Economic Community (EEC) and European Atomic Energy Community (Euratom). Once again Britain was invited to participate but once again withdrew at an early stage.

It became increasingly clear to the British Government that it had to come to terms with the six. The idea of six neighbouring countries forming a customs union with an ever-rising common external tariff alarmed the Government, and British relations with Europe assumed an air of urgency. In 1956 the Paymaster-General, Reginald Maudling, attempted to negotiate a free-trade area which would include the six of the ECSC, the UK and any other member of the Organisation for European Economic Cooperation which wished to join. This proposal was rejected by the French. In response, the British Government set up a rival to the EEC known as EFTA (European Free Trade Association). Western Europe was split between the 'inner six' of the EEC and the 'outer seven' of EFTA.

In 1960 an interdepartmental committee, the Economic Steering Committee, chaired by Sir Frank Lee, reappraised Britain's relations with Europe and considered the options available. The Committee agreed that Britain's future lay in Europe and that it would be to Britain's advantage to be a member of the EEC.

The Conservative Government led by Harold Macmillan announced in 1961 that Britain intended to apply for membership of the EEC. This decision represented a major change in the direction of foreign policy and recognised that Britain was now a regional rather than a global power. Dean Acheson's painful quip that Britain had lost an empire and not yet found a role had been contradicted. Circumstances had led to the loss of empire but now a role had been found, albeit after hesitation, in Europe. Macmillan faced considerable opposition inside the Conservative Party, and the mood of the Labour Party was firmly against British membership of the EEC. The Government was to be humiliated in 1962, when the French President, General de Gaulle, vetoed the British application.

The Labour Government of 1964 largely ignored the European Community (or 'Common Market', as it was then known) issue and pursued a foreign policy which stressed Atlantic and Commonwealth ties. But the problem with this policy was that the US Administration was becoming increasingly involved in Asia rather than Europe, and the Commonwealth was experiencing numerous political difficulties. By 1965 Harold Wilson decided to 'build bridges' between EFTA and the EEC, but the six made it clear that they were not interested in closing the EFTA–EEC gap. In 1966, having followed the same path as Harold Macmillan, Harold Wilson announced that the British Government was to start investigations to discover whether Britain could open negotiations to join the EEC. In 1967 General de Gaulle again vetoed Britain's application.

De Gaulle's retirement from public office removed the major obstacle to British membership of the EEC. In 1969 European governments informed Britain that a third veto was unlikely. A new Conservative Government led by an enthusiastic pro-European PM, Edward Heath, was elected in 1970 and negotiations led to the success fulentry of Britain into the EEC on 1 January 1973.

The Labour Party had once again changed its policy on British membership of the EEC and opposed Edward Heath's negotiations. When a Labour Government was formed in 1974, Harold Wilson inherited a Government that was 'in Europe' but led a party which was 'against Europe'. Labour solved this dilemma by deciding the issue of Britain's continued membership of the EEC through holding a referendum. The Foreign Secretary, James Callaghan, 'renegotiated' the terms of Britain's entry. The Commons voted to endorse continued membership of the EEC by 396 votes to 170, although a majority of Labour MPs voted against. Labour held a Special Conference which also voted against continued membership. However, in the referendum held on 5 June 1974, in a turnout of 63.2 per cent, 17 378 581 voted for continued membership and 8 470 073 voted for withdrawal.

The Institutions of the European Community

The three European Communities – the ECSC, EEC and Euratom – are managed by common institutions and are increasingly referred to as the European Community. The common institutions are the European Commission, the Council of Ministers, the European Council, the European Parliament, the Economic and Social Committee and the Court of Justice, with the support of the Court of Auditors.

The European Commission

The Commission is composed of seventeen members, including at least one from each member-country. The Commission can be described in basic terms as the 'civil service' of the European Community and sees to it that the decisions of the institutions are properly implemented. The Commission ensures that Community rules and principles are respected. The European Community is a highly legalistic institution and it is not difficult for a member to infringe a Treaty obligation or directive. When an investigation concludes that a rule is being broken, the Commission will expect the country concerned to explain and rectify the situation causing concern. If the member-country fails to comply, the Commission may refer the matter to the Court of Justice. Any judgement from the Court of Justice is binding on the member-country and on the European Community. The Commission can impose fines on individuals and companies, notably those which are found to break the Community's rules of free competition. The Commission is responsible for proposing to the Council of Ministers measures which are likely to develop Community policies. The Commission also manages the funds and common policies which account for most of the Community budget.

The Council of Ministers

The Council of Ministers is one of the major decision-making organs of the European Community although its deliberations are largely controlled by the Commission. The Council consists of ministers from the governments of member-countries, with different ministers attending according to the agenda items. For example, Britain would send the Agriculture Minister if the Council was discussing farm prices, but at its next meeting, if the problems of unemployment were on the agenda, the Employment Minister would attend. Foreign ministers play an important role within the Council of Ministers, coordinating the specialised decisions of their colleagues as well as cooperating on foreign policy matters.

Each government of the Community provides the President of the Council of Ministers for six months in rotation, with around seventy-five meetings taking place each year. The Council is assisted in its work by 'Coreper' – the Committee of Permanent Representatives – which coordinates the decisions of the Council.

The Council of Ministers can deal only with proposals emanating from the Commission. Only if Ministers unanimously share the identical view on an issue can they decide on their own authority to defy a Commission proposal.

Otherwise, no decision on an important issue can be reached. Where the Council is split on an issue, the Commission is normally involved in lengthy negotiations between member-states in order to reach a compromise. On most routine issues a majority vote only is necessary within the Council of Ministers although in recent years some important matters, such as annual farm price decisions, have been decided by majority votes.

The Commission is charged with promoting the general interest of the Community, and there is a risk that what is good for the Community as a whole may be against the interests of a particular State. Where a member-country believes that its essential national interest is being eroded by a particular policy proposal, it can exercise a veto and prevent that policy being implemented.

The European Council

The European Council consists of a meeting of Heads of State of the member-countries. These meetings are reported widely in the mass media since they involve the Prime Minister and are presented as 'summit' meetings. The European Council meets two or three times a year.

The European Parliament

Initially the European Parliament was made up from members co-opted to it from the national parliaments of member-countries, but, since June 1979, direct elections have been held to select MEPs. The European Parliament is now elected every five years. Except in August, the Parliament sits for one week in each month, usually in Strasbourg. The European Parliament has 518 members, with Britain electing eighty-one of this total. However, it must be stressed that MEPs do not organise into national sections but into political groupings based on ideological orientations (see Figure 24.1).

The Parliament has eighteen standing committees which meet in private and scrutinise the work of the Commission and the Council of Ministers. These committees are responsible for preparing the European Parliament's 'opinions' on the Commission's proposals to the Council of Ministers. The Commission, then, is answerable to the European Parliament.

The European Parliament does not have legislative powers like those of the British Parliament. So what powers does it have? The European Parliament has what might be thought of as 'all or nothing' powers – which means that if there is a 'nut to crack', all the European Parliament has is a 'sledgehammer' to use. The European Parliament has the power (i) to dismiss the Commission by a two-thirds majority; and (ii) to accept or reject the Community budget. The European Parliament first used this latter power in December 1979.

The European Parliament has become more assertive in recent years and has used its budgetary powers to gain a greater say in the affairs of the

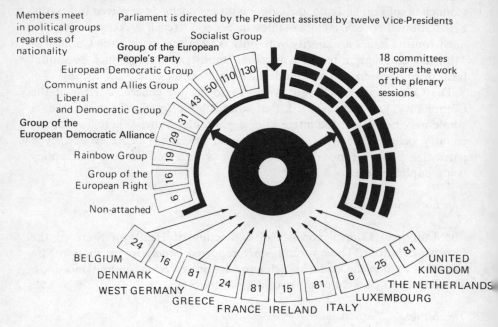

European Parliament

Members meet in political groups regardless of nationality

Parliament is directed by the President assisted by twelve Vice-Presidents

Socialist Group
Group of the European People's Party
European Democratic Group
Communist and Allies Group
Liberal and Democratic Group
Group of the European Democratic Alliance
Rainbow Group
Group of the European Right
Non-attached

130 110 50 43 31 29 19 16 6

18 committees prepare the work of the plenary sessions

BELGIUM 24
DENMARK 16
WEST GERMANY 81
GREECE 24
FRANCE 81
IRELAND 15
ITALY 81
LUXEMBOURG 6
THE NETHERLANDS 25
UNITED KINGDOM 81

Source: Emile Noél: *Working Together: The Institutions of the European Community*, 1985, p. 30.

FIGURE 24.1   *The political composition of the European Parliament (as at 11 February 1985)*

Community. Some MEPs from all countries are keen to reform the Parliament and give it greater powers. At present, the power to enact legislation is held by the Council of Ministers, acting on Commission proposals. Ambitious MEPs want the Parliament and the Council of Ministers to share power to legislate.

The elections to the European Parliament in Britain are characterised by low turn-outs. The 1984 election, for example, produced a 32 per cent turn-out in Britain. It must also be said that Britain is the only Community member to use the first-past-the-post system to vote in its MEPs. Conservatives dominate British representation in the European Assembly with Labour some way behind (see Table 24.1).

TABLE 24.1

Seats won in the 1984 European Assembly Elections for Great Britain (excluding Northern Ireland)

Conservatives	Labour	Alliance	SNP
45	32	0	1

Although the Liberal/SDP Alliance beat Labour to second place in 14 Euro-constituencies, it failed to win a single seat, despite getting nearly 20 per cent of the popular vote. In contrast, the SNP won only 1.7 per cent of the vote but gained a seat. In the German Euro-elections, the Green Party received a far smaller percentage of the popular vote than the Alliance in Britain yet won seats in the Assembly.

The Economic and Social Committee

The Economic and Social Committee provides an opportunity for interest groups to participate in Community affairs. The ESC brings together representatives from various groups selected by their national governments. Britain nominates twenty-four representatives to serve on the 189-strong ESC. Some represent employers' organisations, with current British ESC members coming from British Rail, the Confederation of British Industry and the British Bankers' Association. Some represent trade unions with the TUC, Scottish TUC and large individual trade unions providing members. Other members of the ESC represent a miscellaneous collection of 'various interests', with present members coming from organisations as diverse as the Manpower Services Commission, Brunel University, the Royal Veterinary Service and the Consumers' Association.

The ESC does not exercise great power inside the Community. Indeed, it has to compete with other internal committees and external bodies in its attempts to influence community decision-making. However, the ESC does provide a forum for interest groups to voice their concerns. In order to assist in this, the ESC organises a number of conferences on matters of concern, such as unemployment and the impact of the new technologies.

The Court of Justice

The Community Court of Justice sits in Luxembourg. It consists of thirteen judges who are assisted by six advocates-general. Both groups are appointed for six-year periods of office by mutual consent of the member-countries. To ensure continuity, every three years there is a partial replacement of both the judges and advocates-general.

The Court is the Community's supreme judicial authority, there being no appeal against its rulings. The Court's basic purpose is to ensure the observance of Community law, which it does through outlawing any measures taken by Community institutions or national governments which are incompatible with the Treaties of Rome and Paris which established the European Community. Also, on the request of a national court, the Court of Justice will interpret and clarify Community law. The Court can also give an opinion – which becomes binding – on the agreements made between the Community and non-member-countries.

Through its judgements and interpretations over the years, the Court of Justice has built up a body of Community law. In 1985, for example, the Court dealt with 433 cases and passed 255 judgements.

The Community Process

The decision-making process of the Community and the role of various institutions is shown in Figure 24.2. Amongst the most important decisions made by the Community today are those concerning the financing of the Community. The complex negotiations surrounding the Community's budget – in which Britain is playing an increasingly major role – illustrate how some of the institutions work.

The summit meeting of heads of government – the European Council – was devised as a quick method for the Community to reach agreement, but decisions can be made only when all agree. Britain has made it clear in recent summits that it would use its veto and not allow the Community to increase its budget unconditionally. Faced with a budgetary crisis and the possibility of the Community running out of money, the Commission has made proposals in order to make the necessary financial savings. The Commission places such proposals before the Council of Ministers, which makes the decisions. The Council of Ministers can make unanimous decisions only on major issues, and it is because of this that an individual country such as Britain can exert considerable pressure. The European Parliament has relatively few powers, with the exception that it is able to block the budget. In the past, the European Parliament has voted to freeze Britain's rebate in an attempt to put pressure on member governments to reform the Community. Although this action hurt Britain in the short run, it was actually aimed at bringing about what Britain wanted in the long run. But if Britain was not prepared to accept this action, it could take its grievance to the Court of Justice.

Budgetary and financial problems have long dogged the development of the Community. At the end of 1984, the Community had to make spending cuts in order to avoid running out of cash. In the same year the European Parliament rejected the 1985 draft budget because the Community's estimated revenue would not cover its expenditure. In 1987 a major summit row took place when Britain refused to accept the Community's financial programme. Other member-countries wanted Britain to accept that the Community would run up a £4bn debt by the end of the year, but the British Prime Minister insisted that the Community's financing had to be put on a sound basis.

What is the problem behind the continuing financial crisis which is impairing the Community's development? The answer is found in the enormous costs of the Common Agricultural Policy (CAP) of the Community. The EEC was formed originally to foster free enterprise in Western

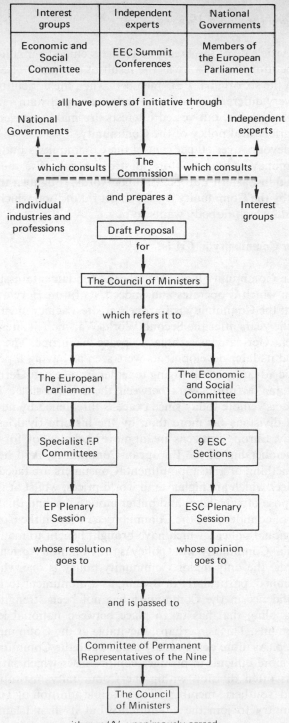

Source: *Observer*, 18 November 1979.

FIGURE 24.2 *How the EEC works.*

Europe, but Article 42 of the Treaty of Rome excluded agriculture from free market competition. The CAP was the result of a compromise drawn up in 1958 between the six original EEC members when the agricultural system in Europe was very different from that of today. From Britain's point of view, the CAP no longer fits, but vested interests are making it very difficult to reform the agricultural policy of the Community.

The CAP devours over 60 per cent of the Community's budget, and over half of this money is used to store, destroy or subsidise the dumping of unwanted food in Eastern Europe. In other words, roughly a third of all the money spent by the Community is used to get rid of food which is expensive to produce and which nobody wants to buy.

The European Community in Crisis?

The European Community faces a number of fundamental issues regarding the manner in which it operates and, indeed, its future development. Some will argue that the Community is Europe's greatest achievement in the cause of peace. In the years after the Second World War many statesmen still saw an independent Germany as a threat to peace in Europe. The formation of the ECSC and its later developments were seen as having a political rather than economic advantage in bringing together France and Germany in ways which would make future wars between them impossible. This political advantage seems remote today since peace is threatened by new ideological and religious divisions far more than by the historic rivalries of Western Europe. Today, Europe's citizens are far more likely to look for the economic benefits of membership of the European Community. And here the Community is something of a disappointment. Consumers are faced with paying European prices which are higher than world prices, whilst at the same time paying to dispose of wine lakes and butter mountains, and this has led to an undermining of confidence in the Community. Although the Community has social and regional policies which have brought benefit to many people, the only substantial Community-wide policy is the Common Agricultural Policy. In other words, the only major Community policy is one which has been widely condemned, particularly in Britain, as a monument to folly.

Public confidence in the Community has not been strengthened by the periodic squabbling that has taken place between national leaders at the European summits. This is, perhaps, inevitable as the Community increases its membership. As more demands are made upon the Community, so it will become ever more difficult to produce compromises which satisfy all members. There is often division within the Community institutions between 'northern' and 'southern' members. The possible addition of Turkey – as the thirteenth country to join the Community but its first Islamic member – would further increase diversity of its membership. Inside Britain the Community does not attract great public interest, as the low turn-out in the

Assembly elections shows. A few countries have expressed a popular wish to exist outside the Community: in a Norwegian referendum a majority voted against membership and somewhat later the small population of Greenland voted against continued membership.

The optimism of the 1950s has given way to a degree of resignation over the future development of the Community. Some of the Community's founding fathers believed that the ECSC, then the EEC and Euratom, were steps along the path of integration which would eventually lead to the establishment of a European Superstate. The process of political union would create a 'United States of Europe' in which France, Germany and Italy would be 'states' in much the same way as Texas, California and Indiana are in the American context. Today, these ambitions seem unrealistic. Although the construction of the European Community is the result of a federalist approach where individual members pool their sovereignty, recent developments have been marked by a move towards a more confederalist approach. This has resulted from a reluctance amongst member-countries to abandon their sovereignty or even at times to agree a common response to events such as the oil crisis of the mid-1970s. Some believe that the Community has lost its early momentum and now faces a crisis over what directions, if any, it should take. There is even a minority view that the European Community is an interesting experiment which failed because it was basically undemocratic, too legalistic, inward-looking and over-bureaucratic. Since the Community seems incapable of reform, lessons could be learned from these shortcomings in the launching of a new organisation to replace the European Community.

SUMMARY

Scottish nationalism and the conflict between Ulster loyalism and Republicanism have raised questions about the permanence of the unitary State structure in the United Kingdom. Whilst some form of devolution might satisfy Scottish demands, the possibility of a constitutional settlement in Northern Ireland seems as remote as ever. Britain's role in the world is now unquestionably a European one, but it has taken many years for successive British governments to accept that the European Community is the appropriate organisation within which to act out this regional role. There are mounting demands for reforming the EC institutions so that they may serve the contemporary needs of member-states more effectively.

FURTHER READING

Birch, A. H. (1977) *Political Integration and Disintegration in the British Isles*, London, Allen & Unwin.

Bulpitt, J. G. (1983) *Territory and Power in the United Kingdom*, Manchester, University Press.

Drucker, H. and Brown, G. (1980) *The Politics of Nationalism and Devolution*, London, Longman.

Gregory, F. E. C. (1983) *Dilemma of Government: Britain and the European Community*, Oxford, Martin Robertson.

Rose, R. (1981) *Understanding the United Kingdom: The Territorial Dimension in Government*, London, Longman.

QUESTIONS

1. In what ways might 'devolution' differ from 'independence' for Scotland and Northern Ireland?
2. To what extent does the so-called 'Doomsday Scenario' affect the legitimacy of Westminster rule over Scotland?
3. How justified is the allegation that the European Community is too bureaucratic?
4. Compare and contrast the functions of the European Parliament with those of the British Parliament.

ASSIGNMENT

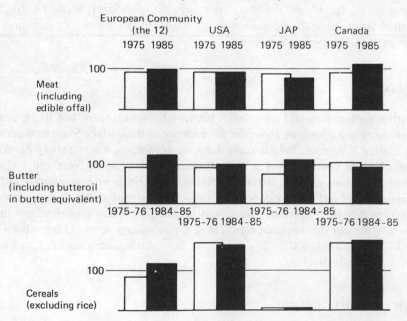

Degree of self-sufficiency (as %)*

* share of internal production in total consumption. Figures in excess of 100% indicate a surplus exists.

Distribution of Community expenditure (as %, 1986)

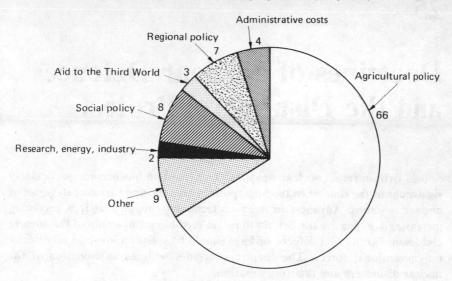

Source. Eurostat and the Community's revenue and expenditure account.

Study the graphs and discuss reasons why the Community's Common Agricultural Policy is such a controversial issue. What arguments might be voiced in support of the CAP? What difficulties might member-countries face in attempts to reform the CAP?

25

Doctrines of Nuclear Defence and the Disarmers' Protest

Should Britain retain nuclear weapons? This question has become particularly significant at the time when the Superpowers are reducing various categories of nuclear weapons. Advances in weapons technology mean that it is becoming increasingly expensive for Britain to retain credible membership of the nuclear club. Some argue that defence budgets should be spent on low-cost missiles or on conventional forces. The chapter concludes with an examination of the nuclear disarmers and their organisation.

DOCTRINES OF NUCLEAR DEFENCE AND THE DISARMERS' PROTEST

The greatest threat to the survival of mankind is posed by the endless arms race between Communist East and Capitalist West. New and emerging technologies mean that both sides are constantly updating and modernising their weaponry – today's 'miracle missile' will be obsolete tomorrow, only to be replaced by an even more awesome system. The overall cost of the Cold War is beyond calculation; the rich nations of the NATO alliance make considerable economies in order to maintain high levels of defence spending, but the poorer countries of the East, led by the Soviet Union, have the political determination to make massive sacrifices in order to keep up.

The new defence possibilities and situations created by technological advance and weapons improvements have an impact on military thinking about how defence is best assured. For example, when America held the monopoly of nuclear weapons, it was thought that 'massive retaliation' would deter Communist States from attacking the Western democracies. But this doctrine was soon rejected because it lacked credibility; no one, including the Soviets, believed that America would launch an all-out nuclear war in response to some possibly minor incident involving action by Warsaw Pact forces. 'Flexible response' evolved as the West's new doctrine, and this involved a graduated response from NATO forces which would reflect the severity of Warsaw Pact belligerence. Flexible response was underpinned by the state of technological development of the time, which resulted in Mutual

Assured Destruction (MAD). In MAD the concept of victory in a nuclear war does not exist, and a war between the two Superpowers is seen as mutual suicide. This produces a stable relationship between the Superpowers since they both know that even if they strike first with nuclear weapons the other side will still be able to deliver a devastating counter-attack.

The doctrine of flexible response was viewed with much suspicion by some of America's European allies in NATO, since it was interpreted as evidence of the USA's declining commitment to the defence of Western Europe. The concept of MAD as deterrence was never popular with conservative strategists in the Pentagon. Today, a new 'war-fighting' strategy has evolved as the orthodox doctrine of the Reagan administration. It is now argued by both the USA and the Soviet Union that a nuclear war could be fought and won. Flexible response lingers on as the most appropriate way to meet a Soviet challenge in Europe, although today the use of tactical nuclear weapons is envisaged at the early stages of any conflict.

BRITAIN'S INDEPENDENT NUCLEAR DETERRENT

The secret wartime Manhattan Project resulted in the successful development and production of the atomic bomb. The Manhattan Project involved an agreement between Britain and the USA to share resources, but in 1946 this collaboration ended as a result of the American McMahon Act. Denied American assistance the British Government, led by Clement Attlee, decided to conduct its own research programme and this resulted in the first independent British atomic bomb being built in 1952. Britain was recognised at the time as being a major global power and it was assumed that Britain would become a nuclear power.

Britain's 'delivery system' in the post-war years came in the shape of the V-bombers – the Vulcan, Victor and Valiant. This was the only period during which Britain had a *truly* independent deterrent – British-made V-bombers carrying British-made nuclear bombs. Advances in technology led to the development of ballistic missiles carrying nuclear warheads and the obsolescence of slow and vulnerable bombers. Britain attempted to maintain its position in the arms race and began to develop its independent missile known as Blue Streak. However, rapidly rising research and development costs, together with the fact that liquid-fuelled rockets such as Blue Streak fell out of favour, led to the cancellation of the project in 1960. The Government was now to rely on the USA for the supply of modern nuclear weapons which formed the independent British deterrent.

The American administration promised to supply Britain with Skybolt missiles as soon as they had been developed. However, the Americans cancelled the Skybolt project in 1962 and for a time Britain's nuclear role seemed in the balance. Finally, President Kennedy offered Britain Polaris nuclear submarines. The Government was pleased with this deal since Polaris was a much more sophisticated system than Skybolt had ever promised to be. From the mid-1960s onwards, the British deterrent is 'independently controlled' but the nature of the deterrent depends entirely on the sort of nuclear weapons that the USA decides to develop and sell.

The four British Polaris submarines have an impressive fire-power. Each of the submarines is equipped with more destructive power than all the munitions fired by both sides in the Second World War. Despite this, improvements in Soviet defences meant that Polaris was becoming less effective and had to be improved if it was to pose a serious threat. Without the knowledge of Parliament, or even of the full Cabinet, Britain embarked upon the expensive Chevaline project. Ministers in Edward Heath's Conservative Government remained silent about Chevaline after their defeat in the 1974 General Election hoping that, if the project were kept secret, the new Labour Government would be able to continue with it. Chevaline involved improvements in the warhead system which would upgrade the effectiveness of Polaris. The Heath Government's estimate for Chevaline was £175m; the Labour Government actually spent £1000m. This spending was hidden from Parliament at the time and only later were details revealed in full by a Conservative administration.

In the late 1970s, the Government began studying the options for the next generation of nuclear deterrent. At first it looked as if Britain would be buying Poseidon to replace Polaris, but the Americans indicated their reluctance to sell since it would have upset the arms limitations talks that were being held with the Soviets.

The British Government was considering the purchase of Trident 1 submarines when the Americans announced that Trident 1 was to be superseded by the more sophisticated Trident 2. Mrs Thatcher negotiated with the US administration and it was decided in 1982 that Britain would buy Trident 2. In making this decision the Government had agreed that Britain should keep up with the USA and Soviets and possess a 'Superpower' weapons system. Trident 2 missiles are fired from submarines 40 feet below the surface and travel 600 miles above the earth before the nose-cone releases a number of re-entry vehicles carrying warheads to as many as seventeen separate targets. Each submarine carries sixteen missiles, and the weapon is accurate to within 400 feet of its target.

The cost of such a sophisticated system as Trident 2 is huge. In 1980 the cost of Trident 1 was put at £4500m–£5000m. By 1982 the cost of Trident 2 had risen to an estimated £7500m and in 1984 this figure was upped to £9285m. If, for any reason the value of the pound was to fall against the dollar, the final cost could rise even faster. Some believe that £12 000m is a reasonable estimate for the final total cost; others believe the final bill will be less than this. Defence estimates are notoriously low and, as with Chevaline, the final cost of a project invariably escalates far above initial estimates.

Those who believe that Trident 2 is going to prove very, very expensive, worry that economies will have to be made in the rest of the defence budget – on matters like the procurement of ships, helicopters, planes and transport vehicles – in order to pay the bill.

When economies have to be made in spending on conventional weapons, and also on spending in the Welfare State, in order to pay for an advanced weapons system, it is to be expected that many will challenge the wisdom of that decision. Does Britain need Trident 2? Is there a cheaper system which is just as effective? Has the time come for Britain to recognise that it can no longer afford to be a nuclear power?

All British Governments have recognised the political and strategic arguments for remaining a nuclear power:

1. Britain's European allies in NATO would not like to see France being the only nuclear power in Western Europe.
2. Without nuclear weapons, the British Government could be at the mercy of a nuclear-armed Third World dictator.
3. Britain cannot rely on sheltering under the American nuclear umbrella because, at some future date, the USA may have an isolationist or Pacific-oriented administration which withdraws its commitment to Europe. British nuclear weapons would then be needed to deter the Soviets.
4. In the event of a nuclear war, British weapons could be used in Britain's national interest rather than in America's national interest.

Although Britain and the USA are close allies, there will be occasions when they have serious disagreements on military decisions. Indeed, this occurred frequently in the Second World War. One example was the low priority given by the Americans to the destruction of the German V-1 and V-2 rocket launching sites. These rockets were reaching London and causing considerable havoc. It did not matter that the Americans were preoccupied with other issues, since the Government was able to send its independent force, the RAF, to attack the German sites.

AMERICAN NUCLEAR WEAPONS

Successive British governments have shared the American assessment of the threat to Western security posed by the USSR and its Warsaw Pact allies. The British and American deterrent are committed to NATO. The American nuclear guarantee involves the siting of American-controlled weapons in Western Europe. There are plans to deploy Tomahawk cruise missiles in Britain, Italy and Germany, with possible sites in Belgium and Holland. Pershing II missiles are to be sited in West Germany.

Cruise missiles are a sophisticated nuclear version of the V-1 rockets developed by the Germans in the Second World War. Basically Cruise is a pilotless aircraft which travels relatively slowly (up to 550 m.p.h.) but hugs the ground (at heights under 200 feet) in order to avoid radar. It can be launched from land (as at Greenham Common and Molesworth), sea or air. Once they are airborne, Cruise missiles are guided to within 100 feet of their targets by an on-board computer-based mapping system which compares their course with that pre-programmed into the computer and adjusts accordingly. The Soviets are probably more concerned about Pershing II than about Cruise. These missiles take little over ten minutes to reach a target 1500 miles away.

Cruise and Pershing II both have the accuracy to hit military targets, such as hardened silos. The American President has sanctioned the development of the neutron bomb, which would be used against Soviet tank formations. Already NATO deploys many tactical nuclear weapons, i.e. 'small' battle-field nuclear weapons, for use in situations where conventional weapons would have been used in the past. All these weapons are manifestations of a 'counterforce' strategy that is designed to attack an enemy's military targets. They are weapons to be fired at the command and control infrastructure as well as at the enemy's weapons installations. They are *not* weapons to be used to destroy the enemy's population and industrial base (the 'countervalue' strategy). Counterforce weapons erode the doctrine of deterrence. The Reagan administration, like the Kremlin, has moved towards adopting a war-fighting strategy. Both Superpowers now believe that a nuclear war could be fought and won rather than ending in the mutual assured destruction.

America's movement towards accepting a war-fighting strategy has been reinforced by the Strategic Defence Initiative, otherwise known as 'Star Wars'. The SDI has its origins in President Reagan's speech of March 1983 in which he called for the development of space-based defence weapons – including lasers – to shoot down Soviet missiles as they headed towards American targets. Although greeted with much scepticism and doubt, the Star Wars programme has already achieved remarkable successes with laser technology. Some analysts, however, do not see the SDI as part of a counterforce strategy. They believe that Star Wars will prove to be the most successful American weapons system, but not necessarily for any reasons concerned with military effectiveness. They argue that the Soviets will feel that they have no option but to follow the Americans and develop their own Star Wars programme. But this will prove to be an intolerable cost on top of an already heavy defence spending burden. The result could be civil unrest and political instability within the Soviet Union, forcing the leadership finally to adopt new and more liberal policies. In short, Star Wars would defeat Communism by bankrupting it.

NEGOTIATIONS TOWARDS A MINIMUM DETERRENT

Despite the ideological differences that separate the Capitalist West from the Communist East, there has been a considerable amount of bargaining and negotiation. There have been exchanges of technical information and agreement on policy which was in the interests of both parties. Mutual suspicion acts as a barrier to rapid progress and each side maximises any propaganda advantage it has over its rival. One of the most significant Superpower agreements was made during the period that MAD was ascendant. If MAD was to hold, each side had to keep its population vulnerable to attack from the other side. If one side deployed effective anti-ballistic missile (ABM) systems around major urban centres, it would result in that side being able to launch a nuclear strike first without the other side having the ability to strike back with a devastating blow. MAD was enshrined in the ABM treaty of 1972. This treaty limited the number of ABM systems to one on each side.

A web of diplomatic conferences and talks have taken place since then. Some have ended in one side walking out; others have made considerable progress towards agreement. The Intermediate Nuclear Force (INF) talks and the Strategic Arms Reduction Talks (START) have spent much time considering whether British and French nuclear weapons should be included alongside American arms or whether the talks should simply concern US–Soviet systems. Furthermore, there has been frequent disagreement on what weapons from each side should be included in the negotiations. Side by side with these talks are the Mutual and Balanced Force Reduction (MBFR) talks, which have been taking place since 1972 and are concerned with the balance of conventional forces in Europe.

A major breakthrough in the arms reduction process was made during 1987 when the Americans and Soviets agreed to eliminate all medium-range nuclear weapons. Although President Reagan remained determined to press ahead with Star Wars, which could be an obstacle to further negotiations, the deal reflects a new age of cooperation and trust between the Superpowers.

THE NUCLEAR OPTION AND PARTY POLITICS

As we have seen with Chevaline, governments may make defence policy decisions of which their own backbench supporters know nothing. When in opposition, political parties may make defence policy decisions that they find impossible to implement once they win an election and form the government. In the late 1950s CND gained a great deal of support at Labour Party Conferences and the party leader, Hugh Gaitskell, was involved in a bitter struggle with the Left wing to prevent Labour adopting a unilateralist and neutralist policy. Labour's 'non-nuclear' defence policy contributed to the party's massive defeat in the 1983 General Election; the issue dominated the campaign for a substantial period and it became clear that there was total confusion amongst the party's leaders on the future of Polaris. Differences within parties are not confined to Labour; for example, amongst Conservative students, there exists the 'Blues against Cruise' group which is opposed by the 'Campaign for Peace through Strength'.

In terms of official party policy, there are substantial differences between the major political parties. The Conservative Party is most committed to maintaining Britain's independent nuclear deterrent. Conservatives are strongly in favour of Trident 2 as the replacement of Polaris and accept the siting of Cruise missiles on British soil. Labour's policies are very different from these and the Party remains sympathetic to the idea of unilateral nuclear disarmament. This would entail scrapping the Polaris fleet, cancelling Trident 2, and requesting the removal of American Cruise missiles, American nuclear-armed aircraft and American submarine bases from Britain. The implications of this policy, should it ever be implemented, are far-reaching and may have many unintended consequences. For example, if Labour got rid of Cruise, this would reduce the bargaining chips held by the Americans in their negotiations with the Soviets to get them to scrap the SS-20 missiles which threaten Western Europe. If there were no American military presence in Britain, the NATO alliance, already in something of a crisis over resources and morale, would suffer an enormous blow. Yet undermining NATO is not part of Labour's defence policy. Indeed, the Party intends making a strong conventional contribution to the alliance.

Social and Liberal Democrat policies had not emerged at the time of writing. In late 1987, the Liberal Party wanted to cancel Trident, but favoured keeping the Polaris fleet as a bargaining chip with the Soviets in arms reduction talks. Liberals were somewhat at odds with their one-time Alliance partners, the Social Democratic Party, which supported the retention of Cruise missiles at their existing numbers. Indeed, the leader of the SDP had long favoured Cruise to replace Polaris and become Britain's independent nuclear deterrent.

THE DISARMERS

The erosion of *détente*, the spiralling arms race, changes towards more dangerous nuclear doctrines, and the acceptance of Cruise and Trident formed the political environment for Britain's 'second wave' of anti-nuclear protest. The 'first wave' protest of the 1950s was a moral rejection of the very idea of nuclear weapons, and the *Campaign for Nuclear Disarmament* (CND) was the only significant anti-nuclear group in Europe. The second wave is very different insofar as CND is only part of a wider European protest movement. Although CND remains a major focus of the peace movement, there are numerous networks of peace groups such as the Women's Peace

Camp and the 'nuclear free' local authorities. However, since 1980 the *European Nuclear Disarmament* group (END) has played a major role alongside CND. The *World Disarmament Campaign* (WDC) is an influential group, but has policies for peace which are different from those of CND or END.

The WDC is multilateralist rather than unilateralist. Multilateralist strategy is to pressure governments to pursue policies for arms control and arms reduction. Unlike CND, which is aiming to influence public opinion, WDC does not really favour large-scale protest rallies. Multilateralists accept that progress towards a nuclear free world will be slow and that there will be many setbacks – this is because negotiations must include both sides and each stage in the bargaining process must preserve a balance between the arms of opposing states. Multilateralists support the START and INF negotiations.

Unilateralists argue that the talks that multilateralists favour have not, in fact, produced a safer world. Despite START and INF, the Superpowers are locked into an arms race which they are both unable to stop. The unilateralist position is that Britain's survival depends upon abandoning nuclear weapons and leaving the military alliances that are part of the Cold War confrontation. Nuclear disarmers argue that deterrence has not kept the peace and provided security since the Second World War, but rather it has locked the Superpowers into a relationship of mutual suspicion and fear. On both sides, millions of people are employed in keeping the Cold War alive. The relationship between the Superpowers becomes one of permanent threat and periodic crises, and this promotes men from military–industrial interests into influential positions in society. As a result, the Cold War becomes self-generating.

In Britain, CND had a maximum national membership of around 100 000 in 1981. Its success alarmed the Ministry of Defence which established a unit, Defence Secretariat 19, especially to counter CND propaganda. There are a number of pressure groups which support the retention of nuclear weapons, although their combined membership is dwarfed by that of CND. *Women and Families for Peace*, the *Committee for Peace with Freedom*, and the *British Atlantic Committee's Peace through NATO* oppose the aims of the disarmers and tend to see the supporters of CND as being misguided by 'Communists, Neutralists and Defeatists'.

SUMMARY

Defence of the realm is an important issue which divides the political parties. The central controversy is whether or not Britain should retain nuclear weapons. The debate featured in the 1987 General Election and was reckoned to be an electoral liability for Labour, the only party to adopt a unilateralist

policy. **The peace movement has also done much to keep the nuclear issue in the public eye, although there is a degree of factionalism which divides 'moderate' multilateralists from harder-line 'unilateralists'.**

FURTHER READING

Bartlett, C. J. (1972) *The Long Retreat: A Short History of British Defence Policy, 1945–70*, London, Macmillan.
Dillon, G. M. (1983) *Dependence and Deterrence*, Aldershot, Gower.
Freedman, L. (ed.) (1983) *The Troubled Alliance: Atlantic Relations in the 1980s*, London, Heinemann.
Minnion, J. and Bolsover, P. (eds) (1983) *The CND Story*, London, Allison & Busby.
Shepherd, A. (1987) 'The Politics of Nuclear Protest in the Fifties: CND and the Early New Left', in L. Robins (ed.) *Topics in British Politics*, London, Political Education Press.

QUESTIONS

1. Evaluate the case (i) for; (ii) against, the retention of Britain's independent nuclear deterrent.

2. Assess the extent to which Britain's nuclear arsenal can be thought of as an 'independent deterrent'.

3. 'The defence of Britain should, above all other policies, be bi-partisan in character.' Why, then, is this not the case in the 1980s?

ASSIGNMENT

Peace movement influenced talks

By Jonathan Steele

The US–Soviet INF deal closes the book on one of the most difficult chapters in the history of Nato, as well as on the first superpower negotiations in which public opinion in the shape of the Western European peace movement was heavily engaged. The peace movements were both actors and spectators, as each superpower tried to outbid the other in making its proposals seem the most constructive to the watching audience.

INF weapons first became a public issue ten years ago when the Carter administration and Mr Helmut Schmidt, then Chancellor of West Germany, first suggested that the United States should deploy ground-launched weapons in Western Europe to reach the Soviet Union. The Soviet Union had long had nuclear weapons targeted on Western Europe but Nato had not felt it necessary to counter them with land-based weapons of similar range. Intercontinental nuclear missiles based in the United States and on submarines, as well as bomb-carrying aircraft, were considered sufficient.

But in the late 1970s strains within Nato as well as fears in some quarters that the US commitment to the defence of Western Europe was declining prompted a debate about "coupling". The United States had to be bound closer to Western Europe, it was argued, and one way to do this would be to deploy a new generation of US nuclear weapons in a number of Western European countries. The debate over "coupling" was sharpened by the Soviet modernisation of its nuclear arsenal with the deployment of the mobile, triple warheaded missile, known as the SS-20. In 1979 Nato took what was known as the twin-track decision to deploy Pershing-2 missiles in West Germany, and Cruise missiles there and in Britain, Belgium, Holland, and Italy from 1983, while also offering to hold talks with the Russians on the issue.

For two years the Russians continued to deploy their SS-20s and declined to talk, apparently in the hope that Nato would unilaterally cancel its decision. In 1981 the Reagan administration came to power with an ideological onslaught on the Soviet Union, and loose talk from some of its officials of a "limited" nuclear war in Europe. At the same time it became clear that the Western peace movements were calling not just for a reversal of the Nato decision but elimination of the SS-20s as well.

The then Soviet leader, Mr Brezhnev, agreed to start talks on the basis of a freeze on future deployments. He did not offer to reverse the Soviet deployments which had already occurred. Shortly afterwards President Reagan offered the so-called "zero option", cancellation of Nato's plans if the Soviet Union eliminated all the SS-20s.

US–Soviet talks began in Geneva in November 1981. In July 1982 the US negotiator, Mr Paul Nitze, and the Soviet negotiator, Mr Yuli Kvitsinsky, during a "walk in the woods" reached a tentative agreement to cut back to 75 missile launchers on each side and the elimination of the Pershing-2s. Both governments rejected the idea.

The Soviet Union, under Mr Brezhnev's successor, Mr Yuri Andropov, made various offers to count its SS-20s against French and British nuclear missiles, but this was considered unacceptable in Paris and London. Massive peace demonstrations throughout

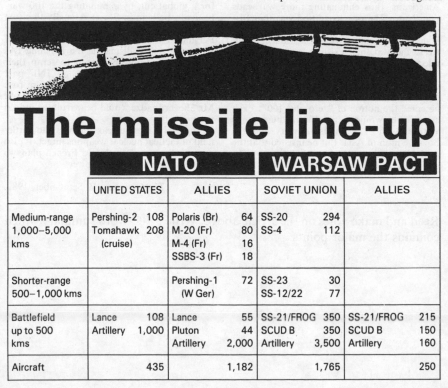

The missile line-up

	NATO		WARSAW PACT	
	UNITED STATES	ALLIES	SOVIET UNION	ALLIES
Medium-range 1,000–5,000 kms	Pershing-2 108 Tomahawk 208 (cruise)	Polaris (Br) 64 M-20 (Fr) 80 M-4 (Fr) 16 SSBS-3 (Fr) 18	SS-20 294 SS-4 112	
Shorter-range 500–1,000 kms		Pershing-1 72 (W Ger)	SS-23 30 SS-12/22 77	
Battlefield up to 500 kms	Lance 108 Artillery 1,000	Lance 55 Pluton 44 Artillery 2,000	SS-21/FROG 350 SCUD B 350 Artillery 3,500	SS-21/FROG 215 SCUD B 150 Artillery 160
Aircraft	435	1,182	1,765	250

Western Europe called on Nato not to go ahead with the deployments, and for the Russians to withdraw their SS-20s. In May 1983 the Russians warned that if Nato went ahead they would add new shorter-range weapons in East Germany and in Czechoslovakia.

In November 1983 Nato started its deployments, prompting the counter-deployments threatened by the Soviet Union and a Soviet walkout in Geneva which it had also threatened. Public opinion polls in all the deploying countries in Western Europe consistently showed majorities against the Nato deployments, thus adding to the crisis for Nato.

In the summer of 1984 the Russians offered to reopen the talks provided that the United States also agreed to discuss its "Star Wars" space programme which was beginning to get under way. Talks resumed in March 1985.

The Belgian and Dutch governments had delayed their decisions on the cruise missiles until the last possible moment because of public pressure against it. But in 1985 by slender majorities they went ahead.

In January 1986 Mr Gorbachev, the new Soviet leader, made the first major shift in the Soviet position by conceding that the Soviet Union would reduce to zero along with the Americans, thus eliminating more warheads than Nato. The only condition was that Britain and France should agree to abandon plans for a large increase in their arsenals and freeze them at their existing levels. This was rejected.

In September Mr Gorbachev gave up the demand for British and French limits, and the following month at the Reykjavik summit accepted the notion of "zero plus 100". Each superpower would retain 100 medium range warheads, the US on its territory and the Soviet Union in Asia. But he insisted that the deal depended on simultaneous agreement to cut strategic and space weapons.

This year came two more concessions. In February, complying with demands from Western governments, he dropped the link between the different sets of talks, and said an INF deal on its own was possible. In April he offered to scrap the shorter-range (500-1,000 kilometres) missiles within a year of an INF agreement. He said this must include the American warheads on the shorter-range West German Pershing-1A missiles.

The offer of cuts in shorter-range missiles surprised Nato since it raised the prospect of the eventual de-nuclearisation of Europe. The British and French Governments feared this could increase the pressure on them to abandon their own nuclear arsenals. The West German Government feared that pressure for the United States to withdraw from Europe might also grow. But with public opinion clearly in favour of a deal which seemed to offer so much by eliminating two categories of weapon, Mrs Thatcher during the British election campaign accepted the deal, as did Dr Kohl shortly afterwards. In June Nato announced its acceptance of "double-zero" in Europe, though not of an end to the Pershing-1A warheads.

In July Mr Gorbachev accepted the US idea for a global cut, by eliminating the 100 warheads to be held in Soviet Asia. By then the major remaining issue had been reduced to the Pershing 1A warheads. In August Chancellor Kohl pledged to dismantle the Pershing-1As once the superpowers agreed to scrap their missiles. Final agreement on an INF pact seemed only weeks away, and optimism rose that the planned talks between Mr Shultz and Mr Shevardnadze would bear fruit, as indeed they now have.

The deal leaves nuclear bombers and battlefield or tactical nuclear weapons intact. It also puts no limit on British and French plans to increase their nuclear firepower.

The Guardian, 19 September, 1987.

Read and make notes on the article above. Write a 400-word summary which contains the major points.

Part IV
British Government and Politics Reconsidered: Theories and Tendencies

26

Power in British Society: Pluralist and Ruling Class Theories

In the two final chapters, we aim to bring the concerns of Parts I–III of our book together, focusing particularly in this chapter upon ideological approaches to *understanding the political system* and in the final chapter on the impact of Thatcherite ideology upon *the working of British politics*. This chapter begins with the question: how important to the interpretation of political behaviour is the social background of the people who make the major political decisions? In broader terms, what are the relations between politics and society? We examine the composition of the élites at the top of major sectors in British society before proceeding to the two main *interpretations* of this evidence – *pluralist* theory in its various forms and *ruling class* theory (a third approach – the theory of a *power élite* – is also discussed briefly). The pluralist approach is broadly associated with *liberalism*; the ruling class model with *Marxist* political theory and ideology. The chapter then considers how these two rival approaches handle the evidence presented in Parts II and III of this book, for which purpose this material is grouped into several broad themes: the Constitution, the political process including the role of parties and groups, and the nature of the State. New Right theories which have come to prominence since the 1970s are discussed where appropriate under pluralism, not separately (as is done by some books on British politics).

BRITISH SOCIAL AND POLITICAL ELITES

Tables 26.1, 26.2 and 26.3 set out the educational and social backgrounds of the British political élite. Elites are the very small minority of people who play the key role in making decisions in their respective sectors and, if they are politicians, for society as a whole. The main point of studying them is to assess to what extent entrance to such positions of social esteem, wealth and power is influenced by the class structure and to what extent such positions are open to all, no matter from what social background. A subsidiary but important question is how far these positions are changing: are they, for

TABLE 26.1

The social background of MPs in the two major parties, 1974–9

	Conservative		Labour	
Professional	154	55%	178	56%
Business	91	32%	27	8%
Working class	2	1%	89	28%

Notes: 1. Percentages do not add up to 100 since some minor occupational categories are omitted;
2. Publisher/Journalist category included in 'professional' classification.

Source: Derived from D. Butler and D. Kavanagh, *The British General Election of October 1974*, p. 215.

example, becoming – however gradually – more open to all comers? The essential context to remember when analysing these tables is the approximate percentage of the population which is privately educated (7 per cent), University-educated (under 10 per cent) and belongs to such occupational groupings as employer/proprietor (2.6 per cent), managerial/administrative (8.6 per cent) and higher professional (3.8 per cent).

The first striking point to notice about Table 26.1 is the predominance of the business and professional groups in Parliament as a whole. These two groups accounted for about 66 per cent of the 'political class' in the 1970s, a proportion which has remained substantially unaltered since. The other significant comment to make about the composition of Parliament in general is the steadily increasing proportion of the University-educated between the inter-war period and the 1980s (Table 26.2). That said, the two main parties present sharp contrasts. The Conservatives have generally had a public school education; Labour MPs normally a State education. Conservative graduates are most likely to have attended Oxford or Cambridge; Labour graduates other universities. In occupations, the Conservatives contain a sizeable proportion of businessmen and managers (about 33 per cent), but an infinitesimal percentage of working-class MPs, whereas Labour contains very few businessmen but a significant proportion (over 25 per cent) with working-class backgrounds. The parties include broadly equal proportions of professions (between 50 and 60 per cent). However, Conservative professionals tend to be predominantly lawyers, with only a sprinkling of people drawn from the armed forces, accountancy, Civil Service, local government and teaching; Labour professionals come overwhelmingly from teaching, the remainder being composed of lawyers, consultants, publishers, and journalists. No Labour MPs have military or farming backgrounds.

Certain important trends are discernible in the post-1945 period. A

TABLE 26.2

The educational background of MPs (percentage of total in the two major parties)

	December 1910		1918–35		1945–74		1979		1983	
	Conservatives	Liberals	Conservatives	Labour	Conservatives	Labour	Conservatives	Labour	Conservatives	Labour
Elementary only	0.3	6.6	2.5	75.5	0.7	20.1	0	4.8	8.2	21.5
Secondary only	8.4	31.9	n.d.	n.d.	5.2	10.1	8.2	14.8	64.1	13.4
Public school	72.0	38.2	78.5	9.0	75.7	17.9	73.0	17.0	64.1	1.0
Eton	33.0	8.4	27.5	1.5	20.2	0.9	15.0	0.4	12.4	
Oxford/Cambridge	46.6	29.7	39.5	7.4	49.6	15.9	49.2	20.4	45.7	14.4
All universities	57.3	51.4	50.1	18.2	61.7	44.0	68.0	57.0	71.7	54.1

Notes: (a) Not all columns sum to 100%, due to missing or omitted data.
(b) 'Public school' indicated by membership of Headmasters' Conference.
(c) n.d. = no data

Source: Extracted from M. Moran, Politics and Society in Britain (Macmillan, 1985) p. 155

TABLE 26.3
Education and class origins of Cabinet Ministers, 1916–84

| | Background of Cabinet Ministers (%) | | | |
| | 1916–1955 | | 1955–1984 | |
	Conservative	*Labour*	*Conservative*	*Labour*
All public schools	76.5	26.1	87.1	32.1
Eton, Harrow	45.9	7.6	36.3	3.5
Oxbridge	63.2	27.6	72.8	42.8
Elem/Sec	4.0	50.7	2.5	37.5
All Universities	71.4	44.6	81.6	62.5
Aristocrat	31.6	6.1	18.1	1.8
Middle Class	65.3	38.4	74.0	44.6
Working Class	3.0	55.3	2.6	41.0
No Data	—	—	4.0	12.6
Number	98	65	77	56

Source: M. Burch and M. Moran, 'The changing British Political Elite, 1945–1983: MPs and Cabinet Ministers', *Parliamentary Affairs*, vol. 38, Winter, 1985.

declining proportion of Conservative MPs have had public school/Oxbridge educations whilst an increasing percentage have been educated at State schools and non-Oxbridge universities. Overall, the Conservative Party has become more open and less privileged in its recruitment. By contrast, Labour in this period became less representative of the social make-up of the population. The proportion of its university-educated, professional MPs increased very considerably with a dramatic decline in the proportion of working-class members with only an elementary education. Over the fifty years from the 1930s to the 1980s, the Parliamentary Labour Party moved strongly away from its working-class origins towards becoming a predominantly white-collar, University-educated, middle-class party. However, this point should not be taken too far. Approximately 50 per cent of the Labour MPs in the new Parliament of 1979 had working-class parents. As Michael Moran writes:

> The Parliamentary Labour Party has thus not simply shifted from working-class to middle-class domination. A more complex mutation has occurred: before the Second World War the typical Labour M.P. achieved mobility out of the working class in his own adult life by entering parliament; in the post-war years the typical Labour M.P. rose out of the working class through education and then capped this social success by election to the House of Commons (Moran, *Politics and Society in Britain*, 1985, p. 158).

The overall trend in all parties over the last half-century has been towards professionalisation in the sense that the great majority of MPs now possess a commitment to politics as a lifelong career. This trend is bolstered by the growing numbers of MPs with experience in local government.

The social composition of the Cabinet (Table 26.3) reveals a tendency towards what may be termed the growing embourgeoisement of party leaderships as well as a continuing pronounced contrast between the two parties. Thus, since the early part of the century, Conservative Cabinets have become more middle class and *less aristocratic*, Labour Cabinets, more middle class and *less working class*. But there are still sharp contrasts. The public school/Oxbridge background of Conservative Cabinet Ministers intensified; between 1955 and 1984, Conservative Cabinets were overwhelmingly composed of people of middle-class *origins*. Labour Cabinets were predominantly middle class in *achieved* status, with over 60 per cent having had University educations. But Labour Cabinets were fairly evenly divided between Ministers with working-class and those with middle-class origins. In this sense, the social composition of Labour Cabinets reflected trends in the parliamentary party over the whole century. The first generation of Labour Cabinet Ministers were predominantly people of working-class origin who achieved middle-class life-styles *through the Labour Movement*. A sizeable, though smaller, proportion of Labour Cabinet Ministers after 1945 were also born into the working class but had already achieved the major prerequisite of middle-class status – a University education before entering the Cabinet. In this sense, the present Labour leader, Neil Kinnock – a labourer's son who went on through grammar school to University – is very typical of recent tendencies in the Labour Party. Mrs Thatcher, however, born into the lower middle class – she is the daughter of a shopkeeper – and educated in the State system, is quite untypical of her own party, except in having had an Oxford education.

We now turn to the educational background of *other élites*. Tables 26.4 and 26.5 show the proportion of a range of élites receiving private education

TABLE 26.4

Social and educational background of 'open-competition' entrants to the administrative class/administrative trainee grade of the home Civil Service

	1921–32 %	1933–9 %	1949–50 %	1961–5 %	1971–5 %	1981 %	1982–3 %
Children of manual/ routine non-manual worker	n.d.	n.d.	27	18	n.d	n.d	n.d
Educated at non-fee-paying schools	20	19	26	29	65	56	n.d.
Oxbridge-educated	84	89	74	80	50	56	66

Sources: Kelsall (1974) for first four columns: House of Commons Expenditure Committee (1977) for 1971–5; Civil Service Commission (1983) for 1980s figures. Cited in Michael Moran, *Politics and Society in Britain* (1985) p. 163.

TABLE 26.5

Percentage of selected administrative élites 1939–83 who had been educated at fee-paying schools

	1939 %	1950 %	1960 %	1970 %	1983 %
Ambassadors	73.5	72.6	82.6	82.5	76.3
High Court Judges	80.0	84.9	82.5	80.2	79.0
Major Generals and above	63.6	71.3	83.2	86.1	78.9
RAF Vice-Marshals and above	66.7	59.1	58.4	62.5	41.1
Civil Servants, Under-Secretary and above	84.5	58.7	65.0	61.7	58.8

Sources: Columns 1–4 calculated from D. Boyd, *Elites and their Education* (1973), pp. 93–5; column 5 from *Whitaker's Almanack* and *Who's Who*. Cited in Michael Moran, *Politics and Society in Britain* (1985) p. 166.

over the last half-century together with the percentage of the administrative élite who had an Oxbridge education over roughly the same period. Whilst remaining biased towards recruitment of people educated at fee-paying schools, the *higher administrative grade of the Civil Service* has drawn gradually decreasing proportions of its entrants from this sector as the century has progressed (Table 26.4). The proportion of its recruits drawn from Oxbridge has also declined, but not uniformly: overall decline is compatible with a recent significant increase in the percentage of entrants drawn from this élite-within-an-élite. In 1982–3 over 66 per cent of entrants were Oxbridge-educated. How is this public-school/Oxbridge predominance possible when recruitment is by a process of rigorous examinations backed by interviews? The evidence is not easy to interpret. A satisfactory answer should include a variety of factors. For instance, educational achievement itself reflects class origins. In addition the bias of recruitment is to some extent self-fulfilling; children from middle- and upper middle-class homes are probably more likely than people from lower middle- and working-class backgrounds actually to consider a career as a top civil servant. Such factors are likely to be more important than social bias in the selectors. Over the half century, moreover, there has been a rise – although a modest one – in the proportion of entrants from the lower middle and working classes and a decrease in the percentage coming from the top public schools.

The Civil Service is more open than all other élites except the Air Force and the Navy. Table 26.5 reveals that, taking education at fee-paying schools as a broad indicator of social origins, the top posts in *the diplomatic service, the judiciary and the army* remain dominated by people educated in the private sector, and in the Army this predominance has actually increased over the past fifty years. In contrast, by 1983, both the Air Force and the Civil Service at the highest levels drew upon State-educated people to a significant extent and, in the Air Force, the majority of its top people were non-public school. Top naval officers (not shown in Table 26.5) also tended not to have had public school educations; in 1970, only 38 per cent had done so, as D. Boyd indicates in *Elites and their Education* (National Foundation for Educational Research, 1973, ch. 5).

The business élite consists of the directors, leading shareholders and top executives of the largest industrial and financial concerns. David Coates provides a valuable description of this élite in *The Context of British Politics* (1984). The business élite not only owns substantial property transferable through inheritance from one generation to the next but also plays a prominent part in finance and business as the chairmen, directors and chief executives of major finance houses and companies. At the centre of this élite are:

1. *families, or closely-knit groups of intermarried families, who own majority shareholdings in major companies*; in 1976, twenty-one companies fell into this category, including Trust House Forte, J. Lyons, George Wimpey, Littlewoods and Associated British Foods, and also *families which are influential (but not controlling) shareholders in large companies*; thirty-five of the top 250 companies in 1976 fell into this category, influential families including Cadbury (Cadbury Schweppes), Colman (Reckitt and Colman), Katz (Unigate), Clore (Sears Holdings) and Marks (Marks and Spencer);
2. *top executives, who serve as managers of leading enterprises at the highest level whilst not themselves possessing significant shareholdings in the companies they manage*;
3. *Directors of boards of leading concerns*; in 1976, it has been calculated, twenty-seven individuals, most of them possessing titles or knighthoods, sat on four or more boards of the leading 250 companies; eleven of the twenty-seven held a total of fifty-seven directorships in the top 250 companies;
4. *a core financial élite, linked at many points and to some extent overlapping with individuals in category 3* and consisting of the chairmen of the Big Four clearing banks and of leading merchant banks, the chairmen of the twelve largest insurance companies and directors of the Bank of England.

As with the other élites, the extent to which members of the business élite had a public school/Oxbridge background varies. According to a study by R. D. Whitley, 'The City and Industry . . .' (1974), the financial sector of the business élite were overwhelmingly privately and Oxbridge educated (a significant proportion having been to Eton and other top public schools); over 80 per cent of the directors of large financial institutions had such educational backgrounds. A rather smaller but still significant proportion (about 66 per cent) of directors of companies had been to fee-paying schools and Oxbridge. In terms of social backgrounds, there were few signs of either sector of the business élite recruiting from the lower middle or working class.

Membership of this élite in general was as narrowly recruited from the upper class (aristocracy/upper middle class) as judges, bishops and army leaders.

The social and educational background of the *trade union élite* stands in total contrast to other élites in British society in being entirely working and lower middle class and entirely educated in State schools. This is the case whether we limit our attention to trade union leaders (general secretaries and presidents) or extend our concern to include the officials who make up trade union bureaucracies. Trade union bureaucracies in any case are small and in the trade union movement as a whole there are only about 3000 full-time officials. The tendency is for trade union leaders and officials to have left school at the minimum leaving age, worked in manual or white-collar jobs and risen to their union posts through work in the union itself. Despite the increasing tendency in some – especially white collar – unions, to look for their officers amongst the university-educated, the overwhelming majority of union leaders and officials in the 1980s still reflect the class and educational experiences of the bulk of the population. Bill Jordan, President of the Amalgamated Engineering Union in 1987, typifies the general norm. Son of a furnaceman in Birmingham, he was educated at secondary modern school, which he left at 15 to take up an apprenticeship with an engineering firm (GKN). He worked there until 1977, when he was elected to the post of Midlands organiser of his union. Thus, from a background of early-school-leaving and manual work on the shop-floor until the age of 40, he moved via his post as union organiser to be president of the AUEW. Only in joining the trade union élite did his experience deviate from that of the working class in general.

RULING CLASS, POWER ELITE OR COMPETING ELITES?

Broadly speaking, there are three distinct approaches to the empirically observable fact that the highest positions in British society and politics are in general recruited from a small and unrepresentative section of the population. These take the form of three models – the 'ruling class' theory (Marxist), the 'power élite' theory (Elitist) and the 'pluralist' theory (Liberal). We consider and criticise each one in turn.

The ruling class theory (Marxist)

'Ruling class' theory holds that a single cohesive ruling class exists in Britain. Its power rests in the control and ownership of capital. Thus, although a number of élites exist in various sectors of society, they are bound together by a set of common interests into a homogeneous ruling class. The main interests they share consist of the maintenance of property, support for the capitalist system, the limitation of effective democratic control and social reform, and the perpetuation of their own wealth and privilege. Divisions of interest may from time to time appear between sections of this ruling class – between finance capital (the City) and manufacturing industry, for example. Ultimately, however, the common interest of such groups in the continued existence and strength of capitalism takes precedence over apparently divergent interests. This ruling class encompasses not only those most obviously involved in the ownership of wealth in all its forms (fixed and liquid assets, land, property and shares) but also those élites (Conservative politicians, judges, ambassadors, military chiefs) which possess a common privileged upper-class origin, education and life-style. Leading civil servants too belong to the upper class since, in the words of the Marxist writer, David Coates, they are 'filtered by a long promotion process' to ensure their identification with the interests of capital (Coates, *Context of British Politics*, 1984, p. 236). The fact that the ruling class is not particularly visible to people as they go about their everyday lives (it does not pose for a group photograph which then appears on television and in the newspapers) does not mean, say Marxists, that it does not exist. On this view, since the State is always and invariably under the domination of a capitalist ruling class, the apparatus of democracy – the holding of periodic elections, party competition for power, the political influence of pressure groups makes no difference to the realities of power. It is a mere façade for the class rule of the big owners of property and capital.

Power élite theories

'Power élite' theories also consider democratic institutions a sham, but for different reasons. Less prone than 'ruling class' theorists to argue the inherent impossibility or to deny the effectiveness of representative govern-ment on principle, they end in a broadly similar position. For power élite theorists, the reason why oligarchy (the rule of the few) always triumphs over democracy is psychological. This theory was developed in the early twentieth century by the Italian sociologists Vilfredo Pareto and Gaetano Mosca and the Swiss sociologist, Robert Michels. The post-war American C. Wright Mills wrote *The Power Elite* (1956) in this tradition. Elite theorists concluded from an examination of the practice of organisations that, whatever the ideals purporting to guide behaviour, power invariably passed away from the control of members into the hands of the few. This was because a small minority simply were more able, ruthless, manipulative and willing to give their time to the organisation than the rest.

During the 1950s, a British version of power élite theory drew attention to the existence in Britain of an 'Establishment', a cohesive political class which pursues its own self-serving ends irrespective of the results of elections. This power élite or Establishment is held together less by shared economic interest (although its members do tend to possess similar socio-economic backgrounds) than by a common culture which separates it sharply from the rest of society. Sheltering behind the traditional rituals, norms of 'moderation' and strong adherence to confidentiality of British political culture, the Establishment governs Britain no matter which party is nominally in power. A permanent and pervasive psychological attitude characterises the 'Establishment'. New people – aspiring working-class and lower middle-class politicians, for example – may enter it but never in sufficient numbers to change or dilute its enduring power and always at the price of the abandonment of radical principles. This is the way in which, historically, Radicals and Socialists who would challenge social inequality have been contained, tamed and ultimately absorbed. In the final analysis, this shared attitude comes down to a determination to remain in political control, come what may.

Pluralist theories

Pluralists disagree with both these theories. According to pluralist theory, what matters about the distribution of power in society is not that it is uneven – since unevenness characterises all societies and is probably inevitable – but three other vital features:

1. Whilst élites undoubtedly exist, they are to varying degrees open and relatively accessible to able people from below, rather than sealed into closed hierarchies. Pluralists do not deny that certain élite groups in Britain – the Conservative Party, the judiciary, the diplomatic service and the financial community in particular – are difficult to enter for those not born into the wealthy upper middle (some would simply say 'upper') class. They argue, however, that élites vary greatly in composition. To set against those parts of society still dominated by upper-class individuals, there are other sectors in which people with working- and lower middle-class backgrounds can reach the top on merit. These include the Labour Party, the Home Civil Service, local government, the police, the Royal Air Force and the trade union movement. Nor is it the case that the Conservative Party, judiciary, diplomatic service and the world of finance are exclusively upper-class preserves at the highest level. Change – however slow it may seem to reformers – has taken place in these sectors, as witness the fact, for example, that the last and present leader of the Conservative Party came from modest social origins.
2. Pluralists maintain no single ruling class or cohesive power élite exists. Rather, they argue, a number of élites compete for influence. Competition *between* a series of power blocs representing diverse interests rather than the rule of a single monolithic Establishment or ruling class is 'the name of the game'. Resources which can be deployed to influence decisions (money, numbers, organisational skills) are in practice widely dispersed. Thus, élite groups representing sectoral and occupational interests

influence policy-making selectively within their specialised fields of concern (industrial, financial, military, academic). Moreover, since disagreements appear from time to time *within* élites, rank-and-file participation is possible as appeals for members' views have to be made. This type of wider appeal beyond the boundaries of the élite itself occurs quite frequently within political parties and trade unions. In parties, it tends to happen in the wake of electoral defeat, as in 1975 when Mrs Thatcher replaced Edward Heath as Conservative leader after he had suffered two successive election defeats within one year. Both the two major parties and trade unions – the first by reforming themselves, the second by legislation – have become more democratic since the 1960s.

3. Pluralists argue that, although many élites can be influential from time to time, the *political* élite, consisting largely of members of the Cabinet and top civil servants, is *supreme*. In their model, the power structure is rather like a range of mountain peaks among which one – the political – is discernibly higher than all the rest. Unlike the other two theories, which tend to locate power with hidden, behind-the-scenes manipulators, for pluralism, real power lies where it ostensibly lies or is supposed to lie – with the political élite. The political élite predominates over the leading business, financial, labour and other groups by virtue of the special authority afforded it by the democratic system of government. Moreover – and this point is fundamental in pluralist analysis – the governing élite acts within the powerful constraints of regular elections, and, between elections, of the countervailing influence of public opinion. Included in public opinion are political institutions such as the Civil Service and the House of Lords and pressure groups, like the CBI, the TUC and the City. Far from considering democratic political machinery a mere façade, pluralists take it seriously. They maintain that although far from perfect it does ensure enough popular control, choice and participation to be regarded as a working or viable system. Whilst it is the case that in some important parts of the system, participation is low – only about 5 per cent of the electorate are members of political parties and an even smaller proportion are party activitists – on the other hand, participation is high elsewhere in the system, and increasing. Minor parties now provide a wider base for political participation than was the case in the 1960s, and there has been a huge upsurge in pressure group activity. In the early 1980s, participation in the environmental, peace and women's movements became a major social phenomenon. Efforts to increase participation should continue to be made – for example, by encouraging people to join parties and generally to play more active parts in trade unions, parent-teacher associations, neighbourhood councils and planning inquiries. But, in the view of pluralists, the present liberal–democratic system, although élitist, is neither deliberately nor irremediably so. Not only are present levels of participation reasonable, they are potentially much higher. And

the system possesses the capacity to change in response to changing social needs and demands – as evidenced by the movement in a quarter of a century from a situation dominated by two major parties with limited pressure-group activity in a relatively minor key to the present multi-party system allied to a broader range of vociferous groups.

Criticisms of 'power élite' and 'ruling class' theories

Since the British variant of power élite theory (the idea of a socially and culturally cohesive Establishment) was first asserted in the 1950s, it has decreased rather than gained in plausibility. This is, first, because British *politics* has become more polarised, more open and more democratic. It became more polarised in the 1970s, as large differences between the major parties displaced consensus. In these circumstances, it became virtually impossible to maintain that elections did not alter things much, and even more difficult after the General Election of 1979. Clearly, the advent of Mrs Thatcher changed things a great deal. Second, British *government* became more open and less secretive. This happened more by inadvertence than design, and it was usually resisted by governments of the day. Nonetheless by the 1980s, the public were far more aware of what went on in the inner counsels of the Cabinet and in the 'Whitehall village' than was the case a generation previously. The publication of politicians' diaries and memoirs (Richard Crossman, Barbara Castle), 'leaks' by civil servants (Clive Ponting) and the revelations of goings-on within the secret services by people like Peter Wright provided fascinating if somewhat selective glimpses of power in the inner sanctums of government and made its 'mysteries' less mysterious. Finally, as we have seen, certain important sectors of British society became more democratic. In political parties, members played an increasing role in the election of leaders and the selection of party candidates; in trade unions, balloting on the choice of leaders and on strike decisions became the norm. The increasing hold of television on society tended to promote both greater openness and greater democracy – not least by providing continual public demonstrations that, far from being cohesive and united, the so-called Establishment spoke with many, often sharply-divergent, voices. The overall count against the notion of an Establishment in Britain is clear: it is neither united, nor – in an age of revelations and media coverage – mysterious, nor – and most important of all – free from popular control. It is a myth.

The views of the European élite theorists of the early twentieth century deserve to be taken more seriously. It can be admitted that there is a tendency in all organisations for power to slide towards a few people – those with more than average commitment, capacity and energy – and for such élites to escape control by the membership. However, it is problematic whether this is inevitable, as Michels suggested with his notion of the 'iron law of oligarchy'. In practice, élite theorists paid too little attention to the leader–follower relationship and to the context, in democratic systems, of that relationship. In effect, leaderships – in parties and trade unions, for example – have to be rather more responsive to the wishes of their memberships than élite theory suggests. The price of disregarding their supporters' and members' opinions is loss of effective power. For in modern organisations leaders are more powerful the more they can carry their followers with them. In democracies, moreover, membership of social organisations is voluntary, and members accordingly expect to be consulted, at least on major decisions.

The assumptions of élite theorists are also relevant. Their starting-point was pessimism about the possibility of democracy. They specifically wrote to refute what they saw as the false Utopianism of the democratic ideal of mass participation in decision-making. Beginning by simply assuming that people were selfish, ignorant and apolitical, they also posed a question – 'Who really rules?' – that invited an answer in terms of an undemocratic élite. It was scarcely surprising that they ended both by finding an élite and by relegating the majority of people to political powerlessness as its dupes. They considered neither the possibility that people would grow in political understanding as society developed nor the possibility that it might make sense for ordinary members of organisations to delegate responsibility for decisions to a few, so long as *ultimate* control remained with the membership. At best, their case remains unproven (perhaps even impossible to establish). At worst, it consists of a sweeping generalisation which requires continual testing by reference to *specific* decisions and often disintegrates when faced by such a test. Empirically, there seem to be better grounds for accepting the pluralist hypothesis – that different élites compete for influence with an over-arching political élite; that élites are to some extent and differentially responsive to memberships; and, above all, that elections matter as a mechanism by which real power may change hands peaceably.

'Ruling class' theory faces a similar methodological problem to 'power élite' theory. This is the difficulty of showing that all decisions are under the control of and in the interests of a specific group – in this case, a capitalist ruling class. How does one prove the existence of power that is by definition *covert*? And if the response is to say 'how does one definitively establish the contrary?' the situation soon becomes one of infinite regress. It would seem fair to argue that the onus of proof ought to lie rather with those who assert such a thesis than with their critics.

The second (pluralist) criticism of ruling class theory is more empirical and concentrates on how Marxists use the evidence. An example of this approach is given by David Coates. The major problem is to establish the precise nature of the damage done to his thesis by certain admissions that appear throughout his book. For example, he does consider 'the impact of democratic pressures, institutional growth and social mobility on the changing position of the privileged in British society' (Coates, *Context of British Politics*, p. 113). Democratic pressures have opened certain élite positions in

Parliament and government to people of lower social background. The growth of government activity and bureaucracy has led to the creation of a new 'service class' beneath the élite, recruited from working-class and lower-middle-class backgrounds. More significant still, particularly gifted or fortunate individuals have risen from these classes to achieve prominence in industry and commerce. Their success, Coates concludes, 'gives the lie to any argument that the British élite structure is totally closed' (ibid, p. 114). Second, the system is not fenced off against working-class influence. Thus, the post-war trade union movement wielded considerable political resources against both employers and the State. Indeed, 'industrial capital . . . found no effective strategy for dealing with that working-class power until the Thatcherite recession became available in the late 1970s' (ibid, p. 54). Under the Labour Government (1974–9) British trade unionism even 'enjoyed a unique and brief period of political ascendancy' (ibid, p. 86). After the war, moreover, politicians responded to working-class pressures by creating a 'broadly-based welfare state' (ibid, p. 233). Pluralists might not put their argument in quite the same terms. They would certainly dissent from language (the Thatcherite recession became 'available' to industrial capital) which suggests that employers welcomed a recession that put many of them out of business and sharply reduced the profits of many who remained in being. But they would agree with the essentials of the analysis – that pluralist bargaining between opposing major interests went on and that accommodation was both possible and mutually advantageous.

However, the thrust of Coates's argument is quite different. Having agreed that the concessions to and the achievements of the trade unions and the working class after 1945 were in a sense real ones, he quickly withdraws into the more familiar Marxist position that they were merely part of ruling-class strategy to incorporate the workers into the capitalist system. Allied with this notion is the idea that the Labour Party collaborated with the capitalists by pursuing a peaceful moderate parliamentary path to political power. The contradiction here seems obvious. On the one hand, the political system is both sufficiently open for lower-class people to penetrate it at the highest levels and as a class to negotiate benefits from it; on the other, such gains are really illusory, since they serve merely to stabilise the system and to consolidate the power of the capitalist class. How does Coates explain the phenomenon of the Conservative working-class vote, then? Why do many workers put nation before class, accept the rights of governments to define the national interest, limit their sense of 'fairness' to fine variations of income and reward rather than challenging the wider inequalities surrounding them? Why do many, also, associate the market with 'freedom' and the State with 'bureaucracy'? The answer is the same in every case. The consciousness of the working class has been deeply penetrated by a whole set of official orthodoxies which reflect 'the interests and preoccupations of the ruling strata' (ibid, pp. 151–2). To liberal pluralists this explanation seem totally contemptuous of the working class, whose actual thoughts and wishes are not seen as in any sense their own but rather as a simple reflection of the ruling-class view. Just as in right-wing European élitist theory, the lower classes end up by being the dupes of an élite, so they do in Marxist theory. In essence, this seems an élitist view itself, with the élitists themselves deciding how people ought to vote and what they should think, and arrogating to themselves also the right to bewail deviations from 'correct' behaviour and opinion (as they see the matter).

Liberal pluralists and Marxists differ not only on the nature, role and accountability of élites but also on the Constitution, the political process (including the parts played by parties and pressure groups) and the role of the State. Their opposed approaches to the central institutions of government were discussed in Chapter 7.

LIBERAL AND MARXIST VIEWS ON THE CONSTITUTION

This book has in general adhered to a liberal conception of the constitution. It has taken seriously the case of the United Kingdom as a unique type of liberal democracy. In doing so, however, it has not ignored the criticisms of and suggested remedies for the defects in the British system of government, many of which themselves emanate from within the liberal tradition. The liberal view of the constitution maintains that Britain has a largely written but uncodified Constitution whose fundamental rules are a mixture of statute law, Crown prerogative, common law and constitutional conventions. A formidable amount of power is concentrated in government which can be exercised over subnational and local government and over social institutions such as churches, businesses, trade unions and the mass media. Checks on this power derive from four sources: public opinion, shaped by the liberal–pluralist values, attitudes and habits instilled through the political culture; legally-established rights; formal constitutional checks as embodied in the two Houses of Parliament; and the resistance of the social institutions and groups themselves. In the 1980s, interest revived in formal constitutional rules as a means of setting limits upon the power of government in the public interest and of guaranteeing individual rights. Concern arose as a consequence of what were generally perceived as centralising trends within the system, notably the erosion of the independence of local government; of the apparently frequent need for UK citizens to have recourse to the European Court to protect their rights; of the evident lack of parliamentary control over the national budget; and of the absence of any formal requirement that a wide variety of authorities (public corporations, quangos, government departments, local government) – many of them non-elected – give reasons for their decisions. Suggested remedies have included the devolution of power upon the regions, the strengthening of local government, the development of procedures enabling more thorough parliamentary consideration of the government's public expenditure proposals and the protection of the liberties of the citizen by a Bill of Rights. These criticisms and suggested remedies have all been designed with the aim of enabling the British system more effectively to live up to its promise of responsible and accountable government. Whether and to what extent these remedies are desirable and, if so, feasible, are matters which are themselves topics for intense debate, as we have seen, between parties, groups and academic experts.

Marxists would dismiss such concerns as mere institutional tinkering. To them, the Constitution is simply a façade concealing the operation of capitalist institutions. To Marxists, the British system of government is more appropriately entitled 'capitalist democracy' than 'liberal democracy'. The stress, moreover, is upon the word 'capitalist' rather than 'democracy'. This is because, in their view, economics takes precedence over politics. For them, the central fact bearing upon the working of the political system derives directly from the nature of the economic system. This is the inequality of wealth and income which flows from the workings of capitalism, a system whose essence is the accumulation of capital in the hands of the few. Such concentrations of wealth, in fact, place massive power in the hands of big financiers, financial institutions and the multinational corporations. What matters for Marxists is not what happens in the sphere labelled 'constitutional' or 'political' but what happens in the spheres of activity labelled 'social' or 'economic'. For constitutional and political rights and freedoms guaranteed to all by the liberal–pluralist system are not really 'rights' and 'freedoms' at all, so long as glaring inequalities exist and the life-chances of the many are so overshadowed by the privileges of the few. Devolution, the strengthening of parliament in relation to the government of the day and Bills of Rights cannot affect the substance of social power and inequality. They cannot give the unemployed jobs, or the low-paid higher incomes, or prune the power of the financial and business élites. On this perspective, 'parliamentarism' is a dirty word, denoting not the gradualist pursuit of political influence by the working class but a process whereby the representatives of the working class have been duped into acceptance of the present unequal distribution of wealth and income.

Liberals reply that Socialists have had over a century to persuade people of the truth of their analysis but have made only modest headway; that mainstream political activity has in the twentieth century improved welfare, resulted in some redistribution of income and enhanced working-class prospects for the acquisition of wealth; and that the organised working class, through the very substantial investments of trade unions, itself participates in the accumulation of capital. Finally, Liberals criticise the Marxist analysis from the standpoint of its method. How reliable, they ask, is an analysis which, on the one hand, speaks of 'capital' as a malign, monolithic interest and, on the other, admits large divisions within it – between finance and industrial capital; between banks and building societies; and banks and insurance companies? When, for example, David Coates maintains that financiers, like industrialists, are 'a hostile band of brothers' (ibid, p. 61), united by common interests but divided by competition and suspicion, why should not the competition and suspicion be regarded as an equally or even a more significant factor than the allegedly common interests which unite them? Liberal–pluralists, of course, would argue that analysts of society should take the divisions between capitalists as seriously as their common interests.

LIBERAL AND MARXIST VIEWS ON THE POLITICAL PROCESS

Liberal–pluralists and Marxists also disagree fundamentally on the workings of the political process itself. To pluralists, competition between parties for office through the ballot-box complemented by the free advocacy of their causes and interests by a variety of pressure groups is the heart of the democratic system. Different terms have been coined to describe the operation of the party struggle at differing phases of its recent history. During the 1960s and early 1970s, relatively minor changes in voting at elections were sufficient to keep the pendulum swinging between two parties whose differences – compared with what was to come later – appeared quite modest. This era of party competition is often described as the *responsible party* phase. In the late 1970s and 1980s, this situation changed dramatically. The two-party consensus broke down with the Conservative Party moving right under Mrs Thatcher and Labour moving left under Michael Foot (see Chapter 27). The party in office acted more blatantly to benefit its own clientele – Labour, the trade unions; Conservatives, the City and the well-off in general. Politics became more ideological. The term *adversary politics* seemed more appropriate to denote the way the system was now working. There were other changes, too. Electorally – with the rise of the nationalist parties and the growing strength of the Liberals in alliance with the newly-formed SDP after Labour's split in 1981 – multipartyism displaced two-party competition. An important effect of this change was to divide the opposition to the Conservatives, with the consequence that after their third consecutive election victory in 1987 they were certain to occupy government for at least twelve years after 1979. The political 'pendulum' appeared to have ceased to swing. Some commentators pointed out that periods of one-party dominance were nothing new in British politics. Historically, a single party had predominated over its major rival from 1846 to 1874 (Whig–Liberals); from 1886 to 1906 (the Conservatives); from 1906 to 1916 (the Liberals); from 1922 to 1945 (the Conservatives); and from 1964 to 1979 (Labour). But, even if not new, how democratic was this situation?

Doubts about the way the British system of representative government was working surfaced increasingly in the 1980s and were not confined to advocates of proportional representation. In the post-war period it was always the case that governments were formed by parties which had received the support of under 50 per cent of voters. But whereas in the 1950s parties took office with only just under 50 per cent of the total vote (49.4 per cent in 1959), in the two elections of the 1980s, the Conservatives gained only just over 40 per cent of the total vote (42.4 per cent and 42.3 per cent respectively). Moreover, as a proportion of the electorate as a whole the position looked even worse, with only about 33 per cent of all electors voting for the winning party. Until recently, it was customary to defend this not very pronounced unrepresentativeness of governments by reference to the stability of the political system in general. The failure of government to reflect public wishes with complete fidelity was more than offset, it was thought, by the fact that at least the system did provide for stable government. During the 1980s, and especially after the 1987 General Election, this view came under increased criticism as complacent. F. F. Ridley, for example, in an article published in *The Guardian*, 10 August 1987, after surveying the proportion of voters which supported the government in the most recent elections in seventeen European countries, concluded that the British Government had less electoral support than any other government in power in a European democracy. In his view the danger was that, when combined with other features of the contemporary constitution including the untrammelled power of the party in government, the exclusion of the major economic interest groups from consultation by government and the Conservatives' rejection of consensus under an authoritarian leader, this situation could bring the legitimacy of government itself into question. The threat to political stability was intensified by the geographical unrepresentativeness of the government; the nation itself was divided between North and South. And there were no constitutional devices such as regional representation in government or a strong system of local government to compel a government whose electoral power-base lay in the South to consider the interests of the rest of the country.

This is, of course, a powerful statement of the adversary thesis of party government. However, other writers have pointed out that this thesis can be exaggerated. In certain important respects, continuities of policy have been as significant as sharp reversals even in the hey-day of so-called adversary government. Thus, Richard Rose has shown that there were no divisions of principle on 77 per cent of the bills introduced by the Labour Governments of 1974–9 and, in the first session of the 1979–83 parliament, 63 per cent of the Acts were passed without divisions of principle (Rose, *Do Parties Make a Difference?*, 1984, p. 80). On public expenditure, there were considerable continuities between 1970s Labour Governments and 1980s Conservative Governments; despite the Conservatives' intention to reduce public expenditure, it remained at a high level both in absolute terms and relative to GNP throughout the first term and well into their second term of office. Finally, in the crucial sphere of economic policy-making, Andrew Gamble argues that the adversary thesis has highlighted certain obvious discontinuities, e.g. the parties' differences on the role of the State and on the boundary between the public and private sectors (the nationalisation/privatisation debate) to the neglect of much more considerable continuities in the post-war period. Thus, in the thirty years after 1945, the two major parties gave priority in broad terms to the integration of the British economy into the US-dominated world economy and, more specifically, to supporting sterling, rectifying balance-of-payments problems and, eventually, joining the EEC (Gamble and Walkland, *The British Party System and Economic Policy 1945–1983* (1984)).

A reasonable conclusion is that the adversary model draws attention to important aspects of the British system of party competition but cannot satisfactorily explain the whole process. In the aftermath of the 1987 election, with the Alliance split and losing support and Labour gaining support and engaged in a policy 'rethink' which at least contained the possibility of some movement towards the Conservative position, the responsible party model might be expected to gain in credibility. In any case, for pluralists, the changing nature of party competition is of less significance than *the fact of party competition itself.*

In pluralist analysis, the activities of pressure groups complement parties in the successful operation of the democratic political process. We have already considered in Chapter 12 the wide range of interest and promotional groups which exist in contemporary Britain. The 'universe' of pressure groups is a constantly changing one but it is probable that many groups discussed in earlier chapters – such as those representing the causes of women, blacks, nuclear disarmament and the protection of the environment – will be active for a long time to come. The major economic groups (business and the trade unions) came to occupy such a central position in national decision-making in the 1970s that a new theory or model was developed. The basis of the *corporatist* system was tripartite bargaining between government, business and unions by which – in return for consultation on economic policy-making – the major producer groups agreed to cooperate with government in keeping price rises down and in moderating wage claims.

Liberal traditionalists criticised the system at the time, first, because bargains struck between government and the major groups in this way bypassed parliament and, second, because it accorded the big producer groups too much influence. Against the first point, it could be legitimately said that the bargains were made with the party which had gained majority support at an election and which could quickly be turned out if the bargains were not to the liking of the electorate.

Against the second point, the principled rejoinder by liberal corporatists was – and still is – that many successful modern European economies (Sweden and West Germany, for example) are based on close government cooperation with representatives of business and the trade unions. They argue that the price of dismantling corporatist arrangements after 1979 has been too high – a level of unemployment which certainly exceeded that of Britain's major competitors in the first half of the 1980s. The termination of corporatism (or 'tripartism') and the adoption of an 'arm's length' attitude towards the major economic groups occurred in the context of the New Right argument that the groups had wielded excessive influence in the 1970s. In the eyes of New Right thinkers, producer group political influence in the 1970s was too great, and needed to be curbed. Britain had reached a point where the veto power of the trade unions acted as a brake on the effort to raise productivity, checked technological innovation and frightened away investment. To the New Right, the corporatist consensus equalled 'pluralist stagnation'. The New Right accords a stronger leadership role to government in its relations with groups than does earlier pluralist theory. But its political analysis is pluralist too, accepting as it does, the legitimacy of the activities of groups over a wide spectrum of interests. Indeed, it would be illogical if this were not the case since the New Right itself – an ideological variant which captured a major party – originated in the activities of a number of 'free market' pressure groups.

To Marxists, elections are simply a ritual which confer neither real power nor even ultimate control on voters, merely the illusion of influence. As Ralph Miliband writes: 'a permanent and fundamental contradiction "exists" between the promise of popular power, enshrined in popular suffrage, and the curbing or denial of that promise in practice' (Miliband, *Capitalist Democracy in Britain*, 1984, p. 1). Capitalism as an economic system requires the containment of 'pressure from below' and whilst the Conservatives might be expected to endorse such a goal enthusiastically, the Labour Party in practice has fallen in behind it also. It is formally committed to internal party democracy but in fact its parliamentary leadership has waged relentless war against the Left-wing activitists in the constituency parties and systematically ignored Conference decisions which it found distasteful. In reality, the word 'labourism' is a more accurate description of its practice than 'Socialism'. In power, Labour has done nothing to weaken, let alone to destroy, capitalism; it exists merely to win concessions for the working class, concessions which, by making for a more contented labour force, strengthen rather than undermine the system. The formal rule by a particular party then is simply that – a formality which serves to conceal the fact that the ruling class is *always* in power. The same analysis is extended to the world of pressure groups. However diverse the character and activities of the groups appear to be, the diversity is only apparent. What seems to be the ebb and flow of influence between government and groups is just shadow-boxing. Behind governments of all complexions stands capitalism, national and international. Ultimately, whatever guise they may assume (the big banks, the finance houses, the insurance companies, the multinationals) capitalists always ensure that the major decisions promote the interests of capital.

LIBERAL PLURALISM AND MARXISM ON THE STATE

Finally, liberal pluralists and Marxists differ on the nature of the social democratic State and the recent history of State intervention. Pluralists support the growth of State intervention since 1945 as a reflection of the advent of a mature stable democracy. Government implementation of a full employment policy and universal welfare benefits were a demonstration for the first time of a national commitment to govern in the interests of the entire community. Once launched, the Welfare State proved popular and, after a phase of relatively slow growth in the 1950s under the Conservatives, public expenditure rose significantly again in the 1960s and 1970s. This rise in State spending was fuelled by three main forces:

1. Rising private living standards (the 'affluent society') raised popular expectations of publicly provided services such as health and education and, with car purchases booming, increased demand for State expenditure on costly capital schemes in new areas such as motorways.
2. Technological advances led to escalating government spending not only on matters like defence (a succession of nuclear weapons culminating in Trident) but also on civil growth industries like aviation (Concorde) and medical breakthroughs (heart transplant surgery, kidney machines).
3. Population growth provided a semi-automatic boost for education (until the 1970s), health and housing.

In the 1970s, the welfare and economic roles of the State underwent severe reappraisal. There were a number of reasons for this including growing public reluctance to countenance ever-increasing levels of taxation, continuing economic difficulties, and demographic and other social changes which prompted a rethink about the direction of public spending. The New Right called for reductions in public expenditure as a proportion of GNP but this goal proved hard to achieve during the first two Thatcher Administrations (see Chapters 17 and 27).

In the broadest sense, the political debate about the role of the State between Conservatives and the centre and centre left (New Right, Conservative 'wets', the Alliance and all except the Labour Left) took place within a pluralist body of thought. The New Right considered that a reduced State sector would provide more room for private initiative in the economy and for the redirection of welfare money where it was most needed; their political opponents felt that State support for industry should be approached pragmatically rather than ideologically (ailing and new industries could need help from time to time) and that with regard to the Welfare State what was needed was reform of the whole system of taxation and welfare, not mere tinkering (tax cuts plus selective welfare cuts). Both sides of the controversy sought the best way to unleash national economic energies and to promote the support of the most needy within a broadly liberal, capitalist and democratic framework: in this sense, both arguments are pluralist.

Marxists perceive the State as inherently biased in favour of the middle class and against the working class. In its most unequivocal expression, this view holds that the State through its agents – judges, policemen and soldiers – is simply an instrument for ruling-class suppression of the working class; according to Marx, it is the executive arm of the bourgeoisie. The liberal or pluralist claim that the law-enforcement agencies are neutral between classes *cannot* be true; the law exists to protect property – hence, by definition, its agents are biased towards the possessing classes and against those with little or no property. Second, the legal profession (judges, barristers and solicitors) largely comes from privileged and wealthy backgrounds and finds it hard to understand or sympathise with ordinary people. Finally, it is expensive to obtain justice; legal fees are high and, since legal aid is granted only to those on very modest incomes, pursuing one's rights in the courts is a privilege largely confined to the rich. 'Equality before the law' and 'the legal rights of the citizen' are mere phrases with scant reference to reality for the majority of the population. Marxists point to contemporary historical experience as further endorsement of their viewpoint. They argue that the recent challenges to the UK State from Roman Catholics in Northern Ireland, from deprived youth and blacks in the inner cities (the 1981 riots) and from the industrial working class (the Miners' Strike, 1984–5) have revealed the hard authoritarian core and the naked class interest of the UK State beneath its veneer of impartiality.

How do Marxists explain the Welfare State which appears to be a benevolent entity? In fact, they argue that the interventionist and providing State is functional to capital which required a better-educated, more docile workforce. Welfarism, they maintain, was explicitly designed to improve the social conditions for capital accumulation. Only by apparently large concessions could capitalist interests preserve social stability and political legitimacy. But the *concessions* were only apparent. In reality, the middle classes – more articulate and more aware of their rights than the working class – have benefited most from the social institutions (NHS, State education) established by the Welfare State. And welfarism has perpetuated an unjust economic system.

The liberal response to this analysis is to put two points:

1. If welfarism is so 'functional' to capital, why was it not introduced over 100 years ago when the working class was suffering a great deal more than it was in the late 1940s? Further, if welfarism is functional to capital, should not true left-wing Socialists applaud the 'cuts' in welfare payments

and services introduced by the Conservative Governments rather than attack them?

In logic, it follows that if welfare is functional to capital, welfare cuts are dysfunctional. In fact, Marxists argue that welfare cuts are designed to 'recapitalise capital' and heavy unemployment is intended to curb working-class militancy. In other words, they argue that *both* welfare (1950–79) and cuts in welfare (from 1979) are functional to capital, which is, as Patrick Dunleavy points out in *Developments in British Politics* (1986), a classic instance of having your intellectual cake and eating it (Chapter 16).

2. Contrary to Marxist analysis, Liberals would be more inclined to argue that the British State since 1945 has been too weak rather than too strong in terms of its ability to achieve intended effects.

This argument is clearly stated in I. Budge *et al.*, *The New British Political System* (1983, Chapter 9). Certainly, the British State spends huge amounts of money and has taken on a massive range of responsibilities. But compared with the French, German and Japanese States, the British State has not managed to create effective links with major social and economic groups – industry, the organised working class, or the scientific Establishment. Policy in the crucial spheres of industry and the economy has been marred by discontinuities and about-turns, by fruitless and counter-productive bouts of in-fighting with one or other of the major producer groups, and by the virtually total failure to mobilise a consensus. The consequence has been a catalogue of missed opportunities and misplaced effort – in particular, failures to stimulate scientific and technological research, to find and back industrial 'winners' and to ensure that industrial investment reaches and remains at a high level. Far from being a powerful State, the British State is a rather loose-jointed, fragmented, uncoordinated one, a paper tiger rather than a Leviathan.

SUMMARY

British élites are in general drawn from predominantly privileged social backgrounds although some élites do contain significant minorities of working-class and lower-middle-class origin. Business and the professions are dominant in parliament, and State-educated persons of mainly working-class origin in the trade unions. Whilst élites have become more open during the twentieth century, change has been only gradual. Both as a general approach to the distribution of power and influence in British society and specifically as an approach to the analysis of the Constitution, the political process and the role of the State, pluralism is preferred to rival theories. The concept of competition for power

between and within élites gets closer to political realities than the idea of a ruling class (or power élite).

Within pluralist analysis, there are important disagreements about the security of civil rights, the working of the political system (the responsible party versus adversary politics debate) and about the nature of the British State. Whilst the New Right seeks to prune what it considers to be the excessive social and economic responsibilities of a 'corporatist' State, some liberal academics do not equate the size of the post-war State with power. They believe it failed to develop authoritative institutions for economic decision-making.

FURTHER READING

Budge, I. *et al.* (1983) *The New British Political System*, London, Longman.
Burch, M. and Moran, M. (1985) 'The Changing British Political Elite, 1945–83: MPs and Cabinet Ministers', *Parliamentary Affairs*, vol. 138, Winter.
Coates, D. (1984) *The Context of British Politics*, London, Hutchinson.
Dunleavy, P. (1986) final two chapters in H. Drucker *et al.*, *Developments in British Politics, 2*, London, Macmillan, 3rd edn.
Gamble, A. M. and Walkland, S. A. (1984) *The British Party System and Economic Policy, 1945–1983*, Oxford, Clarendon Press.
Miliband, R. (1984) *Capitalist Democracy in Britain*, Oxford, University Press.
Moran, R. D. (1985) *Politics and Society in Britain*, London, Macmillan.
Rose, R. (1984) *Do parties make a difference?*, London, Macmillan.
Whitley, R. D. (1974) 'The City and Industry: The Directors of Large Companies, their Characteristics and Connections', in P. Stanworth and A. Giddens (eds) *Elites and Power in British Society*, Cambridge, University Press.

QUESTIONS

1. Critically examine the pluralist approach to the distribution of power in Britain.

2. Discuss the view that variables such as education and social class can tell us little of significance about the nature and outcome of decision-making in Britain.

ASSIGNMENT

It has been said that whichever Party is in power the Civil Service really rules. Collect evidence from your reading and the media news for and against this view.

27

The Consequences of Thatcherism: The End of Consensus, and the Forging of a New Consensus

This book has been written on the assumption that issues in politics are inseparable from institutions and cannot properly be discussed apart. Appropriately, therefore, it ends with the major political question of our times, overarching, including and dominating all others – the overall impact of the Conservative Governments of Mrs Thatcher after 1979 up to 1987 (the start of their third term) and the prospects for the future. In the second half of the 1980s, it was frequently asserted that 'Thatcherism' (a shorthand term for the New Right policies and ideological values of Mrs Thatcher) had broken the political consensus on which Britain had been governed previously, and had inaugurated a new era. This chapter subjects this claim to critical examination, considering in turn the meaning of consensus, the record of the Conservative Governments in the light of their expressed aims and the extent to which the changes they had brought about in British politics by the late 1980s were likely to be permanent. In doing so, it brings together earlier social and economic policy themes in a historical and comparative context.

The word 'consensus' when applied to the politics of the post-war period in Britain (roughly, the era from 1945 to the late 1970s) refers primarily to the broad agreement between the two major parties on the substance of public policy, notably in the key areas of management of the economy, welfare and defence (this chapter focuses on policy in the two first-named areas). The dominant consensus in this period is usually described as 'Butskellite', after R. A. Butler, the Conservative Chancellor of the Exchequer from 1951 to 1955, and Hugh Gaitskell, the Labour Chancellor of the Exchequer from 1950 to 1951, and future party leader. But it is also referred to as 'Keynesian', after the economist, John Maynard Keynes, whose ideas influenced government management of the economy, and as 'Beveridgean' after William Beveridge, the architect of the post-war Welfare State. The substance of the consensus in terms of policy was the general agreement by both parties in government to give high priority to the maintenance of (i) full employment; (ii) a high level of public spending on a wide range of 'universal' benefits and services, and (iii) the broad balance between the public and private sectors attained in the 'mixed economy' of 1950. Many commentators when using the phrase 'consensus politics' with reference to this period also have in mind a 'moderate' political style or approach in which two parties whose ideological and policy differences were not perceived as great by the electors, competed for the centre ground of politics, making no attempt to change the 'Welfare-State/mixed-economy consensus' and few attempts to reverse any policies of their predecessors in government. Characteristic of this attitude was the acceptance by the Conservative Government of 1951–64 of the Labour Governments' initiatives on public ownership, welfare and economic management in the post-war period. This picture can be over-stated – important differences remained between the two parties. However, in the two decades after the war, they remained more differences of emphasis than of substance. Summarised, the major components of the consensus were:

1. a *mixed economy* in which the bulk of industry remained in private ownership but where a set of major industries and services (nationalised by Labour after 1945) were run by public corporations. These were coal, gas, electricity, railways, air transport and the Bank of England;
2. a *Welfare State* in which a wide range of publicly-provided benefits and 'universal' services were available to all on demonstration of need and, in the case of the services, were 'free' at the point of receipt. In historical terms they rested upon a high level of public expenditure, derived predominantly from general taxation. The keystones of the 'Welfare State' were a system of social security and pensions designed to provide a minimum standard 'safety net' in unemployment and old age, the National Health Service (the guiding principle of which was the provision of health care to all regardless of income) and compulsory secondary education to the age of 15;
3. a *Keynesian approach* to economic management in which governments assumed responsibility for running the economy at a high level of demand for goods and services (using fiscal and monetary methods) in order to maintain full employment (3 per cent unemployment was the figure unofficially considered acceptable). To control inflationary pressures, governments relied upon incomes policies (government-set pay 'norms' of either a voluntary or compulsory kind) and increasingly moved into a 'corporatist' style of managing the economy which involved them in close partnership with the 'peak' business and labour organisations, the CBI and TUC;
4. Moderate political parties, with the Conservatives led from the interventionist compassionate centre-left (a position later designated as 'wet' by Mrs Thatcher) by Anthony Eden and Harold Macmillan, and Labour led

from the centre-right by Hugh Gaitskell, Harold Wilson and James Callaghan; and with the parties converging not only on the mixed-economy/Welfare-State, support for NATO, a nuclear defence policy, and the withdrawal from empire, but also on the resolution of policy differences by compromise and agreement.

'Thatcherism' emerged in the late 1970s against a background of intensifying and apparently intractable problems for consensus politics. These centred upon Britain's inferior economic performance compared with other major industrial countries and the related difficulty the country was beginning to experience in paying for the Welfare State. At the root of the economic problem lies a paradox. The economy grew steadily and by historical standards quite rapidly in the post-war epoch. Indeed, living standards (real personal disposable income per head) nearly doubled between 1951 and 1978 (*Social Trends*, 1980, p. 14). At least until 1970, moreover, consensus policies had managed to deliver low inflation (annual average increase 4.5 per cent under Labour 1964–70) and low unemployment (annual average – 335 000, $1\frac{1}{2}$ per cent of workforce in 1950s; 447 000, 2 per cent of workforce in 1960s) as well as economic growth. However, rising prosperity came to be considered as comparative failure because the economies of many other advanced nations grew faster. Between 1962 and 1972, for example, OECD calculated that annual percentage rates of economic growth (GDP) were over one and a half times as fast in West Germany and Italy, over twice as fast in France and over four times as fast in Japan (figures cited in A. Gamble, *Britain in Decline* (1981), p. 19). Although in the 1970s Britain was more prosperous than ever before the country was slipping steadily down the international economic league table: in relative terms, the country was in decline. Of course, it was possible to trace this process back over a hundred years to the late nineteenth century. However, in the post-war period, it came to seem more serious – first, because it was accelerating, second, because it was experienced not in terms of a gradual reduction of advantage but in terms of actually being overtaken by other economies. By the 1970s, living standards in many European countries (West Germany, France, the Scandinavian countries, Luxembourg, Switzerland) as well as in the USA, Canada and Australia, were higher than those in Britain. It was at this time also that economic indicators hitherto favourable took a sharp downward turn: the inflation rate increased, rising from an average annual rate of 9 per cent under the Conservatives (1970–4) to an annual average of 15 per cent under Labour (1974–9). Unemployment rose, too, to an annual average of $\frac{3}{4}$m (1970–4) and then leapt again to an annual average of $1\frac{1}{4}$m (1974–9). The growth rate slowed down. A new term, '*stagflation*', was coined to describe this unprecedented situation of slow growth combined with both rising unemployment and rising inflation.

Against this context, governments attributed inflationary pressures to the excessive wage demands of militant unions and developed incomes policies (statutory, 1972–4) and compulsory non-statutory (1976–9) as a method of curbing price rises. It was the hey-day of the corporatist philosophy of joint economic management between government, employers and unions and this approach characterised the Governments of Edward Heath (1970–4), Harold Wilson (1974–6) and James Callaghan (1976–9). Whatever the final judgement of historians will be on incomes policies, they had the undoubted disadvantage of politicising industrial relations. The Heath Government's clash with the miners (1974) and the Callaghan Government's battle with the public-sector unions in the so-called 'winter of discontent' (1978–9) assisted in bringing about their downfall.

The post-war Welfare State had also come under severe strain by the mid-1970s. The problem was basically one of finance (see Chapters 17 and 18). How was the system to be paid for? The 1950s orthodoxy was that the rapid growth of the economy would enable public expenditure to rise without adding to the tax burden on households. By the 1970s this expectation had been eroded. National income failed to grow as rapidly as hoped. But public expenditure expanded very fast. There were a number of reasons. These included the desire to improve the level of benefits and the quality of services; the adoption of new commitments (for example, grants to the physically and mentally disabled); increases in the numbers of clients of a benefit or service (more pensioners, more unemployed, more students in higher education); and rises in costs (generated, for example, by more advanced medical equipment). This expansion took place against the background of governmental and élite optimism that expenditure on social services could in the not-too-distant future eliminate residual poverty and deprivation and bring about a much greater degree of equality (see Chapter 19). Employment in the public sector rose particularly rapidly in the 1960s and early 1970s: between 1961 and 1978, numbers employed in health, education and social services rose from 6.2 per cent to 12.2 per cent as a proportion of national employment.

In 1975, public expenditure as a proportion of GNP reached a post-war peak of 55 per cent. The gap between public expenditure and tax revenue – which has to be filled by State borrowing (the Public Sector Borrowing Requirement) – increased dramatically. And it did so even though the burden of taxation was at record levels. J. C. Kincaid *et al.* in *To Him Who Hath* (1977) give a clear account of the consequences of these developments. First, the tax system had expanded since 1945 to include virtually the entire population (85%): not only those on average incomes but also those on below average incomes paid tax (Kincaid *et al.*, *To Him Who Hath*, p. 16). In 1975, people officially classified as amongst the poorest in the community (i.e. those qualifying for supplementary benefit and family income supplement) were taxed. Second, the proportion of income taken in tax also increased very considerably. In 1955, a man earning average wages paid 2.5

per cent of his income in income tax and national insurance contributions; in 1975, he paid over 20 per cent (ibid, p. 28). Public expectations were running well in advance of public willingness and national capacity to finance the welfare services at the levels desired. The bipartisan consensus was once again under severe pressure.

Put in broader terms, what was involved in the post-war Butskellite consensus was a compromise between the claims of organised labour and the business sector (see Chapter 20). Under this accommodation, the Labour Party gave qualified endorsement of the accumulation of capital and profits by private business in return for Conservative support for policies of full employment and welfare provision widely considered to be especially beneficial for the working class. This uneasy coalition ran into difficulties in the 1970s as a result of a combination of external pressures – the oil crisis of 1973 – and internal factors which included rapidly rising inflation and unemployment, slow growth, and high and rising levels of public expenditure in circumstances of trade union strength. This situation necessitated policy shifts well before Mrs Thatcher came to power. But it was Mrs Thatcher who, by her wholehearted acceptance and intensification of the new policies, really broke the old political consensus.

The initial changes of policy were carried out under Labour between 1974 and 1979. First, the Labour Chancellor of the Exchequer, Denis Healey, in his 1975 budget, refused to increase demand in the face of rising unemployment, thereby initiating a new emphasis on control of inflation as the major goal of government policy rather than the maintenance of 'high and stable' levels of employment. Dennis Kavanagh has called this policy shift 'a historic breach with one of the main planks of the post-war consensus' (Kavanagh, *Thatcherism and British Politics*, 1987, p. 127). Second, during the sterling crisis of 1976, the Government adopted formal targets for monetary growth (notes and coins in circulation plus sterling current accounts in the private sector and sterling deposit accounts held by British residents) as a way of reducing the rate of inflation. Finally, Labour also began the change from the Public Expenditure Survey Committee (PESC) method of controlling public spending to the use of cash limits. Under PESC, public spending plans were not adjusted according to lower growth or higher inflation than expected when the plans were drawn up. Under the cash limits method, each spending programme received a cash budget for the year and was expected to keep within its budget. Cash limits covered about 60 per cent of public expenditure after 1976. However, if Labour initiated new priorities and methods in economic management and public expenditure control, it was far from launching a new philosophy of government based on these new directions. That was the task Mrs Thatcher set herself to achieve and carry out.

Thatcherism aimed at a radical break with the post-war consensus. In its economic and welfare policies, it had the following main planks:

1. A monetarist economic policy: the aim was the reduction of inflation by tighter control of the money supply and by reductions of government borrowing rather than by agreements with employers and unions over pay norms; wage settlements would be left to free wage bargaining but employers would be encouraged to stand up to militant unionism not least by the government's own firm attitude to public sector pay claims.
2. 'Rolling back the frontiers of the State': this goal involved, first, reductions in public expenditure on benefits and services by the cash limits method with the ultimate aim of lowering the proportion of the GNP spent by government; and second – an aim which emerged only gradually during the first spell of Conservative Government – hiving off public sector services and industries to the private sector. Both targets, it was thought, would stimulate growth in the economy, the former by paving the way for tax cuts which in turn would improve incentives to work harder; the latter by increasing the efficiency of the de-nationalised concerns. New Right Conservatives believed as an article of faith that private enterprise was much more efficient than public enterprise (see Chapters 17 and 18 for fuller discussions).
3. Cutting down the power of the trade unions: proposed reforms included restrictions on secondary picketing, the protection of individuals against closed-shop agreements and the encouragement (by the provision of public money) of secret ballots for union leaders, and on strike decisions (see Chapter 20).

Mrs Thatcher's expectation was that the package of policies entailed by these three major objectives would 'turn Britain round', enabling the country to escape from the vicious circle of low growth, high inflation, high unemployment and balance-of-payments difficulties. The liberalisation of the economy would pave the way for a more prosperous and self-reliant society by restoring personal incentives and diminishing expectations of the State. To what extent did the Conservative Governments after 1979 achieve these specific and more general objectives?

We begin with the Conservatives' record on economic growth. This shows a sharp improvement from the first to the second Administrations, as Table 27.2 reveals. Britain experienced the international recession of the early 1980s with particular severity. Gross Domestic Product (GDP) fell by 4.2 per cent between the second quarter of 1979 and the last quarter of 1982. Industrial production declined by 10.2 per cent and manufacturing production by 17.3 per cent between May 1979 and February 1983. Not until mid-1987 did manufacturing output rise above its 1979 level. Both Labour and the CBI criticised this record. Bryan Gould, Labour's Trade and Industry spokesman claimed that only Barbados, Fiji, Greece, Malawi, South Africa and Gambia had a worse post-1979 record in manufacturing than Britain. As *The Guardian* reported (17 September 1987), John Barham, Director-General of the CBI, compared Britain's 3 per cent *fall* in industrial production between

TABLE 27.1
Britain's economic performance under the Conservatives, 1979–86/7: inflation

	1979	1980	1981	1982	1983	1984	1985	1986	1987 to March
USA	11.3	13.5	10.4	6.1	3.2	4.3	3.5	2.0	1.7
Japan	3.6	8.0	4.9	2.7	1.9	2.2	2.1	0.4	−0.7
Germany	4.1	5.5	6.3	5.3	3.3	2.4	2.2	−0.2	0.2
France	10.8	13.6	13.4	11.8	9.6	7.4	5.8	2.7	1.7
United Kingdom	13.4	18.0	11.9	8.6	4.6	5.0	6.1	3.4	2.3
Italy	14.8	21.2	17.8	16.5	14.6	10.8	9.2	6.1	2.6
Canada	9.2	10.2	12.5	10.8	5.9	4.3	4.0	4.2	2.3
Total average	9.3	12.2	10.0	7.0	4.4	4.5	3.8	2.0	1.3

Source: OECD, cited in *The Guardian*, 29 May 1987.

TABLE 27.2
Britain's economic performance under the Conservatives, 1979–86/7: economic growth

	1979	1980	1981	1982	1983	1984	1985	1986
USA	2.0	0.0	2.1	−2.5	3.4	6.6	2.9	2.75
Japan	5.2	4.4	3.9	2.8	3.2	5.0	4.5	2.25
Germany	4.2	1.4	0.2	−0.6	1.5	2.7	2.6	2.75
France	3.3	1.1	0.5	1.8	0.7	1.5	1.1	2.0
United Kingdom	2.2	−2.3	−1.2	1.0	3.8	2.2	3.7	2.25
Italy	4.9	3.9	0.2	−0.5	−0.2	2.8	2.3	2.5
Canada	3.4	1.0	4.0	−4.3	2.8	5.4	4.0	3.0
Total average	3.0	1.0	1.8	−0.9	2.8	5.0	3.1	2.5

Source: OECD, cited in *The Guardian*, 29 May 1987.

TABLE 27.3
Britain's economic performance under the Conservatives, 1979–86/7: unemployment

	1979	1980	1981	1982	1983	1984	1985	1986
USA	5.8	7.0	7.5	9.5	9.5	7.4	7.1	6.8
Japan	2.1	2.0	2.2	2.4	2.6	2.7	2.6	2.9
Germany	3.2	3.0	4.4	6.1	8.0	8.5	8.6	8.2
France	5.9	6.3	7.4	8.1	8.3	9.7	10.1	10.4
United Kingdom	6.0	6.4	9.8	11.3	12.5	12.8	13.0	
Italy	7.6	7.5	8.3	9.0	9.8	10.2	10.5	10.7
Canada	7.4	7.4	7.5	10.9	11.8	11.2	10.4	9.6
Total average	4.9	5.5	6.4	7.8	8.2	7.6	7.5	

Source: OECD, cited in *The Guardian*, 29 May 1987.

1976 and 1986 with *rises* of 5 per cent in France, 18 per cent in West Germany, 34 per cent in the USA and 56 per cent in Japan over that period. The Government's critics considered that its tight monetary policy and overvaluation of the pound between 1979 and 1982 were largely responsible for driving the country into deeper recession than that experienced in most other industrial countries (Table 27.3). In the second term, however, the economy grew rapidly, averaging 3 per cent per year between 1983 and 1986, a good performance by comparative and by Britain's own historical standards. In that period, Britain's economy grew more rapidly than such successful post-war economies as Japan, West Germany and France.

The consequences of the Conservatives' policy of giving priority to reducing the rate of inflation over decreasing unemployment are revealed in Table 27.1, which shows the inflation rate declining from 13.4 per cent (1979) to 3.4 per cent (1986). But this record does not constitute unalloyed triumph. First, the Conservatives themselves fuelled inflation on coming into office by doubling VAT. Second – and more importantly – in comparative terms, the record looks mediocre. Other leading industrial countries also brought their inflation rates down – many of them more successfully than Britain. Moreover, they did so without raising unemployment or reducing output to the extent that Britain did. Third, there is again a contrast between the record of the first and the second terms of government. Beginning considerably higher than the average of the seven nations (13.4 per cent as against 9.3 per cent) (see Table 27.1), Britain's relative inflation rate came down only slightly (8.6 per cent as compared with 7 per cent) in 1982, but thereafter the difference rose steadily, to 2.3 as against 1.3 per cent by early 1987. Thus, the Government had some success in reducing inflation, although in comparative terms its record was not remarkable.

But its performance on unemployment was poor both by UK and international standards and was heavily criticised. Unemployment, in fact, rose swiftly during the recession, and continued to rise even as the economy improved in the mid-1980s. By January 1986, there were 3.4m unemployed, constituting 14.1 per cent of the labour force. Throughout the period, the British unemployment rate remained obstinately higher than that of other industrial nations (see Table 27.3). The Government blamed excessive pay rises together with over-manning in certain industries for the heavy unemployment and, from 1983, claimed that more jobs were being created in Britain than elsewhere in the European Community. It also pointed to considerable improvements in productivity: in 1986–7, output per person in manufacturing grew by 6.5 per cent and by 1987 broadly the same manufacturing output as in 1979 was being produced by a workforce which was 25 per cent smaller. Critics riposted that manufacturing investment (the 'seedcorn' from which the productivity gains of the future would come) was in fact 20 per cent below its 1979 level in 1987, when, given the benefits of North Sea oil, it ought to have risen by 15 per cent or so in that period.

Tight control of the money supply was the means by which the Government hoped to squeeze inflation out of the system. It was allied with a shift from short-term methods of economic management to the adoption of medium-term targets. The Medium Term Financial Strategy (March 1980) announced targets for monetary growth and the Public Sector Borrowing Requirement for four years in advance. In fact, even though inflation (as already seen) did come down, it was not as a consequence of monetary policy. As Paul Mosley points out, growth of sterling M_3 between 1979 and 1985 was in fact higher than under the preceding Labour Government (Mosley, *Developments in British Politics 2*, 1986, p. 193). Monetarism was quietly abandoned during the Conservatives' second term (Chapter 17). At the time of the 1986 Budget the focus was more upon the exchange rate than upon strict control of money supply as a method of regulating the economy. By 1987, the relationship between control of the money supply and reductions in inflation seemed more problematic than ever with increases in money supply running at an annual 20 per cent but with the inflation rate at a mere 4.2 per cent. The intention had been to bring increases in money supply down to 4–8 per cent annual growth by 1983–4.

The Government also found it hard to achieve its public expenditure objectives. The target for public spending in the Medium Term Financial Strategy (1980) was a 4 per cent fall in total volume by 1983–4; in fact, government spending rose both in real terms (by 7 per cent) and as a proportion of GDP (43.25 per cent to 45.5 per cent) between 1979–80 and 1983–4. The major problem was to establish control over social security spending, which was by far the largest commitment in expenditure terms and which therefore had a massive influence upon total spending. It is one of the areas of government expenditure not subject to cash limits but, in any case, cuts would have been hard to achieve for political reasons in a period of high unemployment. In fact, as a result of increases in the numbers of pensioners and the poor as well as of the jobless, social security spending rose by over one-third between 1979 and 1986 (see Table 27.4).

Some shifts in the direction of public spending *were* achieved – away from housing and support for trade and industry (huge cuts) and education (a very small cutback) towards the Home Office (police) and defence, both of which had very large increases between 1979 and 1986 (see Table 27.4). Moreover, it was also the case that the Government began to experience more success with its public-spending objectives towards the end of its second term. Public spending was estimated actually to have fallen in 1985–6 and a further modest cut (0.5 per cent) was projected for 1986–9. Public borrowing, however, remained obdurately high throughout both terms: the Government intended it to fall to £2½bn by 1983–4 but it was still running at £4bn per year in 1986. Nor did the government achieve its aim of overall tax reductions. In fact, cuts were made in the rates of tax both at the higher and lower end of the scale. But the proportion of income paid in tax (including such things as

TABLE 27.4
Government spending, 1979–86 (after removing inflation effects)

£m base year 1984-5	1978-79	What happened ...							% change from 1979 to 1986	What is planned ...		
		79-80	80-81	81-82	82-83	83-84	84-85	85-86 (est.)		86-87	87-88	88-89
Defence	13 370	14 083	14 397	14 668	16 684	16 174	17 188	17 354	+29.8	16 883	16 570	16 240
Foreign Office	1 874	1 805	1 711	1 692	1 627	1 765	1 804	1 797	−4.1	1 785	1 770	1 780
EEC	1 341	1 285	217	121	829	891	936	761	−43.8	593	1 010	810
Agriculture	1 481	1 589	1 767	1 644	2 045	2 217	2 081	2 408	+62.6	1 977	1 980	1 960
Trade and Ind.	4 244	3 338	3 184	3 886	2 727	2 009	2 124	1 869	−56	1 441	1 110	880
Energy	982	857	809	1 314	983	1 153	2 591	979	−0.3	105	−480	−240
Employment	1 895	1 924	2 627	2 648	2 619	3 031	3 132	3 169	+67.2	3 409	3 340	3 400
Transport	4 745	4 982	5 122	4 971	4 779	4 541	4 583	4 366	−8	4 383	4 270	4 120
DOE/Housing	6 364	6 871	5 729	3 644	2 895	3 242	3 204	2 612	−59	2 508	2 490	2 460
DOE/others	3 963	4 046	3 946	3 624	3 840	3 942	3 979	3 752	−5.3	3 301	3 110	3 040
Home Office	3 595	3 866	4 048	4 328	4 503	4 750	5 039	5 058	+40.7	5 057	4 940	4 870
Education	13 852	13 670	14 024	13 837	13 921	14 040	13 953	13 772	−0.6	13 049	12 680	12 370
Arts	607	617	614	612	652	665	684	688	+13.3	668	660	650
DHSS/Health	13 270	13 608	14 677	14 897	15 144	15 396	15 770	15 889	+19.7	16 152	16 250	16 350
DHSS Soc. Security	29 357	29 673	30 215	33 379	36 423	36 750	38 144	39 258	+33.7	39 125	39 100	39 200

Scotland	6633	6958	6927	6823	6806	7002	7032	7008	+5.7	6901	6530	6350
Wales	2661	2705	2709	2689	2608	2727	2622	2650	-0.4	2647	2590	2560
N. Ireland	3808	3804	3708	3743	3800	3909	4000	4066	+6.8	4120	4120	4110
Chancellor's Dept	1943	1966	2034	2002	2020	1702	1682	1733	-10.8	1830	1800	1770
Other depts.	1415	1458	1353	1626	1585	1022	1174	1264	-10.7	1391	1490	1540
Contingencies										4101	5500	6840
Sale of assets		-576	-521	-577	-533	-1194	-2091	-2497		-4329	-4180	-4060
Adjustments								-143		-365		
TOTAL:	117401	118532	119196	121471	123757	125735	129638	127812	+8.9	126735	126700	127100
% change on previous year		1.0	0.6	1.9	1.9	1.6	3.1	-1.4		-0.8	0.0	0.3
Gross govt. debt interest (not incl. above)	13256	14447	14651	15556	15146	15203	16070	17000	+28.2	17000	16500	16000

Source: *The Guardian*, 16 January 1986.

National Insurance contributions and VAT as well as income tax) – by both the single person, and the married couple with two children, on average earnings – rose between 1979 and 1985. According to OECD (the Organisation for Economic Cooperation and Development) the share of Britain's national income taken in taxation increased by 5.2 per cent between 1979 and 1985. This was the fifth largest increase in twenty-three leading industrial non-Communist countries. But Britain was still not a highly-taxed nation; it was just averagely-taxed, ranking tenth in 1985 (cf. eleventh in 1979); with its tax share of national income at 38.1 per cent it was slightly above the OECD average (37.2 per cent), but well behind the Scandinavian countries, Belgium, the Netherlands, France and three other countries (range – from 50.5 per cent Sweden to 39.1 per cent Ireland).

The Government certainly fulfilled – even exceeded – its intentions in privatisation, sales of council houses and the curbing of trade union powers. The nationalised industries accounted for 10 per cent of GDP in 1979 but by 1988, according to an estimate by *The Economist*, it was probable that their share of GDP would be down to $6\frac{1}{2}$ per cent. Beginning with only modest denationalisation proposals in 1979 (which included aerospace and shipbuilding), the privatisation programme built up slowly during the first term, with asset sales averaging under £0.5bn per year until 1983. Thereafter, sales intensified – they were expected to have raised over £22bn in the decade to 1989, by which year major enterprises such as British Telecom, British Gas, Jaguar cars and British Airways had all passed into private hands (see Chapter 17). Sales of council houses began early in the first Administration with a *Housing Act* 1980 which enabled all council-house tenants with three years' residence to buy their houses at a discount. About 0.5m council dwellings had been sold by the 1983 General Election and a further 300 000 by the end of 1984. Finally, by 1985 a more cautious, carefully prepared legislative and policy attack on trade union powers had brought greater success than the earlier more impetuous Conservative assault under Heath (1970–4). Successive Acts (1980, 1982 and 1984) outlawed secondary picketing, removed the unions' legal immunities from civil actions, required majority support in secret ballot for closed shops, supplied government funds for the election of union officials and decisions on political funds, and provided for pre-strike ballots. Between 1980 and 1982, the steel, rail, Civil Service and Health Service unions were successfully resisted in a series of disputes; in 1984–5, the powerful miners' union was faced down on the issue of pit closures (see Chapter 20). Equally important was the government's stance on economic policy. It abandoned the corporatist incomes-policy approach to economic management which involved constant high-level cooperation with the CBI and TUC in favour of an arm's length attitude to business and the unions. It neither sought their advice nor seemed to pay any attention to it when it was offered. During the early 1980s as businesses collapsed in the recession, it ignored persistent pleas to help troubled industries and to adjust the strong pound which was making it difficult for exporters.

To summarise: Mrs Thatchter's aims were not completely achieved over her first two administrations. It is also true that in many important respects, Conservative policies were anticipated by previous governments. But to say this should not disguise the fact that a radical break with the post-war consensus took place between 1979 and 1987. The final section of this book asks how permanent this break is likely to be. More specifically, how far will the changes made form the basis of a new consensus – to the extent, of course, that this can be discerned at the outset of the Conservatives' third term of office?

THE LATE 1980s AND EARLY 1990s – THE MAKING OF A NEW CONSENSUS?

This last section looks for an answer to this question predominantly in evidence drawn from the public opinion polls and party responses to the 1987 General Election result. A *Marplan Political Attitudes* survey published in September 1986 provides an interesting guide to public opinion on a range of central social and economic issues (see Tables 27.5–27.13). A sizeable 2:1 majority of voters disagreed with the Government's overall economic priority to control inflation rather than to reduce unemployment (Table 27.5). However, there was little support for the Government to tackle unemployment by borrowing money to invest (Table 27.6). Even Labour voters were quite evenly divided on this issue. Responses on incomes policy were ambivalent. On the one hand, there was a sizeable majority against compulsory incomes policy – the control of pay rises by law. On the other hand, a similar majority supported the proposition that the economy would grow faster if pay rises were kept within a government incomes policy (Table 27.7). Presumably, this reflected a perception that pay restraint was necessary if economic growth were to be achieved, together with a preference that it should be pursued by voluntary methods. Nearly half the sample opposed the privatisation of profitable state industries, and they were in a majority. On this issue, there was a clear contrast between Conservative voters – predominantly in favour – and Labour and Alliance voters – largely against (Table 27.8). A very considerable majority (over 3:1) considered it was better to pay higher taxes and have better public services than to have lower taxes but worse services (Table 27.9). It is noticeable that this preference for a decent standard of public services over tax cuts (and a poorer standard of services) is spread right across the political spectrum, with even Conservative voters 2:1 in favour of it. The Government's trade union legislation on pre-strike ballots was very popular, and received heavy endorsement from Labour voters as well as even wider support from Conservatives and the

TABLE 27.5

Public opinion poll, 1986: 'It is more important for the Government to control inflation than to reduce unemployment'

	All			Conservatives			Labour			Alliance		
	1986	1985	1984	1986	1985	1984	1986	1985	1984	1986	1985	1984
Agree	29	32	35	46	51	59	20	23	21	20	28	32
Disagree	59	57	46	39	38	27	72	69	68	71	62	57
Neither	9	8	9	11	9	10	5	5	7	7	8	7
Don't Know	3	3	10	2	2	4	3	3	4	2	2	4

Source: Marplan Survey of Political Attitudes, printed in The Guardian, 2 September and 3 October 1986.

TABLE 27.6

Public opinion poll, 1986: 'The economy would be stronger if the Government borrowed more money and used it for investment'

	All			Conservatives			Labour			Alliance		
	1986	1985	1984	1986	1985	1984	1986	1985	1984	1986	1985	1984
Agree	27	33	28	17	23	24	40	43	41	29	33	33
Disagree	47	42	43	63	58	52	35	33	37	44	40	45
Neither	15	14	10	13	10	11	14	14	10	18	17	11
Don't know	11	11	19	7	9	13	10	10	12	8	10	11

Source: As Table 27.5.

TABLE 27.7

Public opinion poll, 1986: 'The economy would grow faster if (Q1) the Government had the power to control pay rises by law; (Q2) pay rises were kept within a Government incomes policy'

	All		Cons		Labour		Alliance	
	Q1	Q2	Q1	Q2	Q1	Q2	Q1	Q2
Agree	29	49	39	63	28	37	25	57
Disagree	46	26	43	21	49	29	56	25
Neither	15	16	15	13	13	19	14	13
Don't know	9	9	3	4	10	13	5	5

Source: As Table 27.5.

Alliance (Table 27.10). There was also general support across political divisions for worker-participation in the running of industry (Table 27.11). But there was a large majority (58:28) against the idea of *trade unions* having a greater say in running industry, when the question of industrial participation was put in that form by Marplan in 1985 (as reported in *The Guardian*, 26 September 1986). Belief in the effectiveness of government was widely-shared, about 66 per cent of the sample believing that the government could do 'quite a bit' to reduce unemployment against Mrs Thatcher's argument that it could do little (Table 27.12).

These responses do not provide an unequivocal indication of the inroads made by Thatcherism on public opinion. Only pre-strike ballots received massive approval. The majority thought the Government ought to do more about unemployment and wanted to maintain the Welfare State even if it meant no tax cuts. Privatisation was supported by only just over 33 per cent of the sample. On the other hand, certain approaches to controlling inflation and increasing employment often referred to as 'Keynesian' – compulsory incomes policy and government borrowing to invest – got little public support. But anyway such a survey cannot provide the final word. Longer-term trends in opinion and the actual behaviour of electors both need to be considered. And so does the tension Thatcherism can provoke in people between their own self-interest and the public good. Public opinion on certain key questions excluded from Tables 27.5–27.13 needs to be taken into account.

Other evidence – the Gallup Poll surveys cited by D. Kavanagh – points to the popularity of the rejection of corporatist economic management by the Conservatives. When asked the question between 1983 and 1985 whether governments should involve the unions and business when making economic policy or keep them at arm's length, a very large and increasing majority thought the big interest groups should be kept at arm's length (Kavanagh, *Thatcherism and British Politics*, 1987, p. 296). If voters considered that Mrs Thatcher should be more compassionate about unemployment, they also

544

TABLE 27.8

Public opinion poll, 1986: 'Profitable state industries like British Telecom and British Airways should be sold off and run as private companies'

	All			Conservatives			Labour			Alliance		
	1986	1985	1984	1986	1985	1984	1986	1985	1984	1986	1985	1984
Agree	34	39	32	58	66	57	18	17	15	29	38	31
Disagree	48	44	46	26	21	28	66	69	70	53	45	54
Neither	12	10	9	12	7	9	9	9	8	12	12	10
Don't know	7	7	13	4	6	6	7	5	7	5	5	5

Source: As Table 27.5.

TABLE 27.9

Public opinion poll, 1986: 'It is better to pay higher taxes and have better public services than to have lower taxes but worse services'

	All			Conservatives			Labour			Alliance		
	1986	1985	1984	1986	1985	1984	1986	1985	1984	1986	1985	1984
Agree	61	58	54	53	55	58	64	63	61	68	61	60
Disagree	18	19	19	25	22	20	17	17	19	15	19	20
Neither	17	18	15	19	19	16	15	15	12	15	16	15
Don't know	7	5	12	3	4	6	4	5	8	2	4	5

Source: As Table 27.5.

TABLE 27.10

Public opinion poll, 1986: 'It should be illegal for unions to call strikes without first balloting the workers'

	All			Conservatives			Labour			Alliance		
	1986	1985	1984	1986	1985	1984	1986	1985	1984	1986	1985	1984
Agree	78	82	73	86	92	89	73	67	72	81	87	85
Disagree	15	13	15	9	6	8	20	21	28	13	10	10
Neither	5	3	3	3	1	1	5	6	3	5	2	3
Don't know	2	2	9	1	1	2	3	2	5	1	1	2

Source: As Table 27.5.

TABLE 27.11

Public opinion poll, 1986: 'Employees should have more say in the running of industry'

| | All | | Cons | | Labour | | Alliance | |
	1986	1985	1986	1985	1986	1985	1986	1985
Agree	72	74	62	63	84	87	74	73
Disagree	16	15	26	25	7	6	17	16
Neither	8	8	10	10	6	5	7	8
Don't know	3	3	2	2	3	2	1	3

Source: As Table 27.5.

TABLE 27.12

Public opinion poll, 1986: 'Do you think British Governments nowadays can do very little or quite a bit to reduce unemployment?'

| | All | | Cons | | Labour | | Alliance | |
	1986	1985	1986	1985	1986	1985	1986	1985
Very little	29	26	43	41	22	20	23	21
Quite a bit	65	70	50	56	75	76	73	77
Don't know	6	4	6	3	4	3	5	2

Source: As Table 27.5.

welcomed the assertion of government authority in economic management which derived from depending less on gaining the agreement of the major interests. Moreover, taken over the period 1964–83, attitudes in favour of more nationalisation decreased (from 28 per cent to 18 per cent) and attitudes supporting privatisation increased (from 21 per cent to 42 per cent). This point is given additional emphasis by people's behaviour – by 1987, there were over 8m shareholders, treble the number when Mrs Thatcher came to power. Nearly 20 per cent of the adult population had become shareholders, an average of 12 000 in each constituency. Sale of council houses was also extremely popular, 800 000 former tenants having taken the decision to buy their houses by 1985. Finally, attitudes to such matters as tax cuts and public spending clearly depended on whether people were thinking primarily of their own personal interest or of the national interest (Table 27.14). Asked what mattered most to them and their families, a slight majority in March 1987 preferred tax cuts to increases in public spending, but when asked to say which of these two alternatives was better for the country as a whole, a much larger majority endorsed increased public spending. There were significant divisions between Conservatives and Labour/Alliance voters: a majority of Conservatives considered tax cuts superior to increased public spending both for themselves and their families

TABLE 27.13

Public opinion poll, 1986: 'The Government should have power to impose a limit on the amount each council can spend'

	All			Conservatives			Labour			Alliance		
	1986	1985	1984	1986	1985	1984	1986	1985	1984	1986	1985	1984
Agree	49	49	46	70	73	69	40	32	33	48	47	52
Disagree	35	39	36	19	19	23	46	56	55	39	41	37
Neither	11	8	7	9	6	5	10	7	7	10	8	7
Don't know	5	4	11	3	2	3	5	5	5	3	4	4

Source: As Table 27.5.

TABLE 27.14

Tax cuts versus public spending—the personal/public interest division

	All voters	Voting intention			Social class			
		Con	Lab	Alli	AB	C1	C2	DE
What matters more to you and your family?								
To reduce taxes	47 (46)	61 (61)	36 (33)	42 (45)	55 (57)	48 (51)	48 (47)	41 (36)
To increase public spending	45 (46)	30 (32)	57 (59)	53 (48)	38 (38)	46 (41)	44 (44)	50 (54)
What is more important for the country as a whole?								
To reduce taxes	37 (34)	45 (43)	33 (29)	30 (25)	36 (35)	33 (33)	38 (35)	39 (34)
To increase public spending	54 (55)	42 (46)	60 (64)	65 (66)	59 (55)	56 (57)	53 (53)	50 (56)
Whose interests will be more important in determining how you friends vote?								
Theirs and their families'	59	57	63	59	57	60	62	55
The country's as a whole	19	21	16	22	25	18	17	19

Source: Marplan, *The Guardian*, 13 March 1987.

and for the country, a priority reversed by Labour and Alliance voters. A very considerable majority, however, right across the political and social spectrum, thought people put their own and their families' interests above the country's interest when deciding how to vote.

A clearer picture of public opinion on Conservative social and economic policy is now possible. It is a mixed one. Broadly the restoration of the authority of the government in economic policy-making by keeping the big interest groups at arm's length, and by imposing financial discipline on councils (Table 27.13), insisting that unions ballot their members before going on strike, and giving council tenants the opportunity to buy their own houses were popular policies. The response to privatisation was more evenly divided; a majority in the Marplan Survey was against it, but this fact was to some extent offset by people's actual behaviour in buying shares and by the evidence that support for asset sales was increasing. Finally, there was strong and persistent support for government social expenditure (even more pronounced when people were asked what was best in the national interest) and for a more compassionate and active approach to unemployment.

As for the opposition parties, there were signs that policies on central social and economic issues were being adjusted even before defeat in the 1987 election gave further impetus to the process. Only the Labour Left remained committed to reversing the key changes brought about by Thatcherism. Under pressure from the leadership, the Labour Party had already accepted council-house sales, secret ballots on strikes and the election of union leaders by the time of the 1987 General Election, as its manifesto indicated. Afterwards, Neil Kinnock called for a further overhaul of policies. Taxation and renationalisation as well as defence were identified by Roy Hattersley as areas where existing policies had lost votes (the manifesto had called for a 2p rise in income tax). Neil Kinnock wanted a greater realism to prevail on spending commitments. Taking their cue from these remarks, Labour voices were soon to be heard advocating a movement away from the old 'universal' approach to social security benefits towards a more 'selective' one. Others favoured accepting sale of public assets as permanent since share-ownership was not only well-entrenched but also included many potential Labour supporters. David Steel, the Liberal leader, advocated moving on from Thatcherism rather than reversing everything on doctrinaire grounds. It seemed that the Liberal/Alliance grouping (even without Dr Owen) would favour acceptance of at least the Conservative trade union reforms and public asset sales.

On the other hand, both Labour and the Alliance groupings were more 'Statist' than the Conservatives. This implied a greater sympathy for traditional welfare programmes, especially with regard to the protection and improvement of the National Health Service, the public sector of education and benefits and pensions for the poor, the disabled and the old. It also suggested in economic policy – to judge, again, from the 1987 manifestos – a return to a 1970s style of management of the economy, with Labour advocating a 'national economic summit' (presumably in a 'corporatist' way involving tripartite talks between government, management and unions) and the Alliance favouring an incomes strategy to contain inflationary pressures. However, it seemed certain that Labour would have to rethink its collectivist approach to running the economy. As Robert Skidelsky argued in a *Guardian* article on 21 September 1985, the economic and technological assumptions behind the earlier policy no longer applied. The economy was no longer as subject to centralised manipulation as a result of the increasing power of international capital and de-regulation of financial markets. Second, national-level bargaining with the large producer groups was much less appropriate in an economy whose base was shifting from manufacturing to services, in which self-employment was growing (up ¾m between 1976 and 1986, to 2.7m) and the unions had suffered heavy loss of membership (down approximately 3m between 1980 and 1987).

In the final analysis, the opposition parties would inevitably be much influenced on economic policy by the success of the Thatcher economic liberalisation experiment. This meant her success in turning the country round, in regenerating it and placing it on a path to sustained non-inflationary growth. In 1988, it was too early to pronounce on this issue, on which debate still raged. The Government's supporters argued that the economy had been permanently turned round. They pointed to the high growth rates of the second term (in December 1987, growth was estimated to be running at over 5 per cent per annum), increases in productivity, the taming of the unions, the reductions in people's expectations of government, the growth of 'popular capitalism', and the use of oil revenues to build up assets abroad (at £163bn, second only to the foreign assets of Japan). The Government's critics accepted that growth had expanded over the second term but argued that taken over the two terms, the growth rate was poor. Overall, there was no conclusive evidence that British relative decline had been arrested, let alone reversed. There had been policy failures: manufacturing industry was allowed to decline too rapidly in the early 1980s; the extreme severity of the recession was a consequence of the government's policy of allowing the exchange rate to drift too high; the proceeds of North Sea oil were allowed to fuel a consumer boom which sucked in a flood of consumer goods imported from Japan and elsewhere rather than being spent on improving Britain's roads, railways, educational system and, above all, level of industrial investment.

SUMMARY

The outlines of a new consensus were just visible but still incomplete by the second half of the 1980s. If trends identifiable then were confirmed, it would

include a 'mixed economy' with a reduced public and an expanded private sector; a Welfare State sustained by higher levels of spending and in which the moves towards privatisation of education and medicine had gone less far than the Conservative Right would have liked but in which the search was permanently on for economies, value for money and greater efficiency of provision; and finally, economic goals which prioritised control of inflation over the reduction of unemployment.

FURTHER READING

Drucker, H. *et al.* (1986) *Developments in British Politics, 2*, London, Macmillan.

Hall, S. and Jaques, M. (eds) (1983) *The Politics of Thatcherism*, London, Lawrence & Wishart.

Kavanagh, D. (1987) *Thatcherism and British Politics*, Oxford, University Press.

Kirby, S. (1987) 'Contemporary British Politics: The Decline of Consensus?', *Teaching Politics*, 16, 2, May.

For continuing reappraisals of the state of British politics, see the quality dailies – *The Times*, *The Guardian*, *The Independent*, and weeklies such as *The Economist*.

QUESTIONS

1. Assess the view that continuities of policy are more pronounced than discontinuities in recent British party government.

2. What was the post-1945 consensus in Britain? Examine its weaknesses and strengths from the vantage-point of today.

3. Critically examine the 'pros' and 'cons' of 'Thatcherism'. Discuss the impact of Thatcherite political ideas on British politics in the 1980s.

ASSIGNMENT

1. Using Tables 27.5–27.13 inclusive, compare the opinions of party supporters on the main issues of social and economic policy in 1986. Consider the responses under the left-hand column ('all'); in what areas do they show public agreement with Conservative policies, and in what areas do they indicate disagreement with them? According to recent surveys, how far have political attitudes changed since that date and to what extent have they remained the same?

2. Using Table 27.4, analyse the changes in individual items of public spending. Account for the changes in terms of the political ideas of the Thatcher Governments.

28
Postscript

The years 1988 to 1990 saw very considerable changes in British politics. The Conservative Government ran into difficulties; public support for the centre parties collapsed; the Green Party emerged as a political force; and the Labour Party revived after spending most of the decade in the political doldrums. This postscript analyses each of these developments in turn, concluding with a brief review of the Government's response.

THE DECLINE IN POPULARITY OF THE CONSERVATIVE GOVERNMENT

Support for the Conservatives fell substantially in 1989 largely as a result of the re-emergence of economic difficulties. After a brief period of low inflation, falling unemployment and rapid growth, the then Chancellor Nigel Lawson became hemmed in by the consequences of the consumer boom he had fuelled in the preceding years with tax cuts and cheap credit. Rising inflation and a large balance of payments deficit put pressure on sterling. The Chancellor increased the interest rate almost monthly during the summer and autumn of 1988 in an effort to dampen down consumer spending, reduce inflation and boost the strength of sterling on the foreign exchange markets. Interest rate increases continued during 1989.

The very high levels of interest led to concern about the risk of a recession and to the collapse of the housing market, particularly in the South and South-East. The large increase in their mortgage payments reduced the living standards of many home-owners leaving them with less money to spend on other goods. Simultaneously, their homes dropped in value for the first time in recent experience. Many young people had rushed to buy property before changes in mortgage rules which ended double tax relief in summer 1988. They bought when house prices were at their highest and the interest rate was low and were hardest hit when, within months, the position changed dramatically.

Conservative difficulties over the management of the economy were strikingly demonstrated in late October 1989 by Nigel Lawson's sudden resignation as Chancellor of the Exchequer. The reason he gave for his resignation was the continuing presence of Sir Alan Walters as Mrs Thatcher's economic adviser in the Policy Unit at No. 10 Downing Street. A serious disagreement existed between the two men over interest and exchange rate strategy, issues at the heart of Government economic policy. By refusing to repudiate Sir Alan, Mrs Thatcher allowed doubts to remain about her

Government's policy which the Chancellor felt only his resignation could resolve. Sir Alan himself resigned within hours. Lawson's departure forced upon the Prime Minister the second major Cabinet reshuffle in three months. In addition to the damage it did to the credibility of Conservative economic management, the affair brought to the surface again the constitutional question of the extent to which Mrs Thatcher's premiership had undermined collective Cabinet government. Mrs Thatcher's response to queries about her conduct of the Government – 'Advisers advise, Ministers decide' – by no means satisfied her critics.

During 1990, the economic slowdown continued: it was marked by declining consumer spending, falling manufacturing output and rising unemployment. In August, figures were released showing that the current account deficit for the first seven months of the year was £10.25 bn (this deficit had been £19.1 bn in 1989 and February 1987 was the last month when the UK's current account had been in surplus). In September came the news that the annual inflation rate was running at 10.6 per cent. 'Stagflation' – a combination of high inflation with low output – seemed to be returning to Britain. The Government claimed its economic policies were succeeding: 'If it isn't hurting, it isn't working', said the Chancellor of the Exchequer, John Major. It accused its critics of exaggerating the threat of recession. But critics argued that the Government's policy of reducing public expenditure during the 1980s had weakened Britain's infrastructure – its road and railway network – and resulted in an inadequately-educated and trained workforce, thereby undermining Britain's ability to compete successfully in international markets in the 1990s. Further, the Government's unwillingness to control the expansion of *private* credit had fuelled inflation and eroded the effectiveness of its own high interest rate policy.

Other issues have come on to the political agenda to the disadvantage of the Tories. The 'greening' of British politics cut across a number of policy areas – such as health, agriculture and food, water, energy and industry – but also focussed on a general concern about environmental pollution. Green politics places the Government in a dilemma because its free market philosophy does not easily accommodate environmentalism. Thatcherism proclaims freedom in the market-place and the absence of Government controls on commercial activity whereas environmentalism involves more rules, regulations and restrictions to control how individuals and firms behave.

The privatisation of water is an example of Government policy containing the contradictions between Thatcherism and environmental concern. There is already public anxiety about the quality of drinking water provided in many areas of Britain since it is high in levels of lead and nitrates. If the main concern of the newly-privatised water authorities becomes maximising profits for their shareholders, there are fears that the quality of water could deteriorate further. A *Guardian* poll in September 1989 found that only one in five surveyed supported more privatisation, whilst 62 per cent opposed it.

Even 38 per cent of Tory supporters opposed more privatisation.

A Government White Paper entitled 'This Common Inheritance' was published in September 1990. Introducing it, the Environment Secretary, Chris Patten, called it the first really comprehensive statement of Government policy on the environment extending 'from the street corner to the stratosphere'. The White Paper set a target of increasing renewable energy generating capacity ten-fold by the year 2000 and announced a range of environmental promises. These included the encouragement of tree-planting (a new forest was planned for the Midlands), the extension of the tree preservation order system to include hedgerows, the ending of stubble and straw-burning by 1993, a £28 bn investment to bring drinking and bathing water up to standard by the mid-1990s, a ban on the dumping of liquid industrial wastes in the sea by 1992 and on the dumping of sewage sludge by 1998; and measures to recycle 50 per cent of recyclable household waste by 2000. The Paper was praised as a launching-pad for a long-term programme but criticised for failing to support its good intentions with sufficient funding and for failing to impose targets and time-tables for fuel and vehicle efficiency measures.

The future of the National Health Service has also dominated recent political debate. After a swift review of the NHS, a white paper, *Working for Patients*, was published in January 1989, followed in November by the National Health Service and Community Care Bill embodying its proposed reforms. Commentators believed that they saw Mrs Thatcher's personal influence in such proposals as the development of internal markets for treating patients, opportunities for larger hospitals to 'opt out' from health authorities, closer cooperation with the private sector and the direct allocation of budgets to general practices. The British Medical Association mounted a major press campaign against both the White Paper and the Secretary of State, Kenneth Clarke. There is public anxiety that the changes contained in the White Paper would mark the beginning of the end of the NHS with the treatment that patients receive being more influenced by accountants than by doctors. The *Guardian* poll found that only 6 per cent of Conservative supporters now felt that 'the National Health Service is safe in Mrs Thatcher's hands'.

Even policies which the government may have expected to be popular for the time being turned sour. Education is a case in point. The Government produced two major Acts of Parliament in 1986 and 1988. The most recent, the Educational Reform Act, included the introduction of the national curriculum in an effort to raise standards. However, during 1989 this was eclipsed by reports of teacher shortages and pupils being sent home from school and during 1990 by reports of Ministerial back-tracking on certain commitments in the 1988 Act including the national curriculum, which was being slimmed down, and the testing of pupils, which was being reduced. In addition, the policy of encouraging schools to opt out of local authority control gained little response (by September 1990, only 50 out of a possible

6700 schools had opted out) and this prompted the Education Secretary, John MacGregor, to announce to the 1990 Conservative Conference that the opting out facility was to be extended to the remaining 84 per cent of primary and secondary schools.

The issue, however, which may still seal the fate of the Government at the next election is not the economy, the environment, health or education. It is the introduction of the community charge – better known as the poll tax – in England, Scotland and Wales. The announcement of poll tax levels by local authorities in March 1990 revealed that, whilst a minority of households would benefit financially from the introduction of the new charge, the majority would be losers. Popular disturbances followed, culminating in the Trafalgar Square riot of March 31 after which 58 policemen and 86 members of the public were reported as needing hospital treatment. Although its impact was partly alleviated by Government concessions, the tax remained intensely unpopular and showed few signs of achieving its ostensible objectives of extending responsible citizenship and producing more accountable local government. Evasion of payment – encouraged by the Anti-Poll Tax Federation – was rife and by August many councils reported high levels of non-payment. The Government's immediate response – charge-capping 21 Labour councils which it dubbed 'high-spending' – prompted accusations of political bias and by August 1990 it had been forced to promise an additional £3 bn to enable councils to keep expected poll tax increases within bounds in 1991.

The Liberal Democrats

1989 was the year when the damaging consequences of the post-1987 election decision to disband the Liberal-SDP Alliance and merge the two parties became clear. In merging, the two parties had destroyed, at least for the time being, a large part of the popular support which they had commanded when loosely united as the Alliance. From Alliance's 22.6 per cent of the vote at the 1987 General Election, the Social and Liberal Democratic Party (SLD) and the continuing SDP slumped to a combined 6.7 per cent in the Euro elections of June and their support remained broadly at this level after their party conferences later in the year. The centre parties were suffering from a period of confusion in which they had fought each other in national and local elections and signally failed to achieve the by-election victories which continually gave the former Alliance such boosts. By running candidates against each other, the two parties ensured successive by-election successes for the Conservatives, first at Epping Forest (December 1988) – where the two parties' combined vote was within 500 of the victorious Conservative – and then at Richmond (February 1989), where together they polled nearly 9000 votes more than the Tory winner.

After defeating Alan Beith for the SLD leadership by 54 140 votes to 16 202 in July 1988, Paddy Ashdown aimed to commit the party to a multilateralist defence policy and a programme of radical social and political reform. These aims were broadly achieved at the 1989 conference which endorsed a multilateralist policy based on possession of Trident and responded favourably to Ashdown's call for a 'Citizen's Britain' with a fairer electoral system based on proportional representation, a bill of rights, freedom of information, industrial co-partnership and laws to protect the consumer. The party prides itself on having a longer tradition of commitment to Europe and to protection of the environment than the two major parties. But, despite its strength in local politics with over 3000 councillors and about 20 per cent of the vote, the party clearly faces a hard struggle to make itself into a national force again.

The decision in mid-October 1989 by a large majority of the membership to change the party's short name from the Democrats to the Liberal Democrats ended a long drawn-out wrangle and seemed a useful step towards the restoration of political credibility. However, by-election results consistently failed to deliver morale-boosting successes – as they had often done in the past – and only revealed fragmentation and the decline of the centre. At Mid-Staffordshire (March), Bootle (May) and Knowsley South (September) the Liberal Democrats came third. They were handicapped by rival centre party candidates; in the first two by the SDP and in the third by a member of the Liberal Party, which had been re-launched under the leadership of Michael Meadowcroft, the former MP for Leeds West in March 1989. Good local election results in May, though, showed the resilience of the Liberal Democrats in local politics. Their 1990 Conference revealed a clear image of a party committed to constitutional reform, a federal Europe and a cleaner environment. By November, fortified by the collapse of the SDP, a 14% share of support in opinion polls, and a classic mid-term by-election victory in Eastbourne after the murder of the sitting Tory MP, Ian Gow, by the IRA, the Liberal Democrats seemed back on course to exert an influence in the forthcoming general election.

The Social Democratic Party (SDP)

With a mere 3 MPs and only 11 000 members in 1989, the party faced some hard choices. No longer a national force and with its continuing independent viability in doubt, its strategy for survival was to attempt to form an agreement with Labour and the Democrats on electoral reform and electoral pacts. However, by-election disaster overtook the party at Bootle in May 1990 when the SDP candidate polled fewer votes (155) than Lord Sutch of the Monster Raving Loony Cavern Rock Party (418). Ten days later on June 3, influenced both by this electoral humiliation and by rapidly-falling membership (a mere 6200), the SDP national committee voted by a large majority to suspend the constitution and thereby terminate the party. Its three MPs, local councillors and peers would continue as Independent Social

Democrats. Although the decision to end the party was contested by a tiny minority led by John Martin, few doubted that the party's nine year effort to break the mould of British politics was over.

The Green Party

Arguably given its chance by the disappearance of the ecologically-minded Liberal Party into the SLD and by the fierce squabbling of the centre parties, the Green Party's surge in 1989 took political commentators by surprise. Throwing all their resources into the June European election and running candidates in all constituencies, the Greens were rewarded with 2.25m. votes, double their target. They won a higher share of the vote (nearly 15 per cent) than any Green Party in Europe. But whereas elsewhere in Europe, under a system of PR, the party won seats – for instance, 9 in France with just 10.6 per cent of the vote – no Green MEPs were elected in the UK. Understandably, one of the party's spokespersons, Sara Parkin, called for a PR pact with Labour and the Democrats at the 1989 conference.

There is wide agreement that the support for the Greens reflects a general public concern about the environment rather than firm allegiance to the Green Party. Poll evidence suggests that the electorate is ignorant of the Green Party's more radical policies of withdrawal from the European Community, nuclear disarmament and opposition to economic growth. However, with its unprecedented rise in public support, its membership increase to 15 000 (double the 1988 figure) and with the major parties rushing to build environmental concern into their policies, the Green Party was clearly having an impact on the political agenda.

This was further demonstrated in 1990 with the publication of the Government's White Paper on the Environment, which the Greens immediately criticised as lacking in urgency and failing to commit sufficient resources to the tasks it outlined. Whilst membership of the Greens continued to rise during 1990 (to 20 000), the political momentum enjoyed by the party during the previous year slowed down and by October its support in the polls had dropped to a mere 2 per cent. But, despite slender resources, the Greens maintained a significant presence at the political grass-roots, contesting all of the three by-elections between January and September 1990 and averaging 8 per cent in local elections. Although suffering from 'asset-stripping' of its policies by the other parties, by polling 1000-2000 votes in marginals the Greens could still hope to influence the overall outcome of a General Election.

The resurgence of Labour

1989 saw a significant revival of the fortunes of the Labour Party though its explanation must be sought in longer-term factors. The year began with the Conservatives enjoying a four-point lead over Labour, but by May the parties were level and after that public opinion moved strongly in Labour's direction. In June, the party won a significant victory in the European elections, gaining 13 seats from the Conservatives. The results of the election are shown in Table 28.1.

In addition to the difficulties of its political opponents, there were four main factors behind the improvement in Labour's political standing. These were Neil Kinnock's effective leadership; revisions of party policy; the continuing reform of party structure; and sound performances by Labour's front-bench shadow team. Kinnock's overriding aim was to make his party once more into a genuine alternative government by curbing the influence of the hard left and the trade unions within the party. The effectiveness of his own leadership was demonstrated by his success in achieving changes in party policy and organisation.

Immediately after the election defeat of 1987, the Labour leader commissioned a Policy Review which was published in May 1989 and adopted by the October 1989 Labour Party Conference. It gave a clear indication of the range of policies on which Labour would fight the next election:

i One of the most important changes was in defence where a policy of multilateral disarmament replaced the party's former commitment to unilateralism.

ii On the economy, Labour's policy was summed up in the phrase 'supply-side Socialism'. Its programme of economic modernisation stressed heavy investment in new technology and a highly-skilled workforce to be encouraged by a new investment bank and a more powerful Department of Trade and Industry. There would be a return to a more progressive tax system. But there would be no large-scale re-nationalisation of privatised industries: only British Telecom and the water industry would be taken back into public ownership.

iii The party's intention to take 'green' issues seriously was indicated by its

TABLE 28.1   *The election for the European Parliament June 1989*

	Number of Euro seats	Share of the vote (%)
Labour	45	40.1
Conservative	32	34.7
SNP	1	2.6
Green	0	14.9
Democrats	0	6.2
SDP	0	0.5

proposal to set up a Ministry for Environmental Protection and rejection of the case for investing in new nuclear power stations.

iv On trade union law, Labour welcomed ballots before strikes and for the election of trade union executives and was in favour of giving trade union members the right to appeal to an independent tribunal if pre-strike ballots were not held. But the party also accepted that on occasion strikes would occur before ballots could take place; in addition, it cautiously recognised that the law should allow sympathy action where workers had a genuine interest in the outcome of a dispute. It intended to protect unions against the sequestration of their funds if they threatened strikes and to prevent the courts from granting injunctions to employers at a few hours' notice in order to block a strike. A specialist labour tribunal would adjudicate in trade disputes.

The aim of the reforms of the Labour Party constitution was to reduce the entrenched power of the trade unions and of constituency activists. These reforms were under way but still incomplete by late 1990. A start was made in 1987 when, for *the selection of parliamentary candidates*, the party adopted an electoral college method in which the trade unions exercise no more than 40 per cent of the vote in each constitutuency party, the remaining proportion going to ordinary members. However, under this system complaints arose that trade union branches were deciding how to vote without interviewing the short-listed candidates and in 1990 the party decided to abandon the electoral college system. The NEC stated that a new system which would require union members to vote on candidates would be discussed at the 1991 Conference with a view to introducing it after the next General Election. The leadership then turned its attention to reform of the *annual Conference*, first by making the election of the constituency section of the National Executive Committee more democratic, and second, by removing the excessive influence of the trade union block vote on Conference decisions.

In the elections for the seven constituency section NEC representatives in 1989, constituency parties were merely *requested* to ballot their entire membership before casting their NEC votes. Estimates of the number of local parties which did ballot their memberships vary, but many did do so, and the defeat of hard left representative Ken Livingstone was generally seen as the result of wider consultation of local memberships. Full membership ballots for the election of the constituency section of the NEC look certain to be made mandatory in the near future. The party will also consider the introduction of mandatory ballots for the election of constituency officers and of delegates to the party Conference.

Reform of the block vote was widely discussed at the 1989 Conference. At present, the ratio of voting power on Conference policy decisions between trade unions and the constituencies is 90:10. One possibility is that this balance of voting influence will be replaced by a 70:30 ratio before the 1991 Conference. It could even be that the ratio will be 55:45, if Labour succeeds in its aim to double its 270 000 membership by the next election. Whatever the precise system to be adopted, reform of the block vote is imminent.

Finally, the improvement of Labour's public image owed much to effective performances by its front-bench team. Labour's shadow ministers attacked on a broad front including: the damage done to the economy and the harm inflicted on mortgage-holders by the Chancellor's sole reliance on interest rate increases to reduce inflation; the water privatisation plans, including the high expenditure on advertising by the water authorities; the unfairness of the poll tax; the divisiveness of its health and education reforms; and the Government's apparent lack of real commitment to improving the environment.

An *Observer*/Harris poll published on October 28 1990 revealed the progress made by Labour since 1987. It gave the state of the parties as: Labour 48 per cent, Conservatives 32 per cent, Liberal Democrats 4 per cent, Greens 2 per cent. This increased public confidence in Labour, together with the deterioration in their own position, placed the Conservatives under greater pressure in 1989–90 than they had experienced for most of the decade.

The Government's response

Mrs Thatcher's first major response to her Government's sagging fortunes in the polls was a Cabinet reshuffle in July 1989: her twelfth since becoming Prime Minister in 1979. Its nature and extent, if not its timing, took political commentators by surprise. The reshuffle unexpectedly brought the promotion of John Major to be Foreign Secretary in place of Sir Geoffrey Howe, who became Deputy Prime Minister and Leader of the House of Commons. It saw 13 of the 21 Cabinet posts re-shuffled, other important changes being the moving of Kenneth Baker from Education to become Conservative Party Chairman and the promotion of Chris Patten to Environment Secretary. These changes put politicians with good communications skills in posts which would be vital to the next election campaign. This re-shuffle was probably intended to create the Cabinet team which would fight the next election but the Prime Minister was forced to make further changes in late October 1989 by the unexpected resignation of Nigel Lawson. John Major was hurriedly moved again from the Foreign Office to the Treasury, Douglas Hurd became Foreign Secretary and David Waddington, the party's Chief Whip, took Douglas Hurd's place as Home Secretary. During 1990 further unwished-for changes occurred as a result of the voluntary retirements of the Employment Secretary, Norman Fowler, and the Secretary of State for Wales, Peter Walker, the forced resignation of the Trade and Industry Secretary, Nicholas Ridley, after the publication in *The Spectator* of certain anti-German remarks he had made to its editor, and the resignation of Sir Geoffrey Howe.

In late 1989 and during 1990, world events had assisted in a modest revival of Government hopes. First, the collapse of communist regimes in Eastern Europe and the moves to adopt market economies in those countries not only served to inspire Conservative anti-Socialist rhetoric at home but also gave rise to the possibility of significant cuts in the defence budget. Second, although the outcome of the crisis was unforeseeable in October 1990, the Government's firm response along with other countries to the Iraqi invasion of Kuwait in August helped to boost the Prime Minister's public image as a resolute leader. On the eve of the Conservative Conference in October 1990, the Chancellor of the Exchequer, John Major, announced that Britain was to join the ERM (European Exchange Rate Mechanism). This move sharply increased the possibility of a General Election in 1991. To hold an election within a year of joining would enable the Government to profit from the expected short-term benefits – reduced interest rates, lower inflation and an upsurge in economic activity – whilst avoiding the potentially damaging electoral consequences of any longer-term adverse economic effects of membership of the ERM. Then on November 13, following his resignation from the Cabinet, Sir Geoffrey Howe made a severe attack upon the Prime Minister, criticising especially her attitude to Europe. Michael Heseltine immediately challenged for the leadership, gaining 152 votes against the Prime Minister's 204 in the first ballot on November 20. Mrs Thatcher, 4 votes short of outright victory according to Conservative rules, at first declared her intention to fight on. However, with her support crumbling, she was prevailed upon by a significant number of Cabinet ministers to stand down, thereby allowing the two most senior members of the Government, John Major and Douglas Hurd, to enter the contest. The result of the second ballot on November 27 was: John Major, 185 votes; Michael Heseltine, 131 votes; Douglas Hurd, 56 votes. The losing candidates then withdrew, even though John Major was still short by 2 votes of an outright victory, and on November 28 John Major became the new Conservative leader and Prime Minister. His first Cabinet, announced the next day, was as follows:

Prime Minister	John Major
Lord Chancellor	Lord Mackay of Clashfern
Foreign Secretary	Douglas Hurd
Home Secretary	Kenneth Baker
Chancellor of the Exchequer	Norman Lamont
Chief Secretary to the Treasury	David Mellor
Leader of the House of Commons	John MacGregor
Lord Privy Seal, Leader of the House of Lords	David Waddington
Chancellor of the Duchy of Lancaster	Christopher Patten
Environment	Michael Heseltine
Defence	Tom King
Education	Kenneth Clarke

Transport	Malcolm Rifkind
Energy	John Wakeham
Employment	Michael Howard
Trade and Industry	Peter Lilley
Social Security	Tony Newton
Health	William Waldegrave
Agriculture	John Selwyn Gummer
Northern Ireland	Peter Brooke
Wales	David Hunt
Scotland	Ian Lang

Further Reading

Dunleavy, P., Gamble, A. and Peele, G. (eds) (1990) *Developments in British Politics 3*, London, Macmillan.

Savage, S. and Robins, L. (eds) (1990) *Public Policy under Thatcher*, London, Macmillan.

Skidelsky, R. (ed.) (1988) *Thatcherism*, London, Chatto and Windus.

McKie, D. 'Only one in five positively backs Thatcher', a major poll analysis in the *Guardian*, September 18 1989.

Nugent, N. 'The EC and the UK', *Talking Politics*, Autumn 1989 (vol. 2, no. 1).

Wilson, David J., 'More power to the Centre? The changing nature of Central Government /Local Authority relationships', *Talking Politics*, Autumn 1990 (vol. 3, no. 1).

Index